357 Days a Year

Phillip G Mackey

357 Days a Year

Olympia Publishers
London

www.olympiapublishers.com
OLYMPIA PAPERBACK EDITION

A CIP catalogue record for this title is
available from the British Library.

ISBN: 978-1-80439-465-6

This book is memoir. It reflects the author's present recollections of experiences
over time. Some names and characteristics have been changed, some events
have been compressed, and some dialogue has been recreated.

First Published in 2025

Olympia Publishers
Tallis House
2 Tallis Street
London
EC4Y 0AB

Printed in Great Britain

Dedication

To my mam, dad, sister, brother-in-law and nephew; for their unequivocal support and for putting up with my unique brand of nonsense. I am truly grateful.

Acknowledgements

To every friend, traveller, worker, wordsmith, singer, seer, peer, poet, pothead or dickhead that I had the pleasure to meet, converse and hangout with on my travels; regardless of what it was and in what context, you all taught me a lot and helped make all this possible; I thank you.
Special thanks to PADI Aware foundation.
And special acknowledgement and thanks to authors of profound inspiring words;

ID Garuda	Most People Are Nuts
Albie Sachs	The Soft Vengeance of a Freedom Fighter
James Redfield	The Celestine Prophecy
Dalai Lama	The Little Book of Wisdom
Danny Wallace	Yes Man
Anthony De Mello	One Minute Wisdom

Contents

Neehow

'*Neehow*' or to the untrained ear that's Chinese for 'now then' or even 'hello'. My flight was good, I think. Let's face it, when flying, nothing unusual is the norm and just how we like it. Maybe a bit of turbulence? Air stewards run out of booze? Few pissed off passengers? Or scandal of scandals, some rumblings in the mile-high club? Anything more, then people fear the worst and come to the conclusion everything has gone to shit. In this case, though, there was none of that and what the movies were, the food I ate and had to drink, I do not know. I always thought I'd remember some of these details as people always ask about flights. But now after everything, it seems very insignificant. So, no big ups or downs except only the required take-off and landing getting from A to B. The highlight turned out to be the extra space; the plane was at best only a third-full and I managed to acquire a full three-seat row on the right-hand side, instead of just the single seat I'd paid for. I could lie down, put my feet up and stretch out. Some might call it luck or even poor man's first class. Whatever; the nice smooth start I desired came to pass. And felt like instant score.

Starting out, I was already shattered after getting up early just to get to the airport and probably why I think I slept most of the way. This was my first of six flights. A first of many firsts; setting off on a journey that would take me around the globe as a solo traveller. Each flight strategically placed at various cities, heading one way and to be taken within the coming year. My ticket bundled me into cattle class economy; this was not a first as I had been well versed to the leg room and space that would be provided from previous sojourns abroad – a common issue but one which many bare, due to the somewhat absurdly priced first or business class seats. But, in this instance, the fast-thinking chap sat next to me noticed an entire row of empty seats behind us and with the absence of more passengers after take-off, he duly went and occupied, now leaving myself with my own row to stretch out on and fall asleep. Again, this small gesture would be another first where I was to experience the fortune of another person helping someone else where possible. Although grateful, I never actually realised it at the time, how often incidents like this would and do occur and more importantly no matter how small they seem, how amazing they all are.

I woke from a sleep on the plane which didn't feel like I had. I wasn't sure if this aided or hindered the probable jet lag from a ten-hour flight, having never been one to remember when I was or wasn't supposed to sleep when travelling with or against time. Now we were in Chinese airspace and approaching Beijing and near to the start of my adventure. Looking out of the window, the sky was brilliant blue, the horizon's shimmering haze only emphasised a stifling hot illusion. The magnificent yet minuscule mountains slowly subsided and disappeared by the wayside as we approached and landed; safe, sound and I had done it; made the break and was underway.

It was Saturday, 23 August. Ten a.m. We were on time; not only as scheduled but significantly for the last two days of the 2008 Olympic Games. Yet, oddly, I wasn't over excited, despite being in a new city on the other side of the planet when one of the greatest shows on earth was in town. A slight nervous anticipation of what lay ahead and wondering how I was going to cope still gripped me, but now all other worries and fears about what lay ahead were put on the back burner. Because having started, immediate issues came to the fore front. How was I going to get to my hostel? More to the point, avoid being ripped off in the process and should I get there OK? Would the hostel have my reservation? Working my way through customs and immigration, activating my thirty-day visa without any problems, my worries were alleviated when having ascended and descended numerous levels of the arrivals lounge, I eventually found a taxi rank and was surprised to discover that the set price to the city wasn't too expensive and even more surprised that the taxi driver recognised my printout map and knew the address where I wanted to go. Hopping in, we set off. Approaching the city, the sky had dulled from brilliant blue to a hazy smog, testament to the much-publicised air pollution problems of Beijing that were in stark contrast to the ethos of the games. We took the regular car lane next to the official 'Olympic lane only' and its fluttering banners, as we headed straight for the east side, to the district with many shops, restaurants, bars and clubs and, of course, my hostel.

Aware of my reservation, the warm and friendly staff welcomed me upon my arrival. I felt safe. Ambling to my dorm room and finding my bed, any nervous energy gradually dissipated whilst distractedly sorting my things. I momentarily lay down on my top bunk to check how the mattress was. Reassured I was where I was meant to be and despite all the apparent rest and sleep while travelling, I promptly passed out. Again.

Thinking about things, I never actually realised how unhappy I was and it pains me to admit it, being from England as born and bred UK citizen. I had a good job and this allowed money to flow into the bank, a network of friends and was able to treat myself to the nice things in life; holidays, cars, clothes, restaurants, nights out. If I wanted it, within reason, I could flash the cash and make it happen. Also, the UK is a democratic society that provides freedoms many around the world seldom experience; voting, free speech, protesting and human rights etc. Easily taken for granted basic principles of humanity when brought up with them stitched into the societal fabric and, lest I forget to mention as far as Britain is concerned, a free National Health Service that cared for me when I was sick. Born out of the huge sacrifice of so many who fought actual tyranny and died during world wars to preserve the sanctity of the aforementioned. Many less fortunate would themselves die for just a chance at such privilege. And what's more? I was born into a loving and supportive family. We were not wealthy in the *cha-ching* sense but were rich because, as a youngster, food was always on the table, clothes were on my back, a roof adorned my head and education was there ready to teach and allow me to develop as I wished. So, I'd had the sheer luck – and that's what it is – of defying unbelievable odds to gain all of this without lifting a finger and my gratitude and recognition of these facts has not and never would waiver even once.

What more could a person ask for? To put simply, nothing; I had already been given a huge leg up in life. And appreciate the picture I've painted is hardly 'woe is me' and a case for breaking out the violins. Nothing was wrong with that at all either. It's brilliant. It's fantastic. And wish those opportunities could be available to all. But, in my case from the inside looking out, something was wrong. Because regardless of this beautiful bounty, I was not happy.

Apologies for a seemingly typical whinge of having everything and every opportunity, yet it is still not enough. I think despite having all this, I wasn't happy due to the fact that I never really knew what I wanted to do in life or with my life and struggled to find a muse or something that excited me and was passionate about, to give me purpose and direction. I was living in my mind; an ambling existence of not necessarily boring but definite monotony.

What I perceived as making or creating happiness or worth within wasn't working. This perception only solidified the older I got and seriously started to question everything I was doing. I wondered if having money and nice things was the be all and end all. They would only seem to provide fleeting superficial moments to savour. I just knew that they did not have any lasting desired effects. And, frustratingly, didn't know how or what I would need to achieve this.

It felt like I had been sold a bit of a lie by society and started to miss the point of what was expected of me; grow up, get a good education, get a good job, meet someone, get married, have a family, work hard and save all your life, live happily ever after then die. And while you are at it, watch this, like that, eat this, look like that and, by the way, 'you must have this'. Evermore frequently, I asked myself, 'Everyone else is doing this, but why do I have to?' Offered a slow realisation; there had to be more to life.

I had a job running bars. Many would assume a glorious existence of socialising and parties that never stopped. It isn't. I had somewhat fallen into this career from leaving university, but, over time, I eventually grew to hate it. The pay was decent but filled me with dread the thought that this was my life. It interested me for a while but eventually I realised that although a hero and envied by many for providing an escapist's elixir, I still felt unfulfilled and more part of any drinking problem than part of any solution despite the countless training. The bottom line was, all I did was be part of a chain that supplied people with alcoholic beverages and could not see any real value in this whatsoever. I had changed and my values had changed. So this had to change.

At thirty-two, I was living in a beautiful, affluent part of the country but away from most friends and family and I didn't particularly like it. There was nothing wrong with it per say, but it just didn't feel right for me living there. I had moved there four years prior to act as a stepping stone to further my career and now the stepping stones were not the ones I wanted to take any more. My physical and mental health deteriorated and ended up on a negative downward spiral via escape mechanisms such as drink, drugs and gambling that I had fallen into in a vain attempt to deflect the boredom, blot out what was happening and sadly try to induce some form of happiness in my life. It inevitably never worked. And I would then feel worse. I never thought myself an alcoholic. And have never been diagnosed or been to AA, but I would drink all the time; five nights per week and after two night shifts would get home at four a.m., drink a bottle of wine and six beers before ten a.m. This was not good; definite borderline if not definite alcoholism. The drink and lack of activity caused me to be overweight for years and it had taken its toll; cumulating with the need for two operational procedures for a persistent hernia in the space of nine months. By then, I was desperate to find what was missing in my life and wondering even more if what I was doing was all worth it.

First thing was no. It wasn't worth it; despite how things might have looked on the outside, I was miserable and dark inside and all the trimmings and money couldn't change this, there had to be more to life. I wanted to do something fun, something good, be pro-active, a challenge, a test, some excitement, an adventure, I wanted to help people and do positive things. But most of all, I needed to figure out some form of purpose within. I had to change things and simply couldn't go on with this negativity, because that journey did not look fun or adventurous and had an ominously bad inevitability about it. This wasn't me. I had only lost a bit of direction and needed to re-evaluate. Sitting rotting and wasting my life was not an option and decided that being alive was a gift to make the most of. The thing that scared me most was the prospect of being on my death bed, with a huge load of regret about a wasted existence and I simply wasn't going to let that happen.

Fate though had shined a light and somewhat ignited a beacon. I had holidayed and travelled numerous times to various places and continents previously with friends. I loved it and had a great time sampling the different cultures, sights, activities and customs the places had to offer. So the year previous in 2007, I decided to take the plunge and travel on my own to Canada as I'd always wanted to visit there. Being a month or so after my first operation, this was at short notice and a drop of a hat deal; understandably nobody else could go, had other plans or couldn't afford it. But I really wanted a holiday so just bought tickets to Toronto and then decided to make it up from there. It was only for three weeks and in a country regarded as safe, outdoor orientated and customs that wouldn't be too dissimilar to what I was used to. Also, if I ended up in the French-speaking part, I could pull out my dusty old school textbook French I'd learnt some sixteen years prior and give that a whirl. This was the touch paper being lit and what was to be the catalyst for future events.

I loved those three weeks. It invigorated me and filled me with a confidence I had rarely experienced before. Previous excursions abroad always had someone else in tow. Providing companionship, instant conversation and security to help and deal with any issues. But alone, I sampled the first liberating taste of travelling around, where I need not make any set plans and could do what I wanted, when I wanted. I experienced so many things and met so many interesting new people from all walks of life. The Canadian people, psyche, activities and fellow travellers left an indelible mark that wouldn't fade.

On my return, I made a conscious decision that I was going to save as much as possible for a year, and make the break from everyone and everything. The only initial problem was freeing myself from pre-conceived fears of removal from the security blanket of living and residing in a western country with no language barrier and where the money, culture, societal offerings and pleasant surroundings all made sense, lest not mention the warm reassurance of having friends and family all in close quarters that I knew and could rely on. I had to get into the mind-frame of throwing caution to the wind, facing all the fears of giving up a secure job, not earning any money, removing myself from friends and loved ones, being in other countries with different races, religions, societies and cultures and putting all my faith in what life and I had to offer. This seemed a big gamble, but now having done these three weeks I had impetus for change.

With no real commitments, no ties and money that I had saved for ages, made this much easier than expected. Work had taken a further downturn due to circumstances out of my control and resulted in not having a very good time, where I mainly wasn't getting along with my new line manager. Instances were partly my fault but certainly not all. I never drank or was drunk at work because it wasn't allowed and would have been very obvious, so I felt I was still trying my hardest despite the business struggling due to surge in competition that had not been seen before. By now the cracks were well and truly gaping and a parting of ways was almost inevitable. The final issue which nearly jeopardised everything involved having to have a second corrective procedure as the first had now failed. By this point, I was feeling miserable not to mention nervous at the prospect of having another operation which, although routine, made it seem my future was hanging in the balance.

After the successful procedure, although in some pain, I immediately started to feel happier knowing I was recovering. I took time to ensure that I recuperated fully this time and when given the all-clear from the doctors, I handed in my notice. A deed in itself that left a wondrous warm 'things are officially about to change' feeling inside. I had dropped an invisible ball and chain and decided to go for broke and take a chance on life, living and not only being but feeling alive.

I had considered getting another job, but didn't want to. It was pointless and I knew this wouldn't really fix anything as this was *a* problem but not *the* problem. I knew that I had to go travelling; it somehow felt right and was my destiny unfolding, but to where and what? I did not know. I started planning where to go and for how long, making a list of all the places that I'd like to visit and formed a route. The money I had guaranteed about ten months but was tied up in various places, so I would have to count on getting this whilst I was away, but figured it shouldn't be a problem. I never did plan a budget of sorts; I was good with figures but this was mainly due to the fact that I didn't know where to start and didn't want to freak myself out with the price of things and start cost-cutting from the onset, figuring that I would make it up as I went along. It was a risk but in the grand scheme of things everything was a risk, and I was armed with around £13,000 in total. After numerous phone calls and Internet searches, I pretty much had my flight itinerary sorted about where to go; this included China, Hong Kong, Thailand, Malaysia, Singapore, Australia, New Zealand, the USA, South America and Canada. I also had an idea of activities that I really wanted to pursue, some vocational, some educational and some for my own achievement and pleasure, determined not to spend my time away just lounging around on a beach or in the bars and clubs, which, granted, was also definitely on the agenda.

It wasn't easy to make that payment; not only was it a large sum of money to make it happen, but it then offered the stark realisation that everything you know about life is just about to change. It's a piece of piss talking about what you're going to do, but actually doing it? This can be a very different matter. Everything we seem to hold dear has to be given up there and then at that instant, and the security of your known world is to be whipped well and truly from under your feet to face things, people and places that we don't necessarily know anything about. This point is where many would probably fail and not go through with it as the 'what ifs' and 'buts' are in abundance and any amount of planning just doesn't seem enough. But the hardest decisions in life which involve chance and risk invariably offer the biggest rewards; if it works with money, why can't it work with life? With a little bravery, courage, determination, resilience and huge slices of luck, I just may find that niche in life. I was going for it; determined to give myself a new start, learn new things and do something positive for myself and hopefully others. I booked these with a travel company who deal with gap years, and they also dealt with my flights. So with itinerary set and flights booked, I then headed out to get necessary stuff like visas, injections, back pack, sleeping bag, rain jacket, guidebooks and other things.

Despite all this consuming my mind and actions; it still didn't feel like it was happening, probably by now because it was starting to feel like the most natural thing that I should do, although I had seemingly put my departure back by about two months, creating the illusion that it may never happen to others watching from the side lines. I wasn't bothered about this, it didn't matter. The timing had to be right and I prepared as I wanted to undertake such a trip in order for things to turn out as I hoped. Nevertheless, all too quickly the time came around to leave; everything in place, all equipment and things packed, I said my goodbyes with not much fuss or fanfare and headed off to find what I hoped in some way, shape or form was my destiny or at least give me the adventure of a lifetime.

For the first three days, I managed to achieve absolutely nothing. The initial long hours of travelling had wiped me out, so I got up late, met people in the bar and got drunk. This was what those in the hostel visiting Beijing were up to and I fell into the swing of things as easy as instantaneous. Saturday and Sunday spent sleeping and then drinking in Heineken house; the Dutch Olympic party base, although saying that I did manage to get my very own gold medal. After only three days of travelling, I thought it was quite the achievement that not many can claim. OK, granted it was from a night club and for being on the piss. But still, a gold medal from Beijing when the Olympics were on. Over the years, I probably had put in as much time and dedication to training in my specific discipline like the real athletes had.

On Monday, I got up late after the Sunday session and decided this couldn't carry on; the last few days of the Olympics were now done and all I'd really done was savour the atmosphere and a bunch of booze. The possible jetlag, drinking and partying had done me no favours whatsoever and now there were no excuses; I was in a new challenging country, with hundreds of options at my disposal. So, first and foremost on the agenda had to be a visit to one of the ancient world's most monumental structures, so I booked a trekking tour for a couple of days' time as not to miss out, then spent the rest of the day in a relaxed fashion, looking around and checking out my nearby surroundings. Not drinking.

The events had finished; the football and boxing finals over the weekend had come and gone. If better prepared, I could have easily attended one of these events at the 'biggest sporting spectacle on Earth' but decided on fraternisation and inebriation instead. Worse still when I found out that the venue hosting the boxing was literally around the corner from the hostel, right on my doorstep, and I still missed the opportunity through being a lazy dumbass. Also, the closing ceremony on the Sunday was a costly experience, at £200 ticket I figured being a tad on the pricey side so decided again not to bother, even at this fledgling stage of my travels it seemed expensive. I watched the closing ceremony at the Heineken house with the other party revellers. Part of it was the handover for the next Olympics in 2012 which was to be in London, a unique show unfolded that featured British icons; guitar maestro Jimmy Page and pop songstress Leona Lewis. Also non-icon; then Mayor of London Boris Johnson with his trademark 'dragged through a hedge backwards' dishevelled look embarrassingly receiving the handover mantel on behalf of our nation. Again; poor preparation, lack of research or indecision meant 'snooze? – you lose' on all counts. This started a learning curve that would teach me a great lesson about taking chances and opportunities as they would appear.

After the lazy drunken hungover blur of the first three days, on the Tuesday I got up nice and early; this was it, the first day of exploration, discovery, education, excitement, you name it, it was on and I was getting involved. A chance to learn and engulf myself in the travel experience what I'd longed for. I now knew I needed to get out there and do, see and achieve something. So, using the new and improved for the Olympics Beijing subway system – I was whipped to anywhere in the city for a fantastic price of 16p a journey – I headed out. Disembarking and heading back above ground, the first port of call was synonymous with the world over; I crossed the road and immediately walked into Tiananmen Square.

As you would imagine, this is a square; a massive open yet imposing site where everything surrounding can easily be seen. From the Monument to the People's Heroes and the Mausoleum of Mao Zedong within the centre, to The Arrow Tower, Front Gate and National Museum of China that grace the outskirts. Where also, on this particular day outside the Great Hall of the People there was an appearance by many Chinese Olympians; proud fans and well-wishers gathered to greet them and excitedly pose for photos, testimony to their amazing performance and efforts during the games. Away from crowds, the concrete and flat openness of the square was broken by huge floral displays that had been constructed, some specifically to honour the Olympics; including a mock-up of the fabulous Bird's Nest stadium and these features provided an element of beauty in stark contrast to the otherwise ominous, open, grey, vacuous space.

As history dictates though, this was and is no ordinary square. For me, it holds more in the mind from the depictions on TV news I witnessed as a thirteen-year-old lad. Student protests broke out here in 1989, an uprising against the authorities by those who dared to pursue a luxury of the western world; democracy. When they didn't cease and disperse, the demands and people were crushed with military might. Sadly, many died or were imprisoned for the cause, both during and after the large, but determined peaceful protest. And like many, I mostly remember the iconic scene of a lone unarmed man stood in defiance, resolutely, in front of a row of onward-looming tanks, only to be dragged away in fear of his safety. I don't think many know who that man was which is kind of expected; because even if he wasn't found, he surely had to hide away and remain silent. Now here, I wondered if I could ever hold anything so dear as to commit such an act of courage, bravery and bold rebellious resistance? Knowing these very actions would risk certain imprisonment or death from an unforgiving regime. Now nearly twenty years on, there is no talk of what happened here. Officially, it did not happen. And there certainly isn't any memorial. So, I didn't and dared not ask anyone about it and democracy is still not prevalent in China. But it was still difficult to imagine the square – where the name ironically refers to heavenly peace - any different than what it had become to represent from the point of view of an outsider looking in; a place where democracy, its idealistic and some might say 'decadent ways' were brutally quashed and swept away by the singular power of the Chinese authorities. A gentle reminder of this is felt in Tiananmen Square; as gazing out across the whole of the site is a massive portrait of Chairman Mao Zedong. It hangs with an imposing majesty above the gated entrance to the Forbidden City.

With its huge marooned walls and beautiful traditional decoration, the Forbidden City lies in the centre of Beijing. Built as the Chinese imperial palace in the early fifteenth century, the massive double-door gateway is masterfully constructed with the sole purpose of security that would be difficult to breach by a loyal subject or enemy invader now let alone then; designed so it was forbidden to gaze upon an emperor never meant to be found. It truly is city-like in itself where impossible walls interrupt vastness of open courts, buildings and sections in a perfectly designed battalion. A lack of any high vantage point makes it difficult to appreciate the sheer scale of the ancient city where any guideless nomad like myself could easily spend a ridiculous amount of time exploring, foraging and getting lost; which I did. Long walkways in the courtyards connect extensive stairways used by former rulers across history, along with the beautifully crafted and ornately decorated dragon stairway in the centre that was barricaded off from wandering feet; this reserved only for the footsteps of God. Amid the complex lay a wonderful trove of artefacts, many within temples and museums that highlight eras and dynasties of days past; most notable being that which offer an insight into the life of the last emperor made famous in a feature film of the same name.

Understandably from the information within, it seemed life was incredibly dull for last emperor; Puyi. He was a privileged child who lived in a vast palace with lack of friends. This was emphasised by how well he exceeded academically, and the fascination he possessed with western culture that was encapsulated by the spectacles he used to wear before being removed from power at the beginning of the twentieth century at only fourteen years old. Also displayed were fabulous works of art, statues, artefacts and important documentation such as the 1949 proclamation by Chairman Mao to view amid the extensive exploration of many different quarters, temples and museums that included the still-kept courtyards and gardens whereby the last emperor worked within until his death in 1967.

I started to feel inwardly content with my initial efforts of submerging into China's past history and culture. At this point, I'd been about four hours exploring and felt like I'd covered the equivalent of twenty football pitches, yet only visited two places, wandering in and out the countless features on offer in this great cavalcade of information but due to heat, humidity and my severely unfit condition, I was fatigued. But so what? I'd walked a few miles and was a little tired. It would only do me good; and I had finally managed to start to do what I wanted. So, while in the vicinity, I visited

Jingshan Park.

Located the north end of the Forbidden City and the complete opposite end from where I had started, this wasn't on my to-do list, but was first of many instances whereby I had spare time to do something which I didn't know much about, tried to heed a lesson of taking chances as they arose. I was instantly rewarded because inside the park, located in the centre, there was a magnificent pavilion that yielded a now fantastic high up 360-degree ariel view of Beijing and The Forbidden City; where the layered walls within scattered into the distance. Unfortunately, though, the weather had taken a turn for the worse where grey and overcast had now replaced the blue unclouded sky that had greeted me out of the subway; so, the vast sprawl erased into the mist. Nevertheless, post-haste I set about taking photos of the view. I walked around the park, noted the growing myriads of adorning statues and decorations everywhere and started to realise this was to become a focal point of the time spent in China; which was to appreciate the beauty of an ancient culture that I had seldom seen before.

In an open paved area of the park, I watched the locals exercise by tapping a shuttlecock between one another using only their feet like a hacky sack, and then visited the preserved tree site whereby the last emperor of the Ming dynasty was hanged. Harsh treatment for an emperor, some might think? Or an original statistic of finding out how tough it is at the top. Like they say, 'the bigger they are the harder they fall', I guess. I felt sorry for his assistant who had to be hanged with him just because he was in his service; it was probably supposed to be an honour. But hardly a badge, medal or reward, I thought. It seemed pretty shitty deal to me to tag along 'cos some entitled person couldn't put their socks on in the afterlife; and to add insult to injury the assistant was also supposed to be a eunuch, *ouch*!

Returning to the hostel, I was happy. Elated, in fact; finally having a feeling of accomplishment from a full day exploration in a new country, experiencing the culture, seeing historical sights and educating myself. So on the evening I just relaxed, ready with anticipation for the next day, which I hoped would prove memorable given that I was undertaking my first real activity; I wouldn't be disappointed, little realising how memorable it would be.

A six a.m. bus picked us up to visit the Great Wall of China. I should have been excited and raring to go but getting up felt like a chore. I never really slept despite my hours of meandering culture vulture activities the day prior. This was due in part to ridiculous, pneumatically loud snoring in the dorm coupled with not having any means of telling the time or setting an alarm call. My phone died of power and the 'universal' except for Chinese plug sockets adapter I had with me wouldn't fit. So I lay in bed, awake, with my pillow wrapped around my head in a vain attempt to blot out the frustratingly loud, torturous, repetitive rattling of someone's nasal cavity worrying about not getting sleep. After this passed, I then lay there amid the same noxious drone worrying about not waking up. So with about two hours' sleep before reception called to get me, I had felt better.

I'd asked if someone could knock on the door. They did and I heard it as I was already awake. We were picked up on the main road with the bus already quite full of like-minded adventurers wanting to trek on the wall. Everyone was quiet; still slumber-some from the early-hour departure. Light had broken but the air was cold and damp. Even in a busy industrious city like Beijing, the streets were somewhat eerily empty, except for service and sanitation workers and those making early deliveries. As we made our way there, I started to feel sleepy all of a sudden, induced by my in-adverted sleep deprivation. Also, I had nothing to eat since the previous evening and it didn't help the situation. This was more of a conscious decision as I was scheduled to be on a bus; and after five days or so away from blighty the old constitution wasn't holding up very well and the going was definitely good to soft. In other words, I had the shits.

Arriving at the Jinshan Ling and Simatai part of the Great Wall, I was struck with the enormity of this wonder of the world. Straightaway, it was impossible to mistake where we were, even with parts now in a slightly crumbled state created the impression of a formidable defence of Beijing from any potential land threat. Hadrian's wall? Blink and you will miss it. Here, the grey fortress loomed menacingly riding above the hills stretching in either direction. Upon arriving, I could only think of one question; *How the fuck did they build this?* It would be a right ball-ache now never mind back then! Reaching the start point was arduous in itself, the wall was on a mountain and the bus can only take you so far. Then the climbing begins, not exactly crampons and harnesses but initially with one kilometre uphill and steps to reach the wall. There was a cable car, but I decided if you're going do a job, do it properly; I wanted to do the full trek experience and this included scaling up to the top. When everyone reached the start, there was a unified gaze of awe from all in appreciation of the rolling mountains and the seemingly unending snaking wall that defined its contours into the distance. With this, camera shutters fluttered frantically and, with this, it also became apparent how far we actually had to walk.

Starting at around ten thirty a.m., it quickly became obvious that this wasn't going to be easy. In fact, it was going to be hard, very hard. The sun had burned off any cloud cover and was blisteringly hot, especially not having smog protection of Beijing. Also, I was weighing in at about 14 stone or close to 200lbs. The previous six months spent on the couch eating, drinking and not doing much activity due to my hernia recovery had left me overweight and unfit. Not exactly the ideal physical shape to undertake this particular trek; what's more with no food and minimal sleep, I was hardly an advertisement for good preparation.

Even though sections of the wall had been re-built; we walked most of the 10km trek on derelict, crumbling, un-restored parts, away from the tourist hoards. The engravings of soldier names were still etched into the stones from an era long since passed where at times we ambled over rocks, rubble and make-shift stairs of the aged and weather-ravaged ruins. Some bits were OK but some inclines were relentless and brutally steep well over hundred feet high that actually in small parts involved climbing. All elements included, I was quickly starved of energy and literally started dragging myself up the large square boulder steps that had been placed in situ atop the hills of a mountain. No sooner making it to the summit of one peak to then immediately negotiating the declining far side, stepping and clambering down a harsh rugged terrain that was just as painful on the rapidly tiring muscles, in no way helped by the imposing vision of the next inclination to cover. If this wasn't already tough enough, due to severe wall damage and safety issues, at points, trekkers had to get off the wall to instead walk down, along and back up a mountainside trail to the next turret. The little worn track was steep through the shrubbery connecting to where the wall started again. There wasn't much except embankment and ruins on one side and straight down on the other; so without a handrail insight, it made it pretty obvious that with one slip it was goodbye.

About halfway through, I was struggling big time. My lungs heaved hot and heavy, muscles screamed and complained with every step; each sinew had its own personal vendetta with my mind and will as lactic acid ravaged my weak untrained flesh. My skin was soaked cool with glistening unattractive sweat, yet I burnt inside. In desperation to replace energy and fluids to my sapped torso, I started consuming copious amounts of water and fizzy drinks. It didn't work. Rather than being absorbed to soothe the inside, the massive build-up of acid in my stomach reacted with the gulped gallons tipped down my neck to only bloat me and forced a reflex outpouring from my gut, where I had to stop to be sick. Needless to say, this was much to everyone's amusement; those in our group split quickly into the uber-fit and the uber-lame. I fell into the latter category, hardly hiding the fact I was spewing out of a turret window, especially as it happened about six times overall. Despite this, I was purely focused on finishing, not caring about my disgusting state. I was stuck on a massive ancient wall, on a mountain range, in blistering heat, in the middle of China. There was only one thing that was getting me back. That was me, by finishing. I was suffering with the heat, zero sustenance, dehydration, fatigue and lack of stamina. Numerous thoughts tortured my mind; *This is fucking agony! How much further? Am I dying? I dunno how much more I can take! I think I'm dying! Wonder how that woman who had the high heels is getting on? Am I doing better than her? I don't think I am!*

At the start, we were followed by indigenous local folk who act as Sherpas. Day in, day out carrying people's things, offering help and drinks. I was obviously looking like a prime candidate for a tough time as one latched on to me straightaway, knowing the trademark of the unfit tourist and rugged brutality of the wall. I thought it a slight insult at first, but when the harsh reality of the conditions and my physical being kicked in, any help would do as I didn't have a clue who or where our chaperone was or even if there was one for that matter. All I knew was which direction we were going and how bloody tough and torturous it all was.

Here, I was really grateful and happy with this lady's presence and help. Because, in all honesty, I probably wouldn't have made it without her, and at 200 Yuan, her assistance was heaven-sent. She must have been maybe fifty? I couldn't really tell; her sun-worn skin seemed to supersede her age. She helped carry my bag, got drinks for us both, and laughed whenever the signal came for the impending technicolour yawn. Only a shame about the communication due to my woeful, or more like non-existent, Chinese and her lack of English. Here, stark realisation hit and I noticed what others less fortunate have to endure to make a living; climbing every day, rain or shine, in the hope that some hapless sap would require a drink, like to buy a souvenir or even use their services to help carry bags, etc. Even to the extent of grabbing precious sleep in the turrets, as to not waste time getting up and down from the wall. This left me humbled and slightly embarrassed by the fact that someone presumably much older than me, who obviously had endured a much harder existence than me, could negotiate this treacherous terrain far faster, easier and with a lot less effort, moaning, groaning and literally less vomit than me. This was another first.

Upon exiting the wall, I paid and tipped my entertained Sherpa for her invaluable help; this was at the point where my elation of finishing was only surpassed after finding out that to get to the restaurant, I had to walk another 800 yards around a lake or use a massive zip line over it. Here was where my legs got their way; because my arms seemed to be the only part of me that were somewhat functioning now and all that stuff about doing the trek properly went straight out of the window. Regardless, I love zip lines and there was no way I wasn't going on it and was the perfect way to get a knackered fat bloke off an ancient wall; if ever there was one. *Whooosh!*

The Great Wall of China was one of the most amazing experiences I'd ever had. Incredible views from a world-famous historical site, mixing it with the locals and hard, character-building work. Granted, it all but physically destroyed me, and not to put to finer point on it, after finishing I was completely fucked – a weak, tired, aching physical wreck. Nothing short of practically crawling, I hadn't been that exhausted for a very long time and could hardly string two words together, never mind put one foot in front of the other – but loved every minute though. It was what I wanted, my first challenge, what I had travelled for and came through relatively unscathed from literally hiking, scaling and climbing up and down the contours of mountain ridges and peaks. When we reached the restaurant at around two thirty p.m., I still couldn't stomach food and free food at that. Just sitting with a litre of orange juice and half litre of water, within about twenty minutes had started to revitalise me as the vitamins and minerals started to absorb and work their magic rather than settling on the stomach. Honestly, to this day, I don't know how I managed to complete it.

The next few days were spent charging around Beijing; well, truth be told, the charge was more like a shuffle, as my legs were incredibly sore having taken a thorough hammering from the previous days' exertions. I took in some more quickly-growing-on-me Chinese culture at the Heaven and Harvest Temple; again, set in beautiful grounds that encompassed fabulous architecture including massive 360-metered step bridge, a round altar previously used for sacrifice to ensure a good harvest, the music training centre and Nine Dragon Tree which as the name suggests is a tree where the bark has naturally formed to look like dragons. Also, the local residents and other patrons used these grounds; not only for prayer but to perform classical Chinese song and dance, play games, practice Tai chi and exercise; where watching the elderly folk do aerobics, creating some crazy dance moves to music that was pretty much hardcore drum and base, was all very interesting and surreal to witness.

With all these distractions, I found myself not paying much attention to things around me and lucky I didn't end up dead or worse. While walking backwards to take a photo, something stopped me and I dropped my camera, which sent the batteries scattering everywhere and me wobbling backward with my arms outstretched, frantically trying to regain balance. Looking behind offered sharp realisation of how lucky I was. Much like when kids crouch behind an unwitting subject and another then pushes them, I had walked backwards into a wall which was at best only 2ft high but in this case, then offered a 30ft drop on the other side straight down into a dried-up moat; with no guard rail. Put simply, I crapped myself and scurried away to safety while casually reminding myself to be a little more careful.

Temples started to consume large parts of my time; and included Taoism and Confucianism, two of the main religions in Chinese society. I had heard much about the sage Confucius born some 2500 years ago, and was keen to learn some of the teachings or at least about the man himself. The temple was small in comparison to the ever-growing list of temples, but still as beautiful and maintained as any other but serenely calm and tranquil, with a fabulous white statue of Confucius himself adorning the middle of the courtyard. Information quarters provided insights into the teachings, wisdom and life of the man in abundance and I spent much time revering in the information, so much so that I bought a book to take with me from the gift shop, a place I would normally avoid like the plague.

In the Taoist White Clouds Temple, where Ying and Yang teachings come from, the first thing I realised was that I'd forgotten my camera (this would be another first, but certainly not the last). In temples though, and in prayer rooms in particular, it is forbidden to take photos and there were lots of no photography signs around this small, beautiful little temple in particular. I liked the idea of respecting this value, being a foreign man in foreign land, and would hate to cause any offence. Frustratingly though, other visitors happily chose to ignore all this and snapped away. It didn't take long to negotiate my way around the maze of rooms, doorways and corridors, all the time with the fragrant incense burning like at the other temples as a mean of offering by worshippers. After an hour or so and making a donation, I took some of the free literature of the teachings on offer, having the brilliant idea of ensuring they were the ones in English text. Tying up the loose ends in Beijing, I visited the natural history museum, with amazing exhibits of dinosaur bones including the tyrannosaurus rex, diplodocus and triceratops. Knowing that my four-year-old nephew would appreciate them, I took plenty of pictures and marvelled at the excellent exhibits of human evolution, sea life, insects and modern-day mammals.

Obviously coupled in with the day events, a few nights were on the lash. I discovered China's passion for football via the modem of your 'traditional Chinese' Irish pub; why wouldn't there be an Irish bar in the middle of Beijing? English Premier League football was playing and part of the huge football culture growing in China which offered a surprising and unexpected bonus; being able to sit and watch untelevised games from back home at an ungodly hour on the other side of the planet. Made even better by ending up talking to some random bloke who happened to work for a betting company in the UK and he was getting the drinks in having an expense account, which, let's face it, was a blessing and opportunity all rolled into one. Figuring that they owed me for all the money I'd 'invested' with them previously over the years, they wouldn't begrudge me the odd beer or six.

Finishing off, I explored a few random sights of the local area, savouring sculptures and other pieces of art littered around the city, visited the impressive Olympic Park with the Bird's Nest stadium and hypnotically beautiful chameleon that was the swimming venue. Unfortunately, security was tight and it wasn't possible to enter the park without a valid event ticket, and of course the events had ended and was a couple of weeks till the Paralympic Games would start, so had to make do with seeing these only from one particular place outside but were architecturally impressive nevertheless. Besides I had already found my personal favourite venue. It had shocked me to see it in Beijing; in all its glory, a 'traditional Chinese' kebab shop. They were delicious and while I was in town, their business was booming!

Time had inevitably ebbed away and I'd been in Beijing for just over a week so decided to move on. While planning pre-departure, my visa restricted me to only a certain amount of time in China. I'd already decided that my next port of call would be Shanghai, and with no reason to change I asked the lovely ladies behind the tour desk in the hostel to help organise my train journey. So with my new books of Taoism and *Analects of Confucius* to read up on whilst on the move, I packed and was all set for the off.

Joe Shmoes Apartment and the Chinese Mystery Tour

Arriving in Shanghai early, the sun was already blazing, creating a build-up of hot city heat that didn't perturb the locals already avidly bustling around. This really didn't help my state having been on the night train for the best part of twelve hours, and accumulating all of about two-and-a-half hours' sleep. It's not that the sleeper train was bad, cold or uncomfortable, far from it. It was clean, nice, ambient temperature, good food, friendly staff even the Chinese guy sharing the cabin spoke a little English and was kind enough to help me with drinks from the cart. The problem was, even though shattered, I simply couldn't sleep with the rocking of the carriage as we sped south throughout the night. Not being a veteran of this travelling lark and the fun it can entail, I was still well and truly acclimatised to getting some shut eye in stationary means, rather than in a bed that was wobbling all over the place. During the journey, I found myself listening to music, singing 'Night Train' over and over again in the dark and when the urge grasped me, I would get up to have a cigarette by the end doorway in the corridor. With time on my hands and cheap cigarettes at my disposal (within days of setting off from Britain, I started smoking again) coupled with having a bout of insomnia, nothing it would seem could put this bird to rest.

So I was again tired, irritable and not in the best mind-frame to take a taxi in a new metropolis at seven a.m. in the morning. A prime candidate for being ripped off which was precisely what happened. Rationalising it was my own fault, as I could have argued and bartered with the driver as these things were going to happen with a constant inevitability. I knew fine well to be wary, but fatigue disrupted any thought processes and it was actually only a relatively cheap fare, so being overjoyed at the prospects of bed and some sleep, I quickly put this trauma behind me.

After a snooze and some rest at the hostel by midday, I set about finding my bearings by negotiating the subway. Unlike the Olympic-inspired Beijing system, here there were different price tariffs for length of journey, stops required and machines, of course, all in Chinese. But what was becoming apparent was how friendly and helpful the Chinese people were, rendering negotiating the public transport issue null and void, as the staff in the station were only too gracious in offering a helping hand.

When I emerged from the underground station, my eyes were awash with green of the trees, grass and shrubbery at People's Park. This was only a momentary vision, as instantly beyond the flora everywhere you looked there was the ominous surroundings of massive looming grey skyscrapers and could not mistake the hustle and bustle of a city like Shanghai. Using my trusty compass I acquired from a Christmas cracker of all places, I fathomed the direction needed to get to the Huangpu River. Not before stopping off and sampling a 'traditional Chinese' McDonalds. At the fear of being called a heathen, in my defence going was still soft and I was still slowly adjusting foreign foods and I really needed variety in my diet. Unfortunately, this involved shitty western food so make no apologies for this. And besides; I got chatting to a pleasant enough bloke from near San Diego in the USA. We talked about the usual stuff; why you here, what you do, families, music and gave me his card to look him up when I got to the States. I thought it was a really nice and obliging gesture, making friends and contacts a vital part of the travellers' mantra.

Along the river front is The Bund where there are old-style buildings and architecture, not in the traditional Chinese sense, but much more that of a western flavour from a previous era when many countries used Shanghai as trading outpost, they looked a grandiose in design and could have been plucked straight from London, Paris and many other European cities for that matter. The Bund on one side had plush hotels and luxurious shops where the rich and affluent could eat, play and relax; the other was riverside promenade which harboured street stalls, vendors, performers and any amounts of people posing or taking photos, capturing the back drop of mighty, modern skyscrapers reaching majestically to the heavens on the opposite side of the river with scant all else to blot the view.

Walking the streets, I instantly noticed the massive change in Shanghai to Beijing. There were so many more people selling things from makeshift stalls; items ranged from bags to t-shirts to DVDs and even massages. Beggars, many of whom were amputees, were now in abundance here. The con was on with people who approach you claiming to want to learn English or show you some art, and then head to a really expensive tea shop, whereby

31

the unsuspecting victim is landed with an extortionate bill. But from what others had said and reading up on this, I was prepared. All these seemed to come from nowhere to hassle people relentlessly. I'd learnt 'bo shi' or 'no thanks' early on and it came in handy; quite a lot. The traffic was maniacal mayhem and made for real-life game of *Frogger* when crossing the multi-lane streets, and the danger wasn't just confined to the road, as I saw motorbikes frequent the pavement at times during rush hour to hasten their journey, scattering and scaring the shit out of pedestrians waiting to cross at junctions. The smog was terrible and it felt like it permanently brazed the lungs with every breath and visible rubbish littered seemingly everywhere.

As I suspected, with the eyes of the world firmly focused on Beijing due to the Olympics, everything about it was a little too contrived, a fraction too perfect and somewhat too nice, for such a big city with massive population. The amount of cars was cut in half by using odd-and even-numbered registration plates on alternate dates, not that you would notice as the traffic was still chaotic when negotiating crossing the road and just as perilous as in Shanghai, so couldn't even imagine what it would be like on an average day. Even 'Olympic lane only' on the highways suggested how busy the roads still were, to ensure that the competitors got to venues in time hassle-free. Streets were clean and devoid of rubbish and the people there only seemed to be tourists or those who worked in the city. Slightly odd considering that many of the factories within and around Beijing were forcibly closed, a measure along with the traffic restrictions to cut omissions and help keep the air clean as possible for the duration of the games. There were walls in various parts of the city with ornate decorations in the traditional manner which looked really pretty and well kept, possibly too well kept. It was obvious they were new, with fresh grey paint and no wear and tear. I'd peered through a small doorway and behind harboured flimsy shacks and dwellings of the shanties and slums of Beijing's most impoverished residence. The walls keeping the residents and their plight out of direct eye contact of spectators, tourists and revellers, who through no fault of their own, might it seem offend the guests and highlight the less than satisfactory living and sanitation conditions they had to endure. This would, therefore, inevitably cause much embarrassment for the authorities and their keeping up appearances. There were no beggars, no homeless, no abundance of vendors and a lot less con artists trying to liberate tourists from their Yuan. Not to mention the Olympic Park venue, itself apparently built on land reclaimed from those who lived in a shanty town and had to be relocated to other parts of Beijing or even other parts of the country. One of these places was, I suspect, Shanghai. This place seemed to have the poor, impoverished, amputees, beggars, thieves, con artists, trash, traffic and pollution all in abundance and very obvious, as it was impossible to keep them all hidden behind a newly built freshly painted wall.

It may seem more daunting and a grimly painted picture what was happening with the folks of Shanghai, but that's how it was. I thought I got more of an accurate impression of what a Chinese city would normally be like here, and honestly what I'd actually expected. I got pestered and hassled, sure. But these were poor people, looking for an opportunity for quick money; it was nothing that I hadn't experienced before visiting other nations different to my own and nothing which I personally felt I couldn't handle through being aware, learning a few native words and being polite. Saying that, it didn't help venturing outside wearing a football shirt which, not thinking about it meant I would receive lots of attention. Even though I never realised my team were so popular in this part of the world. Fact is, they are not, and it took a while for the penny to drop. The reason for my new-found fame and attention came from the sponsor having numbers 888 embossed on the front; and in China, these particular numbers are very lucky. So as far as any person on the streets of Shanghai that day were concerned, I was 'Emperor Prosperous', from the planet 'Moneymundo'.

At the river, I decided to partake in one of Shanghai's more out their attractions; the tourist tunnel that runs beneath the river, as a way of getting from one side to the other. Whoever designed this went in my opinion above and beyond expectations of what was required, as I can only assume they decided to drop some acid at the same time. Standing in a closed electric cart, I was transported at approximately 10mph under the river, to wonder at all the eclectic and psychedelic images on the walls, glare at the crazy trippy neon lights and bewilder at the day glow, blown-up wavy hand men in the middle of the track that the cart drove over. Strangely though, it was as random as it was cool and I thought that it was over way too soon, leaving me slightly disappointed when the uniquely surreal journey ended.

Stopping on the other side of the river at Pudong provided the opportunity to visit the various attractions there. Primarily, I wanted to head up to the brand new Shanghai World Financial Centre observatory. Only recently opened and shaped like a huge bottle opener, this was now the tallest skyscraper in Asia at just under a whopping 500m in height. Unmissable and, when approaching, its size and grandeur could truly be appreciated, this was only bettered when looking up from the foot of the building to be dwarfed by its shimmering enormity. The queue for the top was really big; fortunately for some, though, this wasn't a problem as they just pushed in, but with my quintessential British penchant for queuing in an orderly fashion, I waited. Entering the express elevator, we were treated to a countdown of how long to reach the top via a massive digital display in the ceiling. Accelerating at vast speed, we soon reached the three viewing platforms at the top and a real tourist trap, especially looking down through the glass floors to the microbial people on the ground, slowly edging about their day-to-day business. Certainly, the view was incredible and provided great scope of the city and surrounding areas, the day itself was clear and sunny, so I was left slightly disappointed by the fact that the smog blotted out the horizon between city, land and sky. Later, I heard an interesting story about the building. Apparently, the hole somewhat resembling a bottle opener fashioned into the architecture wasn't always that shape; originally, it was circular, but this was swiftly changed due to the fact that it could resemble the Japanese flag, a design simply not acceptable around these parts.

Returning back to earth, I ventured to the nearby aquarium to see the piscatorial inhabitants inside; having a fondness for nature trying to take as many opportunities as possible to learn about and see them. The sharks were impressive, and I managed to get some decent photos. Likewise with the massive electric eels which were over 6ft in length and writhed around menacingly within their darkened enclosure; less menacing were the tortoises, amid peering curiously at the more tame sea horses, crustaceans and gastropods to make a really interesting afternoon. Sadly though, some other patrons would lose the ability to read again and put their hands in the water when clearly signed not to. I found this quite brave, especially as the alligators, salamanders and catfish were being fed by their keepers via tongs and a very long pole. I'm assuming there was good reason for this.

The evenings were warm and humid; I spent them out and about around the city with guys from the hostel. Surprisingly, this time Chinese food was on the agenda, with very tasty menus. Most places offered cheap dishes for a bargain price of about £1 for a set meal. Heading down to the river front, we had a few cheeky beers while taking in the dazzling lights of the buildings and the neon advertising banners of the passing boats on the river. I started planning where I wanted to head to next, my guidebook had all but expired as it only covered Beijing and Shanghai, and still be left with about two weeks of my visa left in China. Having talked to other people, it became apparent that Hong Kong, where I was flying out from, would be expensive in comparison and only take about four days to do everything. It would be a shame to waste the opportunity of exploring more of China while I had the chance. So hopping on the Internet, I searched for options. Looking at Nanjing, Xian, Cheng du and Guilin, this would mean moving inland and arching south to Hong Kong. These places offered beautiful scenery, wildlife parks and the chance to see the terracotta army, albeit informed that the view of the sculpted warriors wasn't very good and the majority were in various exhibitions around the world.

Pondering my next move, I went to the park again where lots of others had the same idea; why wouldn't they? Beautiful green scenery amid concrete chaos, the various art works included multi-coloured ants crawling over one of the buildings, the lotus pond, the people fishing using bamboo and line and the complimentary view of locals exercising provided plenty to take in, whilst strolling and relaxing for a couple of hours amid seemingly the only oasis of serenity in the middle of a hectic city.

Despite the hustle and bustle, Shanghai offered some really beautiful spots, like the aforementioned but no more so than the Yu Gardens. Only two trains away on the subway and a couple of blocks' stroll, it was instantly recognisable while approaching. The buildings had changed to only two- or three-storey high and certainly weren't grey or dull. Intricately detailed, colourful, decorated with fabulous Chinese design and patterns, reminiscent of what you would expect to find in a vision of an authentic Chinese town. Within these buildings, there were restaurants and shops offering gifts, textiles, arts and crafts to name but a few. Inside was where I wanted to be, because within the facade of the shopping area lay the actual gardens. A beautifully decorated maze of archways, pristine trees and flowers, walkways and bridges, huge ponds full of fish swimming amiably with the cohabiting turtles and hollowed out rock formations that could be walked through cutting passages unknown where you may end up. Within, revellers peacefully ambled, artists showed exhibits and delicately painted small demijohn bottles using a flexed brush on the inside, without a scam artist in sight and not wanting to miss out on the full cultural experience, I grasped the opportunity to get dressed up in an emperor's regalia of sequined pants, tabard and hat before having my photo professionally taken within the beautiful backdrop.

Returning, I started negotiating the streets back to the subway. As I did, the heavens darkened ominously and within a moment small fragmented rain droplets turned into the mother of all downpours. The warm torrent top trumped the stifling humidity and I was refreshingly saturated. The more sensible and practical-minded locals scattered for cover and looked on at me in bemusement. I wasn't bothered by all the curious stares, which after leaving tourist-laden Beijing was happening more and more. Understandable, I suppose, as not every day the local folk would come across a hefty, white, bald westerner with a strange English accent completely piss wet through and happy about it. I was having a blast, doing what I wanted, seeing cool new things, in places I had never been before. Life indeed was good. How good? My new roommate in the dorm couldn't put me down, even if he was a big fat cockroach, with antennas that twitched frantically amid scurrying in between the walls and furniture. So much so that early one morning, I didn't need my alarm as I was woken by a loud commotion from across the room with one of the others jumping out of bed and screaming about having one of the cheeky *cucarachas* spooning them. I laughed at their plight because, well, it wasn't me, and put it down to an occupational hazard of travelling – after checking my bed first.

I finally arranged my next destination; having talked to people in the hostel and completely confusing the tour desk manager, I'd decided on a place called Yangshuo. The other places weren't really enticing me. There was stuff to do in these places, but it would mean lots of travelling in the space of less than two weeks and leaving immediately. Besides, Yangshuo was a small but tourist town, which having been informed was picturesque, beautiful and with ample things to do there and that pretty much sealed the deal. I was ready to get out of the big cities. Half of the battle or fun with the tour desk in the hostel was communication, the lovely friendly staff spoke good but broken English, which had to be commended as opposed to my smashed to smithereens Chinese. 'Stewart', the operator's adopted English name, did a great job helping me out and I was really grateful. To fill in the rest of my time in Shanghai, I wanted to do and see something different, so decided on a daytrip to Hangzhou.

It was another six a.m. start. People coming and going from the room and the light constantly being turned on ensured that I never nodded off till about four a.m. again, and ushered in another poor night's sleep. More unfortunate, though, was the annoying swollen gland I had acquired in the right side of my jaw. I had managed to sort out the electrical plug adapter conundrum; it turned out that I was just being thick and not pushing it in the wall properly so now I had charged up my phone for the alarm to go off. The day was absolutely miserable, wet and grey and offered a little bit of Britain in an otherwise new and foreign land. Pick up arrived and took me to a hotel. Where? I don't have a clue, but it was in the middle of Shanghai somewhere that seemed to be further into the suburbs as buildings around seemed a little more dilapidated than the ones I was more familiar with. I stood around outside to wait for the others. When everyone else arrived, one thing became apparent. I was the only English-speaking person on this tour.

OK, no problem, I thought. *I can handle this.* Then another thing became apparent. This statistic also included the guide. *Right, this is going to go one of two ways,* I thought. But I figured, *Well, I'm here now; if I wanted an adventure where anything could happen, then this is it.*

Setting off, I quickly started feeling really sleepy, due to the lack of, and I nodded off with my head tucked towards my left shoulder, bouncing rhythmically against the cold window. This was short-lived as soon as leaving the city because I was woken by an unrecognisable loud din, to which I jumped in response with a 'What the fuck is that?' – Not immediately recognising the noise as foreign language; a very loud foreign language. At an educated guess, probably Chinese; from the guide talking elaborately to the rest of the bus, over an exceptionally loud PA system, with what I can only assume was the day's activities and itinerary. Sitting there with a 'Please be quiet' look adorning my dreary face, I swiftly became disenchanted as he talked endlessly for ages, wowing his otherwise literally captive audience. He abruptly stopped and I was quietly relieved at the ensuing hush, as the microphone broke and relative silence ebbed from the struggling speakers.

Sit back, relax, listen to a few tunes, take in the green, yet grey, clouded countryside scenery through the water sprayed windows, and hopefully maybe nod off again, I thought. Our undeterred guide though had other ideas; almost immediately realising the microphone was kaput beyond repair, he swiftly proceeded to whip out a standby 'just in case the mic breaks' megaphone as if he knew this would happen and carried on whaling loudly as the focus of attention. A mad man with the sole aim of destroying any peace and quiet; and he was successful.

On arrival, a really sweet couple called Cliff and Clarissa took pity on me or also liked a challenge and started speaking to me in English. Turns out, they were on holiday from San Francisco. I had visited there before and stayed near China town where they lived, so quickly found common ground. This was really cool, as they explained what some of the guide was saying, and things which were happening. I thought it was a kind gesture and was thankful for their help.

Hangzhou is again another big city and from the brief journey through the centre, what I saw left me quite uninspired, but why we were there does adorn 5Y Chinese bank note. This was the hugely impressive and picturesque West Lake. Donning my 'lucky' number of '88', we were herded like cattle on to one of the boats and took off for a tour around the massive lake; taking snapshots aplenty of the various monuments, boats, wildlife and features surrounding the glass-like water. Despite me not really knowing what many of the features were, I didn't mind. Even with the rubbish weather, this couldn't spoil the beauty within, appreciated as natural scenic treasure the nation was obviously proud of and on a glorious day, I could imagine this would be a highlight being around such an amazingly tranquil and serene setting.

Getting back on our bus, we ventured to the temple of warriors; where stone-carved statues honour warriors gone by, all lined up as if still in regimented formation, protected and hidden by green tree foliage. Then we stopped at a small silk factory. I had seen something similar on previous trips to the Far East and suspected it was more of a shopping exercise for those on the tour, brought there by the tour operator in co-operation with the manufacturers and similarly when visiting a traditional tea factory. Again, I didn't understand a thing, as it mostly involved the host lecturing for what seemed ages about history, where various teas were from and the processes involved. I was obviously briefed afterwards. Being a true Brit, though, while there I made sure I didn't miss out on having a nice cuppa.

By this point, I could hardly remember where we had been and still not a clue as to what was happening or where we would end up next. The tour just seemed to go on relentless, as we scoured the Chinese countryside, making stop after stop as the operators crammed in as much as possible. A visit to Buddhist monastery was actually very impressive. Surrounded by lush green vegetation and scaling the stairs up the hill side, there was temple after temple, one of which featured a huge 50ft wall that had amazingly detailed effigies engraved, but again had to refrain from taking photographs within. This was another very popular stop with many people visiting, paying respects, praying and making offerings of burning incense. Getting dark, our bus tour finally ended up at Good Luck Park. Figuring in for a penny, in for a pound, or a Yuan in this case, I would need some good luck if I was going to get through my travels unscathed, so made monetary offering into in the fountain, and with hindsight of what was ahead this could prove to be a more than worthwhile investment, before we departed back to Shanghai.

On reflection, I enjoyed the tranquillity of the lakes and temples, yet not all the itinerary was to my taste and could quite easily not have visited the silk or tea factory. Not only because I struggled to understand pretty much everything that was said, as these features were detailed with lots of elaborate chatter, but even if this were in English, they just aren't my cup of tea (sorry). I figured this was going to happen as I travelled in a somewhat haphazard fashion. Some things were not going to suit but I rationalised this would just have to form part of the experience.

Weirdly, this also proved to be one of the best features of the day. The fact that everything was in Chinese, I didn't have a clue where we were going, how long we were staying, when we were leaving or what was next, but did get the pleasure of witnessing some really beautiful scenery and interesting places. After the lake had finished, I stopped caring and just went with whatever was going on; as I didn't have much choice. It was very surreal but really liberating all the same. Being the only non-Chinese-speaking person there, I just sort of made my own exploratory itinerary up. Some of the others would translate where we were and what time to be back, making sure I understood what the guide meant by pointing to a time on his watch and then the bus. This was when I found out I had to be back ten minutes before anyone else did. Probably because this allowed time to compensate for the guideless idiot wandering around looking a bit perplexed. The rest of the Chinese-speaking contingency on the bus though this was hilarious. As the day progressed just trying to have some fun, going with the flow and being unfazed with what was happening or where we would end up, the other tourists on the bus became very responsive to this so we talked in broken English and shared cigarettes together while having a good time. All the while, they would chuckle at my plight. I didn't mind; it was a truly unique day which left me overall richer for the sights, being with others on the tour and was glad that I went, if only for the experience that helped prove the analogy; it's not where you are, it's who you're with.

Back at the hostel in Shanghai when I told the guys over a few beers, they were all pissing themselves laughing about what happened, as it turned out I was not the first for this to happen to and got the impression certainly wouldn't be the last.

By this point, I had started meeting loads of cool people and really enjoying my time here. But I lost my camera with all my photos on it. I was gutted and began to frantically recourse my brain as to where it could be. I noticed it missing while out and about with Gareth, a mate I had made from the hostel; we were in a shopping mall and belting out some impromptu 'Over the Hills and Far Away' when he was messing about with a guitar in a music store and I wanted to take a picture. I last remembered seeing it next to the computers in the hostel and hoped no one had picked it up and taken it. Returning, I hastily scoured the computer area; nothing. So I enquired hopefully at reception. A couple of moments later, the staff returned and handed me my camera. Luckily, some honest sort had found it and handed in. I was both relieved and ecstatic at the same time. A wonderful feeling and was really thankful for the honesty and integrity of that person. A couple of celebratory Tsinsyang beers were in order to honour that kind soul, and for a 42p litre bottle the absolute value for money beer was worth celebrating alone, but it tasted even sweeter due to the fortune of my returned camera.

It was great meeting Gareth; he was over there hoping to carve out a career teaching English. We chatted about our respective countries of Britain and America, music, getting older and found out that we were both conspiracy theorists. We both liked them; not because we believed them but more so because of the thought process of 'what if' and thinking outside the box no matter how plausible, outlandish, outrageous, ridiculous or hilarious; 'cos let's face it, with many a conspiracy theory they say more about the people accepting them; both as a truth and spreading as fact rather than the actual conspiracy themselves, especially when claims are usually backed up with zero or completely false evidence. Still, one conversation we had resonated more than any other, because at the time I never once suspected the subject would come back to bite me on the arse and certainly not so quickly.

The Smogless Monster

I left Shanghai the next day again on the night train to Yangshuo, one hour outside the city of Guilin. If someone had asked me to point out on a map where exactly I was going, I wouldn't have a clue. Well, not exactly anyway. The general extent of my knowledge being I was heading in a bit and south a lot. This was a brilliant feeling, true freedom; visiting somewhere I really knew nothing about, sans guidebook, having only a few titbits of information from the tourist desk and Internet, that served up a more tantalising opportunity of excitement, adventure and exploration; let loose from the conventionality of making and adhering to an itinerary, and switching to a lesser known, therefore more intriguing and enticing plan. I was happy about leaving the dirty atmosphere of high-rise urban sprawl and being treated to fresh air, mountains, rivers and green scenery. I also had been told about a little place called Shangri-La. If a mythical place wasn't worth a visit, then I didn't know what was. Heaven on Earth? Yeah? Let's go.

I arrived in Guilin having spent twenty-three hours on a train, to then spend a further one-and-a-half hours on a bus to get to Yangshuo. The train journey proved to be an interesting affair as it ambled slowly throughout the night in its more aged state, much less modern than its Beijing-Shanghai counterpart. The sleeper cabin had four beds and when we set off, two were occupied; one by a nice German fellow, the other by myself. A few stops later, we inherited a couple of Chinese girls in the cabin, who were all curiosity and giggles amid their new foreign roommates and chatted excitedly between themselves, not speaking any of our European dialects; so Marcel Marceau-esque sign language became a productive way of trying to break this barrier. Unfortunately, for me and more appropriately everyone else, for some reason I was farting like it was my job and being in a confined space wasn't the best. So I tried not to make any embarrassing inappropriate noises or smells, while attempting to stifle my flatulent gut. I couldn't help but laugh because at least farting was now an option. A week or so ago, I wouldn't have dared.

Eventually, everyone fell asleep. This was short-lived as we were woken in the night by another passenger wanting a bed. After it was explained they were all taken, he left with no problems. Two minutes later, the door was abruptly flung open again, only this time with an authoritative figure sternly putting the light on and checking our tickets. Waking the two girls, it became apparent that they didn't have these and they were chased out. Cheekily, they had decided to give themselves a free upgrade, so they left quite hurriedly and as one jumped down off the bunk, she managed to drag her large bag with her; which whacked her across the head and nearly knocked her over. I laughed as karma's comical chaos seemed to tell her she maybe shouldn't have done that. Lights off; everything then settled down for all of five minutes, till the guard again burst the door open and shone the light in our faces. An obvious gesture to make sure we weren't shacked up with the two freeloaders, and ensure that everything was in order, probably so he also could get his full quota of sleep on the train. No harm was done and I actually felt rather sorry for the bloke we originally chased as it wasn't his fault, and more so in the morning as he was really nice, sharing his biscuits with us for breakfast – not to mention the carriage reeking of my stale guff.

Getting in to Yangshuo, I had a really good vibe about the place, liking it immediately as one of the local entrepreneurs virtually dragged me inside his bar to have a beer. I only had one as not to seem rude but was tired, so departed swiftly to find my hostel. Approaching early evening, I headed out in to the town. The town centre was really ornately beautiful and offered truer Chinese decor a person would expect and want to see, something that seemed to be lost in the big cities. Wandering round the cobbled streets, there were hanging lanterns, bicycles strewn everywhere and lots of differently styled arched bridges with the central part decorated elaborately, again, barricaded off from meandering mortal feet. These crossed a network of streams to link various shops, bars and restaurants, plus every other establishment seemed to be a tour operator offering various activities, excursions, shows and travel tickets. With the pretty ambient setting and catalogue of things to do; there and then I decided to stick around longer than planned, not that I knew exactly what the plan actually was. Wandering, I met a girl called 'Nina' – now; I'm not that lucky so, yes, she was a guide for her own personal tours, hoping I'd book one of the trips she showed me. Granted the testimonies were glowing but they could've been written by her grandma for all I knew.

Already having an idea of the activities I wanted to do, I sharp came to the realisation I could do these without a guide and for less expense. So I wasn't overly keen with her business pitch. But we chatted and headed down to the river for a drink, eventually exchanging contacts. By now feeling hungry, I went for a dinner. Randomly, whilst eating, two Chinese girls approached me and asked if they could join me. This time, they just wanted to practice their English. Due to the situation, I saw no harm and duly obliged. They were very nice and sweet university students, we chatted about our respective countries and one thing we had in common was how proud we were about our countries' achievements at the games. Great Britain had also exceeded their medal haul expectations, and left the nation and myself very proud. Understandably, this was hot topic of the moment. They also stated how they would love to visit UK someday and learning to speak English was regarded as a strong vocation for a Chinese person. This was really endearing to me, others willing to put in the effort, better themselves and accommodate those of different language and culture; wanting to experience this myself.

The following day, I decided to explore the surroundings, but for a change I chose a bicycle; this being the obvious mode of transport around these parts. The mid-morning sun was already high and blazed away any cloud cover, creating an intense heat. Arming myself with a map of the area and various trails, I headed out. As picturesque as the town centre was, the more modern outskirts were less appealing; fortunately, this lasted only for the main road bypassing the town. It only took five minutes before the countryside opened up offering flat field plains wonderfully interrupted by huge conical pinnacles; unique, grandiose and spectacular. Daubed in vegetation, they randomly towered from the ironed flat, lush landscape. Having visited Vietnam some years earlier the remarkable resemblance to those in Ha Long Bay surely wasn't coincidental.

I decided to head up to the small town of Baisha; approximately 10km north-west from Yangshuo. Not that interested in the town itself but the beautifully scenic Dragon Bridge that spanned the Yulong River close by. Passing through the old stonework village; roads turned into dusty tracks and homes were single storey and basic, chickens ran around with aimless urgency, scavenging dogs roamed and the rural folk quietly shuffled about their business. The very old stone humpbacked bridge was really picturesque. Entwined with age-long foliage, the brilliant sunshine and gentle babbling sound of running water encapsulated its peaceful serenity. Taking in the moment, I proceeded to wheel the bike over the bridge. But when making the descent on the far side, with graceful elegance, I slipped flat on my arse sending the bike clattering further down the old stone arched bridge steps that had been worn smooth over the ages and the cause of my bruising encounter. This was all very much to the amusement of the locals who were already watching with avid curiosity. With only my ego damaged, I picked myself and the bike up, dusted myself down and walked past them; with a subtly embarrassed laugh, I offered a polite "*nee how*". And off I went along another trail further up the river.

Unfortunately, this incident wasn't exactly the end of my troubles. Some thirty minutes later, my excursion was abruptly cut short; the gear cable slipped and the chain jammed. Covering myself in oil, I could only manage to get the bike into a low-speed gear and was left unconvinced about its ability to maintain this, or cover the distance back. Not to mention, the main road used to get there was maniacal mayhem with speeding traffic. So, I forged a cunning plan. Arriving back at Baisha, the villagers by the bridge had previously offered 20ft twined bamboo raft ride, down the river back to Yangshuo for 150 Yuan. A brilliant absolutely fool-proof solution. Now though, the price of taking a raft had rocketed to 210 Yuan; unsurprising as I was obviously riding with some trepidation and the owner figured I was tired on my return. I only had 149 Yuan. But fortunately for me, he wasn't going to miss out on making easy money and this was graciously accepted, so throwing the bike on the back of the raft, we set sail.

The trip back was awesome. Sat in the middle on a wicker chair, sun out, top off, lazily watching the fabulous scenery drift by. Large green reeds and trees adorned the banks which occasionally masked the afternoon sun that was still high, bathing the perfect mountains and scenery in its delicious luminescence. While children played in the river, local men and local kingfishers both vied for the same elusive underwater fishing spoils and these offered ample opportunities for photos, which also included the numerous and varying cascades we had to negotiate over; one I was pre-warned about by my gondola-like captain, who was pushing us along from the stern. I held my chair, my breath and lifted my feet as the front of the cumbersome floating craft plunged down, front first, five feet over the waterfall into the river below. Almost instantly, as if by magic, the super buoyant bamboo craft popped straight back up out of the water, as the rear followed suit, slapping the surface as it too came over the edge before settling with ease gently back on the ambling river; offering the slowest of thrill rides. About forty-five minutes later, we arrived at the riverbank of a rural village close to town, I hopped off to be greeted by a local lady taking photos of my arrival; a lovely warm welcome. This was abruptly cut short though when the guide on the raft informed her, 'I wouldn't bother love, this guy is broke as a joke' or words to that effect anyway which dashed any hopes she had of making a sale. Despite my rubbish translation, this was after all true.

I was up spritely for breakfast and another impromptu English lesson with the staff at a local restaurant; and didn't feel too shabby considering I rewarded my previous day's endeavours with early evening-cum-late night social refreshments. In other words, I had a session on the piss with some Aussies from the hostel with a penchant for drinking games. The hostel provided the bikes free, so it wasn't an issue with the one that broke previously, being put down to wear and tear. So, the next day acquired an upgrade to another one that worked. Again, full of gusto, I set off. But this day was ominously different. Dark grey clouds on the horizon adorned the sky as a huge thunder storm rolled in and torrential rain started to belt down from above, scattering anyone silly enough to be outside into the sanctuary of shelter. Not me this time, having not gotten far; the impending downpour caused me to turn around and head back. The incredible thing was the ladies behind the front desk in the hostel were so apologetic. I couldn't believe it, apologising for the weather. At least five times. Eventually, I had to ask them to stop. It was very sweet of them, though; they wanted their guests to have a good time and enjoy themselves. And be able to do what they wanted to do. But it was hardly their fault. And really harsh to suggest otherwise as these things happen, I'm from Britain, I'm used to it, happens all the time. And at least the rain was warm here.

After some impressive flashes, loud bangs and rolls of thunder, I eventually headed out some two hours later and veered somewhat in the opposite direction from the previous day; due to my trusty map, I knew of plentiful attractions to visit. First stop was Butterfly Spring which had huge ornate model butterfly adorning the cave entrance, but with my agenda full

I refrained from going in and when the road crossed the river, I stopped to take in the scenery and watched the many bamboo rafts launching passengers and tourists on a tranquil saunter that I was now already an aficionado. Approximately 8km up the road was Moon Hill.

An obvious hill; much like any other, apart from it's almost perfectly triangular form and it has a massive hole in it that you can see through. I shit you not. Not peer through, but see through. Even from a far. After a thirty-minute climb, I reached the large distinctive opening. I had to take a breather not being fully acclimatised to what all this exercising and outdoor having fun business brings. My lungs heaved heavy from scaling the treacherously steep, moss-laden, slippery old steps that weaved amid the sticky engulfing forest. The sun had broken out and cleared the skies, without a breath in the air humidity had soared from the previous downpour and caused my skin and clothes to saturate with sweat. Within the middle, rock climbers were scaling the walls of the inner cavity, where it was possible to literally walk through the hill and see the view either side with a turn of the head which was (wait for it) 'holey' unique. I admired the beautiful vista. A sea of green interrupted by towering mountains washed over by brilliant blue. I decided against climbing to the very pinnacle where the mass of rock formed a beautiful archway; the previous storm had made the steep pathway incredibly muddy and slipping a certain formality. Also time was ticking so I needed to set off to reach the Silver Cave; the furthest attraction away was still on the same route, but the road now became more contoured as it wound up and down cutting through the lower land. I peddled hard, or so I thought and after around another 8km or so, I eventually arrived at the resort where it was located.

Finding the Silver Cave was tricky as the garden resort it resided in sprawled with lakes, pathways and random buildings. Other tourists seemed to be sparse and no one appeared to be working there so I wandered aimlessly, wasting time with not being able to fathom the signage. Finding the entrance and some soul to tell me the cost, time and that I had to be on a tour was another surprising arse on. But eventually, our group entered the caves and started ambling through a network of paths to view huge chambers of massive stalagmites, stalactites, mineralised pools, intricate rock patterns and images, somewhat artistically formed over hundreds and thousands of years. Incidentally – with stalagmites and stalactites, remembering which is easy – stalactites (tights as in pants) come down.

Being buried deep inside the mountain, the cave would be dark inside but all the features were wonderfully illuminated by large lighting cannons of differing colours to highlight the intricate detail of curves, points and shadows to enhance the beauty of the images. Again the tour was in Chinese and the batteries in my camera were fading fast. But these were the least of my worries.

The tour started at six p.m. finished at seven p.m., and was a guided tour for conservation, safety purposes and so the lights could be turned on at each individual part as patrons walked through and would subsequently turn off when done. This meant I couldn't go back and couldn't go on ahead. Not good; it would get dark about seven thirty p.m. This left roughly thirty minutes to cover around sixteen kilometres out in the Chinese countryside to get back to town and not being exactly a Tour de France competitor, I knew fine well that this was going to be impossible for me to do. Adding further to my woes, there seemed to be a severe lack of lights from all quarters and this was making me nervous.

Appreciating the caves as I was, this was playing on my mind. As soon as the exit was in sight, I cleared it with the guide and bolted, managing to leave about ten minutes earlier. Outside I jumped on the bike, headed for the exit and started peddling like Lance Armstrong on crack. Strangely, he could probably recommend something better. I needed to cover as much ground as possible before it turned completely dark, knowing fine well I was going to be on a busy road, in rural China, with only the moon as my lantern. At least I had time to get to get back to Moon Hill. I hoped. From there, it wouldn't be too bad. I hoped.

My legs thrashed at the pedals as my arms with steady determination controlled the bike, mind and eyes focused on the road and each individual imaginary check point that brought me that little bit closer to home. Lungs, arm and thigh muscles all ached, screamed and complained; tearing in constant pain at the relentless exertion, yet the headstrong mind ignored those whiny little bitches and continued unabated as my self-preservation instinct kicked in; the eyes glazed steely ahead and relayed a constant visual update of not only what was ahead, but also the light situation. The remaining light etched away and vision receded, eventually leaving me covered by the infinite darkness of a starry universe.

At this point, though, I had passed Moon Hill and was ahead of my own schedule, leaving me encouraged at the good pace I was setting.

Leaving me less encouraged was the fact that I was still about 6km away; no lights on the bike, no lights on the road and certainly no high-visibility attire. The only light I really did have were unfortunately attached to massive trucks, with blinding full beam hurtling towards me on the far side of the single carriage way; and tricked me into thinking I was going to be hit head-on. These were coupled with their opposite, that encroached from behind and usefully highlighted the side road markings only to dramatically disappear as the unabated and unconcerned wagons and their drivers roared past me blearing the horn to belatedly warn of their very obvious, imminent and dangerous presence; leaving behind a trailing gust of shitty swirling air that was difficult to deal with.

Also, just to make things that little bit trickier, people, dogs, chickens and cows all just seemed to find the need to wander out to the road the exact second I was due to pass like a celebratory welcoming party. No flags or fanfare; just curious stares. And if that weren't enough, thrown into the mêlée were endless potholes of the poorly maintained roads. Ever wary of these persistent annoyances, I only could really now use peripheral vision to pre-empt and avoid an accident. This ensured that physical exertion and concentration was immense and I just kept mentally encouraging and willing myself back. This was now one of the hardest bike rides I'd ever had to do and not because of the severity of the trail, but because of the mental anguish caused by the obstacle of things hellbent on making my journey that much harder and that much more perilous.

Eventually, I saw the faint glow of the town and after turning the slow right-hand final corner I had casually taken some six hours prior, a huge wave of relief and elation washed over me like the orange hue from the road lights that signalled civilisation and instantaneously brought me to a more relaxed, slower pace, to cool down and get back to the hostel. I was once again absolutely broken, my thighs smashed to the consistency of jelly and I sported the walk of a roughshod rodeo rider. At the hostel, I again gulped orange juice and water to help revitalise me. Checking the time, it was just past eight fifteen p.m. and I was shocked how fast I had managed to get back and smiled wryly to myself about the cool day I'd had, things I'd seen, the exercise and potential shit show scenario I had ended up in, dealt with and come through unscathed. Admittedly, the smile was mainly from relief but partly was because I felt proud at dealing with what happened and doing what needed to be done, but certainly partly was born out of the un-envisaged excitement of a nerving experience, that had the adrenaline flowing. When this subsided, I was tired so had to rest, yet still needed to eat. I'm not vegetarian but didn't feel the need for meat with dinner that evening; probably due to the ample protein fix I'd already had, from the shit load of unsuspecting insects I scoffed speeding along.

Exhilarated and aching after the previous day's escapades, I decided to dull it down a notch. After breakfast and another English lesson, I was ready. Well, sort of; as now I was virtually unable to walk, never mind cycle, so I headed to the bus station and set off passing Baisha Town up to the fabled Shangri-La resort. Entering the site, I was greeted with a huge lake, beautiful traditional oriental edifices and idyllic scenery that any artist would be enamoured to put on canvas. Straightaway, I was given my own personal English-speaking guide and we set off in a wooden carved boat around the resort. This was sweet; on the water, the resort was enshrouded by beautiful calm tranquillity of the flat yet mountainous scenery. It felt like this really was Shangri-La. We weaved through the waterways of the lake amid the reeds and rushes. It was possible to spot both local folk from the 650-year-old village and cormorants fishing, before we entered through to the Swallow Cave where I was instructed to make a wish and duly obliged. Slowly proceeding inside, the rock formations were nothing out of the ordinary except for a small outcropping which was remarkably like that of a swallow; incredibly easy to identify to justify the name. As we emerged from the other side, the guide informed me that we were entering where the tribal folk lived; not far away, people in loin cloths paraded and ignored our presence. Homes and other structures were manufactured from bamboo amid the trees and long grass; skulls of various livestock hung menacingly from posts. I was instructed to sit in the middle of the boat, when almost immediately one of the tribe members jumped out from the reeds and thrust a spear square at me. Again, I don't mind admitting that I crapped myself, wailed like a bitch at my impending impaling and nearly fell out of the boat. The captain and the guide laughed, as I once again proved good value entertainment for the Chinese.

We then headed back to the main part of the resort where some local folk made linen, clothes, ties, arts, trinkets and wooden carvings and my two left feet even managed to engage in a spot of traditional dancing. Afterwards, I was told to stand in the square outside the workshops that were built up two floors high, a girl had made a traditional good luck pendant of red and gold stitching; a detailed ball embroidered with tassels and was told if I caught it, it would bring good luck. From a balcony she then proceeded to spin the ball by the lace used from where it would be hung. Let go and it flew up and down pretty much straight into my open hands.

With my new good luck charm, I proceeded on my own to explore the gardens, taking in the exquisite ponds that brimmed with fish, as the wooden walkways weaved past, leading up to the printing and papermaking rooms before finishing viewing the astonishingly detailed intricate wood-carved statues of animals, people and mythical figures. I loved it here. So beautiful, peaceful and calm hidden away from the rigours of the modern world and fabulous to see rural people just going about their day-to-day business; although, I was a little unsure how traditionally tribal the people were, or were they just workers or actors? Still, a world away from the mad hustle, bustle and smog of Beijing and Shanghai.

Time pressing, I headed back to town on the local bus; this became a frightening affair only described as utter madness. The roadworks ahead on the left side had caused the majority of it to be coned off, and seemingly unregulated traffic now squeezed by on a narrowed road, directly ahead. An undeterred HGV truck driver bore head-on towards us on our side of the road and at an equally undeterred pace, our bus driver also continued unabated. Neither driver for some inexplicable reason wanted to relent or give way. Closer and closer; this continued until eyes agape, I held my breath in dumbstruck preparedness, the folks behind screamed out loud, equally as aware and to alert everyone to the inevitable impact from the heavy-duty game of chicken. After what must have been fractions of a second, we were left with complete relief and disbelief, as the road works ended on the opposite side allowing the HGV to veer back violently onto his side of the road as the two vehicles diverted from one another like similarly polarised magnets. Sitting shotgun to the driver, I had a front row seat to my own impending vision of death and this bullshit stunt team display which left me dumbfounded with the stupidity of these two clowns. The best they could muster to avoid a serious accident was to blaze horns at one another as the only possible solution. Personally, I thought the safer option was maybe to slow the fuck down? But what did I know? The best I had to offer was common sense. Which, unfortunately, is not very common sometimes. I don't like driving much. A person might be the best driver in the world. It means nothing if everyone else on the road is a complete fucking moron.

The less fraught light show that evening *Impression Liu Sanjie* was set under the cover of darkness on water from the river and used an illuminated mountain backdrop. Set to traditional Chinese music, the audience watched from purpose built stands within the auditorium as rafts, platforms and gangways were systematically put in place and removed for the dancers to perform on. Using stage props, massive lengths of linen, lights and fire both on and off the watery stage and on the costumes of the performers. A really surreal show unfolded, that unfortunately didn't last very long but did create a wondrous illusion of 'how?' I didn't care or try to fathom what was happening. I just sat back, relaxed, watched and enjoyed what could be done. This may not have been my type of thing but I did appreciate seeing something very novel, and have to admit it did look cool as the performers paraded away on a glistening, shimmering, moving viscous stage.

Legs having sufficiently recovered, I was now able to ride a bike again and lord don't slow me down, I was back on it cycling to the Mud Cave. Each day was now seamlessly offering me a new exciting story to enact. Leaving the bike locked at the office, the others visiting and I entered and were then ferried to the cave to get changed with many laughing at anyone trying the 'borrowed costumes'. Luckily, I had sanitary nuance to bring and wear my 'own' swim shorts, so was spared from sporting a horrendous pair of fluorescent budgie smugglers that left nothing to the imagination, let alone the amounts of unknown genitalia that had adorned them previously because, as the name 'Mud Cave' suggests, we were getting dirty. Donning safety hats, a small boat ferried us along a small shallow waterway into a low-lit cave. After disembarking a short walk took us to where the cavernous areas were huge and opened up exponentially; the low light created dark, shadowy, looming effects in contrast to the caves two days previous with no man-made trails or walkways guiding visitors.

Armed with torches on the hardhats, we each took steady, careful steps along a more natural route. Again, there were rock formations which had various names due to the effigy which they depicted; the cat, the butterfly to name but a few. Some obvious and easy to detect; others less so, like a Freudian psychoanalysis test installation. Better still, this was much more natural and eerie than the Silver Cave and it instantly endeared itself to me

51

being trickier to negotiate and also being a smaller group allowed more interactive experience with others. Working our way to the end, we were informed by the guide that we could now have a swim. Top pool was cold due to the water running from the cave roof and was only about a metre deep, but the bottom pool was about 3m deep and warm; heated by a natural gas source from below. A flat but coarse rock formed a ledge to launch in from. The guide was explaining where to jump.

"Be careful when jumping in that part because—"

Before he could finish, I was in. No messing about required not to mention listening. It was really warm and refreshing. Others quickly followed suit. We could clean down using the rushing torrent of a nearby waterfall, but this was kind of redundant as the whole reason to be in the caves were to sample the dirty rich mud pools.

Pressing on a little further toward the end, dripping mud from revellers had been splashed everywhere and created an incredibly slippery hazardous circus and those there couldn't get enough of it. Removing shirts, shoes and gingerly edging over to the not 2ft deep dirty pool, within seconds of entry, everyone was painted from head to toe in sloppy, gritty, brown mud and sludge and offered up the kind of performance to which any piggy would be proud. Hair, ears, nose were caked and it took me straight back to times when as a kid I got dirt in my mouth and tasted exactly the same. It was fucking awesome messing about like a three-year-old, rolling around in filth, chilling and floating on the density of the mud. A makeshift slide had even been formed; a bumpy groove worn into the hard dirt embankment seemingly carved over time by the arse cracks of previous revellers. Finishing; everyone cleaned down in the nearby showers. And the word 'cleaned' is used in the loose sense, because grit was lodged everywhere. I mean everywhere, especially where person really doesn't want grit. But those thirty minutes in the dirty bath had exfoliated, scrubbed and softened my skin to the touch and it felt amazing.

After the day's exploits, I fancied a beer so headed down to reception before heading out. From one minute minding my own business, suddenly I wasn't. An English lad at reception was trying to buy a beer but didn't have change and neither did reception. I'd been getting along well with the hostel staff and decided to butt in and said, "Let him have the beer and if he doesn't pay for it later, then charge me," which they were more than happy with. Having made our impromptu acquaintances, Mark was heading out and invited me along.

We walked straight ahead into the main part of town and stopped outside one of the numerous travel agents to talk to three girls who Mark seemed to know. He made the introductions; Karen, Jane and Chloe. As it turned out, they were all staying in the same dorm room in our hostel. He started talking to the first two who seemed really nice. Chloe blindsided the others from the rear and started chatting to me. She was really nice and friendly; had a beautiful smile and was very pretty.

Can't really remember what we were talking about, probably the usual bullshit; where you from? Where you been? What's good to visit or check out? Standard verses a traveller may engage in to form bonds or find information that may point towards another potential adventure. I was no different. I do remember laughing at the fact that they said they got lost walking around the centre of Yangshuo. Now I'm not saying this is difficult. Well, actually, I am. The place is tiny. You could burp at one end and hear it at the other. Luckily, they weren't offended by our ridicule of their rubbish navigating skills. We all decided to go for food and drinks that turned into bit of a pub crawl where we were eventually entertained by some random guy in a bar 'performing' an acoustic guitar set – who was completely wasted. I think it was meant to be serious, but for us, it only happened to be very funny as he could barely string two words together never mind chords. I couldn't tell you what time we rolled in, but it wasn't ridiculously late and I wasn't ridiculously drunk. But I did have a really good night out, Mark and the girls were lots of fun to be with. Tomorrow was the Mid-Autumn Moon Festival so we knew it was party central in town, and everyone wanted some shut eye and to get up and do some activities and prepare for a big night. Already starting to regale the new faces with my adventures I'd been up to while in town, the girls said that they would like to explore the area too and kindly asked if I'd like to join them on some bikes. I had pretty much visited where I wanted to go but heading out again with some company sounded nice. So that was a resounding "Yes".

The next day, the hostel staff were offering the chance to make Chinese food with them, have it cooked and everyone feast as an inclusive activity for all and sundry as a way of celebrating the festivities. This seemed an opportunity too good to miss; hanging with the locals, learning about the traditional cuisine and sampling it. All for the banqueting bargain of less than a British pound. So obviously didn't need too much coercing.

That was happening later that evening. So, as discussed, we ventured out on the bicycles. The girls had decided that they wanted to visit Moon Hill. Not overly confident on the bikes, especially in the town with the traffic speeding close by and pulling out at random, all with scant regard for anyone or anything, I offered a few handy hints; "Just concentrate and keep your eyes open, don't be afraid to shout and use the bell. It will probably stop you from dying!" Best pearls of wisdom I could come up with for a safety lecture. Déjà vu kicked in as we traversed where I seem to have been countless times already. We stopped at the bridge where the rafts were and took photos before carrying on and headed up to Moon Hill. I showed them where it was; although quite difficult to miss but the hand-drawn map was not exactly to ordinance survey standards of scale, and I was dealing with people who struggled with the few pedestrianised streets of Yangshuo. Having already conquered Moon Hill, I agreed to catch up with them later and set off on my own to explore the Dragon Cave.

The Dragon Cave was similar to the Silver Cave with subtly highlighted rock formations, but didn't need a guide for the tour and could meander around at my own pace, again a designated path guided my route and the smaller grounds from where it was situated were free to explore, incorporating water features, huge statues and icons. While leaving, although glad I went and did something and explored somewhere new, I felt I'd seen it before due to the similarity of the Silver Cave. Upon exiting, my bicycle had been well and truly lodged in by countless other bikes that had seemingly been just dumped randomly, creating an indecipherable mangle of metal; and after what took an age I managed to locate and free my chariot before I headed back to meeting up with the others and saunter back to town. On the ride back, Chloe and I chatted as we hung back from the other two. There seemed to be an instant rapport as we shared much in common with views on life, sense of humour, music, travel and our age; this surprised me most as I could have taken ten years off her easily. I figured she must have had an easy paper round.

One shit, shower, shave later, everyone met up in the reception ready for the Moon Festival. A holiday celebration second only to Chinese New Year, like thanksgiving for the harvests encourages families to get together for food and partying. We proceeded making some traditional style dumplings. Meat and vegetables pressed into pastry parcel and steamed. Mine weren't the exact works of art that the staff were creating and they thought that this was really funny, again not the first time I had amused my hosts with my prowess, or lack of, but I didn't care because I was ravenous and they were getting devoured regardless. There were some vegetables and fish stew on offer also so we gorged on the creations. The buffet was lovely and I really enjoyed and appreciated it having helped with the preparations. More so, it was equally as nice just to hang around and have drinks with the hostel staff, who were having a great time celebrating, showing guests their culture and actively encouraging everyone to get involved.

Later, we headed into the town where restaurants, bars and streets were packed full of people revelling in the festivities. We were in the right place at the right time for this event as many Chinese came here for the holidays. Drinks were flowing and the dance floor got a hammering. Eventually we ended up stumbling into a bar without the tourist hoard and only local clientele who made us feel really welcome despite getting quite late; supplying drinks and spicy noodles, amid more dodgy dancing. Chloe and I decided it would be a good idea to get on stage and mess about with the keyboards and microphones of the now departed band; like a poor man's Milli Vanilli (and that is poor!) trying to sync to some music we didn't know; not necessarily to anyone else's amusement but our own and only make the guy from the night before look legit. It was loads of fun hanging around with the inebriated locals; except when I went to the toilet to relieve myself and another came in and attempted to join in by crossing swords with me. And I don't mean he had a blade, which would've been a lot less threatening.

Daylight had started to dissolve our darkened frivolities before we all went to bed. The night was loads of drunken messing-about fun and I felt it later that morning when getting up to check out, so I went to my now seemingly favourite bar for breakfast noodles again; and once again help administer random English lessons. Returning to the hostel, I wasn't sure where the others were so I just chilled outside, nursing a thick head and dodgy stomach. Chloe, Jane and Karen joined me outside and we laughed about the previous night; drunken antics have a habit of forming bonds as people share the experience as any intense incident. Eventually, we got some bikes and ventured out into the countryside. More by good luck than good management, we found a hotel where a friend of theirs was staying and stopped for a drink. While setting the bikes down, a guy asked me if I would take a photo of him and the two women he was with. I recognised the face, it was familiar, but it was no one I knew.

"Sorry but have I seen you on TV?" I enquired.

"Yes, you have," he replied.

I couldn't remember. "What have you been in? If you don't mind me asking?"

"Lots of different things, too many to mention."

Sensing that he really didn't want to get into it, I just proceeded to take photographs of them all, and then for one of the ladies who was with him; who had asked me to take a photo on her camera. I noticed that she was wearing a team GB t-shirt.

I then sat down with the others, not bothering them. We started talking about the night before and laughing at Jane's 'impression' of Don Johnson, after her self-proclaimed love of Don Johnston when she was little.

I replied, "The only thing I liked about *Miami Vice* was…that's him!"

The girls just looked at me with a blank stare. "What? That's who?" they asked.

"Him, that bloke, he played Miami Vice in the TV series of *Lock, Stock and…*, the spin-off from the movie." Again, blank stares. "His name's Ralf something." Later, it dawned on me that he was also in *Wayne's World 2*. He played the stoner roadie Del who helps Wayne put on the rock concert; his only story to all and sundry is how he had to 'sort out the M&M's or Ozzy wouldn't go on stage'.

We were just about to leave, taking a few photos and admiring the scenery and some hot air balloons which were being inflated when he came wandering past.

I asked, "Did you play Miami Vice in Lock Stock TV series?"

He looked at me either trying to remember or quite shocked by the fact that I knew it. "Yes," he replied.

I carried on, stating that it was a really good show and hardly anyone knew about it, well-written etc. and he agreed. We all chatted for about ten minutes. He told us that he looked at the script for new movie *Rock n Rolla* and said it might as well have been written as an episode of *Lock Stock*. Personally, I haven't seen it, but I have it on good authority that it's really good; and funny. So, I look forward to watching it.

Eventually before we left, I had to ask, "Sorry, I know its Ralf, but can't remember your surname."

"Brown," he said. "Ralf Brown."

Instantly, I recognised the name. It was really surreal and very random meeting a TV and movie personality hanging out in the middle of the

Chinese countryside. Like many others, he was on holiday with his wife and had been taking in the Olympics. He was a really nice bloke and chatted to us without pretention and it was a pleasure to meet him. Eventually, we managed to meet the friend of the girls; he returned while we chatted with our new-found celeb mate, forgetting that he was the reason we had actually gone there in the first place.

Hong Kong Bound

That was our last day; Mark who had also checked out and I used the girls' dorm room to get ready before heading out for one final meal together in the evening. We decided to use one of the restaurants we hadn't been in before and for the first time there were some unusual culinary local delicacies on the menu; namely shark fin soup, snake and dog. I had expected to see this type of thing so was aware and appreciate some cultures eat different things which wouldn't be entertained in others. Sometimes, I don't mind sampling dishes but these were a step too far for me. I prefer my sharks swimming, snakes slithering and dogs walking around on all fours. And not served as an entrée. Call me boring but I gave it a wide birth and stuck to more conventional meat for protein. Thankfully, it wasn't an establishment where things were displayed as I really don't think I could've eaten there.

Before we took the sleeper bus to Hong Kong, the inevitable came where we had to say goodbye; having already agreed to meet up later because we were all eventually heading the same way through Thailand so exchanged contact details and after hugs and kisses, I then made my way to the bus stop. At the bus station, while having a pre-travel cigarette, I noticed a girl also waiting for the bus, and she noticed me.

"Didn't I see you today at the hotel?" I eventually had recognised her as the one of the ladies with Ralf.

"Yes, you did," she replied.

"Did you know Ralf then?" I quizzed.

"No, I didn't have a clue who he was until you mentioned something!"

"Is that why I had to take a photo for you as well then?" I quipped.

"Yeah, as soon as you walked away, I was like 'What have you been in then?'"

I laughed as I had only mustered the courage after he passed us outside the resort when separated from others in his party.

She was really nice; and called Nicole. Turns out, she was an Olympic rower who was travelling after competing. We chatted and she happened to be really pleased when I told her that all the British competitors were heroes back home after their efforts competing and that they had actually installed some national pride. I had seen majority of the games on TV before setting off and witnessed the responses and figured it was a fair comment because credit should be given where credit is due. She continued discussing how hard it is financially for people to train for the Olympics due to lack of funding and sponsorship, whilst having to have job as well. This seemed to make the efforts of the whole team all the more meaningful and hoped give inspiration to future athletes and competitors; with an aim of getting involved and offer openings of potential sponsors to take the initiative to back someone with the desire and ability to achieve their dreams. It did seem strange somewhat but explained why she was, for want of a better word, 'slumming it' with us on what could only be described as a chicken coup of a bus.

There were two isles creating three rows for the beds; two by each side with a window view and one down the middle; each in bunk form. Being 5'10" and about 1'7" shoulder to shoulder, the beds I'm sure were about 5'8" in length and 1'5" wide. You do the math. These buses were definitely built for slimmer, shorter people and not bigger, broader people. The horrible, stale, sweaty blanket provided couldn't have seen any form of cleaning solution or water for that matter in a long time and really wasn't fit for anyone. So, with how uncomfortable I was, it really didn't instil me with much confidence about the journey to be undertaken.

Also, I was gutted to leave Yangshuo having had so much fun there, not to mention the people I met, and started missing the girls; more so Chloe and hoped that I would get to see her again. It reminded me about speaking to Gareth in Shanghai not a week earlier where I'd stated that I didn't know if I could see myself being that attracted to a British woman again. This seemed quite stupid and short-sighted now; as we talked freely, found common ground, made one another laugh and she seemed so much different from anybody I'd met before or at least for very long time. And I was taken aback. But we were now parted and I needed to try and put it out of my mind to concentrate on the weeks ahead. But these thoughts were more amplified due to the fact that I was now pinned in a small confined space, on a really uncomfortable bus with only a smelly blanket for comfort. Worse still; despite getting up early that morning, hung over, exercising and being completely knackered, I still could not fall asleep. Everyone else including Mark and Nicole seemed to be snoring their loaves off. This even included the bus driver who also decided to get some shut eye. At least he decided to pull over to the side of the road and stop first.

I lay hunched up, watching the hours while away, listening to music and when the sun rose, I started to read. The ten hours it was supposed to take to get to the border town of Shenzhen came and went and we seemed to be nowhere near as our surroundings were a river, mountains and patchy dark light green forestation as the scenery instead of usual stifling, dirty, grimy mania of a Chinese city. Testimony to my travel itinerary being in the hands of the gods, or a sleepy bus driver, I was discovering there was absolutely sod all that I could do about this.

Some five hours later, everyone delighted at the amazing experience of getting off the bus and just being able to stretch. Arriving, I had accrued the dizzy heights of around two hours' sleep and was absolutely shattered. Mark, Nicole and I took a cab with others to the train border crossing into Hong Kong. I didn't have any money so needed to find a cash point and left the others. Tired and not thinking properly, there was no reason to do this as it was possible to get money from the ATM through immigration. Now separated from the others, I ended up getting the train into Hong Kong on my own.

On the train, I decided to read the book Chloe had given me prior to leaving; I was happy because I remembered she had written a nice message in the front for me. I looked in my small bag. Then looked again; I couldn't see it. I knew it wasn't in my large backpack as I hadn't opened it and I definitely had it with me at immigration because I could remember putting it down when I filled in my immigration card...

Shit! You fucking idiot! I thought. Immediately, it was obvious; I had left the book in China. At the border, as I sped away on the train towards Hong Kong, I was going to have to tell her I lost her book and look like an ungrateful arsehole. I looked in my wallet for her contact details; these were also missing. *I don't believe this;* I thought and wondered what had happened to the piece of paper? I didn't have a clue where it had gone. More to the point, I wondered if I could remember what was on it.

By now, I was well and truly pissed off with myself; this was largely due to tiredness. Getting to Hong Kong, I came out of the station and jumped in a taxi and told him to take me to where I was staying in Tsim Sta Tsui or TST on the Hong Kong mainland. He tried to tell me it was just round the corner. I didn't care, I couldn't be arsed and I just wanted to get there and get sorted; so insisted he drive me about three hundred yards. I was in no mood.

I spent the rest of the day with a face like thunder. I was on comedown central; from being in a beautiful scenic resort, with tonnes of fun stuff to do, with cool friends who were really nice, meeting Olympians and celebs, to a shitty fifteen hours' bus journey, losing stuff I didn't want to lose, wandering around a metropolis on my own, annoyed with only myself, completely unenthused and absolutely drained mentally and physically. It was made worse by the fact that I had no time or patience for hordes of people who were harassing me to buy a suit every five seconds on Nathan Road where I was staying. The 'mansion' in the loose sense of the word I was staying in was not what I expected, but I didn't know what actually *to* expect. It was a small one-person room, en suite, with countless others in a tower block above a shopping precinct inhabited by any amounts of wheeler dealers trying to flog anything and everything, mind it did harbour some of the most weird and wonderful people there from all sorts of background and the smells from those cooking were incredible. The lot offered a diversity that I hadn't really had the chance to experience yet and I liked it. I had a look around TST, visited the park, ate and went to bed shattered and still feeling utterly pissed off.

It is wonderful what a good night's rest can do for a person; stresses can be miraculously erased, the heart and soul can easily be cleansed and rational thought reinstated by the mind's downtime. Feeling hundred times better, I headed out to get on with things without a clue what to do or where to go, and this for some reason felt brilliant. So I jumped onto the subway, headed straight over to Hong Kong Island and eventually found the tram up to the top of the peak. Here's a good tip; if in doubt of what to do in a new place, head for the highest tourist point and literally have a look around. I dare say that the view here is normally really impressive but wouldn't know, as the clouds hung low and mist swathed a grip on the towering manmade superstructures below. So, not for the first time, I only got an impression of what could be, albeit only from the thousands of postcards in the shops showing what the picture-perfect view skyline would be. Looking down on all the high-rises below though was cool; the modern architecture seemed small and offered the perception that it was possible to reach down and touch them. I wandered around on the peak for a while and read up on the island's development over the years before eventually heading down via the bus on a really steep winding road.

Ambling around the city, I took in the atmosphere and noted all the swanky shops; really affluent and upmarket. This was new for my travels yet I felt unbelievably un-arsed by them to even warrant venturing in, never mind regard purchasing something. So, they were somewhat redundant to me. I figured I might as well take in a different view of the city and decided to venture back to the mainland via the ferry to get ready for the evening. Having already been on the Internet to check the horse racing fixtures, the only chance I was going to get to visit the track was tonight. So that was that; race track it was. I chilled before jumping back onto the subway and took a quick bus journey to the unmissable Happy Valley Racecourse. A big open oval located smack in the middle of Hong Kong Island amid all the high-rise buildings, and at 70p to get in and 70p minimum bet put me straight into the 'I'll have this for an evening of entertainment, thank you' frame of mind. Although this wasn't my betting frame of mind as I should point out that 70p minimum bet certainly wasn't my minimum bet.

Race card? Check. Betting slip? Check. Cigarettes? Check. Beer? Check. I was set for the evening, and started taking in the atmosphere. The track itself was about 1 mile 4-furlong oval with a huge impressive grandstand which was about 300 metres in length stretched out, so it was big with hundreds of corporate boxes running into the thousands for the rich to use and quaff champagne. Trackside was easily good enough for me. Minding my own business, I noticed a couple doing the usual thing of trying to take a photo of themselves together with the stands as the backdrop. I approached and said, "Do you want me to take that for you?"

"Yeah, that would be great!" they replied.

We started talking; the couple were from Ireland and called Steve and Jenny. Explaining why I was in Hong Kong, they told me that they were on their honeymoon and I instantaneously felt like I was gate crashing; who wouldn't? But they said it was fine to join them, as they had only spoke with each other for days so another to converse with was appreciated. They were really nice and friendly. Also, we had plenty in common what with beer, cigarettes, music and, of course, the racing. As the night wore on, hooves relentlessly thundered past us and the finish line; race after race and the luck of the Irish was really working for the happy couple, who had picked four or five winners between them. I on the other hand had nothing.

But eventually managed to bag a winner, just the one; I didn't care, one was enough for me to leave breaking my Happy Valley duck, figuring who goes to the race track to open a savings account anyway? I'd had a tonne of fun, met really nice couple, drank a lot of beer and had, as the Irish would say; 'Good craic'.

So much so that while leaving, they invited me to their hotel bar where we took more drinks and food which was quite upmarket, and certainly not where I would have envisaged ending up with those prices, not to mention the trainers, shorts and t-shirt I was sporting. But they made for an entertaining evening so I obliged as Steve and Jenny were a great couple, I was please to of met them and hung out. Before leaving, we exchanged contacts as they said that they would love to be kept updated with my adventures after explaining the length of time expected to be away for, the things I had planned and had already done. Which I was happy to do. Arriving back on Nathan Road, I had to laugh to myself about my 'mansion' compared to the swank fest I had just been forced, *ahem*, to endure. I went to bed happy after a good day's wandering, a fun night out and especially as my ideas for the next day were already in place.

The previous day, I noticed from the bus stop to the races that I could also get to Ocean Park; so, hopping back onto the subway, I headed over to the island and bought a return bus and entrance ticket for a £17 deal. The twenty-minute bus passed the track which even in the day looked impressive, especially as it managed to smother a mass of prime real estate right in the city. It was only ten a.m. when I entered Ocean Park. A theme park built either side of a mountain pinnacle on the southern coast of Hong Kong Island and included attractions such as rides, sea animals, aquarium and pandas. That seemed to offer enough to entertain me for the day.

The majority of the day felt like it was spent ambling around; negotiating the numerous escalators and cable cars of the park due to the crazy elevated location. I started with least sensible thing; the log flume where getting drenched was inevitable. But there was no queue and it was already red hot, so I figured I would have plenty of time to dry out. I decided then to proceed to venture onto as many of the roller coasters as possible before the queues started to dominate the rides themselves. The rest of the time was viewing the seals and the dolphin show; which engaged the crowds with their flips, tricks and acrobatics. I was entertained but could not escape from the gnawing thoughts about the ethics behind all this. Did they actually enjoy performing for the enthralled masses? Were they not better off free in the ocean? Did they know anything else? I therefore ended up questioning my own role in all this. Never mind everyone else's. Admittedly, they did look well and had lots of room to swim about and play, performing twice a day for twenty minutes. I wondered, and wouldn't be the last time, about these practices; something which I found myself doing more and more with the growing list of experiences I'd had, yet not necessarily only confined to the treatment of animals, but the harsh facts involving the inequalities of life between the 'haves' and 'have nots' now constantly thrown in my face.

The sky turret provided amazing panoramic views from an already high vantage point and a perfect time for my camera batteries to fail. The tropical aquarium with three levels was absolutely massive, harbouring rays, sharks, thousands of fish, moray eels and seahorses. The sturgeon aquarium was very good but short, and the jelly fish feature was a trippy experience; displayed in illuminated tanks and shrouded with darkness, where I somehow almost walked into a full-size mirror; a shocking affair that happened to be only my own reflection. The good thing about the aquarium though was the in-depth information provided in both Chinese and English; and they were a fantastic educational source. I had been unaware that sharks had been on the planet for 4.5 million years, whereas humans only 200,000 years. In much the same way as prior, this made me think about the ethics and in this case, any value in killing these creatures; especially as we don't live in the water, not to mention the whole importance to ecological structure of the oceans. Who knows the untold damage that could happen if they were ever to become extinct and not only that, believing they only have a bad press from hyped media that create an unwarranted fearful mystique. Admittedly, they are bad ass and it would probably be quite unnerving swimming about with sharks in their domain because they win hands down in a Greco-Roman fight with any human and more so in the 'who was here first?' stakes.

On the other side of the hill was the quieter part of the park but had the feature which I really wanted to see, the giant pandas. Having not got the chance to see them in China, I was determined not to leave here disappointed and didn't, well aware of this animal species endangered plight and in this case also being in captivity. There were three separate large enclosures that had at least been made to look like a forest setting;

with grass, plants, trees and logs. In the first, nothing stirred; the second, one was lazing away in the shelter at the far end, but in the third there were two together both chewing on bamboo shoots, wandering, playing and rolling around putting on a bit of a spectacle close by the ever-increasing crowd looking on. I stood and watched them enthralled for about thirty minutes; they were amazing and looked really beautiful but weirdly unnatural as if their markings had just been freshly painted. They seemed content and appeased even with their ample but still confined surroundings and I hoped this was the correct course of action for a species left in jeopardy from a naturally low birth rate and unnatural habitat loss.

It was now getting late and it had been a long but good day; rides, escalators, animals, escalators, views, escalators and felt like I'd actually learnt something, including that escalators are a good way of getting about on steep hillsides. So, I went back to the mainland content with my activity yet still not really the wiser surrounding the morality of some of the practices. Inevitably, my mind wandered and started thinking about next destination at the end of three short-lived days in my more modern, affluent and expensive surroundings.

Never one to shy away from a bit of culture, I took in the museum of fine art and, as luck would have it, it was situated only a short ten minute walk or so down Nathan Road towards the ferry dock and at about £1.50 to get in was an absolute bargain. There were numerous different exhibits but two that I found most intriguing were the main feature of art from Roman times painted on slate, stone and pottery, depicting gods, goddesses, mythical creatures and ancient tales. These were fascinating to see, especially with the history behind the pieces and fine detail still evident. And also, the Chinese ink art; predominantly texts and landscapes painted onto canvas with bold and subtle brush strokes of black ink to form epic scenes of rural life, including mountains and fishing villages of years gone by. Wandering around, other displays included a gallery dedicated to the depiction of horses and how varying art techniques have portrayed them through the ages, plus a vast array of arrangements that showcased beautiful gold artefacts and precious Ming vase ceramics where the intricate pictures and patterns on these were exceptional.

With a little time to kill, I wandered down the avenue of stars along the waterfront. Exactly the same as that of Hollywood, but not in the sense of recognising many of the names due to them being predominantly from the Chinese and Hong Kong film industry, with the exception of Jackie Chan and the legend himself Bruce Lee; of which there was also a statue, plus another featuring a woman reaching up to the sky with cine film covering her hips and breasts, that with a bit of fine tuning I thought might be a good idea for a tattoo design as I pondered along in a world of my own. Until being interrupted by a 'guru' who managed to guess a number and flower I was told to think of and then telling me my fortune, which was all really good news surprisingly. I paid him some money but, more than likely, I got grifted by some random 'mystic' who pulled a snazzy trick catching me off guard in the street. Mind, if he was that good, he would've known I was going to give him less money than what he wanted for payment. So we'll see what happens.

The rest of the day, I sorted my things and treated myself to a take-away kebab. The food in Hong Kong was good and due to the diversity most varieties were available but was now rather expensive than what I'd gotten accustomed to, so wasn't eating big meals, just snacks as these were easy enough to get by and cheaper. That night, I finished the things I wanted to do in Hong Kong by venturing to the harbour to witness the light show emitted from the buildings on the island. The lights of all different strips, cannons, colours and illuminations systematically turn on and off to music. Being told that this show was 'spectacular' was not the word I'd use; it only lasted about fifteen minutes and felt a little disappointed. Don't get me wrong, it was good, but not great, having before seen the bright lights of Las Vegas and Blackpool Pleasure Beach back home; those lights are a dazzling spectacle, and the ones in Vegas are alright as well!

I had been on the road now for nearly a month and all but finished with China and Hong Kong. Overall, I'd had an awesome time. There had already been ups and downs but was fully ready for these as I knew they would inevitably happen; what with the dodgy stomachs, acclimatising to the hot humid weather, keeping a check on scam artists and annoying insect bites: especially the ones on top of my head forming hilarious nipple-esque formations. These weren't bothering me as I was really starting to appreciate new places, cultures and people. But more importantly, for the first time in a long time or possibly ever, a feeling of freedom. Doing what I wanted, when I wanted, with no need for the approval or opinion of others and it felt so good. With this, hand on heart I could say that I wasn't missing anything; not Britain, not the food and not even family or friends. For some reason, I wasn't homesick. The only reasons I could think of for this were that having spent quite a lot of time prior to travelling, living far away from the family circle, I was accustomed to not having close ones at my immediate disposal and that there was a reason and a purpose behind what I was doing. Albeit I didn't know what this actually was.

Personally, I preferred China to Hong Kong. The cultural difference really sold it to me; although, only essentially visiting four places in China and therefore a tiny percentage of what the country has to offer. Just starting out was slow going as I found my travelling feet; honestly, I don't think that I got a true insight into the country, with Beijing being so geared up for the Olympics, Shanghai was manic and possibly felt the overspill from preparing for the games and Hangzhou – I wasn't there long enough. But I loved Yangshuo; it was beautiful and looked authentically Chinese albeit more so for the tourism with loads of things to keep me occupied amid stunning surroundings. But the best thing was how friendly and accommodating the Chinese people were from the few places that I experienced, also very warm and polite. While minding my own business, I was approached many times just to chat which I loved, and they regarded me as helping them. It was an amazing feeling. The culture fascinated me, especially the element of respect each seemed to have for one another, how it was possible for older generations to wander around with no worries or fears about something bad happening as they exercised away in the beautiful ornate parks. All this offered such a different and diverse world from the one I knew, especially as far as the poverty was concerned as I witnessed some things that I found disturbing in reference to the conditions that others not so fortunate have to endure, but I had to willingly accept that I was going to see and be subject to this as I moved from place to place, learn from the experience and possibly try to help whenever I could.

China was different and more of a challenge, that's why it was good and I preferred it to Hong Kong which was all too familiar. Don't get me wrong, I really liked Hong Kong and certainly not the worst place in the world to end up, but it was incredibly commercial and was like Asia's answer to New York. Hustle and bustle, high-rise modern buildings, incredibly upmarket shops and stores where nothing has a price tag, to suit touts and wheeler dealers flogging any amounts of handbags and other fake goods, amid wonderfully efficient subway system, neon for miles, severe lack of Internet cafes presumably because everyone has access to a computer to get online, now paying pounds for things as opposed to pence and lots of people who could speak English, which isn't a pre-requisite of mine as I like the challenge of non-English speaking countries. Even the electric plugs were the same as the UK; another factor emphasising the influence from the years of British Empire, and liberal to the extent that you could buy porno magazines here. Hong Kong was far more multi-cultural, which I truly believe is a fantastic thing and really admirable. People expect to see those from every background and walk of life on the streets here and it was the norm; but in mainland China, it was hilarious. It felt like I was an alien invader at times; not only being stared at with my unfamiliar features and skin tone, but with instances like when I came across the 'squatter' toilet for the first time and had to figure out how to take a dump in the ground without falling over, never mind have any deposited articles drop into my pants for that matter. There was plenty to see and do in Hong Kong and I still probably missed out on some interesting cool things, but three days were easily enough and I felt that I'd done what I wanted and was ready and excited for my next encounter.

Now Then… from Nowheresville

I arrived in Thailand and Bangkok knowing pretty much what to expect and where to go, having been there on two previous occasions. Still, that didn't stop me getting ripped off by a taxi firm outside airport arrivals waiting for a sucker; or rather customer to ferry at an extortionate price into the city centre, because for some reason I decided to take one of the nice swish cabs for triple the fare, rather than using my brain and just collecting a regular taxi at a much cheaper rate. Again, I don't know why I did this, maybe I was feeling good after a short but fantastic flight that I didn't want to get off. But I had also lost my mosquito repellent and sun cream, having had them taken off me by baggage check as I'd forgotten to put them in my check-in luggage; on all counts I was travelling with my old friend stupidity.

I knew where I was going; the arterial highway into downtown Bangkok that is Sukhumvit Road. I'd stayed at the hostel before. Nice and cheap, good facilities, easy to get around being close to the sky train. So, I figured it would easily suffice again. We turned down the soi road it was on and I recognised it instantly, but the driver was struggling to find the place; as was I. Sure we were in the right place and the driver confirmed this with the address and called the hostel. Fair enough, I'd only stayed one night some three years previous but this was ridiculous. Eventually, we turned back around and stopped. Looking closer, I saw a sign indicating that this was the place, but not quite as I remembered it.

Entering, I thought, *Now my memory is not the greatest but this is a totally different place!* And it was. The lounge area stroke reception was half the size, there was no bar, the pool table had gone, very few chairs and it was really grubby. The staff were nice enough though, so I decided to only pay and stay for one night rather than commit myself as I couldn't believe how downtrodden it had become and also, right there and then, I really couldn't be arsed moving and looking for somewhere else. Upstairs resembled that of someone moving home, junk seemed to be everywhere, cupboards, boxes, all sorts just strewn around and when I got to the room, I was put in a twelve-bed dorm, which was OK but again nothing like it was previously.

I met one of the others staying there and have to say he was a complete mess. Clearly, he'd had one or two halves of lager the night before and was now suffering the consequences. We started chatting and he explained that he had also stayed prior and the place had totally downsized due to lack of trade, with more people opting for Khaosan Road part of town nearer to the bars and clubs. Also, he did not forget to mention that the owner was a real mean bastard and didn't think customer care was high on his priority list. Everything started to make sense now.

Si was an Aussie on his last few days before flying back to Melbourne. So, needless to say, was hitting it hard; understandably having a final blow out ahead of his return home. He told me that there were only six others staying on the hostel, and I made seven, but essentially everyone got on well, went out partying together and got wasted, explaining why I hadn't seen anybody else as they were all absolutely done in from the previous nights' drinking activities. Eventually, everyone started to surface, and it was like a scene out of a George A Romero movie with one zombie waking up after the next. And I was pissing myself laughing.

Ade was up next; another Aussie who, hard to believe as it was, looked worse than Si. Then Thom; a cool, chilled out German guy. Followed by Matt and Sam; two English lads also at the end of their travels. Being English we obviously got on to the subject of football, it turned out Matt supported my team and were both from the same area. A strange coincidence as he had moved away as had I, and now, here we were on the other side of the planet, hanging out in this place. Finally, Eddie, a Canadian fella, turned up and the troupe was complete.

Within one hour of arriving in Bangkok and to a shit hole of a hostel, my whole perspective had changed, meeting this bunch of crazed, drunken party animals, who it has to be said were the nicest, most welcoming people you could meet. I decided to stick around for a bit (again, it's not where you are, it's who you are with and all that). Probably also helping explain this further; within that hour someone rolled a joint and we all got stoned. Now I'm not saying that this was the cleverest thing to do, being aware of the harsh penalties imposed by the authorities for possession and use of such substances. Where in some instances can result in the death penalty in Thailand or at the very least a stretch in the Bangkok Hilton, something which the toughest of criminals would be petrified of; and that definitely included me. But we did it anyway, ducking down an alley close by and out of sight. Sitting on the garden furniture outside we were all a little toasted, relaxing with giggling confusion as to what each was talking about, while at the same time staring in disbelief at a full-grown elephant being walked down the street by its owner, with a flashing red light attached to its tail; just in case any motorist behind couldn't see it.

That evening, everyone was going out; again. I tagged along. Starting at a local tavern for food and drinks before heading to Pat Pong district and to one of the go-go bars, where girls parade in skimpy uniforms and are offered to customers; sadly, mostly western men for sexual favours. I've been in these establishments before in Thailand and know what they are all about. Hand on heart, I can say I've never been with a girl from a go-go bar and wasn't about to start, although I'll admit I have been with other women when in Thailand before but not from these establishments. Looking back, I probably only went in because that's where everyone else was heading. I bought the girls a few drinks, hung out with them and had a few laughs but that's it; trying to treat it as an exercise in morality. Now being older and I like to think a fraction wiser, I'm well aware of the dark and sad side of this trade, and didn't want to participate with the exploitative aspect and add to the problem, where even being in the establishment could be argued just as bad. The lady managing the floor obviously realised I wasn't going to take one of the girls, and would usher them away quite hastily to someone more prosperous. So, after a couple of drinks and only slightly less money, I left.

Over the next few days, no other travellers or guests arrived. One by one, the group whittled away as we filled in the time by visiting the markets, getting there via a taxi boat on the canals which run through the city and are one of the fastest and cheapest ways of getting around; only problem being you can only go where the canals go and if you are sitting by the edge, it's a good idea to keep your mouth shut if you do not want to ingest any of the stagnant water, as it splashes up from the speeding vessel. But we mainly just dossed about, smoked the odd joint and watching TV. Sam and Matt were leaving in a couple of days back to Britain and were broke so the others and I helped them out with money for food and drinks. They were really appreciative which was nice to see. I figured it could easily be me in that situation in ten months' time and would like to think that some kind soul would help me, if needed, and it wouldn't do my conscience or karma any harm, so happily obliged with assisting some fellow travellers in need.

71

A good thought process really because at the time I never realised how much help I would need.

I booked into another hostel the day before the last two were due to check out. I'd had a great time albeit where we were staying. Met a brilliant bunch of lads, had plenty of laughs without really achieving much. It seemed like we were in a real-life version of the TV show *Auf Wiedersehen, Pet*, strangers all put together, comradery under less than favourable conditions, but the time had come to move on as there was now nothing to hang around for and I'd also spotted the biggest rat I've ever seen rummaging around in the kitchen.

Tuesday was my birthday; I was struggling to get excited. Generally, I don't seem to make a big deal out of my birthday and don't do anything in particular, and even though I was away travelling this didn't change that fact. On this particular birthday, I spent the morning packing then moving to a better hostel, checked in and met some of the others there; Albert elderly Canadian chap who was in Bangkok on business and another fellow Brit who was also travelling. I returned to meet up with the lads and to say goodbye but not before enjoying a free meal from the rat kitchen. Don't judge; free food is free food so I wasn't complaining. That evening, I took in a couple of beers with my new roommates, talking about the world and travelling different places, but mainly Vietnam. As I'd visited before as had Albert; yet in completely different circumstances – because he was there during the war. And that was my birthday, not that exciting really and not that special but I didn't care, all the things I was doing were making those days exciting, special and like a birthday in their own right anyway. I was aware though that I hadn't done much since arriving, so I booked myself onto a tour of a floating market and crocodile farm.

The next day, the tour bus eventually managed to fight its way through the horrendous Bangkok traffic that perpetually blights the city with noise and smog. After an hour or so, we arrived at the floating market. I hadn't seen one before. The market had lots of stalls both on land and as expected on water. The waterways used by the local traders for hundreds of years snaked and weaved around the green landscape, with homes, shops, exhibits adorning the banks that blotted out the maze-like routes. Where the floating stalls were selling the usual array of traditional food, clothing, hats and souvenirs as expected, but not in this special unique way on a long woven boat, that looked really cool and innovative. The kind of thing you would never see back at home as any health and safety officer would have a coronary at the mere thought, especially the ones selling food with the barbeques on board.

I loved just taking in the atmosphere and having a little chuckle at those gingerly boarding the less-than-stable longboats, offering taxi service up the waterways. I have to say I'd have laughed had someone fell in and would put a large wager on it having happened before to some poor soul. But the most intriguing thing I found at the market was the art exhibition, and was truly fascinated especially by the life-size Darth Vader and Alien sculptures made from recycled metal pieces and parts that had been taken from cars, bicycles or whatever. There were lots of other designs in all sizes, really intricate and exquisite detail. I thought they were amazing and would've loved one for myself, especially the two mentioned, but it figured best not to bother as carting even one around could prove somewhat problematic.

We were taken to an elephant farm where they were offering rides to tourists. I personally wasn't that interested having ridden one before, so just hung around near to where the bus was parked by the entrance and watched, rather unimpressed, as a baby elephant was chained to a post and forced to perform tricks; such as bowing down and standing on his hind legs for the enthralled tourists by the use of a brutal-looking sharp metal hook on a pole. Sadly, people loved the spectacle and couldn't wait to have their photo taken with the poor creature that even looked miserable as its head swayed continuously from side to side.

Before lunch, we visited a woodcraft workshop, again probably intended for the big sell to tourists, but to be fair found it interesting as the craftsmen and women were working on pieces right there and you could walk around in between them as they performed their delicate work. I was really impressed, the level of skill involved creating the carved wooden pictures and landscapes of jungle with complete flora and fauna was fantastic, as it looked seemingly impossible to carve behind the leaves and branches to create the 3D effect of the pictures. The works were also huge, some 10ft long and 3ft deep, begging belief how detailed and flawless they looked, not to mention the time, effort, skill and concentration to make these works of art. They were 'outstanding' both figuratively and literally. I wandered around a showroom of furniture which had been built, left in the rustic style of cut tree logs; the smoothed and varnished works looked really unique, especially due to the fact that they were about four times the size of your average piece of household furniture. These were massive dining tables, chairs and a rocking chair which you could sit in. Not the most comfortable it has to be said, because with something that big you want to lounge out and this wasn't happening with these wooden monstrosities; their design only useful if entertaining an ogre. At least any self-respecting thief would just leave it if you were being burgled, due to the weight alone never mind the trauma of getting it in or out of the house. At the half point of the day, I was hungry and fortunately lunch was provided; a buffet for everyone to help themselves; So mixed it up a little with a concoction of stir-fried noodles, sweet and sour vegetables, spaghetti Bolognese and chicken curry. It was delicious and having it all together became quite the pioneer of fusion food.

The final part of the day was at the crocodile farm. Again, I'd been to one before, but not here. Loving the natural world, I am always intrigued to see animals; but still sceptical of the conditions some are kept in, especially in developing parts of the world where any amounts of quizzing tour agents would be responded with nothing but positives about the habitats. Also this particular farm had more going for it than just our reptilian friends. Set amongst some beautiful gardens, there were lots of huge pens, some over a football pitch in size that was really good to see, harbouring various different-sized crocodiles which would just sit lifeless, basking in the shallow water and soaking up the warm humid weather. They looked almost fake, plastic as if really safe to touch, especially the thirty to forty-year-old salt water crocodiles which were the biggest. This obviously was but only an illusion, shattered when witnessing the ferocity and violence unleashed as one of these prehistoric killing machines would strike with lightning-fast reflexes to take a piece of freshly chopped chicken, which could be bought and thrown in to feed the cool, calm, beautiful, deadly killers.

Bearing this in mind, a lot had to be said for the bravery slash stupidity of the entertainers who put on the crocodile show in a tiled oval arena filled with water on a long island down the centre. Spectators watched in nervous anticipation (not me, I'm expecting carnage and I don't mean that which would provide a new set of boots or handbag) as a crocodile 'tamer' dragged one of the beasts out of the water, much to its annoyance, and proceed to further antagonise the animal with a stick and, when it opens its mouth, put limbs directly into the line of fire. Fair play if you can get away with it, but you can't blame the animal if one day it decides not to play by the rules. Adding to the park, there were numerous other creatures such as fish and birds, but also a large amount of elephants which likewise had their own area and auditorium, and the workers would put on a show for the audience, such as making the elephants dance which I found pointless and boring, especially as the hook on a pole would be used as the steering wheel. This wasn't the only part of the show, they also demonstrated how in ancient times the elephants would be captured and how they were used in battle which was interesting in an educational sense, and the elephants seemed to respond to this as none were obviously harmed and was possibly good exercise for the beasts, which extended to a game of football they all played as well.

I thought that this was one of the better parks that I had visited, nothing was in a small enclosure and all the animals looked in good condition, but wondered about the necessity of the shows. One day, something will go wrong and the animal will suffer through no fault of its own, with man trying to play lord and master, with the most unconventional of pets. Yes, some of it was supposed to be educational, but surely something that can be taught or demonstrated through some other medium. Some parts I thought were ridiculous. What is the point of teaching an animal to dance for human pleasure? Probably though the most disappointing thing is the way people react, like it's really cute and they must have a photo, encouraging the scenario. I was there and paid money to enter and witness it, but now I can say as I saw it with my own eyes that I figure it is pointless and unnecessary. I understand why some animals are in captivity and have come too far now just to release everything back into the wild, but show me an animal running around in a reserve or refuge with a more than adequate enclosure; acting naturally figuring this should easily be enough for any human fascination or entertainment.

It was a long day, especially as at each point we were generally left to our own devices and free to explore as we wished, there were good interesting points and some not so good. By now, people within the group had gotten to know each other, chatting freely on the bus. This involved the Canadian couple sat behind me, where I had severe difficulty not showing any reaction while trying to be as cool as possible, having a conversation with them both; because mid-flow talking, the woman proceeded to get her breast out and feed their baby. She didn't even break sentence in front of a complete stranger. Perfectly natural, I know, but was just not expecting it. They were a lovely pair though. I mean the people. Obviously.

That night, I headed out and took in a few beers at a sports bar close by and unfortunately this time got chatting to another tourist in there. I say unfortunately because his main topic of conversation was the amount of cocaine and prostitutes, he goes through all-in-one session. Let's just say we had slightly different perspectives on life. He was going to some other club that I politely declined going along to, so eventually ended up nattering to another bar fly; a Scot who was working in Bangkok. He was actually kind of normal compared to the aforementioned and we had very similar taste in music, one of my favourite subjects. As the night wore on, we chatted, enjoyed the tunes, got drunk and had a laugh with the staff, so much so, the girl behind the bar ended up asking me to take her to Pattaya. I paused before replying in a slightly sarcastic manner, "No problem, I'll go and get my helicopter." I eventually left about midnight, tired, hungry, pissed and wondering where I'd left my helicopter.

I took a stroll down Sukhumvit Road. Bangkok seems to offer an array of, well, everything. While walking, the senses are overwhelmed as the hot sticky humidity holds you close and doesn't let go, eyes see the most beautiful and disturbing things in one vision, aromatic smells can turn from divine to putrid in one inhalation and the sounds can enchant and terrify from one moment to the next. This was probably the reason I like this place. Every time I wandered around, it offered a mini-adventure, where the unknown would seem to be the only thing I would know. Checking out the shops and stalls, many selling knock-off DVDs and clothing, as well as all the other weird and wonderful things; much of which contraband in many other parts of the world and probably here as well. But with everything it always added up to sensory overload. The main purpose though was administrative for me; kind of boring, I know. This involved putting photos on to disc and getting a large envelope from the post office to send some stuff home, having accrued quite a bit of memorial junk now and wanted to off-load it. I also was checking my emails regularly because as of tomorrow, I was due to start the first of my projects which I had pre-booked, and some others who were doing the same were now already in Bangkok and had been in touch about meeting up. I was hoping to, but my phone sim card didn't work and getting in touch with people using email was slow. So figured I'd just catch up with everyone tomorrow at the hotel. Before the start of another adventure, I went back to the sports bar on the night for a few beers. But prior, I tried out a new bar further up the road. I shouldn't have bothered as nothing much was happening, except for nearly being accosted of a really strung-out ropey looking prostitute who tried to grab me. I pulled my arm away, body swerved out of reach and hastily moved on to my original destination. The bar flies were in when I arrived and carried on as we left off, which was drinking, listening to some boss tunes, talking profound intellectual bollocks and laughing with the bar staff – the one who wanted me to take her to Pattaya, she was lots of fun and called Porn, something I found rather amusing. My smile was sharp removed though when some massive, pissed up, moustachioed German approached and tapped me on the shoulder.

"You fuck him?" he asked, pointing at my Scottish cohort.

"No," I replied hastily.

"You fuck me?" he boldly enquired.

"No, mate, that's not my scene," I added.

He then just stood for about ten seconds, swaying, shit-faced drunk, staring and pondering the situation. I looked at the others and tried not to laugh, just thinking to myself, *Fuckin' hell! Where's Porn and that helicopter?* Eventually, he said goodbye and as did we to him and he left. We burst out laughing and carried on drinking and acting as DJs for the place, enjoying the music that we had pretty much been given full reign of.

Friday had now come around and the next three weeks were sorted; accommodation, food, company and fully itinerary. I got my post sent off and checked out of the hostel to go to the hotel which we were using as the initial meeting point for every one participating on the Thai Experience. But not before having a chat with another who had just moved into the dorm and it turns out that this same prostitute that tried to grab me the night before had actually grabbed him as well but managed to get his phone. Luckily, he realised what she was up to and snatched it straight back. We couldn't quite believe it, as unbelievably plausible as it was, but I thought it was quite random him being in the same room and how you have to be on your guard with this type of thing, as they can happen regularly. I took a taxi to take me to the hotel, checked in and headed down the Khaosan Road which was only five minutes away. It was the first time that I had actually visited the hustle, bustle and hassle of the most tourist-laden part of Bangkok, a semi-pedestrian street of about five hundred yards with lots of shops, restaurants, market stalls, bars, street vendors and compulsory suit tailor touts all hankering for the tourist baht enswathed with vibrant colour, pungent smells, sticky heat and bartering chaos.

Later, everyone participating on the Thai Experience was instructed to meet in reception at seven p.m. I arrived and the group was instantly recognisable.

'I take it you lot are all doing Thai Experience then?"

They stuck out like sore thumbs as everyone congregated in an ever-expanding circle and proceeded with the polite getting to know you small talk. By the time everyone was there, the circle was huge, virtually taking up the full lobby, so only talking to the few in close proximity was really plausible. But there would be plenty of time over the next three weeks to get to know one another. The Thai Experience consisted of two weeks' learning about Thai culture, living in an eco-house, the third week either teaching or trekking and the fourth chilling on a beach island. I had only subscribed to the first three weeks as I'd visited Koh Samet before in 2005 and didn't want to return; not that it was bad far from it; I just had desires to go to and explore other new places.

When everyone had arrived, we headed off down the Khaosan Road to bond over drinks. Expectedly due to there being about twenty-five of us; we split into three groups. Those who had just arrived in Thailand went back early, the acclimatised rest and I stayed out having drinks, where I inevitably ended up in the 'stay up late and get more-than-pissed' group. Another nice, casual getting to know everyone affair.

To kill some time on the Saturday before heading out of Bangkok, three others and I decided to invent our own tour. We hailed a tuk-tuk and set off in our three-wheeled motorised chariot. These are built only for three passengers and it was a squeeze, but still the most fun way to get around the city, but with no meter means you can get ripped off so we negotiated the price first. It was really cheap, yet we did have to endure a trip to the suit shop and a diamond store as random detours. These companies would give gas money to the driver to bring unsuspecting custom to their establishments in the hope of a sale, which, in this case, didn't happen. Tailor-made suits were again not exactly high on our shopping lists. We visited temples including one with beautiful white marble floor courtyard that had baked in the red-hot sun all day and agonisingly seared the soles of compulsory bare feet. The surrounding grounds had large ponds where we released terrapins for luck that we purchased from a vendor, but not sure how lucky for the terrapins due to the massive catfish that were lurking which were whipped into a frenzy by feeding them bread; much like those that congregated around the stilts of the pier at the Chao Phraya River where absolute pandemonium erupted in the water as thousands of fish scrambled over one another in wild mania for a mere morsel of food, thrown in by a gathered crowd to create a mad thrashing spectacle as we finished off our ad-hoc tour. The evening offered a choice; a trip to the lady boy show or the Thai boxing for a price. I didn't bother with either, having seen both before so figured I'd just have a few drinks instead because I've hardly ever done that before.

On the Sunday, everyone met in the lobby ready to head out. Having a cigarette out the front, there was a large protest which marched past the front of the hotel. Apparently, these were the poorest inhabitants of the city who were being force to move to the outskirts so their land could be developed. At first, I thought that this could be part of the previous demonstrations that I had learnt about when in Shanghai, concerning rioting around the Thai parliamentary buildings due to the local displeasure at the government and their apparently corrupt ways. At the time, this was serious and the British government had issued a 'do not travel' warning, yet I wasn't to fazed as it was three weeks before arriving and figured it would all be over by then, which it pretty much was or at least calmed down. I had contacted the company who organised Thai Experience though just to make sure everything was going ahead and as far as they were concerned, it was; as we weren't based in that immediate vicinity and were only spending two days actually in Bangkok. This in front of me now was a large yet peaceful protest, making voices heard and only really disrupting traffic; compared to what had been happening prior.

'The Brown House' was located in the middle of the countryside and there wasn't much around except for dirt tracks and fields. Where exactly? I wasn't sure. But everyone seemed to be pleased with where we were based for the next two weeks. It was easily big enough for the twenty-five of us; a large building that at the front had a covered open communal area with lots of tables and chairs, a kitchen and separate lounge as part of the house while at the back were six dorm rooms, a large grass common and stagnant pond covered in weed that could have harboured any amount of creatures.

Being an eco-house, the facilities we had were basic. Nothing though a person couldn't live without; there were three fans in the room to keep it cool and the water in the shower was only cold, but with the blistering sun and saturating humidity, this was a welcome relief. We were fed breakfast, lunch and dinner at set time each day, in buffet form, so you could eat as much as you like until it was gone, but everything was vegetarian. Although being a carnivore, I figured I could handle not eating meat for a couple of weeks. It would be a challenge and something which I wouldn't mind trying and do have mild admiration for people who choose to eat in an ethical way, rather than someone who just stuffs their face because they can. Other rules were that we all had to wash our own plates and cutlery after eating, due to Buddhist religion had to remove our footwear when inside or in the common area, no relations were allowed (the polite way of telling us no shagging), which was probably not going to be an issue as there was a strictly no alcohol policy as well.

"Are you fucking kidding?" "We are only human!" everyone's panicked cry.

All wasn't totally lost. Directly outside the gate across the dirt track road, a small bamboo bar with a covered seating area had craftily been constructed for people to use; or rather, for those staying at 'The Brown House' to use. Clearly this cornered the market taking advantage of the no-alcohol policy. I was instantly convinced that there was a God or Buddha; and they lived here. Besides, it provided a lucrative income for the local lady running it and one less thing for the owners and organisers to worry about, as they knew where to find us. Also the new influx of our fresh meat would keep the local mosquitos from dying of malnutrition. So we made our acquaintances with the bar owner and settled in for the next two weeks. As a welcome addition to the proceedings as the bar was, personally, one thing had started to become apparent; I was now drinking more than I had initially planned and didn't look like stopping, plus smoking far too many cigarettes which I now regarded as officially having a bad habit.

We had an easy introduction for the first day; initially taking a stroll along the dirt track road by the river to visit some of the inhabitants of the local village, where homes double up as stores or other form of service for those who lived in the countryside of Sing Buri province (as it turned out this is where we were). Upon returning, our first language lesson followed, which I found interesting and useful albeit difficult; granted we didn't learn anything particularly complex, it was more the pronunciation. Yet, I appreciated that now I had few phrases to help me get by should I get stuck. The afternoon was spent meeting travel company co-ordinators for the third week. I opted for a homestay with a local teacher where the kids would go there each day for lessons; I thought this a better and more challenging option than staying at 'The Brown House' and visiting a school each day to teach. As the idea of leaving the comfort zone of this accommodation, entering into the unknown and going somewhere new and different, appealed more.

Early evening, we were treated to a traditional show by the local children performing traditional music, singing and dancing. It was lovely to see as they really made an effort and were very good. We all joined in as well which made the experience all the more fun. What was really cool was that they were all dressed in the traditional clothing too, all beautifully made with superb coloured fabrics. That said, but I'm no fashion expert, still I wasn't too sure about how traditional one lad's attire was though; jeans and black t-shirt with the eye-catchingly funny 'Fuck You' emblazoned across it.

Our first excursion was to Ayutthaya; the former capital from ancient times and now ruins. The site was vast and surrounded by water system, with huge pagodas, steps and walkways leading to various open chambers and rooms. We learnt about the history at the museum and visitor centre and prayed at the large Buddha statue and used a filtration technique of shaking sticks to reveal a lucky number and told a fortune. At the next temple site, there was an impressive huge reclining Buddha approximately seventy feet long; at this point, I was yet to realise the main focal point of our Thai Experience. We stopped at the town close by and a few had a look around; it was full of new builds and quite uninspiring. The main things I remember are the market and in particular where the meat and fish were sold in the open air with not a refrigeration unit in sight. I was repulsed by the smells which lingered sickeningly in the nose and throat. My gratitude at coming from a country where this wouldn't be allowed was insurmountable; here, I imagined being able to afford meat could be a luxury for some. Never mind choosing where it comes from or how it is kept. The smells I could handle; I was more dismayed by the pets for sale that included dogs and rabbits in tiniest of cages and barely able to move; they looked totally miserable being trapped and only hoped that they were actually intended as pets.

As the day pressed on, everyone's arse gradually became numbed because we were being ferried about on the back of two trucks. These had lightly padded benches running down either side and could feel every bump in the road. Of course, there wasn't a seatbelt in sight. The air conditioning was fantastic because when we reached a certain speed, the breeze would just gust through, as there were no coverings down the sides. But this allowed everyone to galvanise by creating the banter of a military truck as we sat in the back together facing one another on our way to the next destination; an elephant sanctuary.

This was really cool, everyone loved it. We all had the opportunity to feed corn to the adult elephants, which they daintily took with their incredibly strong versatile trunk and duly wolfed down. They really are special creatures. So intelligent and majestic yet slightly odd due to the comparatively small eyes compared to the rest of the body and the trunk which seems to move with a mind of its own. One of the adults had unique twisted tusks, which was claimed as the only one in the world like it. The adults were in large enclosures separated by wooden fence rails where they could hang over and interact with visitors, but some baby elephants were running around and playing in the main part of the sanctuary, where people also wandered around in the same proximity. This caused absolute chaos as bodies scrambled to make room for the lolloping baby beasts as they excitedly chased a large ball. The adult elephants were taken out for walks and exercise each day and would pull up to a large platform for washing. This was also where we witnessed two full-grown adults start mating. No one could quite believe it because the mere sight of two such cumbersome mammals going at it was a sight to behold. The Thai staff working there couldn't believe it either because apparently it was such a special and unique moment, being as it's quite rare and they were running around in wild excitement. Not necessarily one guy though who was giving the male on top a 'helping hand' in with a big stick, because the size of the thing he was helping in, well, let's just say every man there felt slightly inferior. All the girls loved it and said we were very much inferior.

After our bout of elephant porn, we were treated to a massive Thai buffet on board a boat cruising up and down the nearby river, the food was awesome and now the beers were being popped open, probably due to the fact that there was a karaoke on board and volunteers would be required. Most obliged, promptly murdering virtually every song, but don't think anyone's ever heard such a fabulous rendition of 'Cotton Eye Joe' before as that was belted out by Rebecca and I. She was also from the north of England and we got on well; she was really cool and we had loads in common. It was her first time visiting the Far East, in particular Thailand. This was for her a trip of a lifetime and was really hoping to visit the JEATH railway which the PoWs build during World War 2. More so as her relatives had built it during the conflict and wanted to pay her respects, so I said that we should visit at the weekend as I had an idea where it was and knew what to expect for the day having taken a tour previously. I didn't mind doing it again as I couldn't really remember the other trip. It would help her to achieve one of her goals whilst on her travels and we now had something to do at the weekend.

We continued the rest of the week with our Thai language lessons, visiting numerous temples, including the laughing Buddha and Wat Praputhabaht. Here, there was a preserved rock of Buddha's footprint in it and had been turned into a shrine inside a temple that we reached via one of three staircases. It was up to the individual to select which; money, health or happiness? I chose happiness because I figured this surely covers all the bases. But the Phra Prang Sam Yot temple in Lopburi really stood out. This temple wasn't inhabited by monks or people for that matter. Upon our arrival into town, the rolled-up plastic covers along the sides and back of the truck were down to keep the rain out. When we stopped, someone looked out.

"Oh my god! There are fucking monkeys everywhere!"

Promptly, we all stuck our heads out to witness something quite surreal. Literally, primates were everywhere. On the pavements, up lamp posts, on ledges and up on the roofs of the buildings; in fact, the whole town was inhabited by monkeys running amok. It looked like we had walked on to the set of *Planet of the Apes*. Parking up, we had our briefing, including that we could go to the temple if anyone wished. Walking to the temple, ironically, there was a sign warning people about the presence of monkeys. 'Really? Where? I hadn't noticed!' It was made even more ironic by the fact that there was a monkey hanging off it. The temple located in the middle of town had only a 6ft high metal fence as its surrounding. It had been vacated by monks centuries ago but the macaques they revered remained and slept in the temple on the evenings; hence why there were monkeys wandering around all over, that had just acclimatising to the town as it grew over time.

83

It wasn't possible to enter the temple and probably for the best. A few others and I entered the grounds where some bought seed and nuts as it was possible to feed them. Another tourist trap but a novel one and the macaques were not pets but clearly used to human contact, especially with the prospect of food on tap. I wasn't too keen on having them grab and jump all over me as I was unsure of their temperament or of any diseases. A decision I felt slightly vindicated of after seeing one fuck another, stop, come all over itself, wipe itself clean and then eat the residue. Totally grossed out, I left pretty much after that and had to laugh at those who it thought it cool to have primates jumping all over them.

Also on the agenda was a visit to a war museum dedicated to local tribal warriors who fought against invading Burmese, a cake factory and the national museum. Again, back in Lopburi, our truck was chased by a Lycra-clad Thai on a racing bike. Everyone was cheering him on and due to his close proximity, we all would have had to pick him up off the truck floor had we hit the brakes. Something that some of us were to get a firsthand experience of. We had handicraft lesson where everyone made bracelets using a variety of beads; mine was a simple black and white, small, slim-beaded pattern, which looked quite boring compared to some of the designs which the others were manufacturing. Still I liked it even though I don't wear accessories like this or any jewellery for that matter, but figured I'd give it to someone who would appreciate it. Throughout the week, the Thai lessons continued. I didn't bother with the final lesson of the week as now I had become chief organiser for the weekend activities. What was initially Rebecca and I going to the JEATH railway was now Sienna as well, who I really liked and got on well with. And due to me missing the language lesson, others found out about our plans and the numbers swelled from casual manageable three to a hectic eighteen.

One thing I wasn't missing out on though was the cookery lesson and involved making a Thai salad with fresh vegetables and Pad Thai noodles. Unfortunately, I'm no top chef, apart from the swearing, and never wrote the recipe down nor can remember what was in it. I would love to try to make it again as mine was a little bland, even the soy and fresh chilli dressing couldn't save it when I tried to compensate lack of flavour with a little heat. I only succeeded in blowing my head off with the littlest and deadliest of the chillies. I like spicy food but call the fire brigade; I was in agony and couldn't complain either as prior, I'd laughed when another never realised and ate a full one. All said, despite the sub-par cookery skills, it was a good fun experience doing something different, practical and working in groups always cause for a giggle, especially when it goes wrong.

Now having a small army in tow for the weekend, believe it or not, made a few things easier. Another helped me put an itinerary together; we chose to go on the JEATH railway as the intended plan then headed to the Erawan National Park to chill out at the waterfalls. Essentially, we chose the easiest things to do within the shortest distance. Others wanted to go to Tiger Temple but I wasn't that keen as I'd heard unfavourable reports about it. Coupled with this, we were also distinctly aware of running behind time on the day, having to relying on Thai train schedule; so, democratically, Rebecca, a few others and I, being the main orchestrators, scratched that idea deciding if anyone didn't like it, then tough. Luckily, most were cool about it. Also, being one large group, we could get everyone there in two mini-vans, which we could hire with drivers for the day and worked out much cheaper.

We had the vans, we had the drivers, we knew the times, we knew the cost about £10 per head and we had the itinerary. So I had the genius idea of writing an idiot guide to put on the notice board with all the information on, because I was already starting to get constant grief from people asking the same questions about what was happening. Problem with idiot guides is they are read by idiots, or you will tell people to read the idiot guide and an idiot will still proceed to ask you their question anyway, or an idiot will read the idiot guide and still ask you their question which is answered on the idiot guide. Being unofficially designated the unofficial organiser, stroke guide, stroke tour operator my brain was well and truly crumbling at this point. So, on the guide I made a point of indicating that everyone had the information and anyone who was going was responsible for themselves. In turn, people just said, "Well, I'll just hang around with you then." I couldn't believe it; out-foxed by idiots.

Saturday was sorted, so with it being Friday night we figured it was drink time, but a few others and I decided to venture to another haunt close by to try it out. On arriving, one thing was apparent; this bar was not used to seeing westerners. It was pretty evident due to the stares, people blatantly coming over for a look and no one spoke a word of English. We sat in a straw hut which was really nice despite the thousands of mosquito gate crashers, while a designated ice lady would constantly put ice in our already really chilled beer and one of the owners' daughters who knew a little bit of

English was now our official translator; she must have only been fourteen, bless her. The ever-curious locals were absolutely fascinated by Sienna's alabaster white skin, Erin's arms and my baldy head. Yet we obliged them, hung out, took loads of photos, got drunk and to everyone in the bars amusement sang karaoke in Thai. How? With subtitles written phonetically in English for some reason. The rural folk loved our crazy Thai singing and were the warmest, welcoming and friendly people you could wish to meet. After we left, we said that we would definitely return and bring the others as well. As it seemed a good idea. At the time.

Saturday was an early start; five thirty a.m. Which idiot organised this? Problem was, we needed to get to Kanchanaburi early enough to get the train; the later one wouldn't really suffice as we would miss the national park, so timing became everything. We got dropped off just after nine a.m. near to the station. The train was due around 10:55 a.m., leaving about an hour-and-a-half to explore. The place was the same as I remembered it; small, easy to negotiate around with a museum, shops and restaurants. The main feature and focus being the bridge immortalised by the movie *The Bridge on the River Kwai*, but it seemed different. Only because it looked like there was more there now; especially market stalls that were selling lots of local-made goods and those of the fake variety; where I treated myself to a pair of flip flops and some 'Ray Ban' sun glasses. These were all located next to the railway line, where people still happily meandered across the tracks, blissfully unconcerned by any oncoming trains. Everyone had a venture onto the bridge, rebuilt after having been destroyed numerous times during World War 2 by the Allies due to its importance for transportation purposes to Burma and infamous in history for having been built by Japan and the Allied PoWs; J for Japan, E for England, A for American, T for Thai and H for Holland, giving it the name JEATH (or death) railway. Countless died in the railway lines construction and subsequent destruction, even binding PoWs to the bridge in the hope of stopping the Allies from destroying it. Some were a little nervous about the prospect of going onto the bridge, not necessarily because the river could be seen through gaps of the narrow sides, but more so because this means being on the actual railway line. So, if a train came, you would have to run to make it to the embankment or nearest safety bay, that were built into the span of the bridge to get out of harm's way. This happened previously and I ended up running with much trepidation, hoping not trip over the boards and rails while trying to find sanctuary. Luckily though, this wasn't the case here, and I had plenty of time to admire the scenery of the town and river front restaurants on one side and the lush forest banks adorning the other as the heavy chocolate brown river washed below.

All this talk of possibly getting hit by a train seemed highly unlikely, as 10.55 came and went without a sniff of a train. People in the group were seemingly getting anxious, as was I, about its non-arrival. I knew it would come but I was more concerned about the fact that this was eating into the day and an already tight schedule. The train rolled into the station at 11.30. Everyone hastily jumped on board. Half the group getting on the first economy coach and the rest on numerous others, splitting us all up with no hope really of getting back together, as the carriages were packed. Setting off for our destination of Nam Tok, the train was old and slow which did allow for good appreciation of the acres of green fields, the mountains and hills in the background and a nice chilled-out ride as the body rocked with hypnotic rhythm of the rails. The seats themselves probably caused the most discomfort, as they were wooden and some were loose, so they would fall though at random moments, but still an enthralling, worthwhile journey. Especially at the points where the driver slowed down as the train passed high up, along a large wooden section that arched around the contour of a cliff face, with an impressive drop down to the river system and jungle below, causing a massive scramble by the passengers on board to get to the left-hand windows to take as many camera shots as possible of the beautiful, lush sweeping view.

Everyone disembarked at Nam Tok followed by a swift head count; miraculously, no one went missing. The mini-vans were also waiting. As planned, we had lunch in the restaurant close by the station, having ridiculously all been ushered into the vehicles to be driven literally about twenty metres when we could have walked; as it took longer to get everyone in and then out again. Lunch took an eternity as time ebbed away and we needed to get to the park for four p.m. before it closed. Eventually, we hit the road and got to Erawan National Park around three-fifty p.m. By now, the weather had taken a turn for the worse and it had started to rain, but we were intent on getting wet anyway. Parking up, we all made a hasty dash for the waterfalls and the swimming lagoon as there was about an hour before we had to leave. Although overcast, it was still warm from the humidity, being enclosed by an army of trees and vegetation, where the rain patted the light green water of the inviting pool below, while a large torrent of cascading white water toppled relentlessly to paint a beautiful picturesque scene. The locals were in and enjoying the water so we decided to join them. I didn't really have much choice anyway after June, a cheeky wee Scot, pushed me in. We swam in the beautiful turquoise water and it was refreshing splashing about; Ellie and I headed to the waterfall to climb the slippery rocks. Not being very high, with relative ease we reached the downpour of water acting as a curtain to the open cavern behind. Although not amazingly powerful, it still created an immense echo in the chamber where we chilled in our moist cut-off sanctuary before walking through the water and immerging on the other side to take turns, jumping 6ft in to the warm oasis below.

We were having a great time messing around in the foaming water around us; senses of sound and vision, as to what was happening, were somewhat dulled. I looked up and noticed the others on the side of the water, some frantically waving their arms and others' hands cupped to their mouths shouting. We could not hear what all the commotion was about. But the frantic pointing revealed the problem. A two-metre-plus-size problem; about twenty feet in front of us where we were jumping, there was huge lizard swimming about and from our close by vantage point looked massive.

"Have you seen the size of that lizard, in the water?" I exclaimed.

"Oh shit! It's blocking our way back!" was her reply.

"Well I'm not getting in the water with it. He looks a right mean bastard! We'll hang here for a couple of minutes and see what happens."

So we waited, peering at the huge reptile, hoping for him to swim off, mindful in the knowledge that we had about five minutes left before we were due back and were already late. We were just looking at each other with a 'what are we gonna do?' look plastered all over our faces.

If I said I dived into water; wrestled the beast and held him whilst the damsel swam past and I calmly made my way to the shore with all the glory, it would be an outrageous lie. Things were a little simpler; I had a good idea the lizard wouldn't hang around because prior to getting in, a very similar-looking reptile had swum across the span of the lagoon, everyone had seen him and freaked out. But he simply got out the other side and wandered off. Then we all ventured into the water. Now, it seemed the creature was only heading back from where it came. And that's what happened; it simply swam to the other side and headed off into the undergrowth. Probably out for a little evening saunter, swim and nosy around. Kind of like ourselves. Relieved, we headed to the water edge and joined the others. Quick change and golf buggy ride back, we made it to the car park and the waiting vans. Everyone was soaked in some way, shape or form from swimming or the rain. As the park closed, we headed back and chatted with our Thai driver about the lizard incident. He said that we did the right thing as they have sharp teeth and claws that if threatened, they can bite and scratch, causing bad cuts.

On the road heading back, I sat with Rebecca and was being employed as a human pillow. Everyone was tired and falling asleep left, right and centre, lined up on the seats like toppled dominoes. Although exhausted with the long day and activities, not to mention pain in the arse stress of organising the trip, I was really happy. Everyone told me they had a great time and really enjoyed the day. I felt good. Feeling I'd made an active contribution and helped give something extra to everyone and was gratified to see everyone have fun and do something different and all it took really was a little effort and planning. The main kudos though came from Rebecca, the reason why we had decided to do this in the first place. She was over the moon and had a fantastic time achieving something which meant so much to her and was really grateful. This made me happiest of all.

It was late when we arrived back at the ranch. We had an invite to another of the project accommodation; 'The Twin House' were hosting a pyjama party but being in the middle of nowhere, we couldn't get transport and were told it was dangerous to walk due to the roaming dogs which scoured the streets in packs, protecting their territories. I couldn't be bothered anyway. Also, I was void of pyjamas and sleeping in my boxers; an awful sight for some unsuspecting stranger. So we stayed local and inevitably ended up drinking till two a.m., playing the classic card game; Ring of Fire, where the drink miraculously made us forget how tired we were.

Feeling bad about not going to 'The Twin House', the following day a few others and I walked along the river to find it and apologise for not going. On the way, we passed some huge beautiful houses, tiny shanty homes, small shops, a small makeshift gym, a bridge spanning the river and an Internet café. At last, we had found some civilisation. And it just happened to be twenty minutes in the opposite direction from where we went on the first day. We had been so busy that no one bothered to explore any more of our local surroundings and we weren't as stranded as we once thought. Although this was at a price; there were some pretty mean dogs on the way and the only form of discouragement from attacking and biting was the prospect of having a rock or stone thrown at them.

'The Twin House' was about 2km away and different to 'The Brown House', even though just another base for patrons to use from the same company. We met with three of the people staying there; they had the party but lots had left that day and the facility was now pretty sparse. No kidding; this housed around a hundred. Nearly four times as many as 'The Brown House' was much more grandiose and better located. There was Internet, hammocks for chilling and a TV area to use at will. We could only use the TV in the private lounge when the owners were not there and if it was OK to do so. We chatted, apologised and explained the no show. The people there were cool with it and even offered some dinner as there was ample. We politely declined, realising the time and ours would be ready. Also we had not stated that we wouldn't be eating and didn't want to be rude and have our food go to waste for no good reason.

Entering the second week of our Thai Experience programme, I was loving it so far and had learnt much about the heritage, culture and language offering a new-found appreciation of Thai life. I was tired though with early mornings and late evenings catching up with me. Monday proved no different; up at five a.m. with the local monks for alms. We walked around the community with the monks to accept kind food offerings from the people. This was humbling as no matter how poor someone was, they all seemed to give something; for some spiritual salvation. And that's what this week was mainly about. Later that morning, we watched a documentary about the Buddhist religion and had a talk on its foundation and belief system. I found this intriguing and paid close attention in the hope of learning something significant, handily we were given paper work and handouts to summarise the main points. I was pleased with this as we could read in our own time, and now had reference because due to being in a tired state, my attention unfortunately kept waning which only amplified my annoyance with others who weren't that interested or bothered, and decided to idly chat amongst themselves instead.

In the afternoon, I was feeling better and more sociable as we visited yet another temple; the features here attracted the most interest yet. The massive statue of a sitting Buddha overlooked a large fish pond brimming with koi carp that constantly broke the surface as they spotted potential benefactors on the jetty who were throwing in offerings of free food. More surreal though amid the beauty and serenity were the many elaborate statues depicting visions of heaven and hell awaiting those on their day of reckoning. Heaven beautifully enchanting light and happy for those who had been good and virtuous. Hell on the other hand torturous, dark and vividly gruesome; a macabre reminder for those wicked and evil how they will bound to eternal damnation; that offered an unexpected and stark reminder from a peaceful religion – you should behave or else…

The others who had gone to Bangkok for the weekend and not joined us on the railway journey still hadn't returned. We were having quiet drinks in the bar on the evening when they eventually did. It didn't stay quiet for long. Dave, one of the youngest at eighteen, was there predominantly to study Thai boxing. I liked Dave and despite our age difference, we got on well. He'd been away over the weekend and returned with a stun gun that he purchased in the markets of downtown Bangkok. Within minutes, chaos ruled. Most of the guys there got a bolt of electricity on various parts of the anatomy. As one had it done, then peer pressure goaded the rest. Seeing Steve get involuntarily zapped and survive, I had a blast to the calf and then to the top of my backside. It didn't hurt too bad with the low amps but I refrained from taking a hit to the head; my few brain cells still quite precious to me. What's worse than a bloke with a stun gun? A pissed up woman; with a stun gun. A slightly refreshed and therefore unhinged Clare got hold of it and proceeded to chase everyone around the bar, zapping bodies at will. People scattered in all directions, furniture uplifted, girls screaming, blokes screaming louder as the horrendously loud crackle of electricity belted out with unnerving regularity. Eventually, Dave got his little toy back and blasted her for her troubles. A very quiet night turned into a very funny night in a strangely perverse and unorthodox way. Amazingly, some good came from this as what had been bought was inadvertently a very effective cure for mosquito bites. A larger version of a click gadget that puts weak pulses of electricity through the site of an insect bite dispersing the histamine that causes swelling. I had a huge, incredibly itchy bite on the inside of my forearm, one blast with the stun gun and the next morning it had all but disappeared. Trademark that motherfucker 'cos it worked like a charm.

Pressing on with our move to things spiritual, we had a question-and-answer session with three local monks. I found this a real privilege as it's not very often that you get to ask questions to those who rigorously practice this religion, in their own country and especially as they couldn't speak English and I couldn't speak Thai. These were interpreted by our co-ordinator. I enquired as to how long the three monks had been practicing? What time scale to adhere fully to the 227 rules of Buddhism? Are monks allowed to study other religious beliefs? And had Buddhism become harder to practice with western influences on the world? They happily answered our questions stating that they had been monks many years since childhood and that there was no time scale but can practice as many of the rules as they wished; which explained why we had witnessed monks enjoying cigarettes when traversing around. Monks can study other religions but remain Buddhist and that the western world had made it harder to practice Buddhism with external influences growing evermore prominent; including celebrity, large corporate chains and the massive influx of tourism.

Then for me came what seemed one of the highlights, experiencing how the Buddhist monks live by spending a day and night within a temple in another nearby town. Arriving in the trucks, the place wasn't exactly what was expected, having been spoilt by visiting some of the most beautiful ornate temples in the country to this; in effect, a building site.

There was timber and tools all over the place, but these places aren't going to build themselves, I rationalised, but the illusion was now already shattered. Especially, as it was on really tatty wooded grounds, along a dirt track with effigies all along the side, looking like something out of *The Blair Witch Project*. Sleeping was split into male and female. Males slept in the big prayer hall and females upstairs in a dorm room of a separate building. Eating was under a long canopy in the courtyard-cum-building site in between both sleeping arrangements. On arrival, we were issued with white pants and white throw over shawls; a standard issue to those visiting the temple for any period of time. The monks wore standard orange full-length robes. Dressed in our snazzy karate suit ensemble, we headed to a beautiful temple within the grounds. After negotiating our way around and through a large ornamental rock feature to enter a tiled prayer room, here we practiced some meditation techniques in its calming serenity. Inside, there wasn't much except white walls, adorned with numerous intricately detailed paintings that depicted the important phases in the life of Buddha.

Meditation techniques involved sitting, standing and walking, unaware there was more than one technique. Predominantly, I was better at the standing, lasting a mere ten minutes and more than half that were thinking and not clearing the mind as instructed. I had always been under the illusion that meditation was thinking about stuff. Not so. Thinking of nothing to cleanse the mind is apparently the way forward. If anyone has tried to do this, you will appreciate just how hard this can be. As reference, remember the end scene of *Ghostbusters* movie where characters are instructed to not think about anything? And now you're thinking about huge marshmallow men. It does take practice. Another thirty minutes meditating were spent on the evening in the main hall, also known as our dorm. This session was with the monks who habituated there. I managed about seven minutes; my mind distracted by squirming in discomfort at the stationary continuous pressure on my bones, from the not-very-familiar position of sitting cross-legged on a hard floor. Others less interested had already started messing around and that didn't help matters either. At the end of the session, it was surreal watching the lead monk seemingly wake from an upright meditative trance and funny, as one of the younger monks looked like he actually woke from nodding off.

After participating in bouts of chanting, we were hungry with every one right up for some dinner. This was sharp squashed though as living with the monks meant living as they live; and included not eating after noon. So we played cards, while some others went out to a bar that didn't exist and ended up drinking from the seven eleven. Staying at the temple, I crashed out on the floor of the meditation room at about ten p.m.; there was a very thin carpet on the concrete floor, only cushioned by our sleeping bags. Even with the hard floor and numerous mosquitoes, I still managed some decent sleep, only waking the five times before eventually getting up at six a.m. to go around the local community to collect alms with the monks. Upon returning, we were asked to help out and tidy up the entrance, removing debris like fallen leaves. Some of the group members decided this was a blatant piss-take by the monks and that they weren't skivvies there to do work. I felt the opposite; at the very least, it was something to do to fill in the time and was a little exercise after a rare night of sobriety so I gave a hand with some sweeping out front. I couldn't really understand not helping out a little because it wasn't as if I was missing out on other more exciting activities. It didn't take long, so I also spent time exploring grounds, taking photos and still had time to crash out on the floor, relaxing till ten o'clock came around and we finally ate.

I loved my time spent with the monks and emphasised a real commitment to that way of life; morning eating only, hard work, praying, meditation and having to maintain this as a respected spiritual figurehead.

Not to mention the other 227 disciplines to abide by if you decide to be the most die-hard of monk; which must require a lot of dedication, as there were a few here smoking too. This was an awakening experience also; the freedoms I take for granted like eating when I want and the use of electrical goods were removed for the dizzy heights of all of twenty-four hours; and I missed them. But it was good for the soul and a brilliant exercise in going without, where the only one complaint being I would have preferred a smaller group of people to be there; and who *actually* wanted to be there. Some were just not into it and their perpetual moaning ensured everyone heard about their woes. Overall though, it was a fantastic unique experience and I was glad of the opportunity to live it.

The rest of the week was spent on more crafts and we fashioned small bamboo wicker pots by the riverside. I started chatting with the locals who were fishing at the time and was left amazed and slightly perplexed when one of them happily jumped into the uninviting beige water to release a snag from his friend's fishing line, without even being asked or offering. We painted small porcelain figurines and went to yet another temple complex where again outside; hellish effigies depicted suffering after passing away for those who live a sinful life, as large-scale models demonstrated the bloody torture to be endured in eternal damnation and another pond stacked full of greedy fish happily whipped into frenzy from thrown bread. Within the actual temple, there were mirrors all over the ceiling and walls and reminded me of the end scene in *Enter the Dragon*. Seemingly hidden by the reflections yet in full view, an embalmed body of the highest most respected monk laid peacefully to rest in a glass cabinet amongst the statues and gongs of the beautifully ornate reflective building.

On our last day in 'The Brown House', the Friday, we spent half of it in Thai Tesco's supermarket; shopping for those trekking before unanimously deciding not to visit the market and head straight for the zoo. Unfortunately, it turned out to be a most unwise and uneducated decision. Here, this included a large Orangutan dressed in shorts and t-shirt sat up posing so people could have their photo taken with him. And it didn't get better; tigers in cages with no or hardly any water to cool off, cubs in small pens and the bears were just locked away. I thought enclosures for large birds were minuscule comparatively to the open area where the smaller species were free to fly about and it was possible to walk inside. There was an iguana and boa which did look well; yet this couldn't take away the images of some of the crappier, miserable and more squalid conditions endured by other, mainly larger animals.

The visit to this park was apparently booked by a subsidiary company in Thailand; they claimed to be eco-friendly – this a tad bullshit. Given how they supported such a poorly maintained facility, I suspect they use this line just for the tourist dollar without actually knowing what it is actually supposed to mean. Annoyingly, as my understanding went, the company was supposed to check on the activities being run, then they could see themselves this was not acceptable and tell the facilitators to improve or stop endorsing it. Much like now, my soap box was well and truly out and I was stood on it ranting; a bunch of others and I complained to the organisers; making our opinions felt verbally and via the feedback sheet that was offered around the group about our programme, the good and bad aspects and how it could be made better. Now, our two weeks were up and we were getting ready to go separate ways. But not before one big piss up.

On Friday night, we all headed into Sing Buri town, to a bar in a hotel on the river front. It was nice but nothing flash, small with warm beer and a few other drink selections, no music except for a dodgy karaoke machine on stage in a fully lit room. The main point being that they sold booze so it was good enough for us. The night got off to a flyer with drinks, bad karaoke and laughing aplenty, but it wasn't long before the pressure cooker that was our last two weeks' existence together erupted in true big brother 'we are all splitting up, I don't care, I've had a drink and I'll say what I like' fashion.

For the last week, I'd begun to notice the fractures within the group. The little splinter cells that split off from the herd as they find common ground with others of their own understanding, or because they had systematically managed to annoy one, two or lots of the others through either something or even nothing they had said or done. Personally, I couldn't be arsed with it all and tried my level best to get along with everyone and refused to take sides as it really wasn't worth it and figured that maybe it was a sort of test to accept how others are different in their own way. Don't get me wrong, I didn't get along with everyone, but I tried to be pleasant enough and not get involved with the bitching and backstabbing as it isn't something I especially revel in. But this particular evening, jokes were said and tricks were played that were obviously not taken in the spirit. These were then followed by arguments, tears, strops, dramatic exits and so on as people got their due attention. Amazing and hilarious drama if you like that sort of thing. I wouldn't care, but we hadn't even got back yet and it was only about nine o'clock.

Back at the ranch, things had calmed down an octave or ten. Everyone was suitably hammered due to the local Thai whisky but amicable enough. One of the girls and I said we should all try the Thai bar we were in the previous Friday with the prospect of karaoke and warm hospitality. Possibly not the best idea, because when there ice started getting thrown about, with fingers pointing to who started it and who was involved; needless to say it all kicked off again, and again, and again, following on from previous arguments. By this point, everyone was involved in some way, shape or form. There were a few of us who decided we should all leave, as we were now causing quite the commotion in the open-air ambience. So everyone left for 'The Brown House' to get some well-deserved shut eye from the excitement of people being well and truly pissed out of their brains, telling everyone else how it was, is or should be. Upon leaving, I tried to apologise to the owners; they thought it was hilarious and were killing themselves laughing at everyone as they shook my hand goodbye. You don't get much more hospitable than that really.

The next day was one of those 'so what happened last night then?' as people woke with stonking hangovers; as expected. Everyone sat down and started talking about the exploits from the night before and laughing about it, even those who were arguing – which I have to say was really funny to listen and also cool with respect to people's acceptance of making a fucking nuisance out of themselves; especially having a good insight into the drunk mentality, from experience of not only with myself but dealing with others in such states. In the cold sober realisation of things, people make mountains out of mole hills; things are gotten off chests which aren't necessarily there and if they are, they always come out the wrong way or straight up say thing they don't mean. As for the rest of Saturday, not an awful lot happened, Internet got used, movies got watched, the obligatory few beers were drunk and the bed was hit. Pretty uneventful really, but it was somewhat needed.

Eventful though was again just loitering with intent around the corner. The next day, we headed off early to a plush hotel resort, located way out in the middle of the countryside, next to nowhere. The facilities though were awesome; swimming pool, horse riding, golf course, masseuse, sports court, bar and buffet restaurant. We were being treated before splitting and heading our own separate ways, trekking, teaching etc. during the third week. For me, it was the end of the line with the group as I wouldn't be meeting back up on the island for the fourth week. I was heading off to do my own thing.

With rooms sorted and everyone settling in, Jake and I decided to put in a not-so-swift eighteen holes on the golf course, playing a flawless round of army golf. Hit it to the left, then to the right, left, right, left, right. Army golf, you see? It was smaller than normal courses but after wandering around the fairways, greens, pastures and somehow a pineapple patch with our caddies, we ended up finishing totally knackered to endure the rabble quizzing us about where we had been for some three hours. I was really pleased about playing not only because the exercise was well and truly needed, but I managed to knock in a fantastic birdie on one of the holes, chipping in from off the green which I'd never achieved before. So that called for one thing; straight to the 19th, let's celebrate.

Inside the bar, there was cool air conditioning and it was a welcome atmosphere from the humid sticky climate of outside. And also respite from the one or two bugs out and about in the early evening witching hour. One or two million, that is. It was absolutely insane and I had never seen so many insects in all my life. They were all over the stairs in the block where we were staying, on the tiled floors, on the windows, and crawling into the rooms through the ill-fitting doors. They were literally everywhere and were attracted by the only fluorescent lights for miles around, that happened to be in the corridors highlighting where our rooms were. So we had to turn the lights off for the whole building. There was that many you couldn't open your mouth for fear of critter ingestion and when walking, they would *crack* and *crunch* as they scavenged under foot. No one could believe what was happening. It was mental and likened to a biblical plague or nightmare horror scenario where all insects had an uprising and were intent on a hostile takeover invasion. That succeeded.

To take the edge off, everyone chilled with drinks away from the rooms. The festivities were quite short-lived as everyone was tired and started to go to bed early at about eleven; more so probably because people were aware of repeating the previous night's misdemeanours. Also, I had a sneaky suspicion that the organisers had a word with the hotel to close early; now knowing the reputation of the group.

The next morning, everyone was up spritely, and hanging around the pool, taking in some sun and playing games in the water. Eventually, the time arrived where we all had to part. Those involved in teaching or other activities said goodbye to the ones who were trekking and departed back to 'The Brown House' to get sorted for school placements or home stays. Driving back, we were all relaxing on the benches of our now customary trucks. I happened to look through the gap ahead over the roof of where the driver was, to see a silver car start to cut across our path as it turned right, and in doing so, completely misjudged our speed, causing our driver to slam on the brakes hard.

In slow-motion split seconds, the dynamic action of our truck coming to a screeching halt catapulted everyone and everything towards the front of the flat bed in the back. Drinks went everywhere, as bodies and bags ended up in a large mangled mass on the truck floor, squashed up against the driver cabin as we all unintentionally crushed one another. And as Sod's law dictates, in these types of instances the smaller ended up on the bottom bearing the brunt of the fourteen people pile-up. Luckily, a few bumps and scrapes aside, everyone gingerly emerged from the garbled heap fine and well, breathing sighs of relief at the close call. How? I do not know, but without seatbelts the bags had definitely helped provide some cushioning. We were lucky; a second earlier and it could have and would have been a totally different story, written about with newspaper headlines involving the words 'tourism car crash carnage'. Right till the very end of being with the group, there was still time for one last bit of drama. Hardly a surprise though.

Homestay

Arriving a tad battered and bruised at 'The Brown House' after our minor incursion, we quickly got our things together and waited for our taxi pick up to take us to our homestay and teaching placement. I chose this because it was the less obvious option. Less obvious in the sense of not having a clue as to what to expect; with living at the teacher's home, how things would work teaching wise and given that I knew 'The Brown House' accommodation was fine and more of the others had opted to stay there to teach at the local school. But I figured I could get more out of the opportunity by taking the less obvious but arguably more interesting option. Plus, there was a small part of me which hankered for new surroundings and after two weeks of vegetarian food, that was nice but a little repetitive, I was looking forward to some more variety and admittedly some meat in my diet.

I was joined by three others; Erin, Clarissa and Jelena. Erin and Clarissa were in our group and I had been with them for the last two weeks; Jelena was from a different group so; therefore, we made our acquaintances. Upon arriving, we were met by the teacher at her home. She was called Mah Lee; a small and slender-looking woman of around fifty with lovely warm smile and friendly nature. Her English was good too so there were minimal problems with communications. She was so pleased that we had chosen to come teach with her and was already really appreciative of the help, so I was immediately endeared to her.

Her home was off a dirt track on the outskirts of Lopburi in the countryside. Entering, there were four separate buildings in the yard area which you could clearly see were classrooms due to the chairs, tables and white boards; these surrounded the drive and pathway to the house. Further up on the left was the garage, then our rooms, a dining area and under a canopy a kitchen and laundry area and our bathrooms. The house was on the right which we never used or ventured into but attached was a separate room that had in it around a dozen computers with Internet access for the children and now us to use. Moving around the back, we were introduced to the family pets; a crazy dog called Tulip whose name came from a former teaching volunteer who was Dutch. Tulip was first and foremost a guard dog, a tan-coloured crossbreed of seemingly endless excitable energy, whose bounding around caused regular havoc, easily disconcerting people with gentle nips and constant pestering to be adorned with attention. More relaxed were two cows in the backyard enclosure that had huge floppy ears and docile look; oddly named Left and Right. Not sure if their names changed if they swapped sides with each other. This was starting to look like a really sweet deal, what with having a lovely hostess and family, nice accommodation, air conditioning, Internet access, basketball hoop and ball to play, meals and laundry. Then it got a tad better being informed that we had mountain bikes at our disposal and an automatic scooter to explore the local surroundings. I had one thought; *If you look in the dictionary under the word 'jackpot', it would say 'see this deal'.* The only thing left was the main reason for being there; this was actually to teach some English to some Thai kids and something that I had never done before.

On the first day, we were up earlier than expected; five thirty a.m. to be exact. This was because it was the final day of lent and Mah Lee took us to the local monastery to give alms to the monks. This time, though, we interacted like the congregation did; sitting in the prayer room where we instantly got involved in the prayers and chanting like the locals. After the ceremony, people flocked to speak to Mah Lee. It was clear she was well-respected and liked within the community and was also actively involved with events and gatherings, bringing the people together, which I thought was great to see and quite inspiring.

As nine o'clock came, we were back at the house and the children started to turn up in their droves, getting dropped off via the school bus, or rather two open trucks with customary benches in the back – an all-too-familiar form of transport for ourselves and in general in Thailand. Others arrived on foot or were dropped off by their parents. About forty-five all together, ages ranging from five to sixteen; apparently these kids (most of them) were in their holidays and came to Mah Lee's house for summer school so the parents could still work and not have to look after them. I wasn't sure where they actually went to school? Or how this affected the others who had gone to the school if it was closed? That said; I didn't give it much thought, because other matters were at hand.

Erin, Jelena and I ended up in the largest classroom together. I was a little bit nervous at this point with a *How the hell am I going to go about this then?* Thought running through my head and felt slightly out of my depth with my new vocation; especially as my 'teaching' in the loose sense of the word now had an audience of a different nationality who could only speak partial English. Many years previous, I had worked with children who had severe mental disabilities as part of work experience when at college, which, as rewarding as it was, wasn't teaching as such, but more helping and interacting with them. But out of my depth, it was what was needed and what I had wanted. It was a challenge, being taken out of my comfort zone, and testing myself and my coping skills, and now I had it. Despite having a booklet of guidance notes at my disposal from handouts, giving hints and tips of how to go about teaching, I had done what I normally would do and not read them thoroughly, having just a brief look through; so I did have a few pointers, but ended up with what felt was more a wing and a prayer notion. Purely because I was now feeling more relaxed about what was happening as my journey unravelled, where virtually every day I could feel confidence grow within and believe in my own abilities, as I seemingly coped with situations and problems with ease, adapted and moved on. Also, I adopted an 'I'll copy off the methods that the others were using and possibly chuck in a few ideas of my own' attitude; foolproof.

The multiple varying sessions were based from nine a.m. till around three p.m. with differing groups of around twelve; aging from five to twelve years old, some of whom could speak decent English already and others only a few words. Surprisingly, it was the younger ones who seemed more prolific in English and would translate any instructions to the older ones, so that they knew what to do and what was happening. I thought this was really kind and interesting to see, as the older ones were actually thankful to their younger classmates, not feeling undermined or embarrassed by their lack of understanding; like they really wanted to learn. We started with the alphabet putting words and pictures to each letter, such as 'A' for apple and a snazzy little diagram showing what it was and were off to a flyer. Next, we moved on to numbers, then colours, body parts, clothing, created maps of where we all live and then tried making sentences using the words which had been learnt; exhibiting the work on the wall for all to admire and clearly envy.

The day was broken up with lunch and breaks, plus they each got a chance to use the computer suite, quite the privilege for some of the children and really nice to see that they were getting this opportunity at all, never mind at such a fledgling age. Mah Lee thought that it would also be a good idea to take all the children outside to play games during some lessons so that they could incorporate exercise and learning English, via throwing a ball to one another and creating sentences such as 'my name is...' and 'I like...' with 'I spy' etc. thrown in for good measure. The various changes in curriculum were frequent as it quickly became apparent that the kids would lose interest in the class without switching regularly to hold their attention, and would inevitably start messing around or the mobile phones would come out. Kids, *eh*? What you going to do? But this also helped us, as it meant we didn't run out of ideas.

That evening, Mah Lee took us to a local temple built into the side of a hill with a festival at the base. Exploring we ventured to the statue at the pinnacle; where a lizard-like giant god held aloft a huge slab of stone. Being quite unique, it was clearly visible for miles around, especially as it was lit up with lighting cannons due to darkness setting in that began to blot any view. Just before the statue summit, there was also a cave with a giant reclining Buddha statue inside and various icons which were impressive and the temple featured the curiosity intensifying remains of a mummified monk resting peacefully in an ornate gold glass sarcophagus. For dinner we headed back down to the festival and we set about negotiating the food which looked nice and edible, giving a wide birth to the meats that looked slightly under cooked, pink and I'm sure still winking.

The traditional Thai dance show featured girls in beautiful traditional costumes performing for the on looking locals. A really colourful, flowing, choreographed spectacle that I unfortunately wasn't fully appreciating as perhaps I should because with the full day, I was feeling rather tired. Eventually, we left at around nine p.m. and was longing for bed only to find that the Thai car parking system wasn't as efficient as back home and we were blocked in. I could feel the annoyance welling up, but I had to remain silent and hold my frustrated tongue. Mah Lee struggled to get the car out and asked that I move it. I wasn't overly keen driving another's car in a foreign country in such circumstances, but managed to get through the narrowest of margins without hitting anything, as Thais frantically moved around dozen scooters and bikes blocking the exit, only to find the track out was obstructed by a 4x4 truck. Once again, Thais frantically bumped and shoved the offending barricade out of the way creating a narrow gap to squeeze through where I hoped not to scrape another vehicle nor put her car in the adjacent ditch. Finally, after around forty-five minutes, we were able to make our way back. I was very tired now and pissed off; mainly due to the long day and the effort to negotiate our way out of the parking debacle, but more so because all Erin and Jelena did to help the situation was laugh and take the piss out of the way Mah Lee would say my name, which I felt incredibly rude and discourteous. If I hadn't held my tongue, they were first in the firing line. One of the reasons I never lost it was because Mah Lee was very grateful for the help and apologetic for the situation which wasn't her fault. On the drive back, I was quiet and just gazed out of the window to witness a shooting star stream across the sky. Never seeing one, thinking about how cool it was, did make me smile though before I went to bed.

The following day was rather odd. We had been teaching (if it could be described as that) for all of one day then had the day off to visit a local waterfall haunt. All organised by Mah Lee; mini-van, driver, itinerary the lot. Awesome, don't mind if I do. Leaving at about nine a.m., Jelena, Erin, Clarissa, Mack – a student of Mah Lee's acting as chaperone and I suspect relishing the chance to hang out with some westerners to practice English – and I jumped into the spacious mini-van to head out. A really bad DVD copy of *Bad Boys* movie played on the entertainment system in the mini-van, so bad was the bootleg that the first twenty minutes of dialogue was exceptionally loud with constant background noise before the sound went off completely and the only other discs to endure for the rest of the day when travelling was Thai karaoke. I should point out that for me, Thai karaoke only is really appealing if words are spelt phonetically on the screen and I'm inebriated.

First point of call was the site of the massive Patok Dam. A huge engineering marvel that wasn't very aesthetically pleasing to the eye; more with functionality in mind, the idea behind it to aid irrigation to the land, so the local folk could farm; an idea that was apparently devised by the king himself. The torrent of water gushing through was loud and spectacular, funnelling from the huge grey concrete flumes of the dam that created a large powerful river system. Occasionally, fish would jump as they battled upstream against the flow which added obvious encouragement to the locals who were fishing on either side. Less encouraging though was, I noticed, that they were all wearing life jackets. Probably a good idea; not hard to fathom one wrong slip and no one would survive the ferocity of white water and undertow. We took in the dam visitor centre and market place that sold mainly souvenirs and items for sun protection before heading to the relaxing waterfalls.

Arriving at the market close by, the place was bustling and we had lunch; the normal concoction of chicken with rice and any amount of hot chilli sauce. Crossing over the footbridge spanning the tree-shrouded river and falls, it quickly became apparent we weren't the only ones with this idea; the rocks, water, pools and riverside were teeming with Thais, making the most of the day and idyllic surroundings, like they too had decided to bunk off work. We found a spot in the shade near to the water. I wanted to be more in the sun as I was still a lovely off-white pasty colour, so I situated myself in an exposed part by the caramel coloured river to try and gather together at least a smearing of tan. That said it wasn't as if I had the chance really to do much sunbathing; everything just seemed quite frantic and I couldn't remember the last time I had a couple of days to chill. I figured this was more than possible when I would inevitably get to a beach resort, but for the minute this would suffice nicely. The water ebbed and ambled its natural way past the stones and boulders while the breeze gently rustled the leaves amid the tall trees. We were just down from where the Thais were casually splashing about, smoking cigarettes and getting drunk on the local whiskey. As the day drew on, they were fascinated by our presence because we had ventured towards a less-worn tourist trail and ended up hanging out together. We basked like local lizards on the rocks in the middle of the river, taking cordial shots of their whiskey when offered, that happened to be quite regular and had pictures taken under the waterfalls with them. It was such a good time and testament to the kindness amid curiosity of strangers and how wonderfully friendly and accommodating Thai people are.

Upon returning, we discovered that the price of the taxi had miraculously gone up 500 baht for petrol. I wasn't that put out; figuring we had experienced a day away from it all on a beat less travelled and sampled unique Thai hospitality. Others argued about the price; then paid it anyway. Again Mah Lee was above and beyond the call of duty apologetic; again, in my opinion, for something that wasn't her fault. This was becoming slightly disturbing yet endearing as she only wanted us to be happy and not upset and it couldn't have been further from the truth as far as I was concerned. Testament to my budget plan, I didn't particularly care about the money and had enjoyed myself immensely, being immersed in the experience of it all. We took dinner, checked the Internet and being tired and a little sozzled, had an early night.

Next day, we actually returned back to why we were there; to teach and was somewhat wondering how much was actually expected of us as we carried on in pretty much the same vain as the previous day; numbers, sentences, vocabulary, hangman and accumulated in a paper aeroplane building contest, which obviously proved to be a great hit. Especially those aimed at someone's head. There were prototype white missiles flying everywhere around the classroom as twenty-plus kids tried their best to manufacture the ideal flying machine. They were built with the idea of distance and time in the air. Or not; as many cases proved. I loved this; it was absolute chaos as the kids shrieked and charged around in excitement at their new fun lesson, but we did stipulate that the planes had to be decorated in some fashion, providing more creativity into the process. This act alone proved a stroke of brilliance as lots of the children were exceptional artists, drawing cartoon characters and intricate designs at remarkably young age. I was amazed at the decorations produced and appreciated their work, coming from the fact that these talents could maybe prove a vocation for some, having honed their skills at a young age, with basic tools that many in more affluent parts of the world may take for granted. The competition reached its climax by the children going outside into the yard to test their creations, furthest flight, longest in the air etc. By the time the kids left for home, there were remnants of destroyed paper planes everywhere; on the roof top, in the trees and littered all over the yard. The others and I did the decent thing and tidied up, where I painfully retrieved the planes that landed high in the thorn tree; too many a joke about big pricks.

After classes, Erin was due to leave and we went to drop her off. That evening, we were treated by Mah Lee to a meal at a local restaurant; more to the point a karaoke restaurant. This could only mean one thing; kicking, screaming or whatever, I was getting up to sing. We ate, had drinks and chatted. Mah Lee took us there and then left to go to the doctor's as she wasn't feeling well. Unbelievably though, she made the effort to return. It was clear she was ill and yet still wanted to accompany us. We said that we could leave so she could rest but, resiliently, she was having none of it. She made the effort; so I did too when I got the inevitable call from the two Thai guys performing classic Thai versions of classic English songs. Egged on by literally everyone in the restaurant – granted this was about two dozen people including staff – I approached the stage and negotiated what songs they had and I knew, and most importantly what songs they had with the lyrics in English. As the two guys were musicians playing guitars to backing tracks and singing along, I settled on singing 'Yesterday Once More' by The Carpenters.

I didn't really know the song that well, but it was Mah Lee's favourite, so I sang it anyway. Not sure how much she likes it now though after I'd finished what could only be described as a massacre. Mind, the Thai ear seemed much less tuned to English songs and compliments are kinder than that of some professional talent show judges and the like. What I'm trying to say is that my efforts went down a storm. Encouraged by my new-found celebrity status, my encore was 'More Than I Can Say' by Leo Sayer; "Whoa, whoa, yeah, yeah" and all that – brilliant fun, a captive audience and free Hong Thong Thai whiskey coming in from all quarters of the ever-appreciative locals.

Friday seemed to come around very quickly. I was slightly tender after the previous night's showmanship, but OK. Again, the curriculum contained the usual sentence forming topics of, jobs, sports, hangman and games. But as this was my official last day teaching there, I had decided to organise a surprise for the children; in the afternoon we had basketball knockout tournament whereby two would get some football shirts I had brought from the UK. Ram and Aat were the two lucky kids who ended up in the final and won a regular branded T-shirt and an official football shirt of my team. Many may argue this was not exactly a prize, given my team are not super-famous and they got walloped at the weekend, but the kids were really happy and I thought it a little something, to offer as a reward and help provide encouragement to those who maybe wouldn't get the opportunity win something as such very often. I also had my prosperous one from China, which was my pride and joy as it commemorated the team's struggle to a first trophy in 128-year history. I gave this to Mah Lee as a small way of saying 'thanks'. The day finished with tears; not from any of us. One of the lads broke his glasses playing basketball and had to do some emergency surgery taping them together, before a manic photo session with all the children outside the house waving, shouting and screaming at the camera for posterity's sake while being presented with a lovely card from Mah Lee, stating that my classes were loved by the children and that they thought I was a really good teacher, which I sort of found uncomfortably hilarious that they would call me that given my haphazard thinking on-the-spot lessons. Nevertheless, I was touched by the kind words and sentiment which were written and felt that I had helped make a difference and started to give something back, rather than just taking what the world had to offer. More so, I really wanted to do something inspiring and pro-active during my travels, to help possibly find the niche in my life that was so far missing, and this definitely helped cover this aspect.

Mah Lee had organised some things to do over the weekend. After which I decided to go straight up to Chiang Mai, the second largest city in Thailand situated in the north. It was a new destination to explore, apparently with plenty to do. Plus I could travel straight up from close by Lopburi saving time and money. It had been discussed I might go to Bangkok for the weekend and then down to Koh Samet to catch up with the others from the Thai Experience for the fourth week. But I felt like relaxing, also as fun as the group were, I'd been before and it seemed pointless to go south to then head back north. So with this I got in contact everyone, apologised, wished them all the best and safe travels in case I didn't get the chance to meet up again. My washing was done and Mah Lee organised my night train ticket up to Chiang Mai. I was grateful; she still wasn't feeling well and had visited the hospital for some tests. It was unbelievable; her thoughtfulness and effort for others was unsurpassed and was still apologetic for being ill. I felt humbled yet again and honoured to meet someone of such a caring nature, and reckoned I couldn't manage that under those difficult circumstances.

On Saturday, we were up and out at nine a.m. to participate in a joint Sing Buri and Lopburi community festival. This happened twice a year along a country roadside in between the two places and residents attending brought food and drinks for all to indulge in for free. The amazing thing about this act of generosity was that it was specifically for the poorer people and monks from each area and it was a real festival with flotillas, music and precessions, organised by those who – from a westerner looking in – would be regarded as poor themselves that showed humanitarianism in its purest form.

Sampling the delicacies on offer included: fish balls, rice soup, deep-fried pastries which were like croissants and the home-made coconut ice cream which was delicious even for me, who's not the biggest coconut fan. We wandered and witnessed the parade of lovely floats depicting Buddha etc. in true flamboyant, beautiful Thai fashion. Mah Lee worked her way around the patrons and again people made headway to talk to her, especially the children. We rested at a marquee where a hundred or so locals had the same idea. I noticed Mah Lee talking to a guy who seemed to be involved in the organisation of the event. I also noticed he was next to a PA system and I also noticed he was holding a microphone.

It was inevitable, I knew it was coming. The foreigners getting lots of stares and attention from the Thais and their 'not being used to seeing western people around these parts' ways, were about to be introduced. Mah Lee asked if we would say a few words to the community as they were very curious about our presence. Jelena and Clarissa immediately looked at me. I was caught between a rock and a hard place, there was no way out of this as Mah Lee had basically already said; 'we would love to say a few words'. Oddly enough, that's literally what it would be in Thai. I thought, not for the first time, *Oh shit, what am I going to do here?* There was only one thing for it really; pass the microphone. We stood at the front of the crowd sitting around the tables, eating and listening to music. Mah Lee took the mic and engaged everyone in Thai as to who we were, why we were in Thailand and notably here. Then the microphone was handed to me.

I said *"sawatdee krap"* or 'hello' in Thai. Before I could say anything else, rapturous applause from the baying audience. I was stunned. They stopped and I continued in English, immediately disappointing the amazed masses initially ecstatic at my opening in Thai. Mah Lee then translated what I was saying. I mentioned that the festival was a wonderful thing, very kind, fabulous people and hospitality and a truly beautiful country of which they should be very proud. I can't really remember exactly what I said due to my two-minute preparation but finished with *"kopkhun krap"* or 'thank you' in Thai. Again to rapturous applause awash with smiling faces. I passed the mic and Jelena and Clarissa repeated my sentiments. The locals were hanging on our every word, or Mah Lee's more to the point. After we finished, they thanked us and patted us on the back. It was amazing and I was quite overwhelmed; never once did I think that I would be giving a speech to random Thai's as part of a local festival during my travels. It was a true privilege, highlight and bizarre experience; all through taking a chance when they came along that I was now starting to appreciate and look for.

Returning from the morning activities, I decided to venture out on the scooter to check out the local countryside area and take in the beautiful green surroundings. All the while, I was hastened along by dogs charging out of their yards in attack mode, desperate to protect their property as I whizzed by, and hindered by nearly running over a massive log in the middle of the road, which after quickly applying the brakes actually turned out to be a lizard catching some midday sun. I was so pleased not to have hit it, not necessarily for the lizard's sake, but mine. I'd have bought a one-way ticket over the handlebars' cos the lazy sod was over 6ft long and built like Godzilla's fucking grandson.

Upon returning, I had to cover up because we were off with Mah Lee to a funeral. This was getting more and more surreal. One of the respected local heads of the community had sadly passed away and pretty much everyone was invited to pay their respects. Being a figure in the community, Mah Lee obviously attended and we were invited along also. Arriving where we had been to give alms at the beginning of the week, the service was being held outside. The amount of people there paying respects was staggering; around five hundred in total, seated and standing in the grounds of the temple. The body was in a casket at the front and after the sermon everybody took it in turn to make an offering of a lotus flower and prayer. Despite the unhappy circumstances I found this another truly uniquely fascinating experience that offered first-hand involvement in the wonderful Thai culture, emphasising the respect they show to fellow men, through something which a foreign traveller would not expect to witness or participate in.

For my final evening, the mood was lightened at (wait for it) the karaoke restaurant; good food, great beer, even better company and rubbish singing once more. Some of Mah Lee's friends joined us and the beers and bottles of Hong Thong were cracked open. English songs by Thais, Thai songs by English – it was great fun and everyone had a good time and the perfect way to finish my homestay. I was leaving on the Sunday evening, having spent the day chilling out and relaxing. Mah Lee and the others dropped me off at Lopburi train station and waited with me, offering one final surprise; by presenting me with a little squashy elephant key ring by way of saying thanks. This was very touching. She had done so much for us all and nothing seemed enough, and I suspected that she didn't have a heavy foot fall of help, so was always really sad to see volunteers leave. I would have loved to stay as Mah Lee was amazing as were the kids and I did enjoy myself, but my short time helping out was at an end and pastures new were calling.

I decided to opt for the teaching instead of trekking as part of the Thai Experience because I knew it was possible to trek in Chang Mai. So instead wanted to do something different, get a feel of what it would like teaching in a foreign country and possibly help those maybe less fortunate than myself, although nervous and apprehensive about the challenge I faced. Finishing, I was happy that I took opportunity to do this and the option to move out of 'The Brown House' and into unknown territory of the homestay. It wasn't as daunting or harrowing as possibly envisaged, I had great fun and had the honour of witnessing and experiencing some truly stand-out distinctive things, which the average tourist or traveller would never be a part of, and left with some amazing memories; from taking a chance on a something a little less obvious, which led me to think of other opportunities which could come my way if I carried on in this manner. I had witnessed how happy people with seemingly less are and this was never more emphasised than through the innocence of the children I 'taught'. It was great to hang around with these guys. They wanted to learn and would help each other; fair enough, this was in short sporadic bursts as attention would wander easily and I still to this day could never actually gauge how much they learnt from me in such a short space of time. Probably not a lot, but I would like to think that it was fun for them 'cos I enjoyed it thoroughly and it underlined how lucky I was to be from a place where everything is provided for. It showed me and started to realise money and wealth may not essentially bring happiness, yet doing good deeds could. I was content and proud with both my sense of achievement and the feeling I'd given something back. But unbeknownst to me at this happy time these choices would come at a price; a price that would change more than I could ever of imagined.

Messing About in the Mountains

I woke around midday after having arrived in Chang Mai at seven a.m., and straightaway after taking cab to the hostel, I immediately crashed out, having not slept much over the ten-hour journey on the train, where the lights were dimmed, but people shuffled around in between stops and the upright hard leather seat and cold air of the unconditioned rocking carriage only persuaded me to sleep a brief few hours at best. After sorting my clothes and belongings, I decided on spending the next couple of days exploring my new surroundings. The central ruined walled remains of the old city and dried moat were now a dilapidated feature of days long since passed but the encrusting rest of Chang Mai smacked of moderate modernity; mostly low-level buildings – bars, shops, banks, tour operators, markets and restaurants – engrossed with busy people-laden streets within the strewn network mess of cables connecting buildings and lampposts around the city, as street vendors created the inviting smells and the sewers below the repulsive. Getting around was another formality with familiar tuk-tuk and taxi operators constantly vying for business on the roadside, but I chose to walk and take in the new ambience and atmosphere to see what was on offer at a more relaxed pace.

I stayed out longer than expected, acquiring a hankering for a few drinks. Living to regret this the next day, I woke with less of a hangover and more of a bad stomach ache instead. I was unsure what from because in my more modernised surroundings, I swiftly returned to eating some shitty western food to add some variety to my diet. My ill feeling could come from anywhere. Who knows how food is prepared or stored regardless of where it is eaten, not to mention the drinks which were from a few different places. Despite this, I headed out to book a three-day trek to the jungle; using one of the countless tour operators in and around the city. Doing this, I came across a zip line activity which looked really interesting and exciting, so I signed up for this on the day after I returned. Still feeling slightly unwell, I ventured back to the hostel to sleep again. Waking, the pain had moved to my kidneys, so I figured I'd picked up a small infection

111

and was working its way through my system. Admittedly, I was still slightly worried about being well enough for the next few day's hiking, but I was confident that a little rest, relaxation and drinking plenty of water would sort me out.

I was up early for a seven a.m. pick-up for the three days and two nights trekking adventure high up in the mountains of Chang Mai; happy and thankful that I now felt fine. First operation of any tour was the customary tour of the city, hopping between various hostels and hotels to pick up of others within the group; once more in the back of a truck with canvass covering and arse numbingly uncomfortable small bench seats, as nine were eventually shoe-horned in the back with bags. At least these were only the small rucksacks provided, filled with few spare clothes and other necessities to see each person over the course of the tour.

First stop was at an orchid resort which I didn't realise was on the agenda; a quick look around at the beautiful array of flowers on show and the countless varying butterflies peacefully resting or fluttering around the netted gardens. This was unguided, allowed to meander around at will and lasted all of fifteen minutes, yet I can't really say that I need much longer. Really this was just a stop to use the bathroom, a chance to stretch the legs and more so, pick up another three people trekking. We now made a full group of twelve; not an issue apart from if we were cramped in the back before, we were like sardines in a mobile can now. The getting to know you banter bounced back and forth, and everyone seemed to be nice enough and getting along, which was a great start considering people from Germany, US, Norway, Israel and Britain had been brought and literally squeezed together.

Approaching the massive cascade of green mountains they imposingly surrounded everywhere the eyes could look; with our now increased elevation in altitude, the climate had changed with more layered white and grey clouds that smeared the view interspersed with breaks of brilliant sunshine. We arrived along a bumpy dirt track to where we were due to start. Our guide for the next three days was named Nam; A Thai national of slender build who had experience of trekking this route for many years, although unsurprisingly was and looked relatively young. We had parked at an elephant reserve and the first priority was to have lunch that was already prepared for us, so within a flash I was back on rice and noodles again. With plenty at hand, every one stocked up, knowing about the imminent long slog ahead to increase the energy reserves. But beforehand, we ventured out onto the backs of elephants for a little soiree into the jungle and river.

My self and another Brit called Dan got on the back of one of the gentle lumbering beasts, who was aptly named Rambo; lucky really as we were both not the lightest of people. We ambled along down a small dirt track in between dense vegetation as our 'driver' ushered Rambo in the relevant direction, keeping his mind on the job at hand with the usual brutal-looking hook to the ear. We sat in a dual seating carriage strapped to the elephant's back, holding on as it rocked from side to side with each deliberately placed step. Reaching the rivers' edge, Rambo took a splodge in relatively shallow part of the muddy uninviting water. I was apprehensive as we entered, not necessarily about venturing too deep or getting stuck because Rambo was clearly a bit of a unit, easily capable of negotiating through, but more so in the instance that if he decided to take in a trunkful of water and shower us in a true comedy fashion. Getting wet was not really the issue either; it was more because the elephants in front and probably all before had decided to unload a massive amount of shit in the water, so I hoped and prayed that I wasn't going to get covered in it if our transport decided to cool off in the humid heat. Saying this, I couldn't help but laugh at those on bamboo rafts coming down the river as they encroached on the area where the vast volumes of elephant dung were being washed into their inevitable pathway.

Returning to the start, we gathered our things and set off on the first part of the trek. Our aim was to reach a village by nightfall high up in the mountains. We soon ventured in to the jungle awash with green from the trees and vines that dangled like unsettling snakes in the peripheral vision. Cooling shade would break the intense sunlight streaming through the dense vegetation that I tried to avoid like a vampire. The terrain was quite easy along a mud track, only having to be careful when attempting to cross the various streams that crossed our path as they wound down the mountain. As we ventured on, the trail changed to being predominantly uphill and the humidity of the trapped air was un-aiding, relentless and overwhelming for the muscles and cardio-vascular system. I had bought bottled water prior to starting and although now warm, it proved its worth as I guzzled it at a high rate. Despite being away two months and living in hot climates; here the exercise, altitude and humidity were a hard task master, not helped by the fact that I was still relatively unfit. My breathing was deep and fast, as sweat teemed from every pore and I was a soaking mess. Throughout, though, the guide Nam was a fountain of information, adding value and worth as he educated us about various flora and fauna, made walking sticks for everyone and allowed for enough rest breaks; where he would treat us to Thai air conditioning – which involved fanning anybody who required it with a gigantic banana leaf – before refreshing relief came while stopping at a waterfall where we were allowed to strip off and cool down in the pool at the base of the crashing water.

Some three hours and seven kilometres later, just before the sun settled beyond the hills, we arrived at our village destination. The uphill slog was hard going and my physiology cried foul as thighs and calves achingly tightened, my arms were weary and the chest heaved at the endurance. There were no roads, just dirt tracks. Dogs and chickens foraged with aimless disposition and children ran around playing games while others stopped to witness our dreary intrusion. Nam took us to our 'hotel'. Sensing the irony in his statement, we arrived at a bamboo hut on stilts, perched on the hillside similar to those in and around the mountain village except much bigger to harbour us all for the night. There were three rooms; a large communal dorm with mosquito nets separating each of the sleeping quarters with blankets and pillows, a dining and relaxing area with real fire and a third room for our guide and host.

We stripped off our sodden clothes, changed into dry ones and hit the beer within microseconds and relaxed out on the large balcony entrance of the hut. It allowed everyone time to take turns showering; a slow process with there being only two cubicles below the balcony area, where the pesky mosquitos were waiting out in force, licking their lips in hungry anticipation – a feeling we all shared gracing the floor mats of the dining area to devour a delicious Thai curry that been had prepared while trying not to scratch our now copious mozzie bites. The rest of the evening we spent drinking, talking and bonding from the few hours' experience together. Nam broke out the guitar and played some songs which he knew and everyone joined in aiding with the singing. The owner was a slender fellow called Bai; he joined us and indulged in a game or two of 'drink the beer'. We had bought plenty from the small shop in the village and plied him with it; as he wished. It was the least we could do and he really seemed to appreciate this, giving us a rendition of traditional Thai song; unfamiliar to us but a cultural delight and we all clapped and cheered. The night wore on by the fire and we indulged in our own traditions; drinking games and having a smoke as someone acquired some weed and a few of us got stoned before crashing around two a.m.; suitably wrecked and therefore clearly (not) well prepared for the next day.

At eight a.m., everyone was up for breakfast and blurry-eyed but still managed to now appreciate the view. The night before, due to tiredness, getting dark quite quickly and in haste to get cleaned up, this had sort of been bypassed. The vast visible area from our balcony vista was fabulous; mountains rolled for miles, enshrouded in thick dense hard forest; parts were bathed in golden morning sunshine and others propped up dark ominous-looking rain clouds, and the patchwork tapestry of the flat lowlands below extended off to an endless horizon. After breakfast and packing unsuccessfully dried clothes, we started out on the second day of our trek. Heading up the tracks of the shanty village, we stopped at one of the local homes-cum-grocers; where a trekking tourist could purchase sugary drinks and treats. Now having an idea of what the days would entail, the successful raid at the shop was a great call as the first hour was straight up the top of one of the countless hills that caused sheer agony on my already minimally recovered weary legs. The torn muscle fibres screamed from the previous day with every push up and now blisters had taken their toll on my feet, due to wrong type of socks being worn and the plasters applied to minimalize the rubbing friction provided scant relief.

Feeling weak and bound by the discomfort of pain made the trek more a war of will and psychological battle that masked the more enjoyable aspects of nature and its surroundings. This also made it difficult to concentrate where I was stepping and my breathing. I couldn't and didn't want to participate in conversation as we trudged higher up through the woods and heat. Descending, I thought, would bring relief; yet this proved just as an equal painful challenge as each impact of the gravity-aided descent provided an energy sapping jolt, as each foot was carefully placed in situ to prevent slipping down the steep, wooded track. Only an instinctive quick grasp by the right outstretched hand around a small tree prevented a serious problem as some loose dirt shifted, causing my feet to slide out from below me and slip precariously down the hill. Shaken, I pulled myself to my feet and I really thought I was heading down the steep embankment a long way the wrong way. I composed myself and attempted to get my concentration back. After a few reassuring words from the others inquiring if I was OK, we carried on.

Unanimously, we decided to not stop for a break so we could arrive early at the camp for lunch; a bit of a masterstroke despite the three hours' trekking on the steep uphill and downhill slopes that had been much tougher and more enduring than the previous day, which increased and aggravated aches and pains. I should point out that we were also asked prior that morning if we wanted to take the easy route or the hard route. Unanimously, we decided on the harder route; less of a masterstroke some may argue by the condition of my weary torso and blistered feet. But this seemed more of a challenge, an adventure and accomplishment knowing the tougher route had been conquered. Also, both these choices hastened our arrival to the campsite where lunch came much faster than expected, so we now had the best part of two-and-a-half hours to chill out and rest by a beautiful jungle stream, with swimming holes supplied by a large waterfall cascading down from the wall of rock towering up in front of us.

After some well-earned eating, swimming and relaxing, we completed the rest of the day's trek. The terrain had now changed from mountainous up down trails to following the stream supplied by our swimming hole that involved slippery moss-addled rocks and stones from the wet humid vegetation. We crossed the water at numerous stepping stone intervals; tricky hops and steps were used to precariously negotiate each gaited move to ensure not slipping or falling from the rocky boulders or steep banks to the shallow water. We arrived after an hour or so at a large opening down from the stream that had formed into a deep pool oasis, carved from a large waterfall that allowed time to refresh ourselves again. The water in the pool was cool and clear, yet venturing in I could start to feel the powerful undertow of moving water from the large 40ft falling flume. It was beautiful and spectacular in its natural simplicity; its illusion seduced me to venture towards it. Fooled by its allure, it first caught me with the spray and droplets, gently peppering and tapping my skin with a seductive massage before venturing too far, to be caught by the hammering torrent and its full weight hit my head, shoulders and back causing me to slip and push me under into the washing machine of white water, that also whipped my shorts down. As I immerged from the watery mire, I fumbled quickly to retrieve my shorts and save my embarrassment and everyone else from my unsightly bare arse.

Pushing on for another hour, we reached camp for the night. I was behind the others due to administering more plasters to searing blisters, which coupled with tired legs were taking their toll and hindering every move. In pain, I was washed with elation to reach the second night camp of wooden huts similar to the previous night but only this time there was no village. We were out in the middle of the jungle enshrouded by tall dense trees; thick shrubbery and the only noise came from the babbling stream which we had followed. Everyone was suffering, not only from the inexperience of trekking and the aches and pains which that inevitably brings, but from the dehydration of sweating out any ingested liquids including those of the previous night's boozing antics. We ate dinner, chilled, played card games and smoked by the campfire, while admiring the vast array of bright stars visible from the opening of the trees that peacefully glistened in the night sky. Learning a lesson and with no means to buy beer; we crashed out for the night at a more respectable time and in much better preparation for the last day.

Eggs and bread had become a staple diet of breakfast in Thailand. Not just on this trek but also at the homestay and on the Thai Experience. Protein, fats, carbs good to go. Also, I was rested and feeling OK; my feet and muscles ached, blisters were sore and had few mosquito bites but generally was OK. Probably the worst thing was my attire; as almost all of my clothes were soaking wet or dirty so looked decidedly a horrible grubby mess. Conversely, so did everyone else but we weren't exactly involved in a fashion parade. But more importantly, we knew the end was near and there wasn't much left, to walk anyway, because there certainly wasn't much left in our tanks.

After packing all of our things, we headed off. An easy morning had a sharp upturn. Proceeding along a two-foot track, we continued to follow the stream at an elevated level, the worn muddy trail offered no real problems, as it was relatively flat and any obstacles were easily negotiable, being kind to the joints and muscles. Halfway along, Nam ordered us to stop and turn left. Where to? There was no turn left? Approaching, he went one way. The only way; that was up. Knowing the group sense of adventure, machete in hand, he started to ascend, slashing away at the bushes, branches and undergrowth like Errol Flynn clearing a winding pathway for us up the steep inclination. In our zig-zagging little droves, unbeknownst to where, we followed behind. With all the thorns, it was a sharp upturn indeed!

After an hour or so of climbing, we reached the top, pausing for ten minutes to catch our gasping breath. One last time, we had taken the hard route to get where we wanted to be; the benchmark of our trek. Each time, the group actively voted for it. The first day was uphill all the way so no option there; but second day on the first hill we chose to go over not around it – where I nearly fell – and then we never stopped for a break, so now Nam had decided to throw in one last little challenge to his weary but relentlessly keen followers.

Trees? Yes. Trail? Yes. View? No. Not at all, dense trees obscured any opportunity for a stunning view. Taking the harder route again, we simply went over a hill rather than around it via a freshly hacked overgrown thorny steep trail. For the whole experience and somewhat sadistically for my wellbeing, I actually enjoyed it. Thriving on the challenge of doing something the harder way as it made the experience a little more of an achievement, plus both mentally and physically I could feel myself growing and getting stronger and more determined as we progressed, overcoming each seemingly deterring obstacle. I loved being in the mountainous jungle and hoped it wouldn't be my last. Nature proved to be fascinating and intriguing with an abundance of cool and interesting plants and wildlife that even included the bugs. We scaled down the embankment, arriving at the now widened river system to a hut and the final part of our tour.

As extreme outdoor activities go, I absolutely love white water rafting. Not sure why, probably because of being with and within nature, pitting yourself against the elements, the unpredictability of it, the danger factor and the team effort required. All these things appeal so I was looking forward to what literally lay ahead. We donned our equipment, had our safety talk and split into two rafting groups to head down the now full-from-the-rain muddy brown river. White water? This was hardly how I remembered it, having been spoilt by crystal fresh summer water in Canada.

For the most part, the seemingly dense river slowly oozed its way in between the trees and hillsides, only occasionally picking up speed when its natural flow was interrupted by grade two and three rapids. We sat on the inflated sides of the rafts, dragging our paddles through the tempestuous water to pull our vessel over rolling broils that splashed and crashed over the front and sides, as we bounced up down and over the submerged obstacles to provide our exercise and excitement. We rafted down the river for approximately forty-five minutes; due to the relatively small rapids, no one ended up in the mire. The worst thing to worry about was swallowing any amounts of earthen water that at times washed over the top, soaking everyone. This was a fun finish to our trek that allowed the arms to do some work and provide welcome relief for shattered legs. Then something strange happened; seemingly in the middle of nowhere we changed vessels; from large rubber dinghies, to large bamboo rafts, like that in Yangshuo but without a chair in the middle. I figured another novel mode of transport to take us to our final destination; especially because with our six and guide on board, the thing could barely float. So we sat on the hard bamboo raft, submerged about two inches under the latte coloured water, and gently ambled towards the end.

One thing then suddenly became apparent – the scenery. I recognised it. But what I particularly recognised was the steep embankment on the other side. And then it dawned on me this was where we were two days prior; the same embankment where the elephants trekked. And the same elephant trek that we had done. And the same place where I laughed unknowingly at people coming down the river on rafts – exactly like we were now doing now, submerged under the surface. And yes, where the elephants happily unload tonnes of shit into the river as we casually drifted past. I should've known.

Obviously, just after here, the rafting finished and we were at the end. Under a small canopied area, we took our last meal together as a group and again unsuccessfully attempted to dry some clothes. After eating, we packed our things, crammed into the back of the truck and took the uncomfortable two-and-a-half-hour journey back to Chang Mai. Upon returning, I felt obliged to give Nam a tip, after putting in such an amazing effort when helping us with river crossings, making walking sticks, educating us, hurtling down the mountain tracks at break-neck speed and encouraging us along the way. All with a cheerful smile and an infectious appetite for fun. He knew the mountain trails and route like the back of his hand, a truly awesome person and guide, a credit to his country and profession – and who, speaking for myself, enhanced my experience beyond expectations. Tipping isn't generally a British trait but I was more than happy to hand over something to him personally, knowing that despite all this effort, his wage would probably be nothing in comparison to what would be expected in other countries. He was really appreciative and accepted with good grace as we shook hands and said goodbye.

At the hostel, I now had new roommates who I started chatting with instantaneously. I had been away for all of three days but it seemed longer, having new personnel about who had made themselves at home. Everyone was heading out and I was hungry, so we ventured out together. In a roof top bar within the city centre, I caught up with the guys from the trek and had some drinks, but I was acutely aware of the time and amount I was drinking, knowing I had to be up at seven a.m. for the next day's activity. Yet that still didn't stop me leaving at two a.m., pissed up. And when you finish off with a signature tequila stuntman, you know things can go wrong.

Morning came all too swiftly and I was up and raring to go; well, I was up and rushing around like an idiot as my seven a.m. pick up was actually at six thirty a.m. and the mini-van was waiting for me. When settled in the bus, the two a.m. boozing was swiftly turning into an episode of when good ideas go bad; for the record, a tequila stuntman is the same as a slammer except you sniff the salt, down the tequila and squirt the lemon in your eye. Big and clever to do? No. Hilarious to watch? Yes.

The bus arrived at the forest where the zip lining took place. This activity involved traversing high up through the trees, hurtling along a course of wire cables from one tree platform to another, attached via a harness, karabiners and using a piece of V-shaped bamboo as a brake. I was initially sold on the idea due to the exciting prospect of speeding precariously at heights, through unknown vegetation, with the possibility of seeing and witnessing some of the wonderful wildlife inhabitants that could hopefully include some gibbons. The idea here was devised by scientists wanting to monitor the wildlife at close quarters and had been then developed into a tourist attraction. My hangover had well and truly kicked in now and I was feeling shitty and tired. That soon passed as we set off. Suspended on wires high in the jungle subdued any lethargy, as blood started to pump, shooting adrenaline through the arteries and veins. It was slow going at first, due to the numbers in the group, and waiting for the people ahead to vacate the subsequent platforms, but the zip lines themselves were awesome as momentum would build from raising the legs, and gravity would then do what gravity does best; have us whizzing along the cable at breakneck speed towards the fast-approaching next station in the trees. The onus was on the person to apply the bamboo brake to the cable, slowing down enough to safely step on to the platform. Brake too early, and you wouldn't make it all the way along. Too late and there was a severe case of performing your very own *George of the Jungle, watch out for that tree!* Impression by crashing into the large trunk in front. Which wasn't advisable.

The day was amazing fun and the views spectacular from 50m high as the jungle foliage, vines and trees passed in a speeding blur as we zipped along through the openings in the now-humid sunshine. Although, personally, I didn't get to see any of the wildlife which some do. I wasn't disappointed as along the trail there were wobbly rope bridges in-between spinning around, bouncing along and hanging upside down on the dozen or so cables, plus there were abseils to negotiate, where the guides would happily drop you from around 20m to the forest floor below. Whether this was to enhance the experience and thrills, or just make you crap yourself at the fast approaching ground, I'm not sure, as I experienced both, especially, when again hanging upside down. The activity finished around noon and all participants took lunch together where, now wide awake, enthusiastic chatter littered the restaurant about the fun we had.

Afterward, we were taken to a nearby waterfall and could explore at our own leisure. I headed out to the peak of the huge cascade that coursed from ledge to ledge and seemed to go on forever. The trail to the top snaked alongside the tumbling water as stone steps, worn slippery from the spray and slimy vegetation, and following the contour of the hillside made them steep and unrelenting. The top was pretty and serene, incurring a feeling of remoteness, with the only real noise coming from the supply of water and falls themselves, yet I left slightly disappointed with my endeavours as any view was obscured by the towering distant trees and there wasn't much else at the summit, but I used it as an excuse to participate in a bit of exercise and exploration into a jungle less known to the likes of myself driven by curiosity of what I might find.

Early in the afternoon, I returned to the hostel, immediately crashing out as it felt like ages since I had rested properly. I now sported numerous cuts, bruises, aches, pains and complimentary mosquito bites. I was mainly suffering mostly though from sleep deprivation and lack of rest from four days' rigorous activity. And I don't need to mention the nocturnal beverage activity. So the next day was a bit of a non-starter; checking up on emails, doing some washing, I had a wander around local shopping mall all the whilst managing to get caught in a thunder storm and I once again was left saturated in warm rain. Drying off for the evening, at the local night market I perused the stalls selling local souvenirs, fabrics, garments, jewellery, accessories, food etc. All sorts of things for all tastes. It was really interesting and the market itself was huge, a whole kilometre street had been closed off to accommodate the regular Sunday evening gathering of stalls in Chang Mai, that was easily worthy of a visit. Especially; as a stage had been constructed down one of the side streets where locals both young and old were performing various talents that included a competition of traditional and modern singing and dance routines, for the excited community. This though was when downpour number two struck and, unfortunately, the event turned into a wash out as organisers, performers and spectators scrambled for the sanctuary of dry cover. Having been soaked by the elements for the second time in a matter of hours, I called it a day and headed back and chilled out at the hostel while plans were being drawn for the next move.

Health and Safety

Some others I had met in the dorm had decided to head up to Pai; a little town in the north-west of Thailand. Having some time before wanting to head south towards the islands and with an invitation, I decided to tag along. We headed to the bus station in Chang Mai; where our short-lived group split up due to spaces available, leaving another Brit called Gaz and I to catch the next bus at around midday. This being a local bus, it was in less than tip-top condition; a good old-fashioned bone shaker in every sense with shot to shit suspension and dirty fumes spluttering out the back. It was crowded with bags strewn in the isles, the fans didn't work and the animals that travelled with us were in boxes poked with holes. A bus envisaged in the true sense of travelling; seemingly less than savoury but a brilliant experience that was also cheap. My seat was OK though and I was lucky enough to have the latest in air conditioning because the window wouldn't close properly; great for breeze in the stifling stuffy humidity, but less so when it provided a free shower driving through interspersed rain. We spent four hours in cramped claustrophobia, squeezed in hard headrest-less seats. I listened to my music and played with my thoughts in between nodding off and waking to appreciate the amazing views of the mountains and valleys as we twisted and turned through the winding roads.

We arrived in the lovely little town of Pai and set about searching for some digs. Five or six places later, we inevitably returned to the first place we looked at; that was, of course, right by the bus station. I met Gaz after zip lining and we had few drinks together so being the first night, we checked out to some of the local bars, the last one in particular on the outskirts of town. It was actually a complex, with a rickety wooden bridge to gain access across a pungent narrow marsh, failing to notice the sturdier more customer friendly version of said bridge some twenty yards further along the road. Being out of season, the bar and open air yard was really quiet, but we made our selves at home anyway, chatting with the locals. The guy bartending was also doubling up as a fire performer and treated us to his ringside show; flaming wooden staves and balls of fire on chord were spun around head and torso at breakneck speed, creating trippy swirls of light which trailed forever in the dark.

We carried on drinking late into the evening; during which we had 'specials' made by some other pissed up friends from Chang Mai who we bumped into. Our drinks were that bit more 'special' as one of our guest bartenders broke her dress strap from some vigorous shaking and involuntarily exposing her boobs in the process; which was nothing short of hilarious, and helped smoke a joint that only aided and abetted a one-way trip to the floor when I fell over, cutting and grazing my hands and knees in an increasingly messed-up state. Gradually, more people arrived and the fire show was once more brought out for the entertainment. Earlier, I'd had a try using with the flaming balls; somewhat successfully managing to spin and twirl and them around my head, torso and in-between my legs. So inevitably much more inebriated; with bravado increased and sound judgement decreased. I decided to have another go. All was fine, until I attempted again to swing the fiery orbs between my legs. Having done this prior I thought it would be easy. But now, I got it wrong; hit my shins, singed the hairs on my legs and nearly set myself on fire. With my moment been had in a more coherent state, I thought I'd better leave these to the expert and put them down. The most sensible thing I'd done all night. Shortly after, I was completely wasted so decided to stumble back to where we were staying. The second most sensible thing I had done all night; to only get caught in yet another all-too-familiar torrential downpour. Bollocks. Fun night though.

The next day proved to be a little more productive. Sporting a black t-shirt, aviator sunglasses and a round piss pot helmet I resembled a poor man's *CHiPS*; as in the motorbike TV cop show from the eighties. Because we decided to hire some scooters for the day; exploring the surrounding area using a photocopy of a hastily hand drawn map. We viewed a local waterfall and then took the ascending hill top roads at breakneck speed, stopping to admire in the breathtaking views of the green valley of Pai's location, protected by the surrounding contours of majestic mountains. We visited the location of an ancient city rather than any actual ruins and smaller indigenous villages, where the locals would stare in wonderment at the sight of 'such cool looking' westerners hurtling past. As we narrowly avoided the free-roaming poultry pecking away at morsels of food on the roadside – that when startled by our presence seemingly tried to commit hara-kiri by running in front of the scooter wheels in a confused daze; they and us both luckily surviving with mad rushes of adrenaline.

This set the tone as a precursor for the evening. We returned to the first bar we started out at the previous night; this was a tiny little shack on the street across from our room. It was so small there was more seating outside on the street. I loved it. The music was great – Ali the proprietor would play traditional rock music; he was a great host and a nice bloke. Upon returning, Gaz and I realised we were locked out and didn't have a clue what to do as no one seemed to be home at reception. He then suggested that we take the scooters out, as we had them for a full twenty-four hours. Not completely wasted but somewhat feeling the effects and against my better judgement, as well as being an idiot, I agreed. So we headed up to the bar from the previous night's drunken escapades. Twenty-minute walk or a five-minute ride was no excuse. We arrived and saw the bartender and explained what had happened. He offered to put us up in the rooms there for a small price, so at least we had somewhere to crash. But first decided to head back and check if someone had returned. Whilst trying to wake the owner, she actually arrived and let us in, which was great and somewhat of a relief.

Brilliant! We were back in around eleven p.m. and could settle for the night, one would think. Yet, inexplicably, we went back to the bar on the scooters. We had a beer and ended up chatting with a totally smashed Aussie guy who was even worse than we were. I was consciously trying to sober up now; feeling compos mentis but I knew I'd had a drink yet this guy was ridiculous. Even more so as when we went to leave, so did he; on his scooter. I thought this could go badly wrong. I held back as Gaz and sir beers-a-lot tore ahead along the small streets; bravado once more started to carry their one-upmanship; speeding, driving close, breaking hard as booze and bollocks overrode the brains. Inevitably, upon arriving at a T-junction and not that far ahead, I noticed red bike lights, but they were not in the position they were supposed to be. As my eyes adjusted to the dim street lighting, I saw the two guys gingerly getting to their feet. It was obvious they had hit each other and scattered both the bikes and themselves ending up on the far side. Dusting themselves down, they assured one another they were OK apart from a few bumps and scrapes. Now it had gone wrong, reality hit that this could've been a hell of a lot worse. Given what had happened, we called it a night and went our own way. Rather fortunate and a lesson learned, as always, the hard way.

This ensured a more conservative approach the next day and we headed out in the opposite direction to the day previous. We passed elephant camps but decided against stopping due to the small unkempt state where the huge beasts were shackled together, harboured under a huge wooden shack, and looked really miserable as their small dark eyes seemed to only tell tales of woe. Leaving me feeling disheartened having witnessed how well they were treated previously. Continuing, we visited some hot springs of steaming pools heated from underground, a World War 2 memorial bridge bringing back memories of the day on the JEATH railway and climbed up Pai canyon to take in the wonderful panoramic views of the harsh dry flat land and more of the beautifully contoured mountain scenery.

Back in Pai, we returned the scooters; one of us slightly more worried about being charged for the bits of damage, but they accepted them back with no problems. Wandering around the relaxed small town, I happened upon a bookstore and ventured in. Rather uninterestingly perusing the shelves, one caught my eye; it was a little red book and nothing which would jump out and scream 'buy me now'. For some reason, I was drawn to it. I picked it up and briefly flicked through the pages. It was full of aphorisms concerning life, people, relationships, spirituality and eternal being wrote in a witty manner due to the author's time spent with various spiritual teachers. Without really thinking or haggling, I immediately bought the book as something about it really resonated with me and I was intrigued by its content.

It was now the end of October. Knowing I was to be travelling for the next few days, I made a conscious effort to ring home. It was going to be my folks' anniversary and nephew's birthday so I hoped to speak with everyone. I spent the time chatting to my mam finding out the party plans and catching up, before being informed that my nephew wasn't there as normal, due to going away for his birthday, so I was left a little disappointed to have missed him and had to do with the big news that apart from the aforementioned, the dog had his balls chopped off and was wandering around feeling sorry for himself. I thought this a strange coincidence, as while walking around town that day I'd noticed some of the knackers the local dogs in the street were swinging about, due to the inability and cost to have them neutered, and I had actually thought of him. Poor thing.

Whilst hanging out here, Gaz had also told me about heading to Laos. Not being close to the border I hadn't planned nor envisaged going but this was another opportunity to visit somewhere new, another adventure and open an unscripted page. Also, some of the things to do there sounded like a shit tonne of fun. So we booked the bus and slow boat to Luang Prabang in Laos. In the early evening, we got picked up by the mini-van to take us to the border crossing at Chiang Khong. The normal winding roads were making it difficult to get some sleep; again, in cramped conditions. Not to mention that one of the others was being rude and inconsiderate, as they insisted on singing along like a strangled cat to their shit music, while everyone else tried to peacefully relax. Selfishly causing much annoyance, even by continuing after all on-board had asked them to be quiet. I did manage to get some shut eye though because I eventually noticed we had picked up a hitch hiker somewhere along the line, as there was an extra body in the front seat that I didn't remember stopping for. Arriving at the accommodation on the night at around two thirty a.m., we crashed out in a room full of single lumpy beds before continuing the journey in the morning when the border opened.

I hadn't slept much and getting up, there wasn't a shower to use, so in true traveller fashion I was stinking by the time we reached the border. It was chaotic and bustling by eight a.m. with travellers, vendors, touts and locals going about their business in the early morning hot sunshine. The passport control official stamping formalities for exiting the country was handled at an unconventional small shack, before being then led down to the muddy shoreline of the Mekong River and the border crossing between Thailand and Laos; which now could be seen on the other side. With care and attention, we boarded narrow long boats which rocked unsteadily, as they ferried people across the river between the two neighbouring countries.

On the other side, the Laos border was just as chaotic, if not more so, as the formalities of entering a country generally outweigh those of leaving. Also, there was actually physically less room, it being a small office at the bottom of the river embankment, and everyone jostled for pens and a place to fill in the paperwork, as the a visa required to enter Laos was obtained for a fee; here at the point of entry. Forty-five minutes later, we got sorted and could carry on our journey. Or so I and everyone else thought, but were now starting to appreciate what thought was worth; absolutely fucking zero. We sat around again for seemingly ages, getting hassled about changing money and buying supplies from the locals, as we waited for our boat to arrive to continue for the next two days down the river to take us to Luang

Prabang. Eventually, the rest of the tourists travelling on the same route and I were herded down to the river, and boarded our boat which gradually became close to being overloaded despite its large 60ft or so length. People complained and got off for another boat that had to be arranged; although, within capacity, due to bags we still ended up with minimal room on the seats of the covered old wooden vessel, as we set off.

Carrying approximately eighty passengers that were strewn randomly on the floor, seats and benches, the breeze cooled through the canopy as we slowly chugged along the river awash with caramel-coloured mud and debris from previous rainfall. The beautiful hills and scenic mountains, now illuminated by searing bright sunshine, created a slow reel vista to inspire and enamour the tedious journey, as we seemed to travel no faster than the water itself. Some played cards, others got drunk. I just sat appreciating the views, reflecting on my time and listening to music. After not seeing any sign of civilisation for about three hours, we stopped for ten minutes at a small port of bamboo huts, adorning the contours of the hills. Local children, some who seemed less than six years old, boarded to sell fruit, snacks and drinks to those on the boat in the hope of making a living from hungry and thirsty tourists. I wondered what it must be like to live this way and work at such an early age to help make ends meet and provide for families. I was glad that it wasn't the life that I experienced or one that lay ahead. It hit home how actually rich I was and the opportunities given to me and maybe taken for granted. It made me appreciative of what I was doing, where I was from and what I had. It also occurred to me that these kids were maybe being exploited? Expected or made to do these chores, to pull heartstrings and purse strings of rich fortunate foreigners. Probably, but being none the wiser, the kids and the society they were living in here, comparative to that of a child in the western world, were vastly different and it only reinforced the notion of how lucky I was, which couldn't be dampened even by the heavy rain we encountered. The tarpaulin covers were deployed down the sides to stop the water running inside which happened anyway and everyone got soaked because the tattered chords holding them in place failed and the plastic flapped open. Meanwhile, I read my little red book and its content started to help put things into context, rationalise and shine new thought-provoking perspective on life.

Early evening we arrived at a tiny little hamlet called Paksong. Disembarking on the muddy shoreline, we hastily scampered up the road to find accommodation ahead of the hoard, although this wasn't really a problem as plenty of guest houses adorned the one-street village; that was a designated overnight stop for the boats travelling through. Gaz a German lad called Henny – who had been playing cards on the boat – and I met some others to eat in one of the many restaurants; perusing and sampling the extra 'happy menu' to that of the regular menu. The aforementioned slightly different to what you would find in any conventional fast food restaurant. Having eaten, we smoked and relaxed with drinks, heading to bed around ten p.m., tired. Staying up was pointless as the town's sparse amenities closed for the evening, plus all the electricity went off and the place was left shrouded in darkness. A small room with three beds draped with coarse mosquito nets became the obvious option, as dogs territorially barked and cricket violin legs croaked – the only noises against the silence as I nodded off.

We were up again at around seven a.m. to continue our journey on the boat. This time, we boarded a different vessel with around only forty passengers on. Others who were with us on the same boat prior hadn't arrived. But we couldn't take any responsibility for their absence so set sail without them and they'd have to take another boat. The journey was the same as the previous day. I kicked back, relaxed and watched the world pass by, thinking about my already-growing catalogue of adventures and pondering what the future would hold on my travels. I wrote my travel log and nodded off at times, only to wake as one of the speeding narrow boats would noisily race past, ferrying those in more of a hurry down the river in the same direction we were lazily taking, only in the space of a day but at a higher cost. Not just in monetary terms – as we had heard stories that they were less safe and more prone to capsizing due to the speed, weight and the unpredictable nature of the river. So I was happy where I was, the price paid and was in no rush whatsoever.

Arriving in Luang Prabang, the second largest city in Laos, we were greeted with the usual hordes of touts baying for tourist money with the offers of accommodation. Having gone through the now-usual ritual of seeing about half a dozen places, we eventually settled on one, which was nice enough for about £2 night each. After heading out for food, I had a slight upset stomach so I headed back home to chill and catch up on some more much-needed rest and sleep.

Feeling better in the morning, I wandered out to look around the town. The French influence here throughout the years was apparent; the architecture of the two-storey buildings was definitely different to that of what we had been experiencing and offered a somewhat European flavour and it certainly didn't feel like being in the middle of Southeast Asia. But it was a lovely quaint place nevertheless and I liked it. The people were friendly, obviously used to the passing traveller, but the hardest part was getting my head around the money situation as they would deal in the national currency kip, Thai baht and American dollar. Depending on what it was, things would be quoted in either of these denominations to make the price sound better. So making purchases became a thinking man's game. Also a novelty was now on the menu; the place was sandwich central with baguettes, the obvious bread of choice that added to the French vibe and all fillings available. It felt a long time since indulging in the earl's creation, having spent so much time in Thailand where they are not readily part of the staple diet and was a welcome addition with my suspect stomach, so I played it safe and essentially started eating these to keep going. The day was miserable and I didn't feel up for visiting local attractions which the others were doing, so decided to spend time in a bar watching football where the premier league was just as renowned as other countries, and carried on wandering around exploring locally whilst booking a bus ticket for the next day to get to where I really wanted to go; Vang Vieng – born out of listening to the excited chatter from other travellers, who had heard about it or already been there. Later, taking it easy I just went back to the bar to watch more football and chill.

Waiting to be picked up from the bus, I was now travelling alone as Gaz and others were heading to different places. This was fair enough and the traveller prerogative; go where you want and do what you want. Suddenly, Jimmy turned up and it turned out that he was staying in the same place as I. While watching the game the previous night, I got chatting to a British guy; this was Jimmy and somehow and for some unknown reason, we ended up snorting vodka with some crazy drunk Swedes. This was quite strange; we never even mentioned where we were staying when talking or where we were heading for that matter. But these things happen. Eventually, I got picked up in packed mini-van and taken to the bus station where I was transferred to another packed mini-van and we set off.

The journey was bumpy and uncomfortable; as no effort whatsoever was made to avoid the massive potholes in the roads. Any attempt though would be futile as the sheer amount of craters in the surface made the word 'road' seem quite the exaggeration and any road markings were, well, non-existent. Pick a side, Mr Driver; left or right – anyone will do. Again though the lush green mountain scenery was spectacular, as we cut through amid low-lying cloud and the random sights kept my attention; in particular, the single lone soldier holding a machine gun by the roadside, that further ahead had the underside of the down slope missing like it had slipped away in a mini-landslide, leaving a treacherous piece of tarmac to drive over and looked like it could follow suit any minute. I was nervous as hell as the van hugged the side closest to the hill - where I could only assume and hope there was earth underneath - to slowly edge our way over the forlorn piece of asphalt. It only took around ten seconds to get across, but it was the longest most breathless ten seconds I felt I'd known.

The humble villages we passed were homes made of pieces of bamboo and wood twined together; often smoke from the inside fire billowed from the sides and the locals either stared or waved at us from their simple abodes. Each occasion offered realisation of the basic clothing and possessions of these folk. The amenities would include an outdoor showering facility fashioned the same as the homes, with a hose lulling over the top, and that was about it. Children had made toys or games for themselves; the livestock ran around at will, so we precariously dodged hitting cows and chickens, and I got the impression that their existence was fleeting as it wouldn't be long before they were to feel the sharp end of a butcher's knife to provide a meal. Real eye-opening journey as it was hard to fathom that the people live like this here; it seemed somewhat not real. Yet it was real and very real to them with probably no idea of how unbelievably differently people in the west live.

Arriving in Vang Vieng, I started chatting to Jimmy and his mates; Colin and Marty. They were transferred to the same bus and we all got dropped off at the same spot. This was now even stranger; not only was he (or rather they) staying in the same hotel, but also that day they were travelling to the same place. Done with the introductions, I asked if it would be OK to tag along with them. Three turned into four and made things easier and cheaper for everyone as far as accommodation was concerned. We stayed in a guest house overlooking the river where the veranda had been washed away by storms previously, but the place was very nice anyway. The guys planned on getting a bungalow on the river but none were available, so we split into two and grabbed rooms. Venturing out for food and drinks, we saw semi-naked people running down the street carrying large rubber rings and laughed at the state they were in, from the obvious day's activities. The three lads seemed good fun, so I was happy tagging along because we had all gone there for the same thing. What everyone had gone there for and where we were heading the next day; tubing.

I had heard lots about this tubing activity from various people as I travelled about and was intrigued by the degree of reports I had heard; amazing fun, crazy, insane, dangerous – all this type of thing, and I concluded to myself that it sounded fucking sweet and I'm putting myself right in the mixer. We were up at around eleven a.m. which still felt early around these parts, and got kitted out with shorts, hat, flip flops, some money and made head way straight to the tube place to get our rubber rings, which were basically large black inner tubes used for tractor tyres or the like. The shop was packed with other revellers and eventually we were sorted to take ourselves and bulky tubes via a truck to the start of the course, and, of course, par course the first bar, where we had the first and certainly not the last drink of the day, before heading down the river in our inflatable rings to the next station or stop; otherwise known as a bar.

Essentially, those participating would jump in the river at the start and get in their tube, allowing themselves to drift along with the current until locals at each bar would throw a plastic bottle attached to a chord and drag you in to shore. There were approximately ten of these bars that were primarily bamboo huts blasting out tunes for everyone to party to whilst getting hammered. It was a bit of pub crawl; but in the jungle, floating on a river, which made it that little bit more absolutely tremendous. If that wasn't enough, each stop had its own activity to take part in; like mud bath volley ball court, Tarzan swings over the water or a zip line to tear arse down. It was really funny watching people on the swings and zip lines inevitably mess it up trying to show off, and end up falling in an ungraceful elaborate fashion into the water. This was made all the more interesting as people floating down the river were now like sitting ducks.

Obviously, I had to have a go – the more beer equals more confidence – so zip lines, no problem; Tarzan swings, easy; but then things got interesting. We approached one of the stops and were dragged over by the thrown lines. I had a beer and was appreciating the music and drunken frivolities. At this one particular bar, though, there was something else apart from the now 'usual' bar activities; this was a large 20ft plus slide with upwards curving end leaving a big arcing drop into the water. With next to no hesitation, before I knew it, I was up the ladder and hurtling down the large wide slippery flume, on my shoulder blades and heels like all the professionals do to reduce friction and build up as much speed and momentum as possible – with as little rational thinking as possible.

Fortunately, this process eventually kicked in but, unfortunately, only after flying off the ramp about 15ft in the air and when I now was about to plummet towards the river. In my haste, I hadn't thought about one thing, a vital thing; how was I going to land? Mid-flight, this dawned on me when I realised my body position was flat, having rotated in the air but essentially not enough, and I now knew how I was going to land; very ungraciously and very hard, in a crumpled heap. And I knew another thing; this was going to hurt.

All my senses seemed dulled for a split-second, and time seemed to cease as I crashed into the river hard on my right, as the sensation of shock reverberated all over my body and water rushed in my nose and mouth. This was immediately overwhelmed by the force my body used to break the water, which caused hot stinging pain to seer down my right side as my full weight slapped against the surface tension. Underwater, my survival instinct kicked in because now I was very aware I had hurt myself, and was very aware I was in deep water, in a river, about forty feet from shore. With immediate effect, I rose to the surface. My side was incredibly sore but the worst thing was that breathing was difficult and this is sort of a necessity; especially when in water. Quickly getting my orientation back, I couldn't swim so began to doggy paddle to the embankment, all the while gasping for air. One of the locals recognising my plight threw me a line which I grabbed and luckily, I was then quickly dragged in, pain seared all down my right and breaths were short and sharp but I was relieved to be out of the water. Within seconds, I knew I would be OK, nothing was broken and I had only winded myself. The local guides were asking if I was OK, to which I replied in a whispered, breathless, "Yes".

Up on the embankment, Jimmy, or Trabbers as he was known, and the others also asked if I was OK. Nodding and breathlessly saying "winded", they had seen it and were laughing as I had at others of a similar fate. I quickly recovered, got my breath back and managed to sort myself out. But in the back of mind, though, I knew I could really have hurt myself or worse. Now I had also broken my flip flops, so I discarded these and was barefoot, my side was still really tender but having got my composure, I carried on down the river in my tube with the others.

We arrived at the last bar and the sun was going down, everyone was suitably wasted at this point and the unconventional 'happy menu' was on offer again. So a couple of silly cigarettes later, we decided to paddle across the river on our tubes to the other side, to the waiting vans that would take us back into town. Midway across the river, the current was really strong, my arms though were not providing enough strength to counteract the water rushing downstream and I could feel myself getting caught up in it. Everyone was ahead of me and had made it over, but I was struggling. Looking right downstream, I saw something which wasn't good; Trabbers was in the same predicament as me, but sat in his tube, and started floating off with the current into the darkness of the river and jungle. Quickly, I thought *Fuck that!* Jumped off, grabbed my tube, headed back to the same side that we came from about thirty yards downstream.

I was worried now; what the fuck had happened to Trabbers? And how was I going to get out of this? Not really thinking again, this time I picked up my tube and put it over my head and started wading across. With nothing on my feet, the rocks and stones were sharp on the soles and caused weakening imbalances, my arms ached holding the tube above my head. I was unable to put it in the water as the current was relentless, especially towards the middle and would wash it and me downstream into the darkness, which I had just witnessed first-hand and really didn't want that to happen. Crossing with every careful, painful step, concentrating intensely on my balance against the pushing waters, I just thought, *Get me the fuck out of here*, and literally willed myself across. Luckily, the water at its deepest came to just below the chest, any further and I believe I would be gone; another wreck-head washed away down the river. Approaching the other side, the water receded and I waded gingerly out, absolutely exhausted and arms aching. The others helped me across the rocks and over to the tuk-tuk; they must have only been waiting around five minutes for me but it felt a hell of a lot longer, escaping my second close call in the space of two hours. I couldn't hide my relief or count how lucky I was. Especially as now we were one missing, and everyone was wondering where the fuck was Trabbers?

Returning to Vang Vieng, we handed our tubes in and headed straight to the bar, which was right by the river. We hung out and shouted his name in the hope that he would float by, but nothing. So decided to wait at the guest house; surely, we thought, this must happen all the time and there would be a contingency plan for these incidents and he would be OK. About an hour or so passed and there was still no sign; Marty, Colin and I were now a bit worried. What if he wasn't, OK? He was absolutely fucked, half naked, in a tube, on a river, in the middle of the jungle, in the pitch black, without a clue to where he was, in a new and foreign land. This didn't look good.

I was sharing with Trabbers, the others had gone to their room to chill, figuring if he doesn't turn up soon then we'll have to report him missing. Almost unexpectedly, the room door flung open. Before me, a wreck of a man entered, covered in cuts and bruises, and looked like he had seen a ghost, not really making much sense and gesticulating wildly. Any other time, I would be really bothered and freaked-out by this; but I was relieved. It was Trabbers.

Hearing the commotion, and not many wouldn't have, Marty and Colin came back to our room. We were all relieved to see him. After what he then told us, he was obviously relieved to see us. Apparently, what happened was this; he got washed down the river as we knew, but managed to get to the riverside. Losing his tube, he clambered through the trees and undergrowth to make it to a field, where the sharp long blades of grass cut into his arms and body. He then bumped into a local man whom he tried to explain what had happened, but the non-understanding local then proceeded to produce a machete and chase Trabbers, who, semi naked, sensibly legged it, eventually making it to a road where a passing tuk-tuk picked him up. He then told the driver what had happened, and the driver explained that the local probably thought he was intent on ruining his crops or (more to the point) a bit of a lunatic therefore chased him. Adding insult to injury, upon arriving in town, the driver had told all of his other tuk-tuk driver mates and now Trabbers was the talk of the town and headline news.

Hearing all this, we were in hysterics, laughing while Trabbers was bordering on a breakdown but we couldn't help asking one thing; "Trabbers, all this happened, yeah?"

"Yeah! Fuckin' right it did, never been so shit scared in all my life!" he replied.

"But it has nothing to do with the shit load of booze and the joints you've had and not to mention the pint of magic mushrooms that you downed?"

By this point, Marty, Colin and I were roaring with laughter. It had occurred to us the predicament that Trabbers was in and this included the copious amount of mind-altering substances he had consumed; next thing, he was telling us all this and had turned out to be a bit of a local celebrity.

"No way! No way! Any fucking shit that I've had is well and truly out of my system, the adrenaline running through my body has gotten rid of all that shit!" he replied. "Go into town, go ask, all the tuk-tuk drivers know, all fuckin 'laughing' at me!" he continued.

We all looked at each other and burst out laughing again. It was a relief to see him, but what a story! We decided that after all that excitement there was only one thing left to do; go have a drink. We headed out and had a few beers and ended up at the bucket bar; one of the bars by the river. Feeling absolutely done in, I left early, shortly followed by the others to have a smoke and laugh some more about the day's activities.

Before tubing, I bought a ticket to the capital of Laos, Vientiane. I hadn't planned on being in Laos too long when, actually, I hadn't planned on even being in Laos. But as I was finding out, that was the beauty of travelling. It was only a week passing through but I was so glad to have visited, witnessing the beautiful scenery, the really friendly people, different culture and run the gauntlet tubing on the river, which lived up to every bit of the thrills and spills from the tales I had heard but also emphasized some of the horror stories that were also told; about how people get hurt, injured or worse on this amazingly insane activity. Figuring I would never get to do this anywhere else in the world, so let's go for it and I was glad I did, despite my close calls and now really bruised right side.

Leaving Trabbers and the others, I set off early at nine thirty a.m., picked up by a van and taken to a waiting bus, again with insufficient room. I chilled and listened to some music. Arriving in Vientiane, the place was really quite uninspiring, confirming the rumours I had heard. At this point, I was travelling with no guidebook, so I talked to people to find things out and asked to have a quick read of their travel guide whenever possible. Getting off the bus, I was chatting to a couple of lads called Ken and Darryl from the UK who let me tag along with them as I didn't have a clue where anything was. The guesthouse we ended up in was a bit of a dump, but it was cheap and for the sake of one night it did the job. So, I booked a ticket back to Bangkok and after a shit, shower and a shave, which were much needed, we went out to meet some friends who the guys knew and ended up going bowling, before heading to a night club on the top of a rather nice hotel – that promptly kicked us out within half an hour as they were shutting. This wasn't a problem as I had the feeling that we weren't missing out on much.

The next day, we were all leaving Vientiane, but I said goodbye to the lads as they left earlier for destination elsewhere. Checking out, I sat chilling in the reception, catching up on my journal. Laos had been a short but eventful soiree; lazing on rivers watching locals going about their business, admiring awesome scenery and beautiful towns, while extreme hardship wandered around in front of my very eyes, not to mention the mad mayhem tubing provided, offering any health and safety officer the chance of a nervous breakdown. I had only covered a fraction of the country and heard of other places that I would really love to visit here, but they would have to wait for another time. The infrastructure within Laos seemed to be lacking behind that of Thailand, but I left happy and at the same time sad, seeing some of its raw infancy and beauty was wonderful, but I knew this would diminish as the inevitable tourist trade grew; yes, this could provide opportunities and jobs for the impoverished but could also drive up greed, westernisation and crime in search of monetary gain and lose its rural untouched charm.

I came here on a whim, unplanned and not knowing what to expect and it didn't disappoint, as it also allowed for a couple of other things; practically, it gave me more time in Thailand as my tourist visa would be renewed, but more so, it provided me with more experience of what it feels like to travel somewhere without an initial plan and only go off what others had told me to guide my guideless itinerary. But this was something I was going to get to experience more than I would or could ever have thought possible.

I eventually got picked up and the group of us headed to the Thai border. In the group was Billy, from the time I spent trekking in Chang Mai; it was really cool to see him again and it gave us chance to catch up. We crossed over the Breeze Bridge which spans over the river separating Laos and Thailand. The formalities at customs and immigration were again a bit of an arse on and involved a lot of waiting around, but the group travelling was pleasant enough and we eventually boarded the night train from Nang Tok to take me full circle back to Bangkok where I didn't plan to hang around too long, having visited there about a month ago, so I could swiftly head south towards the islands.

Island Hopping

Arriving in Bangkok, some of the others, who were travelling on the overnight train, and I headed straight back to the backpacker haven of Khaosan Road. I didn't want to stay overnight, feeling I needed to start heading south to ensure I had enough time to do the things I wanted. Finding a cheap guest house, I arranged a deal to have a room just for the day so I had somewhere to get showered and put my things, while I also headed out to organise some stuff including a night bus and boat to Koh Tao; the first main tourist island in the Thai gulf and a good gateway to the other islands, thus ensuring I was out of Bangkok as soon as possible. One of the other guys I had travelled from Laos with was a keen scuba diver and I found out that this was a great place to dive and to also learn how. I hadn't ever done this before but really fancied the challenge, plus the added bonus of learning possibly some sort of new vocation – why not? I love messing around in the water in its various guises, so heading there could prove quite fruitful, but due to the relatively expensive price and being low on research, I decided not to book there and then but to wait and see what would happen.

Early that evening, the bus headed out of swarming Bangkok later than what time we had been informed it would. The bus ride was OK but again I didn't get as much sleep as I would've liked and arrived at the ferry port around five a.m., aching from the seat, feeling tired and lethargic. We weren't due to set sail until seven a.m., so I had to wait around for a couple of hours. I whiled away the time sat chatting to other travellers, smoking and waiting for a sun rise that would be obscured by dense white and grey uniform clouds, leaving the envisaged blazing sunrise paradise of a Thai coastline a camouflaged dream. But although it was monsoon season, the rising sun uncloaked the darkness around the small ferry port to highlight the beauty of the boat jetty, sandy beach and palm trees that stretched off into the distance.

The large ferry was equipped with TVs that showed movies and had two aisles down the centre of the aeroplane-style seating, but there didn't seem enough room to fit the numerous bags and luggage that were now piled up at the rear, just about not blocking the exits. Thankfully, everyone and everything ended up inside; because venturing out to sea and open water, the warning of forming clouds was ignored and it became much choppier where we hit bad weather. Outside the widows sprayed with rain and sea water as the vessel negotiated the waves of our watery rollercoaster that caused a few on board to start suffering with sea sickness, faces drained to an increasing pale complexion when managing to look up from the inside of a sick bag. I had suffered this before, so I felt lucky to be spared the aching discomfort and quite enjoyed riding with the unrelenting undulations while I chatted to someone about diving, who recommended a dive centre which was close by to the ferry dock.

Arriving on Koh Tao, we docked around eight a.m. and after the organised chaos of retrieving my bag, I headed to the dive shop that was recommended to me; a literal two-minute walk along the beach off the jetty. What was slightly putting me off was the price; it worked out around £150 for the four days' tuition and accommodation, and I thought about other things I could do with the money, but I really wanted to try and experience this and also I knew having my diving certificate would enable me to dive elsewhere along my travels. Besides, other prices quoted weren't that much different in comparison, but would be in other countries around the world, as Thailand is regarded as one of the best and cheapest places to learn. After not a lot deliberation, I came to the conclusion of 'fuck it, I'll do it' and booked, just figuring that's what the plastic fantastic credit card is for. That's right, emergencies. Like this.

The course was starting almost immediately at one p.m. that afternoon. So, I spent the rest of the morning relaxing, watching TV and catching up on sleep. Being there early, I was able to take one of the chalets on the dive resort. A bonus as this allowed for rolling out of bed and being where I was supposed to be. The large bed felt soft and comfortable and I instantly realised how much I had missed this creature comfort; after seemingly travelling sat upright for ages, falling asleep wasn't difficult. That afternoon, there was a group of around twenty-one in the classroom and for the rest of the day we were concentrating on learning the theory behind diving. This involved videos, quizzes and exams with the content focusing on good practice, how pressure of water works, equipment etc. The class was long, not necessarily intense, but there was quite a lot of information to take on board and lasted five-and-a-half hours. Some found this going tough and I caught glimpses of people nodding off, as the heat in the room and the important yet not terribly interesting contents were taking its toll. Unfortunately, staying awake wasn't my only problem. I had another, which could possibly jeopardise my new-found hobby before it had even started.

Prior to the theory lesson, we filled in a declaration of health disclaimer like with any activity such as this. It asked about previous operations including that of a hernia. Now I'm no lawyer understanding legal mumbo jumbo, but that disclaimer statement might have included me; what with having had two operations in the last year-and-a-half for that very thing. I felt OK and fit enough, but figured I should declare it should anything happen with the stresses and strains the body can endure when scuba diving. Knowing my track record of messing up, something would probably go 'pop' under water and it wouldn't be equalising ears. In doing so, I was told that I would have to have a medical and there was a practitioner not too far away. After the class, I headed up to the office to get an examination and fitness certificate, and was sincerely hoping that there wasn't going to be any problems.

Approaching the open shop, there was someone inside behind a desk. I explained why I was there and looked around, wondering where the examination room was. After checking my breathing, blood pressure, ears and chest, I was given the all-clear to proceed; my hernia was apparently fine. Now, I'm no physician or medical expert either but my hernia was in my groin, and I expected to be getting stripped off and examined as before and perform a series of movements and coughs, coupled with various prodding. But seemingly, by looking in a person's ears, you can see through the torso and check everything's all right down by the dangly bits. Brilliant! Medical advances, *eh?* What will they discover next? So, I took my stamped certificate and went on my merry way, not complaining because in the grand scheme of things, the more obvious but very unappealing option would have been to take a look via my arse.

I handed in my certificate and the next day I was ready to start the practical and obviously the most fun part of the course with the rest of the group. For a day-and-a-half, we learnt about the various components of the equipment, how it was to be set up and the checks needed. Then practiced a seemingly endless series of exercises in the pool; these were required skills to master, to ensure comfort and safety should any eventuality or emergency happen when diving. Some of which I struggled with, especially clearing my mask underwater and keeping my buoyancy, as I continually seemed to argue with the physics behind all of this, inevitably fuck it up and lose. But practice makes perfect and with time and patience, I completed what needed to be done. This was all after initially getting my head around the fact that it was now actually possible to breathe underwater, both brain and senses baffled by this very unfamiliar but really cool phenomenon. Finishing, I was happy and didn't feel too fazed by my mistakes as this was my first time with the equipment and practicing skills in this unfamiliar environment, where the psychology of training the brain was an achievement alone and by managing to pass my theory exams, I was feeling good about what was happening and how I was doing.

The best, though, was yet to come; after completing a 200m swim and treading water for ten minutes, our Dive Instructor, a French girl called Maria, and Dive Master assistant, Johnny, took our now condensed group of seven out into the open water for the first time. After setting up our equipment and performing our safety checks, we ventured into the water by falling backwards 4ft off the side of the large boat; which proved quite daunting in itself as the fall was blind, looking up over to allow the tank on our backs to break the surface and provide a smooth entry into the water. We then used the rope of the boat's anchor line to guide ourselves beneath the washing waves to the dive site below; all the while constantly equalising the increasing pressure on our ears, as we submerged into the abyss of the site.

This was incredible; it was like visiting another planet! Oddly enough, I hadn't really thought about what it would be like; what with studying and concentrating on the exercises in the pool. I had seen footage on TV and most recently on the videos in class. But these visuals are nothing compared to actually being submerged underwater; swimming around and being able to breathe in a world unlike anything else I have ever seen or experienced with my own eyes. While there is beauty in diving, it became quickly apparent that media pictures only tell a one-dimensional story of being underwater. Yes; it's possible to see what the camera points at but impossible to appreciate the floating around weightless, the three-dimensional movement, hearing yourself suck air like Darth Vader through a regulator, followed by the rush of exhaled bubbles around your blinkered peripheral vision mask that's restricting nasal inhalation. Not to mention causing a massive accumulation of snot in and around the nose; a truly unbelievable sensation and experience.

The water was a comfortable and warm temperature compared to that experienced on the surface, where it was a little choppy and cold due to the overcast clouds that continued to provide ample rain. Down here, all was calm and serene. Finding clear space, we demonstrated our exercises which we mastered in the pool and followed our instructor via hand signals we also learnt to use for communication, as we explored the beautiful and diverse coral reefs. Fish were our friends as they swam amongst us and Maria pointed out the various species again with the use of hand signals. The dive lasted for around forty minutes before air started to get low in the tanks so we surfaced to the boat.

Boarding, everyone was exhilarated with the experience. Visiting this new alien world was enthralling to all and excited chatter filled the air; 'did you see this?', 'how cool was that?' as my class mates and I offered feedback on what we saw and how we each coped with the dive, as obvious points of discussion. We waited for an hour for the nitrogen which had accrued in our bodies to subside to safe levels. Before we could then start our second training dive.

We moved to another location and donning a full new tank, submerged ourselves once more, this time performing a different set of exercises to prove our capabilities in open water before once more, exploring the area of our new dive site. Again, the beautiful obscure surroundings were encapsulating; the first dive was to 12m, the second only 9m, but visibility was good to 15m that offered surprising comfortable reassurance to be able to see all around. With my experience of the North Sea, I and everyone else assumed that due to the cloudy, dull conditions on the surface, this would be the same underwater. But I never imagined the sea and open water could be so beautifully blue, clear and inviting. We really got the chance to appreciate all that surrounded us. Brain corals, named so because of their cerebral likeness to the human grey matter littered the underwater topography. Beautiful red yellow and blue spiralling Christmas tree worms on the reef would disappear in the blink of an eye, should you approach too close. There were triggerfish that territorially patrolled their domain, unwary of the intrepid novice diver and a moray eel that looked fearsome, opening and closing its mouth of sharp teeth, but only from necessity to push oxygenated water over its gills to breathe. This was in stark contrast to the heart-melting favourite of many; a family of 'Nemo' clown fish living in a designated little sanctuary sectioned off with a ring of rocks; built by divers wanting to protect their habitat and stop people swimming into and damaging it – all of it a real joy, pleasure and privilege to see.

On dry land, Maria was really pleased with how well we all had done. Back safe and sound, we all had an amazing time for our first excursions into the underwater world; for her, though, the vast majority of the exercises taught had been well executed; proving our unfazed adaption from the pool to the daunting salty swathe of the sea and her adept unwavering instruction. Arriving back at the dive centre, we each then spent time cleaning the equipment down with fresh water to prevent salt damage and filled in our divers' log books with; when, where, how long, how deep, what we did and what we saw to keep record of our progress.

The last and final day of the course started early at around six thirty a.m. as we headed out on the boat to the dive site and again descended to show off more skills we had learnt, involving; mask flooding and buoyancy. Also, now we had to perform a mock emergency accent from 9m depth in the event of running out of air and not being close to a dive buddy for help. I initially struggled with this as I couldn't get the slow breathing release right, and would run out of air before reaching the surface; somewhat to the frustration of Maria and my own annoyance for hindering proceedings, that also add extra strains equalising the ears with ascents and descents. Finally, and thankfully on the third attempt, I managed it and could continue with the rest of the dive.

Our fourth and final dive to complete the course was now upon us; we were joined by a cameraman to film our aquatic encounter as we swam around our second dive site, this time again to our maximum of 18 metres' depth, we were lucky enough to see a variety of wildlife that included sleek-looking barracuda, weird but colourful slug-like creature called nudibranch and a stingray. We showed off our now honed skill demonstrations and eventually finished with a grand finale of building an underwater pyramid, stood weightlessly balanced on top of one another's shoulders. Maria said it best, "It's not what you do, it's how cool you look doing it" – too right.

We were back on terra firma before lunch and had finished the course. But more importantly, now we were all officially accredited Open Water divers; able to dive now anywhere in the world; trained to the dizzying heights of 18m or 60ft below. Granted, we weren't exactly going to be scouring every inch of the ocean floor and I dare say some conditions would be slightly less forgiving than the bath like sea we had learnt in, but we were all really happy and pleased with our efforts and achievement; some more than others as they had to overcome real personal fears and anxieties to make this a reality. For this, we were all really proud of one another, having achieved this goal together. For me, though, I love the water; in it or on it, whatever, and this had now given me another string to my bow and opened new avenues when travelling around, allowing me to take opportunities and not miss out. Plus, I had learnt and experienced how wonderfully fragile and beautifully dangerous the ocean could be and appreciation of the staggering array of life it harbours, gaining a newfound awareness and respect for the world's most powerful element.

After filling in the final two dives of our log books and getting our official stamps, I took the opportunity to sign up and buy a project aware conservation card which would be sent to my home address, stating my Open Water Diver status; proof to other operators of my ability to dive; much like a driving licence, plus rather than standard card this type made a donation to the protection of sharks, figuring this would make a worthwhile cause as I had remembered what I had learnt when in Ocean Park in Hong Kong and wanted to help contribute in saving of this most misunderstood animal, how could I not? Quiet easily, if you're an irrational idiot, because you'd think I'd get eaten through saving them and be in more peril being a diver. But this notion would be an over-exaggerated ridiculous nonsense to say the least; probably born out from bullshit Hollywood movies and the like about sharks that are a load of bollocks, where any truth couldn't possibly get in the way of a good (but usually stupid) story and are only made to frighten people. Just because sharks are bigger and naturally more adept at hunting and killing than any human in water, they have somewhat been made an unfair scapegoat, to play on unwarranted fears that certainly does not mean they should be destroyed. In fact, it should be the opposite; we don't live in a shark's environment and are not part of its natural food source or diet so therefore this makes us generally pretty safe. Furthermore they play a pivotal role keeping life in the oceans in a healthy balance, something which is essential for the maintenance of life on Earth. I figured now I had bought into a moral obligation to the sea and its wildlife conservation and that included the coolest creature of all, so I would take my chances. What's more rather than any shark, being in a place like this people are more likely to be killed by another silent deadly assassin; one on

144

land. Little did I realise; I was just about to meet my real arch-enemy and nearly my maker.

We now had the rest of the day to while away as we pleased and there was only one option really; a few others and I went to a nearby bar. On the way there, a huge coconut fell from one of the trees and crashed to the floor with a massive thud right in front of me. If I had been a second or so earlier, it would've smashed flush onto the top of my head. With its green outer shell this thing was as big as a bowling ball and just as heavy and, frankly, it more than likely would have killed me outright. Dead as fuck. I couldn't believe my luck and was grateful for the closest of close calls that left me relieved and cursing the coconut; my real mortal enemy.

To celebrate a day of death-defying brilliance, we carried on having something to eat and early afternoon mojitos indoors. The weather was continuing as it had for the last three days by raining hard. Not really an issue when spending your time in the water but now on land this was torrential. The slopping streets of the town were now turned into running rivers from the excessive downpour, and rolling blinds had to be brought down to keep the rain from blowing in and washing out the open bar. We followed on in the same fashion that evening, with everyone else who participated including the instructors, as we watched the video footage of us all underwater, gracefully gliding around performing our skills, accumulating with our spectacular pyramid – that was in no way as spectacular as the vein bulging from my head as I unknowingly suffered from the pressure below. We moved on for an evening meal and had the drinks that were generously paid for by those who had accrued bar fines for the bad practice and mistakes made during the course. I paid two for leaving my mask on my forehead; twice. But still I got off quite cheap compared to some.

Rising the next morning, I checked out of the resort and was now again ready to move on. The course and instructors were fantastic and I had loved every minute of learning to dive and was slightly disappointed to leave, but it had definitely been worthwhile. I'd had a great time and learnt so much, not only how to dive but about the sea and the wonderful wildlife that it harbours; it really opened my eyes and enthralled me. Plus I now had a new skill set and opened opportunities to further my adventures though I never really sat and reflected on what I'd achieved that much and never realised at the time what it meant. This had kept me preoccupied and busy so there wasn't time to think about much else. But now, I was again on the move and thinking ahead. And this paid thoughts to what was going to happen when heading to Koh Pha Ngan; the next main island south and infamous for its full moon parties.

Chloe had been in touch and she was going to be in Koh Pha Ngan for the full moon party. She had messaged me when I arrived back in Bangkok after I'd luckily managed to remember her email. From messaging back and forth a few times, our paths were destined to cross again and we arranged to meet up here, having not seen each other since Yangshuo. She provided details of where she was to be staying and after checking it out I decided to go somewhere else. Jane had gone home leaving Chloe and Karen, but the resort where they were staying at was expensive for my needs and I didn't have anyone to share the cost with. Also with the full moon party looming and thousands of people coming over at that time of the month, proprietors had the chance to take the piss and charge whatever they wanted. So I opted for something a bit more budget worthy as I wasn't planning on spending that much time in the accommodation anyway.

Taking the ferry in the morning from Koh Tao to Koh Pha Ngan was an experience in itself; the weather hadn't let up and the boat across was much worse than that from the main land, creating a much larger roller coaster. The journey over was also longer and lasted approximately two hours. I just sat back, relaxed, listened to music and enjoyed watching the watery horizon rhythmically disappear and reappear from the top and bottom of the window, constantly changing from dark sea green to light sky grey as we dipped up and down with the contours of each passing crest. Less could be said for other passengers though; people were drained to pale green, skin washed out through sea sickness, sat hunched over with their sick bag security blanket stuck to their chins. Their eyes pined for the relentless movement to stop, torture etched across the face due to the inability to adapt to the unfamiliar circumstance of a constantly moving surface. But there was no let up and they had to ride it out like the rest. But surely it would be worth it.

Arriving at the port, everyone hastily disembarked to embrace the reassurance of stable earth. I wandered aimlessly down the peer and happened upon some locals offering chalets on the beach. The accommodation I had booked prior wasn't beach-side, and nor was I too confident with my reservation as the person on the phone had very poor

146

English. Rightly or wrongly, I decided to take the offer in front of me, which was also 100 baht cheaper and they took me there straightaway. The place was about a fifteen-minute drive from the port following the road straight along the coastline; before eventually taking a right down a track towards the ocean, which seemed promising. The complex wasn't that tidy, as the trees left lots of debris on the ground and as now normal the domestic fowl and dogs foraged around freely at will. With only sandy trails, there was no paths or terracing as such except for what was the owner's home and reception, but beyond that, about thirty yards on was the beach and sea as promised. So I took a wooden chalet raised up on stilts with a porch and hammock, that inside had a double bed, fan and a doorway leading to the bathroom with cold shower. Not being one for airs and graces, decided this would do just nicely for a few nights.

In an attempt to meet with Chloe and Karen, I headed out. They knew I was arriving but didn't know when, so I ventured up the main road to the resort where they were staying. Calling at reception, I explained who I was looking for and told their room number. Knocking, Karen answered and it was really nice to see her again and made with the greetings, explaining that I'd just arrived and where I was staying. Chloe was apparently using the Internet. I had missed where the computer facility was, having sort of meandered off the track and ended up next door, so I had to perform some impromptu cross country to get back to the actual resort. Karen and I wandered down and she showed me where it was. Chloe finished on the computer and I was greeted with a big hug. It was great to see her and Karen again after what had been some six weeks that felt much longer due to the things that I had been up to in-between. We then spent the afternoon having a few beers and catching up; Chloe went for a dip in the sea with the neighbours' Rottweiler. Ill prepared without swimwear, I just watched from the shoreline. We had a stroll along the beach; her tall slender frame, short blonde hair and petty face were exactly as I had remembered. We chatted and laughed about what we had been doing and things that had happened.

I asked, "What's your plan for this evening?"

"Getting pissed with you!" her abrupt reply.

That evening was the night prior to the full moon party and there was a warm up party event on Haad Rin beach, situated on the other side of the peninsula at the south of the island. We headed over there by flagging down some bloke in a 4x4 truck to take us. There was no room for me inside the truck as Chloe, Karen and the two of girls who they were now travelling and sharing room with got inside. So I jumped into the back of the flat bed and held on. The road was winding and took an up and downhill course as it caressed its way along the craggy coastline. The driver, clearly a rally fan was enamoured with speed. My hands and legs ached as I had to lower my centre of gravity to avoid tumbling around on the dirty base of the truck having changed from sitting on the edge, as it was only a matter of time before I would end up over the side, bouncing off the tarmac to roll into the nearest seedy go-go bar; where the girls outside were still beckoning me in, as we hurtled past at about fifty miles per hour.

Upon arriving, we had dinner and hit the beach area laden with makeshift bars selling all sorts of bucket drinks in their various guises, designed for every taste including; SangSom, vodka, Jack Daniels, gin, coke, lemonade but all pretty much laced with the lethal Thai energy drink to keep revellers going. We each got armed with one and set about, as they say, 'getting on it'.

Drinking, fire being thrown around, dancing on tables, people painted in fluorescent body paint – this place was mental and wasn't even the full party. This was a dry run, the pre-party. Needless to say, I don't remember an awful lot about the night but the next day's hangover told the story when we just spent the time relaxing by the pool where the girls were staying. That evening, it was the main event but due to the previous night's antics, for once I really wasn't in the mood for going out and struggled to get a beer inside me. But this was why I was here, and is an event that is etched into traveller folklore, so lethargically put my arse into gear and headed once more to Haad Rin beach, this time for the big one; the monthly event that draws people not only from Koh Pha Ngan, but like myself from the surrounding islands and from all parts of the world. Just a few thousand revellers were expected to be adorning the beach due to the time of year. During high season, I had heard that this number could triple, swelling to an insane ten thousand.

Upon arriving, I armed myself with a bucket of SangSom and potent Thai energy drink, the poison to reinvigorate me; part one job done. Everyone was getting body paint put on and I opted for a huge spider web and spider painted in fluorescent orange and green on the top of my head. It looked awesome glowing in the dark of night; part two mission accomplished. I proceeded to party. Two buckets later, I was feeling good, but part three was something else as I trudged off up the beach.

Some of the guys who were staying in the same complex as the girls had mentioned a place called Mushroom Mountain. Here, as the name suggests, it is possible to get a blended drink of magic mushrooms by the beach. It was discussed at the time about what a bad idea it would be to have one of these while out at a place like the full moon party and I agreed. But that was then and this was now; my new-found boozed up train of thought was something along the lines of 'the best thing I could possibly have right now is a mushroom shake – I'd be stupid not to' self-destruct button; here we come. Off I went walking twenty minutes up to the top of the beach. Somehow managing to find where it was, I bought one and walked back. Arriving at where everyone was, Karen asked as to what I was drinking. And I don't remember an awful lot after that.

Literally from that point, I lost at least two hours of my life and was pretty much oblivious to who or what was around me. I do remember getting told that I couldn't get on the bar to dance; probably a good thing because I was completely fucked and would have easily fallen off into all the bottles. I'd already whacked my head on a low ceiling and nearly knocked myself out going up some stairs, in-between being bought a beer by a random person who was suitably impressed at the state I was in and standing on a footbridge above everyone else, dancing around whilst I was rushing off my tits. As the night wore on, the mushrooms started to wear off and I decided enough was enough. So I went back up the beach to go get another.

Upon returning to where we were, I didn't have a clue where anyone else was, or how long I had been away, but it must have been a while, cos I stopped at some random bar to listen to some music by The Doors. Far out, man! Next thing (a few hours later) from out of nowhere, Dave appeared; the younger lad who was on the Thai Experience. We chatted, kind of, and he was laughing at the state I was in. Then anyone and everyone seemed to just start appearing out of the wood work. Charlotte, a Canadian girl who was on the diving course, was asking if I had seen her friend Sharon, who then turned up. Joanne who was also on the dive course was then asking if I had seen her friend Hailey. I really don't know what made these people think I'd know where people were? I hardly knew where I was! Or what the fuck was is going on for that matter, as I was barely able to stand or string two words together. Just as they disappeared, I was still 'talking' to Dave and his mate, when Hailey came stumbling past, I tried shouting her, but she was completely gone, totally out of her tree, wobbling about all over the place and making me look fucking sober; and that sent me over the edge as I couldn't stop laughing. I think I can only remember these bits because of that moment. It was definitely late (more to the point early!) now, as we had a couple of beers and knocked out a few shapes on the beach, as the sun rose, with the other die hards. Come daylight, I was fading fast so decided to head back. I somehow found a lift, jumping in the back of a random truck which happened to be heading my way, with a dozen or so others in an equally sorry state.

Waking later at around noon, I got up and wandered into the bathroom and nearly got the shock of my life at the vision staring back at me. My face absolutely covered in paint, I looked like some sort of tribal warrior who had been to battle; red, orange, green and blue streaks across my cheeks, forehead and chin, along with the still intact spider and web on my head that I had had done at the very start of the evening. I burst out laughing to myself. I knew some random girls with body paint were coating me throughout the night but I had no idea how much or what it looked like; nor did I care. But now the evidence was staring back at me in the cold light of day. It looked like I'd a good night. I'd say; and not bad for someone who 'wasn't quite feeling it' beforehand.

I showered and went to see the girls, bumping into Chloe halfway down the track to their complex. She told me that she was just about to come looking for me. Which was quite thoughtful, considering I went off on one, and for what I can remember, I hardly saw them all night. The rest of the day was spent chilling and recovering amid taking a ride down to Haad Rin, where videos were playing of the drunken debauched evening on the beach. Fortunately, due to the numbers, I don't think I featured but I wasn't really feeling like reliving what happened, as I was already feeling rough enough as it was. The day ebbed away relaxing in the bars, watching comedy videos and dining to provide some sort of adequate sustenance, while haphazardly piecing together the previous night's shenanigans.

The next morning, the two girls who were with Chloe and Karen went their own way, so the girls moved out of their chalet to more affordable digs, or more precisely where I was staying. The day after, we were all due to leave as Koh Pha Ngan as well, as it had served its purpose and we had booked tickets to head out. They were going to Koh Phi Phi. I was sticking to my plan and heading to Koh Samui. Still, we with a day to kill we hired a jeep to explore the island.

Setting off, we headed north with Chloe driving and me navigating in the back, stopping at various resorts and waterfalls to admire the scenery. We each took it in turn to drive. That said; I lasted all of five minutes behind the wheel before Chloe insisted on driving which I conceded to. It wasn't that I was driving badly or that fast, just that as she put it, "I'm a really bad passenger" or, as I preferred, "a crazy neurotic". Carrying on, we ventured about until we saw one amazing vision of loveliness which we all realised we would have to stop and admire. In the middle of Koh Pha Ngan, a tropical island in the Thai gulf, there stood in all its glory a country pub exactly like what you would find anywhere in rural England. We nearly broke the brakes on the jeep let alone the front doors of the establishment to get in. Kind of stupid considering that not two hours prior, we were all commenting on how good it was to be chilling out in bars made of bamboo on the sunny shoreline. Next thing here we were in a mock Tudor, ye olde pub, in the afternoon, drinking pints of cider, admiring the traditional English pub grub menu and playing darts; typical Brits abroad and so much for experiencing other cultures.

We then attempted to get to numerous waterfalls within the island but albeit in a jeep, the terrain was really tricky on the soft muddy track roads and our plans subsided like time did in the same fashion. Chloe did a good job handling the vehicle, so I'll give her dues, amid the poor terrain and shroud of dense forest that only aided in masking the increasingly poor light and it was dark when we arrived back at Haad Rin, where I gorged on the most sensational chicken and bacon Caesar salad I'd ever tasted. Someone had ordered it the night before and I wanted one as it was massive and laden with grilled chicken. It looked awesome but tasting it was even better and was a good ten minutes before anyone got even so much as a murmur out of me until I finished, being left ravenous by the lack of sustenance of the past few days. Eventually, we filled the jeep back up with fuel, returned it and headed back to the chalets – theirs now next to mine. We exchanged hugs and goodbyes as we were leaving at separate times and would miss each other the following morning.

Moving On

Having organised a taxi to pick me up from the main road to take me back to the ferry port, at six a.m., I waited with my things by the roadside. I waited, waited and waited a little more yet nothing arrived. So, I started to get a fraction concerned about missing the ferry as cars, bikes and other taxis roared past me with hasty motorised contempt. Randomly, out of the blue, a scooter pulled over and the guy on board asked in a thick German accent where I was going. It turns out, he was also heading towards the ferry so he said, jump on. I was a little apprehensive; not necessarily because of the situation of accepting lifts of strangers, but having my large back pack and small bag making me unsure of the weight and more to the point my balancing skills. Being in a situation though, I put on my back pack and attached the smaller one to my chest and away we went.

Arriving at the port all was fine and I thanked the guy, who brushed it off nonchalantly saying it was not a problem and went on his way as if an everyday occurrence. I was really happy and thankful for this; such a simple gesture on his behalf but it really helped me out and saved a bunch of hassle should I have missed the ferry. Under the circumstances, he didn't have to stop or help as he was on a little scooter and I was carrying all my things and looking a little cumbersome to say the least; so, to this man I salute and wish him the best. Armed with my pre-bought ticket, I arrived at the jetty ready to board but ended up resuming with some more waiting. Hailey, Joanne and Ella arrived who I'd met on the diving course. The girls were on their way to Koh Samui also, so we chatted and inevitably laughed about our full moon party high jinks. Also, the weather had taken an upturn and was really warm and sunny; finally and somewhat typically as we were now travelling and not necessarily lounging around to appreciate it.

With the good weather, the ferry journey this time was nice and relatively smooth. Arriving, I went straight to the main resort of Chaweng, and managed to get myself a place at the north end of the town for a reasonable price by the beach. Deciding that I wanted to make the most of my time, I hired a scooter, grabbed a map and headed out. First point of call was to one of the lookout points and then I continued up the coast road to see if the girls from the ferry were up to anything exciting. This turned out to be nothing as they were still feeling worse for wear recovering from the previous night and I had woken them. Never mind. The afternoon was getting late so I decided to go for a quick exploration of the local area, finding some places that I wanted to visit having planned on spending the next day racing around the island.

This though nearly never happened, as I proceeded to have what we'll call a slight mishap. Just about ready to set off, my hand slipped on the twist accelerator of the automatic scooter and it went from under me. The more I held on, the more it applied the gas and the bike squirmed uncontrollably ahead of me, as my grasp seemed to tighten in a knee jerk reaction. Somehow, I luckily managed to get the bike under control and stop it just before going head-first straight into a wall, but not before injuring my leg and toe in the motorised mêlée. After my near-miss, I wasn't hurt too bad; my ego the main casualty being damaged more than my actual self, from shitting myself up with another good comedy moment for anyone who witnessed it. I headed back and parked the bike up for the evening as a good idea, and instead ventured out on foot to one of the local bars to watch some football, to then get verbally harassed by the local lady boy prostitutes on the way home. This another sorry downside to the culture and tourism that is prevalent in Thailand; not just because of the harassment that I might get or possibility of being robbed or the like, as I knew that I needed to have my wits about me. But this runs much darker in the sense of the unfortunate and possibly desperate situation people such as those are in, what they have to endure and what they may or may not have to do to try and make a living, which therefore makes them very susceptible to dangers and exploitation. I didn't stop to enquire or find out any specific details, but surely it couldn't be a healthy or safe existence for someone to live. I quickly made it back to my room – I'm hasten to add, alone.

It was hot and sunny the next day. One of the best I'd had for seemingly ages and certainly whilst being on the islands. Sticking to the plan, I made like *Easy Rider* and headed off out on my scooter, this time with camera to snap away. I stopped at the view point; looking down below, I took a shot of Chaweng bay as it swept round to the far peninsula, small parallels of white water waves steadily encroached the shoreline from a deep blue sea that was all beautifully illuminated by the bright overhead sky. I never actually realised how big the island was; vast compared to the others and my hand drawn rough map seemed to have features smattered all over the place. Off the main road cutting through the island and heading up towards the hills was one of the many waterfalls featured, so I took my trusty steel steed to go and see it as my speed allowed warm air to whip over me to help keep cool.

Parking halfway up the road at the small shop entrance, I started heading down a steep little track through trees and vegetation to make it to the waterfall. I knew I was close as the murmurs of cascading water became more and more apparent and through the green of the trees and bushes white water could be spotted. This truly was quite a secluded spot; and how. Arriving at the edge of the water with trees enclosed on either side, I started looking around the narrow opening which let sunshine fall down on the water and rocks from the not so high yet serene and pretty falls. There were two couples sunbathing further upstream in the water. Ignoring them, I started to take a couple of photos. Just as I went to do so, they decided to get up and venture about, not minding my presence. It seems I wasn't the only one who had realised the secluded-ness of the spot as I didn't realise until that moment that they were completely naked.

Unfortunately, this was the blokes; the women kept some of their dignity intact by having their bikini bottoms on. Life just isn't fair. Yet, they proceeded to wander around whilst I was trying to take photos. Now I'm no prude and if you want to run around with no clothes on and be all kinds of 'nekkid', then go for it, I couldn't care less, but I don't want to be labelled a pervert either. So, I tried my very best to take photos with a nonchalant demeanour without getting some random fella's love hammer in the shot, never mind incur his wrath or whatever else for that matter by having him think I was happily snapping his missus' boobs; which were very nice as it turned out. I thought best not to intrude any longer and made a hasty exit back up the hill. I couldn't help but laugh though, especially as an elderly American couple passed and they asked me the way and what it was like.

"Just down there. Beautiful, lovely views" my not quite divulging the full details reply.

I tried looking for a particular Buddhist temple but couldn't seem to locate it as my map was again less than accurate. Obviously, this wasn't down to my crappy navigating skills, as reading a map becomes kind of a chore when trying to steer and ride on a scooter at the same time. I had wasted enough fuel messing around, resulting in another aimless wild goose chase, so I headed to another waterfall which wasn't that far from where I had left the initial one. This, though, was much busier and had shops and stalls supplying goods to those visiting. And it was obvious why when I actually got to the falls, as they were tall and impressive. Many stood and had their pictures taken in front of them whilst those there for any period of time swam in the lagoon. I didn't bother; just using the time to increase my own photo portfolio. It reminded me very much of ones I'd seen prior, minus the masses of people. So left soon after, not feeling the need to hang around too long, apart from taking time to watch a couple of locals wash an elephant in the boulder strewn river further downstream which actually looked like they were having loads of fun. Both handlers and elephant alike really seemed to be enjoying themselves, and created a wonderfully scenic view with having the bathing sunlight, soft rippling river and dense thick green foliage in the background.

Heading to the far side of the island, I visited the big Buddha Temple, which as you might have guessed had a massive statue of Buddha within; impressive and beautifully ornate. Surrounding the temple, there were various statues on land and in the water of a lagoon, depicting fables and stories that proved an interesting and worthwhile look before then heading to the crocodile farm near to the scene of my misdemeanour the previous day. It seemed expensive for what it was and didn't look too inviting so I didn't bother, so decided to head back, plus another reason was that by now, I'd been out riding for about five hours without a shirt on and I could feel my skin beginning to tighten.

Returning to the room and looking in the mirror, I found that I had turned a lovely shade of pink after spending all day out in the sun. Thankfully, it didn't hurt, yet that wasn't really the problem. The problem was I had big pink patches covering my back, one side of my body and arm, where they were all adequately cooked, but the rest was still rare and off white, having not gotten full coverage from being hunched over on the scooter the majority of the day. With this, you have to admit that when you get a patchy tan, it does leave you looking – for want of a better word – a bit of a 'twat'. Like when skiers or fishermen get a white ring around the eyes from their shades; that's right, they 'look a bit of a twat'. It wasn't too horrendous though and thankfully wasn't sore. At least I had a fair idea I would be getting the chance to top it up over the next few weeks. And for the moment, I still had the option to cover up.

Being due to be picked up at six a.m. in the morning was no problem except that I woke up at five forty-five having forgotten to set my alarm. I quickly dashed around and got my things together, feeling a little jaded. I need not have worried because in what was now becoming the norm, my transport was late and I ended up waiting around in reception for the van. Eventually, it turned up and we made a few more calls to other residencies, picking up other travellers, but by the way the driver was driving he must have thought he was late. This was one of the craziest rides I'd been on; absolutely thrashing the vehicle to the ferry port, attempting mad overtaking manoeuvres and not bothering to slow down for humps in the road. I was sat at the back and must have banged my head at least three times on the ceiling from being catapulted upwards when driving over the larger speed bumps that failed miserably to stop this maniac driver; one of which was hit really hard and left me rubbing and holding my head. Not quite hung over but more concussed thanks to Thailand's answer to Lewis Hamilton. We made it to the ferry port to take us back to the mainland in plenty of time, making the *Wacky Races* and my bruised scalp a somewhat pointless exercise.

The ferry was huge and had fixed seats which reclined, so I caught up on some sleep as although the bus journey had certainly kept my attention, I was still tired and feeling the effects of a few beers from the night before. On the mainland, we changed buses twice before getting to the transport office, where we then waited around again for another bus to come along and take us across the mainland to the ferry port on the west coast. Some other backpackers were complaining and moaning about the less than efficient service being provided. Tired, I just figured 'so what?' and went with the organised chaos, before eventually getting on the bus to doze off again. At the ferry port, I started chatting with three girls from the UK; Brianna, Dina and Dora. They had been on the initial mad ride bus. I hadn't really spoke to them being somewhat focused on hoping we wouldn't be killed. But now, rested and recovered, I made an effort. As was the order of the day, the boat was late and around a hundred people waited patiently for it to arrive and take us to Koh Phi Phi.

After the mad scramble to get on the board, we all sat on the bow as lines were released and we set off, chilling and chatting while watching the mainland drift away, as the smaller islands we approached silhouetted to a setting sun. When we arrived, it was now almost dark and had taken nearly eleven hours in total to get there. Unfortunately, it hadn't finished, as we still had to find accommodation. Most of the places were full and couldn't fit the now-acquainted four of us in; so I split and found a place which offered a room for one night with the option to extend at a lower rate should I wish to stay. The Thai bloke telling me about the room was hanging out at the end of the pier with his picture display cards, so he took me to the place and saved me the effort of carrying my large bag as he took it on his bicycle, which was good of him but just in case I decided to keep my smaller more valuable pack with myself.

Getting sorted with a room quickly, I dropped my bags in and headed back into town with the same guy. He told me that he knew a dive shop and I wanted to chat with them about the possibility of doing a few dives or gaining my advanced diver's certificate depending on price. But rather than walking, the Thai bloke offered me the use of his bike to use. With such a kind gesture I obliged, but not wanting to see him stuck I insisted on giving him a ride on the bike seat, as he was going back to the pier which he duly accepted.

Now the town on Phi Phi is very small and doesn't have cars or traffic and as the streets go, some are cobbled and some are just dirt tracks but generally busy with people, creating a very beautiful, chilled out, ambient place. Apart from when you have some idiot speeding along these small narrow streets on a boneshaker of a bike that was in its prime during World War 2 and a Thai bloke on the back holding on for grim death; where it could only end in tears. Actually, not quite tears but a few bumps and scrapes as we fell off, narrowly avoiding crashing into someone else coming the other way; each wobbling erratically from side to side to avoid one another in a head-on collision. Fortunately, the innocent parties were unharmed and my Thai co-pilot and I got up and laughed while dusting the debris down. Luckily, we were also about two doors away from the dive shop, so we shook hands and each went our own way, having signalled my arrival in style.

Unconvinced of what to do, I decided to get back to the people in the dive shop. In the meantime, I checked the Internet. It wasn't good news. My dad had emailed me and generally only did so if major things were going on or something had happened. Unfortunately, it had. I'm really close to my brother-in-law, his mother, whom I also knew, had passed away and it made me sad. I knew she had not been in the best of health but this was sudden and I really felt for him and my sister. Also adding to the woes, their son and my nephew, who was only four, was not very well. He had flu and was not helping matters under the circumstances. All this accumulating, I felt quite useless being away and sort of guilty for not being around. Not my fault, I know, but a person still cannot help the way something like that makes you feel; especially when it's your nearest and dearest involved. This was one of them times when travelling puts you out of the loop and at a disadvantage of not being there for people when it matters. Unfortunately, I knew this could be a case at some point and a fact that had to be accepted. The night was getting on now so I met up with Brianna, Dina and Dora as we said that we would get together for a drink, prior to leaving each other at the pier. I had a good time with Brianna who was a police officer and had a great sense of humour. Although she didn't realise, she played her part in cheering me up, helping take my mind off things and was something I was thankful for.

In the morning, I went to the guest house where Chloe and Karen were staying. They had headed over here while I was getting an uneven tan on Koh Samui. It was good to see them again as we failed to meet up the previous night when out and about. We chatted and one of the topics on the agenda was that they were now both sporting new tattoos. I'd never had a tattoo before but liked them and while away travelling thought I might get one, as it seemed as good a time as ever. The subject had arisen when we talked in China and I was still up for getting one or possibly more; I had an idea of about four which I wanted but hadn't really put much thought into exactly what or where. So far, the situation never arose when I was going to get one done. All of a sudden now, it had and it had jumped right to the front of the queue, so it felt like the pressure was on slightly. As they were saying that I should get one done and that the place that they used the previous night was really good. I agreed, thinking, *What the hell!* or was it, *What the hell am I going to do?* or *What the hell am I going to get?*

We were just about to leave for breakfast when the door opposite their room opened and Jenny emerged, I'd met her the night previous, after somehow ending up on the beach with a bunch of other people, where we chatted for what seemed ages about things I can't quite recall. It was late and I was drunk, so, therefore, in those instances I tend to babble a load of shit I don't remember. It was randomly strange, her being next door to Chloe and Karen. But made the introductions and then she joined us for breakfast in a little restaurant down the pathway. After we had eaten, the others were discussing what they were going to do for the rest of the day. By this point, I was feeling the effects from the evening refreshments and a hangover was kicking in, unaided by the sapping hot sun. I bailed out and went back to the room to get some more sleep and hope for some quick inspiration in regards to getting a tattoo.

Upon waking, I was still not one hundred per cent on getting a tattoo as I pondered that this wasn't exactly off my own steam, but eventually decided that this was the opportunity to shut up and put up and I did really want to get one. So, it was on. Thinking about it more, I'd made some executive decisions and definitely knew what I would get and where. Admittedly, though, I did have slight reservation about the pain I'd have to endure.

Arriving at their room on the night, they didn't bother to ask if I was still getting one, it was more a case of "Are you ready for your tattoo?" "Are you nervous?" with obvious smirks as they spoke wondering if I would have the bottle to go through with it. We arrived at the tattoo place which was essentially in-between where we both were staying. I decided on a font, colour, size and position and the price was good costing around £100. Stupid really, as I was debating paying for a dive course that actually had means to an end – offering learning, activity and education plus included accommodation for a little more – yet, now I was willing to have my body permanently etched by a piece of bamboo with a needle tied to the end, all done freehand for around the same price that didn't offer any of those things, except included a few hours of pain and grimace instead. I lay on the open shop floor with my left arm outstretched, hand pointing up over as we began.

Chloe asked, "How is it?"

"Is that the pain?" I asked back.

"Yes," she replied.

"No problem, I'll see you in couple of hours. Can ya get me a beer, please?" She did, with a straw which was very useful and equally as thoughtful; she also bought me a sandwich.

Honestly, I didn't think that the needle was providing that much pain, especially as everyone was saying that where I was getting tattooed was one of the most painful areas; on the inside of my bicep. I lay there listening to the tunes, occasionally chatting to people as they sporadically came and went to see how things were going. The worst thing was the position my arm was in; after the two hours on the floor, my shoulder and elbow having been held up and out over, in that position, for that long were now killing me. Upon finishing, I was so relieved to be able to move my aching arm down again, where with blood flowing properly and in a more natural position, the motion in the joints soon returned. Now, though, the inside of my arm was incredibly sore, having been punctured what felt like a million times with various-sized needles. I looked in the mirror and was very happy with the result. I thought it looked cool and was just what I wanted; written in black ink going down the inside of my left bicep. I wanted something which would remind me of my time travelling and also meant something, so took the title of a favourite song which seemed to encompass all these ideas. I was really happy with the end product and glad I had it done, especially as it was a design personal to me and not just something from the tattoo artist book.

A group of us were hanging around now; Chloe, Karen, Jenny and I. Also Joey and Aide who I met through the girls on Koh Pha Ngan, who cropped up sporadically, and I was introduced to Cale and Stephy who were a couple they had also met whilst travelling around. The next two days were whiled away in pretty uneventful fashion; spending them eating, drinking and relaxing at the beach. I had to avoid the salt water due to my newly acquired body art. I did randomly bump into Trabbers in the street; the legend that he is with his usual funny cheery self, full of banter and stories of chaos caused between Laos and getting here. Yet, needing to be places and despite saying we would, unfortunately, we failed to catch up again on an obligatory night out, which I was disappointed with.

The day before we were due to leave, it was decided that we should do something; I definitely wanted and needed to. Relaxing on the beach and getting pissed is all fine and well but I can't do this for long, as I get bored easily and start to crave at least a little excitement. I had mentioned to Chloe about going cliff jumping and she said that Joey and Aide were up for going too. So, Chloe, Karen, Jenny, Aide, Joey, two girls they knew called Sindy and Caroline and I headed out on a boat. There was also more to the day than just doing the jumps, so it offered a little something for everyone.

Stopping first at monkey beach, we got out of the boat and went on the sand to witness, in very close proximity, the wild monkeys that live there amongst the trees of the sheer grey rock face. Whole families of primates; male, female, young and old would approach, bold as brass in their search for food – nurtured now to be comfortable with human presence from the countless tours which pass and the food that people bring. Care had to be taken where this was concerned, as some had a tendency to be quite aggressive in their search for the bananas we'd been provided with; snatching frantically from people's hands. It proved fascinating to observe their behaviour with each other and visiting boats. I did wonder about the cost of human encroachment on their society, but in turn also had to laugh at their random, surprise sex antics with one another other; the kind of etiquette and behaviour that sees humans arrested and thrown in jail – and rightly so.

Rather quickly on our boat trip, we were up next. The people who were cliff jumping, that is. The boat was anchored with a 25m swim to the rock face, Joey, Aide, Sindy, Caroline and I were already kitted out with rubber shoes and gloves, so with our guide we jumped overboard and swam to the rocky shore line. Climbing out, the iron shore rocks were peppered with holes from years of abrasion and were extremely jagged and sharp, easily answering the question; why the gloves and footwear? Steadily, one by one, we followed the guide up to the top; very aware that one slip would result in severe injury or worse before even having had the chance to voluntarily jump from the cliff.

Climbing to the initial point of 8m, we all jumped and made it leaping rather un-apprehensively from the seemingly higher than anticipated vantage point out into the blue, providing a good rush for a start. Then we swam back around to climb again; this time to the 12m point. We all jumped like lemmings. And thankfully; all made the leap. Even though it was only four metres more, there looked and was a huge difference now between jumping and the eternity that it seemed to take hitting the water. Time seemed suspended, yet the body not so, within the gravity accelerated warp. How we entered the water now was critical; it was obviously deep enough, but with the speed accrued from falling meant that arms must be by the side and not flailing around, and the body had to be straight or things were going to get painful.

Here though, one of the girls got it slightly wrong on entering, and the flesh on the back of the leg made a loud *crack* as it broke the surface tension of the water. The sound was enough to tell you it hurt, but thankfully she was OK. We then went again; this time to the 14m point. Only Aide, Joey and I ventured up to it and peered over the edge. It was high and worse, there was a ledge to consciously jump out over. I don't mind admitting it was scary and I was a bit nervous; but driven once more by bravado and not brains, with a one, two, three, we each took turns, all jumping out over to land far enough away from the cliff and out into the water. The fall seemed suspended for a fraction before the body came thundering towards the water. The scant time allowed for quick thought to get any moving arms and legs into a correct, ridged and straight position in line with the body, as nanoseconds later, feet first the body crashed through the liquid line. Salt water raced the nose and a rushing plumed bubbling fizz engulfed the body from air pushed below the surface, with such ferocity that allowed it to dissipate with steady tickling regularity as the water's density slowed the speeding torso. When all momentum had subsided, with a few kicks of the legs, it was possible to slowly swim up to the surface.

After this, it was unanimous that we weren't bothering to do the 20m jump; I know this doesn't sound that high, but when you are up there and look down, it is. Think of it as a four-storey building. When one backed out, the others followed like dominoes. Part of me wanted to look at it though, and in hindsight I wish I had, because I might have done it and it felt like I bottled it, chickened out and never completed the course. But, conversely though, I wasn't in competition with anyone, I had nothing to prove and knowing me, I would've fucked it up at the critical moment, and more than likely fucked myself up too. At 14m, it felt high and it was already the highest thing that I'd ever jumped off, without having something to stop me splattering into an unrecognisable mess. So I didn't push my luck and left it at that.

Back on the boat, everyone said well done. We moved on stopping for a more relaxing moment splashing about in the lagoon, before heading around to the other side of the island, jumping into deeper open water with the snorkelling gear on to admire the beautiful corals and fish that would saunter amongst us as our ever wary accomplices. The next part of the day was at a famous movie haunt; visiting the beach where aptly named *The Beach* was filmed. We relaxed and lolled about in the sea amid numerous other revellers and boats. Unfortunately; the popularity had started to take its toll now and create a bit of a tourism mess, where any secluded idealism portrayed looked way off the mark. As each vessel and person's carbon footprint was left well and truly behind, to the slow but sure degradation of the natural environment. We were now part of this and despite seeing a beautiful cinematic location, the hour spent there was enough to tell me to not bother going back. For a finale, once again the snorkelling gear went on, as we ventured into the deep to swim with some sharks. Sounds brilliant and would have been, if there actually were any, so was a slight let down, but still provided a nice saunter with our other aquatic friends. I really enjoyed the day out as we toured the smaller islands of Phi Phi; where despite the environmental implications, it was good to see new interesting scenery, finally be active, check out the local wildlife and get buzzed off some adrenaline. So I was tired on the way back, yet still appreciated our amazing setting being highlighted by the beautiful backdrop of a mellowing, electrified sun, ebbing away to silhouette the densely formed clouds of a long day. After finishing and although managing to make it out on the night, I decided to cut mine short.

Nothing had been heard from home. Dad had explained that everyone was a bit preoccupied with what was going on and said that I may not hear from them, but it was bothering me and having a few beers, I felt the urge to ring home. I was glad I did as I managed to get to speak to everyone, especially my brother-in-law as he was at my parents' home and although upsetting, obviously, more so for him, we had a good chat about what had happened. But I didn't mind talking about this kind of thing if the other person wants to and was only too willing to listen, offer some support and reassurance even from the other side of the planet. To lighten the mood, everyone was laughing at my antics, so I thought I'd use the opportunity to tell them about my new body art; this cheered the brother-in-law up no end; he, like me, knew my mam hates tattoos and couldn't wait for her to find out. I felt better after the call and decided to join the others for last beers as it was getting late and we were leaving in the morning.

Chloe, Karen, Jenny, Cale, Stephy and I had decided that we had been on Phi Phi long enough now and as we were all heading in the same direction, mainly towards Singapore, we took the ferry to the next island south; the much larger Koh Lanta. It was a relaxed journey, sitting on the bow of the boat, I just listened to music as we cut through the waters and watched the waves roll by, quietly thinking to myself while resting on the railings not saying much. Upon arriving, we jumped in the back of a truck with the bags and headed for the accommodation we arranged with some touts on the dock. The place we were first taken to was poor; the cabanas had no locks on the doors and the water was putrid brown. Furthermore, there wasn't much around by way of amenities. Chloe and Karen had already moved further down the coast by a few kilometres and needless to say; it wasn't long before we followed suit.

We managed to get into the same place as Chloe and Karen and compared to where we were initially, this was a palace. They had a hut sorted and the owners said we could have a two double-bed room for the night which the four of us took, being short of options at this point. But this was fine for one night as it was really nice and clean. We ate and chilled out, the girls had an early night while Cale and I headed out to watch some uninspiring football with a few beers in a local bar; where the most entertainment happened to be a gecko making an absolute racket that I can only assume was a war cry, because with no right whatsoever it then proceeded to attack and devour a massive cockroach that was far bigger than itself. Mr Gecko was not to be fucked with. Wonderful nature at its finest!

We switched to the complex next door the next day; I shared with Jenny while Cale and Stephy got themselves a room. In fact, everyone did as Chloe and Karen's cabin was infested with cockroaches and didn't want to hang around in their cabin another night. If I'd known I would have asked Mr Gecko to pop round and 'have a quiet word'. But we were all sorted with a decent place to stay for the next two days on a nice little complex with pool, bar and restaurant on the beach, which is pretty much where we hung out for the duration, whereby chilling and playing with a football, allowed myself to turn a further shade of red in the intermittent sun. At this point, I had decided I was smoking too much and needed to get some exercise; especially with not many activities to preoccupy myself with. So tried cutting down on the cigs, started running up and down on the beach and swimming in the sea. Also I'd began to read upon some of my future endeavours and knew I would need to lose more weight and get fitter, or things could prove to be a little difficult otherwise. Here was pretty much relaxed affair, with nothing happening and after two full days on Koh Lanta, we needed to make headway and move on to our next destination; Malaysia.

I was really going to miss being in Thailand, I had been here before, but this time, I thought I really got to know the place that much more.

Mainly due to participating on the Thai Experience and teaching; where I learned so much about the religion, culture and customs. It offered me the chance to get immersed within the psyche and have some truly unique experiences, through interacting with regular everyday Thais. I ended up in places and situations where many would not; from collecting alms and staying in a temple with monks to hanging out and making speeches at rural festivals. No more so, than when staying with Mah Lee; her involvement in the community opened up a level of inclusion I never imagined possible and created everlasting memories, along with those that made me very proud to of helped her and the children. These times were such a privilege and highlight making it a stand-out part of my travels so far, which extended to amazing rewarding activities such as trekking and diving that allowed me to learn, both in an educational sense and about myself too. It offered a whole new outlook, respect and appreciation as I felt like I'd really invested in the country. Therefore this left me that bit more humbled, empathetic and concerned at the hardships with the infrastructure; especially regarding the political unrest that dominated the headlines, where I hoped a peaceful resolution could be brokered between protesters and the government. Not being anything to do with tourists, I was lucky and grateful that my own personal plans weren't affected. But it shouldn't be forgotten about the many people who were disrupted when airports got closed down, something which I also empathised with. Unfortunately, internal troubles can happen in any country, at any time so sincerely hope that this wouldn't stop others coming here. It really is beautiful; the people, religion, the culture, the splendid scenery – everything – and it would be such a shame if tourists were put off, due to internal strife that was only intended as a means to hopefully invoke change and make things better for everyone who lives in such an amazing place, where the inhabitants are friendly, warm and welcoming, to the thousands of revellers who do come here each year; and I'll testify to that.

Cale and Stephy stayed, so the four of us now travelled to Malaysia; Chloe, Karen, Jenny and myself. We took a ferry from Koh Lanta to the mainland then a bus to Trang, then another bus south to Satin. It wasn't all plain sailing as we got dropped off somewhere but not where we were supposed to be. I really didn't have a clue as I'd fallen asleep on the back of the bus and was woken by the others when we stopped. Chloe managed to get a taxi to take us to the port which was round a twenty-minute drive away from where we were. Getting the formalities of passport stamps out of the way, we jumped aboard the ferry from the southernmost tip of Thailand and sped to Malaysia and the island of Langkawi, situated in the Indian Ocean off mainland North-West Malaysia. And, yes, I also had to check where it was.

If You're Going to Oz-tray-lia…

Arriving in Langkawi, we headed straight for Penang Centai; a beach resort away from the main town and ferry port. Having travelled pretty much all day to get there, it was night by the time we arrived. With guide book pages fluttering, we checked out a couple of places for accommodation with no success, as they were already taken and we had not booked in advance. Persistence does pay off as we eventually landed an apartment just off the main road and across from the beach and being our own place, it felt more like a home; with its little lounge area, sofas, self-contained kitchen, shower and three rooms with twin beds. Jenny and I took one room, Karen and Chloe the other. Third room was left unoccupied as this was intended for others to use if someone else arrived and needed somewhere to stay, but for the moment, with no invaders to ruin our ambient circle, it was just us and it felt like our place. We settled in for the evening, relaxing and watching the novel experience that was TV. I got some beers from the shop at the end of the dirt track that led to the main road, to take advantage of Langkawi's tax-free status working out about 40p a can; this was a deal, considering we had entered a Muslim country and figured beer was going to be quite expensive from now on compared to what I had grown accustomed to.

The following days were ebbed away doing mainly nothing. This involved relaxing on the beach, interrupted only at various points to continue with my new exercise regime of running and swimming. Karen and I did venture for a long walk along the main street, where it was slowly being developed to incorporate drainage, utilities and sidewalks. Unfortunately, this littered the roadside with dangerous un-marked holes that person could easily disappear down, as we ambled towards the aquarium. Inside, we gazed in the darkened passageways, peering through the glass displays at each of the weird and wonderful marine life there; small blacktip sharks would gracefully glide around, huge electric eels hid menacingly in the darkness and beautifully illuminated sea horses swayed almost lifeless clinging to branch-like perches of their habitats. Again, I did get the feeling that I had seen some of these before, which I had, but it allowed for the chance of further education concerning the aquatic life when reading about the various creatures within; albeit not sure why, especially the larger species, needed to be there in the first place. Now being a diver, this only reinforced my opinion that surely the ocean would suffice?

New foods were also now on the agenda. A smorgasbord of new cuisines and flavours there for the tasting. Almost instantaneously, I got addicted to falafel kebabs which they were selling in a nearby restaurant; the mint yoghurt dressing incorporated within and the flat bread was divine. On an evening at the open market, there was a ridiculous variety of local homemade delicacies on offer. The walk had worked up an appetite and I was ravenous upon arriving. I split immediately from the others as the smells sent my senses wild and floodgates of saliva in my mouth burst, as I greedily set about trying pretty much anything on offer; noodles, rice, chicken, fish, sweet, spicy – if it looked good, I tried it. Everything was made fresh there and then encapsulated with delirious scents of delicious taste at a crazy cheap price. The walk home was as slow as a snail. A fat stuffed snail at that.

Cale and Stephy caught up with us. Unfortunately, the spare room in our apartment was now occupied so they were unable to share our little pad. Some random intruders had taken it that day; putting paid to a carefully co-ordinated plan for them to move in with us. A few days in the weather had taken a turn for the worse, which for the time of year was not uncommon and any sun chasing had to be put on hiatus due to the cloud cover and intermittent rain. With this, we hired a car which had to be a large saloon to cram everyone in, and in an obvious un-argued dictatorship, Chloe decided she was driving, taking us to visit the local tourist haunt that was Seven Wells Waterfall. At the bottom of the waterfall, monkeys scaled the trees and eagerly scavenged for scraps of food while we gingerly stepped across the slippery stones to pose for a group photo with the high and impressive falls thundering relentlessly in the background. The many steps to reach the top were worth the trek up to only provide a lovely view if the weather been better, as cloud and mist became the shroud to our vista. Despite the conditions, everyone laughed as Chloe lost one of her sandals in the water and in a blink over the edge of the cascade it went; meaning she wasn't getting it back. It was funny for a few reasons; not only because she was now at the top of a really high water fall with only one sandal and a few hundred steps to negotiate down, but also because these were her favourite

– nicely designed and comfortably worn in to the contours of her feet. But strangely, they were fixed not two days prior by taking the liberty of using a full tube of super glue a kind shop keep had lent her to re-attach the sole back on and neither herself nor anybody else did the decent thing and bought anything from the shop, let alone the glue. Never mind, karma, *eh*? Or was it destiny? I wasn't sure but with the circumstances it was both funny, *ha-ha*, and peculiar.

It was now end of November and I had been travelling now for just over three months; it seemed time was flying by within an occupied whirlwind and I wasn't even halfway through my travels. The day prior, we had missed the travel agent as it had closed by the time we returned so never got the chance to get ferry and bus tickets. That morning, Chloe came into my room and said that both she and Karen wanted to change their flights from Singapore to Australia by putting them back, so that they could stay here in Langkawi longer and asked if was up for doing the same. I paused for a second's thought before resolutely saying "no"; reasons being I had already put my flight back to Australia once when I was on Koh Tao because of going to Laos; which I hadn't planned to do and had put me back a week. Also, returning to Thailand had renewed my visa, so it allowed more time to do the things on the islands like the diving. With the added bonus that Asia was cheaper, so the original six weeks I had in Australia, which would be nowhere near as cheap, were now only four weeks and would be easier on the budget (whatever that was. I was spending like it was going out of fashion, and not paying attention like I was supposed to). Yet, four weeks was still enough time to do what I wanted. Any less time in Australia, especially over Christmas wouldn't do it justice. So I told them to change their flights if they wanted to, but I was keeping mine as scheduled. Besides that, I also had another reason why I didn't want to change my flight.

Whilst having a cigarette outside, I flicked through the pages of my small uncomprehensive Malaysia guidebook thinking about where to go next. I only had a week left before flying out from Singapore, so was definitely leaving that day. Chloe came out and said that they were now not going to change their flights, stating that we had agreed to travel together and that we would go through together, sticking to the original plan. I asked 'if they were sure', she said 'yes'. She had family waiting for her to arrive and didn't want to mess them around either. So it was back to plan A. This was actually quite funny; I'd asked 'if they were sure' not only to double check they were OK with moving on, but also - and more so - because I didn't even realise (or hadn't remembered) that we *had* agreed to travel through to Singapore together, I thought we were travelling along till - whenever. So I just kept schtum. We booked tickets to leave that evening on the ferry and bus to Kota Bharu. Jenny wasn't joining us as she had longer to spend in Malaysia before her flight, so she stayed with the intermittent sun and beach. Chloe, Karen and I were heading for the jungle. We took the ferry over to the mainland and then a night bus across to the north-eastern side of the country.

The night bus was comfortable and air conditioned with hardly any passengers on board which was fine and allowed for stretching out. But there was one problem; notably from a select few that included two middle-aged Australian couples and in particular one male, who felt it necessary to voice his choice racist remarks about the people from Malaysia and derogatorily slur the colour and culture like he was some authority on the matter. His ashamed wife slowly shrank next to him, squirming with aching embarrassment, pleading with him to be quiet. And when I looked around at this bigoted moron, it seemed as if he expected me to laugh and agree. Far from it; this was a look of derision as I shook my head. Being middle-aged and follicly challenged means I'm bald. Only because nature dictated my hair would fall out in my early twenties. But being of Caucasian skin, this age and having this hairdo I didn't realise would qualify me for membership to this tosser's tiny mind set, which included his braindead, backward and ignorant thought process. I actually like to think I have a brain underneath my shiny dome, not like this moron. I was less than impressed, annoyed and abhorred his words. He was visiting their country; which begged the question, why bother coming here if you feel like this? Shouldn't people judge others on their actions and like in this case, what they say as opposed to any skin tone, nationality or ethnicity? Who has the right to say these things when they do not know someone or what type of person they are? Colour, beliefs or where people are from or live have nothing to do with this and it is impossible to know a person by these judgements alone. The world is becoming a smaller and smaller place, metaphorically speaking, these days; people are mixing more than ever and cultures blending with our interactions. Many embrace this and bloom; others sadly stay bigoted and poisoned with no good reason, but it left me wondering as to why this particular bloke acted as he did, thinking it appropriate to voice his vile bullshit opinion, as if others really wanted or needed to hear it or worst would agree with him. Heeding his words, I judged him… a fucking dumb racist idiot and seriously doubted he would have had the bollocks to be so vocal had there been any actual Malaysians on board.

We arrived at the bus stop and took a short taxi ride to the train station. Discussing the remarks, we were all in agreement. He was a bigoted idiot and pitied his wife who did seem to be genuinely horrified by his ignorant backward statements. Not dwelling on this, we arrived at Kota Bharu station and hung around for a few hours, chilling on the platform till the train arrived early in the morning. The train was old and relatively slow, but this didn't matter; it provided ample time to catch up on some sleep, chat and mess about hanging out of the doors of the carriages when the train stopped, striking poses as we took photos of one another against the bright green wash of vegetation that bristled in bright sunshine as the journey headed straight down the centre of the country. Lush window views of the forests, jungle and mountains that Malaysia had to offer were hurriedly passed by as we relentlessly chugged along, but we were intent on experiencing these at even more close quarters anyway.

Arriving in Jerantut, we then caught another bus to Taman Negara National Park and travelled for the best part of twenty-four hours powering through to get there. We wanted to experience the train ride and relish the adventure, so knowing what had to be done, we just got on with it. Finally getting to the small town entrance of the national park there was a smattering of restaurants and a few convenience stores. Locating some dorm digs, we then ate at one of the array floating restaurants made of wood and bamboo that rhythmically rocked with the wake of passing river traffic, before preparing our things for the next day ahead. I also browsed small book store in the hope of getting some maps of the area but for the second time, I randomly found a book that I wanted to buy.

It was warm and humid in the jungle, really sticky and clammy. Getting up that morning, we prepared for our trek with the aim of making it to a hide; a designated cabin in the middle of the jungle where it was possible to stay overnight. We crossed the river, bought our park entry permits and then stocked up on supplies; water, snacks and bug spray. I also bought a hat, knowing the prevalent mosquitoes would be merciless and ravage relentlessly, and a new torch because looking the night before for the one which I thought was in my bag had now disappeared. So, naturally I assumed some fucker had stolen it, but I couldn't recall where or when I had it last so it was more likely I lost it or left it somewhere. We knew there was a long day ahead, as we had 11km to cover high atop the banks of the river system in about seven hours before dark.

Starting the trek, the route was easy, very easy. Using a walkway purpose built to enter the jungle the first stop was early into the trail to experience a canopy tour. A series of wire rope bridges high up throughout the tree tops; this was a tourist activity for young and old alike where clouded daylight broke through the fluttering leaves and branches as we gently swayed on the gangways. There were about twenty bridges in total offering various views of the trees, river and surrounding area, as we trudged steadily from tree post to tree post with the expectation of seeing some rare or very cool creatures; which, unfortunately, we never did before we disembarked further up the hill.

We ambled down to the 'real' start of the trail. This was much different and harder than the relative ease of the start, apparent now that the walkway was only built for access to the canopy. Here we were on the actual route and essentially as nature would intend, except for the narrow, mud trail worn away by the trudge of trekking boots. Now there were tree roots to negotiate, stones, rocks, boulders, muddy embankments, streams and slippery passages with steep drops to the river below; where at times this would be obscured by the thick dense forest which in turn would blot out any sunshine, yet hold in the heat to create a stifling, hot, humid environment that uncomfortably wrapped around the whole of the body.

Starting spritely, everything was fine for the first 6km, the most obvious discomfort being that clothes were drenched in streaming sweat within what seemed a matter of minutes; hat, t-shirt, shorts, bag, all a sodden mess as the humidity and exercise took a quick hold. Steadily, we negotiated the course that ran up and down with the contour of the elevated pathway, climbing past the various moss-laden obstacles and flora that had grown wild over time. Wildlife was in abundance; monkeys skipped with effortless agility around the tops of trees and the insects were plentiful, especially beautifully mesmerising butterflies. Less welcome were gruesome leeches, blindly writhing around on the ground until successfully attaching themselves to shoes and make their way on to the skin for a blood-sucking feast. This happened to Chloe and she had to endure the pain of a lit cigarette lighter to burn them off, and the mosquitoes swarmed in their masses during pauses for water, where no amount of repellent would seem to deter them. With these and time working vigorously against us, breaks were frequent but very short.

As we pressed on, the trail seemed endless and monotonously similar; with streams to cross, climbing up and down dirty treacherous slopes that became more and more frequent so the effort started to take its toll. Tiredness sapped weary limbs and joints, and humidity robbed the body of vital fluids, leaving a mind waning on concentration that no amount of water could seemingly replenish. Walking in single file, Karen was in the centre and suddenly slipped down into the shrubbery of the embankment, she pulled herself up and we asked if she was OK. Just as Chloe spoke, she also slipped; thankfully, she too was fine. But at about 8km along, Karen's feet really started being a source of pain due to the forces of excessive steep inclines and declines. She stopped to complain that she couldn't go on; the tears streaming down her face only masked by intermingling with many beads of sweat.

At this point, Chloe and I had to offer words of encouragement to continue, as we were stuck and no one would come to get us. We were here now and the only way out was to push on. I didn't say anything at the time, but I was worried. Not for myself as such. I was determined to finish and wouldn't be beaten and was pretty sure Chloe would also be OK; she like me had a tough stoic determination about her, but Karen was now a problem. It was clear she was in pain and I seriously doubted her ability and will to carry on, and if need be, we would have to carry her because I really didn't fancy spending the night in the open jungle. I love animals and nature but don't want to sleep in such close quarters with it, especially here knowing that there were some big creatures on the prowl and where the little ones were bad enough. There was some hope; I felt though that if we made it to the bridge which crossed the river, the hide wouldn't be too far away. Purely because looking at the map, I realised early on that it was not to scale and was indicated as a shorter distance than it looked. I hoped I was right.

Pressing on, the trail disappeared and we seemed to be just stranded in the jungle. Things were not looking good on our mission. The area had overgrown with no clear way through, so we set about looking for the pathway pushing through wiry branches and thick undergrowth, first having

173

the common sense to place a marker so that we knew where we were as a point of reference. After about five minutes, Chloe called out. She had found it. Not only the connecting trail, but the bridge spanning the small gorge and our check point. She had done well and the wash of relief was as welcome as any shower would have been. Time was now at a critical point; we had been trekking for around six hours and it was due to get dark within the hour.

We crossed the footbridge and came to a split in the trail. Right would take us to the river and the boat pick-up point, left to the hide. As I suspected, the hide was sign posted as only 1.5km away and not the distance feared on the map. We headed left, with a newfound spring in our step. Karen cheered up as she realised the distance was doable now, due to the flatter and more manageable trail, and didn't have to try to take a boat back that evening as her feet were painfully sore; not that I knew if there would even be a boat to take her. Something I kept quiet about. Trudging through the boggy mud and still climbing over the massive tree roots, we all breathed a sigh of relief as the trail opened up to a small deforested area and in front of us was a wooden cabin, about 20ft off the ground on huge stilts. It was blatantly obvious what it was. We had made it to the hide.

It was like victory, but a tired, sullen victory. All washed with oppressed happiness at the relief of locating our sanctuary, after hours of effort and avoiding the threat of the imposing dangerous night-time jungle. The sun hadn't quite set and the seven hours' walking were now over and although exhausted, wet and smelling bad, the main thing was we were all relatively OK apart from aching, weary limbs and few bumps, cuts and scrapes. We headed up the stairs to make ourselves home for the evening.

Inside, there were about six wooden bunk beds with a distinct lack of mattress, fixed seating was placed front of large open viewing windows to encourage the hope of spotting any wildlife. And that was it. The toilet was located in a cubicle outside the door at the top of the stairs. It was broken and infested with bugs and a disgusting stench, as others had used it previous despite no water for flushing. This now posed another problem; we were running out of drinking water. I initially, prior to starting, decided on taking two litres; Chloe and Karen had a litre each and this was a serious underestimation of our task, having drunk much more than anticipated due to the overwhelming humidity in an attempt to replace the vital fluids lost. We now had about half a litre left between three of us for the evening.

This simply wasn't enough. The mind and body clamoured, pleading for proper rehydrating refreshment that was agonisingly rationed as occasional gulps between us. Changing into spare clothing, we settled down. The entertainment involved sitting quietly at the window, eagerly watching the jungle in anticipation of seeing maybe a leopard, tiger or something equally as majestic. Unfortunately, nothing such appeared, except for a large lizard on a tree and birds settling amid masses of green trees and foliage that gradually changed to shadowed silhouettes as light etched away to douse us in darkness, where we watched mesmerising little fire flies brightly zip around as glowing little natural embers of night.

With the lack of electricity, we used our torches and went to bed early. Chloe and I pulled faces at one another with our electric lanterns strategically placed under our chins, as we messed around, unwinding from the day's slog, having kindly let me use her mosquito net with her, which was literally draped over the both of us to help prevent a torrent of bites. Sleeping though was difficult, not only because I liked her, but more so because of the real discomfort of lying on incredibly hard wooden boards with interspersed small gaps in-between; this caused me persistent uncomfortable fidgeting that seemed to eventually wind Chloe up, and even more so when I turned over and hit her with a flailing arm. In the end, I decided to get out from under the net as it felt restrictive and took my chances by applying a ton of mosquito repellent, to lay less bound before I eventually succumbed to tiredness and fell into asleep of sorts. Waking the next day, Chloe said she was getting annoyed. I was sorry but being a dickhead, I mouthed silently to Karen that I wasn't; it was a joke but she seemed to take it the wrong way.

Upon leaving, I was last on the way out and left the door slightly open and she abruptly said, "Shut the door!"

I abruptly told her "OK" and called her a "bossy cow". Tempers somewhat frayed.

Setting off just after daylight, we trekked 2km back the way that we had come. My feet and joints were very sore, my clothes tatty and dishevelled, but my thirst was torturing me the most. We passed the turn off for the bridge and headed straight on down to the main river system. Arriving at the jetty, we waited; thankfully for only ten minutes before the long speed boat turned up to whisk us back to Taman Negara, by following the river back along the steep forested gradients we had traversed over the

175

day previous. The boat was fast and loved crashing through the waves created by the shallow rapids that offered a bumpy, wet, refreshing, invigorating ride, speeding along the twisting, winding river. Despite the enjoyment, luckily, it didn't last long, as it was a slight piss-take having all the water splashing round us that we couldn't drink.

Arriving back at the floating restaurants, we had breakfast and I felt relieved to be back. The trek was hard work both physically and mentally, also not to put fine point on it, the humidity was a real motherfucker. In hindsight, I personally feel that we should've been better prepared; especially as we had *just* enough water. It is a vital resource and the four litres between us went quickly and could have been a big problem, so upon returning, I was ecstatic at the prospect of replenishing copious amounts of vital fluids. We came through unscathed apart from tiredness, sore feet and limbs but learnt a harsh lesson about having enough to drink for these types of activities. On the whole, I was really glad we did the trek and it was a fantastic adventure, especially as we went out and did it on our own without a guide, seeing and experiencing some really cool things along the way. But mainly, I felt I learnt a lot about my own personal resilience to completing a task when things do not go too well, plus how we all stuck together and never gave up. So, I was also really pleased for Chloe as the idea was hers as something she really wanted to accomplish and it was made possible, but probably slightly more so for Karen as I felt quite proud of her efforts; having to dig deep, from being terrorised and tortured by the jungle and put through the wringer somewhat.

We had completed what we came to do in the national park, so got a room at the hostel for the day to chill, shower, sort our belongings and have a snooze. We were ready to head over to Kuala Lumpur. Time was still against us to make it to Singapore whilst doing things that we wanted. The bus was leaving back for Jerantut in late afternoon but being back at the hostel by mid-morning allowed a visit to the book store to make my purchase. After catching a total of three different buses, we arrived in Kuala Lumpur at around eight p.m. It was dark and as we drove through it, one sight became apparent; shining brightly amid the skyline, the world-famous Petronas Towers. The twin towers looked beautiful, as the white lights that illuminated them dazzled a shimmering glow high up over everything else, pointing majestically into darkness. I was excited about going and seeing them at close quarters, not to mention the view of the city from a height.

Finding a hostel that wasn't our original choice, we decided it would do just for the night as it wasn't the best. And being back in civilization, we did the only decent thing and headed out for a few drinks. Unfortunately, these were now the most expensive I had experienced in months – an outrageous £3 for a small beer. But where needs must I indulged; while residing in a cool reggae bar that we spotted arriving into town. We were joined by a couple who Chloe and Karen knew from previous travels. We chatted, ate and drank before heading back and crashing out. Being on the go and barely stopping for the last three days had taken its toll, especially as we were planning a whirlwind tour of the city for the next two days to see the sights.

The next morning, we checked out of the hostel having found the one that we originally wanted to stay at. Ironically, we had walked past and missed it, about three times, and more ironic that it was situated directly opposite the bar we were in. But that's tiredness for you. After checking in, we headed out, taking the sky train to near the Petronas Towers. It felt strange being in a metropolis again and life looked that much more frantic in and around the buildings, shops, traffic and people that also just billowed noise all around the ears. Everywhere, there was movement of colour and objects loomed large, close and unforgiving and initially provided a confusing mess of information to the senses that had become accustomed to a somewhat more subdued life around beaches and jungles. But within the modern world, I was allowed to check the Internet and was rather pleased that a friend who I used to work with had messaged me, saying she was going to be in Singapore when we were due to arrive, and felt excited at the prospect of meeting up with a familiar face.

The Petronas Towers offered the chance of witnessing some fabulous views of the city from the vantage point of the observation deck which spans the two towers; unfortunately, on our arrival, this wasn't going to happen this day. Everything was perfectly fine with the towers, but bureaucracy dictated there were only four hundred free tickets, issued each day to go up, and we had missed them and would have to try again the next day. Instead, we explored around the magnificent and ever-so-swanky shopping complex at the foot of the towers. I split from Chloe and Karen as they were in their type of stores and I fancied exploring on my own.

After a largely uninspiring wander around the shops that granted would have been a hell of a lot more productive if I was incredibly rich and on a spending spree, I met back up with the girls and we headed back to the hostel, and met up with Kenny – the girls' friend from the Reggae bar – and another girl, Jas, who had moved into the six-bed dorm room with us. After making introductions and chatting for a while, we all headed out to the large outdoor market area which was in China Town and literally round the corner from where we were now staying. We ate in one of the arrays of outdoor restaurants, and after Chloe and Karen decided to spend time at the stalls in the market, Kenny, Jas and I wanted to visit the KL Tower and the observation deck to view the city at night.

Once again taking the sky train, we inadvertently got off at the wrong stop. We thought it correct as we could see the large spike-shaped tower seemingly looming close by, but perspective can be a funny thing. Large objects always seem to be nearer than they actually are; something we found out while walking for around forty-five minutes to get there, only for the second time that day to again not be allowed access, as the observation deck closed at eight p.m. and was only accessible to those with restaurant reservations. We had just eaten, weren't exactly dressed for the occasion and no way able to afford the prices. So, we decided to head back after another unsuccessful excursion on a day where things just didn't seem to happen.

The next day was the Petronas Towers; take two. We had Kenny with us as he wanted to visit the towers and experience the views. This time, we managed to get our free ticket passes, had our things scanned through security and headed up. The observation deck spanned the distance between the two monumental columns at about halfway and is easily visible from the outside. I had hoped that it would be possible to go further up one of the towers for a higher view like that of the tower in Shanghai. But this wasn't possible, so felt slightly disappointed by having to make do with the spanning bridge, which felt wasn't nearly as high as what an observation deck could be, as on either side, each tower endlessly continued towards the heavens when looking up. That said, the views provided were still impressive, allowing a view of a good cross section of the city to peer down on the gardens, parks and minuscule folk below, also let's not forget this was free to do; you just had to be keen and eager to get there early enough for a ticket. So, it wasn't really a wasted excursion and at least another box ticked.

I was now somewhat at a loose end, having finished the viewing platform. Chloe and Karen had plans which possibly involved the mall, as did Kenny. From consulting a guide book in the hostel, I decided on some culture vulture activity; opting for the national art gallery to do something a little different and invest time within the interest of the arts. Upon arriving, I noticed the building was quite new and there were various sections dedicated to different types such as sculptures, modern and classical art and those specifically by national and local artists. There were some fantastic pieces that really caught the eye, involving an artist's self-portrait swimming under water, which looked truly like a photo due to the fabulous detail of the air bubbles, light refraction and the artist's hair floating when submerged below; two large separate oil works of a tiger and elephant which from up close didn't look much but from a distance provided an amazing illusion made up from the intricate brush work. It left me marvelling at how pieces like these are ever created from such close quarters to flourish into such grandiose works. I was in awe of something that I would love just to be able to purchase, never mind paint. I perused the gallery for about two hours in admiration, thinking away the time amid the tranquillity that was as welcome as the works themselves before heading back. I stopped off at the bus station to buy bus tickets for the next day to take us to Singapore where we now would only have one night to spend, but whilst doing so managed for the first time in a while to get caught in a massive sudden downpour. Shit.

Returning, Jas had left, but we were joined in the room by a lovely American girl called Lauren; so as is with hostels, one person replaces another. That evening, we attempted the KL tower again. This time, we made it with enough time and actually managed to get off at the correct station and the five of us were allowed to take the elevator to the observation deck. Circulating the 360-degree platform provided better views of the city, where lights illuminated for miles into the distance of night. The Petronas Towers were in full majestic view, but only offered a side profile due to the positioning of both towers in relation to each other. Earlier on in the day, we couldn't even see the KL tower as it was to the side of the Petronas Towers and not within the viewing scope of the observation deck in the middle. We took time to use the binoculars to find land marks such as China Town and the market area and I marvelled at what looked like a UFO in the sky; only to realise that it was a motorway in the far off distance which snaked up a hillside and the lights from the traffic created a ring where the road swept round, like it was forming the outer edge of a space ship. A cool optical illusion or close encounters of the turd kind? I couldn't decide.

Checking out, we made our way to the bus station to take our bus through to Singapore. On the way, I read my book. I'd bought *The Celestine Prophecy* in Taman Negara, but I lent this to Chloe to read, as I had already read it before and thought that she might like it and also because I was still finishing reading a book called *Soft Vengeance of a Freedom Fighter*. I had bought this in Langkawi and concerned the struggle back to health of a lawyer who suffered a bomb assassination attempt whilst fighting apartheid in South Africa; a wonderful and humbling story of how despite all the odds a man can rebuild his life after such horrific injuries – harrowing yet inspirational stuff. I listened to music, gazed out of the window and again pondered what had been and what would lie ahead. With an idea of what I wanted to do and where I wanted to go, but nothing booked or set in stone, or at least for a while anyway. So, this was quite an exciting prospect of what could happen – that was interrupted by seeing an overturned truck on the highway and witnessing what was happening at an office block, as all the workers had congregated in the car park after what I assumed was a fire alarm. I was leaving Chloe and Karen the next day, they were heading straight to Sydney while I was going to Brisbane, leaving us only one night and part of the next day together.

Having crossed the border while going through immigration, I filled the goods declaration card out with the wrong colour pen and had to do it all again which caused a delay. Eventually, we set off. Unbeknownst to me, this wouldn't be the first time I'd have problems at immigration and be mild in comparison. We soon arrived in Singapore and the sun was shining in the hot bustling city. The first thing that struck me was how unbelievably clean it was; the streets were immaculate with hardly any debris at all along the tree-strewn avenues. Getting a cab, we headed for Little India district. Most of the hostels we tried were full, largely due to the majority of travellers arriving in Singapore and Kuala Lumpur. The gateway airport to Southeast Asia in Bangkok had been closed down, due to protests, so more than average amounts of people were flying in here. Eventually, we found a guest house which was quite cheap and nice. We headed out for something to eat, deciding on a curry and then checked the Internet where I was able to call Helen; the friend who I had arranged to meet up with.

We agreed a prominent place would be down the marina, near the

Merlion Statue. Chloe and Karen were heading down there and were also OK with meeting up with Helen. Coming out of the subway station, the weather took a turn for the worse and was raining heavily. Getting to a nearby hotel, I asked the concierge if I could use an umbrella which he kindly gave me. Chloe and Karen seemed really pleased with my practical acquisition as they were now able to carry on to the marina without getting wet. Arriving there, Helen was late so we waited and after about twenty minutes she arrived; completely drenched.

Grabbing a coffee, we chatted; it was great to see her again, she was still working where I'd left and our conversation inevitably turned to my former place of work and how things had and hadn't changed. It was nice to hear about what was happening, but in all honesty I didn't really care much. I was glad I had left and didn't miss the place in the slightest and was having the time of my life travelling around, doing what I wanted to do. We all took a look around the marina; snapping away feverishly at the beautifully illuminated mermaid stroke lion statue feature, as it spouted water. We then continued to some bars and had drinks, where the price had rocketed to a whopping £7 per drink. I nearly passed out, but not from consumption; there was fat chance of that or so I reckoned. Unperturbed, I managed to acquire some free shots, had a bunch of expensive drinks and ended up on the bar dancing around, unable to stop myself banging my head on a large concrete beam across the ceiling before then heading to a club to finish the night off. Having a cigarette outside, I ended up chatting to some random stranger, a middle-aged business man, about what I was doing and he stated how he envied me – a man of wealth and prosperity envying me? How come? Couldn't money buy everything? And if this was the case, was he so trapped that it was impossible to do something like I was doing? I found it bizarre and hard to fathom yet not hard to understand. Also, during the encounter, we talked about religion, money, freedom and fears and there and then I pretty much made up my mind on something I was going to do. Upon leaving, we grabbed a taxi back; the girls got out to get some food. I wasn't hungry and needed some time to think so headed back on my own.

The next morning, we got up, packed and headed on the subway to Helen's hotel; she was there on her own waiting for her sister to arrive later and had very kindly offered us the use of her room. Here, we could store our things during the day and freshen up before our flights that evening, which was great having spent a small fortune over the night. We wandered around during the day; feeding ourselves to feel better and returning to the scene of the crime as it were, to see if the things left in the bar were still there; which they weren't. So some sunglasses and an umbrella became a nice acquisition by someone. We returned to the room and I got ready to go to the airport, saying goodbye to Chloe and Karen, mentioning the possibility of meeting up at some point in Australia. I was sad to be leaving them; yet, it was obvious that we had had our time together and now had to move on. Helen was due to meet her sister at the airport, so she came with me and after a swift twenty-four-hour catch up, we said our goodbyes, as I went to departures and she headed to arrivals.

It was awesome seeing Helen again, totally unexpected and out of the blue. I didn't give it much thought as to why we randomly met up especially at such short notice and on the other side of the planet. I was pondering other things as I boarded the flight to Brisbane, where I sat thinking and feeling like I really never made the most of my time in Singapore or Kuala Lumpur for that matter. I did what I wanted but left feeling like they both had more to offer and I missed out. That said, I'd had beach, jungle, metropolis, action, adventure and culture – all in the space of a week, what more could I want? After only what seemed moments in my seat, I passed out with lack of sleep from the night before.

Landing after the six-hour- or-so flight, I disembarked as usual and passed through immigration without any problem with my electronic visa activated. Minding my own business, I waited to collect my bag from the baggage carousel when I was approached by a customs officer who proceeded to ask me questions concerning my arrival, where I had been and the contents of my bag. All the while, he scrutinised my arrival and goods declaration card that indicated certain items subject to quarantine. Eventually, I was questioned about the possible things I might have brought in from the countries I had visited. I happened to mention that I had bought a carved statuette of the Hindu god Ganesh. When asked what this was made of, I replied that I thought it was wood. That was it, all that the customs needed; he pointed out that this was subject to declaration and that I had ticked 'No' on the declaration. He marked my card with a code and asked me to take the customs line with everyone else when I had my bag.

I started racking my brains as to what could happen; I was certain I was going to be searched, why would the card be marked with an ambiguous code? Immediately, I started reading the card for anything else not declared.

I had hastily filled in the card on the plane as we arrived, waking from my slumber and not really paying much attention to what was on the form as I had filled in these cards before. I was not carrying anything illegal, no problem, and so I ticked 'No' to the criteria listed. A big mistake! I suddenly had a bad feeling; where was I not four days prior? In the jungle. And what was in my bag? My shoes, my stinking unclean shoes, with half the jungle still attached to them. *Oh shit,* I thought, *I could be in trouble here.*

My turn arrived at the customs line, the officer took one look at the card and summoned the officer in question and was taken to a private area screened off from the queues. I was asked if I realised that the form I had filled in was a legal document; which I didn't. But surprise, surprise; where I had signed, it said in very small words that I understood this was a legal declaration. I was now rather worried. The officer began searching my bag, all the while asking me questions again about its content, where I had been prior and what I had been up to. He came across my toiletries and found non-prescription medication; again not declared on the list, he found the little weaved basket that I had made in Thailand on the Thai Experience; a wooden plant product, again not declared. By now, I was starting to think that they aren't going to let me in and I'm on the next plane out of here 'cos they haven't even come across the shoes yet.

Continuing the search, the officer opened a plastic bag and peered inside. He looked at me and asked, "Is this a joke? You are taking the mick now; these shoes are a mess! There's half of the jungle on these!"

I apologised and said that I only just remembered that they hadn't been cleaned. He was not impressed, not in the slightest, and continued his search. Whilst questioning, I'd said that I had a pair of scissors in my bag, which he couldn't find and repeatedly asked me where they were, which honestly, I didn't know; I just knew they were in there somewhere. What was I supposed to do? Memorise where everything was in my bag after opening it and emptying it every two or so days. With all my things now on the table, he found my statuette which had caused the concern in the first place. Examining it, he said that he didn't think that it was made of wood and didn't know what it was made from. I couldn't believe it.

So entering the country; I was carrying three items subject to quarantine which I was legally obliged to declare and I hadn't done so. It wasn't looking to good. But we weren't done there; I was questioned whether I had taken any drugs whilst on my travels, which I had. Reluctantly saying "yes", I figured I might as well own up to admitting to smoking some weed. Then I was asked if I knew what the device was which he was holding. I guessed that it was a drug swab. I was correct and the bag was screened, but nothing came back. The officer asked if I had any food with me. I replied that I left a bag of crisps on the plane. Chloe had bought me these to have as a snack but I never did; which now luckily, I had forgotten and left behind. Finally, he said that I was able to put my things back in my bag. I felt light at the end of the tunnel as my turmoil was almost finished, but he continued; due to the state of my shoes and the other undeclared items, I was looking at a $250 fine and that the shoes would have to be cleaned by quarantine. *That's just fucking marvellous,* I thought. *I'm not even out of the airport and haven't been in the country literally five minutes and I've already incurred a big fine.*

But fucking marvellous was just that; a few minutes later, the quarantine officer turned up for the shoes, having been called for by customs. She was in her late twenties but the one thing that struck me most was the way she spoke. "Morning!" she said in a spritely happy-go-lucky Aussie accent. "You have some shoes to be cleaned? Be back in a minute." And off she went with the offending articles. I wasn't the only person surprised by this bubbly character. The customs officer was stunned.

"Mate, today's your lucky day; you have happened to get the happiest quarantine officer I've known; I don't know whether it's because it's a Sunday or she had a good night or what? But they haven't fined you. Pack your bag and wait over there."

Hastily, I packed whilst getting a warning about form declaration should I return to Australia. I apologised again and headed away to one side, away from any more grilling to wait for my shoes to be returned.

Finally outside, having a cigarette and waiting for the bus, I was again awash with relief as the stress was cleansed away like all the dirt from my now-sparkling clean shoes. I couldn't help but laugh to myself, not because of what had happened, but how unbelievably lucky I had been. Another bullet dodged; what with being let in and not being fined, through something which was my own stupid fault, getting away with nothing more than a severe bollocking and slap on the wrist. And in hindsight, it could have been much worse if they had decided to snap on the rubber gloves and ask me to bend over for a closer inspection. Not that they would have found anything.

I arrived at the hostel but had to wait till one p.m. to check in, but with everything that had already happened, I didn't mind, so I happily chilled in the reception area, caught up on some sleep and ventured out for breakfast; which happened to be a fresh doner kebab roll from a takeaway with lashings of chilli and garlic sauce. Just like I could get back home, but this was at ten a.m. on a Sunday morning. I thought, *This is fucking amazing! I like Australia!*

Garden Creeping, Dingoes and the Wild West

The following day, I started to make plans for my time in Australia, but one of the problems facing me was the fact that Australian summer time had attracted countless other travellers there, and I had met many en route travelling through Asia. Not only that, but it was the beginning of December and those people were preparing for Christmas; therefore, hostels and tours were getting booked up fast as people readied themselves for the festivities. Back in Thailand, I had the common sense to book my hostel in Sydney for between 22 to 27 December. That was sorted, but New Year wasn't, nor anything else for that matter. I wanted to visit Fraser Island, having heard loads of things about it and those who I talked with raved about how much fun and amazing it was, making it sound like my type of place. This would have to be sooner rather than later, because it was further north in Queensland; and therefore in the opposite direction. This meant going up before heading down towards Sydney and my final destination of Melbourne. I booked my tour and bus so instantaneously knew where I would be heading to next.

Brisbane was lovely; a really nice city that seemed to have lots to see and do. Also not being very big in comparison to the size of some cities, this readily made things easier to get about. I actually seemed to stop and take a look around at a more relaxed pace. Wandering about, a couple of things became apparent; It felt I had been out of the modern loop for a while and was sort of strange and alien not having bamboo huts, temples or greenery at every turn, as the architecture of the buildings towered from the ground into the sky, reaching further than three stories. I had been in Kuala Lumpur and was frenetic rushing about on sky train and Singapore was an overnight jolly on the piss. I could see all the large buildings and was even in some, but in such a short time never appreciated them from below and as being a constant surrounding until I landed here; now a third city in a row in a somewhat short space of time. More so, it gradually dawned on me I was now back in an English-speaking country, with all the cultural trimmings (pies!) which could explain this further. In comparison to

Singapore, what struck me was how immaculate it seemed here, especially the city centre. Somewhat miraculously devoid of any rubbish or debris on the ground as if constantly cleaned and maintained; like how a person would take care of a prized possession and this only highlighted how everything seemed new, brand new; and I can only presume this is what helped emphasise Australia's relative short modern history as it seemingly became apparent through its well cared for newer-city infancy.

To help while away some time, I visited a gallery on the other side of the river, having a chance marvel at the Rodin statues, Picasso paintings and other fabulous art including original aboriginal works, by dousing myself in some quiet-time cultural activity for a few hours. A past time now, I was really starting to appreciate having never really done this type of thing before, yet finding the peace and quiet equally as fundamental as the artworks themselves in the process. Upon returning, I spent the evening in the bar and bumped into Hailey, Joanne and Ella, the Geordie girls I met whilst scuba diving and at the full moon party, who were also randomly staying at the hostel which was really cool, giving us time to catch up over drinks and re-live our jollies together. Meeting with people who I had previously met had happened on numerous occasions now and was brilliant, either through contacting them and they happened to be in the same place or more so just out of coincidence. It was starting to really emphasise a beautiful aspect of travelling and left me wondering who I could meet again next and where; especially those just left to chance, creating that much more of a surprise.

The late nights and beer were taking their toll and I woke later than I wanted, having plans for the day to visit Lone Pine Koala Sanctuary. Getting there by bus from city centre proved to be an enjoyable experience; touring around the suburbs on public transport was liberating, allowing a cheap look around, but also because the bus driver proved to be a great patron of customer care and general common sense, by letting me onto the bus and pay a little later as he and I both didn't have any change, and we sorted the fair out when he did. It was a really nice thing to do and left a very good impression on me; especially as I couldn't imagine this happening in many other places, where I'd have to go get change that would invariably also mean; get the next bus.

Lone Pine was far bigger and had much wider variety of animals and wildlife than expected. All seemed to be inhabited in large and open enclosures which were clean and they looked in excellent health, also the information about the animals and the aim of the sanctuary was extensive and offered a good learning experience; a credit to Australian culture. The inhabitants there ranged from birds, lizards and snakes, plus the kind of ones traditionally associated with Australia such as wombats, wallabies and kangaroos which hopped around in a massive open field where people could wander in amongst them and view the creatures at very close quarters and take photos, especially of the ones which at random opportunities would provide another free sex show for the stunned, yet laughing spectators who all seemed to have cameras at the ready.

As the name suggested, the place was a reserve for koalas, and there were lots of them in specially designed sections, with an array of branches to hang on to or off and copious amounts of eucalyptus to dine on. Although not the most exciting or dynamic of creatures, they are very beautiful and do look incredibly cute with their docile, somewhat sleepy-looking features. It was fantastic to see them for the first time, so I sat and watched them for ages. I discovered that they aren't bears either as some people call them. Bears being mammals and Koalas are marsupials as they have a pouch like a kangaroo to shelter their young; you learn something new every day, well, I did that day. Also on offer was the opportunity to hold one, a chance which I wasn't going to pass up. Supervised constantly by the keeper, the koala was passed to me and it clung to my arms and torso like a new born baby; a baby with twenty, long, razor-sharp claws on each of its extremities that dug with an uncomfortable reassurance into the skin as it grasped despite being cradled. The fur was really soft like its placid temperament and with the talons on show this was kind of a relief. The surprising thing was how much they weighed; this one wasn't exactly little, being an adult of around 10kg or 22lbs, though I suspect it was slightly less when I handed it back, because as a parting gesture for the special one minute bond which had formed between us and as a term of affection, it shit on me.

I returned back to the city centre and hastily set about completing some other things which were on my itinerary, before continuing my travels and heading out the following day. I took the opportunity to see the city, suburbs and the horizon from on high via the giant Ferris wheel by the river bank, and then undertook a somewhat all-too-brief visit to the museum. This offered only a whistle stop tour of the various attractions that included an array of dinosaur bones, marine life fossils and aboriginal history, because I arrived only fifteen minutes prior to closing for the day and it left me feeling slightly disappointed, having missed out knowing there wouldn't really be time to return.

My disappointment was short-lived though, as I had managed to get in contact with a girl who I'd met whilst travelling; I met Jessie on my first day in China in the hostel bar with some others and had drinks, got pissed and saw her the next morning looking like shit, as she was about to leave really hung over and far from prepared to get her flight back to Aus. But we swapped contact details and kept in touch, having told her I was to visit Brisbane and she offered to show me around; a very nice gesture having known her for all of twelve hours. Jessie had agreed to come to the hostel to meet me for a drink, I was excited to see her again as she was really bubbly, fun and a great to be around. Well, that was from what I could remember.

In reception, I looked round just as the door opened and there was Jessie; small and slender, tanned skin, short dark hair and a big beaming smile. We recognised each other immediately. I had wondered if I would remember what she looked like, or her me due to our brief, drunken time together on my first night and her last in Beijing. But it was cool, we did and she complimented me on the weight that I'd lost. It immediately made me feel good. We headed straight to the bar and started with the beers and banter, creating laughs that came as easy as natural when talking to her. It was a Tuesday and nothing special was happening so we took part in the quiz to no avail. We didn't expect to win and weren't taking it too seriously; it was more of an exercise in proving how stupid we were. We discussed the prospect of possibly doing a small road trip when I got back to Brisbane on Sunday from touring Fraser Island. This depended on when I returned and how things played out for her over the weekend. Leaving it at that to let fate take its course, I thought it would be cool and good fun if it happened. We had quite a lot to drink in the end before Jessie left; she had also brought the car, but wisely left it, cursing me for having to get it in the morning with a huge hangover that she would have to endure all day; I just laughed at her predicament. I didn't know why because I also had to be up early to leave for my next adventure. But at least I wouldn't be suffering at work.

Arriving later the next day at Hervey Bay bus station, I was picked up and taken to the hostel where I would stay, before meeting with others in the group to go to Fraser Island the following morning. The place was a nice little complex with pool, bar and food. Lucky really as it seemed to be located in a quiet, residential area and there wasn't much else around. I ate in the bar and had a few drinks with some of the Irish contingency already there, but I was quiet, keeping myself to myself and needed to use the Internet.

On the bus heading there that day, I sat and did my usual thing of reading, listening to music and mulling things over in my head. One thing in particular playing on my mind was Chloe. I was attracted to her in China, the feelings I had for her had extenuated over the weeks or so that we travelled together. It had been bothering me for some time now how I felt about her and felt I needed to clear things up and get things out in the open. When I was talking to the business man that I met in Singapore and with the things that we discussed, I decided pretty much there and then to tell her. Unfortunately, the opportunity never really arose before we parted, and I hated the fact that couldn't put myself on the line to say something to her when together, and remembered how we barely looked at one another when we said goodbye in the doorway of Helen's hotel room because for me, it was awkward, yet more so inevitable. Right or wrong, I wasn't sure, but I decided to send her an email, explaining. This was for two reasons; one being that the chance that she may have felt the same, albeit deep down I didn't think that she did, which was one of the reasons that I was willing to walk away when she asked about staying on in Langkawi. Obviously now with this course of action, I could be setting myself up for a fall. I was willing to accept this, whatever her reply, and deal with the consequences. Secondly; at least I would know and be free to move on and get on with my travels and not leave myself wondering what possibly could've been, especially as we had discussed the possibility of meeting again in Australia; although, due to circumstances involving our plans, I didn't think this likely to happen.

It was an early start at seven a.m.; meeting in the bar, names were read out by the organisers to check everyone was present and at the same time we were put into groups of ten for our tour of Fraser Island. I was placed in with a group with four other brits; Paul and his mate Ron, another Paul and his girlfriend Shelly, there were three Danes; Amy and Enya who were travelling together and their fellow countryman Mich, a Swiss girl called

Joss and a German girl called Sophie, making the other nine.

First task of the day was to nominate a lead driver for the insurance, and someone with a credit card to provide their details should anything go wrong. Paul and Ron volunteered their services respectively for this. The next thing was to decide a shopping list of food and drink and two people to go and get the supplies; we chose things obviously which people liked and each were given their chance to have their input, that involved also taking into consideration items which weren't easily perishable, as they had to last three days and we only had a couple of ice boxes to keep things in. Then there was the important stuff; the booze. We unanimously decided on couple of boxes of red and white wine; coming to the conclusion that wine wouldn't necessarily have to be kept cold, it was cheaper, would take up less room, you could get pissed on it easier and everyone liked wine; so we left weighty, space-consuming, lower alcohol, soon warm beer on the shelf with a brilliant display of completely rational democratic decision making at its finest. Amy and Enya stepped forward and headed off to the supermarket with the money we all chipped in for the supplies, while we went to the car hire store to pick up the 4x4.

A list was drafted for all those people who wanted to take a turn driving from the group whilst on Fraser Island. Most put their name down. I never did. Normally, I would have but I didn't have my driving license therefore couldn't prove my eligibility to drive (I'd actually forgotten about this small fact for the five or so seconds I was allowed to drive on Koh Pha Ngan and with hindsight probably for the best I didn't drive). I just gave it a miss and honestly wasn't that bothered. After a close call at the airport, I wasn't going to risk driving illegally on an island with police patrol, so was happy to be ferried about in the back doing a spot of map reading. And not worry whether I was going to end up wrecking the vehicle, injuring someone or both while on an off-road safari. Myself I was willing to risk injuring, others not so much, especially without my licence.

Paul and Ron got the 4x4 Jeep, equipment and utensils that included everything we would need; these were things like tents, pots, plates, cool boxes, map, and itinerary, all signed for as all present and correct after inspection. The rest of us sat and watched a safety DVD in respect to driving the 4x4 dos and don'ts, laws on the island and hazardous wildlife which we could encounter. This painted a grim yet rather exciting picture. The Danish girls returned with the groceries and we headed to the ferry port about a twenty-minute drive away. A drive which we nearly never made after Paul misjudged a tight corner too fast and we skidded around like something out of a cop movie; the back end sliding out and snaking from side to side as we straightened up, with the eight people holding on for grim death in the back. A good start and another reason to not have beer; as it, like us, would have arrived at the ferry port literally shaken. The 4x4 was driven aboard and strategically placed in a very neat and tidy fashion to allow room for the other vehicles, before the passengers walked on to take some seats in the sun for the crossing.

Fraser Island is one of, if not the largest sand island in the world off the east coast of Queensland, and a popular safari tour for those wanting to get away from it all in search of adventure, beautiful views, wildlife and a smattering of fun. With this in mind, we were all really excited by the prospect of the next few days ahead, especially as the itinerary suggested all these things were possible.

Arriving at the port on the island, we disembarked and immediately hit the dirt roads that loosely networked around the island, surrounded by trees, forest and vegetation. The going quickly became very slow and bumpy, as these roads then turned to tracks of mud and sand the further inland we headed, seemingly hitting every possible pot hole that threw and bounced everyone in the back around like freelance jack in the box. Guided by our map and list of itineraries, we each took turns to voice our opinion on the course of direction. One navigator and eight back seat drivers? What could go wrong? Well; after about two hours or so of driving and getting lost numerous times, we finally arrived at our first point of call – Lake Wabby.

We parked the car and headed along the sandy pathway that was now agonisingly hot on the feet in the midday sun. Flip flops were useless as the searing, powdery sand coated the tops of feet as well as trapping underfoot. The only real way to stop this was to not standstill for too long; and it just made everyone hop and jig around looking like they needed to take a piss. The viewpoint was not too far away and allowed us to peer down on a gorgeous emerald lagoon, which was encased by the surrounding lush trees and had a huge yellow sandy beach embankment to the inviting water. It beckoned with seductive refreshment. But unfortunately, we had wasted a lot of time arriving to the lake with some questionable navigating, and was a further thirty minute or so walk downhill to the inland oasis where we had planned to take lunch. Unanimously, everyone felt that this would take up too much time to get down to, set up and get back and therefore compromise some of the other activities for the day. Also, people were already hungry, so we returned to the 4x4 and ate out of the back, dining on sandwiches we hastily made from the shopping items and was hardly the picnic memory anyone envisaged.

Fed and watered, we then ventured on to the next point of call; this was a blessing as we left the dirt tracks of the forest and emerged on the east side of the island at the beach, which was classed as a road (not to mention runway for aircraft) that literally stretched for miles far into the distance, as the golden strip disappeared into the horizon. We started to drive north on the wet sand, maximising our speed, avoiding the softer sand higher up that would slow us down and the actual sea water full of salt, which would damage the body work. We had been warned about this and could be charged for it so preceded with caution, especially as water channels that ran from the land to the sea carved deep cut gullies across the beach that sporadically crept up unsuspectingly. We had to be wary and negotiate these carefully to avoid damaging the suspension, as there wasn't a warning or road sign or any sign for that matter in sight. And we did drop down into one channel quite hard; much to everyone in the back's chagrin. No damage but lots of complaining and one swift driver change later, we continued.

Our next point of call was easy to find; a place called Eli Creek. It was easy to find not because it was right on the beach and we had to pass it, but masses had congregated there already and wasn't hard to fathom why; a lush, deep, freshwater creek running from the forest bush to the beach and down into the ocean. After parking, we grabbed our gear and headed up the purpose-built walkways to make our way to the start point. Having missed out on the first water stop, by now we were hot, sweaty and ready to jump in to the welcoming, cool, refreshing water. The waist-high crystal clear ambling flume allowed us to drift along with the current. Trees and bushes created shading and the sandy bottom only made the experience more relaxing and enjoyable in the blazing sunshine. With time now pressing on, we headed further up the beach, stopping at the shipwrecked *SS Maheno* by the shoreline. It was an old yet large vessel, wrecked during a storm when the tow chain snapped. Now a dilapidated and rusty outer shell with nothing left inside as the elements had taken their toll. Here though, signs warned of the dangers of entering or climbing on the wreckage and it was quite obvious why. So obvious that we armed each other with another's camera, and proceeded in turn to enter the rusting wreck and peer through the port holes to have our pictures taken with warning signs in full view.

Late in the afternoon, we arrived at camp for the evening. First thing was a pep talk from the owner, an old-ish, but nice enough Aussie bloke called Lance who recited the camps dos and don'ts and emphasised the wildlife warnings that mainly involved snakes, spiders and dingoes. Safety lecture over, we proceeded to get our pitch and put up the tents; they were dome-shaped and slept three to four, and unlike the map were surprisingly easy to fathom, as it had been years since I had done this sort of thing. Accommodation swiftly sorted, the next important thing on the agenda was eating. Making a beeline for the barbeque and seating area on the camp site where Lance had provided his words of wisdom, the couple travelling together – Paul and Shelly – stepped up and proceeded to make a delicious pasta dish for everyone, despite our cooking utensils being of such poor quality stone age man would throw them away. Within nanoseconds of sitting, the wine was cracked open and was coursing like water in the creek; the boys predominantly red, while the girls tackled the white. As the evening progressed, more and more people from the other groups arrived around the tables to use the stoves. And like us, they proceeded to eat and get royally pissed up via the vital modem of ye olde drinking game. Our choice was again; ring of fire. At nine p.m., as Lance promised, all the lights went out on the camp. With torches at the ready and completely unperturbed, everyone carried on drinking before eventually we, or rather the guys, finished off our full quota of red wine; that was intended for both days.

Everyone seemed to be getting on well within the group and it was fun. The two Danish girls Amy and Enya were great to be around. Both were nurses, in their early twenties with a good sense of humour and we seemed to click instantly. They would call me 'little man' and threaten to beat me after I started making fun of them; in the nicest possible way as they were both 6ft tall. I wasn't threatened at all; in fact two, lovely looking twenty-two-year-old Danish nurses threatening me? It was the kind of thing some dreams are made of and being 5′10″, any rumours about being 'little' were just wicked speculation. The British guys' Paul and Ron were lively and good for a laugh too like first day unelected group organisers Paul and Shelly, which I was happy for them to do; my attitude was go with the flow, sit back, relax, have some fun; if something needed doing, I'll do it. The others in the group seemed a little more reserved, but, I just figured sometimes it can take a while for people to come out of their shell.

We were up quite spritely the next morning to get on with the rest of the itinerary around the island, despite nursing a dubious headache from the night-time refreshment escapades. This was a small price to pay because if it wasn't for intoxication, sleep would have been nigh-on-impossible due to the sporadic roar that was Paul snoring. Heading further north up the beach in an attempt to find Indian point, we stopped and were perplexed by the lack of trail leading there compared to that on the map. Or again, we were just perplexed by the map and our shit skills at reading it. Rather than hanging around, we headed off to the champagne pools instead, as this was the furthest point away and where we wanted to take lunch; not that we had much choice hanging around, as waiting and wandering on the sand was again another nigh-on-impossibility, below it was already blisteringly hot on the feet and moving was the only option to keep the extremities cool and avoid scorching pain. Arriving at the point of the champagne pools, we all grabbed the cool boxes, equipment and our personal belongings to settle in for a few hours.

To make life easy, there was a purpose-built wooden trail which lead up and over the rocky peninsula down to the beach area. Immediately, it became apparent why this area was called the champagne pools. In front of the open ocean, there was a large line of jagged rocks acting as breaker offering protection from the onslaught of the mighty waves on the far side. Being at high tide, the waves fiercely crashed into and over the natural barrier, forming fabulous cool deep refreshing pools of sea water on the sandy beach to swim and relax in. Every few minutes or so, the calm pool was violently disrupted as a wave of white water toppled over the barnacle-encrusted rocky defence, causing an invigorating fizz of foam in the otherwise tranquil oasis, that bubbled around the body like a million tiny masseuses arrived all at once to revitalise the skin.

Needless to say, it was somewhat of a masterstroke heading here to have as much time as possible messing about in the pools and enjoying the sun. And mess about we did, or I did rather as Amy was fascinated by the strange weird sea life on the rocks. There were thousands of peculiar-looking sphincters amid the algae and barnacles that released trickles of water as they were washed by the waves. When she was examining them closely and not paying attention, I decided to shock her where she promptly screamed out loud, crapping herself in the process to my own and everyone else's amusement. She vowed revenge and duly took it later, by dumping a mass of soggy sand all over my head when I wasn't watching. As unassuming as these little sphincters were, they proved lethal enough to stop a full-grown man in his tracks as Paul decided to start pounding them with clenched fists like a Neanderthal for some unknown reason, only for one to somehow squirt a jet of sea water directly at his face. It was quite a brilliant hit, one easily worthy of applause and we all burst out laughing as he reeled back over, having taken a money shot of sea water straight in the eye; one quick lesson in instant karma from a very unsuspecting and unlikely source.

We whiled away the rest of the time at the pools before heading back, only this time to actually stop at Indian point and find where we needed to go. Naturally, this wasn't where we were previous, but this time the eight passenger-drivers had somehow by hook or crook got it right and found the trail to the top. The high craggy point offered vast sweeping views of the beaches either side; to the north from where we had come and south to where we were now heading that etched away into the distance. Those there were not that interested in this view as lovely as it was, it was the 100ft or so below where people were gazing most. Here offered a chance to spot lots of different wildlife in the ocean, most notably the prospect of seeing one of the many sharks which patrolled along the coastline of Fraser Island. As part of the induction, we had been warned about this and told not to venture into the water because a shark attack was more than a possibility. As I and everyone else fancied leaving here alive and with all faculties intact, there was very little activity involving anyone playing about in the actual sea; albeit Paul and I did have to show off like twats and go for a little splodge earlier just to say we had done it – we were waist high for about ten seconds. Like sensible shithouses.

From the breezy rock-addled ridge, we managed to spot rays and turtles that were cool to see in the wild. Also, intriguingly, two large, ominous, torpedo-shaped objects cruising around together. They were deep so it was impossible to make out exactly what they were, but also just as intriguing was the thin stream of red on the surface of the water, that looked like something had been killed and dragged along yet no evidence of what. We pondered what had possibly occurred in the depths. After pausing for the compulsory photographs and taking in the vast 180-degree shimmering and glistening horizon of the ocean, we headed back to camp for the evening.

The previous night's plan of eating and drinking, followed by more drinking, followed by drinking games seemed a winning formula so we stuck with it. As the lads had finished off the two-day quota of wine in one night, we hit the shop on site and to our relief were able to buy more. Easing past the scary five-minute prospect of having no booze, we promptly got on with the job at hand. By the end of the evening, we were again left nattering in the dark; both Ron and I, suitably oiled, decided to stumble to the tent and retire for the evening. On the way back, we heard something in the dark to our left as we vacated the dining area. Shining torches, we immediately saw dog-like creatures; illuminated white eyes staring directly back at us with the glare from the light. These weren't dogs; well, they were but not the ordinary domestic kind. These were dingoes, the wild dogs that scavenge around the island. Again, we had been warned about dingoes; they're pack animals and there have been prior reports of them attacking people. Luckily, in this case, they just looked away and carried on hunting for food by the bins. Oddly enough, I personally didn't feel threatened and it was a bit of a thrill to see them at close hand, having also been told that they can be quite elusive. Also the fact that we were three sheets to the wind helped ensure the encounter wasn't so traumatic or nerve wracking as booze provided the bollocks nulling the brains.

I must have been pissed that night as when everyone woke, I had initially forgotten about our encounter, only remembering when Ron mentioned it; needless to say, everyone took the piss saying we were full of shit as they knew we stayed up late drinking. My case wasn't helped by the fact that I couldn't remember climbing on top of the 4x4 either to put the equipment on the roof, to be ready to leave that morning which I was also reminded of by Ron when I was wondering where it all was. And Paul's snoring also went unnoticed. But the dingoes were there; that brief moment of clarity I do recall.

After finishing, packing the tents and the rest of the gear away, we headed off down the road or rather the beach to find central station, the old logging site in the middle of the island; now tourist museum and information centre. Truth be told, I felt that we had wasted too much time here; yes, it was good and informative and I enjoyed the walking trails in the forest, it was really picturesque, but not half as picturesque as our final stop; Lake Mackenzie. Arriving again via the bumpy, sand dirt tracks and after a short walk, a large beautiful watery oasis opened up, surrounded by a large line of lush green vegetation on the distant horizon. The water was truly inviting and it took seconds for us to disrobe and join the other people already there splashing around. It was more overcast than the previous days so the powdery white sand was cooler, forming a beach area relaxation point that delicately caressed the feet; coupled with the tepid warm lake, this created the illusion that you had just entered the sea even though you hadn't, due the lack of waves and the strange sensation of not experiencing the burning bitterness of the sea salt on the palate as we happily swam and splashed about in fresh water. This was a highlight and I only wished that we could stayed longer as its beauty and serenity was amazing as everyone had told us and I wished that we had heeded their words more carefully. Unfortunately, the ferry was calling to take us back to the main land as our island safari was coming to a close and could not be missed.

Dashing back, we had lunch waiting in the long line of vehicles to board the ferry, I relaxed and took advantage of the now smooth asphalt roads of the mainland. We dropped the vehicle and equipment off without any fines or hassle before saying goodbye to half of the group that was leaving to other destinations straightaway. The rest of the afternoon and evening was spent with Paul, Ron, Amy and Enya in the pool and bar of the hostel, getting lectured for about three hours on the dangers of smoking as Amy worked with cancer patients and saw the horrid effects of a ridiculous bad habit on a day-to-day basis. I was interested in what she had to say so I didn't mind; yet, it still failed to correct the error of my addicted ways.

Also, that evening, something was bothering me; I had checked my emails and had received a reply from Chloe. I didn't open it, not really looking forward to its contents; fearing it would affect my mood and didn't want to spoil the atmosphere. Problem was, though, I was concerned about this email for obvious reasons and this distracted me from another I'd received. I didn't pay much attention to this other email. But this less significant and somewhat disregarded email was unbeknownst to me at the time important. In fact, very important; so much so that if Chloe's email could change things, this would definitely change things. And the things that this would change was; a lot.

I headed to the bus station at five thirty a.m. to catch the bus to my next destination of Surfers Paradise further south back down the coast. I was really tired but managed to get plenty of sleep on the bus despite wondering what was written in Chloe's email. I arrived at Surfers Paradise mid-afternoon, got sorted at my hostel and settled for the evening – my priority – then find a computer. Opening Chloe's reply, I found its content short, sweet and pretty much to the point, essentially saying that she was sorry for not feeling the same as I did about her, and wished me the best. I spent the night mulling over what was written and what had happened. For the first time in ages, I felt lonely, yet I wasn't in the mood for talking or socialising with anyone anyway. One thing became apparent: everything said and done now seemed to have an ominous inevitability about it all; from saying something to Helen in the taxi on our way to the airport when leaving Singapore, where although she didn't say so, it was obvious she knew it wasn't happening, to going way back where I myself lost Chloe's contact details and book at the border. But despite me knowing this and knowing I had brought it upon myself, it still cut, and I was now going to have to pull myself around, put any feelings aside and move on. As there was sod all else I could do about it.

Surfers Paradise was new; everything about it. It was a city purpose-built on the gold coast, with high-rises and fashionable shops set back from the miles of beach which stretched up and down the coast line. There was plenty to do but nothing which really stood out, knowing I wasn't going to hang around long and could do these things in other places. At least, it was hot and sunny, so I whiled away the time looking about around the shops and down at the beach, topping up my tan in-between trying to find accommodation at my next destination of Byron Bay. This alone was proving to be a distraction-cum-headache now, as reservations for the Christmas period were at a premium and I hadn't pre-booked places, not wanting to be tied down to being somewhere at a certain time. This was obviously not the best way to go about things, creating a huge element of uncertainty and unease about whether I was going to have a roof over my head from night to night. But adversity comes in many forms and was now just another challenging distraction, but most of all it made things that little bit more exciting.

I left Surfers Paradise after two days, feeling that I could happily not bother going. This was made all the more ironic by the fact that in Chloe's email, she had suggested going to Noosa, claiming it was beautiful. And Ron, Paul, Amy and Enya had all gone there after Fraser Island. They suggested that I tag along, but I decided to stick to my plan instead. Maybe

I should've taken life's opportunity? If I had opened the email earlier, would I have done so? But conversely, would it have changed my mood when there? Who knows? Maybe yes to all those things, but still I never once wished I had gone to Noosa even though those guys were good fun. What was done was done and with the decisions I'd made, I was grateful of the time and space to think and relax, despite Surfers Paradise not really being my kind of place, but I did acquire some sun and a lovely little thought-provoking book by the Dalai Lama to muse over.

By now, I was feeling better about things. I'd emailed Chloe back and told her that it was fine and there were no hard feelings. At least now I knew where we both stood and figured that we both had lots of travelling and adventures ahead, not knowing where these would take us. I did feel that it was for the best that we now were not going to meet up, as I didn't even know if we would be in the same place at the same time together. A shame, but at least this would make things less awkward and easier to move on, which, in all sense of the word, is exactly what I did.

I finally got accommodation sorted in the popular traveller resort of Byron Bay. Unfortunately, the four days I wanted to stay there prior to moving on to Sydney were unavailable and was only able to get in three of the four, so I decided to book the third night at hostel further inland in Nimbin, and then return to Byron for one night before leaving to head south. Arriving in Byron, the hostel was a really cool resort on the outskirts of the town that incorporated facilities like pool, Internet, catering and entertainments as you would normally expect but there was also camping, arts and crafts sessions, yoga classes and their very own bush survival man would turn up to give walking tours for those interested in finding out about how to survive in the Aussie outback. These features really appealed, making the hostel unique and stand-out, as well as having a nice, fun vibe too.

Instantly loving where I had ended up, that evening a few others and I went to the bar on the complex before heading to one of more notorious bars in town, which was packed. Notorious was the right word, for as soon as we entered, I looked to the stage and there was a wet t-shirt competition going on. *Brilliant,* I thought, *here we go!* Emily who I was with was less impressed, not because she disapproved; quite the contrary as this was just down to the fact that women weren't her thing, because she sharp changed her tune when the men were dragged on stage and started stripping. She was an Aussie herself, having a little staycation from where she lived, and we were now in the same room together. From the outset, she was really bubbly, always smiling and laughing; I liked this about her and we got on well straightaway, so proceeded to get drunk together, leaving the place with our footprints well and truly embedded on the table tops.

The day I'd arrived, I had taken the free sample tour of the bush walk around the complex with many others, it was really interesting and educational stuff. This was in part due to our host and guide 'Wallaby Pete' also being very funny with it as he would mercilessly take the piss out of people, including himself; having a sense of humour trait that resonates easily between Brits and Aussies. Afterwards, I found out that there was a half day tour in and around Byron with Pete the next day. Whereby, I signed up immediately. So here I was; hangover in hand, ready to head out and learn how to survive in the rugged harsh Australian bush, within the comfortable, neighbourly suburbs of Byron Bay.

We walked around for the best part of three hours, yet managed not to venture to far from the hostel which was situated in a residential area, and before we even left were promptly told off by some yoga instructor for talking too loudly; interrupting the peace, tranquillity and zen ambience of her session. *Ohm*. We headed out to a large field where we dug for water, spent time learning how to make rope from reeds, which we dried out and some fashioned into bracelets, picked various plants that you can eat, didn't pick the various plants that would poison you, studied spiders, learnt how to kill ticks using WD40, ate sugary residue from grubs, tasted nectar from flowers and ended up on the front lawn of a local resident, with Pete enthusiastically explaining the healing properties of one of the trees growing in the garden. I couldn't believe it. Even more so when the owner came out to find out why there was a group of random strangers stood on his grass, watching some bloke rape leaves off his tree. Pete apologised and promptly carried on telling us and now the owner how cool his tree was like he was his best mate. I thought that it was going to kick off but the owner was immediately enthralled as much as we were, it was so surreal and amazingly funny, I just thought to myself that if this had happened back home, there would have been hell on, the rozzers would have been called with blue lights and sirens wailing; the lot. And at the very least, we would all be getting done for trespassing.

Finally, we finished off on a field in a local park, where we were given the opportunity to throw aboriginal spears; these were about 6ft in length and could be launched long distances, as they would be used to hunt with. Some managed to throw these quite far. I, on the other hand, was shit and mine went only a couple of yards, ending up with a thick ear for my trouble, having brought the launch stick past my head in a throwing motion to only whack my right ear hard. Any prey would've been in no peril whatsoever and just wandered off and yes, it fucking hurt. Lastly, we tried the age old art of starting a fire by rubbing two sticks together. This actually worked a treat. Our hands were sore afterwards from the friction, but it was cool to start a fire from next to nothing; couple of sticks and some dry kindling. Again, this is the kind of thing people would call the cops for back home; chucking lethal objects around in public and starting random fires in the park like yobbos. Not here though, this is really useful, need to know, educational stuff.

I'd had a really good day and learnt so much. Pete's enthusiasm for his work was really endearing, making the exercise worthwhile, informative and lots of fun. Upon returning, I was greeted by the dorm room being turned upside down by the others staying in there. Not exactly what I was expecting. Under the circumstances though, I understood. Some of Australia's natural residents had decided to pay the room a visit with the presence of a large huntsman spider and like most of the nature in Australia; it is kind of dangerous with the potential to dish out a nasty bite. So cue clothes and bed mattresses being thrown everywhere, as the wily little fella or in this case rather big fella scurried about, rapidly avoiding capture. Although not petrified of spiders, I'll admit that chasing and catching them is not my forte; particularly when they're big, hairy, fast and can bite. So, I was less than enamoured about the prospect of having to do so. But what are you going to do? Only one thing to do in such instances; get some crazy stoned Dutch bloke to sort it out. After more frantic running around the room with a plastic bag on his hand, he caught and released it unharmed outside the dorm; excitement over. As a way of saying thanks, everyone in the room promptly decided we should get pissed and stoned with him.

I chilled out and relaxed on my bunk, wearily looking about now for large spiders. A big storm was on the horizon and you could hear the rumblings and roars in the distance. The storm was moving fast and rain started with smattering of gentle tings on the corrugated roof, before building into a crescendo that lashed to a deafening din, until out of nowhere, *BANG!* Thunder broke from the night sky right above and was so loud that it actually shook the room. I'd never heard anything like it in all my life. It was like a bomb going off and not expecting it, I totally crapped myself, as natural instinct injected adrenaline right through the body and sent my heart racing, leaving me instantly wondering what was happening, likened to being under attack. When calmed down, I was minding my own business, listening to music in my own little world when suddenly I was under attack; as I was hit on the head by a renegade half full bottle of water.

I looked up, Emily was pissing herself laughing. "I've just heard that… at the bar tonight, there's a wet t-shirt contest on…"

"What the fuck?" I retorted. "Fuck off, its eleven thirty, absolutely pissing down, thunder and lightning and I'm fucked! And so will you be if you throw that again!" I said as I launched it back.

She pretended to look shocked but wasn't, because she instantly burst out laughing, I was pissing myself laughing at her too. She was mental and Aussie mental at that, but in a nice way and I liked her a lot.

I had to check out of the hostel the next day; my two days were up in Byron and I was due to head to Nimbin. Unfortunately, Emily and some of the others were also checking out but heading off in their different directions, so I wasn't going to get to see them or her upon my return. Which was a shame, especially as Emily was heading further north in the opposite direction to me, but as I'd already found out; travelling life changes fast and I, like everyone else, was doing my own thing. Still I did want to go see the next place as I had heard so much about it.

The bus took about an hour-and-a-half inland to reach Nimbin; pretty much a one street town, with loads of psychedelic art work everywhere. Apparently, hippies had arrived here in the sixties for a festival and never left. You could tell. Rather than immediately exploring, I stayed on the bus which dropped me off at the hostel that was situated on the outskirts of the town; a small secluded resort with beautiful views of scenic mountains and trees. There weren't any facilities as such there, so a few others, who I started chatting with, and I headed into town having ourselves a cheeky joint as we ambled down the hill.

Getting into town, I thought that the place was like the Wild West. Time had seemingly stood still here and I half expected someone to come crashing through a window at some point due to a bar brawl, and there were some really out there characters adorning the streets. It kind of felt quite intimidating, probably due to a little bit of paranoia creeping in from having a smoke prior. Every one of the people we saw seemed to be stoned off their nut or on magic mushrooms or both, I hadn't seen anything like it. It sorts of reminded me of Royston Vasey from *The League of Gentlemen* for some reason; we had a quick wander about checking out the stalls, shops and having something to eat. Acquiring ourselves some weed, we headed back to the sanctuary of our hostel retreat, whereby we spent the rest of the day relaxing and getting baked in nature's more serene surroundings.

The bus back the next day wasn't till three p.m. so I took the opportunity to head back into town, visiting the infamous weed museum, using the word 'museum' in the loose sense of the word as it just looked like someone's house with loads of shite on the walls and paraphernalia thrown in. There was, however, information about the origins of weed and in one of the rooms a video playing, showing the last time that the cops had raided the place as they searched for evidence. I went for a beer in the pub with a few of the others before heading back.

One day in Nimbin was easily enough. I had seen what everyone had told me about the place and done what I wanted; basically, have a look around and get high. Mission accomplished, leaving no real desire to hang around much longer. I'm an advocate of the herb and it is readily available here, but I have no desire to continually get baked out of my tree; much like not getting completely pissed every night, in the sense that moderation is key. Admittedly, a key that seemed to be getting used quite a lot.

I couldn't help but feel there was a somewhat seedy undertone to the place and that something wasn't quite right. Probably due to the scores of doped up drug dealers patrolling the streets, or the fact that the vast majority of people seemed to wander around out of their tree. It felt like those there had just sort of given up on life and wanted to drop out altogether, to live a perpetual state of minimalistic drugged bliss, away from the real world, yet, be where paranoia runs throughout the place. I myself, was accused on the streets of being a cop by some strung out local; hilarious irony. Don't get me wrong, I was glad I went and the experience was a real eye opener, or just about anyway. But I think that the love, peace and harmony of any sixties-inspired ethos was now long gone, and those there was just intent on disregarding normal society, except for their own little bubble, and/or making money dealing knowing that visitors would come drawn by the reputation of the town. Like me.

Despite this, I couldn't help but feel that I was supposed to come here, as course of fate as it were. This wasn't anything to do with the place itself or the copious amounts of weed I smoked, but something else – a strange thing that happened. While chilling in the hostel prior to departure, I was looking though the book exchange, immediately spotting one which caught my eye; *The Celestine Prophecy*. I had read this book a couple of years back, given to me by a friend. A fictional story that concerns man's evolution and achieving a higher state of spiritual insight; I enjoyed it but didn't really understand its content too much. I wanted to read it again, intrigued and interested with its message so swapped my *Soft Vengeance of a Freedom Fighter* book for it, but that wasn't the real point. Back in Malaysia, after finishing the trek in Taman Nagara with Chloe and Karen, I went to a book store and had actually already bought the book, but because I was reading the aforementioned at the time, I lent it to Chloe to read, with the intention of getting it back when we hopefully met up in Australia. Obviously, now this wasn't going to happen and the book I bought was with her, and I wasn't going to chase after it. But now by fate of not getting a place in Byron for one night, staying over in Nimbin instead which I wasn't going to do and staying in this hostel, I had now come into the possession of the book again. It felt like I was supposed to have this book and read it. Being a firm believer in things both good and bad happening for a reason, which oddly enough is what the contents of the book deals with, and as I was finding out, was happening to me seemingly more and more, and now knowing what was about to happen provide another instance that I should bear this in mind.

Arriving back in Byron Bay, it was about four thirty p.m. and I checked into my hostel, a different one this time. Good news: whilst there, I bumped into Amy and Enya, it was great to see them again. We had barbeque dinner (obviously, it was Australia) and caught up. I told them about Nimbin and its druggy ways. Although Danish, turns out they actually lived and worked in the Netherlands; so this was nothing new.

I checked out the next morning, ate breakfast and fell asleep on the sofa in the hostel reception for the best part of two hours to catch up on sleep from the late night and early checkout. One last thing to do before my bus to Sydney was visit the point to the south of the bay. I set off in the blazing heat and the trail took me along the cliffs before arriving at the lighthouse which offered a fabulous sweeping view of the bay and the sea, which dazzled in the sunlight. I was now officially at the most easterly point of

Australia and the furthest distance I had ever been away from home. It was a cool moment I found difficult to comprehend – travelling now seemed to be ingrained within – distances had become irrelevant and I still never missed home; the view was spectacular though unfortunately, all I had to take were precious memories, as three quarters of the way there in my still-bleary state, I realised that I'd forgotten my camera.

I managed to catch up with Amy and Enya before I left; they had been surfing that morning. We said our goodbyes and after a short and all-too-brief encounter, we went our separate ways again. I seemed to click with Amy, as we talked, laughed and took the piss out of each other constantly but felt that I had more in common with Enya. She was a little quieter but when we spoke, it was always good, enthralling conversation, probably enhanced in part as she had the most amazing, hypnotic emerald green eyes that in turn made her ridiculously pretty. The girls were brilliant fun to be around. I hoped to see them again sometime soon as we agreed to stay in touch. Boarding the night bus to Sydney, I treated myself by eating some space chocolates to ensure a good sleep on the long journey. So couple these with my hangovers, what was all that nonsense about some moderation and some keys?

That Was a Merry Christmas...
Everybody Had Fun

It was now 22 December and I arrived for the Christmas holidays in Sydney early in the morning, having slept like a baby on the bus; so much so, I had woken as we pulled up and had missed coming into town over the fabled Sydney Harbour Bridge. I never even realised until someone mentioned it later and thought to myself, *I don't remember seeing that. Did we come over the Sydney Harbour Bridge?* With it not being very inconspicuous, I must have been out for the count as the space chocolates seemed to have really done the trick. I got to my hostel and checked in to the large sixteen-bed dorm which was about half full; being still early, I dumped my bag, climbed onto the top bunk bed and fell asleep.

I woke around eleven a.m. Dozing; I could hear others in the room talking and offering reference to who was now occupying the once vacant top bunk. I raised my head, looked across and said 'Hello' with a fleeting wave, eventually waking enough to start chatting with them, finding out that they were all casualties suffering from the frequent traveller phenomenon of a hangover. Collette and Sara were from the UK and Aaron was from Ireland. From the way they were talking they had been in the hostel for a while, but were very pleasant and amiable with a good sense of humour. And there were more of them in a group scattered around the various rooms of the hostel.

There wasn't a plan really for the day ahead. I knew some of the things which I wanted to do, but was feeling sociable so these were put on hiatus and I decided to take up Sara and Collette's offer of heading to Bondi Beach with them, figuring that at least it was a chance to visit the world-famous site which was something I actually did want to do, and could now chilling with some new-found mates. It was about three p.m. before we finally got our arses into gear and set off on the bus; which was cramped with people going about their day-to-day business but offered another public tour of the city that I was more than happy to go along with.

Arriving on the promenade, I was hungry so we stopped at a burger joint for a quick bite. Munching away outside, I looked round and *boom!* There was Joanne and Hailey again; from Koh Tao to Koh Pha Ngan to Koh Samui to Brisbane and now here. I just seemed to bump into them at every turn and it was as welcome as it was random. They were in Sydney to find work and just out for the day, enjoying the sun, and not looking for work. A trap that many travellers were falling into until the funds became really desperate. I could see why though; fun place, hot weather and away from home. Why not make the most of it? I was lucky, having saved a good amount and had the luxury of not having to find a job or work to top up the funds. Even if I wanted to, I would have had problems as I was over the age limit to apply for a traveller's working visa. The experience would have been good, but I was more interested in doing voluntary work in various guises anyway, and didn't want to commit to staying in one particular place for a long period of time, although working out of the UK was something which I had ambitions for in the future.

I introduced the girls and they seemed to get on, Joanne and Hailey had other plans though and they headed off their own way, but not before I got a contact number for them as they were up for meeting in a few days, when we knew our plans over Christmas. We headed to the beach. First thing I noticed when we sat down was that despite how busy it was or seemed, the sand was remarkably clean, which was great; then, it was explained that essentially there was strictly no smoking or drinking on the beach and no littering. And, shockingly, people were abiding by the rules, helping to keep this world famous site nice and pristine for all to enjoy. Probably in part due to the signs plastered around and that it was also being patrolled relentlessly; nevertheless, something to be proud of and much respect, making the hours we whiled away lazing in the sun interspersed by taking dips in the sea very enjoyable.

Upon returning after a rocky ride on the public bendy bus, the rest of the evening was essentially sat chilling and getting to know everyone. The Tuesday, though, I had a plan; out and about, having a look at what Sydney had to offer, so I headed off down George Street with the intent of booking myself on the bridge walk, having heard that it was possible to climb to the very top of the iconic Sydney Harbour Bridge; which apparently was around here somewhere. Again, this falls right under the jurisdiction of the box ticking brigade, having been there, done that blah blah blah, but if you didn't do any of these things, then what are memories, stories and experiences made of? And what would you actually achieve? And how could you overcome any fears? And most importantly, what the fuck are you going to brag about? So for me, I say, tick away.

Minding my own business, I ambled down the road to the harbour, off in a world of my own and not really paying attention to anything. This state of unreadiness was to be my downfall. Without a moment's notice and from nowhere, I was set upon. My first reaction was to panic as one's natural fight or flight instinct would automatically take over, and a charge of adrenaline was pumped immediately into the blood system. But almost instantaneously, I knew that I was OK; the flurry of expected blows to liberate me of my possessions wasn't happening, nor was I being wrestled to the ground, but what I did have was someone hanging off me. Gaining my senses, I looked at my bouncing, cuddly assailant. It was June; from the Thai Experience. She had seen me walking down the street and without a second thought had run up to me and literally dived onto me from the front, flung her arms around and started hastily cuddling me.

Looking at her and laughing, I said, "You fucking stupid cow! I absolutely shit myself there!"

She was in hysterics. "I could nee help it; I saw yee in a world of yee own so I thought I'd say hullo!" she retorted in her staunch Glaswegian accent.

It was lovely to see her cheery smile again, despite June's Judo-style assault in the middle of the street, right out of the blue and not having a clue what was happening. One minute I was happily strolling, minding my own, next thing I'm brought back to this world by being pounced on, where the relief of it being a friendly face was definitely part of the euphoria of seeing her again.

She was with Lydia, who I also knew from Thailand but being a slightly more reserved character than June, she just watched and laughed as I got accosted off a mad jock. Gaining my composure, I stopped and chatted. At this point, I had to wonder if everyone I'd met was now going to pop up in Sydney. Again, I didn't realise they were here but should have expected it really. Seemed like every bugger else was. We caught up with where we had been, what we had been up to and our plans for Christmas; that led on to another exchange of contacts in the hope that we could catch up on Christmas day as I was still unsure of any plans. I carried on warm and happy at being assaulted in the best possible way and chuckled to myself about the whole incident, the only saving grace being that I didn't scream like a big shithouse, but it must have looked funny to any passer-by who witnessed it on one of the busiest commercial streets in Australia that day.

Just up from the harbour shore line and under the bridge itself was the bridge climb information centre. I purchased a ticket for the following day on Christmas Eve and felt it would be worthwhile and a nice little present to myself. Leaving, I proceeded to explore around the rocks and circular quay area which possessed a beautiful old-world feel, with the architecture and cobbled streets seemingly unchanged from the 19th century of yesteryear, and a welcome change from a modern buzzing metropolis only a short walk away, that included the view and modern architecture of the renowned Sydney Opera House synonymous in stature alongside the magnificent bridge itself, before finishing off with a leisurely walk around the lush green botanical gardens. Arriving back at the hostel, everyone had a plan, a simple but effective one; get the drinks in, we're getting on it.

The next day, I was rough; twenty-four carats of self-inflicted woe. Not the first time, certainly wouldn't be the last; we had a good night out in one of the Irish bars which was just around the corner, handily enough. I rose about noon, giving myself enough time to grab some sustenance, clear my head and get to the bridge for the climb. I was really excited at the prospect of climbing to the top of such a world-renowned landmark structure and witnessing the views that would be on offer.

Upon arriving, I felt fine, checked in and waited. Eventually, we were shown to a room to fill out the complimentary legal forms and disclaimers, no problem. Then a problem, a problem which would change my plans; not necessarily totally but one I had brushed off rather nonchalantly the day before having been warned about. We all were then submitted to provide a breathalyser test to ensure our suitability and safety to climb the bridge. I failed it in spectacular fashion; twice.

I was kept back as the rest of the group headed off to get kitted out. Straightaway, I knew what the problem was; someone had spent the night getting more than adequately refreshed, and the little gizmo that the cops use for testing for a drunk driver was being maxed out by someone's boozy breath from the night before.

The staff member quizzed, "Have you had a beer or two for lunch?"

"No, that's from last night," I answered.

"Bloody hell! You had a lot to drink then, yeah?"

"It looks that way, according to your little machine – I can't quite remember!" Bearing in mind that this was now half past two in the afternoon, they were obviously concerned about my condition. After the second attempt and consultation with various staff members, it was deemed that they could not and would not let me make the climb. I thought, *What a knob end I am; imagine if I'd driven here!*

In all sincerity, this was all of my own doing. I knew about it, but brushed it off the day prior and got caught up in the moment of partying hard and never gave the breathalyser another thought, and rules are rules so I had to grin and bear it. I was advised that it wasn't possible to climb there and then, but was told that if I went away, had some food, walked about in fresh air then should be all right to complete the climb later in the late afternoon, obviously subject to rescheduling fee. Problem though was that I had to take this time slot if I wanted to do it; it was Christmas Eve, and not being open on Christmas Day and Boxing Day, with me being due to leave on the day after, it left me hoping and praying that within the next couple of hours, I could sober up enough to be allowed to climb.

For once, I heeded the advice and went and had some more to eat and figured I'd head back to the hostel and see the others. Also, I could use the time to get some stuff sorted to send back to the UK. I wandered back into the hostel as the booze brigade looked at me in bewilderment.

"What are you doing here? Aren't you supposed to be doing the bridge climb?" Collette quizzed.

"Can't, they won't let me at the minute. I failed the breathalyser test." Cue raucous laughter.

The weather had become more overcast now as I arrived back at the bridge climb centre; for take two. I was greeted by a member of staff asking me if I was the guy who failed the breathalyser. Oddly enough, all of the staff working there seemed to know me, or at least who I was. I don't know how often this happens, but I seemed to provide entertainment for the staff on duty that day, as they all had knowing smiles or nice little quips, in true Aussie fashion. I didn't mind and sort of revelled in the notoriety of it all, but really though I was just happy to be allowed on to complete the climb, as I now passed the breath test at the third time; which as they say is a charm.

We were kitted out with our boiler suits, headphones, and safety lines before then given the lowdown about the dos and don'ts from our guide Samantha, who was really nice and funny, also pretty too; so things were looking up – which was incidentally where we were heading. We walked under the bridge and up through the massive steel girders and thousands of rivets, standing out like pimples holding the magnificent structure together. Birds flew in and out of the bridge from nests and the wind whipped through but still couldn't drown out the noise of the countless cars roaring past from above.

Passing through the stone pylons, and up beyond the road, we then climbed up four separate narrow ladders to the starting point. This was where we joined the huge arch that crosses over the top of the bridge. The gradient wasn't that steep and proved easy, taking a steady pace to the centre of the arch way. I say it was easy, but that was my personal opinion not being scared of heights, but there were some gingerly taken apprehensive steps by some others up there. As you can imagine, it was very high, especially looking down at the road below where the relaying traffic noise was now completely blotted out by the wind and breeze. We were safe and didn't feel fazed by the climb; easy to say when attached and on a purpose-built walkway and steps. Unfortunately, this was not the case for the countless construction and maintenance workers, who built and looked after the bridge in the past before these paths and steps were constructed for tourism and the health and safety executive got a grip. Ropes and an acute sense of balance being the only things to save these brave souls, as they went about their day-to-day work in the quest for building and maintaining engineering excellence, and needless to say many paid the ultimate price in doing so. It was fascinating and really interesting hearing about the history of the bridge; the effort and problems which had to be overcome to ensure its successful construction, one point being how if there was a millimetre discrepancy when starting on either side this would mean that by the time the bridge met in the middle, this would be amplified to over a metre and wouldn't connect together; a true appreciation for the scale of master engineering for the time.

We eventually reached the top of the archway which spanned across the harbour, and stopped to admire the view; a 360-degree spectacular that offered the high rises of downtown Sydney to the south, the residential areas and industries inland and to the north and of course, a bird's eye view down over the world famous opera house which now seemed quite small at our elevated height. Not to mention the countless boats and ferries patrolling the waterways below, where we exchanged waves with pissed up revellers in Santa hats at numerous Christmas parties. As you would expect, this provided excellent photo opportunities; unfortunately though, no cameras were allowed to be taken up by climbers. For any cynic out there, this was so the company could sell you the photos that they were taking, but I like to think that this was on the sole basis of people's safety, as you could imagine people would insist on carting up four tonnes of equipment, take forever finding the elusive ideal snapshot, obviously become distracted and end up taking a one-way trip to the tarmac or water below; that wouldn't just be confined to the camera. So thinking about the implications, it made sense not to let Joe public have any cameras, and was happy to let our guide take individual and group photos from various points of interest, also as part of the price we were able to have one of the pictures free and any others could be bought. There was a distinct breeze at the top and the overcast weather wasn't helping or enhancing the view either, which was a shame but these things can't be guaranteed. We crossed over to the other side of the bridge when the group ahead of us had moved on, and then headed back down to where we had come from. We had been out for a few hours now, and the excursion was good value for money as dusk fell. I couldn't wait to get back though, not necessarily back to the hostel but back to the centre; there wasn't anything in particular happening, but I was in a boiler suit and there was also understandably a severe lack of facilities on the bridge, and after three-and-a-half hours, I was absolutely bursting to go. Apparently, having a wiz over the side was a bit of a no-no. So after one mad dash to use the toilet, everything was good.

Melanie was on the climb with me. Upon finishing, we chatted about how much fun the bridge climb was amid other things, and decided to make the most of it by stopping off for a few celebratory drinks. She was really nice and on holiday from Chicago. Later, when we came to go our own separate ways, I told her of my plans of visiting Chicago in the USA as part of my travels later in the New Year, saying I would keep in touch which she was happy with. I hoped to see her again as I had done with lots of others on my travels, as my catalogue of correspondences and contacts increased.

Christmas day was now actually here; oddly though, it didn't feel like Christmas. It was a strange feeling celebrating the festivities in the southern hemisphere. It was hot, the sky was blue and people were wandering around in shorts and t-shirt, although it was possible to hear people performing carols amid scant few decorations in the high streets and up in shops, but that was about it in comparison to the UK. The weather was probably the most obvious factor in what I felt was a subdued festive period, even the hostel wasn't full. Good news though as I had managed to extend my stay to 30 December. Also factored into this; being from the UK, I was conditioned to have Christmas thrust upon, from all angles at the beginning of November where it is all quite blown out of proportion by TV, advertising, companies and corporations vying for money and increasing the psychological pressure for people to feel that they must have a happy, elaborate and expensive Christmas.

Because of this, I wasn't really a big fan of Christmas; essentially over-indulging to the max. Getting smashed, eating too much and buying lots of gifts to prove how much you love someone seemed to have taken precedence, so for me the holidays had become false and completely detracted from any true meaning. So this year, I was happy to be away from it all, not having everything festive heaped upon me, no pressure to have a good time (times were already good and it could be argued that most days were like Christmas day anyway), not worry about getting or giving presents and just hanging out enjoying the company of friends, having drinks, traditional KFC Christmas meal before heading down to Coogee for a party on the beach.

Needless to say, we arrived late afternoon after fannying around for what seemed an eternity. Getting there, the grass verges were packed even before getting onto the beach. We were then joined by June and Lydia and by Joanne and Hailey, and ended up sitting with some of Collette's mates, so we had a nice little reunion going on. The super cheap goons of wine were swiftly bust open, allowing everyone to laugh and chat easily; aided by the drinking Olympics and (another) classic game of ring of fire. Time seemed to fly by before it got dark and we were moved on by the cops; who were also sporting snazzy Santa hats where we couldn't resist the opportunity for photos, which they kindly obliged with in the true Christmas spirit. The night wasn't over, most people had left and whilst getting something to eat a random bloke invited us all back to his. Probably because he fancied Colette but when we got there, he passed out and left us to drink his booze, eat his chocolates, smoke his marijuana and make an absolute shit load of noise. Cheers mate, Merry Christmas.

We left at around four a.m. with Joanne pretty much a dead weight; wiped out by the drink and smoke and Hailey so shit-faced she fell down the stairwell and nearly knocked herself out. Deciding we'd had enough, we headed back to our respective digs, except for me; I needed to do one last thing. It was five a.m. so I stumbled to the 24-hour Internet cafe and called home to drunkenly try and wish everyone there a Merry Christmas; who were some eleven hours behind me in the partying stakes.

As was now the norm, Boxing Day was a slow start, surfacing at around one p.m.; I was quite excited though as Aaron, George and I had decided to go to the day fixture at Sydney race course. We jumped on the bus and headed to the track. Arriving, the place was packed, as was expected, with all and sundry unsurprisingly enjoying the sunny weather and the holiday racing. We headed straight to the bar and then the tote to get the bets on.

We were eventually joined by Colette and Sara, and continued gambling and drinking into the late afternoon, savouring the packed raucous atmosphere as people urged their expected equine to the finish line. What quickly became apparent though was that my betting skills had not improved from Hong Kong; loss followed loss followed loss. Well, win some lose lots. Wasn't the first time I'd been grifted at the races and hazard a guess that it wouldn't be the last. Aaron on the other hand though was having a right time of it as two $10 bets left him $300 better off and really chuffed to boot. Fair play; you pay your money and take your chances. He also got the beers in, a true gent. Everyone left suitably oiled having a skin full and really just topping up from the previous day, before deciding on a cheap night in cuddling a goon of wine, chilling and laughing at our late evening haunt of the roof top terrace.

I now had three days left in Sydney or rather three days left in the hostel, which meant that I was getting kicked out on the 30th. Initially, I hadn't planned to stay in Sydney and was going to go to Melbourne for New Year. I'd managed to extend my stay in the hostel for three days but now that New Year was nigh; the place became instantly booked up, as people flocked into the city. It left me sort of stranded; not having a ticket to get to Melbourne or a place in the hostel or anywhere else for that matter. But lady luck was about to smile on me once more.

The next few days were spent visiting Manly Beach, which I didn't think was as good or nice as Coogee or Bondi, doing a spot of shopping and finishing exploring whereby I got a chance to see the various works of art scattered around the city, ride the monorail, visit darling harbour and a walk around the quay. I also found out that there was a museum dedicated to the construction of the bridge within one of its stone pylons, which I had a vested interest in not just because of my climbing exploits but the fact that the construction company responsible for building it was called Dorman, Long and Co. from Teesside, where I am from. This strangely made me feel rather proud of my roots, as I read the large steel cast sign which had been embedded within the towering stones column, describing the who's, whys and where of the bridge's construction; a more grandiose version of the Tyne Bridge in Newcastle. I was aware of the strong steel construction history that the Tees region provided, but it was really cool to see such a worldwide iconic image in all its glory made possible by a company from my area, for the world to admire and do so for many years to come.

Not only that, when I visited the beautiful Hyde Park, there was the lake of reflections and the Anzac war memorial commemorating fallen soldiers. But also within was testimony to Britain's sea faring past; a statue of Captain James Cook who sailed the *HMS Endeavour* in 18th century and for want of better phrase credited for discovering Australia. He was also from Teesside. Again, I knew of the history and it left another reminder how Australia, Sydney and the Teesside region would be intrinsically linked. But I don't think discover is the exact phrase. It wasn't exactly lost; just unknown to foreign explorers and colonial invaders at the time, something I'm sure any native aboriginal would testify to and any statue of sorts must only serve as a dark reminder of this.

The 30th came around all too quickly and I had to vacate the hostel. I now wanted to hang around in Sydney to see in the New Year, pretty much because it was one of those things which I decided I should do, as countless people told me what a great experience it was and really wanted to witness it, especially having made it this far. Unfortunately, I had nowhere to stay, so it was looking like crashing on the beach. Fortunately for me, the no hostel situation disappeared with my sandy bed because during one of my frequent boozy excursions out with Joanne and Hailey, they offered to let me crash at the place they were staying for a couple of nights, allowing me to hang out with them, meet up with the others and witness the Sydney New Year. This was brilliant. I was really grateful and jumped at the chance.

They were staying in Kogarah near Botany Bay. Friends of theirs were away and let them use the house; this was ideal. Arriving, I dumped my stuff and we got ready and headed off to Coogee Beach to meet up with the others again, and did the all-too-familiar ritual of getting pissed up and arsing about in the sea, before heading home where Joanne and Hailey, unbeknownst to me at the time had a punch up in the back of the taxi over money and the fare. Geordies, *eh?* Can't take them anywhere; at least the bridge was behaving itself and doing what it was supposed to.

New Year's Eve was now here, we had arranged to meet the others at the hostel. Arriving again late afternoon, George was already absolutely shit-faced on Jack Daniel's, propping himself up against a wall in the middle of the street. He was a bit of a mess and distinctly unaware of people talking to him, laughing and rolling their eyes at his all-too-familiar state, even at such early stage of proceedings. Everyone decided that they wanted to be on his planet or at least halfway there so hit the liquor store and headed off mob-handed to observation point. Getting down to the harbour was easy; due to the sheer volume of people expected on the streets, most of the roads were closed off, making pretty much everywhere pedestrianised.

Friends of Aaron had made a pitch on the grassy verge of observation point, which faced north looking out to the back of the bridge on the opposite side to the opera house, providing an ample view for the spectacular display. We were heading to meet them in the hope that we too could sit down without too much trouble. It was about five p.m. and there were already hundreds of people arriving at the harbour, getting good spots to witness the fireworks. Eventually, we found where Aaron's friends were at and squeezed in to the rapidly filling spaces. For the next six or seven hours, we sat, drinking and having craic (the vast majority amongst us being Irish), patiently waiting. The children's fireworks were set off just before dusk and night rolled in, like the swelling crowds the anticipation just grew and grew, news reports suggested that there were approximately 1.5 million people who were there witnessing the event. Whether it was because of the good time or because of the drink, it seemed that within an instant the time was nigh and everyone started to count down.

"Ten, nine, eight, seven, six, five, four, three, two, one, HAPPY NEW YEAR!" rung out in unison with a massive cheer, instantly followed by the first of many beautiful, bright, colourful explosions as the fireworks were triggered from the steel girders of the bridge. People started the usual ritual of hugs, kisses and issuing best wishes for the forthcoming annum, to those they loved, knew or were in the vicinity of. It was a really cool experience and certainly one of the best New Years that I'd witnessed. Albeit, I don't get that excited by watching fireworks, yet this meant so much more as the whole camaraderie of being with those from the hostel made this all the more special, being that we all were essentially strangers in a strange place. I was made to feel welcome from the start and those staying there and those who I had met back up with all got on brilliantly. The hostel was a bit of a shit tip but that didn't matter, the warning we received on the door of our dorm about the noise, smoking and drinking within the first forty-eight hours of my arrival only cemented everyone's resolve to party hard; it was a traveller's dream.

The midnight sky was adorned for the next ten minutes with brilliant flashes and sonic booms, as the various fireworks were sent in screaming streams high up above the famous harbour setting, and the revellers watched in awe with various '*OOOhs!*' and *AAAhs!*' at the differing displays. Then, as suddenly as it had started, it was over. Everyone began to disperse, heading to various pubs, clubs and parties and we were no different, where even though we weren't staying there, still went back to the hostel to party together on the rooftop for one last hurrah. Once again, time had slowly but surely moved on; so now I too needed to move on and was due to take my bus to Melbourne the following afternoon. Because, let's face it, there was no way I was getting up in the morning.

All Sorts of Carry On!

The bus to Melbourne left at approximately three p.m. I'd once again said my goodbyes to Joanne and Hailey and thanked them for their kindness in putting me up, as to enjoy the New Year celebrations in Sydney, and now was preparing myself for a fifteen-hour bus journey. I'd had a brilliant time and it left me wondering what else was in store. I wasn't sad or down about leaving because it was time to head for pastures new and had heard that Melbourne was a fantastic place with a different vibe to Sydney. Also, I had the chance to catch up with an old acquaintance.

I arrived in the early morning, and headed to the hostel, checked in and was given a now all-too-familiar shit tip of a room, with other people's stuff strewn all over the place. But I wasn't going to be in there much and it was only for few days before flying out. Due to the fact I didn't get much quality sleep on the bus, the bed was once again the only thing calling so I crashed for another couple of hours.

Melbourne was different to Sydney; it seemed somewhat more relaxed and less manic as I strolled around the city in the lovely sunshine, exploring the various sights and districts, including Federation Square, Southbank Promenade, the huge Queen Victoria Market which was at least the size of a football pitch, Carlton Gardens that harboured the exhibition centre and museum before heading down Smith Street at Fitzroy. I really liked it there, having a kind of bohemian feel to it, as the artisans would hang out in the cool-looking cafes, shops and bars, presenting a really laid-back ambience; compared to that of St Kilda, that I also liked but got the impression it was a lot more exclusive and expensive, where elite would want to hang out and be seen. Although not necessarily my scene, I did appreciate the various artworks and sculptures which adorned the shops that made them unique and stand out.

I'd had a couple of days wandering sort of aimlessly, achieving nothing, deciding to take it easy for a few days as there wasn't anything that I was desperate to do in particular here, except for one thing; I was really hopeful of meeting my mate Ben who lived in Melbourne, I had met him the year previous when in Canada, and we ended up travelling around together with a bunch of others for a couple of weeks. Unfortunately, though, he wasn't around during the New Year holiday, which was one of the reasons why I ended up staying in Sydney but was due back in town on the fourth, when I was due to fly to New Zealand. He had also kindly offered to take me on a road trip up the Great Ocean Road if we could sort out catching up.

Unfortunately, I never got chance to meet up with Jessie again, so that road trip didn't work out and I moved on. With this in mind, I couldn't resist, also coming all this way would be a crime if we never caught up, especially as we got on well, having had a riot together in Canada and Ben was the kind of guy who didn't take life or things too seriously and liked doing the same sort of stuff as me including; fishing, being scared shitless in dumb haunted houses and we both did our first bungee jump together in Ottawa; where beforehand we both nervously took the piss out of one another, while crapping ourselves prior to taking the elasticated plunge. For the record, I went first, so he had to jump or wouldn't be able to live with himself knowing a Pommy had one over on him. So it had to be done; I postponed my flight for a few days and on the fourth when he returned to Melbourne, we met up.

The other thing that we had in common; we both weren't shy about getting on the beer, which unsurprisingly was the first thing we did. He arrived at the hostel and we met in the bar, it was great seeing him again and looked just as I remembered; tanned, wavy dark hair and big daft grin. The banter just started almost instantaneously. He checked into the dorm where I'd reserved a place for him and we got straight on it. He suggested that we head up into Fitzroy to the bars there, as he knew the area and I'd patrolled the streets the days previous, liked it and was happy to go along with that idea. We proceeded to get wasted; the night wasn't the busiest but that didn't matter, because it was only a case of 'when' not 'if' before Ben was somehow challenged to a dance off and I knew what was coming; his signature trump card – when all else fails to impress – full on hand stand, legs in the air, bouncing around the dance floor. I was thankful because it could have been lot worse; as he had been known to dabble in amateur penis puppetry, using his knob to mimic watch strap around his wrist which was always disturbing and gross. We had a good time laughing while catching up despite unsuccessfully chatting to girls when playing pool. This wasn't surprising as by this point, we could hardly see the balls on the table let alone string any coherent words together.

The next morning, we were up around eight thirty a.m. and headed to Ben's place to grab some gear for the next few days on the road. Approaching a row of cars parked up, he asked, "See if ya can guess which is ma ride?"

I looked along the line as we walked, spotting a large 4x4 3.2 litre truck, with bull bars, the lot. "I sincerely hope this is it?" I enquired.

"Good guess!" was his reply.

I thought, *You beauty, we'll have no problems with this thing!* It wasn't that hard to guess. Ben really doesn't come across as the little run around or saloon sort, he worked for the fisheries agency in Australia and this thing could cart anything around, which included the hunting, fishing and camping gear that I knew he would have with him when out and about. Arriving at his place, I met his girlfriend Lottie who was really nice and we got sorted with the gear that we needed before freshening up. Ben decided to cook up a 3kg lobster he had caught. I hadn't seen anything like this; it was massive, almost filling the bottom of the cool box where it was being kept on ice in a docile state. Something which I appreciated because its size, dark armoured shell, protruding gnarled limbs and spikes made this thing looked pretty fucking menacing. Ben's hands were testimony to this as they were already cut to ribbons from the large jagged antenna that it had dug in from displeasure at being removed from its watery home in the ocean. The tail thrashed as Ben stuffed the large crustacean in a big metal pan and boiling water splashed perilously around the kitchen, as it was placed reluctantly into its own personal scalding hot tub to meet its maker. I honestly thought it was going to topple over during the mêlée that gradually saw the resistance subside, as the large creature succumbed. Being second nature, Ben wasn't too bothered. He just picked out another lobster of about 2kg from the fridge which he had also caught and cooked in a true 'here's one I prepared earlier' fashion. He decided we should take it to have for dinner later and ever the gent, left the other in Lottie's capable hands, in the pan, on the stove, as we finished packing and headed off.

The Great Ocean Road is a long winding road along the coastline of Victoria heading westwards towards Adelaide. The sea was a beautiful blue hue in the sunlight and the road stretched for miles ahead of us as it snaked along the contour of the hilled coastline. We stopped off at a lay by about

221

20m up from the rocks and where the waves were crashing below.

Ben asked, "Do you fancy doing a spot of lobster fishing?"

I was a bit apprehensive as the sea was choppy and the rocks looked less than inviting, and I knew absolutely nothing about catching lobsters.

Ben picked up on this. "Look, it will be okay, we'll get the snorkelling gear on, get out there and have a look around for half an hour and see if we can catch some," he said optimistically.

I thought, *What's the worst that could happen? Smashed to bits by the waves and rocks? Hands turned to that of Freddie Krueger by an irate lobster? Sod it, why not?* I said, "I don't know anything about catching a lobster, how to do it?"

"Don't worry about it. If you catch a lobster, I'll eat my fucking hat!" he confidently replied.

I laughed, figuring he more than probably had a point.

We headed down through the bushes on the steep hillside to the smoothed rock area below and started preparing. On with the wet suits, masks, snorkels and fins, we entered the rock pool formation to swim to the inlet and where the waves were breaking over the shallow rocks to the open sea. Just before we headed out, two lads in their early teens were spear fishing in the deep yet calmer pool where we were. They were with their families and Ben asked why they were in here and not out further; they said they wanted to go into the open sea but their parents had said 'no', as there was one older to go out with them.

Ben being Ben said, "Well, why don't ya come out with us? I'll look after ya. I've got my Pommy mate here; he'll be more trouble than you!" I thought, *Cheers, thanks for that. Cheeky bastard.* Again, though, he more than probably had a point. It was a really nice gesture and the lads went and asked their parents and returned all mask, snorkel and speared up, ready to go.

We set off swimming for the gap where the waves were breaking in between the rocks. As we approached, the current became more and more intense, but the instructions were clear; just keep swimming, and when you think you're through, keep swimming. The waves were quite hard to swim against, but being just below the surface of the water, we were missing the breaks, so it made it easier and from learning to dive I also knew the drill of what to do when I inevitably got a mouthful of salt water.

The water shallowed as we headed through the surf, the brown kelp waved frantically back and forth, all that was visible looking down in the torrent of white water. I just kept kicking as hard as I could, and I realised what Ben had meant when seemingly the pressure eased, but this was just a brief few seconds before another wave came crashing through and everything went white again, as the awesome weight of water tried to force us back. I was just as relentless, though, with my efforts, and eventually we made it out far enough into deeper open water where the waves weren't rising up stop us swimming forward. Settling on the calmer surface to find our bearings and each other, we all made it through OK as Ben reassuringly asked to confirm everyone was all right.

We set up a marker buoy and started peering down into the water to orientate ourselves; the lads were doing their own thing but close by. Ben headed straight down about 10m or so, looking under the rock shelves for the elusive lobsters and I followed. Well, sort of; unfortunately, I couldn't get down as far or stay down as long, due to the fact that he was easily more practiced and adept at holding his breath, so my excursions underwater were much briefer, that bit shallower and involved having to come up for air on a more regular basis. Still, there was plenty of fish to admire and swim about with while submerged, and the bright sun from above cut streams of light through the glistening blue water, highlighting the kelp and rocks. The one thing I did notice though, and it was hard not to, was how cold the Southern Ocean was. It was fucking freezing being out here, compared to being in shallow, calm water by a sandy beach and was thankful for the use of the wet suit.

After around twenty minutes or so of swimming around, we both met up, surfacing at the same time. Ben had only managed to find about two small crayfish (lobster) and due to the regulations had to put them back being undersize. Needless to say, having problems getting down and staying down, I never even found one never mind had the opportunity to take one. I realised now that his hat was looking pretty safe and wouldn't be an entrée. I started asking about the various types of fish there.

Ben said, "Tell ya what, I'll catch ya one."

Within seconds, he had borrowed the four-pronged spear that the lads were using and was gone. I watched though the water as he swam down and almost instantaneously jabbed the spikes at a passing fish and brought it up to the surface, where he then proceeded to tell us about a particular hamlet fish. The two lads and I sat in the water, bobbing up and down, listening to every word he was saying, and I have to admit he did know his stuff and it was really interesting and fascinating watching him. He was the proverbial fish out of water and you could tell that his job was his passion, where both work and pleasure were one and the same; an ideal that has to be part of any person's dream. Despite the merciless fish-spearing exercise to prove a point of education, this specimen apparently "tasted like shit", so was left for dead to be foraged upon by the rest of the ocean dwellers.

Feeling the cold after around half an hour, we decided to head in. The only matter now was the waves that would be carrying us. And we had to hit the small opening where we entered to safely get back or there would be trouble as waves crashed hard against the uninviting rocks everywhere else. Ben checked that the lads would be OK; then grabbing my hood as not to go off course, we swam back in. For the ten minutes that it took to get out, it was a fraction of that to get in, I could feel the waves pick us up as each one roared and rolled past. Each time, I expected to hit the rocky bottom as we lowered, again visibility was nil and honestly, I didn't have a clue what was happening or where we were. Despite all this, I didn't feel nervous; I was calm and just kept swimming, trying to concentrate on what I was doing and probably why I wasn't panicking in the uncontrollable thrashing white water all around us.

As expected, we quickly made it back through to the large rock pool and the calmer shallower water, safe and injury-free. Ben had guided us well and yes, I was relieved. But I was really glad that we went out, as this was a new experience and one many wouldn't get to do; actually hunting for lobster by hand. Granted, I was totally rubbish at it, only managing to catch a glimpse of some antenna sticking out from under a ledge on one of my brief excursions free diving down that Ben had shown me, but at least I got to have a go, doing something that never even occurred to me as an activity or imagined that I would do. I was really pleased and thanked Ben for the chance, where the danger factor and thrill of the conditions only seemed to sweeten the deal.

We packed up the gear and carried on to our evening destination. Passing through the beautiful town of Lorne and stopping to see wild koalas lazing in the trees, along the scenic coastline that was becoming a real joy as we chilled, listening to music, chatting and laughing. Arriving at Apollo Bay, we got our digs and headed to the beach to give us a chance to kick back, relax and occasionally mess around in the sea with the body board. Ben grabbed a quick snooze, recovering from the previous night; which was understandable because apart from terrorising lobsters, he had been up early and pretty much driving all day.

After our down time, we bought some chips and beer to have with our gourmet lobster, which I don't recall ever trying before; scoffing as we sat fishing for squid in the harbour. I'd never done this before either, but one thing I had done before, was catch fuck all. The signs were encouraging; there must have been squid there because there was black ink splattered all over the decking. But we struggled; I didn't doubt Ben's credentials what with the job, pictures of him on a fishing magazine front cover, let alone the tattered hands and I at least had an idea of what I was doing from fishing in various guises back in Britain. But nothing was happening. We ate our delicious feast and had few beers while peering down into the water to see the squid's arch nemesis; a huge stingray patrolling around beneath us, and a probable reasonable for not catching anything. People came over to talk about the fishing or lack of; where I couldn't stop laughing at Ben being halfway down the dock ladder, while they just nattered away to him oblivious that he was taking a piss. Enough was enough now, three hours down the line and still nothing. So we went to the pub.

The next day, we were up early and hastily on the road for nine a.m., when an hour down the road I realised I had forgotten my towel and sleeping bag. This was an annoying nuisance especially as I knew they were gone, because due to commitments we were not going back that way upon our return. But at least they weren't too expensive to replace, I wouldn't care, I'd once already had to quickly dash back remembering I had forgotten my trainers. We headed to our next and furthest destination point along the coast; the twelve apostles.

These were a collection of massive limestone columns, left standing along the shoreline due to the erosion of the cliffs over thousands of years and are a huge tourist draw. We made our way along the purpose-built trails over the cliff tops to get the best views and take photos with the other visitors. The weather on this particular day was overcast and drizzly, so unfortunately the snapshots didn't do the structures the justice of clear sun or better still an amazing sunset; yet, they looked really awesome and seemed to be defying physics as they towered hundreds of feet up from the sea. Some were large and more of a mound, others thinner and looked ready to topple any time, each though detailed with beautiful, layered, colourful rock that provided a safe haven for birds on the top. I wondered how long these would have taken to form? How long some had left before the relentless ocean would eventually claim them? And how spectacular it must be when they eventually collapsed, especially arches from the mainland crashing to the ground to leave one of these columns. I loved this being a big fan of natural wonders and was so pleased being given the chance to come and see these magnificent structures.

Now around midday, we then headed back, but this time we moved inland, cutting out Apollo Bay and the coast road and headed for the rainforest skywalk. This was a series of walkways within the forests which incorporated higher, large metal gangways, set 50ft up in the trees. This had been devised to give people a chance to spot wildlife in the lush vegetation, it reminded me very much of those at Taman Negara in Malaysia, but these were much sturdier, although there was some sway on the tallest tower platform which scaled to about a hundred feet high. The resort was for all ages with lots of information regarding the various creatures, plants and trees of the surrounding area, plus the chance to spot the many model dinosaurs scattered all over the trails and at extra cost an abseiling facility. This was good but not great, I thought I had already experienced better and was more for families, but it served a purpose adding something to the growing itinerary and killed a bit of time, which was exactly what happened on the way back; by taking the C159 that was the windiest road ever through the forest, leaving us unable to get over 20mph especially when stuck behind trucks and other traffic. The road though did pretty much lead us back to the picturesque coastal town of Lorne where we had passed the previous day and where we were going to spend the night, as Ben had arranged to meet up with a friend of his, who was also called Ben, from their time in university together as his parents had a place there.

As we had some time before we were to meet up with the other Ben, upon our arrival, we first went to the beach. The sun was now blazing so we chilled and I again spent time getting acquainted with the body board. Ben gave tips in spotting where the big rollers would be out back and the best timing for good clean ride on the breaking waves, in between checking out and beckoning some *chicas* in frilly bikinis to no avail. While at the beach, we noticed a couple of ambulances hastily go past and at the time we thought nothing of it. Unfortunately, when we got back into town, there was an obvious reason why. The main road through was closed off, because apparently a car had mounted the pavement, hit approximately eight people, some of whom were children, and ended up overturned down an embankment into a car park. We arrived to see the aftermath of the wreckage and the police investigation enquiries start as numerous injured had been taken to the hospital. This was awful news and you just wouldn't expect this type of thing to happen anywhere, never mind in such an idyllic place, but it does and did. I remember hoping that everyone affected was OK, as details at the time were still unclear.

We met up with Ben's (Ben's friend) family, his mum Fiona and dad Chaz. They were a really lovely couple and not to mention extremely hospitable and friendly, as they put us up in the guestroom, before we headed out to a friend of theirs' house situated on the seafront of the Great Ocean Road to have a barbeque of delicious kebabs. Not wanting to impose too much, Ben and I decided to head into town and have a couple of beers while checking out the nightlife. Hitting a roof top bar, we sat down at a large table where two girls were already, who then, almost instantaneously got up and left. We just looked at each other as if to say 'that was your fault!' even though we hadn't even opened our mouths or said anything to them. Momentarily, they then both returned and apologised, saying that their actions seemed incredibly rude. We laughed and said it was OK, and proceeded to chat with them, eventually realising they were the two girls in the frilly bikinis from earlier in the day. After a few laughs and drinks, it was kicking out time and they were heading back to their place, with no invite forthcoming, we said our goodbyes and for the third time in the space of about nine hours, we were binned off by the same two girls, quite the unwanted record.

It wasn't that much of a big deal due to the fact it was now midnight, and we had already made plans to meet back up with the others from the barbeque, who were up for a spot of night fishing off the pier to attempt to catch at least one squid. Ben had taken quite a lot of flak from his mate Ben, his dad Chaz and the others about what he hadn't been catching and the gauntlet was thrown down. He was determined to prove his ridiculers wrong, so we grabbed the gear and headed down to the pier. We found a pitch with the others and started fishing with jigs, to try and snag some elusive squid. An hour or two later, Chaz had managed to get ink on the deck by catching one and Ben had landed two, but not my mate Ben; he like me drew a blank again. Finishing the famous Aussie sledging was even more relentless as his scratch record continued, he wasn't a happy bunny.

We returned back to Ben's parents' house and had a night cap of whisky with some fresh crab and to really take the piss, some pickled squid before retiring for the evening, which was when I realised something else was missing.

My mobile phone! I knew exactly where it was; I had also left it in Apollo Bay, the last place I had it was on charge in the room and I knew I hadn't picked it up, fucking bastard. I couldn't believe it; well, I could; this was typical of me and my blasé attitude. Towel gone, sleeping bag gone and now mobile phone also gone. If I'd realised the phone was forgotten earlier, we could have gone back, as it wasn't too bad losing towel and sleeping bag, but the phone would have made a difference and now we definitely didn't have time to go and get it. Stupid idiot now I had to do without or get new one. Little did I realise at the time, although losing these things was annoying and frustrating, it was going to pale into insignificance with the problems I was about to encounter.

In the morning, we were presented with a lovely full breakfast prepared by Fiona, to ready us for our journey. We said our thanks and goodbyes to Ben and his family, and took the same route back to Melbourne. At Ben's place I grabbed the rest of my gear that hadn't been taken or forgotten and he drove me to the airport, where once again I was saying goodbye. After a whirlwind three days of activity and amazing fun, before I departed, I thanked him and vowed to meet up again sometime in the future.

My month over Christmas in Australia was now over, and it was a new year. I'd had a fabulous time. Especially as much of it was made up on a wing and a prayer, with some help from an eight-year-old out-of-date travel guide that I exchanged for my China and Malaysia guides in Brisbane that now seemed ages ago. I remembered at first arriving how everything felt odd being out of westernised countries for three months prior, everyone spoke the same language, the buildings were new and modern, with things harder to sort out over the busy holiday period, yet they just worked out for me, maybe I got lucky, it certainly felt that way. The cost of travelling had gone through the roof as it was just as expensive as back home, the weather was obviously much better but the things that I got up to created good character building scenarios, not to mention lasting memories. The best being though was the people that I had met who truly made the month special. Each and every one played their part in enhancing the experience and for this, I was exceptionally thankful. Continuously bumping into

Joanne and Hailey was a godsend and they helped make Christmas, plus I couldn't thank them enough for not having me sleeping rough over New Year; that was a true blessing and I was extremely grateful to them for helping me out. Ben was a legend; true to his word, from Canada, that if I ever showed up in Aus to give him a bell and he would show me about, which he didn't have to do, especially straight after New Year and people do say this type of thing yet they don't mean it or never follow through; but he did, at relatively short notice and we had a blast where all it really cost me was halving the petrol; which for the experience was a small price. One day, I would like to think that I could return the favour; especially if he fancies coming over to the UK, we could do a similar sort of thing or go watch England batter the Aussies at cricket, that shouldn't be a problem apart from maybe the weather. Ben though just seemed to encapsulate the Aussie perspective of being open, friendly and having relaxed attitude to life. I had experienced this in various guises from bus drivers, to hostel staff and more recently how welcome and looked after we both were by Ben's mate's family in Lorne. At times it seemed quite alien to me, as I'd perceive there may be more an element of mistrust in Britain, where it could be argued that it would take much more time to get to know someone, certainly before welcoming them to stay overnight in the family home and then be so open and generous; especially in this case to some random riff raff who just rocked up from the north of England.

We touched down in Auckland at around one thirty a.m. This time, having learnt my lesson, I filled out my goods declaration card properly. I got searched but there weren't any problems and I was through with minimal fuss. Buying a bus ticket to the city, I sat and waited as it was due about two thirty which came and went. I rechecked the time table; yep, two thirty in the afternoon. Fucking idiot; the first bus wasn't till six a.m. I thought it was a bit quiet. Rather than hanging around, "Taxi!"

I checked in early in the morning as there was a bed available, so essentially, I had two nights for one which was a bonus; but rather than use it, I was wide awake at silly o'clock in the a.m. so I headed out for a few beers. After a couple hours' sleep, I was up and about, using the information from the hostel to take a look around at various places, including Harbour Park that had some really interesting sculptures and to see the view from the sky tower which was on the way to the bus station, as I'd decided to leave the next day and not hang around, having realised I had cut my time shorter in NZ due to the extra days with Ben in Aus. Also, I had another prearranged meeting with an old acquaintance.

One thing was now starting to concern me; I was due to fly to the USA at the end of my month as part of my flight itinerary, then get connecting flights to South America. But back at the beginning of December, I had received an email from the travel company in the UK that I used to pre-book various projects such as the Thai Experience and my flights. This was the email that I received at the same time as Chloe's reply. I had opened it but not really paid much attention to what it was referencing, being more concerned about her words. I knew it was about visas so it was important. Although at the time I never realised the full impact of what it was and what was going to happen; but it was about to stop me dead in my tracks and change virtually all my plans and everything ahead.

I took the opportunity of a quieter day to read the email properly. Whilst away, I wasn't exactly keeping up with current affairs at home, let alone anywhere else in the world; but now part of the visa waiver programme to gain entry to the USA, which UK residents such as myself were permitted to use, called for pre-flight approval. This was called an ESTA and just a matter of filling in a quick online application, no problem; or so I thought.

Clicking onto the website, my heart sank. I just gazed at the screen reading but not quite believing what was in front of me. I had to double check it. Hands cupped together, supporting my face, as a physical indicator to something being wrong. Which it was; basically, it stated that anyone who had been arrested in their country of origin for certain criteria now had to apply for a visa. Essentially, I couldn't make the criteria for the ESTA application, having been arrested and issued with a caution by the police in the UK a few years prior and would now need an actual approved visa to continue on with my travels. I sat just staring at the screen, not knowing what to do. Initially, I contemplated lying and filling in the form. In the end, I couldn't do it as I had a horrible feeling it would turn around and bite me on the arse. So, I just left it. Now suitably worried, I had to think as I really did not know what I was going to do. All my plans and ideas for the next six months or so had been thrown into jeopardy. Making any towel, sleeping bag and phone worries seemly evaporate in an instant.

The next day, I made my short bus journey to a place called Bombay, where I was due to be picked up to meet with another friend. Brenda and I knew one another also from the time in Canada, from where, as part of the group travelling together, she also knew Ben. I was looking forward to meeting her, as I had been invited to her stepdad's 60th and step sister's 21st joint birthday party, and like Ben, I hadn't seen her since we travelled in Canada where she was like our mum keeping us in check when out and about. I didn't wait long before I was approached by an elderly fellow who introduced himself as Barry; Brenda's step dad. I jumped in the lorry which he was driving as he had a haulage firm and we headed off into the middle of nowhere to the ranch where they lived.

Upon arriving, I was introduced to everyone; mum, sisters, brother, friends the lot, as they were preparing feverishly for the party the next day. It all seemed really manic as they had made a real effort to make the day special. A marquee had been set up with full working bar, ribbons, balloons, tables and chairs the lot. Space wasn't an issue as there was green field and surrounding trees for miles, some people were even camping there. That evening, we all got together for the pre-party piss up.

The day of the party, I was woken by Brenda about at seven thirty, who was off to town and asking if I wanted to go. I asked if she didn't mind if I didn't as I'd stayed up later with her brother and friends and was a bit rough. The next thing, I was woken again by Brenda. It was about noon. I thought, *Oh shit!* I never had an alarm (lost phone) and had slept in, I felt really bad as the others had already started the set up and were working away feverishly; needless to say, I copped a fair amount of ribbing for my lazy-ass antics, with everyone else up around three hours or so prior. After apologising, I set about helping to sort of redeem myself.

When the party started in the early evening, people just seemed to turn up from everywhere. There was a fabulous spread on, that allowed everyone to eat like a king, with amazing pork and lamb barbeque and all the trimmings on offer. Brenda, her mum and sisters had really pulled out the stops, the drink was teeming from the bar and the music was pumping, it was great being out in the middle of the country, with a marquee and the stars above partying away. Everyone was really nice and friendly; although, I have to admit, at times I did struggle with what people were saying to me, as they spoke really fast and this was worse when inebriated, but people had the same problem with me so I could hardly complain and for a moment though, I let go and managed to forget about my visa predicament and enjoyed myself before crashing at about three a.m.

231

I redeemed myself the next morning by actually getting up at around nine, pretty much the same as everyone else, but still had the piss ripped out of me for the exploits of the day before. I wasn't getting off lightly. Never mind, I had thick skin so I could easily take the banter. There was a clean-up operation and we all chipped in, cumbersomely carrying our thick heads. After a late breakfast, Brenda gave me a lift back to Bombay to get my bus, as I had to keep moving to do all the things that I wanted and didn't want to impose too much. It was great to see her again too and the hospitality ethos in Australia clearly stretched to New Zealand as her family were just as welcoming, which was awesome, so I also took the opportunity to thank them for another great experience that a traveller wouldn't normally get. The only unfortunate thing was that I think the only time Brenda and I really had time to catch up was when we were in the car to the bus station.

Heading south through the centre of the North Island, my next destination was Rotorua. Whilst in Auckland, I had consulted a traveller bus service, which was a hop on, hop off bus specifically for those to travel on with set designated routes and destinations. I was contemplating using this as I was short of time with about three weeks to do everything I wanted, but I felt the price wasn't right and would be cheaper to do it on my own, especially with this visa problem pending that could prove costly to sort out. So, I essentially built my itinerary on the information that they had.

Rotorua was small, but did offer some cool things which I wanted to do. Unfortunately, the running around and late nights were taking their toll and I surfaced quite late at one p.m. So, I instantly started making moves. I visited the hot springs at the park as you entered the town. This was free to walk around to see the natural vents all over in the ground, where thick grey mud sloppily bubbled away as sulphurous gas and steam released from the earth, which subsequently caused the lake to harbour virtually no life and added a weird jade hue to the water, that both looked and smelled like something from another planet. Through being naturally polluted by the noxious gases this put paid to any notion of a cool, relaxing dip or swim; any idea of such a dangerous impossibility.

There was also a facility out of town to go Zorbing; or rather jump inside a large inflatable and tear arse down a big hill, like a human hamster ball. This was right up my street, getting rolled and flung about uncontrollably with minimal chance of injury, absolutely brilliant, couldn't wait. I arrived with the intention of doing the dry run; that involved being strapped in the ball and rolling down the steep hill straight to the bottom. One problem was when I got there, the only available activity was the wet Zorb; because the wind was too high for the straight dry Zorb (albeit seemed perfectly calm to me) so I now required some swim shorts that I didn't have with me. But I really wanted to do it so I paid and informed the staff I would return to complete the activity.

I had to wait longer than expected as I missed the bus back when I briefly went to the toilet. Eventually, another bus turned up. I headed back, got my swimmers and returned. On my arrival, both wet and dry activities were now on. I just thought, *Someone is taking the piss out of me.* I still decided to do the wet Zorb though, as those whom I had spoken to said it was more fun and lasted longer. Taken to the top of the winding course in a jeep, we waited for the ball to be moderately filled with water and then dived inside through the hole in a superman fashion. When ready, the ball was set rolling. I managed to stay in a fixed position and surf down the course for about five metres till I hit the first bend where it was game over, and was promptly flung around in my mobile washing machine for the net forty-five seconds or so, as the gravity-powered inflatable ball slalomed from left to right along the course. It was eventually stopped by the staff at the bottom, preventing it from careering out of control, causing untold mayhem. In the traditional sense of these activities, there was a company photographer taking the most unflattering photos of participants as they flopped back out of the hole; now a soggy mess, looking like some alien life form had just given birth.

The Zorb was good fun; but it was short and expensive for what it was, and apparently the dry run was even quicker, but I did enjoy it though. Later in the day, a less taxing activity finished off my time in Rotorua; I really wanted to get involved in some cultural activity so took it upon myself to visit a Maori experience resort that entailed an evening of education and activity. Maoris arrived via a small stream on traditional boats into the auditorium, where we watched them re-enacting the way in which a chief would be elected, how battle and dance routines were performed to the beat of drums that included the world famous Haka. This was brilliant, very informative and a good insight into the lives of the Maori. There was audience participation and it was laced with humour, all adding up to keep everyone enthralled. After we were then treated to a traditional Hangi meal;

that had been prepared by baking meat and potatoes using hot coals in a hole in the ground acting like an oven, and then offered as an all you could eat buffet, where the really succulent tender meat was mercilessly and appreciatively devoured by all. Suitably stuffed, we finished the experience by taking a short walk through the forest and vegetation on purpose-built trails, where a guide would explain how the Maori would use the components of the land for weapons, food and medicines; it wasn't so strange that they waited till dark to do this, as on the trail there was the opportunity to see the tiny glow worms that inhabited there, delicately highlighting the way, which topped off a stomping, yet enriching, informative and interesting evening.

Due to leave the next day, I had an easy night, to get some decent shut eye because what I had planned over the next couple of days, things were going to get interesting. Considering I was still stuck with this visa issue, if I'm honest, I was concentrating more on having a good time and kept putting off making a plan of exactly what I was going to do. One; because I was nervous about the prospects of what I *was* actually going to do and what *was* going to happen and two; also because I figured if I chilled and relaxed, the answers would come within these interesting times. Unwittingly, I didn't have to go anywhere or do anything in particular to have these interesting times intensified.

At a loose end, I called home. Dad answered and told me that everyone else was out; fair enough. No problem. But then he said that he had been meaning to have a word with me. I sensed the tone. I wasn't wrong. He proceeded to tell me that he and my mam now knew that I had been arrested and issued with a police caution. I just sat and thought, *Awe fucking hell, what next?*

This came about because I had a criminal record check done prior to leaving, so that I could be eligible to teach the children in Thailand. I was worried about it at the time when dealing with the travel company and explained the circumstances, as it was only a caution and nothing to do with harming kids or others. I was told it was fine, happy days no problem, so went ahead with the application, swanned off to the other side of the world and had a great time helping the children and Mah Lee in Thailand.

Unfortunately, both the company and I received a copy of my criminal record check; I received mine in September when I was away. And even more unfortunate was the fact that I was living at my parents prior to leaving and I'm named after my dad; so it went to their house and they opened it. There it was in black and white for my parents to see and in unfortunate circumstances find out how I had been in trouble with the law. Unhappy days; yes, problem.

I felt awful, knowing I had let them and myself down, and is something which I regret and am not proud of. Dad explained that my mam was upset when she opened it, and then somewhat understandably furious. And hearing about that was something which I felt worse about than the actual incident itself. I said that I had learnt my lesson, offered to explain myself and stated that I had beaten myself up over it a thousand times prior but had now put it behind me, forgiven myself and moved on, as there was absolutely nothing that I could do about it, much like them finding out. Although hurting my mam is the last thing that I ever want to do and was gutted I had. I was disappointed that they found out in such a way and that I never had the courage to tell them myself.

They had decided to mention it now as it was a new year and wanted to get it out in the open, which I appreciated. I found it odd that they never said anything earlier, I presume it was because I was having a good time and they didn't want to disrupt that or take time to divulge in the fact that there only son isn't as morally upstanding or clean cut as once thought. Strangely, I was glad it was out in the open. I hated the fact that I hadn't told them; it was a strange twist that it had come about now when I had this whole visa problem to deal with, which it was directly correlated to. I never mentioned the visa predicament at the time. I didn't see the point until I knew what was what. Dad and I finished on a good note, we chatted about what I'd been up to, what was happening back home and in closing, I said, "Speaking of not telling you things, I'll let you know now. I'm planning on jumping out of a plane in a few days - don't tell mam!"

I couldn't believe that they had kept this away from me for so long without mentioning it. I had called home every two–three weeks. The last time being when I was in Auckland and I had spoken to my mam, where I mentioned about meeting up with Ben and Brenda. She asked if I was also planning on catching up with Troy; an old friend from college and university, who had moved to New Zealand following his travels. Before I set off, I'd sent him an email but not had a reply. So, while on the phone my mam had passed on his mam's number to try get in touch with him.

After finishing talking to dad, I decided to ring Gia; Troy's mam.

Answering, I explained who I was and how I knew Troy. Her reply was a little surprising; "I know you! How are you? What are you up to?" she said with immediate recognition in her usual, uplifting, bubbly persona, yet quite shocked and surprised at the random phone call.

Proceeding to explain that I was in New Zealand and hoped to contact Troy only enhanced her excitement. She explained that he would be really chuffed with the chance of meeting up again, as he never got to see any of the old crowd any more, which was hardly surprising with him being on the other side of the planet. We chatted, having a quick catch up; it was easy talking to his mam as we had gotten on well when she and Larry – Troy's dad – both came to visit our student house when we all lived together at university and it was just like then, which was cool. I was informed not to bother ringing at the moment, as she had just got off the phone with him and he was on nights at work and tomorrow would be in bed, so I took his mobile number, intent on calling very soon.

Finishing, she said, "Look, I won't say anything to Troy so it's a surprise and just in case you don't get to meet up with him," which was fair enough, I thought.

I woke at ten thirty a.m. in the hostel and checked out at eleven a.m., some two hours late; the owner was less than impressed. My lack of alarm was fast becoming an issue, having to be up for things and being on the move, so I decided at the next opportunity to buy an alarm clock as it was cheaper than a new phone and the alarm was pretty much the only thing, I was using my phone for, as my UK sim wouldn't work and had to buy a local one make calls or send texts. I headed to the bus terminal and further south. Taupo was only a couple of hours away and I arrived on the bus with plenty of the day left and headed straight for the tourist information centre, deciding that it was now or never to do a skydive; so I booked it there and then for the following day. It was on. My first ever tandem skydive from 15000ft. This was something that I'd always wanted to do; I was nervously excited.

The rest of the day I spent wandering around Taupo, the day was overcast. But it still didn't take away the inherent beauty of the place; loads of shops, bars and restaurants, it was small enough to get around while offering a catalogue of things to do for the outdoors sort of person, not to mention the beautifully serene crystal-clear lake, which was huge in size, adorned by a spectacular array of white snow-capped mountains on the horizon. Taupo was my type of location, I liked it a lot. On the outskirts of town, I wandered by the river system that was fed from the lake, on purpose-built trail throughout the forest. Halfway along, there was a thermal spring churning out steaming hot water which followed a small channel to the river. As the two waters met, it offered a more ambient temperature. People bathed and I took the opportunity to put my feet in, more so out of curiosity just to see how hot the water would be, and let it sooth my skin for a few moments. I continued further, eventually making it to the Huka Falls, a massive raging torrent of water, caused by a narrowing channel from either embankment that literally squeezed the river funnelling it. The white water looked like what it was, incredibly dangerous and was hard to imagine anyone being able to ride the water in a kayak or the like, as it spewed out into a misty waterfall at the other end where the embankment again widened. I was pleased at the end of the day, having taken a bunch of scenic photos and walked about eight kilometres in total to prepare for the death-defying antics (hopefully) of the next day.

With this in mind, rightly, I had an easy evening with literally only a couple of beers and a movie; and also decided to ring Troy. He answered but with not quite the reaction I was expecting from someone whom I hadn't seen for well over seven years.

"Now then! Me mam said you were going to ring. In New Zealand, aren't ya?"

I started laughing, explaining what his mam had said and he said that she had rung him straight back and told him. So, any surprise was right out of the window. We chatted for a few minutes and agreed that I would make my way to his on the South Island; it had to be done. It had been so long and we always had a good laugh while at college and uni. I couldn't wait, so said that I was going to finish off on the North Island in the next couple of days and then make my way to his. Within moments, I had scrapped any ideas, plans or notions and was heading to Dunedin.

I still never had an alarm clock and was woken at seven thirty a.m. by my roommates who were getting up anyway around that time. I was told to ring in the morning for confirmation that the jump was on in case the conditions were adverse. With blue sky and not a cloud in sight, this didn't look very adverse to me and I wasn't wrong; it was party time in the sky. The mini-van arrived to pick me up and I was taken to the airbase.

Arriving, I saw I wasn't the only jumper. There were a few others. We picked which package we wanted, such as height, DVD, stills, t-shirt etc. and were then briefed. I had chosen to jump from 15000ft, the highest for a tandem with all extras chucked in. It cost $500 but figured it was my first jump; I was in a stunning location, so do it properly. Next, we were fitted with jump suits, harnesses, goggles and assigned a jump instructor, who we were to be attached to; mine, a cool Kiwi called Geoff, who was an engineer but did tandem skydives as a bit of fun on the side, as a hobby, nice thrilling work – if you can get it. He was really relaxed and friendly, helping put any nerves at ease as these were now starting to jangle a little at the prospect of what was ahead. Oddly, though, I didn't feel half as bad as I thought I would. Having a final briefing and presenting ourselves to the camera, we all boarded the plane in a pre-set order of those who were to jump, those at a lower altitude in last and going first.

There were approximately five pairs of people jumping, fifteen in total with each duo having a cameraman. So, the plane was crowded as we sat interlocked between the legs of one other, on either side of the fuselage. The plane engine roared and we gathered speed and took off. Gradually, we increased in elevation, climbing higher and higher in a circular motion, to get to the desired heights. The trees shrank away into oblivion, as they became undistinguishable patches of dark green against light green and the lake looked just like a blue cloth that had been laid across the land, and the mountains were now more visible and somewhat bigger as they became more majestically exposed. Suddenly, the door was opened as we reached 12000ft and the first lot of jumpers were all jettisoned. The noise was deafening as the wind rushed with gale force around the inside of the plane. Strangely, this sort of made the thought of jumping easier, as I now knew what to expect, with the noise and wind, but also emphasised very much now how real this all now was.

The door was again closed, causing a sudden lull in the wind and noise after the last of the jumpers had gone, and the plane continued to climb. We had a little more room to manoeuvre and Geoff asked if I was OK; but for a few butterflies I was good. The plane turned around and I saw one of the coolest things I'd ever seen. We were approaching 15000ft and the sky was radiant blue, impeccable conditions. I was told to look left out of the window and he pointed out a thin line which I could see; this was the west coast of the North Island. He then said to look out of the right-hand side, another thin line. This was the east coast of the island. I couldn't believe it;

I was looking at both the east and west coasts of the island by turning my head 180 degrees. Amazing. After the final pep talk, the door was opened again.

I was second last to jump, Geoff asked if I still wanted to go; I was ready. He said, "Good, because there's only one way down and the planes not an option!" We shuffled to the edge of the open hatch, and dangled my legs over the side. The violent wind grabbed the jump suit and the material flapped ferociously, it felt like we would be dragged out. I smiled for the camera, grabbed the harness by crossing my arms, tipped my head back and rolled out.

For a few second, I was totally disorientated as we somersaulted into position, plummeting to earth. But in what seemed like a matter of moments, I was flat facing the ground with arms out and legs raised. This was incredible, we cut through the air at approximately 200kph; both our weights combined were pretty much ideal for reaching top speed in free fall. Not that it felt that we were falling; it felt like we were flying, the wind roared past my ears and the noise was unbelievable. Our camera man had caught up, having hung onto the wing to film our exit from the plane. And like our diving video, the pre-requisite was to look cool, so I promptly started shaking his hand, some high fives, few dance moves, a spot of swimming and pulled out some good old-fashioned devil horn. Well, at the time I thought it was cool, plummeting to earth at that speed. I wasn't going to try posing and pouting, it could have been my last moments, so might as well have a bit of fun.

The time like us went fast, I looked down and the ground was a hell off a lot nearer now, things were distinguishable, the messing around for the camera had distracted me enough to forget about the effect that gravity was having and the pesky laws of physics wouldn't be denied. At around 4000ft and a minute of freefalling, the chute was released. We immediately slowed and got ragged into a vertical position as my body straightened with the sudden increase in resistance, that caused the straps to dig in around the groin, we fell for a few more seconds, before all of a sudden there was a final jolt as we came to an abrupt halt in the sky; when the parachute fully opened.

YES! Get in there, it was all good, we had done it, everything was OK, I was euphoric. Geoff then released a couple of straps to move my body away from his so he could pilot the parachute; I dropped down, falling about a foot – crapping myself in the process at the sudden release and not expecting it.

It had worked, I was safe, I was gonna be OK, any fretting over, fucking brilliant, *you beauty! I love you, physics, you're my best friend, giving me so much fun.* I just hung there in the air, some 4000ft up, absolutely thrilled. Relaxing, I just gazed out and admired the view on what was now an even more perfect day, as everything went to plan and I was alive. My chaffed fucked up groin suddenly not an issue any more. We circled around, gracefully descending through the atmosphere, all the while the earth grew larger and more apparent as we glided to destination terra firma, and some five minutes later we swooped down, raised my legs in preparation for our return to earth.

Our camera man was already on the ground in a field next to the hangar, to film us coming in for our landing; which I did with text book grace, skidding along on my arse. Back down, safe and sound, Geoff was chatting with the camera man and said a strange thing; he thought there was going to be a problem with the chute and was going to have to use the reserve, as the main seemed to tangle. I was oblivious. Honestly, at that moment I didn't care. I was down in one piece, had conquered one of my fears and done something which I had always wanted to do, especially as few years ago I never thought that I would have the bottle; now, it was done. I wasn't ecstatic and there wasn't any adrenaline that had been and gone. I was happy and content, extremely proud of myself. I had now joined the skydive club of been there done that. Ready at any given opportunity to brag unashamedly about my thrilling endeavours to the 'would never dare' brigade. I didn't know exactly if there was or wasn't a problem with the chute but it did seem to take a while from straightening up and slowing right down to actually coming to a stop, but I didn't know any better either. Regardless, there's always a chance things like that could happen and it added a bit more dramatic effect to an already death defying tale.

We returned to the hangar and watched the DVDs and collected our things, including our T-shirts, and then paid. I supposed it would be a bit of an insult if something went wrong and they'd charged you for it. Naturally, everyone else who took part was also buzzing; chatting enthusiastically about their particular jump. It was very cool to see so many elated and relieved faces. I finally thanked Geoff again for providing one of the most exhilarating experiences of my life before being whisked back via an uneventful boring old bus ride, to where we were staying.

It was now about ten a.m. in the morning and the rest of the day was my oyster, being wide awake after such a high octane start. I hired a bicycle and headed into town. I went and admired some people doing bungee, sunbathed by the lake and took a really invigorating and refreshing swim in its perfectly clear waters, and perused around the harbour at the boats moored there. I also sorted some things; I emailed Troy about my arrival in Dunedin, emailed the travel agency about my visa predicament, figuring that I needed some advice and equally as important, bought an alarm clock. The next day, I checked out on time and took the six-hour- or-so bus to wellington.

Getting to wellington late, I never really achieved anything except that I had received a reply from the travel company and they suggested doing the honest thing and not trying to blag it and see if I could get a visa. Which I sort of knew was inevitable, so it didn't really help me out. One thing I did know was that if I was going to get this sorted, it would have to be soon. So this meant it was going to be a brief visit to Wellington; in, look around, out. I was churning up the miles. I checked out the next morning, put my stuff in storage and had the full day exploring before my evening ferry.

Visiting the impressive Te Papa museum, it had interactive exhibits of earthquakes and tsunamis where patrons could learn about the incredible forces that Mother Nature can wreak and brought home a realisation of how devastating they could be; luckily, having never experienced one of these personally. There was giant squid of about 15ft preserved in a huge glass case that had been captured from the deep, Maori artefacts and art works. I was fascinated and spent about three hours in there before realising the time and moving on. I headed to the harbour for a look around and came across an exhibition of Leonardo Da Vinci inventions that had been made into working replicas from the original drawings.

I had to go in; I was a huge fan of Da Vinci. A true genius in every sense of the word; excelling as artist, anatomist, scientist, engineer and inventor to name but few; you name it he seemed to be a forerunner in virtually every discipline that was the renaissance. The word 'genius' seems to get bound around far too free and easy these days; usually by people seriously underqualified to be deciding who is a 'genius'. Therefore; those who are labelled 'genius' many in my opinion are found wanting, and I consider most to be an insult to any real multi-talented forward thinking pioneer. Da Vinci's work is generally regarded as being four hundred years before his time; devising inventions like flying machines when people probably thought the earth was flat (Some people now still do! I can only laugh at these 'geniuses'). This exhibit proved just how much of an amazing innovator he was with other working replicas of water pumps, bridges, armoured vehicles and parachutes using just the basic materials at his disposal. It was fascinating and I was enthralled, just as much as the countless others who were in there.

I continued in culture vulture mode, by taking the tram to the top of the hill to get a great panoramic view overlooking the city, where then I spent the rest of the afternoon getting lost, wandering around the steep trails and paths of the botanical gardens, admiring countless sculptured artworks amid the beautiful floral and green surroundings. I'd had another brilliant and educational day to tire me out before heading back to the hostel to prepare for twenty hours or so of travelling that now lay ahead. Regardless of this, I was excited because I was sure it would be worth it.

Bak 2 Skool and the Winning Combinations

I hadn't planned on visiting Dunedin; the city located in the south-east corner of the South Island. Troy lived there and kindly offered to put me up for a few days, so that's where I headed. I was only going to charge around the South Island at breakneck speed and didn't really know exactly where I was going to go anyway. Queenstown was definitely on the agenda, but that was about it. One thing was for certain; I was going to need time to sort out this visa problem to the USA. But I was really excited about seeing my mate again; so decided to head straight to his and hopefully arrange some form of solution.

I arrived after a night on the ferry from Wellington to Picton and slept on the floor of the terminal whilst waiting for a bus to get me through to Christchurch; after a two-hour stopover there, I had a connecting bus to Dunedin, arriving around six thirty in the evening.

Troy was waiting for me at the bus stop. I recognised him instantly and he me; we obviously hadn't changed much and that extended to our behaviour; as I did the honourable thing of banging on the window, pointing, laughing and making a wanker gesture at him, which he just started laughing at. It had been the best part of eight years since I had seen him last; he had come over to the UK with his then girlfriend Jen who was also the mother of his daughter. Getting off the bus, it was brilliant to see him again; forgetting any aches and pains from long hours of travel, I was made up we had gotten in touch. We had a brief chat before jumping in the car to head back to his place. There was only one thing for it; into town and on the lash.

The town was eerily quiet; few cars and not many people milling around. I found this odd. Troy explained that Dunedin had a large student populous, but it was January and they were all away on summer holidays and not due back till beginning of February. He should know as he now worked as a fireman there, because apparently it was complete chaos when they returned; having call outs every evening for a settee fire or something alike that they would inevitably start. This was just the tip of the information iceberg, as we chatted for ages about his job, Dunedin, moving to New Zealand, what happened with him and Jen, the fact that he was now a dad with a young girl, living with another woman who had a daughter herself too and how things had totally changed for him. Obviously, he was curious about my escapades, so was harping on about why I was travelling, where I'd been and what I'd done. The old bullshit banter flowed and it certainly didn't seem or feel like we hadn't seen each other for those years while being on either side of the planet. This only increased more reminiscing about the times at college and university, when we started with the 'remember when' stories. "Oh! Shit yeah!" and the "fucking hell, I forgot all about that!", "what are so and so up to" and generally ended with us roaring with laughter about previous exploits and people past.

The next morning, we were up early; Troy's place was situated in a residential area up a steep hill on the outskirts of the city so it already had an excellent view of the urban sprawl, the harbour and peninsula from the kitchen window and balcony. It was quiet and peaceful up high with a cooling summer breeze. The rest of the family had stayed out overnight and the tranquillity was soon broken as the flock arrived back at the nest. I met Helen who was really friendly and welcomed me to their home. I thanked her for letting me stay and she said it was no problem; which it certainly wasn't for me, as I had the guestroom downstairs with a large double bed, small lounge and own bathroom and, frankly, was an unbelievable creature comfort. I thought that she was lovely and a very warm, nice, person. Troy was a lucky man. I was then introduced to Aria who was Troy's daughter, and to the somewhat quieter Frankie; Helen's daughter.

We then proceeded with the getting-to-know-you chit chat. Troy had obviously told Helen quite a lot about me and why some random for the other side of the world was coming for a visit. And I also explained my predicament; Troy and Helen were only too willing to help saying that I could use the Internet and phone whenever needed. I was exceptionally thankful. They also informed me that there was a branch in town of the company that was used to book my flights through. This all was a god-sent gift and great news; not only having a comfortable base among friends to sort this out, but I could speak to someone directly about my flights and make necessary changes with a person face to face should the need arise.

First thing was that I managed to get in touch with the US embassy, which happened to be back in Auckland. I was informed that I would need a visa, no surprise; but to obtain one, I would have to go there in person with an appointment. So, I couldn't just turn up anyway whilst I was in the vicinity. Not that it would have done me much good, as the amount of paperwork I had to produce to obtain a visa was ridiculous, to the point that you would think I was trying to emigrate; they wanted ID, bank statements, references, two application forms filled out to exact criteria and other paperwork, not to mention the fee of around two hundred and fifty dollars which would not be refunded should the application not be successful. This wasn't looking good. I was at the other end of the country, didn't have an appointment and had zero chance of getting any of the paperwork or documents they needed. I decided there and then that I simply wasn't going to the USA, and any plans to do so were now officially dead in the water.

This left me in a slight predicament. I had to take my next flight from New Zealand to Los Angeles, but not having a visa I wouldn't be allowed on the plane; but if I missed the flight, that would render the rest of my flights null and void and leave me stranded in New Zealand. I also had extra flights booked from LA into South America that now I couldn't take and a hotel reservation in LA that I didn't need. Also, to top it all off, I had to be in Ecuador in ten days' time for the first of February, because I had things already booked there; that were paid for at great expense back in the UK. It's fair to say things could have been better.

But they could have been much worse too. I was with friends, in a lovely home, with amenities at my disposal; the weather was good, some money to play with, my passport and my health. I hadn't come this far to be stopped now. I had passed worrying, even though leaving it too long had put the pressure on to re-organise things, especially with time being short. Things were exciting, made all the more so by them being out of my control, in this case, posthumously of my own doing. This, as I was fast learning, was what travelling was all about as I had already experienced, but certainly not of this magnitude. Yet, this was what I wanted; excitement, adventure were what I yearned for. Although I never once envisaged this, but I was now presented with a good test of resolve, so I was determined to get these issues sorted. I had learnt so much already about self-determination and resilience. In short, I decided there and then that there was no way I was going to stop. I had got to here; yes, any plans for the North America were scuppered, so what? I thought, *Right, fuck this! I'll make new plans.*

Next point of call was in town. Luckily, I'd been booked through a global company with offices worldwide, and more luckily, I now had a branch on my doorstep. Heading in, I explained my predicament. They immediately cancelled my Auckland to LA flight and the other remaining flight from New York back to the UK, as I definitely couldn't use them. Due to the nature of these flight packages, the price paid was calculated on the amount of miles you are travelling. So I was only able to be offered equal to what I already had and where the flight paths go to. Flights didn't go from Auckland direct to Quito in Ecuador, the nearest I could get to was Santiago in Chile. At least, I was on the right continent. But I still needed to get back to the UK. The only plausible option due to distance now was to leave from Rio de Janeiro. I accepted the flight changes. That was it; the rest of my time travelling was to be now spent wandering around South America for potentially the next six months.

After a bit of contemplation and trying to get my head around what was happening, this threw up a couple of silver linings. Firstly, I was going to learn Spanish and now would have ample opportunity to continue to learn and practise as I was to be in the environment much longer; therefore, I had the opportunity to become more fluent. I had toyed with the thought about possibly heading down to Mexico upon my return to LA to continue practicing the Spanish that I was going to learn. Now Mexico was not realistically going to happen, but Spanish would now be prevalent in any of the countries which I wished to visit except, of course, for Brazil. Also, I was pretty sure the cost of living and travel would be a hell of a lot cheaper than in North America; therefore, I would be able to travel for a longer duration of time before the funds ran low, or it would get to 21 August, the last day my return flight could be taken, a year later from setting off.

If I was serious about having a full travel experience, wanted a challenge, experience new cultures, thinking on my feet, making it up as I went along, well, I now had it. Call it circumstance, call it fate, or whatever; essentially, life and circumstance dealt a hand and said 'You want it? Well, sort this out and you can have it. By the way, you have ten days to prepare.' With everything that had happened, I called it fate, and fate had dictated this was how my travelling adventure was to be defined and if it was exciting before, it had now just taken some drugs and hit the overdrive button.

I had to pay a rescheduling fee for the flights, dates could be changed which I had already done before, but not destinations; that was £200. Also, I still had to get to Quito so I booked a flight from Santiago in Chile to

Quito in Ecuador to arrive on 31 January to be in time, leaving me two days in Santiago; another £500. £700 total to sort everything out; *ouch*. But I was sorted that was the main thing. I was ecstatic. I was finally on the move. Some other good news was managing to cancel the hotel in LA, that cost me nothing but time on the net. Also, even better involved the extra flights booked to get me from LA into South America and back again; these were through a separate online company and when I explained to them that I needed to cancel the flights because of circumstances out of my control, I got a full refund with no fuss or hassle that left me astounded, yet again though, thankful.

Done and dusted, I could move on. Happiness radiated as the pressure valve of tension had been opened and I could feel anxiety alleviate from my whole being that I actually felt lighter; mentally, physically and spiritually that seemed to put a new vigour and spring in my step. I wasn't even thinking about what or where lay ahead. The problem was solved, that was the main thing. I felt like the seasick who found dry land, a defendant judged not guilty or a captive released and the wash of relief was a more exhilarating, powerful sensation than any drug could provide.

Despite my parents knowing about my arrest, they didn't know about the subsequent consequences of not being able to obtain a visa or entry to the USA. I decided to call home and tell them. My mam answered and I explained what had happened. The conversation went really well as I revealed the full facts. Mam was understanding and agreed with my course of action, adopting a what's done is done attitude and now move on; figuratively and now literally the case for me. I knew I had hurt and disappointed her, but there was no point hiding from it now. We chatted and she suggested that I could come home after finishing my planned events in South America. This wasn't surprising; considering that while away, I knew she had worried about my wellbeing, what was happening and what I was doing. Unfortunately, I had other ideas. I now wanted to make the most of the opportunity; visit other countries which prior I wasn't going to get the chance to see, do some more worthwhile activities, and now have a true adventure with a book of blank pages, or at least the vast majority. But I had to ask a favour, I mentioned the cost of rescheduling and asked if I should need it, would my parents later lend me the money, as I could repay them from my tied-up savings when I returned.

She said, "I'll pay the money into your account tomorrow."

This was an amazing help and although I didn't need the money straightaway, I gratefully accepted, giving me one less thing to worry about as £700 was a chunk out of my reserves and the flight money I got back was in no way going to match or cover this; plus, I was still going to have to reschedule part of those flights as I still needed to get elsewhere in South America. I thought about everything that had happened and really brought home how lucky I was to have such loving, understanding, supportive parents and emphasised how unreserved this was. I wrote them a long email, explaining my gratitude, why I was travelling and apologised for letting them down.

Amid the emails, phone calls and back and forth into town, I actually got to appreciate some of the sights of Dunedin. We headed out to the surrounding area and I was taken up to the hills, where on a blustery day the wind whipped hard looking down on the city. We visited some bunkers-cum-gun turrets that had been placed as protection during World War 2, but were now dilapidated, graffiti-laden, trash strewn hovels, still nevertheless were interesting to see, not realising the geographical extent which the war reached as they perched in prime vantage point, atop a marvellous view over the beautiful blue ocean below. I then got to see the ocean at closer quarters one morning down at the beach; where the kids revelled in the water more than the adults, who were happier to spectate basking in the considerably warmer sun to the sharp contrasting freezing cold sea. This was rectified later at the local pool where Troy and I appreciated the warmer water and slides far more, entertaining the girls by jumping high off the boards, doing flips, dives, bombing, splashing water everywhere and generally carrying on like big kids; the real kids were really impressed with this and egged us on relentlessly. Not that it took much.

I was still hopeful of visiting Queenstown. Troy was off work over the weekend and been given a pass out, so we headed for a bit of a boys jolly getting out of the way of the family. Especially after a rowdy night in, where we made a little slash way too much noise. We drove through the mountains, passing numerous rivers and lakes, which provided stunning picturesque scenery and it was not hard to realise why this would make for many a stunning backdrop in the movies. After about four hours, we arrived in Queenstown; a popular and pleasant little town on beautiful Lake Wakatipu shrouded by more snow-capped mountains. Queenstown is a mecca for those visiting New Zealand and especially adrenaline junkies and seemed to offer so much to do; AJ Hackett introduced the world to the very first bungee jump here, there was skydiving over the majestic scenery, jet boating on the lake and white water rafting to name but a few. Our activities though were predominantly inside the bars. One thing was apparent, due to the popularity of the place and it being a tourist trap, it was expensive so this put paid to any ideas of bungee jumping. Not only that but considering the money I had just spent on flights and the small fortune over the last two months in Australia and New Zealand. I didn't want to be seen taking the piss somewhat, by spending money frivolously, frittering it away with more thrill seeking, especially having just completed my skydive.

Thing was, just being here in Queenstown itself was proving nearly very costly anyway; not only with the tourist prices, but because tourists themselves attract thieves and I was nearly pick-pocketed, only stopped by Troy turning round to notice someone trying take my wallet out of my back pocket. Then in the hostel after a few beers, I got up in the dark to go to the toilet, tripped over and fell face-first against the corner edge of a protruding wall; that hurt like hell. I was so lucky not to end up in hospital as my full face fall never broke the skin let alone any bone, and amazingly only left minimal bruising and slight swelling on my cheekbone and forehead for a few days after.

We did manage to head up to the top of the mountain on the cable car, to appreciate the stunning view of other surrounding precipices shrouding the fabulous blue lake, witnessing the now tiny town from above and its minuscule inhabitants scurrying around. Before also having a go on the cart track where we raced down against each other with reckless abandon, Troy winning each time. He had about 3st (42lbs) extra weight than me and therefore more mass and gravitational pull, helping propel him down the hill faster; my excuse. Heading back, we stopped off and visited Arrowtown; a small but beautiful little place which was formed as part of the gold rush some 150 years previous, it was still possible to pan for gold there, down by the river. But we decided against trying to strike it rich, our short time was hardly likely to yield the bountiful gold nuggets required for any retirement plan. The place was enchanting as the shops and buildings were made of wood and retained the charming old architecture of days past, and learnt about the Chinese miner settlements and the harsh conditions that they had to endure to earn a living there; where, like us, they had scant hope of striking it rich.

Our Queenstown visit only lasted literally one day and two nights. It was a really nice picturesque place and any other time maybe I would've hung around a little longer, but Troy had to get back. Nevertheless, I was just happy to actually manage to visit the place, with a good mate that made the time that much better. I did leave feeling maybe I missed out doing at least one of the famous activities, but under the circumstances I never regretted it. This was born out of the fact that I was in a situation where many future set plans and ideas were torn up and thrown into complete disarray. They needed sorting and reorganising in a very short space of time. This was achieved but only possible with the kindness and help of good friends and family, and I simply couldn't have done this so easily or readily without their assistance. From this alone, I felt like I was winning and left me with a sensation that I had nothing to prove, as all the adrenaline and stress had been used on this rather than in any duel with gravity.

On our return, I had three days left before I was to fly to Santiago, so it was obvious that I wasn't going to get to do much else. I still had the length of the country to cover to get my flight to South America, and hadn't been to buy the supplies that I needed having now run short of a few things. I decided to fly back to Auckland rather than spend the time on a bus, as it just made life easier and Troy and Helen said that it was still OK to stay, this allowed time for buying travel essentials like mosquito spray, sun lotion, painkillers, new shades, shit tablets and as I was heading to a completely different continent, I bit the bullet and bought a travel guide.

So far, I had coped by using a guide to Australia 2000 and two good, but not very comprehensive guides that covered Beijing, Shanghai and Malaysia. The rest of my travels I had pretty much blagged my way through without having any information at hand. I now really didn't have much of a clue where I was going and what I was doing; especially after my pre-planned events were finished. So, I thought it best to invest in a guidebook and could read up on what was potentially in store and help prepare. This would provide a good safety blanket for information, hints and tips. Rather than turning up at an unknown (to me) continent blind. It added a couple more pounds (lbs) and being quite big, took up valuable real estate in my already jam-packed bag; but I knew it would be a worthwhile investment.

Before I left, Troy arranged a spot of fishing off the tip of the peninsula, where he landed two and I caught sod all; again. This time, I'm going to blame the seals that were there, scaring off the big fish I was about to catch.

250

It was really cool looking down watching them dart about in the water with incredibly nimble agility, occasionally popping their heads out of the water to have a breath and brief look about to see what's happening on the surface, before seemingly giving me 'the finger' and ducking back under to scare off my catch, but nevertheless a privilege to see beautiful carefree creatures in the wild.

Quickly, the time came round for me to leave, I had been at Troy's for about a week with the couple of days in Queenstown. My flight to Auckland was from Christchurch so I took the bus there. I left on the evening having eaten at the fire station with Troy; where again like a big kid, I got to have a look and play inside the fire engine, being shown what all the various buttons and things were for. I bought a gift to say thanks for the real kindness and hospitality that he and Helen had shown. I'd had a really great time staying there, especially at such short notice and the fact that they let me use the house as I would at home, with Internet, phone, laundry at my disposal and also feeding me. It was fantastic catching up with an old friend whom I hadn't seen in years and meeting his new family. I was truly grateful. It would have been so much more of a struggle to sort things out if it wasn't for them and they really helped me out and made things that much easier. It was amazing the assistance they offered and one day I really hope that I can repay the favour in some way, shape or form as it would never be forgotten.

In traditional fashion, I fell asleep on the bus to Christchurch and realised I had missed the stop for the airport and had to pay $30 for a taxi back; another fine performance. I eventually took my flight to Auckland, safe in the knowledge I was landing where I needed to be before leaving the country. Waiting at the airport allowed time for reflection about the time that I had had in New Zealand. I charged through the country at what seemed breakneck speed; hastily doing this, that and the other, but oddly didn't have many if any regrets. I had managed to complete my tandem parachute jump and would remember that always by finally overcoming fears and achieving a personal goal. But I also got immersed in some of the culture, which I also wanted to do as much as the exhilarating stuff. I witnessed beautiful scenery from gorgeous snow-capped mountains to lush green forests and moon-like landscapes, the natives were fantastic and again I met with old friends who showed kindness beyond compare and made me want to behave in such a manner. It was now blatantly obvious why so many people come here to travel and love it, some not leaving; Troy being the example, who couldn't say enough positive things about the place. It was plain to see why; he had carved out a life for himself, with a good job, fantastic partner and beautiful children. It had been hard work, but he was now settled and doing well. I was exceptionally pleased for him, as he is a top bloke, who many years earlier took a chance and went travelling and his destiny unfolded. Despite initial early hardships of not being able to work which he told me about; it was now paying off as he looked to a bright future with Helen and the girls. I'll take this opportunity to wish them all the best.

Granted, I didn't get to do some of the things which I had wanted; a bit of adrenaline-fuelled activity in Queenstown which many including myself would've thought was an obvious given. Nor see the glaciers or other places New Zealand had to offer. Travel plans and itinerary having to be changed and reconfigured was a big problem, so I ended up rationalising that the country isn't going anywhere and left me with the excuse that I would definitely have to return at some point in the future. It was arguably the most difficult and stressful time travelling, as the visa debacle caused a real headache. The time spent had been shorter than what was originally planned, with changing flights, and to say things hadn't quite gone to plan was putting it mildly. But what did I expect? Lots of things hadn't gone to plan so far, some of its circumstance, some of it my own doing, but I had dealt with everything that had been thrown up so far and I was still in one piece. I was moving on, I felt like the experiences and adventure I was craving had definitely been thrust upon me, but I was starting to realise that these were going to come in various guises, both good and bad and regardless of what it was, they both had to be dealt with in the same manner – positive and proactive – if I wanted to learn and grow from them.

Now I was sure South America was going to be no different. I was excited about what the future months had in store and realised now that I was more than ready to tackle such a challenge with the majority of my time being an open book. I cannot lie by saying that I wasn't a little nervous about the prospect of being in South America due to things that I had heard, read and seen on TV, plus starting all over in a foreign-speaking country, with different culture and customs. But I couldn't help but wonder if there was a reason for all of this; was I supposed to come here? But that would've been like saying, was there a reason for everything that had happened so far on my travels? And, therefore, was there a reason for everything that had happened so far in my life? Thinking about this too much though would subsequently send my brain in to meltdown, so I decided to just take a deep breath, hold on tight and enjoy the ride.

The sun was absolutely blazing when I arrived in Santiago. It was 30°C plus. One thing dawned on me in the taxi to the hostel; I had crossed the International Date Line and it was Thursday, the 29th again; *Groundhog Day*. I thought; *Get the lottery on – it's in the bag!* Unsurprisingly, there was no time for this as I was completely knackered. Yet I felt like I'd slept pretty much all the way on the plane, also upon landing, I noticed that my feet and ankles had swollen to twice the size. Normally, a person might freak out about this scary phenomenon, but rightly or wrongly, I was not bothered about it in the slightest, being so tired. It didn't hurt, so I thought, *Fuck it.* I got to the hostel and promptly passed out, any plans I had for the day which mainly involved looking around were scratched. I was suffering from twelve-hour flight and the fact that since Dunedin; I'd been travelling in total for the best part of thirty-six hours. I was completely jet lagged, which also doubled up as rhyming slang for my state of being.

I woke in the evening; it was dark but still warm and humid. The hostel was a large old colonial-style building. I wandered outside into the back garden and decided to have a beer at the bar. Problem was, I decided to have more than one and ending up having a lot and got completely pissed. It must have been gone two before I eventually went back to bed in the dorm, but honestly, I can't remember. I woke the next day and looked at my clock, it was ten past twelve; then seemingly in an instant, the next thing I looked and it was six o'clock, and I was still wrecked, barely had the energy to lift may head off the pillow. Then the same again; this time it was now nine o'clock. I had missed the full day sleeping off a jet-lagged hangover. I couldn't believe I had wasted the full day!

I ventured out, people were talking to me who I barely recognised, saying, "Good night last night, wasn't it?"

I replied, "Err, yeah! Was it?" with a confused 'how do I know you?' look on my face.

Amazingly, I still managed to get some sleep and woke the next morning at eleven thirty a.m. I felt great, bright-eyed, raring to go and full of energy. Also, I had spent that much time in a supine position that my feet and ankles had now returned to their original size. I sorted out my things and prepared to go to the airport. I had been in Santiago for nearly two full days and achieved absolutely fuck all. The furthest I ventured was to look in the garage across the road outside to see if they had anything to eat, which was a no. I was disappointed with myself for not making more of an effort, I wasn't sure when I was going to be back and had missed an opportunity. Unfortunately, not the getting pissed opportunity which had done me no favours whatsoever. I headed back to the airport to catch my connecting flight to Ecuador.

In the taxi, a few things were now apparent and I was noticing much more. I was in a completely different environment; firstly, my English didn't hold much sway, and secondly, I couldn't get my head around how much the pesos were worth. The buildings were old, some decrepit and rundown, the sidewalks were unclean and damaged, rubbish was littered everywhere, graffiti adorned most open spaces on buildings and structures, and there was smog, lots of it. This was a far cry from the last two months or so in clean, well-kept Australia and New Zealand. It was immediately obvious that I was now back in a developing country, and it reminded me somewhat of the first time that I had visited Thailand some seven years prior. Interestingly, by comparing both instances though it didn't seem that it was anything strange.

At the airport, I had a meal and it was hard work eating it, not because it wasn't very nice, it was fine but simply because I now hadn't eaten since I got to Auckland some three days prior. My stomach had shrunk and body surviving off its reserves. It was crazy. I had gone onto auto-pilot and forgot or hadn't bothered to eat, apart from a bag of crisps and beer calories. And that was my short and brief experience of Santiago, I'm afraid to say. I figured I would at least accomplish something. Whatever that may be, but sadly now it would have to wait till another time.

The flight to Quito, the capital of Ecuador was approximately five hours with stop-over in Ecuador's largest city Guayaquil. Approaching, there were dark black clouds harbouring an electrical storm that made our descent here somewhat squeaky bum time, as the plane bounced and dipped erratically before we came in to land. Thankfully, we did safely and everything was OK. After dropping off and picking up other passengers here, we continued on to our final destination.

I was now to be based in Quito for four weeks, where I was due to spend the duration at Spanish school. I had booked this back in the UK so it was an already pre-planned activity that I was to participate in. This was for a few reasons: I didn't want to just spend my time partying and going on excursions or activities, which it seemed I had already done in abundance; I wanted to try and do something educational so learning another language seemed to fit this ideal, plus I had already studied Spanish to GCSE level at school therefore already – albeit some seventeen years prior – had a very basic understanding. Also, learning a language was vocational and fit in nicely with my love of travel, and I felt it very important to at least try learn a foreign language – to aid in bridging the gap between cultures and show some respect to other people, feeling it rather shameful to rely on other nationalities to learn English just because most of the modern world seems to speak it. With all this in mind, the next four weeks I was to undertake with my newly acquired extended stay in South America now seemed a very shrewd investment.

It was already dark when we landed. I was collected from the airport by a representative who was acting on behalf of the travel company here in Ecuador and they arranged for me to be dropped off where I was going to be living for the next four weeks. This was at a home stay, living with an Ecuadorian family. It was paid for inclusive of the Spanish lessons, with two meals per day also thrown in. So not only was I saving by not having to pay for accommodation, but food as well. And now I had the opportunity to witness what it would be like to live with a regular family, in another country, and experience their culture and customs first-hand; that created an engaging and exciting prospect ahead.

It was about nine p.m. when I arrived, a large set of steel gates and high walls barricaded off a porched area of a semi-detached three-storey house. I was met by Hector; the owner's grandson who welcomed me in. I chatted with him for a while; the actual lady whose house it was and my contact for staying there was out, as was everyone else. He spoke good English and he showed me where we were on the map, due to it being dark and me not being able to witness any of the surrounding landmarks upon my arrival, and pointed out various places of interest to visit, that happened to be mainly bars. Also, he warned me about certain areas where muggers operated; something I had read countless times whilst swotting up with my guidebook and now having a local verifying left me a little disconcerted. It was getting late and with no one else around, I decided to chill in my room, that I was pleasantly surprised with being large, having a double bed, TV and ensuite bathroom which was great; until I took a shower that had an electric coil element shower head; this heated the water before cascading down and when I went to turn off the water, I got an electric shock from the metal tap. Now I'm no electrician, but I do know that water and electricity don't mix; not exactly a winning combination.

In the early hours, I eventually fell asleep; which was poor at best, waking numerous times. Mid-morning, around nine a.m., I made my way into the living quarters; which was decorated with elaborate furniture and laden with ornaments, trinkets and pictures of nearest and dearest. I met my hostess, Marcia; a lovely elderly lady. She also spoke to a good standard of English, we chatted and she told me about the house and the fact that her immediate family lived in the flat upstairs; including her daughter, son-in-law and grandchildren. This turned out to be the norm and nothing unusual for this part of the world, as it kept the cost of living down, plus was somewhat endearing as it maintained family values and allowed to easily be at hand to help each other. It could be argued these had started to go missing in various other parts of the world as families would live separately being possibly derided as unusual or lame to live as a multi-generational family together. Not here; it was practical and worked well. I liked Marcia immediately; she was warm and friendly, speaking slightly broken English with a lovely Spanish accent. Nothing seemed too much trouble and would happily potter around the house whilst whistling or singing in a chirpy manner.

Eventually as we talked, others entered the room; Gina, Sasha, and Kay. They were all from England. We chatted and got acquainted. Kay spoke to Marcia impressively in Spanish, which was encouraging as she had said that she didn't speak a word of the lingo prior to her arrival, and was now waffling on somewhat fluently some four weeks later. We ventured out to the Mariscal Sucre area of the city, which was predominantly bars, restaurants, hotels and littered with tourism agencies. This area was the main hub for travellers and tourists. Being a Sunday, we were informed it was quieter than normal, but nevertheless the area which I had been warned about to be on guard against thieves and pick pockets, due to the nature of the clientele it attracted. I was surprised how westernised many places in the Mariscal were, with some really nice establishments, and there was a large square in the centre which was pedestrianised, allowing for sitting outside to enjoy a drink or meal in the sun, and it was where we were to be spending the majority of our time as the Spanish school was also located here.

We took lunch in the square, and had a wander around one of the markets which was close by, selling a large array of indigenous clothing such as ponchos and hats made from llama wool, each with elaborate colours and designs, plus artworks and crafts by local trades people, all vying for the money that tourists bring, which was a much more familiar currency now due the depreciation of the Ecuadorian sucre in 2000, as this lead the country to switch to using the US dollar.

I resisted any temptation to buy anything, and we headed back. Now daylight allowing some bearings, I noticed our home was situated at an elevated level, rising up to the west of the city towards the foothill of a ranging Andean mountain ridge. It loomed majestically with lush green vegetation, protective of the long narrow capital, situated in a valley some 3000m above sea level. Now arguably the highest I had been living at whilst travelling. Many visitors have had trouble with altitude sickness at this height; air being somewhat thin on the ground and exasperated by horrendous black smog that spewed from numerous vehicles. The altitude I put down to the reason why I was having trouble sleeping; leaving me whiling the midnight hours away reading, writing and doodling new tattoo designs before eventually claiming at least a few hours' sleep.

Gina, Sasha and I were each studying Spanish at the same school for four weeks; Kay had finished her stint and with a swift 'hello' and 'goodbye', moved on. On the Monday after practically zero sleep, we headed there for our first day, starting at eight thirty in the morning. Both starting from scratch, I was placed with Gina and was literally just me and her in our class. This made the teaching and learning process a whole lot easier, as it was much more up close and personal with our tutor Susan, who was really friendly and helped us where needed with patience and diligence. Straightaway; the main rule was 'no English'. This was reasonable considering we were there to learn Spanish; and immediately began at a pretty fast pace. I recognised some words and phrases but most was predominantly alien to me and it was like starting all over again.

I had really enjoyed my first lesson and was excited about the rest of the time there; especially as after a few hours' things had started coming back to me. The class finished at twelve thirty p.m. and were Monday to Friday that left afternoons and weekends free to do as we pleased. This was great news; all work and no play makes Jack a dull boy. We also started to meet and mingle with the other students; who ranged from all walks of life, were of all age ranges and they had mentioned some of the cool things that there was to do in and around the city. Plus, the school also provided extra-curricular activities such as salsa classes, afternoon excursions and cookery lessons which students were free to participate in.

I was really loving now being in unfamiliar surroundings, in a foreign country, with a whole new culture to embrace; it felt like I was a fish out of water as my adventures seemed to be starting all over again, with the challenges and experiences of being out of the western world at the forefront, yet had already accumulated a network of people and contacts at my disposal to help out where needed. I was excited about the next few months ahead. But, less excited about the copious amounts of homework that we had been given on our first day; which straightaway took pay to the tonnes of free time we seemingly had. Oh well, nothing ventured nothing gained.

El Conquistador

The Spanish lessons continued in much the same vein, practicing conjugating verbs, increasing vocabulary and trying to fathom what all this masculine and feminine business was all about; with it being a non-existent concept in the English language. It was intense but good fun at the same time. The mornings were taken up with our study and the rest of the day was our own, which was great. Although, I have to admit, I found it quite difficult to motivate myself to do the homework that we were now getting after every class; because it was more fun to involve ourselves with the other cultural and recreational activities available.

Tuesday afternoons offered free salsa lessons; while chatting beforehand, it didn't take long to come to the conclusion that the few new *amigos* and I were all born with two left feet, so thought it would be good idea to participate. Located around the corner from school, we took our place in the dance studio and started with simple warm up steps. *Uno, dos, tres* over and over again; as everyone repeatedly got them wrong. I couldn't help but laugh; using the mirror to try and concentrate on the necessary foot movements only played havoc with my co-ordination as left foot would move instead of right and vice versa. All the while though it made it reassuringly possible to see who else was messing up as much as me. Finishing; everyone was hot and sweaty after a full hour of aerobic exercise that consisted of about four different basic dance steps over and over again. We all agreed it had been a blast and loads of fun, excitedly bragging about how rubbish we were. But practice makes perfect so pretty much there and then decided we would be back next week to continue with salsa 101. Not quite ready to set any dance floors on fire.

Activities cropped up thick and fast; Susan gave us the opportunity to visit the local supermarket, to practise some of our Spanish out on an unsuspecting public when shopping for ingredients that would be used during the weekly cookery lesson we had signed up for. On the menu were *llapingachos*; essentially a big fry up involving *chorizo* that Gina and I bought. Other ingredients included fried potato with cheese, salsa, salad, avocado and a fried egg to complete the meal. I appreciate that this may not sound like the most complimentary of ingredients, but it was really delicious and in various guises formed part of the staple diet in Ecuador. The good thing about the cookery lesson was that we each helped Patricia, one of the teachers, to prepare by chipping in with a spot of peeling, chopping, slicing and dicing as everything was made from scratch. There was a small kitchen on the premises of the school that we used; which was nice and cosy with ten or so people working in there. Nothing was wasted, as the food was intended for all including the teachers, so meal time became an excellent getting-to-know-everyone affair, as we all sat outside in the front yard of the premises and ate together; encased by large metal railings and an electric gate. We later found out these were installed because someone had previously tried to gain entry with a gun intent on robbing the place; which unnervingly only helped reaffirm no matter how normal things seemed in South America, something crazy could happen at any time.

Days were jam-packed; lessons, doing this, doing that, and of course homework. I really made the effort to do as much as possible, wanting to get the most out of the school and cultural experience as I possibly could, and the fact that Gina and I were both house and class mates allowed us to help and coerce each other which made life easier. Conversely though; this didn't stop us going on the drink after we had class, eaten and then carry on drinking whilst doing our homework, before heading into town to meet with the others on the Wednesday evening (otherwise known as start of the weekend) for more drinks to see the Mariscal in full swing at night.

The next day wasn't good; both Gina and I had massive hangovers. It was heads on desk time and we both struggled to string any form of legible sentences together in English, let alone Spanish. Susan was laughing at our antics as she quizzed us about what had happened and we had to reply in native tongue. I think the only thing that I learnt that day were the words *borracho* which meant 'drunk' and *chuchaqui* which was 'hangover'. Things didn't improve on the afternoon either, when we all visited an orchid expo and I was late to meet everyone, and all the taxis to the centre had gone various routes and Patricia said that she was going to kill me for (her) losing everyone. Don't exactly know how it was my fault, but I was late so I apologised; because I was busy planning the weekend excursion which would turn out to be more like exertion. Everything worked out though as eventually all those attending met up at the exhibition centre, a large glass modern building located in Itchimbia Park; which was at an elevated level to the east and offered a spectacular panoramic view of the city and the adorning mountains. At this point, I really wasn't feeling the orchid expo experience. Granted, it was very popular as there were hundreds of people visiting to gaze upon the really beautiful displays, where apparently some of the floral exhibits could fetch thousands of dollars. But I was tired, unenthused and still slightly worse for wear.

The day though seemed to go on forever; returning home, Marcia had already offered to take us all out for the evening, which prior to monster hangovers we'd accepted. She spoke in very high regard about the Panecillo that translated as little bread loaf. It was a hill near the central old town and divided northern Quito and the city where we were based, with southern Quito where most of the populous lived and regarded as more dangerous part due to drugs, crime and poverty. The Panecillo was special because adorning the top was a huge statue of La Virgen de El Panecillo which was possible to see from miles around in both daylight and at night, when it was beautifully lit up.

Marcia drove us there and on our arrival at the top, we were greeted with a spectacular glittering sight of the city flickering away at night, made all the more impressive by the clearly visible Basilica and San Francisco square. The lights stretched as far as the eyes could see in either direction as the length of the city became apparent and I was surprised with how narrow a city Quito actually was; as the blackness of the surrounding uninhabited mountains encased the many thousand twinkling illuminations below. We checked out the small selection of stalls selling souvenirs and indigenous clothing before heading down to the gorgeous old colonial town where we sampled the local fire water, or *Canelazo* – its more common name; a head blowing spiced rum concoction flavoured with hot orange to warm any cockles on a cold evening. Heading back, I was absolutely knackered with the effects from the previous night and couldn't wait for bed, only to still have to do my homework.

I seemed to be constantly on the go. There seemed to be so much going on. It was relentless; but I wanted to do it. Having got my bearings, I'd started walking to school and the thirty-minute walk to the Mariscal could only do me good, especially at altitude. Also, I again made a conscious effort to start exercising as this had casually gone on the back burner throughout Aus and New Zealand; doing press ups and crunches to aid me

261

in getting into shape and prepare for the rigours of what South America had to offer. Little did I know, I was on the verge of taking on what was to be one of the most rigorous activities I was to embark on – not only on my travels, but ever.

It was now Friday and the week had flown by; after school and lunch, a few others and I headed down to the Centro Historico or old town to explore during the day where we had been the night prior. Beautiful white-washed buildings, tiled roofs and cobbled streets were a far cry from the rest the city; the beautiful Plaza Grande overlooked by the presidential palace had fantastic ornate statues for the hoard of visitors to admire, as they whiled away the hours and close by was La Compania de Jesus; a church of incredible beauty with amazingly carved stone facade adorning the front, only bettered on the inside as it was gilded in gold; with fabulous old paintings that looked stunning, offering little wonder why it was regarded as the most beautiful church in the country. We again passed the Plaza de San Francisco and headed down La Ronda, to sample some more fire water. We took the trolley to return back to the new town, that was basically a tram service and decided I was done for the day; figuring it best to relax for the evening, have an early night to conserve some energy, as the weekend was here and once again, I was finding myself going up in the world.

Sasha's study partner was a guy called Steve. He was cool, good fun and loud, but this was easily over-looked having an endearing positive attitude and a generally happy persona. We got on well and had started hanging about together as part of our group. Earlier on in the week, he had mentioned that he wanted to attempt to climb Cotopaxi, located some 55km south of Quito. On Thursday, before the hungover orchid expo we had visited one of the local tour operators to discuss the possibility of doing this. I was slightly apprehensive as this was quite expensive, but with the pair of us both participating, it made it somewhat cheaper.

Also more importantly my apprehension was due to the nature of what we were about to undertake; Cotopaxi is some 5897m above sea level, we were already at just under 3000m in Quito and altitude sickness was already an issue so this was potentially dangerous being the second-highest peak in Ecuador. Also, Cotopaxi was one of the few equatorial glaciers in the world and, therefore, specialist equipment is required to reach the summit. And to top it off, it is regarded as one of the worlds' highest active volcanos. Taking these facts into consideration, I thought about whether it was worth it, because with the cost I seriously doubted my ability to complete it. The altitude was an issue with only six days at 3000m to acclimatise, I hadn't done anything like this before where the highest peak in the UK is Ben Nevis at 1344m and I had been nowhere near it. And as for glaciers? Frozen drinks with shots in; about my level of experience there, so certainly haven't climbed anything with snow and ice on it, let alone used any of the necessary equipment. It was fair to say I had my reservations. But again opportunity had come my way; this could either make or break me. I decided there was only one thing for it; drink a bucket of concrete – harden the fuck up and go for it.

I met Steve early on the Saturday morning at the *terminal terrestre*, which was the bus station serving transport for destinations south of Quito; where for a very reasonable 75c bus journey our destination town of Machachi lay. From there, we took a taxi to our meeting point of Papagayo; a lovely hostel resort in the countryside that people used as a quiet getaway and to prepare to climb Cotopaxi in the nearby national park. Here, after waiting around and exploring the grounds, we met our guide; Oso de la Montaña or 'Mountain Bear' as the translation goes. He had been highly recommended by the tour operator who had apparently previously climbed with him before and had vast experience of scaling the peak; this filled us both with confidence. Because let's face it, you don't get a name like that by sitting on your arse in an office messing about on a computer.

We headed to the outside shed where we were then both kitted out; thermal bottoms, thermal top, wind-resistant jacket, wind-resistant pants, heavy duty walking boots, harness, hard hat, crampons and ice axe. At least, I was going to look the part and give the impression I knew what I was doing. The previous day, I had purchased some thick woollen socks and hired some anti-glare shades, gloves and a balaclava as these weren't provided. Unlike Steve who had most of these things because living in Denver provided ample opportunity and experience to hike and climb the Rocky Mountains. So was a fraction more an aficionado than myself.

Prepping and packing our gear, we headed back to Machachi to buy supplies. Water, energy drinks, peanuts, chocolate and biscuits were on the menu; anything that was laced with energy and easy to carry, we bought. Now ready, we set off in Oso's small 4x4, along a very bumpy track littered with stones, rocks and potholes hindering the already slow process as the inclinations and gradients were steep in parts, heading high into the Andes to reach the national park. But looking out the dirty rear windows provided glorious uninterrupted views of the green landscape in the valleys of rolling hills and mountains. The intersected little villages below that we had passed through were now tiny hovels that slowly disappeared as we twisted around corners and ventured into the encroaching clouds.

Approaching the national park, we paid our $10 entry fee. The terrain had plateaued as we made our way across the barren mountains. There was less green vegetation due to the more hostile conditions and thinner air at 4200m for plant life to grow; trees were sparse with only few resilient bushes and long grass as the trail cut towards our destination. Seemingly from nowhere, we were able to see Cotopaxi; majestically towering an extra 1700m from the flat land that we were on. It looked amazing as a stand-alone volcano; perfectly conical in shape, encrusted with brilliant white ice and snow glacier scaling down from the pinnacle. It looked easy from a distance; the sloping gradient didn't look too difficult. But I realised how deceptive appearances could be, as things do look easier and less intimidating from afar so I wasn't taking it for granted as the task ahead was now in full blinding view.

Towards the foot of the volcano, boulders scattered all around the ground, varying in size; some small, some the size of a car. Oso explained that they'd come from the volcano from previous eruptions. The last major one being in 1904 that ferociously blasted out debris for miles. I couldn't fathom the magnitude of this, let alone try to imagine what it must have been like as massive rocks of red hot debris showered down, surely something reminiscent of what Armageddon would be like; deadly to the extent that a major eruption could destroy the local town of Latacunga and reach suburbs of Quito. Debris from the last major eruption was reported to have reached the coast some 100km away; easy to believe as even the smallest particles can cause havoc for thousands of miles if the wind blows in the wrong direction. Also, somewhat worryingly, we were informed that the volcano was now overdue for an eruption.

In the distance, just off the edge of the glacier, there was a tiny yellow building. This was our destination for the night and brought in to perspective how absolutely massive the volcano was. We followed the winding dirt trail up to about 4300m before parking the car. Unloading, we changed footwear and put on extra layers. It was now cold and misty from the clouds. Picking up our bags and supplies, we started the ascent to base camp at 4800m on the steep gravel track. The stones underfoot gave way and slowed an already snail-like progress, that combined with the extra weight of the equipment and lower oxygen levels caused every step to sap energy and make matters worse. Breathing became heavy and deep as lungs and body clamoured for more oxygen from the increasingly unforgiving environment, only enhancing the seemingly getting nowhere fast hike. I put my head down, concentrated on breathing and timing. Approximately an hour later, with cold sweat on my face and steam billowing from my insulating jacket, wearily I was greeted with the welcoming sight of base camp.

Oso had powered ahead to prepare, not only was he our guide but was also cooking our meal prior. Him leaving us wasn't an issue, it was obvious where we were going and there were plenty of people about as many had also come to scale the summit; while others were downhill mountain biking or simply looking around and admiring the views. Steve was behind me and struggling; he had already dropped his sleeping bag which had rolled far down the hill that Oso had kindly gone and retrieved. It was obvious he was feeling the effects, especially as he had complained earlier of a sore throat and feeling slightly under the weather.

Base camp was bustling and busy with those preparing to climb. We spent the time relaxing, checking out the surroundings and taking photos of the stunning view where a mountain fox curiously scavenged by the edge of the now very close glacier. Inside were tables and chairs by the kitchen area, while upstairs were multiple triple bunk beds to rest in. We loaded up on a protein and carb fix of chicken, potato, vegetable soup and bread. We had our final pep talk from Oso about the preparation for the climb, he informed us that the conditions were good; some cloud around but calm with minimal wind. If it had snowed, no one could climb, due to it being fresh and the risk of it moving a serious hazard. A fellow climber told us it was his second attempt; he failed the first time due to this. We had to prep our small bags with drinks and snacks and then told to rest and get some sleep. It was six p.m. and we were due to start the ascent at about one a.m. to reach the summit to see sun rise at around five thirty a.m. This would also allow enough time to get off the glacier before the intense equatorial sun would be right overhead, melting ice and making it incredibly dangerous.

The dorm room was noisy upstairs as people wandered in and out, sorted their equipment, chatted loudly and constantly turned the light on and off with scant regard for any one even dreaming of getting any sleep. For me, this was somewhat impossible with all the ruckus; I might have dozed for a few moments but had nothing that resembled sound sleep. I chuckled to myself though as I rested, thinking about the task ahead, what I had gotten myself into and mainly because I'd developed another bout of smelly rasping flatulence from the food we had eaten. Steve couldn't sleep either and now he had got worse, the glands in his neck had swollen and he was feeling feverish. He said that he didn't think that he could climb.

Twelve midnight seemed to arrive far too soon, considering the lack of sleep, but the time had now come to make the climb to the summit. After eating a light breakfast; I put on the rest of my clothing and equipment in preparation for the ascent. Steve had woken and told us he had decided that he wasn't fit enough to climb. Honestly; I was slightly concerned about his health and ability to take part, I had no doubt that he would be able to make it if he was fit and raring to go, but he wasn't; far from it. It was obvious he was sick; looking at him he was as white as the glacier. The problem was; if he did attempt to climb and couldn't make it, we all would have to return, putting an end to both our chances, as he wouldn't be allowed down the glacier without the guide. This was why Oso never took more than two people up at any one time as it minimalized the risk of people failing through no fault of their own. I felt bad for Steve having essentially coerced me to this. I knew how much he wanted to do it and having come this far only to fall ill. He made the correct call to not jeopardise himself or the climb, it must have been a difficult decision to make and a bitter pill to swallow. I had to thank him for the courage in this decision and increasing my chances of completion. Now the only person stopping me reaching the summit was me.

Oso and I made the short walk to the edge of the glacier; we put on our crampons to dig into the ice we were to walk on, and he tethered us together with about ten feet of climbing rope. Armed with hard hat, ice axe and looking like Scott of the Antarctic, we set off.

The ice cracked and crunched from the large metal spikes under the weight of pressure from each step of our trudging feet; the ice axe was a godsend as it helped provide balance and leverage, much like a walking stick, and aided in keeping time – something that Oso emphasised the importance of. "One, breathe, two, breathe, get the rhythm, is a machine!" he kept repeating his analogy; it was right as it helped keep time, making the ascent easier and conserve energy. The gradients we were climbing ranged between 35 and 45 degree steep slopes; and continually steep so there was no let up. Due to the severity, we scaled a zig-zag fashion to ease the assent on the limbs and joints; and set the speed of the steps we were taking, which was a nice and steady pace that wasn't too fast nor to slow. This was dictated by me due to my fitness level and inexperience where I did my level best to maintain a constant tempo. I tried to refrain from looking up; this just emphasised the severity of the slope and the top was nowhere in sight, we had a total of just over a kilometre to climb.

Within the hour, I was feeling good. We had caught up to the larger parties ahead of us and passed them, the system was working and we were powering on up; stopping at regular ten-minute intervals for two minutes to have a breather and for Oso to check how I was doing. This allowed time to have a brief look around. Despite being dark, the view was incredible; the mountains around us were silhouetted black against the somewhat lighter night sky, we had now broken through the clouds that blanketed the near world below from view; they looked soft and inviting as if you could just jump onto them. Out towards the west in the far-off distance, an electrical storm was raging and it was possible to see the clouds light up and the occasional bolt of lightning crash across the sky, and tiny yellow dots smattered the ground allowing civilization to have light during the night. It was very beautiful but there wasn't too much time to hang around due to the increasingly cold weather and the need to keep moving.

After approximately three hours, the hard, continuous exertions, increasingly lower oxygen levels and unforgiving terrain were starting to take their toll; everywhere hurt but in particular my thighs, calves and ankles were now burning hot as ligaments, tendons and muscles formed tiny tears within that wreaked unrelenting havoc from the stresses and strains demanding that I stop. But my argumentative brain fought hard, even as I found it difficult to cope when we walked across the steep fresh part of the glacier to continue on the trail; my ankles bore the aching brunt of my full weight, balancing and walking along the severely slanted, uneven, slippery surface. Pausing, Oso was concerned too because I had slowed and said that if I continued in such a manner, we would have to return. I heeded his words, knowing he was serious. But this galvanised my resilience and made me more determined as now I knew that the summit wasn't much further with about an hour climbing left to accomplish. I ate some peanuts and a biscuit to try and get some energy into my weary body, but this just sat in my stomach on the fast-accruing lactic acid.

We reached part of the glacier with a small but sheer concave gap to pass through. We now had to literally climb. Oso went first to show me the way and providing the technique to get up the 15ft high wall. Aided by Oso, holding rope from the top, I kicked hard, digging the spikes on the front of the crampons into the ice, and using the ice axe and rope, I climbed and dragged myself up and through. I was relieved as this was a tricky part for an already tired body, but provided opportunity for other muscle groups to work in a different manner to help alleviate some discomfort. Although not yet at the summit, I now knew it wasn't far, because the glacier wasn't as unforgiving now, the gradient had receded and we plodded on. Eventually, though, I succumbed and had to stop again, the acid build up in my stomach took its toll and was sick regurgitating the biscuit and peanuts I had eaten. Oso didn't look back; he just ignored me and after finishing emptying the contents of my stomach, I said OK and wearily continued. Unbeknownst to me, thankfully, this happened when we were about three hundred yards from the summit. Oso had exaggerated the time required to reach the very pinnacle and the gradient rescinded rapidly to a nearly flat level. I found some reserves of energy and plodded on the final few yards to scale the top. I had made it!

Elation drowned me and although not showing it, I was ecstatic. Yet no jumping up and down, no shouting and cheering. I was literally running on empty. Relief was as much a welcome feeling as that of achievement. The pain and discomfort of walking on 45-degree slope had subsided and the earth below my limbs was at a more satisfactory level plane. My legs felt like lead and I could barely lift my arms in a celebratory photo pose. But the constant huge grin on my face clearly said all the words and superlatives that my broken lungs could not relay. At the top, it was cold; very cold at about -5°C, and the thin air coupled with exhaustion made breathing difficult. It was possible to see a large group of yellow shimmering lights in the distance; that was the southern suburbs of Quito some 50km away. I took time to peer over the edge into the ominous black abyss of the crater, it was huge and uninviting, a sinister black hole on earth that was impossible to look down into and see anything. I thanked Oso and asked the time; it was four forty-five a.m. and had taken us just over three-and three-quarter hours to scale the summit. I was astounded the average time for completing was around four-and-a-half hours to be in time to see sun rise from the top. This would have been spectacular; unfortunately, we would have had to wait around forty-five minutes for this to occur. Due to my state and the freezing conditions, this wasn't going to happen. We were the only ones there and had passed all before us on the way up. I was really pleased with my performance and the time for completion; I expectedly hoped I could do it, and certainly expected to be subject to some pain and agony, but certainly didn't expect to finish this fast. Oso said it was a very good time.

We experienced the beautiful views amid snowy, barren and harsh conditions at the top for approximately ten minutes. Then, as adrenaline subsided, harsh reality kicked in; the cold was biting now, heat was escaping rapidly from ourselves due to stopping and we weren't being kept warm from the exertions. Also, more importantly, we were only half done and not finished; what goes up must come down and I was in pain and very weary.

On the descent we went the same route and it started to prove just as difficult. I was struggling to stay vertical; my legs had gone and had to stop every five minutes to rest and gain my composure as the impact of every step was taking its toll on pretty much every inch of my fibre. We passed other parties still on their way up, as we trudged down. And managed to get through the pass where we previously climbed and then across the slippery fresh part of the glacier. I had taken a break and sat on the ice and was now struggling bad, daunted by the prospect of the further time ahead descending and the punishment that my body would have to endure. Then came salvation; not in the form of a helicopter or a lift – that would be ridiculous; handy, but still ridiculous – this was more inspirational; Oso suggested that I slide down. I didn't need asking twice as it was obvious. We were tethered together; so the idea was why not let gravity and the somewhat soft slippery surface do the work? I had spent ages fighting and working against it and was now starting to lose. So now was time to work with it. Tucking myself in, I sat on my arse and started sliding vertically down the glacier, with Oso running behind.

This was not exactly orthodox but it was the means to an end. We were now flying down the steep slope; me on my backside using the ice axe as a brake and Oso to the rear, keeping the line connecting us somehow taught; like an Eskimo with a husky dog. We stopped sporadically when those still coming up were in the way; so that we didn't crash into them and send them tumbling down the glacier. We were receiving some very odd looks. Halfway down, we paused to appreciate the sun rise break beyond the horizon and take photos before carrying on. Our mode of descent was allowing us to get off the volcano glacier in record speed but had its downside; the ice was accruing up inside the back of my jacket and it wasn't as soft as it looked or once thought. It was cold and uncomfortable, as it pushed the clothing up over and the build-up of the hard crystals scrapped my back. Also, I could feel bruising start to form on my arse and legs where I continuously hit larger lumps of ice as I bounced and slid down the deceptively uneven surface.

After hour or so of descent, we were finally at the edge of the glacier and I just sat there trying to recover. Every part of me seemed now to be in pain; ankles, calves, knees, thighs, arms, back, arse and now groin from the harness being pulled up as we slid down. Not one part of my anatomy had escaped punishment. With the total exertion, maximum concentration, minimal sustenance, depleted oxygen and freezing cold on a slanted, unforgiving terrain for five hours, I was mentally and physically drained. I just sat on the edge of the ice for about fifteen minutes, not wanting to move, slowly drinking a can of energy drink in the hope that the vitamins, sugar and rocking caffeine content would help bring me round. Removing my crampons, I wearily trudged back to base camp.

"Did you make it?" Steve asked when I got there.

"Yeah, I made it, but I'm absolutely fucked, mate; that was the hardest thing I've ever done in my life" was my short, somewhat curt reply.

As I started packing up the rest of my gear, news was filtering through about those that didn't make it and had turned back. It started to dawn on me the realisation of what I had accomplished and enhance my sense of achievement. The energy drink tonic started to kick in and I could feel myself starting to pull round. It was a strange sensation as I became more invigorated and had energy to finish trudging back down to the car; probably more so now because I had rested and knew I had achieved what I wanted, where the satisfaction of such was unbelievably rewarding. We put the kit in the back and I crashed on the back seat. It was now about six a.m. as we drove away. I looked at what I had just climbed and conquered with great pride. I couldn't see anyone on the glacier, it was too far, but couldn't believe I had just been stood on the top of this magnificent, conical, natural wonder which now looked more impressive; there were no clouds and as the sun rose, it was brilliantly illuminated against a gorgeous blue Andean backdrop sky.

We took the car straight back to Papagayo where we sorted the equipment and said our thanks and goodbyes to Oso. He was a legend and pushed me to my physical limits. He had to or I wouldn't have made it. I couldn't help feel respect for the man who scales this monster approximately four times a week, truly remarkable and fair to say he was as super healthy and fit as a butcher's dog. He would have to be. I had made it – just – but was feeling the effects; these would wear off yet the achievement would be with me now forever. I was thrilled. Granted, I never got to see the sun rise at the top, which would have been spectacular, but just getting to the summit was the goal and I had made it – somehow. Especially as climbing in this sense; was something I'd never done before. It was a bit surreal and I totally appreciate how it was a slight piss-take by myself to some extent; people can train for months to prepare for this and circumstance really dictates how successful they will be, and I'd just decided to do it on a whim. Weirdly, if I had researched and looked into it more, I probably wouldn't have done it. Enid the girl behind the travel desk initially tried to talk us out of it, but Steve was adamant he wanted to climb this one. Yet, unfortunately for him it never got to happen; whereas I got the full experience that included being at the highest point I've ever stood on Planet Earth and feeling like I was on top of the world.

The rest of the day we just relaxed at Papagayo, watching movies and eating, before a tour bus there offered to take us back to Quito, which as a bonus was a free ride. From Quito, I said my goodbyes to Steve and he said that he probably wouldn't be in school the next day, as he was still feeling unwell. I got a taxi back home where I tried to regale the taxi driver in my finest broken Spanish about my accomplishments. Getting in about eight thirty p.m., everyone had been wondering what had happened to me, thinking that something had possibly gone wrong. I spent about ten minutes enthusiastically explaining the incidents and the adventure I'd been on, before crashing into a welcoming bed where I fell asleep in an instant.

Walking into school the next day was an ordeal in itself; my legs ached from top to bottom and I had some choice bruising on the backs of my legs and arse. Arriving, people were already waiting outside and wanted to know instantly how it had gone. I was congratulated for the achievement and felt proud, but people also shared with me the disappointment of Steve not being able to complete the climb; it was nice to see the empathy as they knew it was his project. As good as I felt, the fact that he could not participate was a downer but his unselfish attitude allowed me to complete it. As stated, he wasn't at school still as he was not feeling well. Now even the Spanish lessons were hard work as I struggled to remember what I had learnt previously, as everything prior seemed to have been pushed out of my brain by the excitement and ordeal from the weekends' endeavours.

Luckily, the rest of the week I was more focused and things improved again in class, which I was happy with as that was the main reason why I was there. The same could be said for the salsa lessons; word must have gotten around because more people were taking part and the dance studio was much fuller, making it harder to narrowly avoid treading on people's toes, as we daintily incorporated more steps to again get wrong. The excursion was to the Guayasamin Museum; further up the residential east side of the city at the former home of Ecuador's most celebrated artist who died back in 1999. The museum had some fantastic pieces of his works and was really worth the time going. I loved it as we were allowed to peruse at our pleasure the various stages of his life's work, which centralised on the indigenous people and their plight. The former home was on lavish grounds, so much so the site was being extended by construction workers outside and had an envious collection of old model cars in the garage.

Wandering out onto the veranda, a large passenger plane came past. It was close by at eye level with myself, and had buildings and houses in the back ground from the far side of the valley; this really intensified the illusion that it was severely off course and about to crash. Forgetting I was up high and the airport much further down in the city centre. But still being able to wave at the pilot as he came to land was pretty bizarre.

Ceviche was on the menu for this week's culinary lesson; cold soup traditionally made with sea food, but on this occasion, chicken; which at the risk of sounding a heathen appealed more, but still incorporated more of my other favourite flavours like lime, onions and tomatoes. This time, I had the easy task of providing some plantain chips to accompany as a side dish. I loved the cookery lessons; they were good fun and a chance to work and play together with others. Plus, we got to eat a delicious plentiful meal for a very minimal price. Afterwards, Gina, Steve and I decided to get out and about and have some fun. As the country name suggests, Ecuador has the equator running straight through it and north of the city just past the suburbs is where it lies. This was an opportunity too good to miss. We had mentioned it to Susan and she told us how to get there via public transport rather than taxi, as it would cost less and induce more sense of an adventure. We had heard so much about the equator and what was there from those at school. Trouble is, here, there are two.

What? Hold on; I don't know much about geography but I'm pretty sure there is only one equator? How can there be two? At the bus stop, we took the Mitad del Mundo or 'middle of the world' bus from Avenida America for 25c, determined to find out. The final stop was our destination and impossible to miss. A large complex where we paid the $2 entrance fee and started walking around. There were shops and a museum, plus restaurants and was a really lovely attraction; central focus being the famous towering monument with a globe on the top that we had seen so many times already on pictures and souvenirs. In front of the monument was a line with north and south on either side of it. Here we were on the equator, smack in the centre of the earth, stood one second in the northern hemisphere the next in the southern. Or were we?

We had spoken to friends and they told us about the real equator. We were intrigued and wanted to find out what they were on about, so left the Mitad del Mundo complex, having only been in less than an hour. Making the short walk next door, we then saw the sign post for the Museo Solar Intiñan. Along a dirt track, were then greeted by a beautiful little resort surrounded by green vegetation. Paying $3 entrance fee, we were given a complimentary English-speaking guide (me being clearly keen to practise Spanish at any given opportunity was not evident here) to show us round and explain about the exhibits on offer. This was an indigenous park and concentrated on teaching and educating about how the native folk used to live, how some still do and the various wildlife encountered in the Amazon.

We were shown a mock hut that was an indigenous 'pub' fashioned from stone, mud and wood and had live guinea pigs in the corner to warn if bad spirits entered and showed how the local tipple was made from spit. A native home had been constructed in the same manner which was laced with artefacts; like tools and crafts highlighting a simple yet industrious nature. There were exhibits of enormous snakes and spiders amongst other things, these obviously now deceased were displayed for educational purposes. But the most unsettling was a jar with the dreaded candiru fish inside; these live in the Amazon River and are attracted by urine, so should any unfortunate soul relieve themselves in the water, the fish can swim up the stream and lodge itself inside the urethra of the penis to feed off blood. The only way of removal is via surgery as it can't be dispelled because of backward-facing spiked gills, leaving us wincing at just the thought. We carried on.

Things then got more macabre; a picture display showed how tribes used to make shrunken heads; this was a step by step guide. Like how you would build flat pack furniture but, in this case, shrink a head. Step one, take a fresh head; step two, scoop out insides etc. etc. but then things took a weirder turn as there was an actual exhibit. It looked strange and somewhat fabricated, which in essence it was; a head that had been shrunk to just bigger than a tennis ball. The eyes and mouth were sewn shut, said to preserve the soul of the individual inside. It was hard to fathom it was real, but hoped and believed it was, because even though it was being kept in a small glass case, we weren't allowed to touch it. The shrunken sloth we were allowed to handle. There were instances of tribal kings' burial chambers and explained the rituals involved, that included the unfortunate spouses who had to be buried along with them. Cacti were displayed and shown how they were used for medicinal and hallucinogenic properties. Before we finished our whirlwind tour of indigenous life with the opportunity to fire a blow pipe and dart at a hanging cactus; the same way it used to be done when hunting. Steve managed to hit it, I missed. This was brilliant, a fabulous little outdoor museum crammed with strange, weird artefacts and information. I loved it; being so interesting, interactive and fun yet hadn't even touched on the reason why we were there.

Just as we entered the resort before the museum, there was a red line in our way; a sign read Latitude 00, 00', 00" measured with GPS. We had now crossed from the southern hemisphere to the northern hemisphere, this time for real. The next part of the tour was fascinating. After having our photos taken straddling the equatorial line, it was time for our science lesson. Starting first with the Coriolis Effect; a sink filled with water was placed with the plug hole directly over the line and a leaf put in the water. Removing the plug, the water fell straight out to the bucket below. Next, it was placed above the line in the northern hemisphere and on the plug's removal, the leaf and water drained out spinning anti-clock-wise. Finally, it was placed below the line in the southern hemisphere and the same again, yet this time the sink having been moved just a couple of yards the water drained out spinning clockwise. It was so cool to witness; the Coriolis Effect was apparently true. I'd previously been told that it was a myth and I believed so with mechanical instruments like toilets, but where the only factors are water and gravity, it seemed to work. And we had witnessed it first hand; my belief that we were now standing on the real equator was fast being confirmed. The science didn't end there; experiments demonstrated how you are weaker on the equator, how it is harder to balance on the equator, yet it is possible to balance an egg on the top of a nail. This after a little perseverance I was successful with and received a certificate. An amazing interactive lesson and absolutely fascinating, I never realised that messing around on the equator could be so much fun. We all had a great time and learnt so much in the gorgeous surroundings, I was really impressed how they managed to incorporate cultural history and natural science together, at a very cheap rate, and kept us entertained for hours. Our guide was so enthusiastic and helpful that we had to tip him handsomely.

Incidentally, there are two equators because as the story goes; apparently French explorers over two hundred and fifty years ago marked the equator but got their calculations wrong, yet despite knowing this nearly two hundred years later the Mitad del Mundo was built in the wrong place to commemorate the event; a lovely celebration of the equator that isn't on the equator, it's about 250 yards further South from where it should be. A big monument to celebrate a big fuck up. The indigenous folk on the other hand seemed to know a little better and from their own calculations using the stars had it marked and then confirmed with GPS at Museo Solar Intiñan; Absolute genius.

Again, the weekend was fast approaching; I had plans to do, well, nothing. I was happy with this; finally, time for a spot of rest and relaxation. With school finished on the Friday and the weather a fine, beautiful Andean afternoon, to fill in the time a group, including Gina, Steve, Sasha and Caroline – another American improving her Spanish whilst visiting her sister – and I took the opportunity to head back towards the old town and explore the Basilica; a huge church at over 130m long, stands alone in-between the historical and modern-style towns and was constructed over a hundred years ago. The frontal towers resembled that of Notre Dame and reach well over a hundred metres into the sky, ensuring that it is visible from many areas of elevation in and around the city. We wanted to visit the Basilica as according to our guide books and talking to others, it offered a nerve-wracking view of the city from on high.

On closer inspection, the gothic grey structure loomed with the many gargoyle busts leering from the sides. We entered the main chapel to look around. The ceiling towered inside to about 35m high and graced pews were overlooked by ornate stain glass windows from the sides, depicting numerous biblical figures. The towers were separate from the main part of the church as there was an entry charge with it not being a part of where people go for worship. Paying the minimal fee, we started ascending the stairs of the tower. First stop was a balcony which stretched over the back of the church, giving a wonderful elevated view. Exploring, we ended up outside on the side terrace, as one of the doors was open and took the opportunity to have photos with the city as our background. But for myself, Steve and Caroline, this wasn't quite cutting it. We wanted the scary view. Heading further up the left tower, we came out to a loft-like room. From here, a thin rickety wooden gangway stretched across the top of the ceiling the full length of the church below, we now in effect were in the attic. It was strange because what looked solid roof just either side of the planks probably wasn't, and because of the height climbed, we knew was the best part of a 120ft drop with nothing soft to land on should you fall through. At the end, there was an un-sturdy metal ladder about ten metres high which in turn led outside to the base of the spire at the back of the church. If this wasn't bad enough; the ladder to the top of the spire was vertical and haphazardly attached to the outside. Now we were the best part of fifty metres up, outside on a ladder that wobbled about in its unmaintained, rusting state and looked like it could fall off or collapse at any moment. One large breath and quick scramble straight up the side of the spire, we each made it to the top. The view itself wasn't scary. It was getting there.

Jangling the nerves was well worth the risk. Quito looked fabulous from here, offering the fantastic array of buildings from the various quarters. Also straight ahead looking through the two towers at the opposite end was the glorious Panecillo and where we had been up a few days earlier. There were some quick complimentary snapshots as the unpredictable weather in the Andes started to quickly turn for the worse, and it inevitably started to rain. This hastened our departure down, as up here was not a place you would want to be with adverse conditions.

I was looking forward to the weekend; we had made plans to head out on the Friday night. Ending up in a salsa club that made the lessons more worthwhile as I was able to cut some decent rug with the many people spinning around. More likely, it was because I was pissed and didn't care while Steve and Caroline couldn't cut anything being completely wasted. Saturday continued in the same fashion; pub in the afternoon and night in the Mariscal, with the small tables inside a Beatles theme bar bearing the brunt of a wild night as we drunkenly surfed on them to the tune of 'Low Rider'. As expected, the Sunday being a more sombre affair recovering from the weekend and the fact that we had to say goodbye to my non-climb buddy Steve as he was leaving the next day to continue his travels elsewhere, which was a shame but he wouldn't be forgotten for inadvertently providing me with one of the most incredible experiences of my life.

Graduation, Marcia and Condor Man

Quito was proving a fabulous place to be based. I loved it here. There was so much to see and do, and the people I was meeting only enhanced the experience. The time was flying by and my Spanish just seemed to be improving with every lesson; where now with two weeks left, I was concentrating on more and more to get the most out of it. Also carnival was approaching and this meant that the weekend was going to be full of people partying and we were to miss the Monday at school due to the holiday.

Even so, the extra-curricular activities continued unabated; in the salsa classes, I was still learning and practicing the same very basic moves as before to induce some muscle memory, whilst trying to incorporate some new ones to add a little flair. By now, I actually thought I was OK; I probably wasn't but I just thought I was when drunk. Still using the sessions as a new form of exercise, coupled with the walking to school and continuing with my routine of crunches and push ups really started to help my fitness. A real positive having also decided to quit smoking two days prior to climbing Cotopaxi, but negatively I promptly started again with the demon sticks a few days after, making quitting somewhat pointless. We made *empanadas* in the cookery class; a shallow fried pastry dish which can come with various fillings. Our two types were with meat and vegetables like a *Cornish pasty* and a cheese option; making a tasty snack or accompaniment to a meal. This in turn created another chance to practise our Spanish on the unsuspecting world with another excursion to a large undercover market with Susan to buy ingredients. The market offered an array of weird sights and smells to stimulate the senses. It seemed possible to buy everything here; from whole barbequed pigs (head, trotters the lot) to the more regular supermarket ingredients plus flowers, clothing and trinket stalls that compliment any market. It was busy with the local folk suggesting that this place was much cheaper than the other; a fascinating experience wandering around as every turn could offer a unique surprise. We also managed to take an afternoon excursion back up to the Panecillo to see the splendour of the city in day light. Viewing the city from above was easily possible in Quito; its geographical location offered vantage points from an abundance of different places and directions that easily pulled a person away from the hustle and bustle below. I was rapidly getting through the things I wanted to do, this also included something somewhat more personal on the agenda.

One thing was bothering me; I had noticed it and when in New Zealand, Troy had also noticed. On the inside of my arm where I had my tattoo etched a couple of months prior, there was a faint blue hue to my skin from the ink. The tattoo itself was fine but I wasn't sure why the skin around had stained blue. Wiping excess ink away maybe? I didn't know. What I did know was it looked shit and brought home the pit falls of getting a tattoo abroad, as I could hardly head back and have it fixed. At least I hadn't caught any nasty diseases. Or any I knew of, anyway. Fortunately, I wanted to expand the tattoo, putting some form of border around the text. There was a tattoo parlour in the Mariscal which had come highly recommended, so I set about designing some patterns, wanting something individual that wasn't from a book and therefore be the only one with it. Eventually, after numerous designs, I settled on a rising sun to sit above the text and an effigy of a condor underneath. The idea being that this would now all represent my time travelling, following the most powerful entity in our solar system and a reason for life to thrive, coupled with an endangered species that represents the fragility of life and is also the emblem of South America, that had now unexpectedly formed the basis for the rest of my travels.

When I went to the tattoo parlour, Alberto the tattoo artist didn't speak any English. As I was talking about something with specific vocabulary, I struggled to explain in Spanish what the problem was and what I wanted. Coming to the conclusion that if this is going to fuck up, then this is a sure fire way for it to happen, and end up with another botch job of a botch job. Help was at hand; I explained to Susan what the issues were and she agreed to come along and help me, which was very kind. After about an hour of consultation, I managed to get the condor design right and positioned correctly and was relatively straight forward. The problem was the rising sun. When it was redesigned, it was a folded design, that when opened was too big and the flames that emulated were symmetrical, which I didn't want as it wouldn't look right; flames are unique and no two would look the same. In the end of course; after plenty of faffing, Alberto eventually just took the template I had sketched; it fit perfectly and looked how I wanted.

To this day, I still don't know why we didn't just do that in the first place. So all set, *BBBBBZZZZZZZZZZ* under the needle I went. Again.

This was different to how I had the tattoo done in Thailand; this was with a conventional tattoo gun, as oppose to bamboo. It didn't make much difference to me as I wanted it doing. So once again, I lay patiently while my body got permanently pigmented. Listening away to Alberto's Mexican rap music and trying to have the occasional chat to deflect from the pain which was reminiscent of the bamboo, but certainly more, as the mechanical needle punctured and hammered the skin that much faster than any lone hand. I looked at the work in progress and got the shock of my life seeing that he had done it red! I couldn't believe it; I didn't want red. I wanted it black to match the writing.

'*Es rojo*?' (It's red?) I enquired worryingly.

'No, *es sangre*' he replied. (No, it's blood.)

Relieved, I thought, *Thank fuck for that. I'm only bleeding quite profusely*. So much so, I actually couldn't see what he had drawn.

When finished, it looked too clearly defined. By putting some shading in and around the flames, in between the letters and around the condor, this blended more of the stained skin while adding depth and substance to the final design. After an hour-and-a-quarter in the chair, I was finished and bandaged up and told this time to keep the area clean and moisturised with cream. The pain wasn't too bad while I lay down, but when I stood up, the blood rushed back into my arm and was really aching and sore. But this would pass. Moreover, though, it was done and I loved the result. I had now what looked like my very own personalised emblem emblazoned on my inner left arm; safe in the knowledge it was unique to me. I couldn't wait for the bruising to subside and for the ink to settle, so I could see it in its full glory, now complete and stain-free.

Gina had turned up by this point to have a nosy, where after finishing and probably against better judgement, we decided to go for a few beers; and then again on the evening also. A couple of hours later, I'd removed my bandage and bound my arm with cream and cling film to protect it. People were curious to what it was and I proudly showed them. Although obviously during the course of the evening, some drunken twat grabbed my arm to get my attention and with the pain, my attention they certainly did get.

It was third weekend of February and the carnival was in full swing; many from the city had headed out to various parts of the country and those not from the city headed in. The others in the house decided to go to festival celebration elsewhere, but I didn't fancy what they had planned and couldn't be bothered with the hassle, as these events were notorious for people having things stolen through distraction of water or foam to help liberate someone from their things. Inevitably, with booze involved, it made things that much easier for any thieving bandit. Also, I wanted to let my arm rest. So, apart from heading into town to book a trip for the next day, I put myself into study mode using opportunity of quiet time in the house to get the most out of what I was learning.

Quilotoa is another volcano close to Cotopaxi, forming part of the notorious ring of fire that encircles around the Pacific Ocean. It seemed a nice day out and could provide some cool sights. Although I was with Gina, Sasha and others from the house, I wasn't feeling sociable on the bus and couldn't be arsed talking or listening to anyone for that matter, and just wanted to watch the world go by and savour the scenery whilst listening to some music. We were heading south again on the road we had taken two weeks earlier to get to Cotopaxi, before veering off to the west to head for another part of the Andean mountains.

First stop was the town of Pujili – a small dusty place that allowed for wandering around the market, where more of the normal, then weird, then wonderful things were on offer; fruit, vegetables, clothing, souvenirs, arts and crafts and dodgy DVDs. But the meat stalls though were something else. These were certainly not like in UK or seen in Quito for that matter; cow jaw bones, bloodied with flesh, teeth still intact, with snout attached, all types of various hooves, intestines, entrails and body parts from many an animal – it looked like a bit of a massacre – all displayed on a stall in the open and unrefrigerated. It was a vegetarian nightmare; bad by any carnivore's standards and to any western onlooker looked quite disgusting coming straight from the sharp end of a knife. But here things weren't ready-prepared in packaging, nothing wasted as it could ill afford to be and regarded that everything can be used in some way or another. A butcher back home may never use these parts for general consumption as is, but saying that who knows what ends up in some of those cheap shit sausages you can buy.

On Cotopaxi, due to the prospect of the climb, the darkness of night and then mentally and physically being torn up within, I never really had the time to sit and gaze and savour where I was. The road up to Quilotoa was narrow and winding, as it shifted with the contoured hills and edge of the endless rugged mountains. The scenery was a panoramic beautiful ancient vista, as old as time that had hardly changed throughout the eons; majestic and bold, having been slowly pushed up from the slowest ever crash in history, as tectonic plates collided to create an unfathomable mass. It made me feel good to see the earth in such natural wonder, knowing this wasn't or couldn't be man-made. Being out of the way of civilisation, wild llamas grazed on the harsh shrubbery roadside, where their sole intention of feeding was unperturbed even when we stopped to take photos.

Yet when we passed native farms and villages, the children would run out and throw water at the bus as part of the carnival celebrations; and it made me laugh when someone on the other side foolishly left a window open. I was again left humbled by the way that they entertained themselves; granted, at our expense. As the poverty here in these rural areas was much more evident, I hadn't seen or more to the point realised it for a while; the last to this extent was back in Asia. Housing was simple shanties, children ran around in old clothes and barefoot, trying to avoid the scavenging fowl or dogs in less-than-clean conditions, as rubbish was strewn consistently and littered the ground everywhere. Human presence, poverty and inaccessibility to services spoilt an undeserving land. But never the wiser, rural folk and in particular children waved happily, before swilling the bus with water like tiny smiling assassins.

Quilotoa last erupted some 350 years ago and we were informed it was so violent that it caused a huge earthquake, the obvious remnants of which could be seen from the bus; a wide canyon in the mountains where the land to the side of the road had literally cracked open and dropped down, creating a huge, long trench which splintered in many directions. I hadn't seen anything like it. It looked like it could have been excavated due to the sheer sides, but the size of the gap would have taken thousands of people forever, and was so random it would have been pointless, serving no purpose, and the land at the bottom had now regrown and was fertile again. It looked amazing and once more I found myself trying to comprehend the magnitude and force of such an incident to literally cause the crust of the earth to split.

Reaching an elevation of 3800m, we arrived at Volcán Quilotoa; there were a few shops, guest houses and market stalls just away from the edge of the volcano for the convenience of tourists and people wishing to stay. Approaching the rim was spectacular as the volcano's vastness opened up. The edge was craggy and jagged, circling back round to where I stood and was huge, approximately 3km wide. Looking into the crater, the massive mineralised water lagoon below was illuminated to a fantastic emerald green as the sun shone; only changing when the clouds regularly encroached over and around us to occasionally steal some of the marvellous view in front.

From the top people looked small and insignificant some 400ft below. I wanted to experience the view from inside, so began trudging down the steep volcanic ash rubble trail that snaked to the bottom and was well worn by the footfall. Some twenty minutes later, reaching the shoreline I relaxed; unenthused about taking the kayaks for hire out onto the water. The rim now loomed high and impressive, encapsulating around the enormous volcanic basin we were in, yet despite where we were and the potential destructive ferocity beneath the feet, it felt very calming and serene with its uniqueness, so I happily watched the world go by sitting on a boulder waiting for the others to arrive and savouring the ambience. After around half an hour, I decided to make my ascent back up. Local folk offered mules to ferry visitors both up and down the steep trails, but when watching numerous people take advantage of the humorously touted 'natural taxi', this made me feel sorry for the beasts and being more than fit and able, decided to again walk on the soft loose ash, which coupled with gravity and altitude increased the difficulty of the trail, where some thirty minutes later I arrived again back up at the top of the rim. I was nicely out of breath and sweating, but content with my exercise and endeavour, knowing I'd spared a beast of its burden. Granted, I also spared a local a few dollars for the fare, but we did take lunch in one of the nearby restaurants; not that there were many places to choose from to have the obvious concoction of chicken rice and beans for nourishment, but at least it put some money into the community before heading back.

Returning, the clouds rolled in and everything darkened; visibility became reduced for the scenic views, but more so for the driver, as the rain started and people sitting in the coach seats had worry etched on their faces as this was to make the conditions for the winding descent more treacherous. Strangely; despite the looming adverse weather, just before we started to head down from the higher elevated mountains, the bus stopped to admire the vista. We stood at a prominent ledge on the mountain; to the left, it was raining ferociously and any sights were obscured by the sheer volume of water and large bolts of lightning hitting the ground intersected by loud *roars* of rolling thunder. Above us and on the edge of the mire, black clouds sparsely hit us with large rain drops but from centre to right, brilliant bright sunshine broke from over the thick cloud, to gracefully illuminate the lower patchwork miles of land that stretched off into the distance. Far off on the horizon, Volcán Tungurahua erupted, constantly spewing out plumes of ash and smoke that floated high into the sunny blue the sky. The two totally contrasting weather conditions and a destructive natural wonder of nature created a truly spectacular scene from on high. *Click.*

The bus continued precariously down the winding mountain road before we got back to Pujili, the roads awash with a torrent of caramel water running downhill that caused the traffic to slow considerably. Finally making it back to the highway, we carried on, slowly trundling back to Quito because now hail stones had started carpeting the ground, capping off the varying seasonal weather in one day that offered a sight that I never imagined possible, considering we were in the tropics and only a few kilometres from the equator. After a long, tiring journey, due to the weather and a crash on the road that caused a detour, we arrived back in Quito some two hours late.

There was no school on the Monday. I studied on the rooftop terrace of Marcia's place and basked in the sunshine. As the weather was unpredictably good, Gina, Sasha, Sabine (Swiss girl who had moved in) and I decided to take advantage of the conditions, ditch the studies and have a ride up the *Teleférico* cable car for an elevated view of our surroundings. Marcia's home was at the foot of the mountain and only a twenty-minute uphill walk away. But one, short, five-minute, costing next to nothing cab ride later, we arrived at the *Teleférico*. At its base was a theme park but we left it till after, opting to take the cable car to the top first. We paid extra to skip the holiday queue (which was extra for being foreign anyway) and set off up the mountain. Increasingly more and more of the urban sprawl came into view, and tried to spot local landmarks around the increasingly shrinking sliver of a city as we elevated to 4100m; the higher and more prominent Panecillo and Basilica were easy to spot, then the very obvious airport came into view and we all curiously tried to locate the now unobvious Mariscal Sucre as it had blended within the concrete edifices. The city looked spectacular from the top as it stretched panoramically, as an uneven mosaic mass in either direction, only obscured by the close uneven contour of the mountain ridge.

Wandering around the harsh grassy top of the mountain plateau, I stopped to peer over the side. It was a long way down and thankfully not too windy, as the only thing stopping someone going over the edge was a thin piece of barrier tape held up by a few flimsy sticks in the ground. Up here, indigenous folk were offering horse treks and also had a barbeque set up selling food. I was ravenous, so scoffed skewer kebabs of beef, *chorizo*, potato and plantains doused in *aji*; the local spicy garlic condiment I was fast becoming addicted to.

Volcano Pichincha had now become visible up here; it wasn't from lower down in the city due to the mountain edge and it being set back. A trail lead towards it, and I started walking but got only so far before deciding to turn back as ominous black clouds started to loom. This though really gave me the impetus to want to return to complete the trek. I met Gina who had crashed within long grass and we returned to the *Teleférico* to take the cable car back down, but just before doing so managed to time it perfectly to get caught outside in a squall of heavy rain for the first time in a while. At the bottom, we had a quick look around the fun park, it was more for kids with no adult rides, so gave it a miss to get back and finish off the homework and studies. Normally, I wouldn't be in such haste but despite the small amount of time in the rain, it lashed hard and we were all piss wet through as well at this point anyway.

Tuesday was the last remnants of carnival and back to school for start of my final week in Quito. After class, returning back to the house, the neighbours were throwing buckets of water from rooftops, trying to drench unsuspecting passers-by, and kids were having running battles in the streets with eggs and water bombs as their weapons of choice; this just created a run the gauntlet mad dash to get inside before the inevitable splattering; targeting an *extranjero* (foreigner) was worth a lot of points and kudos to any local.

Marcia had previously hired some home help; a young girl called Margie who was good fun yet seemed quiet. Appearances though can be deceptive, as upon our return, Spencer – another new addition – and I were promptly ambushed by Margie with some suspect yellow spray foam from a can, that unintentionally stained clothes and when it went in my mouth tasted fucking awful, all the while coerced by our hostess Marcia; sixty years plus and the ring leader in all of this. We were not taking it lightly; swiftly stealing the can of illuminous 'I really don't know what' spray foam off her, she got absolutely covered – much like the rest of the house, as more cans of this weird radioactive looking substance appeared – and a running battle of chaos ensued as we scrambled around spraying one another. Marcia took a can and pointed it at me. I was stood facing down the barrel of a spray can at point blank range; mine all gone, used up – I was doomed. As she mercilessly pressed the top, I had an ace up my sleeve. I somehow failed to mention that the nozzle was facing the wrong way. So, she promptly unloaded a load of horrible-tasting shitty foam straight into her own face. I was in tears laughing.

We weren't done. Margie's sister was visiting yet hiding amid all the commotion but was due to leave, so Marcia took Margie and her sister to the bus stop in the car. In that time, I went to the corner shop at the end of the road and bought a packet of water bombs. I filled them and went to the roof terrace. When Marcia and Margie returned, I had a full cache and launched them at will, so water bombs rained down on Margie as she had to get out and open the gates. All the while, Marcia cheering wildly inside the car as they erupted on Margie and the vehicle. It was absolutely insane.

At school, we had to give Susan the usual update of what we had been doing, and in Spanish told her what had happened; and in Spanish, she told me that you can go to jail for three days for that; construed as wasting water. I thought, *What? Really? Must have some pretty big jails around here 'cos half the city has been carrying on like 'Red' Adair, chucking water around ad hoc for the last four days.*

Lessons were now quite intense as we had moved onto different tenses and constantly regurgitating verbs so that we knew them on instinct as Susan knew we were to leave and wanted us as best prepared as possible; which was in our interests so we obliged and tried our hardest; but respite was at hand through our weekly cookery class where we made a final meal of corn, cheese, beans and potatoes and tonnes of homemade *aji*.

Marcia also knew that we were soon to depart, so she treated us to another night out in the old town again at La Ronda. It was great being out and about with a local who spoke so fondly of the city and was very proud of the beautiful old town; and rightly so. We sampled the 50c *Canelazo* fire water again for a cheap warming shot, before relaxing on the rooftop terrace of Marcia's favourite restaurant that offered a fabulous view of the Centro Historico with the golden lights glittering around, interrupting the dark. It was so good to see her happy and she seemed to really make an effort with everyone who stayed with her.

Our last day at school came around all too quickly. I was sad to be leaving, yet felt ready to move on and knew the time was right to get out of

Quito. For better integration, Susan had prepared some key phrases for us that were essentially phrases and sayings in Spanish that the locals would use; that means, this wasn't textbook lingo we were learning, but local slang and an ideal opportunity to try out and learn some swear words, that provided lots of fun and laughter on a very relaxed last lesson. Before leaving, we had the complementary photo session for posterity with Susan, Patricia and the rest of the staff who we had got to know that had provided such a memorable experience while we were there.

Obviously, there was still time to cut some rug on the last night; showing off our now not fantastic but not too disgraceful salsa skills. Less could be said though for our early-hour singing. Returning home, we played Euro name that tune; Sabine singing along from head phones as Gina and I tried to guess the song. Being five a.m. and sober, Spencer didn't see the funny side, waking him with much pissed up laughter and utterly shite singing. The next morning, I woke feeling a little worse for wear. Gina and Sabine were a lot worse for wear. Sorry to leave, I gingerly packed my things, said goodbyes and headed for the bus station to get to my next destination, as once again I had plans and needed to be somewhere.

Four weeks in Quito were brilliant and I had a fantastic time, the people who I met through either living with or being at school were amazing and I had a blast. I learnt and saw so much; the city provided an endless list of entertaining and interesting things to see and do and I left feeling like I'd really made the most of my time there. This also extended past the city, as Ecuador's location on the planet had already provided some of my best adventures so far, with the endeavour, stunning scenery and generally just out there strange, cool things which I never imagined I would see or do. Some of which was absolutely thrilling and so exciting that created and left unbelievable memories. I wanted to immerse myself as much as possible, while trying to be focused on learning Spanish. When I left school I thought I was now more than able to get by, week by week my confidence increased as I naturally found myself communicating more and more with the locals, in shops, bars, restaurants and taxis, who on numerous occasions had to decipher my sometimes more than garbled Spanish, as baffled individuals returned me with quizzical looks. I wasn't bothered about getting things wrong, practise was making perfect and I coped with the laughter it sometimes brought with good humour. Majority of the time, a person would correct me, after eventually getting what I was trying to ask and always seemingly impressed and happy that I had bothered to learn their language, or at least made an effort. It was a bit like learning to drive; the lessons gave you the basics and then you really start to learn after you finish and practise in the real world, in real situations. I now had a strong foothold with Spanish to stand me in good stead for the forthcoming months. There were many schools like the one I studied at and it provided so much more; with cultural activities on offer and the fact that you instantly got to meet new people from around the world and effortlessly made new friends, which was a great comfort being alone in a new country. That in itself made it a really good call deciding to make the effort to learn another language.

I never had any problems in Quito, but some of the comments in the guidebooks about the crime were founded. We heard unsettling first-hand reports about criminal activity that Susan witnessed and these were apparently worse in the south of the city where she lived, plus numerous people studying were the victims of pick pockets in and around the Mariscal Sucre, and that was while we were there. But the same could be said for every city in the world and it was just a question of keeping wits about you and taking necessary precautions. The most random part of the time spent there was the weather; usually hot and sunny in the morning, black clouds and pissing down with rain in the afternoons, yet it always seemed to be a lottery what you were going to get, leaving you either overdressed in baking humid heat to getting drenched numerous times from heading out without a rain jacket or suitable footwear. This all just added up to how brilliantly unpredictable the place could be.

The best memories though came from having a home stay; our 'Ecui'mama' (Ecuadorian mother) Marcia was one of the most fantastic persons I've had the pleasure to meet. She had such a wonderful, warm, kind persona, welcoming total strangers into her home and sharing her life with them, making a real effort to show people around and help them out. This extended to the community, including the security guard for the street, who she would feed every night when she didn't have to. Her lust for life was unrepentant, and as unpredictable and chaotic as the weather; Gina and I would be in stitches laughing at her, not only for the spray can and water incidents but when she would roll her eyes and pull faces if one of us tried to speak to her in Spanish, especially if it was a little incorrect or with an odd accent. In the house, we had to speak English because she wanted to learn it better. She would venture on to the terrace to shout and heckle people in the street; even noisy dogs were subject to abuse. Or would forget to give us parts of our meals, lose safety deposit box keys with our passports and bankcards in, sing and dance continuously around the house, go out partying for whole weekends (we never saw her over carnival), dabbled in a spot of belly dancing and seemed to have suitors in every direction. Which probably explained why she went missing over carnival and seemed to know anyone and everyone when out and about; she was like the godfather not even having to get out of the car when going to the shops, the owners would come out to her. And the journeys in the car themselves were hilariously unsettling, because when she lost her prescription driving glasses, she just drove without them or used her friend's glasses instead. A truly remarkable lady, with such a zest for life it was inspiring. I loved spending my time at her place and she made the month in Quito truly a wonderful experience. The only regret was that I never got to say goodbye the morning I had to leave; as she had gone out.

I was going to spend the weekend in Baños, having heard so many good things about it and seeing wonderful pictures of the place, plus it was on the way to where I needed to be the following week. Once again, I took a bus and headed back south on the road where I felt I had been so many times already. We eventually ventured east into the mountains and weaved along roads which cut though the Andes that were easy on the eye for around four hours, before arriving late in the afternoon. After a brief wander around the lovely streets and plaza, that still had decorative remnants of carnival hanging, I had a couple of beers with my meal on the evening and crashed out in my hostel completely knackered from the journey, and more so the previous late night frivolities.

Baños was small, quaint, picturesque town that had lots to offer, but I was going to be in town for only a day-and-a-half, so I didn't really have time to book or experience some of the countless activities like rafting, rappelling and quad biking. I leaned towards the cheaper option of hiring a mountain bike and exploring the local area, being more beneficial to both wallet and health. Heading east out of town, I had been given a map that wasn't very comprehensive, so I ended up just making it up as I went along. This was predominantly at speed as the road leaving eastward was a downward slope and got as far as the hydro dam in the valley of the mountain, before deciding to turn around to find something a little more interesting; this was when I realised this was the only road and I'd covered about 5km and had to cycle back up. Exercise already proving beneficial to the health indeed.

Laden with trees and greenery, the hills and mountain seemed to circle around Baños; beautifully located sitting on a mid-mountainside plateau, in a steep valley with a gorge cutting through. Looking up, huge birds circled round here and I wondered if these could be condors, or a type of. They were majestic and graceful in flight as they scavenged for food. Putting faith in the map, I started the steep road ascent up the mountain around the back of town; passing the beautiful Ulba falls, this let me know I was on the right track. I had seen many a waterfall so wasn't the reason why I was heading up. But I really didn't know how long it was going to take and some two gruelling hours later, I eventually reached the top, where a dirt track eventually lead me to the edge of the mountain with the town below. It was hard work but worth it; as the view overlooking Baños and the valley it sat in was stunning. The incredibly steep, lush green mountain I stood on circled round to the left, and acted as a protective backdrop for the town and a source of the waterfall and hot pools that Baños was famous for. To the right-hand side was the deep gorge and river that flows through the valley. I sat on the benches provided to admire the scenery and get my breath back.

Up here at the edge of the mountain precipice, a huge cross was situated. This was lit up at night and from below looked quite small; it's now-huge size emphasised how far up I had come. I was just about to head back down when something caught my eye. The mountains which encircled Baños had initially obscured the view, but I noticed thick clouds moving in the sky. But these weren't clouds. It was hot volcanic white smoke billowing out from the top of the very active Volcán Tungurahua and the source of heat for the hot springs. Sitting just behind the town and conical in stereotypical stature, it looked incredible. I had never seen a volcano in action before this close (I hadn't seen a volcano period, till few weeks ago; now they were fucking everywhere and was totally oblivious to the fact Lake Taupo is actually a super volcano as well!). The view was amazing and I stared at it in wonderment. I'd seen it from afar on the day trip but now here, I was at its feet and mercy. I tried to imagine what it would be like nearer the top or for that matter what it would be like with lava spewing out; as was the case when it erupted back to life in 1999 and Baños had to be partially evacuated.

Heading back down, the journey was considerably quicker; gravity was now my friend and the two hour trip up took a fractional ten minutes to get down and I stopped to watch a local game of football from the grass verge on the roadside for a while. I hadn't seen any football for a long time, hardly a big game classic but a game in South America nevertheless, so this would suffice. Back in town, I decided to take a look over the gorge and headed to the bridge which crossed it. The road upwards on the far side gave another tremendous perspective view of the town, mountainous wall background and now in full sight the still-smoking Tungurahua. Yet heading back, I passed up the opportunity to complete the last thing I wanted to do before I left.

The next morning before leaving, I headed straight back to the bridge over the ravine and met the guys who were going to prepare me to bridge jump. I had heard about being able to do this and felt really up for it, especially having missed out in Queenstown. Here, this was much cheaper than the bungee jump and it was little more exhilarating, having never done this type of jump before so I had no excuses. But the day prior, I seemed to have every excuse in the book because when crossing, a company was setting up and I watched as a Kiwi jumper went for it and leapt off. Chatting beforehand, he said, "If ya want to do it, just bung these guys $10 and do it now." I had no adequate footwear, not enough money (he offered to lend it to me) and I was nervous. So, essentially, I bottled it and backed out. But when I returned the bike, I decided not to be beaten and booked it for the next morning; so here I was.

The rope was anchored to the railing on the far side of the bridge and then fed underneath and to the other side where I was harnessed up. And a platform was placed over the railing where I was to jump from; the railing that was there to stop idiots from jumping or falling off. It was about 60m to the bottom; granted, I wasn't going to fall that far; well, not unless something went wrong. I was nervous but not as scared as the day prior, which I found slightly odd and figured I had now psyched myself up and prepared mentally. Also, I had been in this situation before bungee jumping in Canada but with one big difference; here, I was attached by a climbing rope and there was significantly less give in this rope compared to the elasticity of bungee. Therefore, it was imperative to jump out over as far as possible to create a pendulum effect reducing the hard pull of the rope when it took hold and help avoid the chance of injury. With bungee, you can take a tentative step and fall off the edge and the elastic will slow the fall, caress and take care of the jumper. Not here. I had thought about this and visualised that I had to literally throw myself out into the void.

Looking straight out at the valley in front of me, I was counted down:

3, 2, 1…

My legs pushed as hard as they could. My arms thrust forwards and then spread out over as I fired myself off the platform at a ninety-degree angle and I soared like a bird. For the briefest second, I was horizontal still looking at the valley, then almost instantaneously I started to tilt down over as I looked to the river and trees below and the air started to rush past my head as I built up momentum in free fall. Before my mind could really process what was happening, and after a matter of what felt like seconds, there was a sudden jolt around my body from the harness as the rope unexpectedly snapped.

Into action, that is. This seemed so quick to take effect, I could only have fallen 20m before being uncomfortably hurtled underneath the high bridge at fast speed to the other side, dangling from the end of a rope and swing back and forth out of my control. Shouts and *whoops* of exhilarated excitement echoed under the bridge as everything had gone well, I was OK; apart from the familiar strangulated crotch. After five or six passes and when the momentum had ceased, I dangled helplessly before the guys on the bridge lowered me down where the rope jerked and lurched as I was manoeuvred into position, reminding me that the harness was digging in the groin Eventually when I leached a low-enough level; a rope was thrown to me which I caught and was dragged back to the safety of the embankment.

Thrilled to have completed the jump, I headed back up to thank the guys; now happy and content having proven a point to myself before heading to the hostel, pack my things and take the relatively short bus journey to my next intriguingly 'wild' encounter…

Jungly, Jungly… the Jungle is Massive

The local bus from Baños headed eastward along the road I followed the day before on the mountain bike. It was crowded and people swayed uniformly onto to one another as our carriage hastily negotiated the twists and turns demanded by the mountainside of the valley. We had started at an elevation of 1800m in Baños and headed steeply downhill; after an hour or so, the mountains subsided and before me a fabulous ocean as far as the eye could see. The vista was similar yet different to that I had seen before. This time, no blue rippling rhythmic motion, no white cap waves; a different kind of ocean; dimpled and mottled luscious green; vast and expansive with a flat horizon touching an overcast sky above. Yet, as much as you wouldn't want to get lost at sea, you wouldn't want to get lost in here as it could be just as deadly; the Amazon jungle.

My destination was a small town called Puyo. Prior to departure along with learning Spanish, I booked two weeks of volunteer work at an animal rescue centre; wanting the experience of working in an environment at close quarters with nature having a keen interest in the natural world and wildlife, also I had never done anything like this before. This I hoped would provide the chance to do something worthwhile, give to a cause, help make a difference and keep me occupied while not just self-absorb with my own personal leisure activities and goals, further more hopefully learn something and have a good time in doing so. In Quito, I had a meeting with a group who were the agents for these activities, I was due at a different place but due to political issues, the location had been changed which I was fine with, having not really known about where I was going or what to expect anyway. My contact here was a British guy called Don; who was the volunteer co-ordinator for the rescue centre. I arrived in Puyo and called him; unfortunately, he was returning from Quito and not in the immediate vicinity, so I arranged to meet him and I took lunch while I waited for his arrival.

Wandering close by to the bus stop, I noticed a guy crossing the main road. He also noticed me. Immediately, I knew this was Don, my contact;

essentially because he stuck out like a sore thumb being European-looking. And in Puyo, I had realised there seemed to be a severe lack of tourists, so my chances of being wrong were slim, and I wasn't. Conversely, he knew who I was for the exact same reason. Having made our introductions, we headed do get some supplies; I only really needed some rubber boots, as I had been pre-empted on the things required when in Quito and had acquired medicines, plenty mosquito repellent, and more importantly a mosquito net while there.

We headed ten minutes out of town in a cab and followed a really bumpy track off the main road into the greenery of the surrounding trees and countryside. Though this was soon sharp forgotten as I was astounded by what I saw when I got there. The rescue centre was incredibly beautiful and picturesque; way beyond any expectations. Soft wood chipping trails carved the way around, an uninterrupted view of trees, plant life, flowers, water channels, large pens and enclosures creating a sprawling utopia in the middle of the jungle. Don set about showing me around; explaining the different types of wildlife inhabiting there and using the opportunity to find the other workers, getting an update of occurrences in his absence and making the necessary introductions.

There were over a hundred animals being cared for and weren't specialising in one particular species; these included various monkeys, parrots, macaws, toucan, cats, kinkajous, agoutis, coatis, tayras, an anteater, a wild pig, caiman, snakes, turtles and tortoises to name a few. I immediately started getting a good vibe about the place, albeit not for the first time I was slightly nervous and apprehensive about the prospect of the unknown; more over not knowing how or if I could cope having to work with a somewhat unpredictable nature of these animals, which were wild and hardly there under their own duress, but more from necessity for their own protection and rehabilitation.

The daily work routine involved being up around seven thirty a.m. for breakfast; straight after which, we prepared breakfast of various feed for the day-time animals and then head out to clean, feed and interact with them, check on their wellbeing and any report issues if anything unusual. The rest of the time was downtime when the volunteers could relax and do as they pleased, until next feeding and cleaning, but more so it was an opportunity to be involved with project work throughout the centre; such as maintenance and making improvements to the facility which was interspersed with taking lunch. Then at four p.m. late afternoon was preparing, feeding and cleaning again involving the nocturnal animals before finishing around six p.m. in the early evening. This was fine, I was more than prepared for long hours and hard work and now quite looking forward to it, being given the opportunity to do something pro-active and trying something new. I'd decided that the free time shouldn't be wasted and I wanted to help as much as possible, immersing myself with anything and everything required.

For the first couple of days, I shadowed either Don or another volunteer; an American called Colin who was there as part of his college studies that required some field work experience. There were only five of us working at the centre. Don and two indigenous workers who only spoke Spanish and Quichua, the native language; these were the full-time staff and with my arrival made two volunteers. There was also our little mascot; a gorgeous little baby capuchin monkey called Frederica who was too young to go in with the other monkeys as there was a real danger that if they rejected her, she could be injured or killed being so fragile. So, she hung around with us (mainly Don) and generally just inquisitively foraged around in her infantile state, getting into mischief that mostly involved having a piss or dump on anyone and everything that she interacted with.

It was slightly daunting at first, the prospect of five people being responsible for the whole centre; it was big and the property easily covered the same space as a couple of football fields. It was owned by a local well-to-do family, but they didn't actively get involved yet, understandably, had a say and vested interest with what was happening in and around the place. Quickly, I started to get to grips with the different types of animals and what they were. This was all brand new to me and some of the species I hadn't even heard of, never mind what the dietary requirements were. Fortunately, in the food preparation area, there as a chart with the different animals listed and what type of thing they would eat. This would generally be a mixture of fresh fruit and vegetables chopped up into manageable portions. Some days, certain types of animals would be given something different as a treat to supplement the diet. This was slightly confusing at first as it seemed there were so many animals to take into consideration, ensuring everything was getting fed was bad enough, let alone that there was plenty for each group or species and it was the right food source.

Some were much easier to feed than others for various reasons, but each seemed to pose a potential challenge in some way, shape or form; some of the creatures could roam free around the centre, some were in cages, some in enclosures, others hung around on their own islands surrounded by water, some were placid, some not so placid and some had the potential to be downright dangerous. And I was very aware that each should be treated with the utmost respect. Easier tasks were feeding the agoutis; a small rodent-like creature where the only real challenge was making sure that they never made a break for freedom through the doorway on entry. This was even less so in the case of the tortoises, who would slowly saunter over when the various leaves and fruit would be placed in their pen and it was rather amusing watching the humorously named Flash and Lightning try to chase someone when entering the enclosure to clean away any uneaten food or debris. Around this time was where I'd oddly find myself constantly humming the theme tune to *One Foot in the Grave* as the ambling tortoises menacingly ventured towards me at an alarmingly slow rate.

Others were more of a challenge; the capuchin monkeys were housed in a large cage. They constantly engaged the small door upon feeding time, having learnt exactly where the food would be coming from, and crouching to get inside had to be a quick, meticulous operation, involving distraction of pushing some bananas through the wire mesh further away. Yet, still one in particular called Beba was the house Houdini, hell bent on escaping. Being in the cage could prove hazardous at times as the capuchin would take exception of you being in there, and on more than one occasion I found myself being pelted with fruit from the above branches while cleaning table tops and floor. The much smaller and less disruptive squirrel monkeys were free roaming around the site, but carry in a bucket of food and they would appear in an instant and were suddenly your best friend; jumping all over head and shoulders with the only intention of liberating pieces of fruit for themselves. With them being quiet little it was no problem or bother, more fun than intimidating as I had envisioned it could be much worse, but I quickly started to gain a greater understanding and respect for each of the various species of monkey. Just watching them swing and climb was a great spectacle; as they would leap and jump around with such agility and dexterity, using the tail like a fifth limb increased balance and mobility, providing a strength to move that was somewhat hypnotic and effortlessly amazing.

The woolly monkey, Thomas, occupied his own island surrounded by water. This meant he was out in the open and had lots of tall tree trunks and branches inter-connected with rope to play and exercise on, yet couldn't go anywhere because of the dislike of water. Thomas was much larger than the others and much stronger; about third size of an average human with fluffy dark fur, that probably made him look bigger that he was but with his size and strength was possible to break a persons' arm with ease should he get upset enough. He was intimidating. So, with some trepidation, I tried to be mindful of this when going to feed him, this was done in pairs by balancing on a rickety ladder placed over the water to reach the island and distracting him by throwing pieces of banana to the far side. Fortunately, Thomas had a kindly nature and would come over to say 'hello' and actively jump onto your back whilst trying to put the food down or clean his area; only once did he have an episode when I tried to clear a piece of debris and he still wanted it and started howling and screeching with menacing eyes. I dropped it real quick. It was pretty scary; a large primate pissed off over a rotten banana skin. But this was dealing with nature and why two people would go onto the island together; one acting as security for the other person that had just filled their pants.

Other larger primate was Manuel; a spider monkey who was really sweet and timid. He was slender with longer arms and legs than the others that made his appearance spider-esque. He made lovely little high-pitched cooing noises at the prospect of being fed and when having interaction with visitors. He was in his own separate enclosure and squirrel monkeys would occasionally pay a little visit to come and see him; or rather steal his food. He was again not one for missing out on mischief; when I was cleaning his enclosure, I found myself the target of him dropping the contents of his bowls on me from a height.

Parrots and macaws provided a different challenge, as they also largely inhabited their own islands out in the open that involved another tricky balancing act to get over to, either that or a good 6ft leap to the far embankment, but this tactic always ran the possibility of an impromptu swim. The plumage were beautiful colours of vivid green, red and blue that stood out; if they weren't easy enough to spot, they could be heard from all over the centre, as loud screeches and squawks would regularly break the ambience. Their unfortunate contact with humans had enabled some with the ability to talk and could mimic certain words. It did bring a smile when you would be surprised with a spontaneous '*Hola*' if nearby or interacting with them, as they seemed to offer the chance to build a rapport. Entertaining as this was, it didn't distract from the fact it was unnatural for the birds to do this; human pleasure through teaching them bad habits, maybe? I suppose as it's not necessary, but when as pets people want to bond and the parrots naturally just pick up noises and sounds and start mimicking them as part of the biology. It's difficult; for example, who doesn't talk to their dog? I always talked to all the animals and was even harder not to talk to the parrots.

Worse still was the harm caused to them and reason for being brought to the rescue centre; all having had their wings clipped as pets. This meant they couldn't fly or at least not very far; a practice that had left them in perilous danger from attack. Their most natural defence had been removed and would be a long time before they would re-grow. Knowing this made me glad they now had their own little sanctuary to live on and recuperate. They loved corn and would hastily shuffle along the branches where it was placed for them carefully as not to get bitten off the incredibly strong and razor-sharp bill. They would then pick a piece up with a claw and start munching away. Much like the toucan who was just as overzealous at feeding time, his gorgeous large yellow and blue bill clacked expectantly and signalled danger; another who had to be distracted with morsels of food elsewhere prior to getting his main course.

Others though weren't so straightforward; the coatis were a curious-looking mammal with striations on the tail like a raccoon and a long snout, yet, generally easy to work as they didn't pose much of a danger sniffing around; difficulties being they would constantly be at the door waiting, making it quite tricky getting in and out of the enclosure and easily ransack any food before it could be placed down having a really curious and inquisitive nature, so would constantly get in the way when trying to scoop up the copious amounts of really pungent smelly shit that they seemed to produce on demand, all the while looking on wondering why you were tidying up their mess, also being adept climbers and diggers had to be constantly aware of looking for and filling in the holes they'd hollow out with their sharp claws. I quickly grew to love the coatis though as they were really friendly and you just knew they'd be up to something. And the same could be said of the tayras.

These resembled a large stoat, similar in nature to the coatis but were much quicker and watching them dart back and forward, jumping onto the branches, swinging in their tyres and wrestle with each other with athletic ease was great entertainment and another hypnotic spectacle. Incredibly possessive of their food, it would have to be put in separate piles for them both to indulge in at the same time to stop them fighting over one single amount. They too were quite friendly but had to be very wary of where they were; bending over, they would happily jump onto a person's back and claws would dig in as they sniffed around the neck a little too close for comfort with their sharp teeth; that were easily adept at demolishing a treat of raw chicken or eggs, devouring them as if going out of fashion.

I was enjoying dealing with the animals and being in such close quarters, I always tried to focus on what was required and take nothing for granted, notably with the tayras who provided a more unpredictable and volatile nature. Especially having been informed another previous volunteer had allowed one to escape where it made a beeline straight for an unsuspecting macaw and tore the poor bird to pieces. So I tried to bear this in mind with what I was doing and the prospect of what could happen.

The most disconcerting job though came from dealing with the kinkajous. These are incredibly cute-looking mammals, small and bear-like with little round ears, big eyes, and a lovely furry coat; almost as if butter wouldn't melt. Yet, these were incredibly vicious with big teeth and bigger claws, and certainly didn't appreciate people encroaching on their territory. Good thing though was they were nocturnal so it was possible to feed and clean them during the day. Being very stealthy and quiet, we ensured that none were hiding in hollow tubes. This meant they were in their hutches and the doors of where they slept could be blocked off with wood. Safely locked inside, it was possible to clean and put food down, but time and a keen eye was always of the essence, as they would usually wake and could hear them knocking against the makeshift door blocking them inside. When finished, the wood was removed where they would then sleepily wander out for a look around to see what was happening and like proverbial bear with a sore head, provide a knowing stare and growl to anyone still the vicinity. Don told me he had previously been attacked off one in a lapse of concentration and it put its claws straight through his rubber boot. These were the only animal that the indigenous workers Miguel and Carlos who had years of experience were nervous about working with. This spoke volumes about the nature of these beautiful but potentially dangerous little critters.

Animals such as the margay cats, the caiman and snakes we didn't feed or clean. The full-time workers did this and Miguel looked after the snakes like they were his own personal pets, but we were actively encouraged to watch or help. The cats were only small in comparison to say a tiger; about three times the size of a domestic pet but nevertheless extremely beautiful with spotted markings, piercing eyes that wouldn't move from watching a person and a sinister under tone of constant growl, to emphasise the contempt that they had for anyone thinking of entering or putting hands too close, as these still weren't your average kitty. It was quite a spectacle seeing two of Carlos, Miguel or Don enter and have to use a sweeping brush as a cat deterrent while cleaning at the same time, to then hastily throw a diet of raw chicken through the door, as they impatiently patrolled back and forth waiting for their feed or just to menacingly deter any more antagonising behaviour. I never got to see them actually eat as they were quite private in such a manner, as they always waited till everyone had left before settling enough to dine. Much like the caiman, who could be elusive during the day, submerged within the murky pond of the enclosure and only became more visible under the cover of darkness. We'd often go for a walk around the park to check on the nocturnal animals in the pitch black, using torches as the only light source and they would reflect back from the caiman's eyes, having now made their way to the waters' surface or the land at the edge of the enclosure.

Picking up the feeding and cleaning procedures in the space of a few days aided me so much and I quickly found myself growing with confidence when dealing with the animals and was enjoying it immensely. They were all beautiful creatures in their own special way and the fact I was getting to interact and provide for them at such a close quarters only helped enhance the experience. But as the saying goes, 'never work with animals and children', I was also realising how apt this could be. Seemingly every day, something would happen that would put the day activities on hold or delay the cleaning and feeding procedures and could manifest in what seemed in any way, shape or form.

Animals could easily escape given the slightest of chance. Beba the capuchin monkey was very adept at this and she managed to escape because I hadn't closed the cage door properly; I felt bad about the fact that she had gotten out but was assured that it happened on a regular basis and she never went far, knowing that she could get fed very easily being somewhere in the vicinity of the cage and also she would miss the company of the others; so much so, she would regularly be seen interacting with those still-inside from the outside. Problem was, she was very disruptive with other animals; easily getting onto the islands and upsetting the parrots or chasing Thomas and antagonising him. Which was why, the capuchins were captive; if they all were loose, it would be absolute bedlam. Being in a forested area and spending time up in the trees ensured catching Beba was easier said than done. On more than one occasion, at the end of the day, a team of us would have to chase around to bring her in, yet finding ourselves wanting more times than successful, as she would recognise each person and know the outcome of getting too near. Eventually though, she would be captured by getting tired, too close or distracted. More successfully though was the safe return of the tayra which got out when being cleaned and fed by Don and I. I got blindsided by the male as I was about to leave and within a flash of silky black fur, he was out. He didn't go far, hastily exploring his newly expanded surroundings; I quickly grabbed some fruit from the ground and Don ushered him in the right direction; being a typical male thinking with his stomach, he ended up back safe inside the cage after some nifty broom work and chasing the fruit thrown inside. Luckily, there was no one else around to spook him and was returned some five minutes later with minimal fuss; especially bearing in mind what had happened previously to the macaw.

On many occasions, running repairs had to be made to the cages or enclosures, such as fixing leaking water bowls or the fencing, as animals would dig and we constantly had to look for holes or damage. Also, there were also 'unwanted' visitors as two local dogs had found the benefits of the rescue centre with the plentiful amounts of food on offer; they would turn up each day and follow people around the park making a nuisance out of themselves and disrupting the animals, this made catching Beba a nigh on impossibility as they would want to chase and play with her; granted, this was reciprocated. It was a situation which had manifested over time before my arrival; the dogs' owner never looked after them and they were allowed to roam free, so obviously headed where there was food, fun and attention. With the nature of the place, it was difficult to just get rid, as they were really good-natured and just doing what dogs do. Even though it wasn't the responsibility of the centre to take care of them; they still sort of did.

People visiting could also be an issue; for a small fee, parties were welcome to wander round, interact and learn about the animals. This was great and I was happy that people wanted to take an interest feeling that it was important especially for children but also had its downside, as lots of screaming and unsupervised youngsters would disrupt some of the animals and on more than one occasion, found people feeding them; which could have terrible consequences. Point and case being that on the day I arrived, apparently the vet had been and another woolly monkey had died. This was due to a blockage in the intestines from eating a bread or pastry product that someone had thrown. The emphasis of 'do not feed the animals' couldn't be more overstated; they have strict diets and food which we eat are potentially harmful to animals because things like bread and pastries are not readily available in the wild, so they naturally struggle with digestion to the extent that they can be fatal.

People were also a danger to themselves as they would also put their fingers in to the cages of the tayras to try to stroke them or put hands near the beaks of a wandering parrot; where it is plain to see the beaks, claws and teeth on offer are more than capable of causing damage, especially to a youngster, yet parents would seem oblivious to this. Despite any obvious implications, the main problem was that it wasn't organised properly for them to be taken around with someone responsible to act as guide; Don, Miguel and Carlos may not have been available at their arrival and Colin's and my Spanish or knowledge wasn't good enough to provide a comprehensive tour. One positive though was that strangers offered a good foil for Beba; she trusted them to get food and would happily forage closer and let a small boy pick her up, who only handed her back to Don. Back in the cage she went; again.

Regardless, I was having a wonderful time working with the animals in beautiful surroundings. I was living in a custom-built wooden cabin in the middle of the refuge that had hammocks on the porch; much to the really cute squirrel monkeys' delight, I regularly caught them playing in there and used it more than I. All the time surrounded by the weird and wonderful creatures and the noises that they bring, not to mention learning so much. They were long hours and it was hard work; rain or shine, we were up and out doing the necessary, all for the benefit of the animals. On more than one occasion, I was caught in a torrential storm, as the weather was still predictably unpredictable but all the while stiflingly humid.

During the days when it was quieter, time was spent on construction. I helped Carlos build a wooden gate as part of a dam, for the lake out the back; chopping pieces of wood with only the basic tool of a machete. It was hard and tiring, so I think he was happy when I returned to carry on helping him after lunch, as he thought that I was going to quit and leave him to it. I was pleased to prove him wrong. The job needed doing so I helped till it was finished. I also spent a couple of days working with Miguel; lugging wheelbarrow after wheelbarrow of heavy rocks and gravel about 100m from the front of the centre to the caiman pen, as a new and improved lagoon was being constructed for them, with the beady eyes of the larger 2m long caiman watching on, all the while my beady eyes were on him to make sure he was still where I thought he was. Finishing, I had the privilege of holding the smaller of the two and even at just under a metre in length, I could feel the power within its smooth-scaled armour and admired the rows of tiny flesh-ripping teeth; which looked like they'd had a go at my legs, having been cut to ribbons off tiny sharp barbs on the long grass when fixing the pipe blockage of the natural water supply to the pen.

Also trails were built in the forest out the back; in my case by adopting a stance comparable to that of a drunken woodsman, as we slashed and hacked at the undergrowth with a machete to create clearances for people to walk around and appreciate the natural surroundings of the jungle vegetation, as well as a spot of logging and carrying loads of large, needless to say weighty, fresh cut tree trunks to make pathways throughout the park.

Yet with all the good endeavour, there was bad news; the saddest part of the experience was having to dig metre-deep holes to bury two animals that perished. The ant eater was amazing; a beautiful creature of curious nature, another brilliant climber and digger with large hooked front claws. I had never seen one, never mind worked with one before. And an armadillo that was brought in sick. Despite best efforts looking after them and the vet being unavailable to come out in time, they both passed away from causes unknown and in quick succession. I was gutted and felt like these creatures had been failed. Don was also upset and both instances acted as a real downer on everybody there.

In the second week, we were joined by another volunteer that I thought would ease the workload somewhat. But what did I know? Because it never. Another had to be shown the procedures and Carlos had now also finished working there, so effectively we lost an experienced member of staff for an inexperienced volunteer. Despite this, there was always a great team spirit; with Don at the heart of everything. He had come to Ecuador having studied zoology at university and got involved with a bear project in the Andes; tracking, tagging and monitoring them before hearing about and taking the job here. I thought that this was a really excellent ethos; he had left Britain to pursue his dream and the job he loved and was passionate about. Despite the fact this was in a foreign country and he never spoke a word of Spanish on his arrival, whereas now he was pretty much fluent without having a single lesson.

We worked as a team; dividing the jobs up, we all cooked, ate and cleaned up together in the communal area for three meals a day, and when everything was done, we relaxed together. It was fantastic that we got to work with local indigenous people who were warm and friendly, which provided the opportunity for me to practise my Spanish that was mainly let down by my lack of vocabulary, but a great experience, as I discovered a work ethic of a high relentless standard, in what was purveyed such a worthy cause, indicative of all the people who were involved there.

Where people work hard, they tend to play hard and here was no different. Just down the lane before arriving at the refuge centre, there were a couple of houses inhabited by locals; the first house had dogs, who would bark wildly and run out as if to bite. It was worth it to negotiate past these as the second property operated as a small shop, the elderly lady who lived there sold our beloved Kryptonite; beer and cigarettes. This allowed us to unwind. Unfortunately, this was to the annoyance of the owners, which was slightly disappointing as we weren't completely wasted, having a massive party or making lots of noise till the early hours; we were up the next day doing what was required, feeding, cleaning and working. They spotted the empties later the following day and we were made to feel like we had done something wrong. Something I then felt slightly hypocritical, when the owner's wife decided to have a party for her friends and colleagues one lunch time at the centre, took over the whole kitchen and food preparation area and wanted us to join in, allowing us to drink beers in the middle of the afternoon. I can't complain too much though as we had a fresh lunch prepared for us as well; barbequed fish with rice and my fast-becoming new favourite root vegetable yucca. It tasted somewhat like a potato when fried. I thought it was delicious and so did the animals, so who was I to argue. After our fill, a strange thing happened; instead of going back to work, the owner's wife then insisted that we all have a bit of a dance about with her and her friends. Again, we all obliged and started making shapes around our communal area in our rubber boots, which everyone thought was brilliant; me also as I never quite envisaged this. It was too much fun dancing around in the jungle.

The weekends were our own after Saturday feed and clean, finishing around midday; this allowed time to head into Puyo, to use the computer or buy some supplies. I took the opportunity to chill out and relax after a heavy workload and long working weekdays. I also had to obviously help Miguel drink some beer.

All-too-soon, my time to leave had come around, I had put in two weeks' work which was the pretty much the minimum for volunteers; I felt disappointed to be leaving. I had had such a wonderful time helping out there and wanted to give more. I felt invigorated by the fact that I had worked incredibly hard and was now covered in cuts, scratches, insect bites, large bruises, and was aching all over, completely knackered from my endeavours. I didn't care, it was all worthwhile, leaving me feeling really good about myself and was pleased when Don acknowledged so and thanked me, saying that he and the animals were really appreciative. I mentioned that plans had changed somewhat, and there could be an opportunity for me to return now because of spending the rest of my time in South America. Don was hopeful, but I was undecided about future plans so I didn't want to commit or make a promise that I may not keep and we left it at that. I had made good friends with Don; a fellow northerner from Britain and we got on famously, having similar accent, way of talking and an interest in football. He taught me so much and helped me out with my lack of experience dealing with animals, and were generally a really bad influence on each other with regards to drinking and the fact that we both were trying, and failing miserably, to stop smoking.

The place itself was fabulous. A beautiful serene natural setting that offered so much education, endeavour and fun that even extended to having a shaman hut (who I hoped would come and visit!). But primarily a sanctuary for the poor animals that ended up there, mainly from the abuse of man or neglectful owners. It was really heart-warming to know that they were now safe and I was proud to have helped with the refuge mission; feeling really privileged that I had got to work with such beautiful creatures and yet it was also more than that. Due to the fact there was only a few of us, we were all ultimately responsible and it felt like being part of a unique collective, working as one to achieve something really good and positive for the local wildlife and environment. It created unity and comradery; like when the water supply went off, no showers were available and needing to get cleaned up at the end of the day, we just took turns bathing in the small fresh water river that cascaded through the centre, much to the amusement of passing visitors looking on in bewilderment. Small sacrifices like this helped galvanise us. Knowing we were in it together, to make us get it done for the animals. Albeit a work in progress, Don had made massive strides already and had some good plans for the place and I left feeling really happy and confident about its future.

I was due to leave but not before there was still time for some fun which involved beers and pool in town on my last night, to messing about on the Tarzan swings that were strung up in the trees, at the back of our communal kitchen area, they were ridiculously high when swinging out; so much so that you had to make sure you got off on return to the steep embankment, as it was a good 10m drop should you lose momentum. Finally before taking my bus, we spent a couple of hours at a local outdoor water park; blazing down the really fast kamikaze slide, that effectively removed any dirt or grime that was on me from the last two weeks, acting as a high-speed power wash. Inevitably, all good things have to come to an end and I had to get back to Quito; again to catch up with someone where together we would embark on lifelong dream.

Incas Have Purple Thumbs

After a rather uneventful journey returning to Quito, I once again realised the pit falls of the Ecuadorian public transport system as the traffic was horrendous and slowed considerably on the approach to the city. It took ages to negotiate our way to the terminal and with a severe lack of toilets, I found myself completely bursting at the seams. In the end, the discomfort of my full bladder was unrepentant and when you got to go; you got to go. So, I had to take a wiz into a bottle there and then on the bus; I have to apologise for this but it was absolutely necessary. Luckily, the bus was quiet and I was discreetly tucked away in the rear seats, not stood mid-aisle, wailing a satisfying *'aaah'* so was happily relieved; that also included not making a mess, causing a commotion or being arrested and yes, I did the decent thing and took the offending bottle with me to throw away when I left.

My flight was the next day and I stayed in a centrally located hostel as I had some things to sort out before leaving; firstly washing. All my clothes were either wringing wet, stinking and/or absolutely pitted with dirt from the activities at the refuge and they needed cleaning badly. Also, I had to get money to pay the airport tax upon departure, something that I'd initially forgotten about. While waiting around for my washing, I took lunch and wandered aimlessly around the Mariscal Sucre but did venture into one of the bookstores I knew of. There, I chatted to the owner; an ex-pat who moved here to be with his wife. He kindly made me a cup of tea and I couldn't remember the last time I had a brew so enjoyed it immensely, as a change from the coffee frequently available everywhere. Perusing through, I happened upon a book. *Yes Man* had just been made into a movie and I was intrigued by it. The basis of the story being a social experiment that the writer himself had undertaken; where anything asked of him, he would have to say yes to. It sounded interesting as that sort of thing could land you in any amounts of trouble yet had the potential to open any amounts of interesting adventures and could take your life anywhere. I had been looking for a while for my next read so with an instinctive 'yes' bought the book there and then (see what I did there!).

At the airport, my Spanish failed me again, after somehow managing to have my baggage wrapped in swathes of plastic, this was at a cost when I didn't want it doing so, I demanded that they remove it; they weren't best pleased. But were far too overzealous in trying to make a quick buck by wrapping before I could utter any form of discouragement. My destination was Lima in Peru and then onto Cusco. During my month studying Spanish, I'd had to buy flights to get me to the destinations where I had more of the pre-planned things scheduled; which were all in a relatively short space of time. The flights I had initially were now cancelled, as they involved coming from the USA, to Quito, then to Cusco and from Lima back to the states. Now I still needed to travel some distance which wasn't possible overland in the time frame required.

I spent the night on the floor in Lima airport as we arrived late, sleeping with one bag attached and one as a pillow to keep them close; not that anyone had much chance of stealing anything due to the security around and I use the word 'sleep' in the loosest sense, before then taking my early morning connecting flight to Cusco. On my arrival, the Andean sun was blazing in the early morning. I was picked up and taken to my hotel accommodation, included as part of the four-day trek to the mystical and world-famous Machu Picchu. This was always on my itinerary as something that I wanted to do as part of my travels, and participate in as a long-time dream; that now had come to fruition. But I hoped it would be more than that because when I organised the trek some nine months prior, my cousin had got wind of my plans, and was equally as keen to visit the site and decided to come out to meet me. I was really excited as I hadn't seen him for over a year, and knew that there would be good/chaotic times having been on holiday and travelled together before. I wouldn't be wrong.

He had arrived the day previous and told me the hostel he was staying at. After checking where it was, I headed straight there to catch up with him, finding Dan in the bar area taking breakfast. It was amazing to see him again. He looked just as I'd remembered, apart from now missing the hair on his head, having shaved off the few wisps that remained, as the onset of becoming follicly challenged like myself had arrived. We chatted hastily about what I had been up to, what was happening back home and proudly showed off my new body art when curiosity got the better of him and he demanded to see what I'd had scrawled upon my persona.

He checked out of his hostel and I helped carry some of his things, as now he was also moving into the hotel where I was. We wasted no time in looking around the Centro Historico of Cusco; the former Incan capital of the Andes. Yet it was difficult to tell nowadays as this place was incredibly touristy with western travellers and holiday makers everywhere you looked, much more so than anywhere I had been in South America so far; granted this wasn't many places. But being the central base town for visitors to the ever-increasing popularity of Machu Picchu, what else was to be expected? And where there are tourists, there is money to be made. The Plaza de Armas (main square) was just down from where we were staying; touts for tours, vendors, market stalls, bars, restaurants and massage offerings adorned the sidewalks around the edge of the square; one after the other would approach to offer their services, to only politely decline each and keep on walking. Despite the commercialism, it was a charming place adorned with architecture from old colonial times, so I quite liked it.

We headed to one of the bars with a balcony overlooking the plaza, and over a couple of early afternoon beers continued catching up, invariably talking shit while watching the world go by and a runaway llama nearly get knocked down by a car in the street. As great as it would have been getting hammered all day, we couldn't, as supplies were needed having received our information packs at the hotel and had to sort our bags before meeting our guide later, to be prepped for the start next day.

Chatting with the guide, everything was fine when discussing what we would be doing and the itinerary. Then problems; firstly, we were told that we would have to pay an extra subsidy to be able to take part in the trek, a new tax of sorts or park fee that wasn't in place when we booked, so we had to pay the difference or wouldn't be allowed to participate. As we were due to start the next day, we were held over a barrel somewhat so had to pay. Fortunately, it wasn't too expensive but we got receipts, with the intention of taking it up with the tour operators that we had booked with. Next documentation required was our insurance; I had mine, no problem. Dan on the other hand never had. He had travel insurance from his girlfriend's bank but no written documentation or copy to hand over. Cue hastily calling home and emails being sent. I just thought, *Here we go; chaos rules.*

The next morning, we were up for six thirty a.m. and loaded up on the free breakfast at the hotel before meeting again with Manuel the guide and setting off. Arriving in Ollantaytambo – a small gateway town to the Inca trails – was a quaint, charming little cobbled street former Incan town, seemingly unchanged for centuries where locals were selling their traditional merchandise of llama wool jumpers and head wear to the trekking hoards. We stayed for a small snack and stocked up on supplies of coca products and purchased walking sticks, as from previous experience we knew how helpful these could be for the impending terrain.

A short drive later, we arrived at a car park at Km 82 and our start point. Disembarking, we were introduced to our three porters and most importantly our chef, which was quite unexpected. I hadn't actually thought about where we were going to sleep or how we were going to be fed, let alone where any of the equipment was coming from. All I knew was it was provided for. In all these instances, it was coming with us. Crossing the railway line and heading down to the passport control, our tickets were checked and passports received an official stamp for the national park; one of only five hundred issued to the trail per day. Again, the sun was high and seared in a cloudless Andean sky, as we set off crossing a wobbling bridge over raging river below and proceeded to following the gravel track along the river system. This newer trail was easy and offered a pleasant walking pace, with time to admire the beautiful surrounding area of the green valleys and far stretching mountains. I was loving being out here and felt invigorated with nature's wilderness. One thing had become apparent; our group was easily one of the smallest on the Inca trails, as there was just the three of us (guide included). This was fine; but I liked the idea of having the opportunity to meet and interact with new people on such activities, and was expecting the same again like the times before, but it never happened for whatever reason, probably because we booked back home and not in Cusco where the idea would be; why take few when you can take many? As expected, there were lots of others in different and larger groups to interact with anyway.

After an hour or so, the trail took a steeper turn and a more rugged terrain, as it started to wind up over along the hill and mountain edge, giving the opportunity to work a sweat and clasp at the thinner air. Eventually, we took lunch in a grassy opening just off the trail. The porters were carrying lots of equipment, including tents, table, chairs, cooking utensils and food for the three-day trek, and they hastily pressed ahead to get to each rest point. set up and prepare for our arrival. I was just starting to appreciate how difficult this would be, not only the fact that they did this quickly, on inclining and declining trails so participants could be fed and watered in relative comfort, high up in the mountains, but also on a regular basis, as this was their job and days off were very few and far between. We headed off after lunch and I pressed on slightly ahead, leaving Dan talking to the guide as he was taking it easier, being wary of the possible onset of altitude sickness.

The relatively placid first-day walking finished after a total of around 11km. And we stopped for the evening in a field of a local indigenous village called Wayllabamba, encased by steep mountains that seemed to hold clouds in place and offer vital shelter from the elements. Other groups stayed there also and allowed time to meet and chat with folk while having a couple of beers before dinner.

The first day's trek was easy. It seemed that walking around most places over the months had put me in a healthy good stead, not to mention the benefits of hanging around in the Andes over the last six weeks had ensured altitude sickness wasn't causing many problems. Also, Dan was faring well so far and despite being at such an elevated level for only a short time wasn't having any problems either. But we couldn't be allowed to fall into a false sense of security, and not distract from the severity of the trail and what the 3000m plus elevation could have on the body; as we found out talking to a Swedish gentleman who was having difficulties with his heart from the course and altitude already, and unfortunately had to return unable to complete the trail, as it was now only going to get worse.

If the first day was somewhat of a gentle introduction, then things were just about to get a bit more difficult. Camp was at the foot of a valley that divided two mountains; we were heading along these and up over to Dead Woman's Pass, which interconnected both of the peaks. Unfortunately, this was around 8km uphill, elevating further to around 4200m. We took breakfast at six thirty a.m. and set off at around seven thirty a.m. Within minutes, I was changing clothes, the incline and effort started to warm the body so I ditched the tracksuit bottoms and waterproof jacket, used as cover from the cold morning air, for shorts and t-shirt, because with the increasing exertion and rising sun it was only going to get hotter. The trail was long and winding, stretching far into the distance following the left-hand-side mountain. The flatter inclines were easy to cope with, but now I started to experience a more expectant trail, one that had been placed by Inca hundreds of years prior, that of harsh rugged stone steps. Some were in remarkably good condition, others not so, but each were much larger than the average stairwell step, and legs had to push hard to elevate the body up over.

For a while, this wasn't too bad, but the relenting frequency eventually caused an all-too-familiar tearing pain throughout the leg muscles, as the body was slowly hoisted up the seemingly never-ending steps. I couldn't help but wonder why these blocks needed to be so big! The Inca weren't giants, were they? Surely not? Because if so, the future generations that included our porters had taken a downturn in stature over the years. Yet, those guys were still running this gauntlet with what looked an effortless ease, while carrying packs of equipment that spoke volumes for their fitness levels at altitude, all the while with much less puffing and panting, moaning and groaning than ourselves in the process.

We ventured higher and higher before eventually stopping at an open plain. Here, we could take on more water, have a toilet break, relax and recover, yet only briefly as it was advisable to keep moving so that the legs wouldn't stiffen up. Also, the view was starting to become more and more prominent; now looking down through the valley from where we had come, peaks stretched off into the distance and the faint trail below disappeared around the corners and within the vegetation of the majestic mountains. Having photos taken of the vistas allowed more interaction with fellow revellers and start engaging in running banter battles with Aussies who insisted I was old and were going to finish before me; me insisting that they were the usual gob shite and full of shit, plus the American girl who was completing the trail in a bikini for a dare; although seemingly impossible, she managed to improve the view.

The trail carried on relentless, as each turn and corner provided an energy-sapping disappointment, as it carried on up over with no end in sight. Four times, I got my hopes up thinking I had reached the intersection between the two mountain sides, yet the steep steps kept coming regardless, with each one almost intrinsically designed to painfully drain the ever-tiring muscles and limbs. Eventually, the trees and stones subsided and the hillsides opened up at 4200m where we reached the opening of Dead Woman's Pass.

Air was much cooler now as the clouds closed in around the elevated mountain tops and blotted the searing sun, creating a misty atmosphere that was refreshing on a heated, sweaty torso. The air was noticeably thinner and less oxygenated to prolong the recovery period of regaining breath, as the lungs clamoured from the upwards exertions. I stopped and relaxed with others already there and despite the lower oxygen levels, I eventually decided I needed to have a cigarette. I was glad I did, the astonished look on the faces of others there was priceless, shocked at my audacity. It was fucking hilarious; some even asked if they could have a photo. The air was thin; sure, but we were still on Planet Earth as far as I was aware, and had perfectly reasonable excuse due to the activity and a raging addiction. Eventually, Dan and the guide joined us to relax, take on board some fluids and precious memory photos. But what goes up must come down and on the other side of the relatively small pass, the trail continued with large stone steps winding steeply downhill into another valley. Clouds still masked the vastness in front of us, with smatterings of green vegetation showing through, but our attention wasn't on the scenery. We had trekked nearly 8km uphill and fatigue was becoming an issue, the walking stick proving vital for balance and helping with sure footing, as weary legs suffered with each of the continuing large steps. Even the Aussies weren't sounding off or giving out shit and we actually managed to have a civilised conversation instead of the usual bullshit, bravado piss taking, all while trying to stop ourselves taking a painful tumbling fall.

The steep descent was luckily only an extra 3km before reaching second night base camp. It was only two p.m. upon arrival yet due to weariness, it felt like we had been up and hiking for a lot longer. The early arrival was great, allowing plenty of downtime to recover in the tents and take both lunch and dinner. The surroundings were superb. Looking back from where we had come, it was now clearly visible why Dead Woman's Pass was named so; as the contours of the rocks formed the silhouette shape of a woman in a supine position – possibly dead? A sea of green shrouded around us as the mountains helped provide shelter from the wind, and a small waterfall ran from high through the camp and down into the valley, where the clouds still hung like a carpet below us and ones higher briefly moved to reveal the elevated task ahead.

We set off again the next day at seven thirty and were greeted by two hours straight uphill slog along dirt tracks, more huge Inca steps and wooden bridges to fill the gaps of eroded trails. The early morning weather was cloudy with slightly drizzly rain but was still warm. As we pressed on, the altitude and elevation increased again but now we noticeably started to see more ruins. On the first day, we had looked down upon a large Incan site that graced the base of a mountainside with homes, places of work and cascading terraces. The second day, there wasn't many cutting along the side of the hill and mountain but now we approached them with a frequency that started to give the feeling that the end was nearing, including that of age-old stone outposts and larger impressive site of Sayacmarca, where it was possible to walk around and explore; seeing a large stone carving of an Incan warrior in the wall which tantalisingly and expectantly whet the appetite for our arrival at Machu Picchu.

The terrain eased somewhat from inclines and descents to allow welcome rest for the legs as the trail followed along a mountain ridge. Unfortunately, visibility was poor, as thick clouds engulfed the surroundings, yet it always gave the impression we were extremely high up with sheer drop just a few feet to the left. Having stopped for brief lunch and recuperation, we all carried on together, as previously I would trudge off in a world of my own with the tunes on. We were now heading steeply downhill through jungle, and the worn away stones were extremely slippery due to moss and water running from the mountain side, which we took advantage of by putting our heads under for some natural refreshment. Eventually, the trail split; right would take us to camp and left would still take us to camp but via a longer trail passing down and through massive Incan farming terraces. Still feeling OK, we decided on the longer option, which I felt was worth it getting to see more; much to the despair of our flagging guide who was probably used to the less-traumatic option. But he quickly felt better when approaching the camp site from the opposite side to everyone else, as there was a small shop and we bought ourselves and him a beer. When we entered camp from the forest, the *cervezas* provided quizzical looks from other trekkers and questions of "where the hell did you get that from?"

The hard work was now done, three days and approximately 30km of sometimes tough, challenging, but always beautiful terrain amid some of the most spectacular scenery on Earth. Because of our detour, the tents were already pitched and food was being prepared. The camp at Winay Wayna was arguably the most welcome for those trekking; not only was it the start of the final furlong, but there was the opportunity to take a hot shower and like before buy beer, with both seemingly top of the agenda for everyone. After relaxing, we and our guide Manuel headed to another close by Incan ruin to explore the steep rooms and terraces, offering ample photo opportunities to our increasingly impressive collection that Dan was taking and were in no way thanks to me. My camera wasn't the best and after months of constant wear and tear, had finally given up the will to live on the last few days of the animal rescue centre. I now needed to purchase another one before Dan left to return back to the UK, and unfortunately due to the tourist nature of Cusco, the ones there were obviously very expensive for what they were. So, for the minute, we were sharing a camera. Yet somehow, with everything that had happened, and the way situations tend to pan out, I should've realised at the time that this was an ominous sign of events to come.

After a riotous dinner, the topic of conversation among Dan, Manuel, the porters, the chef and I had somehow gotten on to wanking and shaved balls (must have been the altitude) and to anyone passing who heard must have been slightly disturbing. We took photos and said a pre-emptive goodbye to the porters and chef, as they were starting to pack up the gear and were due to leave early in the morning to start all over with a new group. We were so grateful of the effort that they had put in, making sure that our trek was a memorable experience, and really brought home how hard and how much they had to endure when working to earn a living. Another humbling experience likened to that of the lady on the Great Wall of China, with the effort required to earn a comparatively small wage to the visitors on the trails, who they assisted in making dreams a reality, and the small fortune spent to participate was probably a sum these could only dream and wish for themselves. We tipped them handsomely as they deserved it, just on the sheer load that they had to carry alone.

Despite the hard work and effort at least my cousin was providing some reliable entertainment by systematically trying to ruin his meals mistaking salt for parmesan cheese, and stuffing copious amounts of tissue paper up his nostrils at dinner to stem the nose bleeds probably caused by altitude; shenanigans of which were much to every one's amusement. Despite being due a very early start, Dan and I hit the makeshift bar that opened on the evening and carried on drinking while playing card game shithead with Aussie Elise, bikini girl Jena and her two friends Rich and Trent; the ones who had dared her.

It was still dark when we got up, unsurprising considering that it was four a.m., and we actually still got to see the porters as they kindly prepared us breakfast. The check point didn't open though till five thirty a.m. so we chilled in the bar till everyone had left and eventually Manuel came and got us; not seeing the point of hanging around waiting on the trail in the cold dark mountainous forest. We weren't hellbent being there first. Just before the checkpoint opened, we joined the back of the waiting queue, and slowly we shuffled ahead to venture through on to the last leg of our intrepid trek.

Knowing the end was in sight, we had a spring in our step, and like the days previous once again left the guide trailing behind, quickly passing those who were walking at a slower pace, as many now were really suffering from the last three days. The sun started to rise, lighting up the valley and mountains to our right, where a low-lying cloud in the middle created a white hung river in between. The foliage, undergrowth and morning dew caused the trail to be slippery underfoot as we headed along the now-familiar-looking mountain side for approximately 4km before negotiating an uneven, exceptionally steep set of old Incan stairs which at the top continued with a slight incline pathway that met an abrupt end and an ancient stone wall. This had a doorway at the pinnacle of the mountain; the Sun Gate.

Venturing through the doorway on to the stone terrace, we looked down over; to the far side of the adjoining mountain, there lay the awe-inspiring and spectacular site of the 'lost' city of the Incas; Machu Picchu. It was rediscovered back in 1911 by Hiram Bingham and reintroduced to the world. Again, to the local indigenous folk, it was probably never 'lost', just a bit overgrown by a reclaiming jungle, despite its elevated mountain perch. Now cleared, it created a truly wonderful sight that had adorned many a picture postcard and the same vision graced my very own eyes. A stunning view to behold and this alone made the last three days all the more worthwhile.

The sun was now up high enough in the sky to adorn the beautiful, green, expansive peaks, and bask the famous old ruins in glorious sunshine, to only be occasionally interrupted by clouds making a brief claim to the view, that made the scene and experience all the more beautiful as they would quickly roll by, and the stunning vision in front would reappear. With the spectacular world-renowned iconic Incan site in the background, we frantically started taking photos with each and both together in shot. It felt though these would only be for the benefit of others, as I couldn't ever imagine forgetting this moment and vision of a massive cascading stone city high in the Andean mountains, as it permanently etched into the conscious. It was amazing and another idealistic dream had come to fruition, leaving a joyous warm feeling of accomplishment that was hard to envisage or emulate.

There was a final 1km walk downhill along the still notoriously slippery pathway. Descending, we stopped at the huge stepped stone terraces which formed what would have been the outskirts of the city. They were now laden with short grass being carefully manicured by llama as they lazily munched away. Now the size of the place started to come into perspective, having looked somewhat smaller than imagined when at distance and elevated level of the sun gate. Hastily, we continued with our descent before finally reaching the site itself and proceeded to explore the somewhat maze-like ancient stone citadel. It was confusing looking around the various open chambers, plazas, temples and rooms which were all interconnected with a series of pathways and steps, yet made exciting exploration in discovering where the next turn or set of stairs would lead. The masonry of the stone had stood the test of time and still looked superb due to a quality craftsmanship of massive seamless joined blocks with smooth edges that would be hard to surpass even now; and only reinforced the age-old question of how? Or even, why here? This would have been hard enough work on a more forgiving terrain, let alone shifting the huge cumbersome boulders from some 35km away, up to a high-ridge precipice in the Andes, and then take the time to have them fit perfectly together, using no mortars or adhesives. A concept that was both intriguing and baffling at the same time.

After an hour or so of us exploring aimlessly, Manuel came along and gave us a full guided tour and shed some light on the various components of the site. These included the sacred plaza, royal palace, various temples, ceremonial baths, residential and industrial sectors to name but a few and we were given an insight into how each area was used and how the Inca used to live. I found myself enthralled in learning about the place and tried hard to imagine life in those days. We seemed to wander around for hours at our own free will, exploring and even just finding points to sit and relax and take in the whole experience. I loved the fact that much of the reasoning behind Machu Picchu is still largely unknown and open to much conjecture; was it a sacred city? Was it a hideaway from the conquistadors? I didn't know and could only take an (un)informed guess, but this only added to the

317

mysticism surrounding it and whether there were any secrets still locked within.

It was almost energising being here; three days of aches, pains and general tiredness of early mornings and mountainous terrain trails were forgotten, having now reached our mystical goal appreciating its splendour with our own eyes and not to mention the stunning setting pitched high in the mountains, allowing for some of the most incredible sights on Earth. The steep, large dome-shape mountain of Wayna Picchu towered majestically over the site, providing a picture postcard view. Unfortunately, we couldn't experience this as only four hundred tickets were available per day to the summit and these went quickly and we were too late. Although tired, I was elated within. Proud of my efforts, but also for Dan too, whose first real time of travelling out alone and being in an unknown country could yield such a reward, as he kept telling me how much he had enjoyed the whole experience and it was clear to see.

Eventually, approaching midday after some five hours, we decided to get the much-sought-after passport stamp for the site and head down the mountain. Our descent and return to civilisation was to be a much more relaxing affair and part of the reason why this was described as an 'idealistic dream' earlier. In my head, this place was remote. Hard to get to and a reward for the day's endeavour of following the paths and trails laid hundreds of years prior. But these were paths well-worn on a regular basis by those like us, in search of adventure to this famous 'remote' place. But also more unfortunate was that this historical site wasn't only accessible to those who had trekked; it was open to many on day trips, via bus and train, that made much more of an appealing prospect to many more people and had become inundated with swarming groups of tourists. And sadly for me, this stole any idealism of a spiritual seclusion I'd envisaged prior to being here. More so, it had been reported that the vital architecture and stonework was being constantly damaged due to its popularity and the countless thousands visiting from the now very easy access to all and sundry, who didn't want to or couldn't for whatever reason participate in completing the trails to get here, and now apparently to the detriment of this UNESCO World Heritage Site. I myself unfortunately was now part of this sorry statistic; even the trail itself was in constant state of maintenance, hence the five-hundred-person cap allowed on per day and it also closes completely during February. I was thankful I had done and experienced it now, before it would succumb to tourists and damaged beyond repair or become too unsafe to go and witness which would be an absolute tragedy. And like *the beach,* it certainly would now make me think twice before returning, albeit there are lots of other less-travelled trails to arrive there which now seem more appealing, but still the problem would remain for the main site as it slowly but surely would lose its lustre.

Aguas Calientes was the town at the bottom of the winding steep mountain road to Machu Picchu. A bus ferried us off the mountainside and into civilisation. Many people bustled around and we took lunch in one of the vast amounts of restaurants with others from the trek, who seemed to be appearing in their droves. Like all the people who arrived earlier in the day or stayed overnight to get directly up to Machu Picchu, the train that brought many of them here, would also be our mode of transport back. On board, amid the comedown of completing the experience, I physically couldn't engage in any conversation with anyone about the last four days and nodded off, totally exhausted.

That evening back in Cusco, Dan and I had a little dilemma; whether to hang around and appreciate what Cusco had to offer or head out of town. So we thought the best thing to do would be to go out and get pissed whilst we pondered the next move. Not that it got much thought; we met some of the others in a 'traditional Peruvian' Irish boozer before heading to a club, only deciding to leave when suitably oiled in the wee hours and after Dan had been sick.

Our conundrum had been solved by the cold light of the next morning, figuring best to make a move; not only armed with our bags but stonking hangovers as well, we made for the bus terminal. I was still half cut when we got to the station and Dan was really feeling the effects; he was white as a sheet and just slumped in the chair waiting whilst I used my finest Spanish to sort the bus tickets. I thought I would have some fun and decided to put his name down as 'Little Danny', but when the tickets came back on inspection, it said 'Little Donny'. Still pissed, I was in absolute hysterics at his new moniker. Now turning pale green and having picked up a cold of some sort, he proceeded to give himself his new moniker of 'Snotsville' due to the copious amounts of illuminous mucus he was producing. This nearly sent me over the edge. 'Little Donny Snotsville', I loved it. I couldn't understand why he wasn't on the phone changing his name by deed poll. It had a lovely ring to it, and right there and then it suited him to a tee.

I chuckled away to myself on the bus as we headed out of town. The lack of air conditioning inside coupled with stifling heat and hangover wasn't a good combination. 'Donny Snotsville' was now seasick green; just sitting quietly suffering in silence, except for the occasional groan and profanity to emphasise how rough he was. Not that I was really listening, as I put my headphones on and started staring out of the widow at the beautiful scenery. The road cut between green mountain hillsides and pastures as we headed away from Cusco and were daubed with huge ambiguous notices; ambiguous to me anyway. Political statement, love for a town, person, God or anything really seemed to be the subject of these huge natural billboards, which looked like someone had just grabbed a lawn mower and shaved their particular message onto the monumental grassy hillside. It made interesting viewing nevertheless.

Bus journeys were fast becoming a real experience in themselves. Not knowing what was going to happen or what would be seen next and this journey was no different, as we passed people on the roadside of a mountain after their bus had veered off the road and was now just teetering over the edge saved only by a tree. Obviously, everyone made a move to the right-hand-side of the bus, to get a closer view and gawp as we didn't stop to offer aid or assistance. There was a huge argument amongst locals over seating at our stop-over point of Sicuani, where a little girl ended up in floods of tears due to over the top, fanatical berating between two waring families and finally on the flatter plains towards our destination Puno, the clouds darkened and an angry thunderstorm raged, with massive bolts of lightning regularly crashing down, discharging on the earth below. I just sat eagerly staring out of the window, waiting in anticipation for the next spectacular bright blue arc flash and subsequent bang. All the while 'Little Donny Snotsville' was still a groaning fucked-up mess.

Arriving in Puno on the shore of Lake Titicaca, the world's highest and South America's biggest lake, we quickly found accommodation from a waiting tout at the bus stop. The price was right and seemed nice enough, so saving time we headed there. It was late so we headed out to eat before returning to grab some much-needed rest from the previous night and day travelling. Dan's condition hadn't really improved; I thought that he'd contracted a cold or virus of sorts and was being amplified by a hangover, but now the booze had worn off, he wasn't eating and was now looking genuinely ill. I figured it could because of a variety of sources; exertion, fatigue, altitude, long travel journey, being in new country, something eaten or drank. An endless list sprung to mind, but adding all these together would explain a lot as his body's immune system had taken a battering over the last six or so days and a slower pace with some rest and relaxation would help bring him round. I hoped.

Visiting the lake was the focus of our time in Puno; more over the floating islands and the inhabitants there. Although Dan had only been in the country for five days, time was quickly becoming an issue, as he was only here for just under two weeks and we wanted to get around and see as much as possible, before he had to fly back to the UK. The next day after breakfast, we were told about a half day tour of the lake that was leaving from the hostel. With about twenty minutes to prepare, we jumped into action, grabbed our things and headed out.

The lake was massive and created the illusion of being at a costal port. We were given a brief introduction and explained about the safety issues when on the boat before setting off. The water seemed shallow as we headed out of the harbour and cut through large patches of rushes and reeds.

The wooden gang plank was placed off the side of the boat and we disembarked onto a floating island. It was hard to believe that people could live on these. Not that it was bad or inhospitable; far from it, but mostly because it was so unique. I hadn't seen anything like it. They were made from layers of totora reeds which we had passed in abundance when the boat headed out. This allowed for a constant replenishment of the handmade floating islands, as they would disintegrate overtime from the water below but the sheer amount bundled together created a really soft bouncy underfoot experience. We gathered in a large semicircle where it was demonstrated and explained how the islands were formed, weaving the reeds with the same process as centuries ago, when the Uros tribes devised the system to isolate themselves from other tribes such as the Incas, showcasing how the reeds formed the whole basis for the lives of the inhabiting indigenous folk, allowing them to make woven homes, boats and arts and crafts. It really was a fascinating tour, where people who lived there had carved a unique society from their natural surroundings, passed down through the ages, that was still going strong. With a distinct lack of modernised materialism, it may have looked like they lived in abject poverty. But this was just a different existence and way of thinking, that used the raw materials around to their benefit and what made the place so charming, as it seemed the must-have items of the world had never even been invented.

After the presentation, we had the privilege to wander around the island. It wasn't too big; maybe just over half the size of a football pitch, yet big enough considering it was floating and anchored down. There was a hole in the middle where stores of fish were kept to be eaten at a later date. We were invited into one of the homes of an indigenous lady, who showed us her basic accommodation made from the interwoven reeds that formed the wall structure and tight thatched roof. It was a single-room abode for parents and children to live in, with little furniture and some bed linen that all used for sleeping. Dan bought a present to take back from the arts and crafts available, before having a venture up the rickety wooden watch tower in the centre, so we could catch a view overlooking the ocean-like flat shimmering lake. Our visit proved an exceptional eye-opening experience, where I mused about how long before I could cope without all my twenty-first century luxuries if I was miraculously transported here; figuring it probably wouldn't take long. It again made me grateful for my own comfortable existence. It did, though, leave me encouraged to test myself; maybe take a longer trip in future to see if I could live out here, in one of the huts to get a truer, more natural feel of day-to-day life, cut myself off from modern life and live on these fascinating floating abodes, or at least in a similar sort of circumstance.

We boarded the boat to head to another larger island just across the water way, and were serenaded when departing by a performance from the indigenous children who waved us off. The larger island was much the same but had actual restaurants and shops on board to buy supplies before we headed back. The trip itself was short and sweet, only a half day getting out, looking around and heading back to Puno. It was a much-needed casual, relaxing affair and was really worth it. I was glad that I got to witness something quite unique; although, now it was geared to greet tourism and provide an opportunity to make a living from visitors. This was understandable. Everything was or is, and I indulged in this machine countless times everywhere. Everyone needs to earn money in some way, shape or form to survive, that even stretched to those showing how they live in surreal meekness.

Back in Puno, after something to eat and with nothing else to keep us there, we made the decision to head out and press on. Even though Dan still wasn't feeling too clever with his stomach and I had eaten something which, without getting too graphic, went straight through me. We still took another bus for an eight-hour journey to Peru's second largest city Arequipa. Deciding on this after reading, it seemed to offer lots of things to do; there were canyons nearby to explore, an encompassing terrain that created plenty of outdoor activity and the city centre was of old colonial architecture, all overlooked by two impressive volcanoes of El Misti and Chachani. This seemed perfect with an abundance of options. Arriving late, I headed out for a look around the area and grab some sustenance, while Dan was just happy to roll into a foetal position on the bed after relapsing and now having a really bad stomach.

The hot sunny weather continued to be with us and feeling somewhat better, the next morning we had a look around the city centre; the Plaza de Armas proved a beautiful photogenic square of trees where people sat watching the world go by, encompassed by large cathedral and countless shops within the colonial architecture to while away a few hours. During this, we took the opportunity to book a rafting expedition for the next day, hoping to provide some activity and excitement for our time in Arequipa. Dan wasn't too sure about how he was going to feel, but took a chance on being better so we booked it anyway as he had improved, yet like most when travelling now had the shits and was struggling to hold anything in. But I was really happy about the prospect; I loved rafting, having had a fantastic experience before in Canada plus the time in Thailand. It was possibly my favourite outdoor activity, so I was excited. Our exploration of the city also offered up a chance meeting with two people we had partied with in Cusco. Pete and Barry were also from the UK and travelling around in much the same way as ourselves. It was good to see them again and we all agreed to meet up later in the evening for a couple of beers while that afternoon, Dan and I headed back to chill on the roof terrace and have an easy day relaxing, grabbing some tropical sun. Unbeknown to me at the time, I was going to have much more time to grab some sun, and any plans were just about to be thrown into turmoil.

That evening, we met up with Pete and Barry as planned, having a few beers. Being a Monday, the place was quiet with only a handful of places open, let alone busy. A couple of bars in, we entered up the stairs of an establishment, drinking, laughing and joking as we had been, but upon exiting the bar, the steps used to descend down to the street below were old stone and worn concave smooth from the hundreds and thousands of footsteps beforehand. Reminiscent of the Dragon Bridge in China, halfway down, my feet shot out from beneath me as I slipped and fell straight onto the rock-hard stone. My arse bone (or coccyx as its more technical name goes) *cracked* hard on the edge and I felt the intense pain immediately. And this was only detracted from by the incredible pain ravaging through my hands and thumbs. Whilst falling, I had instinctively put my hands down to break my fall, but my thumbs only caught the lip of the stairs and my full weight bent both of them right back to my forearms and I was in agony. Immediately, I knew I was in trouble; I could hardly move my hands and the top of my backside wasn't too clever either. The good news was that I knew that my thumbs weren't broken or dislocated as I could still move them. Just. But every ligament and tendon in the thumbs, hands, wrists and forearms felt like it had been shredded. I couldn't blame the booze as I hadn't had an awful lot to drink, so I wasn't anaesthetised by alcohol either. If I hadn't put my hands down and fell with full weight force onto my arse, I probably would have broken my tail bone but my thumbs had basically lessened the fall, stopping just short of breaking or dislocating themselves. One thing immediately sprung to mind; there was no way in the creation of cow shit I was now going to be able to raft the next day. Not in a million years.

Only being able to sleep in certain positions, I woke up numerous times during the night, as turning over would apply pressure on my hands or backside, even the soft bed caused sharp pain on my heavily bruised appendages and would wake me in an instant. I tried to sleep as much as possible, eventually getting up around ten a.m. This wasn't good, so I said to Dan, "I can't raft, there's no way, I can't even move my thumbs now, never mind hold anything, nor sit down properly,"

He replied, "Well, I don't fancy it either, 'cos I still can't hold my stomach and don't think I fancy having to wear a nappy!"

We were both now two fucked up messes.

Remembering about his dodgy stomach meant he wasn't over keen anyway, but I could only laugh at our bumbling, chaotic antics; as we seemed a right pair of fuckwits. The rafting would have been good fun, but it wasn't to be so I was disappointed; especially as Pete and Barry had decided to join us, after I had encouraged them to get involved. I was gutted but more so with the predicament I was now in. Never take for granted how much you use your thumbs during the day – this is basically all the time – and for the smallest, simplest of tasks. Now it was like they had been removed and I was left stricken and unable to do anything with them. I had to hold pens, knives and forks in my fingers, and had to pick up drinks carefully using only the palms of both hands, while taking care not to knock or move my swollen, increasingly bruised and incredibly sore tender digits. Travelling around, I had witnessed lots of people who were amputees, and tried to imagine how awful this would be and the difficulties and challenges each day would bring. Especially those who live in poorer nations where healthcare is not so readily available as my own. Now I had been given the opportunity to marginally feel for myself how it would be to deal with an affliction as this. Yet, I had the consolation that the pain would rescind and strength and movement would eventually return, so bandaging my hands I was determined to carry on, and cope as best as possible with what was actually a minor, although somewhat painful, setback of my own fault. Especially as with hindsight, this was not going to be the only thing which I would be left reeling from, that was also going to be completely my own fault.

We got in touch with Barry and Pete, explaining that we were no longer rafting, which they understood as we had been out with them the previous night and bore first-hand witness to my tumble and painful predicament. Thankfully, though, they still participated and gave Dan and I the money as they hadn't paid and just took our place instead, which I found very noble and really kind as we were unable to get a refund. Even though it was me who encouraged them and despite reservations, they still went along and participated, it showed great character and emphasised how they were willing to help out fellow travellers, for which we were very grateful.

Instead, we again spent the rest of the day chilling and resting, as any grand ideas for Arequipa had gone out of the window via falling down the stairs. I hoped to return to make more of the place and experience it better, but didn't know how or when. Not being too disheartened, we left again on the night bus, looking forward to our next destination as we had also managed to book another must-do activity; as we tried to make the most of our short, yet what was turning out to be very eventful, time together in Peru. All the while, I wasn't looking forward to the best part of ten hours sitting on a bus, with my less-than-comfortable bruised backside.

Amazingly, I awoke just as we were arriving into Nazca. I couldn't believe that I had managed to sleep on my side pretty much all the way, only waking when painfully turning over. I was bemused that I had actually managed to get so much sleep, but grateful nevertheless. We went straight to the tour agency which was handily right next door to the bus station, to participate in witnessing the world-famous Nazca lines. I really wanted to see these, probably just as much as Machu Picchu; holding a similar mystique that intrigued me as again not much is known as to who exactly built them or why. Were they an astrological calendar of sorts? Spiritual representations? Some kind of offering or message? And being so large, were they only meant to be viewed from way up high? By aliens maybe? The whole aura surrounding them had me fascinated, so I wanted to see them properly and the only way to do this was via an aeroplane. It wasn't cheap, but the only way for a true appreciation.

Trading in our pre-bought vouchers at the tour shop, we were then hastily taken to the airport that operated flights to revellers over the lines and allowed the best possible viewing. We approached our small plane, boarded, donned the noise-reducing headphones and early in the morning sun we set off down the runway. Within moments, we were airborne and heading to the site, armed with my new camera I bought in Arequipa (the opportunity to buy one arose, that was one positive). I was looking forward to putting it into action for the first time and especially at such an impressive sight, although the Cessna provided a somewhat bumpy flight from hitting the rising thermals, coupled with my damaged digits and achy-brakey arse made this a tad trickier than first thought.

Flying to an altitude of around 1km, we quickly approached the first of the lines, and the five of us in the plane eagerly peered out of the window as it banked to the left, passing the whale. Then turning around and banking to the right, so that people on either side could get the chance to appreciate each of the depictions and take photos. The images looked somewhat smaller than what I imagined; yet so did Machu Picchu from afar, but they were still impressive, carved by moving darker stones from the surface and exposing the lighter ones underneath. The famous astronaut on the hillside, the curly tailed monkey, the dog, humming bird, spider and of course the condor but to name a few, all enigmatically smattered on the scorched earth with the hundreds of other geoglyphs passing below us, where huge straight line trapezoid stretched far off into the distance and I could only come to the conclusion that this would be an alien landing strip. Definitely; couldn't be for anything else really.

At times, the images looked hard to distinguish; especially where the rough grey dirt seemed to of shifted and obscured them. Yet, when you could make out what was actually being represented, they were obvious and impressive. I was very glad at having witnessed the lines and another famous UNESCO World Heritage Site, and wished that it could have lasted longer, having been airborne for around thirty minutes, but was still a worthy investment to marvel at these mysterious effigies that left me none the wiser about the origins and reasoning, having now seen them with my own eyes. I was really happy that I had made the effort, despite my damaged appendages acting as a psychological drain that easily superseded any monetary cost; but I knew I would've regretted it if I'd skipped doing it because now, I had contentment at realising another 'bucket list' dream, where the depictions below were not the only form of entertainment.

When we landed, Dan was looking decidedly green.

"What's the matter?" I enquired, cottoning on that his stomach still wasn't in top shape.

"I've been sick," he announced.

"What? Where?" I retorted in a surprised fashion, totally oblivious to his predicament having been sat in front of him.

"In this bag." He proceeded to show me a bag of horrible bile wretched from his stomach, as we stood next to the plane on the tarmac. I just started laughing, thinking, *What next?*

"That flight was horrendous," he carried on.

I was still laughing. I knew it had been a bit bumpy, but I was too busy glaring out of the window to notice what was happening behind me. I said, "You must have looked a right picture for that girl sat next to ya! By the way, did you notice the wing?"

"Eh? Why? What are you on about?" He was the one now confused.

"Probably best you didn't notice. But the stanchion wasn't connected to the wing properly," I said. "Here, look at this." I proceeded to show him a photograph I had took in flight, as you could see clear daylight through a gap between the angled stanchion and underside of the wing, where I can only presume rivets were supposed to be and then one of the other wing which was tightly bolted. "I thought it best not to say anything until we landed, and judging by you in that state, I was right," I said as Dan hastily proceeded to go and inspect the wing.

"Fucking hell!" His abrupt summarisation said it all.

We headed to the exit to head back to the tour shop. Waiting for the bus, an old shaman approached and started talking to us. He was dressed in a native poncho, had all the feathers, trinkets and amulets attached. I was fascinated by his presence; I know that he was probably after some tourist soles (Peruvian money), but I didn't mind and we both had our photos taken with him. When he was just about to shake my hand, I had to refuse. I physically couldn't and apologetically explained about my hands and what had happened, while at the same time also apologising about my Spanish. But he understood and proceeded to hold my hands and run his own lightly over mine, all the while chanting; as if drawing the badness from my hands.

Was I slightly sceptical about this unorthodox treatment? Yes, but only because I was nervous about my hands being hurt, yet I was more than willing to let him try to help cure my ailment – why not? I didn't know any better. Plus a few of the things that fascinate me are power of the mind, psychology and spirituality, usually I may consider these separate from one another but in this instance, I wondered how or if they could intertwine, feeling there is so much unknown about the human brain, our consciousness and the potential energies within that could be unlocked, so I thought this was an opportunity not to miss out on and it surely couldn't make them any worse. Leaving, I gave him some soles for his troubles and Dan asked if my hands felt better. Honestly, at the time, I didn't think so, yet it only enhanced my curiosity surrounding these mystical figures, to find out about their beliefs and teachings and I was pleased with our encounter. I was hoping to meet the one who Don knew in Ecuador but the chance didn't arise, yet now with busted hands this one had come to me. I have never visited a faith healer, clairvoyant or tarot reader, nor do I want to. This is down to scepticism, as I don't think that there is much in it, like the guy in Hong Kong, but mainly as I have no interest in knowing my future, nor my destiny. Purely because I think that this could change decisions you make and affect your way of thinking, to try and forge positive outcomes which might not be the right choice and affect your true place to be in life; which I was starting to believe could be achieved through your own intuition and doing the right things, even though these may seem difficult and not worthwhile at the time. With this in mind as I travelled, I learned that the element of the unknown was fast becoming just an unfamiliar friend as opposed to a feared entity; helping me along the way with each challenge, both good and bad. And these again would be words which I would learn to heed.

We headed back to the shop in town and booked ourselves on to another bus, as we were not too bothered about staying in Nazca. We had been there and done what we wanted, so we took a short two-hour bus journey up to Ica, which was closer to our final destination of Lima before Dan was due to leave. And I also had heard about a lovely little place just on the outskirts called Huacachina, which we decided on visiting for a few days to experience the desert and the activities available.

After taking a taxi from the bus terminal in Ica, we arrived at the beautiful resort of Huacachina. It was tiny but picturesque, very calm and serene, with a big lagoon in the middle that adorns the 50 soles note of the Peruvian currency. Walking around the shops and homes, bars and restaurants could be done in the space of half an hour, but what we had now swapped was towering mountains for towering sand dunes, that enclosed around the town. This provided the allure for many as they were used for most of the activities there; including sand boarding, quad biking and dune buggy tours where by revellers would be taken on crazy white knuckle scrambles up and down the huge shifting embankments.

Unfortunately, I wasn't able to participate in any of these to compound my frustration with my condition, even though my hands had begun to gain more range of motion, leaving me wondering; had the Shaman actually started to hasten my recovery? But at the same time recognising any involvement was just another accident waiting to happen. Therefore I spent the time relaxing by the hostel pool, while Dan, now feeling much better and an avid motor sports fan, went out on a guided quad bike tour that he enjoyed immensely. I was really pleased that he had actually gone out and experienced something for himself. My activities were pretty much restricted to hiking up the massive 300ft mounds of sand, proving to be much harder work than it actually looked; with each step up shortened by the loose shifting granules. Reaching the top was worth it though, as from here it was possible to see for miles around, gazing at the distant mountains, the town and the unfathomable rolling ocean of shifting dunes which stretched far as the eyes could see, creating the illusion of being stuck square in the middle of the desert.

After literally a two-day break, here we made the last leg of our journey together, getting to Lima for one last night, before Dan had to take his return flight back home. I'd had a brilliant time travelling with him again and had so much fun together, getting into adventures and the trouble and chaos that these endeavours usually bring. We weren't affectionately referred to as Laurel and Hardy amongst friends for nothing; due to the fact that things like this had happened so many times before in the past, when we previously travelled together; shit would always seem to go wrong. Yet there was still time for one last incident.

After the short six-hour trip north to Lima, we booked ourselves into a hostel close by the tourist part of Miraflores. One quick shit, shower and shave later, we headed out on the piss and started caning the drinks. Moving between bars, we happened upon a guy who started talking about tattoos; which I was interested in. Alarm bells should have been ringing, but this was more of a dull clang due to the booze and when we went for more drinks, he joined us; only for his mate to come along and start offering us drugs which we refused. Things were not looking good as the tone changed.

I never took my camera on a night out, I thought about it here, but decided not to. Dan, though, did and while he went to the toilet he gave it to me thinking the guy was up to no good. Who in turn realised that I now had the camera, so when I went to the toilet, he subsequently followed me. Hearing someone behind me I stopped and turned around; he just looked at me, glanced down and said nothing. I looked down to see that he had produced a knife with retractable blade. Bastard. There was only one thing for it. I was handing the camera over, or suffer the consequences.

I gave him the camera. In an instant, he was gone and as I came out of the toilets; I caught only a brief glimpse of him and his mate as they fled out of the bar door. I couldn't believe that I had been so stupid and let my guard down, falling for such a trick and now had fucked up. All I could say to Dan was, "It's gone, the camera has gone."

I felt awful. This was all my doing, interacting with him in the first place and by the time I realised it was a set-up, it was too late. I figure he must have clocked us taking photos prior and being inebriated, we became obvious marks. Thankfully, Dan was very philosophical about the whole incident. His attitude was that at least no one got hurt. Cameras and such things can be replaced, whereas people can't; which was kind and I hoped that one day in retrospect I could learn from this and adopt a similar attitude, should it happen to me with roles reversed. But it still didn't take away the fact that I fucked up and felt really bad; more so because someone else lost out due to my actions, or lack of.

Strangely though, not twenty-four hours earlier in Huacachina, Dan had insisted on getting the photos that we had taken so far downloaded on to disc. This happened to be a real arse on and seemed to take ages as we both were not so up-to-date with the technology business, but persevered and in the end finally managed it. It now turned out to be a masterstroke as we never lost any of the amazing pictures that we had taken. Again, these were something that were not necessarily irreplaceable, but very tricky and costly to emulate, so having some actual forethought provided one silver lining.

The next morning, we woke and I apologised again before he left for the airport. Dan asked if I could go to the tourist police to get a report for the insurance; which I did, as it was the least I could do. Here, this seemed another, all-too-familiar stupid gringo tourist getting mugged scenario and they couldn't get me out of the place fast enough, hastily writing a report of what happened, having ruined their lazy Sunday ambience with my predicament. Returning to the hostel, I found myself not for the first time sending another apologetic email while contemplating my next move.

The Waterboy

It was fair to say that I'd had the wind knocked out of my sails; not necessarily because of the fact that I had a knife pulled on me and was now scared and apprehensive of heading outside. No one got hurt, so I didn't have to cope with the trauma of a wound or injury, nor the dilapidating physiological and psychological effects that would cause, so I was thankful for the mercy of not having to deal with that scenario. But my guidebook and others warned me profusely about getting robbed and I knew it could easily happen; especially being in a new city, at night and in unfamiliar surroundings. This should have made me more wary, yet I let my guard down. Stupid, I know, but maybe I was prepared for the inevitability of it? I was taken aback more so because it was someone else who ended up suffering the consequences of something that was my fault and I belatedly saw it coming, yet didn't act appropriately before things went too far. I was caught up with the invincibility factor that everything had been going so well and adopting an 'I can handle any situation' kind of attitude and this was ultimately my downfall.

It would have been very easy to blame the drink which created bravado at the time, but I had now fallen foul of the escape mechanism that enhanced my own inflated ego. I didn't know it all, I could easily fall into bad situations and I might not be able to handle them and when out and about in a new place and being drunk would only exacerbate any vulnerability; so now I had to learn a harsh lesson – as always, the hard way. I still needed to be on guard and wary, and this hard line realisation was now a positive thing to come out of the incident, plus the fact that thankfully no one did get hurt.

Oddly, I found it hard to blame the guy who pulled the knife and stole the camera. We or I, were just another tourist target and I made us obvious pickings. I thought about his motives and reasoning; did he do the same thing day in day out? To get by? And to feed his children? Or drug habit? Or was it only at certain time of the month when bills needed paying? Extra to subsidise his regular income? It being low? That said, he never asked for cash either and the camera was also money. But it must've been too easy an opportunity to turn down. Whatever; I figured it could be all or any of these things, but he was carrying a blade and that sort of made it premeditated. Anyway far from me to judge; though it did seem he was taking an easy but risky option in life, by pursuing crime and preying on the weaker and vulnerable (in this case drunk and stupid). He gambled by playing with higher consequences and ultimately by the law of averages could end up one day with a less profitable, sorrier or even tragic ending. I would never want to live like this or never want to feel that I should or have to. Bearing this in mind, I did feel an element of pity for him.

After the frantic last two weeks of seemingly endless travelling about, trying to cram in as much as possible, getting injured and ultimately robbed, I now had a week before I was due to fly out of Peru. I toyed with a few ideas about what to do for the week, but one thing was for certain; I wasn't too enamoured with Lima and wanted to go somewhere else. I decided to head north for a week of rest and relaxation, but first I had to hang around the best part of half a day waiting, to spend the night on a bus. My destination was Trujillo; a large unspectacular city just inland off the northern coastline and from here I took a taxi to the little coastal town of Huanchaco.

With a pleasant, long-sweeping coastal front over the road from a large beach, I now had the welcoming smell of the sea air and I found a nice, cheap enough hostel just up one of the side streets. Heading out, I wandered along the sea front for a look around; there were restaurants and plenty of them, unsurprisingly serving mainly sea food, harvested from the nearest and most obvious source. There were the usual amenities; grocery stores, shops and banks but plenty of surf shops too, taking advantage of the large swells the Pacific Ocean provided. And that was it; really peaceful and quiet, not providing much else apart from the pre-Colombian archaeological site of Chan Chan that we passed on the way into town. But this was ideal and I wasn't looking for much else anyway.

I sat and had something to eat in one of the restaurants, minding my own business a passer-by offered me some smoke. With nothing else doing really, apart from possibly surfing later on in the week, I bought some and promptly spent the next four days in an idle, relaxed state on a dark, sandy, somewhat pebble-strewn beach, eating and pondering things that I'd done and what was next on the agenda. Trying not to make too many plans as I just rested, whiling away the hours, taking in some sun and getting, in all sense of the word; baked.

My hands and thumbs had pretty much regained full range of motion and the strength had started to return since I'd slipped on the stairs a week or so prior. Managing to draw myself away from a perpetually stoned state, I finally booked myself in to do some surfing. It was an ideal opportunity with some tremendous waves rolling and allowed me to get involved in some activity. I had tried it once before down in Newquay, the UK's surfing mecca, and had fun doing so, although only managing to stand a couple of times before falling in the water. But I knew what to expect and it would serve a purpose of being out and about, active and in the sea, which I loved yet hadn't experienced for a while. The lesson lasted around two hours and really only managed to confirm what I already knew; that I am shit at surfing. Managing to stand up for all of about five seconds before losing balance and splashing in the ocean. On the plus side though, I was getting much better.

The constant effort of swimming, standing, falling in and battling with the relentless waves left me exhausted afterward and also injured, as I'd damaged my right shoulder, probably from the tonnes of inefficient paddling and my chest from the countless times I heaved myself back onto the board; both now ached badly in each area. At this point, I was a physical wreck, what with the thumbs and bruised backside which granted were healing nicely. This was one of the reasons for not surfing earlier in the week, as I could move my thumbs and hold things OK, but the ligaments were still strained in my digits and would hurt if I pressed on something, and now with a body hammered for a couple of hours by relentless waves and a severe lack of balance, just added to a growing list of ailments. That said I did have fun and was pleased to be doing something; also, I got to meet a really nice couple of Canadians who happened to be brother and sister. Neville and Sharon were from Vancouver and we met up for drinks later, having a good chat about their native country, having been before and stating my desire to venture out west at some point which they encouraged me to do. I had initially pondered the possibility of still going to Canada, but wasn't sure if I could get there with costs being a factor. Plus, I had already decided where my next port of call was going to be, still they kindly gave me their details to keep in touch, and I hoped that I would see them again in the future as they were friendly and good fun.

Unfortunately, I had to leave the next day; my week of getting 'really relaxed' had left me even more battered and bruised, but felt like it was just what the doctor ordered. I was ready to move on now and took the bus back down to Lima where, upon my arrival, I headed straight to the airport. I sent some post home which included paperwork and receipts that were now weighing me down and a memory card with photos on for the folks back home to enjoy, as I no longer needed this with having a new camera. Plus, I sent the police report for Dan about the stolen camera to claim on his insurance.

Having boarded the plane, I had a couple of hours' stopover in Quito airport, before then taking a connecting flight to Bogota in Colombia. While at Spanish school, I decided to come here because when booking my additional flights from Quito to Lima then Cusco, it somehow was £80 cheaper to then have an extra flight to Bogota rather than just the straight return flight back to Quito and even just a one-way journey was about the same. Fuck knows how? The airlines pretty much seem to make it up as they go along – which was exactly what I was starting to do. This cheaper deal made up my mind where I would be heading. I would have now been due to head back to the USA if I were finishing my original plan of just visiting Ecuador and Peru. This was it; from now on, my plans were not set. I could make it up as I wished for the next four-and-a-half months and all I had to do was get to Rio by August to take my flight back to the UK.

For some reason, I had this preconceived idea about Colombia; dangerous, kidnappings, drugs and guns everywhere and not the type of place that you would really want to visit. This had come directly from what was reported in the media back home and also whilst staying with Marcia, because an English bloke had come to visit her, all battered and bruised and said that it had happened in Colombia. This didn't look good or instil much confidence in my choice. But as the story unfolded, it emerged that the police had done it, as he was classed as illegal immigrant having not got his passport stamped with there being no one at border control late at night, so just entered the country anyway. Now, one thing I wouldn't do was cross a border without the correct accreditation to be in a country, as this could only lead to trouble. So, when he was stopped by police, they arrested him and gave him a pasting. I had heard about police corruption all over South America due to poor wages and being largely unregulated. So he seemingly had given them an excuse; especially not having any money to pay them off. Despite this not being right and over the top, I realised why they would do it. That was his story anyway and had left me a little weary of my destination. Although, that said, I did also get the impression that there was more to it than he was letting on and was just his version of events.

Now with this in mind, I was heading to somewhere I never once envisaged I would be heading to and have to admit I did have my reservations. But I wanted to come here, face this unknown and possibly unfounded fear, see the place and experience it myself before I could really pass judgement. Also, more positively while on the plane travelling, there were numerous advertisements from the Colombian tourism board, showing how beautiful and cultural the place was, with the slogan 'the only danger is wanting to leave' – the government now after years of negative press, making a big play for the tourism trade and this was backed up in my guidebook as it emphasised how many parts had done their utmost to clean the place up, and were regarded as much safer for travel now, that filled me with much more confidence and optimism.

Arriving in Bogota, the weather had changed to something more like what I was accustomed to; cloudy and drizzling with rain being back at an elevated level of just over 2500m up in the Andes. I made my way to the hostel in La Candelaria area, elevated to the east of the city close by the historical downtown. The people who were already in the dorm were going out to get breakfast and I was invited to join them, so I took this as a good opportunity to have a look around and get to know some of those staying there, before in the early afternoon taking the local trolley and then a bus to the Salt Cathedral in Zapiquira, a town north of Bogota.

I had wanted to get out and about straightaway and start doing some activities again, as I had heard about this but hadn't really planned to go. I took advantage of the situation as it was the idea of few of those in the hostel so I headed out with them. The salt cathedral was underground, built into a salt mine. We entered as part of a group with a guide who proceeded to show us around and explain the history, the church, the exhibits and the fact that this still is an actual operational mine as well. The cathedral and mine tour only covered approximately five per cent of the total excavation and is kept separate, blocked off from the main industrial part where we could still see equipment on the far side. Yet the ceremonial area of worship was massive covering about three levels, displaying an unmissable huge illuminated white cross at the far end. Inside was really beautiful with ornate black salt carvings, religious icons and various other subtly lit surrounding features. Apparently the place had been used to stage concerts and fashion shows due to the incredible acoustics, also it was said parts of the movie *Zorro* had been filmed there. This was certainly one of the most surreal churches I had ever been in, as it was so interesting and unique. Especially considering outside it just offered a normal hillside charade, where apart from the cross on entering through the tunnel you would never guess a church dwelt within. Finishing we treated ourselves to an amazing off the bone, smoked barbeque from a local stall close by, the ample cheap portions were delicious, making the journey all the more worthwhile. That evening, I chilled at the hostel watching a really thought-provoking Colombian movie *Maria Full of Grace*, concerning the plight of desperate people who become drug mules and the dangers it entails just in the hope of making some money, before retiring to bed knackered but really happy with my first day's endeavours in Colombia.

Walking around the city the next day everywhere was packed and by the historical centre, things got even worse. There was no traffic on the roads and the streets and plazas were crammed full of people. There was a very good reason for this, as I hadn't realised it was Easter weekend and a public holiday. Countless revellers lined the streets to celebrate and there were massive queues for anyone wanting to go to church. This was an awesome spectacle to see, so many locals and people from out of town, flocking in droves to witness the religious parades, street performers and take advantage of cheap trinkets, artefacts and souvenirs, not to mention the endless food and drink on offer. Over the two days, I seemed to just wander around savouring the atmosphere, not really doing an awful lot. This was mainly due to most things such as the gold and Botero museum being shut for the holidays. It was even hard work finding an Internet cafe that was open with everywhere being closed and people downing tools. But I happily sacrificed these for the fact that even though not a religious person myself, I got to witness what the Easter holidays or Semana Santa was like and how they were celebrated here in a completely different fashion to how I was used to.

The great thing about this was that I got to mingle more with the locals, sharp realising how unbelievably nice and friendly the Colombians were. It was truly remarkable and made for an amazing first impression of the country; everywhere I looked, people seemed to be happy and smiling, which made it all the more unbelievable taking into consideration the troublesome past and reputation that the place had, and was loving the completely different psyche one might expect – in shops, on the street and even just watching how they interacted with each other. Sitting in a restaurant, there was a family together and the younger son of about seven slipped off his chair while messing around and not paying attention. The father, instead of berating or fussing over the child, burst out laughing at him, ruffled his hair in a 'you crazy little scamp' fashion and sat him back down before returning back to the company and conversation he was enjoying. I smiled with amusement at what happened; while I watched the world and the happiness it exuded go by.

After my third day in Bogota, I decided to leave the city, wanting to get out and about to explore the country in search of more of what was on offer. Consulting my trusty guidebook, I'd decided on a visit to the small colonial town of Villa de Leyva to the north-east of Bogota; enticed by the prospect of its reported chilled-out feel and the fact that there was no modern architecture. Booking onto a six a.m. bus was stupid. I inevitably woke at five forty-five a.m. the next morning after communal meal in the hostel followed by a subsequent night on the piss. So sharp realised the bus booked 'why so early?' was going to be missed. Luckily, one of the guys working in the hostel checked and there was another at the more sensible time of ten a.m. which, having said my goodbyes again, I then took.

Now used to incredibly winding roads, hanging off the edges of steep cliffs and seeing spectacular rolling mountain views as far as the eye could see, this journey was no different. Except here, there were many Army check points included along the way. Compared to other places, in Bogota I noticed a vast increase in military and police presence that were all heavily armed; essentially to help ward off any paramilitary or guerrilla attacks, and this applied when travelling around the country, used to look for people who may have been intent on causing harm. This made me a little edgy because it brought home the fact that there was still an element of trouble within the country and that things could still happen, yet it also reassured knowing there was a presence patrolling the towns and highways to help keep innocent people safe. Given that, I probably should've been more concerned with the driver's antics of steering the bus with his knees; freeing up his hands so he could happily munch on a packet of crisps.

Getting to the bus terminal at Tunja, I immediately took another smaller *colectivo* bus further and higher into the mountains, to the national monument of Villa de Leyva – a title awarded because of its untouched status. The place was exactly how it was described; stone-clad, white-washed buildings, no more than two-storeys high and all with a colonial design. It looked fantastic, incredibly ornate, still holding its centuries' old beauty. Tarmac roads stopped on entry and only started again as I exited the town centre in a taxi, heading to the outskirts of town, up a dirt track and passing a military base to find my hostel in the countryside. Getting late, travelling all day and being a tad hungover, left me really hungry. So after settling in, I headed back into town for something to eat while precariously trying not to fall and break my neck on the large, age-old cobble stone streets, then spent the rest of the evening relaxing outside in the hostel garden, hanging out with others staying there.

There was a range of activities on offer from the hostel, but I had to try and keep it cheap and cheerful as it was impossible to get money from the ATM. The revellers over the Easter weekend had cleaned it out. So, I opted to take a mountain bike and explore the local area. Once more armed with a 'not necessarily accurate' hand-drawn map, I headed to local places of interest which were described on it. Higher mountains in the distance adorned the horizon in every direction surrounding the town and farmland flat plains of the shallow valley we were situated in. Now in the rural countryside, I cycled on dirt tracks with limited signage that made finding the places I wanted to visit trickier, and instigated many a wrong turn to create a challenging yet more fun adventure trying to locate them.

My first stop was at a heritage site full of large stones; laid out to form an ancient calendar. Not exactly in the Gregorian sense but familiar nevertheless. Even though dating from around four hundred years old, some stood up straight, some lay on the grass, some thick, some thin, but with one similarity throughout; all of them carved and shaped as huge monolith penises, ranging anywhere from 3m to 10m in length. Not that I was measuring. It looked really surreal and I didn't expect in a million years to be standing, staring at massive stone phallic works in a valley in the middle of the Andes in Colombia. Apparently, they were carved by indigenous folk who inhabited the area, also as an offering to ensure that the ground would remain fertile and provide good yields for the farming there. It made sense, I suppose; with a knob that size, the mind boggled at the amount of what could be yielded.

Before reaching my next destination, the weather had changed and not for the better. Starting out, I had been basking in sunshine and wasted some of this having to return to change batteries in the camera, but now after faffing around, getting lost and checking out some big stone cocks, it was overcast. Behind me towards town, there were black clouds; in front of me over the mountains; black clouds and to my left, guess what? Black clouds – where occasional bolts of lightning would strike the higher hill tops. Yet surrounded by this ominous spectacle of dark and sinister weather, I was thankfully bone dry. So I hastily pressed on. Arriving at the Museo Paleontologico, I locked the bike up, wary of a horde of marauding kids who might liberate me from my steed, and headed in to see El Fosil; which believe it or not translates as 'the fossil' and oddly is an almost complete fossil. A Kronosaurus was a marine reptile that dated back 120 million years from when the area was a seabed. It looked fascinating to see at around 10m plus in length and the detail of the bones and teeth incredibly preserved as they were laid out in its natural state from when it died, was then discovered and subsequently uncovered. I wandered around the small but exhibit-laded museum for seemingly ages, looking at and reading up on the other artefacts, predominantly wondering and trying to piece together what the fragments were, amid all the scientific information, but more so, trying to comprehend that all these and at this level used to be underwater at some point.

Pressing on, I found the ostrich farm but decided not to venture in as time was getting on and I wanted to visit the blue pools, where I hoped to take in a spot of swimming before heading back. But my map reading and rubbish navigational skills brought me out by the main road into town. Now numerous times lost and left head scratching, I just ventured back. But I didn't have to wait long before getting wet. As I approached town, I approached the rain. Having managed to stay dry so far, the inevitable happened and I got absolutely drenched. The cobbled streets ran as babbling beige rivers, newly formed waterfalls cascaded down the tracks of the mountain that sheltered the town from behind, while interspersed *cracks* of lightning and *roars* of thunder reigned over-head. I took refuge under an overhanging balcony in the hope that it would subside. No chance; this was set in and I was out in the rain with the huge rain drops belting down and was getting soaked. Cycling up to the hostel, the now really muddy track was awash with streams of water. The military guards on duty just looked perplexed, as I smiled and said '*Hola*' before getting back into some sanctuary to dry off and change clothes.

The rain was unrelenting, so I hung out with some of the others sharing the dorm; they were making dinner and kindly asked if I wanted to join them. This solved the problem of not having to venture back out in the unfavourable conditions, so chipped in and we made a pasta, vegetable and *chorizo* dish, spending the rest of the night chilling out together. I'd had a good day on the bike and thoroughly enjoyed myself and the exercise had served me well. The next morning, the early sun had dried out my things, which was good because I was now intent on making a move again; that was the plan anyway if I could get my hands on some cash or I wasn't going anywhere. To my dismay, the ATM still hadn't been filled. I was now kind of stuck with hardly any money and an increasing hostel bill to pay. The bank here though had the same laid-back approach to life as the town itself portrayed, and I was early; so fortunately I only had to wait around half an hour for it to open and the machine to be filled. One of the cashier clerks even gave me a hand, as it was only in Spanish and I didn't understand some instructions, an act that just helped reinforce the lovely, friendly nature of the Colombian people I was experiencing.

Relieved to be finally sorted with some funds, I settled my dues and headed for my next destination. The more I read, the more I wanted to do and experience, as I ventured around this unforeseen entity of my travels, so I started to move with some vigour even though still a little beaten up. But my ailments were healing and I started to appreciate getting back to an ache and pain-free physical state. On a small mini-bus that took around seven hours, I whiled away the time studying Spanish, listening to music and gazing at the soaring birds over the spectacular mountains, valleys and plains before I reached San Gil; a larger town known for its reputation of offering sports and adventure activities that I now wanted to get immersed in. Despite not being a hundred per cent full fitness, this place looked ideal and I figured I could base myself here for a while and give it a go.

Next day, just down the steep hill from the hostel, a football game from the UK was being shown, so I watched with a couple of guys called Mark and Rob from the hostel; it was worth it as two of the big guns served up an eight-goal thriller finishing 4-4. While there, we talked about a caving tour available. It sounded fun so later in the afternoon we booked up, headed out of town to where it was, met our guide and got kitted out. Not being able to remember the last time that I went proper caving, I was excited by the prospect, so I cast any injury woes aside because this was different to the caves earlier on in my travels; as it involved hard hats, headlamps and flotation jackets and seemed more the real deal, as opposed to wandering around looking at beautiful rock formations.

The entrance was something out of Indiana Jones; covered by dense undergrowth of a reclaiming forest that featured a rusting, old, disused cable car from previous industrial period. The cave mouth was quite large where light was already diminishing, due to the surrounding vegetation and this slowly started to etch into darkness as we ventured within. Caution had to be taken where to step, as walking through the cold stream allowed water to rush into the trainers making the way inevitably more slippery underfoot as we progressed. After only about 150ft inside, the guide stopped us and pointed towards the ceiling. Looking up using only one head light, we saw there were dark patches everywhere. On closer inspection, these were bats and there were hundreds of them in clusters hanging upside down. They looked unnervingly cool as I pondered the chaos; should they all get spooked, starting a feverish rapture flying around the cave, having never seen a spectacle like these before in the wild. There was a strong musky smell that filled the cavern and nasal cavity from the copious amounts of *guano* (bat shit) accumulated on the floor, which we disrupted when walking through. Having a waterproof case to put cameras in, we took some quick photos and not wanting to disrupt them in their habitat, we hastily pressed on.

The cave narrowed and the ceiling closed in as we ventured further inside the earth; seemingly up and down through the disorientating passageways, with only the focused glow of the headlamps guiding the way in the blackness. Inside the air was cold and offered what was like a faint echoing hum, where at times we ended up on hands and knees trying to get through 2ft crawl spaces; thinking how it must be an thrilling prospect for someone exploring an undiscovered cave for the first time, as it would surely get the blood and adrenaline pumping, wondering what's lurking through an unexplored gap? Is it going to open up on the other side? Or is there another passage? Or just a dead end? Obviously, this wasn't the case here and it was quite easy to shuffle our way through before once again being able to stand up properly. Despite our torches it was still dark, moist and dingy, having to tread carefully to avoid slips and trips especially as we approached an edge where the pathway stopped abruptly.

From here down over was a metal ladder heading into the dark. One at a time, we slowly descended. At the bottom, there was another ledge and a platform. We waited for the guide and when he arrived, he announced that to carry on now we had to jump.

What? Jump? Jump where?

Looking warily with the headlamp, about 25ft away was a wall of rock. But looking down, it was pitch black and extremely difficult to make out what was there. Our guide assured us that below was deep water, I could hear the unmistakable torrent of water rumbling in the cavern but couldn't see it. Now he wanted us to jump into the darkness and hope everything would be OK. If this wasn't bad enough, then came the finer details; make sure not to jump too far out or you will hit the wall, while making sure you jump far enough as to land in the deepest part. *Are you fucking kidding me?* Not only was it impossible to tell how high up the jump was, whether there was water there or not and if so, where actually the deep part of it was. It all added up to shit scary blind jump.

I have to admit I was slightly apprehensive and somewhat wary of the guide's reassurances, but came to a rational conclusion this must be a 'thing' to, do as turning people into crippled heaps in caves hardly bodes well for any company who ventures within. Also, as before, I found the more you stand worrying about these things, the more nervous you become. I just thought *Fuck this* and jumped straight out. There was a flash of rock wall from the headlamp as time seemed to slowly suspend and I fell further than expected or possibly hoped, before I crashed and was fully immersed in the cold water. On entry, as a natural reaction, I lifted my legs up, just in case. The momentum of the fall carried me under and my sole hit the rocky bottom but not hard to cause any injury. Popping up, I was relieved to be OK. The water where I'd hit was around 7ft deep and refreshing, expecting it to be much colder than it was. Wading into the shallower part, I waited for Mark and Rob to jump; which now looking up was about a 20ft drop. Eventually, they did after much swearing and blasphemy. We then had our photos taken by the guide in the water pleased with our leaps of faith; after he casually had taken some steps down, failing to mention they were there, while taking great pleasure in watching us shitting ourselves.

Finishing the final part, we followed the water, ending up swimming for the last hundred yards that brought us back to the cave mouth then out into the open forest. Even though it was starting to turn dusk, it still offered a slight relief to see daylight again from these events, as it meant not being trapped in the belly of the earth; however unlikely. Trudging soggily up a trail in the forest, we made our way back to the guide centre. The caving only lasted approximately an hour, but it was really interesting and an exhilarating activity that seemed to provide good team-building fun. We chatted excitedly on the way back, only interrupted about six times as the guy driving the cab thought he was a professional stunt racer, speeding, swerving in-and-out of traffic and being an absolute maniac on the road, providing an experience scarier than the actual caving itself.

The manager of the hostel knew some of the locals who organised the expeditions, and they regularly played football together once a week. This week was no exception, as he managed to get good numbers from those staying at the hostel who wanted to play, and that evening they were going for a bit of a kick around. This was at one of the community five-a-side courts that seemed to be everywhere; not just in Colombia, but Peru and Ecuador as well. With the prospect of a bit of exercise and not drinking for thirty seconds, I decided to bring myself out of retirement and join in. Unfortunately, I hadn't kicked a ball in anger in over three years, never mind a street football that they were playing with. It was like a solid plastic rock, that didn't bounce and was hard on my precious European toes. But this was the least of my worries, as I never actually thought to warm up properly and after about fifteen minutes, my short-lived comeback was over. I turned to get the ball and strained the ligaments in my left knee. With stinging pain inside the joint, straightaway I knew I was done; so, I spent the rest of the time sitting by the side, watching, as to not aggravate it further. I was gutted, not about the football but the fact that I had now picked up another injury. My arse was fine, my thumbs were still a little weak but no problems, my sore shoulder had eased, my chest was good; but now there was this. I had safely negotiated caving weighing up the risks yet was blasé about the footy and never gave it a second thought. But what was pissing me off even more was I had booked to go white water rafting the very next day.

It just seemed to be one thing after another picking up silly injuries all the time and it was becoming quite annoying. This time wasn't as bad as Peru; there was no chance at all of rafting there. But here, there was a chance. Apprehensively; I decided to still go for it as it had been cancelled due to the conditions over the last few days and today it was happening, plus we had the numbers; whereas, if I dropped out, later on in the week there may not be enough people to go. Also I loved rafting and really wanted to do it and now I was more determined with what had happened previous.

There were five rafting in total; myself, Rob and Mark who had been caving, plus two others; Kevin and Rachel. The rest of the boat was made up of the guide Jorge and Harry from the company plus a friend of theirs and Sergio was in the safety kayak. We had already met some of these guys as they played football the night previous. We headed out of town into the dense jungle about an hour away, and apparently this was into potentially dangerous territory as it had been explained previously that companies as such, had to pay off those who live outside the law as paramilitary or guerrillas and control these regions in exchange for safe passage without fear of being attacked or kidnapped as hostages. How ethically right or wrong this practice was, that was up for debate. But it was means to an end. And probably offered a reason why tourism was allowed to grow within the country.

Stopping at a bridge spanning the river, we donned our life jackets, helmets and were given paddles as the raft was set up. The river was again an uninviting mocha colour and raging through, awash from the heavy rainfall from higher up in the mountains. It was touch and go whether we were actually going to raft as it had the potential to be very dangerous, but the good news was that the guys who we rafted with were some of the best, apparently being part of the Colombian national team. We were given our briefing about instructions, safety and what to do in the event of falling in etc., before we all got in the boat and had practice drills of the various instructions. Before I knew it, we were off and I purposely sat on the left of the boat, jamming my left ankle under the inflated rubber section across the centre to shore up my somewhat sore left knee.

The initial rapids were quite timid, allowing us to roll with ease past the few grade threes, but the subsequent rougher grade fours required some hard paddling towards; this built up speed and momentum to smash over and through them. The raft bobbed and rolled up and down frantically, causing an invigorating white spray of water that soaked continuously in the process. Only after the frenetic stretch eased, celebratory paddles were loft in the air; a victory over our naturally enigmatic, raging nemesis that would momentarily be calm where we could also relax and conserve energy, letting ourselves lazily drift along. After about an hour of numerous passages and exhilarating work, we took our included pack lunches along the muddy silt banks of the thickly dense jungle river, providing a cooling shade away from the intense sun.

Carrying down the course, we were expertly steered by Jorge and avidly listened for his instructions: "Hard left!" "Hard right!" "Back left!" "Back right!" "Hard ahead!" would be bellowed in a specific order, which everyone was expected to act upon to get the raft in the correct position, allowing for maximum performance going into each rapid; especially as we soon hit a big grade five. We powered into it hard and as the raft crashed into the huge broiling water; 'GET DOWN!' Everyone ducked down; wedging themselves inside the raft to avoid being washed over the side, as the inevitable torrent came thunderously sweeping over everyone. I was loving it as was everyone else. The adrenaline was all consuming and saturating as the wild water itself. So far during the day, we had only lost one over the side. It was always expected for someone to get washed over with these activities, but we just hauled them back in with ease and carried on. Doing really well, we took time for a swim in the river when it was calm for a few brief moments, before dragging ourselves back inside for the last run.

Breathing heavily with the exertions, everyone concentrated approaching the last series of rapids; paddling hard through the grade fours. Then as everything was fine; suddenly, we weren't fine, not in the slightest. The fours turned into a monstrous grade five of heaving, thrashing, relentless water and within seconds and seemingly out of control, the raft unexpectedly turned, letting the mighty flow take hold and we hit the last rapid wrong. Now side on, we had a big problem. Before I knew anything, all I could see was the blue inside of the raft as it was lifted up by the water and bodies went everywhere. I tipped backwards over the side and the raft flipped over onto me. We had been smashed by a huge rapid and I ended up underneath, trapped in the maelstrom of massive swells.

This was unchartered territory for me, it hadn't happened before. I was in trouble and knew I had to get from beneath our stricken craft. Thankfully, I wasn't panicking, just trying to remember what I needed to do; instinctively I started to pull myself toward what I thought was the outside, where thankfully, after what felt like only a matter of seconds, I popped up at the surface. Looking around, I got my bearings to find where the raft and everyone else was. I'd ended up ahead of it with Rob close by. The river was now deeper and out of the way of the dangerous shallow boulders causing the rapids, but the constant splashing of the speeding tempestuous water was consuming me as I bobbed uncontrollably between the underneath and surface. Swimming was useless and I ended up clamouring; just trying to keep on my back so the face was out of the unrelenting water; this was not good. In fact, it was pretty nerve-racking as bodies were literally everywhere and the whole incident was a blurred mass of exertion in the frantic conditions. Luckily, one thing I had remembered to do was hold onto my paddle and this was my life line; Rob had gotten hold of the guide rope around the side of the raft and I used the paddle handle to hook myself to him and he pulled me towards it; where we held on. In almost an instant, Jorge had then gotten on top and with one pull managed to flip the raft back over to the correct position and in turn started a chain reaction of bodies, including Rob and myself, being hauled in.

The raging pass of river had now subsided and everyone had their own crazy version of events. But we were missing three; two were picked up by ourselves a couple of moments later, but one had a more interesting experience and was brought back on the front of the rescue kayak having thought that they were just about to drown after hitting their knee hard on a boulder in the water. As relieved as we all were, we still had issues; we only had three paddles between us. Sergio headed out in the kayak and hastily started to find and retrieve another three before we had enough to get us to the bank of the river and the end of the course.

Back on the riverside, everyone was elated at surviving being smashed over by the grade five rapid and how insane it all was; buzzing of the adrenaline of having successfully dealt with such an occurrence. I overheard the raft guides talking, saying 'muy peligroso' which I knew meant 'very dangerous', but we all lived to tell the tale and were so proud of our selves, having braved such an experience and survived an amazing adventure that turned pretty wild. I loved it! Yes, it was dangerous, but that's what these activities are and there is always a chance that something could go wrong, especially when you are battling against the elements. But for me and many others, that's the rush; having to put yourself against the uncertainty and unpredictability of it all and come through unscathed, yet when it does go wrong, being good enough and confident enough to recognise what to do and how to come through safe – which was testimony to the fact that everyone listened when instructed and did what they were told, so our faith in the guides' expertise that were with us paid off. This was now another crazy incident amongst many which went wrong but ended with no real damage done. Would I go again? In an instant. Having now experiencing what it's like to go over in a wild river reinforced I was capable of handling what it was like and what I needed to do, which only reinforced my resolve to want to go again. And in the same breath, it made me respect the elements to be dealt with that much more, and it has to be said always worthwhile paying a little more also and using reputable top professional outfits when doing these types of adrenaline-fuelled activities. It really can make the difference. That evening, we carried on the team bonding with the slightly less fraught activity of drinking some well-earned beer.

Like the river; everyone else at the hostel and I was in full flow and we continued to try and finish ourselves off with gusto. My knee had eased somewhat and was pain-free but tender when twisting and turning, but I refused to let this stop me. Confident after having survived the rafting activities, Mark, Rachel and I headed to a local bridge to do a spot of bungee jumping the next morning. I had no reservations about this, having done it before and the bridge swing jump, plus this was not very high with a 25m drop to the river below. The guys set up and we were donned with harnesses and helmets. Here, the elastic was attached just below the sternum and not at the ankles; that I assumed was due to the relatively small height we were jumping from. Climbing on to the edge of the bridge and without much thought or hesitation, after a three, two, one, I leapt off and out into the yonder, putting my faith in physics and some thick elasticated rubber. Jumping out was fine and after a short fall that lasted seconds, I was slowed by the increasing tension to within a metre avoiding the water, before in turn bouncing straight back up with increasing velocity to slow and stop about a metre from the fast-approaching underside of the bridge. I again fell as gravity took another hold, but on the second bounce I jolted my relaxed leg and felt a sharp pain. Not realising I wouldn't be attached by the ankles, the midriff harness attachment allowed my legs to flail and tweak my already sore ligament in the knee. Bastard. I wasn't in too much pain, but it would set me back and leave me limping again with an emphasis it hadn't healed properly and that sometimes I simply wouldn't learn.

After being dragged back up to the bridge by a car winch, I was unhooked and watched as the others then had their turn. This was entertaining; Rachel was no problem diving straight out like a consummate professional. Mark on the other hand was already petrified by the prospect of his first jump. He eventually went for it by just falling off the bridge rather than jumping out and ended up running down what looked like an invisible wall, the speed he mustered from a direct drop caused the bungee to elongate further, especially having been stretched by us prior, and he didn't quite slow enough to stop before splashing into the river, soaking him. He bounced the usual five or six times, wailing, shouting, screaming and swearing profusely before eventually coming to a stop. Although we were laughing because well, let's face it, it was funny as fuck and he was fine. He really wanted to do it and jumped, overcoming one of his fears. This was the main thing and must be commended for that. So again, we all left, chuffed with one another after what some might say more stupid exploits.

Once again, I was fast running out of cash. Most places here only dealt with hard currency so I had to regularly use the ATM. I was having trouble getting money out and ended up having to call my bank to get my card reactivated; as it had been stopped from working due to the fact that the bank didn't realise that I was in Colombia, thinking I was in the USA. So after the usual bit of bureaucratic hassle, I was eventually then able to withdraw some funds and carry on having fun; especially as the things that I was able to do here were working out to be much cheaper than other places. With such great value for money, I was making the most of it.

With our jumping off bridges, getting bank cards reactivated excitement done and dusted by lunch. We were all back at the hostel for the early afternoon where we had our next activity booked. It was relentless as we were heading out back into the close by hills and mountains for a spot of paragliding. This was another activity I hadn't tried before and possibly because of my knee I wasn't exactly raring to go, but it was already organised along with the bungee so thought, *Fuck it, I'll be sitting down,* and went along anyway. There were around ten of us in total ready to participate; with two flights in tandem at the same time lifting off from the high-up plains.

It was windy at the top on the grassy verge where we were to take off from and return to after the flight. Everyone was having a good giggle at those coming in to land; finding themselves either swept back up or funnier still dragged along the grass. Harnessed up again, I sat in what could only be described as a cradle, with the pilot behind. Instructions were pretty clear; run, lift your legs and admire the view. By the way, scream if you want to go faster.

We set off with textbook grace, as my knee held firm and the ground below immediately subsided. We were instantaneously soaring in the air by the opened canopy caught by the blustery wind. The trees fell away as we ventured off into the sunny skies carried along by the now very much noisier air streams that shattered the illusion of calm and serenity when watching. The views were incredible and the horizon stretched away far into the distance, as the earth turned to white haze then brilliant blue from the clear sun-drenched sky. We never ventured far from where we had taken off, but with our elevation it was still easy to see a canyon that broke the ground below about a kilometre away from where we were sailing.

Due to our amazing vantage point, I was fully armed with camera in hand and from my strapped seat was able to take photos, gliding above the rolling patchwork of mountainous land below, reaching much higher than I expected. This allowed the pilot to put us into some amazing and gravity-defying spins, G-force pulled on the body and I looked up to see the top of the canopy, yet instead of blue sky behind it was green shrubbery as we span around virtually horizontal with centrifugal force keeping us pinned into the cradle, flashing past seemingly ever-closer trees and foliage. It was amazing, yet I couldn't help but feel that it was wholly unnatural, expecting to crash any second due to our flimsy craft and the seemingly reckless abandon with which it was being used, creating some heart-stopping moments where all trust and faith were put in the hands of the pilot and his god-like manipulation of physics. But this was the rush and why it was exciting; I had no control and had to sit back and enjoy the ride – which I did, immensely – before we came back into land, skidding along the grass of the take-off area on my arse.

Having spent the first three days like a man on a mission, getting immersed with as many sports activities as possible, the last three days in San Gil were a little more of a relaxed affair, as the hostel cronies and I headed to a local resort to relax. The Pozo Azul was on the river system out of town and let us chill out in the sun and swim in a huge natural pool and we explored the forest area looking over elevated waterfalls out at the vast sea of green jungle, stretching out in front of us and there was a visit to the very beautiful Parque General in town which had carved pathways throughout and the trailing vines and bridges that all encompassed the place's natural beauty and serenity.

I was preparing to leave and had a fantastic array of experiences here, which one by one were slowly dwindling away as gradually I ticked them of the to do list. But before departing, I had one last excursion I wanted to experience. Villa de Leyva where I stayed previously left a lasting impression on me. It may have been small, but its elegant beauty was unsurpassed, and I loved the fact that it was tranquil, yet seemed to provide everything a person could want and this was fast becoming my type of place. The cities were good and they served a purpose, but being in less populated, beautiful, untouched places, high up in the mountains held an unparalleled mystique; so I spent an afternoon visiting the close by gorgeous little town of Barichara.

The local bus was a cheap and inexpensive way of getting there that offered another chance of travelling and interacting with the locals. A worthwhile endeavour in itself; where my Spanish would have to come to the forefront and provide ample opportunity to practise. Arriving, I again wasn't disappointed by cobbled streets and colonial architecture. Granted, it had been rebuilt over the last few years but it was really difficult to tell as it had been done in a very befitting manner. We whiled away the hours just exploring around, taking in a gallery exhibition of local artist's works, before dining in a restaurant that served up a local delicacy of ants. Here, these were in a sauce on a steak which one of the others had bought, but I'd tried them earlier from a packet, eating them like they were peanuts. They were quiet crispy having been fried but still soft in the middle. Honestly, I can say they were nice and I liked them. Certainly not disgusting at all and was told that they are good for you being full of protein. So munch away.

Carrying on exploring, we sat on a hill side by the edge of town gazing out at the countryside. The mountains in the distance were shadowed by low cloud cover, yet bright light streamed through less-dense gaps to bathe the valley below in radiant beams. It had a certain divinity about it as if someone was purposely trying to highlight an already beautiful picturesque landscape of an already idyllic place. Little wonder when we arrived back at the town square to get the bus, there was a TV company there filming an episode of one of the popular soaps outside the church. Still I resisted the call to possibly become Colombia's newest gringo soap star.

The six days or so I had spent in San Gil were fantastic and they flew by, in a non-stop whirlwind and certainly felt that way; so much so that my travelogue was the only real way to un-blur what happened in such a short period of time, as I had seemingly done way more than what was anticipated, because on my arrival at the hostel there seemed to be a wide variety of activities I was interested in compared to what my guidebook informed. But I was fast learning this; it was only a guide. Information regarding something that can evolve from when it is written about, so the best way to find out what things were on offer was to actually go there, see and do it myself. San Gil had served a purpose and an extremely adventurous one at that which provided ample opportunity to meet and interact with some amazing other travellers and have a tonne of fun together; that also allowed me to find out some disturbing news about my next port of call and subsequent adventure.

Jacque Cousteau, Muddy Waters
and the Lost City

It was the first time in Colombia, I travelled from one destination to another on the overnight bus when I left San Gil to head north to Santa Marta on the Caribbean coast; the guidebooks advised not to due to safety implications, but I decided against this as those who I had spoken to said it was fine and hadn't experienced any problems. Also, this meant that money could be saved on a night's accommodation and a day travelling could be spent doing other things, rather than sat on a bus albeit at the expense of witnessing the beautiful scenery and surroundings. I actually arrived in Ciénaga on the outskirts of Santa Marta and then took another bus into Santa Marta itself although this still wasn't my destination. En route, I met two cousins who were travelling together, Janette and Marlou, who were going to Taganga; a relaxed fishing village over the hills a few miles further up the coast. This happened to be where I was heading. Again, having spoken to other travellers who had come from there, they informed me it was a much better place to be based rather than the bigger bustling concrete jungle of Santa Marta.

When we arrived at the hostel where I intended to stay, it was now full. But they offered Janette, Marlou and I a chalet for the evening close by, as there would be rooms and dorm beds available the next day. So, for the sake of one night and not having to search around, we accepted. Hostels were easy to come by in Colombia. Most where I was staying formed part of a network in different destinations, so travellers could find one they liked where they were heading next and reserve from the hostel pre-departure. The best being that they would only be recommended if they were reputable; providing security in the knowledge that you were getting a safe, decent place to stay at a good peso price, which seemed to be cheaper than the other countries – another factor testimony to Colombia's fledgling tourist trade and draw for people to go there.

Taganga was lovely and really chilled out, a place where nothing seemed to happen in a hurry. It was ideal; small and easy to walk around, with plenty of restaurants, bars and street vendors serving fresh fish and deliciously refreshing fruit smoothies, cooling temperatures in the now 30°C plus heat of the Caribbean sun. Not to mention the fact that there were beaches to while away the hours on. But here also carried a good reputation for scuba diving. Something I now could do having learnt and getting my certification some six months prior back in Thailand that when I reflected on, seemed a very long time ago. Being a somewhat expensive hobby, here the prices were good. So, I decided to immerse myself once more into the blue.

I had bumped into an Aussie who I had met in San Gil called Dave and he informed me that coming up at the weekend was *Dia de la Tierra*; or 'Earth Day'. This involved getting as many scuba divers, snorkelers and volunteers as possible into the water in and around the bay of Taganga, to clean up and remove rubbish and debris from the beaches, coral and sea. Straightaway, I wanted to get involved. It seemed such a worthy cause. It was only one day and I figured it my moral duty to help; being in such a privileged position now that I could dive, I should help. I had loved learning to scuba dive and it had given me a certain affinity with the sea. I learnt so much about the importance of helping preserve the wildlife and coral vital to the ecosystem, not to mention the lively hoods of people who used the water as vital tourism and employment resource, and this would aid me in giving something back to the local area.

One slight problem; it had been a while since I set up, put on the equipment, used it and squeezed myself into an amazingly unflattering wetsuit. So I figured it would be a good idea if I had a couple of fun dives the day prior, to familiarise myself with what was going on; therefore, I wouldn't look a complete 'Johnny no-stars' berk on the actual day of the clean-up and I'd be able to operate quicker, more efficiently and therefore be more effective. For once, some actual sound thought and planning going through my head. This was surprising really as I had some news from back home that left me somewhat annoyed, frustrated, put out and in need of a worthy distraction.

The next morning, I headed to the dive centre for eight a.m. I was sized up and given the necessary equipment; BCD, regulator, mask, fins, weight belt and still unflattering wet suit and started feeling at ease immediately, as I recognised the various components and how they come together with the tank to be able to dive. My dive master and guide was a laid-back Asian fellow called Hossain who seemed to have good knowledge of the job and area, having worked at the dive centre for some time. With paperwork and payment sorted and a bright sun overhead, we headed to the beach, where we launched on to the water in a small, long skiff to venture out of the bay on the calm blue sea and sped to the first dive site of Calichan.

When we arrived, the anchor was set and we prepared our equipment. We were then briefed about the dive site, the expected conditions, our dive time, maximum depth, the cool things we could expect to see and various safety procedures. But gearing up, there was another problem. The boat was too small to put the equipment on inside, like we had done in Thailand. This meant that the bulky Buoyancy Control Device; a jacket that inflates and has the air tank and regulator (where you breath from) attached was to be primed and thrown into the sea, chased after by myself with fins, weight belt, mask and snorkel on. Then I was to put the BCD on in the water. Unfortunately, I'd only done this once before as a training exercise in the pool. There was only going to be one way to find out how successful I was going to be doing this; so in it went, as did I after it. At least, it would sharpen some skills and I figured I'd rather have a go now as oppose to the day after.

Bobbing about in the ocean, having clasped the inflated BCD, I somewhat floundered before eventually managing to roll over and get my arms inside, probably not quite textbook but at least I was half way there. Then I fastened the Velcro strap, *clicked* the clasp on the front so it was attached and pulled the chest straps down to shore it up. Job done. I was surprised it had turned out to be quite easy, the trickiest part was fumbling for the various hoses and finding where to tuck them away, all the while wobbling around ungracefully in the sea. Fortunately, Hossain knew that I was still a relative novice and hadn't used or had much experience with the equipment so checked everything was OK. No real problems and now I knew what to expect when there would be more people diving the next day, as opposed to myself and one other which was happening here. Although a little different, I could see how this method of entry was useful and not only when diving from a small boat. Out of water the equipment was quite heavy, so would also be beneficial for those participating if they had any physical issues, as it didn't involve any lifting.

Slowly, we descended by deflating the air from the BCD into the blue abyss of the earth's second world under the sea; with just the slight *click* and *hiss* of the regulator from the inhaled air and the subsequent *rattle* of bubbles when exhaled. You are never really conscious of breathing in a normal day-to-day existence, but here it is very obvious and relevant. The brain fully aware you are unnaturally breathing underwater, because all your life as a natural reflex it has told you; if the face goes in water - hold your breath. Now underwater, this action would be very dangerous. You cannot hold your breath, as doing so from depth would cause the air in the lungs to take you up, and the subsequent less pressure of shallower water around the body, would cause trapped air in the lungs to expand, and this could tear the tissues inside and result in severe injury or death. This is one of the reasons why diving is classed as an extreme sport; because when manipulating physics and messing with gasses under pressure, the dangers are abundant and all precautions *must* be adhered to. The allure though is overwhelmingly amazing – being able to escape the surface and explore the intriguing beauty of a whole new world opening up before your eyes. As this was a fun dive, there were no exercises or skills to complete, so we swam about admiring a new less-visited, more untouched, wholly more natural and unique environment at 18m deep. Fan corals and soft sponges swayed gently as water moved with the surge and eagerly gazed upon the swarms of fish life; including the queen angel fish with fantastic neon yellow and blue colours standing out, and oddly shaped puffer fish with fluttering fins and puppy dog eyes, that casually sauntered away as we patrolled around the formations, floating neutrally buoyant in a world where gravity didn't exist, and to move up and down was now as natural as left and right. We checked our air regularly and as the first person started to run low, after around forty minutes we made our return, swimming slowly up to the surface.

Back on the boat, we exchanged air cylinders from the used one to another that was full, while we had our surface interval. We had to wait in between dives to allow the nitrogen absorbed in our bodies during the first dive to release. This was because the heavier water had exerted pressure on the body while breathing below. Getting back in again too soon would mean that during the second dive, the nitrogen in the body would build up too much, too quickly and we'd have to end the dive early. We only have certain amount of time at certain depths – the deeper we go, the shorter the time before nitrogen builds up too much to return to the surface safely. If this isn't adhered to and is overextended; the diver has to come up very slowly and can take a long time, increasing the risk of running out of air, but coming up to the surface too early or faster than allowed, the nitrogen will release from the body tissues quickly and can cause decompression sickness, more commonly known as 'the bends'. Again; another life-threatening condition, therefore, times (and depth) both underwater and during the surface interval *must* be monitored. Highlighting another reason why diving is classed as extreme sport, albeit a very lazy one.

This time though gave us the opportunity to relax, chat, take on board some refreshments and move to another location. The next dive site was called Punta Granate; entering the water some one hour and twenty-five minutes later allowed enough nitrogen to be released from the body. Our guide used a recreational dive planner to work this out, indicating that we were now safe to re-enter. We were briefed again about the dive; and splashed back in.

The body is predominantly made out of water, so isn't affected by the pressure of heavy water that surrounds it when diving. But we have a few air spaces in the body that are susceptible to this pressure, these are; the lungs, ears, sinuses and mask. To counteract this, we have to 'equalise' or push more air into these spaces, so the air inside doesn't get squeezed when down below, causing discomfort or pain; the lungs take care of themselves by simply breathing slowly, deeply, in and out, continuously without holding the breath. The ears, however, are a little trickier; by pinching the nose through the mask and blowing gently, this can push extra air into the ears and sinuses, thus equalling the pressure to the water outside. This must be done often during the descent, as the water pressure increases quickly. Being mainly a land lubber all my life, I would find this difficult, so would have to make sure I did this often, yet it would still take time; having to descend very slowly for the equalising to happen. I had gone too far down on one occasion and the pain was a relentless crushing on the inside. Signalling I had a problem, I then had to ascend to relieve the pain and pressure then re-equalise. The mask covering the eyes and nose forms an air pocket and is somewhat easier; all this involves is blowing out through the nose to push air inside the mask to equalise it, still important nevertheless because failure to do so will squeeze the mask to the face and break the soft blood vessels around the eyes. Again, this will become uncomfortable then painful. If that's not bad enough; it can cause big black panda eyes that not only make a person look stupid but also gives the impression they haven't necessarily been diving, but more likely involved in a punch up.

It's fair to say there's a lot going on when diving, what with the trying not to kill yourself, getting injured, looking stupid, all the equipment, safety procedures and that's before you get distracted by all the cool stuff down there. Strangely, most people who don't know about diving seem to be more worried about getting eaten by sharks. Fucking hardly; this concept is easily least of any worries, despite having so few dives under my belt, I hadn't seen one swimming around in the wild and was sharp realising they weren't exactly patrolling around everywhere. But still I hoped we would; figuring it to be a thrilling experience as we again headed down to 18m maximum depth to explore the fantastic rich coral, and were joined by the pretty black and yellow 'Rock Beauty' and many other fish species sauntering around in front of us, including another moray eel, that like in Thailand, was stationary amongst the reef naturally opening and closing its mouth to breathe. Most fish swim to do this, but unfortunately the eel sort of creates a wrongly assumed fierce persona, just like the sharks that we unfortunately never saw again while gently gliding around. I was loving being back under water, it really brought home how much I actually enjoyed it; swimming around in a whole new environment, amid the relaxing, calm serenity, where the only communications are by hand signals and no one can bother you with inane chatter, so you don't have to listen to someone talk utter bollocks. Feeling like your cut off and a million miles from the constant stream of crazy nonsense that happens above the surface. Unfortunately, though, some forty-five minutes later, running on low on air and bottom time, we inevitably had to re-emerge and return to the manic chaos that is life on land.

Finishing, I thanked our guide; he really helped me being chilled and relaxed. This was nice, putting me at ease and increasing my confidence for the next day's activity ahead. That afternoon, I had to go to Santa Marta to get some money; as the overdue ATM in Taganga hadn't been installed and the diving wasn't going to pay for itself. The following day's dives for *Dia de la Tierra* were again an early start; there was a team of twenty-four divers in total which I assumed was a pretty good turn out and more so, as it involved people from all parts of the world. They had seemingly heeded the call, come together in this one spot, with the sole aim of giving something back for the past time, vocation, ocean and earth that they loved and I was no different. It felt very cool and I was proud to be part of something like this.

After briefing, we headed out in the boats to the dive site that happened to be Punta Granate where I had dived the previous day. I didn't mind though, as it was nice just to be diving for a cause and figured it would help being somewhere that I was kind of familiar with. We were buddied up as not to be diving solo, given refuse sacks and headed down to the dive site; but this time in a shallower part at around 12m so it already felt like I was diving a different site anyway, as this part wasn't explored the day prior and I struggled to recognise any of the features or topography that could give aid to any navigation. In my novice state, it wasn't like I knew where I was going, so we sauntered along, loosely following the direction of the group and dive professionals. The objective of the first dive was to pick up and remove any rubbish and debris of a man-made nature that wasn't supposed to be there, been discarded and left lying in and about the coral reef as we made our way around the peninsula, before exiting the water. The first dive lasted approximately thirty-five minutes and was relatively successful. But not for the reasons that one may expect, as we collected virtually no trash; myself personally removing two plastic bags caught amongst the reef that I carefully untangled so as to not damage any of the sharp but brittle coral. When added to what the rest had collected, it didn't amount to much at all. This was a good sign in a strange way, as it indicated that the reefs were in a good condition and waste hazards from man were not affecting the underwater world here too much. Yet I did wonder if we had picked a site which was less vulnerable to human impact, as it was out of the way of the town's actual bay area. But during our surface interval, we stopped for an early lunch at one of the nearby beaches, where we made up for this with gusto; collecting heaps of discarded cans, bottles, food wrappers, paper and plastics that were strewn all over, littering the sand and surroundings. Not only was it a real shame to see such pristine shoreline in such an unnecessary mess, but with instances like this, it would only be a matter of time before the trash would inevitably make its way into the ocean. So we happily removed the offending articles at the source before the waves would inevitably and unfortunately claim it.

Back in the water for the second dive, all involved headed down to the sandy sea bed for a promotional photo opportunity, behind a large banner which promoted the *Dia de la Tierra*, I presume it wasn't left down there as it would have been quite the PR stunt gone wrong, because I was late arriving due to this time having trouble equalising my ears, and didn't nor couldn't make a hasty descent, knowing the dangerous implications and somewhat feeling the pain. We were still encouraged to pick up trash, but the main objective of this dive was for everyone to perform a coral watch. This fortunately wasn't staring at the coral waiting for it to grow at an unbelievably slow rate, but in our buddy pairs and armed with a chart, pencil and torch, we then navigated around the various coral, identifying what type it was; such as boulder, branching or plate and highlighted its natural colour by shining the light onto it, then matched this to the corresponding colour on the chart to indicate how healthy it was. It was really easy to do and I never realised I was to be involved with this type of research and data collection, which would help identify instances of coral bleaching. This is where coral, that are actually living creatures with an exoskeleton, lose their algae or pigment due to high water temperatures and can put them in danger of dying off if sustained too long. They are vitally important to the underwater world, providing food and shelter to thousands of the creatures which live on the shallow reef of our oceans, acting as protective barriers for the land and sustain thousands around the globe through source of food and tourism to name but a few.

Some forty minutes later, we resurfaced to return back to the main beach in Taganga. It was odd returning; I felt somewhat that maybe we had failed, although we did collect a tonne of crap from the nearby beach. We were the divers, yet didn't collect much from under the sea? And maybe we had wasted our time? Obviously, we hadn't, as the simple matter of fact being there wasn't much to collect. It was a good thing, emphasised by the corals examined that were in a really healthy condition. Also, we were on an actual designated dive site, where divers would be inclined to go because of the beautiful and interesting features there, and it was nice to see that at least there was little impact of human footprint evident. But back in the murkier waters of the bay away from the dive sites and closer to human intervention, it was obvious that those on land and snorkelling had been involved in a somewhat more rigorous operation. And probably what made me feel like we may have failed or certainly more inferior, as we gazed upon the massive pile of rubbish and junk that had been retrieved from the beach and underwater. An incredible mound that would have easily fit in a couple of dumper trucks and was hard to believe or comprehend that so much shite had been thrown away and discarded to litter the local area.

Now left with a massive pile of smelly trash, the organisers were incredibly pleased with our efforts and were ecstatic with the rotten fruits of everyone's labour, and the positive outcome which had ensued. As everyone could only be a winner from the project. The environment, the wildlife, the people who lived there and the tourists, which all added to a sense of pride and achievement due to a fabulous coming together of people from all walks of life, both young and old with one common goal. It created a can-do spirit amongst the hundreds involved, from divers, snorkelers to those who patrolled up and down the beaches picking up and clearing the area of waste. All it took was people to care enough, get off their arses and be willing to spend a little time and effort, all in aid of the greater good. The event also raised a greater awareness of what it was trying to achieve and the profile of Taganga on the whole, as it attracted national news with both TV and paper press coverage following the proceedings. Adding to the certificate of recognition everyone received, all participants finished the day by having a large photo together on the beach, where we were joined by some Colombian models standing in front of the huge mound of smelly garbage, just what every *señorita* wanted for their portfolio.

Once again, I was left with an amazing feeling of self-satisfaction and achievement that I had done my bit and helped in some small way, shape or form. This had happened to me a couple of times throughout my journey, and was becoming one of the best things about travelling for me, with the only rewards coming from the thanks and gratitude shown, but the sense of wellbeing and pride from within being a real reward. It was one thing having fun, partying, meeting new people and even achieving feats pushing myself to physical limits – these were all easy as they were for my own personal self-esteem, accomplishments, overcoming fears and it has to be said bragging rights – but these type of events were much more for others and making a difference in their lives and communities, those who hadn't had the opportunities that I was lucky to have had, and was now starting to appreciate this so much more. Especially as it is so easy to sit around moaning how crap things are, yet not actively setting an example and trying to make a difference yourself.

I needed this. Both days helped provide a worthwhile distraction and put some things into perspective. A couple of days prior, I had found out that some photos that I'd sent home had gone missing. Or rather, all the photos that I had sent home in the package from Lima airport, involving the last week in Australia, all of New Zealand and Ecuador had been thrown out and were gone. This was because I put the memory card in and taped it to an envelope with other receipts and memorabilia inside, ironically so it wouldn't get mixed up and lost amid the stuff inside or accidentally fall out, and that was then placed in within a larger airmail envelope. When opened, it wasn't checked properly and the envelope inside with the photo card attached was discarded and now gone forever.

Initially, I was annoyed that it had happened, more so because I had called home from Huanchaco in Peru and explained what I was doing, but this information went out of the window and the card was discarded. Obviously, this was an error and a stupid mistake, which people tend to make. And who was I to start pointing the finger, start shouting and balling especially considering my antics and what had happened on the last night in Lima. Upon reflection, I realised it would have been awfully hypocritical of me, plus I never had the good sense like Dan to back up the photos and this was always a risk, and fate bit me on the arse as I just thought that there would be no problem having done so previously. Due to Dan's forethought, I never lost the Peru photos, but I had now lost two-and-a-half months of other stuff. There seemed to be an inevitability of it all with my camera breaking, having to buy a new one and then getting robbed, so after my days distracted underwater and focused on the tasks at hand, I concluded that shit happens and there was no use blaming anyone, as what's done was done and especially as I had been so well-supported from back home despite my previous misdemeanours, something which I was exceptionally grateful for. So, I let it go, realising it wasn't the end of the world and that those responsible would be feeling really bad about the incident. But little did I realise at the time that fate was going to offer me a small helping hand in rectifying this, but like anything it was going to come at a price.

Having done the 'Earth Day' dives with Dave, we both had separately headed to Taganga for ultimately the same reason. That being a trek we had heard about in the close by Sierra Nevada Mountains called the *Ciudad Perdida* or 'Lost City'. This was mentioned and included as a highlight in my guidebook and sounded really interesting, also the only way to access it was via a five or six-day hike through mountains and jungle. Seeing a lost city just sent my imagination wild, envisaging discovery and adventure;

swashbuckling through the dense jungle, while searching for Eldorado the fabled lost city of gold, but in much the same sense, this unfortunately could also mean danger.

I had talked to Mark about it in San Gil; he had come from the 'Lost City' not a week prior. He loved it, saying how amazing it was, but then his revelations of what happened after was the problem; the story going as such:

Apparently after finishing the trek, on the way down the mountains in the bus that the group was carried in, they were stopped by two armed men who ordered them all out of the vehicle, leave their belongings and told to make on foot and run away down the track, which they all did. Getting around the corner, they heard shots and needless to say sprinted for their lives until they reached the army check point at the bottom, where they explained what had happened. The military took them back up to the point of the incident. On their arrival, they found the bus had been tipped over the side and worse still the driver of their vehicle shot dead. The military went and retrieved their things out of the bus and placed them, their belongings and the dead driver into the back of the military truck and headed back down the mountain. It was treated as a really big deal by the authorities and government officials had ended up apologising to those on the trek and apparently later in the day, they arrested two men for the killing; where it came about that the group had been targeted by the paramilitaries because the company whom they went with had not paid them so that they could pass safely through the region, so the unfortunate driver paid this price with his life. The worst thing apparently being that the guy didn't actually work for the company and was only driving on that particular day as a favour.

A horrible and scary end to what he described as a brilliant time. Whilst in Taganga, this was a hot topic amongst the travelling fraternity, many having their own version of events with conjecture taking over from facts. Much like my version; although mine the testimony of a person who was on the tour that was affected. One thing for sure was that an innocent person was brutally killed and it left me wondering how scared he must have been at the time and how his family must now be feeling or coping due to the circumstances.

I thought about the dilemma in front of me, evaluating that as far as I knew, the paramilitaries never hurt tourists; they killed someone local in a dreadful act of retribution due to non-payment of moneys, an act which all companies seemed to be doing for safe passage on guerrilla territory in most places; the same as the rafting. Deciding in the end that I would risk going as the 'Lost City' trek was something I wanted to experience. Granted this could've been a bad decision and have serious repercussions, never mind whether it was ethically wrong or right which I again pondered, especially now as most of the tour agencies were offering the trip for a special offer cheap price, to keep the tourism interest. One thing was for certain; I wasn't using the company that Mark had used. Yet, oddly, they were recommended to me on three separate occasions when talking to people at the dive centre and in and around Taganga. "Err… *no, gracias.*"

Dave and I booked onto the tour the day after our dives with another friend of his he had met travelling, whom I had yet to meet. The idea was essentially the same as the Incas; trekking with guide and porters for three days to the historical site, but this time we would stay there overnight then return by trekking the first three days, in only two to get back, giving five days in total. But the way we started was a minor miracle that we even got there in the first place.

Meeting at the office in Santa Marta, there were eight others on the trek in our group; Bobby, Dale, Chris, Art, Katie, Cass, Dave and Veronica who was Dave's friend, plus myself made nine in total. It seemed a good group on first impressions; a mix of Aussie, Kiwi and Europeans, offering plenty of people to chat with and get to know. As soon as we set off, the problems started. Firstly, the small old bus, which had open sides with really funky colours and tricked out with shiny chrome, got a flat tyre before even leaving Santa Marta. So the driver fixed this and we carried on. Then just after, someone remembered that they forgot some vital medication, so they had to go back in a taxi to get it while we waited just on the outskirts of town. Eventually, we got going, and headed into the countryside but were brought to another grinding halt as traffic was backed up for half an hour, as road markings were being repainted. Then, unbelievably, we got another flat tyre, which the driver again had to fix; who incidentally was absolutely livid at this point. And then after all that, we had to stop for gas of all things, and we hadn't even reached the national park. All this fucking around leaving us about two hours behind schedule and the prospect of not finishing in time and trekking in the dark.

We passed the military checkpoint; where the paper work and

documents were checked before we spent the next hour driving up the long, winding, bumpy dirt track with steep drops down from the edge, without a barricade in sight up into the mountains and the part that most of us had already heard so much about.

Eventually, we stopped at a pleasant little village to start the trek. Beforehand, our guide Esteban and porters prepared the equipment; we stocked up on supplies and took a quick lunch. From here, we started walking, heading out of town by proceeding along the single asphalt road, that then turned to dirt trail eventually crossing three small rivers, as we started to venture amid the forest before coming to a steep but small track, that was almost sand-like in its consistency; you could feel energy sap as we began to ascend. An hour and some 800m up over later, the terrain flattened off and everyone waited for the others to catch up; the fitter and healthier had pushed ahead which was always inevitable. We were now at around 1200m above sea level so getting altitude sickness wasn't really an issue; but tiring nevertheless, and apparent it was just going to be full-on, hard slog to get to each of our destinations over the days. The trails were small, thin pathways, through shrubbery and flora with views that allowed for some excellent vistas of the rolling hills and cascading valleys, awash with varying shades of green, stretching as far as the eye could see. It was welcome news being slightly overcast, allowing a cool breeze instead of a stifling sun, as we trekked for another few kilometres or so, passing an army checkpoint on the way, before starting the long descent into base camp for the evening smack in the middle of the jungle and mountains.

Luckily, we covered the distance in good time and it was about half an hour before dark on our arrival. This allowed time to quickly head off to the jungle-shrouded local watering hole for some swimming and jumping into the deep water from the high rocks of the accompanying cascade; not only did this help relax tired muscles, but also provided a natural bath, ridding the body of the day's build-up of sticky sweat and grime prior to the onset of night. The camp was more than what I imagined; as we had a designated canopy, with hammocks tied to the posts and mosquito net draped over to sleep in, plus a seating and cookery area where the food was prepared over an open fire. It was wonderful chilling and relaxing in the jungle, with the sounds of the insects and the water from the idling stream that ran just past the camp. There were other canopies for other groups and some local homes there had set up shop to provide trekkers with energy drinks, chocolate, snacks and obviously beer.

The next morning, we were up early and after breakfast set off through the jungle at around eight a.m.; the day previous, we hadn't walked very far in total, it was just hard work up and down, which was again the theme for the day ahead. Tackling another uphill gradient, we crossed the elevated earth, giving the opportunity to gaze upon the scenery, although this time under a blazing sun which made the day's trekking all the more difficult and uncomfortable due to the rapid onset of sweat and the constant replenishment of fluids. But what goes up generally has to come down and we were no different, descending along the dirt tracks again into one of the local villages, occupied by the indigenous folk who still inhabited the rugged precipitous region as they had done for centuries.

It was absolutely fascinating and a privilege to see how these people still lived, almost identical to how they always had; the homes were cylindrical made from earth with a thatched conical roof, a few children dressed in basic covering cloths gazed at our alien intrusion. Our guide proceeded to inform us about the village and that the parents were out working and farming in the pastures close by. We were treated to a locally grown banana from the harvest there; it tasted fantastic, perfectly ripe with rich flavour and being weary from the hours' walking, I was appreciating the natural sugars of my snack even more during our rest period.

Pressing on further, we had the awkward pleasure of having to wade across a relatively small yet thigh-deep stream, gingerly negotiating the invisible rocks and stones underfoot, as not to stumble and face plant in. We had been warned about the prospect of getting wet throughout and on a regular basis; as the trail followed along the more accessible sides of a river system, but this was a welcome break, giving a chance to cool off in the crisp refreshing waters, but being in a sodden state did make our way that much more hazardous and slippery around the boulders and rocks at the side of the river. We arrived mid-afternoon at our second night's camp; situated on a cleared plain just up the embankment of the river. Where again, we messed around and got cleaned up in the cooling waters, jumping from the craggy heights into the deeper parts and drifting down in the current, to lie on a sun-heated smooth rock in the centre of the river, surrounded by walls of towering, lush peaks. Second base camp was another covered shelter, but yet this time had actual bunk beds at our disposal. After eating, we whiled away the time playing card games by candlelight, where we adorned faces with black soot tribal markings, issued to anyone who lost a particular game before eventually crashing out around nine p.m. to prepare for our last day push to reach the 'Lost City'.

Before setting off in the morning, the guide gave us a briefing that what we were to embark on was arguably not the most gruelling, but was the more technical and dangerous day so far, to reach our goal. Following along the trail up the right-hand bank of the river, we passed the deep water that we had enjoyed on the afternoon, but it wasn't long before we realised why the briefing. The trail cut away and to continue, we were faced with the prospect of edging along a rock face, with only a jagged, narrow, six-inch ledge as a foot hold, from the 10m fall to the rocky river edge below. 'Steady as you go, one wrong move here and you are in for a really bad fuckin day.'

I'd kind of forgotten about this part, with all the stories about guerrilla activity, but had been warned about it. And very apparent why; with the fall pretty much guaranteed to cause severe injury if not death should the worst happen, especially being stuck up in the mountains with no immediate rescue available. Again, allegedly, this had happened once before to a tourist, who slipped due to being still pissed and stoned from the previous night and had to be taken out on a makeshift stretcher, carried by the guide and some locals who lived there. Under the circumstances, this sounded more than plausible to me. Thankfully, I was feeling compos mentis, concentrating and taking nothing for granted. Hugging the slopped rock face, I slowly edged my way across.

I had sure footing and shuffled my way over the 5m-long, narrow ledge, where it then widened again and I was relieved but only for a brief few moments; to my dismay, the small ledge continued in virtually the same manner, broken into two parts and I had to pretty much do the same again. Once again, with full concentration, I steadily edged my way across. Having nervously negotiated the trickiest part, I was happy as our standard trail continued, and we made our way down to the huge boulders and stones of the river system that cut through the valley which we crossed. Next was the same drill as the two previous days. Up, up and then up a bit more for an hour, which left legs burning from the exerted effort on top of that from the two days prior. Reaching a clearing at the top, we rested at another small village, that had a 'we know what you need very convenient store' and indulged in fluids to replace those lost, that now drenched my clothes as hot humidified processed sweat. Carrying on, we made our way back down the other side to meet up with the river again, where we relaxed on the stones taking a lunch of fresh fruit and sandwiches.

In the afternoon was the final furlong of the trek and wasn't particularly hard work, but we had to watch our step as we were going to get wet for this involved following the river further up into the mountains and due to its course, we had to cross it some eight times. The only available route was the dry rocks and boulders interspersed on either side due to the winding nature of the river. The water came up to waist-height in parts, making feet, shoes and clothing heavy and soaking wet, that dripped water everywhere, making slips not only possible, but an inevitability; especially having to pay particular attention when skipping over large boulders and step stones that again increased the concentration and co-ordination levels during the effort and balance to avoid a painful fall. After an hour or so, we crossed the river for the last time, to the seemingly nowhere of small, sparse opening in the thick trees and vegetation of the steep embankment on the far side.

Sure-footed, wading across and fighting against the current, each one of us scrambled up the muddy bank into the jungle, where unexpectedly we were greeted by steep, narrow, wet, moss-laden steps that were cumbersome and uneven. Easily laid eons ago, this was the unassuming entrance up to the 'Lost City' perched somewhere beyond the thick mass of green surroundings. I don't know what I was expecting – especially as Machu Picchu had the sun gate – maybe an entrance that indicated you had arrived? Here though was just a gap in the trees and probably why it was left undiscovered until 1975 when it was accidentally found by tomb robbers, and testimony to its much-less-trampled state. The steps were tricky to negotiate, but the worst thing was there were about 1200 of them in a seemingly never-ending pursuit to the top. Eventually, we arrived with heaving breath to an opening in the trees; a stone pathway circled a raised grass terrace. We stopped and waited for the others and the guide. Here now was the first terrace and entrance to the *Ciudad Perdida* or 'Lost City'.

With the chance to catch our breath, Dale, Bobby the Irish contingency, token Kiwi Katie and I were joined by the rest. We thought it best to wait for the guide, as this looked like a place where you could easily get 'lost'. Pathways lead from the terrace in different directions, all shrouded by tall trees. The route we took treated us to a further few hundred more steps up as the main stairwell; these were three stones wide with a more forgiving gradient, so made the going somewhat easier to arrive at another open terrace; where it was thought the shaman temple used to stand. As we looked around, there was another elevated terrace above, and that offered a spectacular view of the prolific summits and valleys, increasingly engulfed in cloud and mist from the deteriorating weather.

Peering in towards the hillside, there was a small ravine. Amid the jungle, it was possible to make out a tall hut on stilts. We continued following a path around to get there, this was our base camp for the evening. We were the first group to arrive, so we set up our beds as more were expected. The guide said that we were not going to tour the site till morning, as it was late in the afternoon and now pouring down, but we were more than welcome to have a look around if we wanted. With the shit weather and after a long day, a few others and I decided not to bother; opting for the drier guided version in the morning. Also, after the exertions and being in such a place, our main aim was getting all kinds of super stoned.

People drifted off and eventually came back. Other groups arrived and set up. Soldiers turned up for some human interaction, chit chat and a bite to eat, while we just got baked, admiring the view up in the middle of the mountains – in a pre-Colombian settlement; in the rain; surrounded by the military – that had taken us three days to get to. It was surreally unreal. If I was ever going to get stoned, it was here.

Along the way, we had managed to buy some smoke from the locals to relax, take the edge off the nights and it worked brilliantly. The army were there to protect the site and those trekking from any possibility of paramilitary or guerrilla incursions, with each soldier having to spend six months up there at a time away from friends, family and civilisation. Like the place itself, chance of action seemed remote due to their numbers, so for the vast majority of the time spent there, they were bored out of their minds. When a new group came to see the place, they were excited for the interaction with new faces and the chance to get some cigarettes, chocolate or anything offered really. Subsequently, they didn't seem to enforce any regulations about smoking weed, as we asked our guide and he said it was OK but we were still discreet about it.

As night darkened, we spent the evening laughing and joking after dinner, playing cards by candlelight which was fast becoming a really cool thing, being in such a good, friendly group, hanging out in the fresh open air of nature's wilderness. Later, everyone made a hasty retreat to their bed, as there were now over forty staying on the second and third floors of the hut, where mattresses and mosquito nets quickly maxed out the premium floor space.

The hut was vacated early by all the different groups. Grabbing still wet clothing from the washing lines on the grassed area, we headed back over to the main ceremonial terraces where we had come from the day prior, to begin our tour of the site with the guide. The sun was shining early in the morning, as it breached the towering trees above, and we took the opportunity to have collective photos together with the terraces and mountains in the background which looked incredible. Leaving our things with our cooks and porters, we proceeded to navigate around the network of 150 or so terraces, most hidden from eye by the overgrowing vegetation, but all interlinked by stone pathways; including where pottery products were forged, the farming area, living section and the baths. We stepped onto the earthen site where young shaman were selected, given insight about the different rituals involved and told of how stones were cut using the acid from plants. It was truly fascinating learning how the Tayronas lived and hard to imagine the full scale of the place, due to its elevated level lying engulfed within the shroud of trees. It was thought that at the time it would have been a much more open plan, due to the volume of people living there, plus the terraces were just that; flat, round, stone-walled plateaus, most were empty with nothing on them except grass, but some had mock buildings constructed to highlight the type of buildings that may have been expected, but unlike the Incas there were no actual buildings, as time and nature had destroyed these akin to the tomb robbers who had stolen many of the artefacts left over.

Perusing the site for an hour or so, we eventually returned to the large stilted hut to pack our belongings and start our return to the campsite from the second night, negotiating our way steadily down the now treacherously slippery 1200 steps that we had come up. Due to the vast amount of rain overnight, these were even more precarious and a couple of times my feet nearly went from under me; only a quick clasp of vines nearby saved me from a harrowing and painful fall. Now having to trek back from where we came was proving to be a bit of a psychological mind fuck, because we knew what to expect; river crossing, getting wet, up steep hills and then down, not falling or slipping over and how far we had to go which sort of made the journey more difficult, recognising landmarks and how far away they still were, plus what was lying ahead, but slowly and steadily we passed each checkpoint that brought us closer and closer to the notorious narrow cliff face that was oddly a welcome sight, indicating that after coordinating and concentrating hard one last time, camp and rest for the evening would only be a few hundred yards away.

The final day was a big push, as we had to cover the first two days in one. We rose with the sun, leaving the camp and another group on their second night, at seven a.m. The terrain was even harder returning, as conditions had deteriorated more on the dirt tracks with the rainfall. Heading uphill took longer, as footholds couldn't be found and feet would easily slip from under with the force being pushed down. Mud was deep, cut up and sludge-like, that made heading downhill just as perilous, where I found myself on my backside on numerous occasions, getting caked in dirt, before we made it back to the camp site location from the first night. Here, we rested and took lunch to replenish some much-needed energy, as the final part involved once again heading straight uphill, on the less-than-firm terrain. Bobby, Dale, Katie and myself with Cesar the chef and porter were making good time though, crossing the top of the mountain and virtually bounced down the huge winding first hill from the first day, like some out of season lost slalom skiers.

When reaching the bottom, we just followed the trail back. There was a small but deep pool from the large stream en route to the town; passing it on the way up, I thought it would be really nice for a dip. Others had the same idea and we asked if it was safe to go for a swim. Cesar didn't see why not, so left us to it while we jumped in from the rock-side into the cool water, sending the heaps of patrolling fish in their hundreds scattering everywhere. It was just what was needed before the others were to turn up, which they never did. So, we swam around and cleansed ourselves before finishing the rest of the much longer than envisaged journey back to the town, absolutely knackered after some seven hours of walking. But this was probably explained better due to the celebratory joint we toked on, as we trudged back.

We waited at the restaurant where we had eaten before starting. We had the good sense and decency to get the beers in, so were in full relaxed mode as the others arrived and duly joined us. There were congratulations and celebrations all round for a job well done by each and every one of us; it was a fantastic group to work with and everyone got along, which was great as this was not necessarily the case on other similar type of adventures. This made the event much more worthwhile and pleasurable, but that's the luck of the draw. Obviously, there were differences, but egos and selfishness never got in the way here, and everyone just accepted one another and got on with the job in hand and after hard, difficult days' trekking, socialised and had fun together. It was a pleasure to see and be part of. Everyone loved the whole experience; the stunning views, the terrain, the wildlife, sleeping in hammocks, drinking the mountain water, dodging mules and horses on the steep banks, crossing rivers, cutting through jungle, seeing the real-life indigenous villages, never mind visiting the 'Lost City' itself and the fact that you have to trek there to see it and then trek back, in what is regarded as dangerous territory, in a new tourist haven country, many would maybe avoid. Some including myself were even privileged to see a demonstration of how cocaine was manufactured; getting up early one morning, meeting and following a native who showed us to his makeshift factory deep in the jungle, and the step by step petroleum, chemical laden, dangerous disgusting process of deriving the powder that is such a scourge on societies and lives; which was a real eye-opener. Especially when we rubbed a bit of 'here's some I made earlier' on the gums that put a right spring in the step. Yet not once did I feel like anything untoward was going to happen and completely forgot about any of the things told prior. This all just added to the mystique and adventure of it all for me, knowing that not many have done this before, let alone heard of it and as tourism grew in turn would only grow in popularity. This set it apart from the Inca trail; although the goal not as impressive, but everything else encompassed possibly made this the best trekking adventure I had been on so far.

A good time was had by all and our guide and porters were all fantastic, whom we got on well with and learnt so much from; showing once again how hard they actually work for our pleasure and relatively small pay. So much so that then we were sitting around having beers, another tour group turned up from the same company and were short of a porter. Cesar just picked up the equipment and headed off to do the five days again. I could not believe it. We were all exhausted and he just set off straightaway. It really brought home how hard people have to work in these parts of the world, to make ends meet and provide for families, true dedication making somewhat of a mockery out of a double-shift back home, with no double pay or the health and safety executive to protect people by laying the law down. Once more, although I was elated with my own and the group's achievement, I left feeling humbled.

Everyone was in good spirits as we headed back down the dirt road track, even though we were getting bounced around all over the place. We arrived back in Santa Marta and everyone went their own way; I myself back to Taganga to check back in to the hostel where I had left my large bag in storage and to just chill and have an early night.

I woke in the dorm the next morning and went into the bathroom. Looking in the mirror, I couldn't believe what I saw; I looked different. All over my torso and arms, there were big, red swollen dots and blotches. The mosquitoes in the night had a real feast; counting the ones I could see had about thirty-seven bites in total. I had come back from the *Ciudad Perdida* with about five and overnight I was the main course. My particular favourites were the six that formed a row from my forehead over to the back of my head. I now looked like a fucking Klingon; marvellous, 'beam me up Scotty'. I wouldn't care but I used the mosquito net provided, yet failed to notice that it had two large holes in it and being so tired never applied any repellent. Adding insult to injury, the greedy little bastards were still in there; dabbing their mouths with napkins and loosening their belt buckles. I hadn't really been bitten an awful lot but seemed to have a regular one or two with the application of repellents; this though was ridiculous. Unperturbed, I decided to show off my new look around town, as I headed up past the peninsula to chill out on the beach at Playa Grande for the day, where I lapped up the sun. Unfortunately, I lapped a little too much and that evening had turned myself a hellish shade of red. I now looked like a sunburnt Klingon. 'Piss off, Scotty, I'm not in the mood.'

It was quite funny, yet disturbing for anyone who I interacted with. Fortunately though, on my travels I'd had these things happen to me and had grown accustomed to dealing with them, although not so severe or at the same time. The next day, I had now changed in colour, as the fire had gone from my skin and was a nice shade of brown, plus the swellings particularly on my head had gone down; this was due to a bit of mental training I'd learnt by resisting the urge to scratch or even touch mosquito bites, so they were less likely to itch bad, therefore not get inflamed and last longer. Granted, this was tantamount to resisting the urge to breathe. But I did find that it seemed to work and they would disappear quickly; especially not having a mad woman with a stun gun at my disposal, like in Thailand.

The time though had now come to depart; with the completion of the 'Lost City' being the main thing that I wanted to do in Taganga. I loved it here; small, beautiful and relaxed, my kind of place. Although unfortunately, I never got to go to the Tayrona National Park along the coast which I had heard was postcard picturesque, lounging on hammocks over white powdery sands and vivid blue waters. But never mind, it was impossible to do everything and I could let that go, feeling that the other things I had done were more worthwhile. But not being a fan of the big cities after what I'd been reading, I was strangely excited about my next destination south-west along the coast at Cartagena.

After a short bus journey; whereby I continued practicing my Español by chatting with a lovely Colombian girl, who unfortunately got off halfway in Barranquilla, I arrived in the famously beautiful city of Cartagena. Booking into the hostel, I met up with Dave and Katie from the *Ciudad Perdida*. I'd arranged to meet them here; where we chilled and had a few beers in the courtyard of the newly opened, still with wet paint, pretty colonial hostel. Unfortunately, this was a fleeting catch up as they were to depart soon, yet the next day we headed out together, visiting the site of a Volcán de Lodo El Totumo just up the coastline out of town. This is actually a volcano; differing from that of a regular volcano in the sense that it was only about 25ft high, and you can actually climb into it and rather than be seared by red hot lava, it is possible to bathe in the therapeutic warm mud that bubbles all around the body and nether regions due to the gases from underneath and within. An opportunity not to be missed and after stripping off, negotiating the perilously slippery wooden stairs to the top, we plopped in.

The mud was dark grey with a thick, slightly gritty texture and felt really good on the skin as it exfoliated with every move. So dense you could just suspend yourself upright and float at neck level; it was quite a surreal experience and what it must be like to be stuck in quick sand yet more relaxing, aided by the people working in the mud who offered rubdown massages where the benefits of the fifty-one different minerals could be felt. It was really funny also watching the people getting in and covered from head to toe in the warm sludge, with the occasional giggle from someone surprised by a big bubble, tickling them in all the right places on the way to the surface to expel as sulphurous smelly gas; only bettered when people getting out of the crater would lose their underwear from the weight of the mud lodged in their pants, looking like they had shit themselves; very much to the amusement of those still wallowing.

As we got out, we were all coated from head to toe, again with mud where mud really shouldn't be. But it felt great, despite knowing that I would be still finding it for weeks to come, and I don't just mean in the crevices of my shorts. We washed off in the nearby lagoon, left clouded by the countless others doing the same before us. A brilliant experience and something that you don't get to do every day. After a stroll along the beach, we took lunch at a nearby small fishing village where unsurprisingly fish was on the menu. Not really a big piscatorial-eater back home, here I'd grown to like it, having it served to me on so many occasions, being the cheapest most readily available source of meat for protein and especially as there was rarely any other option available. That evening, we chilled out and ate together over a few beers as Katie was leaving in the morning and Dave later in the day. Quite the relaxed affair, surrounded by gorgeous buildings in the beautiful Centro Historico of Cartagena after the rigours and exertions of the last few days; despite the incredibly loud, wandering musical entertainment of the mariachis in all the garb as they serenaded in-between the dining revellers; who afterwards, I suspect, were ever so slightly deaf.

Unfinished Business

I was woken the next day with two police officers inside the dorm room. Not exactly what I was used to as my cheap $1 alarm clock usually sufficed. After the initial shock of having two uniformed cops mooching around, I realised everyone else was up with them and had a good idea what it was about. The day prior, Dave whom I was sharing a dorm with had been out and changed some money into dollars to pay the captain of a boat that he was due to sail on to get to Central America. Later that evening, before we went out, he had checked his wallet and it was short a few hundred dollars, which I'd found out about as Katie and I had to wait for him while he went to check in the room. When he couldn't find the money, this started a wave of numerous theories as to where it could have gone.

That morning, he had got up early, reported it to the police for insurance purposes and they decided to investigate; first point of call being the dorm where he was staying and wanting to check everyone's belongings. My conscience clear, I didn't have a problem with this and was OK with them to doing so. Also, I had an alibi; being with Dave the day prior and when he went into town, I spent the afternoon with Katie and we didn't even know he had returned with any money, never mind where it was. Plus, I would never steal from anyone let alone a friend, reasoning these actions the lowest of the low and could only deal a severe blow to my mental karma status, let alone the perils of what may happen if you got caught, and I had no need either as I was still good for cash. Unfortunately, the three others in the room were feeling like they were having the finger pointed at them; which didn't help matters with the fact that the four were all due to set sail together that day.

It also immerged that one of them was apparently in the room when the money went missing (I didn't know these guys) which only enhanced suspicions, as the police only really checked that particular person's bags which escalated the paranoia. More unfortunate being a dorm, the door to our room was never locked properly as people came and went throughout the day; so, it could be argued that anyone could have gone in and took it as there were a lot of people working in and around the rooms, due to the hostel not yet being fully completed. This in turn put the hostel staff on edge, thinking there could be a problem with internal stealing and really didn't want bad press for a business at such a fledgling stage of just opening.

Sadly, the loser in all this was Dave; I had known him from San Gil and we had gotten up to cool things together in Taganga, and shared my camera at the 'Lost City'. He was a top bloke and we got on well and although I didn't know him as a long-standing friend, the way he spoke, his actions and mannerisms did nothing to raise any red flags of mistrust. He was only trying to do the right thing to recoup the money lost, but inadvertently had caused a whirlwind of suspicion amongst staff and people he was to travel with; saying himself that all he wanted was a police report so he could claim money back – which, I believed.

I didn't want to believe that anyone in the room had stolen it either. There is an unwritten rule among the travelling fraternity that you don't touch or take anything belonging to anyone else; without their consent. You are all alike, kindred spirits if you will, there to support and help each other wherever possible, therefore you don't do anything that would purposefully jeopardise this. It was something that I really believed in. On occasions, others had taken my things, they were only small but it was annoying nevertheless; but also, I knew what I was like and was equally as likely to have lost or left these things somewhere. My theories were that someone else had been in the room, but everyone else's things were fine and seemingly untouched, like the rest of his stuff or as I pointed out to Dave, he could possibly have been grifted by the person who he changed the money with, via a slight of hand showing him certain notes but when handing them over swapping them for others of less value, because apparently he said himself only the larger notes were missing and was common knowledge that there were many unscrupulous people working in the money exchange business in South America. But he insisted that he had checked it.

Unfortunately, who knew and what was done was done but hopefully he could now claim the money back. That was a 'fun' start to the day and sadly, I had to say goodbye to Dave under less than excellent circumstances, but I knew that he would be OK as he came across as a genuine person who optimised a traveller's ethos and way of thinking with a friendly Aussie nature. Wishing him well and safe travels, I hoped our paths would cross again sometime when travelling in the future.

I spent the rest of my time in Colombia's biggest port Cartagena, not really doing an awful lot, except wandering around the incredibly picturesque, historical centre encased by a huge wall built hundreds of years ago to protect the port from invasion; notably from the England's Sir Francis Drake back in the sixteenth century. The architecture was really vibrant with colour, compared to many that I had seen of the usual white but still garnished with lots of overhanging balconies looking onto the narrow streets, plazas, historical statues, churches and museums. I ventured into the Palacio de la Inquisición; a museum dedicated to the display of brutal instruments of torture, used during the Spanish inquisition to flush out and find heretics and witches. Grisly examples of the gallows, the rack and an array of weapons were all here, each with a gruesome description of their use. I had to admire the less than scientific list of questions used to by inquisitors to determine whether a person was a witch or not, that gave me the impression if you were being asked these questions, there was a pretty good chance you would be getting some first-hand experience of the sharp end of these instruments regardless of your answer. On a less macabre note, the museum also had pottery artefacts from pre-Colombian times and detailed portrait artworks of colonial generals and their battleships; some of whom probably had first-hand use of some of the aforementioned weapons.

As I never got to visit the Tayrona National Park and sample the fine, secluded beaches, while in Cartagena I took the opportunity to visit Playa Blanca National Park, on la Isla de Barú hoping to spend the night there relaxing in a hammock by the water. The beach was strewn with wooden cabins, beautiful soft white sand and lagoon blue sea where I wasted the day just relaxing and watching the world go by. Unfortunately, I was told by the tour company that I could use my ticket to return the next day, but while there I found out that I would have to pay again for the return. It kind of ruined my plans as without an ATM in sight, I didn't have enough money, which was annoying and put the spoilers on an otherwise lovely relaxing time and I had to return the same day. When I arrived back at the port, I told the rep about my displeasure, having felt that I'd been miss-sold a trip; who in turn as a gesture of goodwill and means of compensation, offered me the chance to go back the next day for the same price; A deal which, oddly enough, I decided to decline.

On the island, I spent much time pondering about where next? Central America was an idea; intrigued by the five-day sailing adventure that Dave was embarking upon, but the boat was expensive and was virtually impossible to get to Panama overland, plus I now had only about three months maximum to get to Rio and would then involve getting a flight back to South America. It was a possibility; although I was still good for money, I didn't want to waste it on expensive travel. Also, I was quite enjoying the bus journeys as they were easy, cheap and allowed the chance to see some of the most amazing sights on earth. Thinking about all this pretty much made my mind for me. Stay in South America, get the bus and head south. I would be glad I did.

A strange notion came over me on the bus as I was wondering about what could have been, if I had headed back to the USA as originally planned and then headed into Mexico, to practise my Spanish. All over the news, there were stories about the outbreak of swine flu in Mexico. I realised that had my fortunes been different, I may have been there when this was happening and thought that I was quite lucky being here now. I didn't know what the chance of catching the virus were or how I would have been affected, but envisaged that it would have caused me any amounts of hassle at the very least when trying to travel on from there. That left me thinking more about how some things were just not meant to be, as I wasn't going into Central America at all but I wasn't that bothered, it would have to be another journey to add to the travel list.

Another thing I realised was that I was starting to get tired. I know that sounds odd and a bit of a piss-take but the more I travelled, the more hectic things became; and in South America more so. Finding myself having to take more time to relax and recoup for a few days; from the bus journeys, the treks, going here, doing this, seeing that, the voluntary work and, of course, the odd party here and there. Everything just seemed relentless, with a new opportunity at every turn that I wanted to get immersed in, to embrace as much as I could and the shorter time became the more, I found myself wanting to make the most of it. Thing is though, I was loving it; every minute – good and bad. The challenge still was as exciting as nine months ago; especially not knowing what was round the corner or what would happen next and overall I would not have swapped places for what I was doing with anyone in the world, whoever they were. And I realised there and then that to feel like that was a true gift; a feeling which cannot easily be bought and was possibly the greatest feeling in the world.

After my overnight musings, I arrived early morning in Medellín.

Finding my hostel, it was quickly established that this was quite the party city with every night seeming to offer a tear up in some way, shape or form. Although I did spend the first evening out and about with some from the hostel in a getting to know you, let's have a look about drinking reconnaissance mission. I really was feeling quite uninspired and as good as it was, I couldn't be arsed going out all the time, getting hammered, rising at three in the afternoon hung over just to do it all again. But everyone in the hostel was a friendly sort, good laugh and usually either completely wrecked from the night or day before, which created a sort of community spirit. The hostel was ideal with bar, pool table, games yard, TV and DVD room, which offered plenty of opportunities to hang out with everyone. So, I took the opportunity to recharge, smoke some weed, have a little time out and relax, not worrying about anything that I wanted to do.

To be honest, this was just a pit stop as there wasn't much that I wanted to do in Medellín; a large sprawling city and home to thousands including that of former world's most wanted man Pablo Escobar. I didn't want to visit the notorious drug baron's grave, feeling I had no need to pay any respects or revel in any sort of notoriety, as I wouldn't class him as a hero figure, having a few years back read the book *Killing Pablo*, even though around the city, many revered him as a sort of modern-day Robin Hood providing for the poor, despite this being via a massive criminal underworld that involved a lot of pain and misery in every aspect; so for me, it would have been just a case of been there, seen that and some sort of crass photo opportunity. But I did visit the Museo de Antioquia whilst venturing into the city centre which offered the chance to see another of Medellín's famous sons; the artist Fernando Botero – where even outside the plaza was graced with two dozen or so obscure yet brilliant sculptures of his work, giving a precursor for the pieces inside which were just as fascinating and interesting. I wandered around in silent admiration, especially where I was also lucky enough to see more works by Picasso and sculptures by Rodin offering an unexpected treat much like the other modern, colonial and pre-Hispanic artworks and the gold artefacts exhibited there.

Some five days later, I was recharged and ready to go as I could feel myself getting itchy feet, wanting to experience a new place, new things, new people and get out of the comfortable little rut that I had carved for myself, which was mainly sleeping, eating, drinking, getting stoned and watching movies. So, I arrived in Cali – Colombia's third largest city – As

I made my way south and back into Ecuador. Again, I didn't want to spend much time here, wanting to keep moving, but still intended to at least have a look around. The hostel was more like someone's house, but it was cool enough and the people who owned it were really welcoming. Getting there early in the morning ensured that nowhere was open to get breakfast, so I just chilled. Other backpackers turned up; Robbie, Wesley and Johnny which was good as it had struck me that the place was quite quiet. They all seemed friendly and chatty. So, it was easy to get along with them. Robbie was older than me and from the UK, Johnny younger also from the UK and Wesley slightly younger still, from Canada. As seemed to be the unwritten law now; first night, new place, out we went, hammered we got. Starting off in the bars and pubs at the bottom of the street, where we met up with some girls whom Robbie knew from travelling before jumping in taxis to the local Salsateca; a salsa nightclub where we received a few strange looks from the regulars there as the gringos had turned up – the only gringos. There wasn't any problems and were given a table where we caned some bottles of vodka and sambuca between us, beefing up the confidence to knock out some salsa shapes on the dance floor whilst trying not to knock the person next to us, as they openly shared a shovel full of Colombia's most potent powder right there in the club.

The next day, everyone was worse for wear and got up really late in the afternoon and could not be arsed to do anything. So, all singing from the same page, we were happy to relax and watch movies. The day after and suitably recovered, Robbie, two of the girls Vanessa and Patty who had been out with us and I decided to visit the zoo. Obviously, I had an interest in animals but was slightly dubious of what to expect with regards to how they are being kept. I had read that it was Colombia's best zoo but wanted to see for myself before passing judgement. In Beijing reports had stated that habitats there were quite horrific, so I gave it a miss and the less-than-savoury conditions at the end of the Thai Experience added to my dubiousness. I wasn't sure on whether zoos were ethically or morally correct, but understood if their purpose for safe housing and protection of certain species but again would much preferred to see animals in their natural habitat, in a refuge or somewhere they were not necessarily subject to being caged up, with no other purpose real purpose than human entertainment, providing some information and making money.

Wandering around, I saw there were flamingos in an open lagoon and some condors in a big aviary. I'd now seen a condor but in a very underwhelming and crap way, where thought it inappropriate for such large birds to be cooped up as such not giving them the opportunity to stretch their wings and fly. Other parts were much better as crocodiles, leopards and tigers also had enclosures with plenty of room to wander around and sizable pools to play in, away from the 35°C heat which the brown bear took advantage of being constantly submerged. There were capuchin monkeys like I had worked with earlier, plus a separate aquarium harbouring varying species of fish. It was a large zoo, with plenty of animals to see and a good educational tool for finding out about them. Although we did have fun together taking photos and admiring the various species I thought it unnecessary to rant and complain too much about what I perceived as some less-than-favourable habitats and used the experience to educate and increase my awareness about these things. I left feeling that some of the enclosures were maybe too small for larger animals and smaller creatures in larger enclosures; it was good to see with my own eyes but felt it could have been better, which from my point of view would always be a contentious issue when concerning animals in captivity and whether they should be there at all.

Robbie and Wesley were intent on leaving for Ecuador that evening and I wanted to move on also. So, we took another night bus down to Ipiales; the Colombian border town with Ecuador. I couldn't really sleep on the night bus. But neither could anyone else as we were stopped by the military and everyone was dragged off to be searched. Stood on the roadside in the middle of nowhere, we were questioned by the officers with fully loaded machine guns about; who we were, where we had been and where we were going. Our bags were searched and we had to put our hands on the hood of the bus to be patted down. Fortunately, there were no problems and under the circumstances there was no way I was going to cause one, before eventually they allowed us to carry on. I had heard that the military were more prevalent on the routes towards the borders as they would stop anyone or anything, with the intention of apprehending paramilitaries, guerrillas, those trying to smuggle drugs or whatever. So, it was somewhat expected but intense nevertheless.

Early morning, the border at Ipiales didn't open for a couple of hours. With not much to do, we decided to visit a church on the outskirts of the town. The Basilica of Our Lady of Las Lajas was no ordinary church as it was famous throughout South America, having been built around the image of the Virgin Mary on a cliff-face and attracted visitors from all over the continent. Needless to say, as we approached it was very easy to spot; white, gothic-style in appearance and built onto the side of a gorge with a large arched bridge spanning the chasm. It looked beautiful and impressive in its unique state and with no real reason other than the discovery of a profound religious iconic image, would anyone use this location to build anything; let alone a church.

Stopping at the nearby small town, we made our way on foot down the path into the gorge, passing thousands of plaques on the way which people had cemented into the walls that gave blessings, thanks and prayers, each indicating who and when they visited. The church itself looked somewhat smaller than when looked down on, yet still as impressive with its fabulous ornate decorations. We took the opportunity to go inside and witness the rock with the image on. Embedded at the altar, there was a shrine that surrounded part of the cliff wall; yet peering inside, I couldn't make out the effigy or even where it was. But I also didn't want to start asking others as to what I was looking at either; people were inside giving prayers and I didn't fancy upsetting, offending or causing a commotion by messing with people's beliefs due to my un-keen eye. So, I left none the wiser to exactly what I had witnessed. We looked around outside and the stone arched bridge was wide and stretched to the other side of the deep chasm, where the waters of the river rushed by some 200ft below. On the other side, there were more plaques, plus offerings that people had left on the statues and winding trails down to picnic areas deep within the gorge. It was yet another beautiful but bizarre church due to the seemingly implausible site, where we all agreed it was definitely worth the look around, giving the chance for all of us to see something which was quite rare and unique; even in my case if that didn't involve fathoming the Virgin Mary's actual image.

Back at Ipiales we prepared to cross the border. Getting our passports stamped and changing the last few pesos into dollars, I was quite excited. Having been in South America now for nearly three-and-a-half months, this was the first time that I crossed a border overland, the last time being Malaysia into Singapore. Putting our bags on our backs, we trudged across the bridge over a ravine that separated both countries passing under the large 'Welcome to Ecuador' sign.

Completing the passport and immigration formalities that now included declaration about swine flu symptoms, we jumped in one of the regular, yet crammed *colectivo* buses to ferry us to the nearest main town of Tulcán, where we then jumped on another bus to head south down to Quito. I thought that the transition from country to country had gone rather smoothly. I need not have worried though as it wasn't long after leaving the town that the police stopped the bus and asked us to get off, to search our bags that also included the large bags in the hold. As there were only about half a dozen people on the bus and obvious with stamped passports we had come from Colombia, it was definitely a case of 'search the gringos' – which was fine and kind of understandable with the checks that happened over the border; except here, the dog was going absolutely berserk, barking like he knew something and was grassing on everyone. Fearfully, I hoped he couldn't smell anything. Not that I suspected he did as I was damn certain I wasn't going to be stupid enough to bring any illegal substances over the border, but I couldn't necessarily vouch for anyone else. Anyway, about thirty seconds and one very un-thorough search later, we were on our way.

Leaving, I was really pleased that I'd took everything that I had ever heard, read or seen about Colombia with a huge pinch of salt and decided to come, see and experience this beautiful country. Don't get me wrong, I still had some reservations, but seeing things for myself now I wasn't disappointed. I'd had a fabulous time and absolutely loved it, mixing action and adventure with culture and relaxation. It offered everything that I was looking for my own personal gains from travel. It was a really vibrant and colourful place and not what I was expecting at all. But that's what happens if you believe all that is reported. The other main factor for me was the people that I had met, nearly all travelling around were having an amazing time and loving the place too, with a travel industry still somewhat in its infancy. It couldn't have been a coincidence and it wasn't. This was also largely due to the Colombian people who were some of the most friendly and happy people I'd had the pleasure to meet. With the country's former problems, it would have had been understandable if they were slightly apprehensive or not very welcoming, but it was exactly the opposite, and they seemed to not take things too seriously and had a true love for life, which was a real endearing quality and plus some of the women were the most beautiful that I had ever seen. It was obvious that there were still problems within the infrastructure of the place regarding security from terrorist activity, but my personal opinion is that this is still ongoing and could still take many years to sort out, but massive steps had been taken already to eradicate this and had clearly come along way with making Colombia much safer so it's beautiful sights, scenery, architecture, climate, culture and people could be visited and appreciated by the outside world and given the recognition it deserves, and this had to be commended. I for one would love to return sometime, a true pleasure and highlight. That left me pleased that despite going against what I thought or thought I knew, I had opened my mind, took a chance and it paid dividends.

Robbie and Wesley's plan was head to Quito for a couple of days and then head straight over to the coast for some beach and sun. That sounded like a brilliant plan to me. I could go to Quito with them, show them around the best bits so as not to waste too much time, feeling like I was practically a native. There was method in my kind madness; as all the while I could take photos that I had lost in the post from the first time around. Excellent. Then it dawned on me; provided the weather was OK, I could climb Pichincha – the volcano that I somehow in the space of four weeks never had the chance to climb and most importantly as she lived close by, I could visit Marcia, not having the opportunity to say goodbye to her. That would be amazing. I was really excited; like Hannibal from *The A-Team*, 'I love it when a plan comes together'. Once again, though, my plans were going to change very soon and not how I would have imagined.

The six-hour- or-so bus journey from Tulcán to Quito was uncomfortable. I was tired through not sleeping much; this really wasn't an option due to the loud audio from the movie and Spanish CD on after. Again, the only consolation being the vast valleys and mountainous scenery that I couldn't get enough of, and working out my plans which pretty much involved getting though Ecuador, Peru and heading into Bolivia; brilliant. Job done. The first hour-and-a-half we spent in Quito involved being stuck in a traffic jam, before eventually getting to the bus terminal. Robbie picked out a hostel that he heard was really nice. I had thought about trying to stay at Marcia's place, but there was no guarantee that I could get in there, not knowing how many students she would have staying. So, with no complaints, we headed straight to the hostel and gate crashed the pre-prepared curry dinner that was on offer, that we duly washed down with a few beers on the rooftop bar, before passing out absolutely knackered having been on the road for the best part of twenty-four hours.

Our plans were sorted for the next day. First to the close by Basilica; Wesley and myself crossed the thin planks through the loft in the roof to scale the outside wobbly loose ladder to get to the top of the spire; Robbie declined with a polite 'fuck that'. '*Click*' photos. Second; to the Centro Historico and the Compania de Jesus gold church – '*Click*' photos. Third; San Fransisco Square – '*Click*' photos. Fourth; beautiful La Ronda – '*Click*' photos. Five; take the trolley to the Mariscal Sucre for a look around, food and beer before finally, the bus stop to head up to the Mitad del Mundo or rather the real one for some more arsing around on the equator action; where I managed to balance the egg on the nail again getting myself another certificate. '*Click*' photos.

We had a brilliant day and a good laugh, managing to see so much. Granted, I had seen it before and was playing tour guide, but I didn't care; I was getting to take the shots of some of the things that had been lost. But it made life for Robbie and Wesley loads easier and they said thanks which was nice and appreciative of them, before we returned back to the hostel just after sun down to get involved in a game of drink the beer.

Drink the beer got very interesting as soon as I walked onto the rooftop bar. Not paying any attention, from behind me in a thick northern accent, I heard, "Hey. 'Ow ya doin'?" Turning around, I was startled to see Don from the rescue centre in front of me. Totally unexpected; but I was really chuffed to see him. Starting to grill him as to why he was here of all places, it turned out that he had come up to Quito from Puyo for a few days on a recruitment drive for volunteers to work, as they had no one at that present time. He was staying at his girlfriends' place who lived in Quito. But he was in this particular hostel spreading the good word, as he knew the people who owned it from staying there previously. Fair enough; well, there was only one thing for it; one swift phone call to his missus later it was, beer, beer, beer.

After a few drinks, Don asked the inevitable question; whether I fancied going back to work there again, as I had said previous, I'd like to return at some point. I wanted to, but had set my heart on working at another similar place that I had heard about in Bolivia; which was why I was heading there to get experience of another site and how they operated. Being a reasonable bloke, Don appreciated this. Having said that, I really got on well with Don and I admired the fact that he was passionate about the job he loved, which to me was also really worthwhile. I loved being at the rescue centre and the work being done there, but I did ask if I could have a slight concession in the price hoping that he knew I would be good for the work and wouldn't need any training, as now money could start to become an issue, not to mention the time as this could take up another week or so. He said that he would have to ask the owner; but it would be great if I could come back.

I thought about it for about half a nanosecond and said, "Fuck it; yeah, I'll come back again, definitely. Let's celebrate. Oh look, here's some beer." I pretty much decided there and then, sod it. I didn't care about the price, and I didn't care if it took out another week or so out of my 'oh so hectic schedule'. Seeing the fact that I had randomly bumped into Don, in a place where I necessarily wasn't meant to be and he was actively looking to recruit volunteers. I regarded it as one of those twists of fate that was meant to happen, much like ones that already had; like the fact that I wasn't supposed to be going to his rescue centre in the first instance or staying in South America afterwards at all. Plus, more weirdly, it felt like I was somehow being tested, as if I actually wanted to do voluntary work of this type or could I be arsed enough to actually still care, having been there and done that and now was tired, knowing that it would be long hours and hard work. What resonated most was that it wasn't for me but for others, it was in a good cause and this was what I had loved about it, and also had given me so much confidence, self-pride and energy in return without even realising it at the time. The answer was a simple 'Yes, yes, I could be arsed'. Also, I could take more photos similar to those I had lost; another bonus.

There was another clause though in my increasingly boozed up verbal contract; "I'm here for a couple of days, then off to Montañita for a few days with these guys. I'll be with you in about a week?"

"No problem, it's a nice place," he said, really pleased that I decided to return, as was I.

Contracts negotiated; to seal the deal, we had some rum that desperately needed drinking with Robbie and Wesley; also, a girl called Sharon who was from the north-east of England was with us, as she had just finished volunteering with Don and was aiming to get some work in Quito. But for that evening, everyone was free and at a loose end, so decided the best thing to do would be to get drunk.

I got up late the next day. By the time I sorted my things and checked out, it was about eleven a.m. putting my bag in storage, I had a mission;

Volcán Pichincha, but I also had a really bad head. Before a full-blown hangover could kick in, I got some supplies and set-off for the cable car *Teleférico* to get to the top of the mountain where previously I had been with Gina. Despite my induced fragile state, it was now or never to have a crack at climbing this; I felt quite determined, adopting a 'right, let's fucking have it' attitude. Probably because I was still a bit pissed.

Following the track as I had done before; I made my way up towards the pinnacle. Problem was, because it was so big it looked much nearer than it actually was. Each time clearing a brow, I would find a dip in the terrain that would lead to another brow and was around 6km before I actually made it to the right-hand side of where the volcano seemed to start. It was easy to walk on, with long reed grass either side of the trail, just hard work not helped by the blustery conditions of the less-oxygenated thin air, but at least being above the smog of the city, the briskness cleared my headache rather quickly and I started to feel good. The further I scaled, the trickier the path became and I found myself having to negotiate across some steep sloped passes. Turning around now, I had a majestic view of Quito, as I towered above Ecuador's metropolis helped by the fact that the clouds were rolling by really quickly, so I was getting to appreciate it bathed in sunshine, then shade and then sometimes not at all, because I myself at times became engulfed by the cold mist of cloud.

Eventually, I made it to a loose section where underfoot it was soft and gravel-like and I found myself having to scramble approximately 300ft up to the next part, where I had to clamber further up and over large boulders, before eventually reaching the ridge summit some two hours plus later at an altitude of around 4700 metres. I stood and admired the view, getting to briefly see the valley on the other side which looked really far and distant. Views were fleeting more so now due to the increased thickening cloud being much higher up, and it was also much colder and time was quickly becoming a factor before the sun went down and more importantly the *Teleférico* stopped working. After some snap shots, I hastily made my way back.

I was so pleased that I had made the effort, accomplishing what I had set out to do. Especially as it would been very easy not to bother with the way I was feeling in the morning, and it was only because we were supposed to be checking out of the hostel that I got up. I didn't have a clue what Robbie and Wesley had been up to or whether they had checked out either. There was an unexpected bonus before getting the *Teleférico* back down; the clouds were still moving past quickly and from one of the observation points, I saw it in the far-off distance. In all its snow-capped glory, some 55km south was Cotopaxi. I set about taking photos of it at opportunities where the clouds moved and sun gleamed against it; I could have done with a better camera in this instance to actually do it justice, but now this was the only evidence that I had of actually seeing it. There was no chance of climbing it again, if for only one reason being that climbing Pichincha with its purpose worn trails was a complete piece of piss compared to the brutality of climbing that thing.

There was one thing left to do and it would be done. At the bottom of the mountain, I made my way along an all-too-familiar street. I rang the doorbell for the yard; Marcia's daughter who recognised me let me in, but proceeded to say that Marcia was out and not sure when she would return. I was disappointed but not altogether shocked. I was introduced to some other the students who were staying at Marcia's and proceeded to chat to them. Then her daughter returned to tell me that she was on her way home and should be about ten minutes. I was over the moon as she had called Marcia and told her that I had turned up (unexpectedly) to see her.

I knew straightaway when the door went it was Marcia; you could just tell. Singing, whistling, whatever, she came in to the lounge area with a huge grin on her face and it was incredibly warming to see her again. She was exactly the same; looks, speech, quirky little mannerisms. I knew it had only been two-and-a-half months since I had seen her, but it felt a lot longer. We chatted; Marcia giving me the gossip about what had been going on in and around the street, telling me how the family was getting on and some trouble that she had been having with the security guard. It was my own private Spanish soap opera. I loved it though as she spoke so passionately and elaborately about everything. I explained what I had been up to and where I had been; mentioning the fact that I knew Don, because 'what a surprise' he knew Marcia as well. It was great fun and I was so glad that I got to catch up with her, especially as something odd had happened; without realising it, I was having my first full conversation in Spanish. Chatting away to her like it was normal, picking up so much on the way as I had travelled about, yet hadn't realised how much I had improved. I was talking with people in everyday life but this was my first full conversation. Marcia commented on how much better my Spanish now was which made me feel good.

I'd like to think that Marcia was as pleased to see me as I was to see her, I was so glad to have made the effort, as she brought me so many good memories and was a truly genuine, nice person who optimised life and how to live it, despite the ups and downs, and was glad to call her a friend. Unfortunately, I had to say goodbye, but this time I had managed it properly though as I had to leave to catch a bus; again, though, before I left, we exchanged contact details and promised I would visit her again when I would inevitably return to Quito sometime, and we posed as one of her other student guests took my camera to capture a photo of us together.

Although I had spent the most time of my travels in Quito, I really needed these few days just to sort some things out. I was now officially done and things had been put to rest as it were and I could move on without feeling that something was left unfinished. So, I was grateful for the time there and making an effort. Getting back to the hostel, I found Robbie, Wesley and Sharon who was now tagging along with us to Montañita. I had no problem with this; the more the merrier, so in the early evening off we went once more to the bus terminal; where sitting on the bus I was offered the polite assistance of someone wanting to put my bag up on the rack above my head for me. With a glazed look, I said "no", safe in the knowledge that if he got my bag, it would not go onto the rack. It would go straight out the door and off the bus at 100mph with him attached to it. I shouldn't be too sceptical but he wasn't on board when we left. A common scam; on the other hand, if I'd had a couple of beers, knowing me I'd have probably handed it over whilst asking him politely to take my photo. But, not this time, *amigo*.

The sun was roasting without a cloud in the sky when we got to Montañita. A beautiful little town that was easy to negotiate your way around, with buildings made from wood and straw with sand occupying the pedestrian streets from the nearby beach. Eventually, we found a hostel five-minute walk out of town that was quiet and secluded, compared to those in the close proximity of the banging music of the hub, especially on the weekend which it now was. We were glad to get here and sorted as the bus journeys were hard work; stopping at two towns, changing three different buses, over roads at best described in parts as pot-holed dirt tracks that epitomised the fun of travelling and for me was worth it.

I fell in love with Montañita straightaway, it was brilliant. Lovely relaxed ambience, excellent restaurants, bars, clubs, hot weather, gorgeous sandy beaches and nice clean sea water to mess around in, plus endless stalls selling delicious fruit smoothies and cocktails laced to the max with booze. It was the idealistic ocean-side retreat. We just hung around there for a few days or so, not really doing much, with the beach the place to be during the day and getting pissed and high the place to be on a night.

Wesley had left us at this point, citing various reasons of wanting to move on because he didn't like the vibe and accusing everyone of talking about him, which simply wasn't true. Unfortunately, this was after a time where lots of booze and drugs were involved, and I fear they may have taken their toll, scrambling his thought process somewhat. While there, though, Robbie bumped into a young couple who he had also met previously; John and Rebecca were from the UK and fun to be around. So, the five of us just lived the life of Riley eating, drinking, sunbathing, swimming in the sea, partying and taking in a spot of body boarding for good measure in a beautiful little haven on the pacific coast. When after some five days and numerous drinks and joints later, all good things must come to an end and we all had to go our separate ways, where I had to get on the bus again carrying some disappointing news from home.

Hey, Hey We're the Monkeys

It was now official; after eleven years in the top flight of English football, my team had a terrible season, where wins were scarce and succumbed to inevitable relegation. Despite being thousands of miles away, it was disappointing, but as I wasn't in the immediate vicinity of what was happening made the news easier to bear, not having media or gloating rivals shoving it in my face, listening to the endless critique and analysis of how bad the team were and what went wrong. Being away travelling, I seemed to be living a right here right now moment; allowing me to subconsciously become somewhat disengaged with things like football and started to realise the escapist distraction of it all. I concluded, as I had no influence over it, there was nothing I could do about it, so I just took the news on the chin. I liked the game and was still valid entertainment, but could only associate with it as an interest and because it affected those who I cared about more, where being in closer quarters they would be let down to the point of devastation. This was the only thing which put a slight downer on the time in Montañita. But if my team were to get relegated, I figured I may as well have been here, distracted through other more positive means instead of suffering back home.

To get to the refuge, I had to take three different buses as there was no direct route from the coast to Puyo. This involved a three hour bus over to Ecuador's largest city Guayaquil, then eight-and-a-half hour bus to Baños, where I arrived late in the evening so took a room in the guest house next to the bus terminal. It was the nearest and I only needed a room for the night, so I would be ready to move on in the morning.

Due to the twelve hours of travelling and late arrival, I slept through my eight a.m. alarm, eventually surfacing at ten a.m. Quickly, I headed out to cross the ravine where I had done the bridge swing jump and carried on up the road to take some elevated pictures. Unfortunately, these weren't quite as good as the previous ones; not having time to get to the high precipice where I had the fantastic views looking down on the town and also the conditions weren't particularly great, meaning Volcán Tungurahua was obscured by cloud. But beggars can't be choosers and I was happy to continue replenishing my photo portfolio, getting some shots of this lovely place, before taking a late morning bus to Puyo, arriving an hour-and-a-half later. Now knowing where to go and what to do, I took a cab and headed straight to the rescue centre.

It had been almost two-and-a-half months since I had left the animal refuge centre and wondered if things were the same. I knew Don wasn't going to be there as I had been in contact with him; this didn't bother me as he told Miguel about my arrival and said to just get on with things like normal. Arriving, I dumped my bag in the canopied kitchen and dining area and headed into the refuge to find Miguel and familiarise myself with the place again before setting about doing the daily jobs. It was good to see him, and he in turn was happy to see me back at the place, which gave me a warm feeling inside and a nice sense of appreciation. We had a chat in Spanish, now being able to communicate with him much better, which surprised Miguel somewhat as we could interact more in conversation due to my improved linguistic skills. After quickly changing and putting on the rubber boots that I'd left, I set about giving him a hand with the maintenance issues he was dealing with.

There were large woven sacks that I'd passed in the car park which as it turned out were full of sawdust and chippings. So, I set about carrying these to the trails close by the Tarzan swings and tipped each one out and spread the contents about; bag after bag, I was straight back into the fold and quickly started to work up a sweat. Some two hours later, we had laid pathways around the majority of the hill and swing area. The time had flown by, so then we set about preparing the feed for the nocturnal animals and cleaning down those fed from that morning. Taking a little longer than I had in the past, having to re-familiarise myself with the different buckets of fruit and vegetable feed, I headed into the park only to get caught in a torrential downpour. The weather in the jungle was now once again really unpredictable and a far cry from sun-kissed beaches I had gotten used to over the last month or so. Also, the only key that could be found was for the first cabin of two along the trail in the middle of the park. Even being the only volunteer; I still never had the choice of which to stay in, and of course the one I was getting was notorious for having a cockroach infestation. Given the choice, I would have probably chosen the other, but I had stayed in this one on my last stint so now didn't mind having had countless encounters with creepy crawlies throughout my travels. Besides, the cockroaches in the room were going to be the least of my worries.

The next day, I carried on with the usual duties; feeding and cleaning the animals and then helping Miguel. The owner's son Fernando had also now started working at the place. In the time I was away, apparently, he had lost his job and now worked at the centre making improvements and repairs, much in the same way that Miguel did and made me feel really welcome when chatting as we all ate our meals together. During the five o'clock early evening feed, Don returned with another volunteer; a Welsh lad called Paul.

Within what seemed like a split-second of his arrival, we were getting pissed again. It was Friday evening, after all. Heading up the lane to the elderly lady's place to keep her pockets lined, we sat in her yard and sculled the beers that she sold us from a hatch-cum-window, before heading into Puyo to have drinks with some of Don's friends that he was due to meet. Then after feeding and cleaning on Saturday, we went to the water park, chilling in the sun, laughing at the reckless Ecuadorian approach to playing on the slides, where it was a case of send as many down in one go and worry about the carnage when hitting the water at the bottom. More worrying considering it looked like many couldn't swim very well, if at all. Sunday was a full day off and Don being a legend brought breakfast to the cabin; Paul had to temporarily move in with me and the cockroaches, as the key to the other cabin was still lost, but at least there were two beds otherwise he was in the hammock with the squirrel monkeys. Being a beautiful day, we took the bus up to a jungle resort, which catered for visitors with chalets, steam rooms and restaurant within the forest. The owner was another friend of Don's who after much struggling with a leaky old boat, set sail across the river to drop us off on the far side sandy embankment, to spend time chilling and swimming in the river; where I did remember to refrain from having a piss in the water, paranoid about the possibility of candiru fish and wanting to avoid the unfortunate issue of one swimming up my knob end. After whiling away the afternoon in the middle of the jungle, we headed back across via a rusting old cable car that stretched across the river to gorge on a dish of fresh fried fish and rice kindly prepared by the owner, before then taking the incredibly cramped, early Sunday evening bus back.

Paul couldn't believe his luck at how much fun and easy this volunteering lark was; he had been here two-and-a-half days and had only managed to do the Saturday morning feed and spent the rest of the time out and about, seeing the local sights, having fun and getting pissed with the rest of us. But that was going to change really quickly.

It took a while to see but there were subtle changes that had happened in and around the rescue centre that I hadn't initially noticed. Some were easier to spot like the island with the woolly monkeys on, this had been refurbished with new framework, ropes and tyres. But the main difference being that Thomas now had a new friend with him, he was called Junior. Same species but he was much bigger and more dominant; therefore, he more possessive of food and territory. This meant feeding now was definitely a two-person job, helping ensure that they were both distracted and nothing untoward occurred. Extra food had to be prepared for the both of them and now placed in two separate areas on the island, so both had opportunity to feed without one getting riled up and taking the lion share if not all from the other.

There were few more extra inhabitants; these were mainly snakes that again we didn't have to deal with, as Miguel again adopted them as his own pets. What was more apparent was who was missing; there were now no dogs running around the park. Raki and Flaco, the troublesome twosome who followed everyone around eating the spare food were now gone. Homes had been found for them with better surroundings and new owners who wanted to take care of them, which was good to hear. As nice as it was to having them around, it was always a cause for concern that although placid, their disruptive nature was not helpful in and about the centre with the other animals, and they would follow everyone to such an extent that Flaco, the smaller mix breed, was almost killed in front of us previously when he ventured to the main road, pulling his nose out of the way of a speeding truck at the very last second. Someone else was missing, it took me a while to realise, but Frederica the capuchin monkey and rescue centre's little mascot, was now no longer inhabiting the canopied dining area or attaching herself to one of us.

Passing the large capuchin cage, I noticed a small dark ball of fur huddled up high, on one of the platforms under the sheltered area; when it moved, I realised this was Frederica. She had now been successfully integrated with the other larger capuchins. Also, she had noticeably grown and looked happier and healthier than ever. It was initially a worry that she was too small to be with the others, but as she grew the staff would continuously find her on top of the cage as she would inquisitively venture out; so they decided to put her amongst her own kind as she seemed to integrate well. So well, in fact, that Beba carried her around on her back like she was her own. It was really sweet and heart-warming to see her adoptive methods. Although, to do this, she did have to be in the cage, and any instincts of motherhood would swiftly be abandoned at the first chance to make a break for freedom, leaving Frederica to play happily in the cage with the others or on her own.

The more I integrated in and around the centre, there were other noticeable differences; the caiman pen was now completely finished with fully functioning lagoon that I had helped build with Miguel, carting wheelbarrow after wheelbarrow of heavy boulders and gravel to the site over two afternoons. It brought back memories of how hard the work could be and the effort required; problem was, I didn't need this to bring back the memories, as we were going to get some fresh first-hand experience.

Out the back towards the lake, the majority of the land had been excavated by hand. This was where Fernando was predominantly working, forming log pathways for easier passage of visitors and channels creating a flowing river supply of water to the centre. It was also now much less perilous to clean and feed the kinkajous as lockable doors had been placed onto the nesting cupboards where they slept during the day; so from the outside, it was possible to pull some thick twine and tie them shut whilst they were asleep, allowing entry. Safe in the knowledge that they couldn't get out, all pissed off ready to attach themselves to someone's appendages. Regardless, a good preliminary check was still in order to ensure they all were actually in the cupboards and hadn't slept elsewhere outside. This pleased me and was good to see; as I had initially put forward the idea of having some form of actual door and locking system for them, rather than covering the hatches with a broom that precariously held wooden boards in place over the entrance. Now this was much safer and efficient as it could be done by one person as opposed to two, and it felt good that my comments and ideas had been taken on board and developed.

One thing that I never realised until Don mentioned it was that although the feeding was essentially the same, it was aided by new diagrams and instructions on the white board that now logged the cleaning routine, which had also been changed. Everything now got cleaned at the morning feeding time; this was to make it easier to remember the basics of what, where and when due to the constantly changing stream of volunteers passing though.

This in turn made life easier as nearly everything was now done in the morning, with only feed to be taken care of towards late afternoon and meant one less thing to do in the wake of hard day's work.

The new project being started as part of the centre's rejuvenation was to build a new tayra enclosure; the one they were in was adequate, yet still left them wanting slightly for plenty of actual space to run, climb and exercise for such a speedy and agile animal. So this was another step forward. A clearing had already been cut in the forest at the back close by Pancha the wild pig, where we were to construct a 4m high cage, formed by putting huge posts in the ground, to couple up with the trunks of larger trees still left in the clearing.

First, the posts used had to be transferred up to the site, as the materials had been left at the car park entrance. The materials in question were 5m lengths of solid timber, some cylindrical and some square. With no machinery or form of transportation to move these, there was only one rather obvious but daunting option; to be carried manually by hand and sheer hard work because they were not light in weight. In fact, they were heavy as fuck. Even after moving just one with Miguel some 300m up to the forest, it left my right shoulder aching badly from the weight bearing down; yet this was still the easiest and most efficient way to shift them and I found myself breathing heavily and sweating profusely, finding it better not to stop and break the inertia to finally drop the load at the site. With another thirteen to go, I looked at the rest of the task with trepidation. Others were busy doing various other jobs like mending one of the cages, as a rotten frame had broken, causing a gap to appear in the mesh and needed urgent attention. So, it was left to Miguel and I to move the cumbersome wooden beams. We managed to move around eight pieces over the course of around two-and-a-half hours, before deciding that was enough for the day. Fatigue had now set in and I was weary and crippled with aches in the arms, legs, back and most notably in the shoulder; where scratches and bruising had developed due to bearing the brunt of weight and friction from moving an awkward, heavy load, only to be told we could resume moving the rest the next day.

My shoulder was still in pain when we restarted. I wasn't looking forward to the job ahead, but I had bought into this and knew what to expect. It wasn't easy work; it was hard, physical and mental graft that called for extra reserves of effort, so I shut up and got on with what was required.

Fortunately, the others were available on the second day and after numerous bouts of moaning, groaning and complaints about the weight and pain inflicted – that I knew all too well about – we competed moving the heavy logs. In fairness to Miguel, due to his shorter stature, he actually found it harder to move with others helping, so he started carrying one at a time on his own. This might have been South American male macho bravado showing the soft European folk how weak they were, but it also demonstrated how hard he actually worked for the refuge to get jobs done. All the while, nearing the end of the heavy pile with two other and myself carrying one, my shoulder at this point was in absolute tatters.

It was hard work come rain or shine, that happened to be notably less shine. Preparing the site, holes a metre deep were dug out to hold the massive lengths of timber upright, forming the posts for the cage. The old broken shovel could only go down so far, before the rest of the sodden dirt had to be loosened and scooped out by hand, where I found myself lying on the wet forest floor and getting covered head to toe in mud. The posts were then lifted, tipped and wedged into the holes as the new cage frame work started to take shape. The square logs were then hoisted up 4m high, using rickety wooden ladders and nailed to the top of the upstanding posts and trees, connecting them all together and forming where the roof was to sit.

Money (like most places) was an issue here; centres as such, in these countries are unable to receive any government funding or state handouts. So, they rely on the owner's purse strings, charitable donations and contributions from the visitors and volunteers, such as myself paying to work and help out. Therefore, they have to make use of all resources available as a cost necessity. Pancha the wild pig had a large enclosure that for some reason was divided into two halves within the wooded part of the refuge. She was moved to the top half and the metal mesh surrounding the bottom half covered around 40m; this was ripped out, rolled up and then taken to the top site to be placed around the newly constructed framework. Again, at the time this sounded easier than what it was; with sharp spikes, the huge metal roll grew heavier, cumbersome and more awkward to move, as we deconstructed the fence. To avoid cuts, we slogged carefully to shift and work it into place, rolling it around to create the new enclosure. The project work done for that week was hard and gruelling, but again left me with warm self-gratification concerning my efforts and not having shirked any responsibilities and given my all – something that I was finding others weren't as willing to do; especially when the harsh reality of not being able to lie back in a hammock or play with cute animals all the time kicked in. I'd already learnt a while back that being in these places unfortunately wasn't all about that, as other things less pleasant also need doing as they were equally as important for the benefit of the furry inhabitants.

If the hard slog wasn't enough, the elements made these activities less enticing. During the week, the rain returned with a vengeance and was something which I hadn't been subject to for a while. Not only being constantly wet, the terrain became much more slippery and treacherous. Also because of the sheer volume coming from the mountains, the water supply to the local town of Las Americas had been shut off due to contamination and this was also the provider for the refuge; so the water was off here as well. Providing for the animals wasn't a problem due to the network of water channels now teeming throughout the park and we cooked using natural mineral water bought in to drink, but showering wasn't possible, so we found ourselves having to go to the nearby river again to get scrubbed clean after the rigors of work, but having really muddy embankments to negotiate would still leave hands and feet dirty and a sense of frustration at not being able to get clean properly, especially as there was still no water after four days.

Obviously, all of this would be too easy without the inevitable; the animals getting out, making a break for freedom or just making a nuisance out of themselves in general. It wasn't long before Beba was out and about once more. As much as she loved looking after Frederica, this simply wasn't a substitute for the chance to escape and the exciting freedom of causing havoc around the place, and usually took advantage of having new volunteers not lock up the gate tightly; as I did previously. This would cause another team effort to have her captured again. One of the tayras escaped during the clean again and I just managed to catch the aftermath of Don grabbing it, as it was just about to scurry up a tree and be out of reach and gone. Seemingly every day, there was a break for it and people were swiftly finding out that every care and attention had to be taken when dealing with these creatures to ensure their and the other animals' safety.

The cabins had their own cause for concern; during the day, the door would be padlocked to stop people wandering past from entering where we slept, keeping our belongings safe. Although it was unlikely that someone would attempt to break in, let alone have the opportunity to do so. One afternoon, I went back into the cabin to find that the place had been trashed. On first sight, it seemed that we had been burgled, with clothes strewn everywhere, and both mine and Paul's bags ransacked. I was annoyed that someone had done this, yet baffled. The door was still locked with no way a person could enter without key or causing damage. *Eh? What the fuck's going on?* My thoughts. Initially, perplexed as to what happened. It wasn't anything to do with me; so, *Has Paul lost something and been through the things?* Was my next assumption. Paul arrived and I showed him the mess; he knew nothing about it and was as stunned as I was.

With a little detective work, all became apparent. Nothing of value was missing, the tiny rip in the tough mesh over the windows to keep mosquitoes out was now larger and food debris was scattered all over the floor and beds. The plot thickened. There was no way a human did this unless they were a very small human, lightweight, with excellent climbing capabilities and intent on finding one thing in particular; food. Small muddy little footprints all over the beds and mosquito net towards the ripped mesh all but confirming one thing; the mischievous squirrel monkeys – who roamed free, played happily in the hammock outside and used the roof as a launch pad to nearby trees, creating the patter of tiny feet scrambling across the corrugated metal that regularly woke those inside – had been in. The guilt suddenly fell squarely at their feet; their muddy little feet, that is.

Paul and I set about tidying the room, suring up the mesh and removing the remnants of crisps scattered around; which caused another delay in the day's work activities. But also, I had to see Don as it was quite urgent.

Finding him, I said, "Don, it looks like the squirrel monkeys have been in our cabin and have trashed the place."

"Really?" he asked, bemused. I proceeded to explain what had happened and what had been found and he started laughing, adding, "The little fuckers, sorry about that."

I would have laughed myself, but carried on, "The thing is, though, they have been through my medicines as well, opening the foil packs, there are pills on the floor."

"Shit, what were they? Are there any missing?" was his now concerned retort.

"Malaria, headache and diarrhoea tablets; I can't tell exactly what's missing though because I don't know how many I've used, but there are only a few on the floor and it looks like maybe one or two have been chewed." I continued.

"Which ones?" he enquired. "There's definitely half an Imodium missing."

"OK, we'll have to keep an eye on them, but chances are they spat it out, cos they'd have realised it wasn't food and tastes like shit," he said.

"I'm just relieved that there wasn't a major cause for concern," I said hopefully.

"We'll have to be a bit more careful in future, though," he said and I happily agreed.

He continued, "I wouldn't care, but the other week one stole my bottle of aftershave and my girlfriend's razor from the house." I burst out laughing.

"So, we're looking for a monkey getting ready for a night out, that can't shit? Yeah?"

He laughed. "Yeah, seems that way."

Fortunately, over the next few days, there wasn't any repercussion through the behaviour of the animals and they carried on as normal with no ill effects, so it was a relief. Despite the fact that the squirrel monkeys had also discovered the kitchen area, so were now prone to visiting there while people weren't around, and had started rummaging through cupboards in the hope of finding food. Thing is, though, as we knew, monkeys aren't very good at tidying up after themselves, so regularly now we started to find some form of mess in the kitchen and dining area. We in turn ended up tidying after them, and to prevent this, we therefore, had to be good at tidying up after ourselves and leave nothing lying about.

The worst was yet to come when inspecting the kinkajous one night; it was found that five of the six had gotten out. Those responsible for feeding them had insisted that the door was shut and tied up properly. I personally hadn't inspected if this was correct or not, as it was a possibility that they could have chewed or dug their way out. But now five of the six – beautiful, cuddly, but potentially dangerous little beasties – were at large. One was captured almost immediately, as Miguel with much trepidation coerced one of the smaller ones from the roof of the kitchen area after hearing strange noises as we sat and ate. But where were the other four? This created a cause for concern especially when walking around the place in the pitch black of night with them being nocturnal and having darkness as their cover.

It was Fernando who found that the kinkajous had gotten out and he was furious. But then proceeded to blame Don solely for the escape, citing that he should be checking every animal and cage at the end of every day – which I felt a tad unreasonable, as the simple fact was that we all were responsible; including himself for checking each of the cages and the animals. Not just one person, because that would mean that he would have to inspect every animal, which he did during the course of the day and par for the course would, therefore, have to inspect every cage after someone else had been inside, as incidents like these were not confined to just on a night-time. Plus, Don did go around feeding and cleaning each of the animals with any new volunteers, who would be shown the procedures and any special requirements needed, and then he trusted those to carry out the job, not having to watch over and micromanage the people volunteering; which he should not have to do as the tasks were rudimentary enough and not exactly rocket science, and I personally had no problem with what was being asked, despite having a couple of escapees to my record.

The grey area I couldn't work out being that Don's official role was that of volunteer co-ordinator. Yet, what seemed to me was that he was actually expected to run the place as manager; essentially getting fully involved with everything that was happening and something he happily did. Things like; recruiting and organising the volunteers, training, feeding, cleaning, maintenance, construction, cooking meals, dealing with administration and providing information in English and Spanish for the website to name but a few. Even I could see it was a lot and appreciated all that he did; as it was all only really for benefit of the animals within his care and he took great pride in his job. The simple thing was, for a place this size it was understaffed with only three full-time members and two other volunteers maximum at any one time when I was there. Plus, it was still a work in progress; Don had only recently taken over some four months previously and was just trying to start implementing the changes that he wanted to make for the improvements to the animal welfare; inheriting a place that was apparently not in very good order, and I got the impression that the owners wanted him to work miracles straightaway, seven days a week with minimal staff and minimal budget. As much as I loved the place, this was quite apparent as a drawback.

With never a dull moment, the week flew by and come the weekend, around four of the kinkajous had been returned before once more I was due to leave on the Monday. I celebrated my last shift on the Saturday morning by having to get off the parrot island without the use of the rickety ladder. This meant one thing; I was getting wet or rather wetter because I had already fallen in thigh deep in the surrounding water after losing my balance on the sunken log. So, with what Don dubbed as new ritual for anyone leaving, I made my speech and took the plunge into the water. Miguel wanted me to do it head-first rather than just jump. So, in the spirit of doing a job properly and getting filthy, I obliged and dived head-first into the thick sediment water with my clothes, hat and rubber boots on, much to everyone's amusement. When finished on the Saturday, everyone pretty much stayed up drinking till Sunday. Some started, stopped, went to bed, got up and started drinking again, but blurrily in between this time we incorporated a spot of dancing around the front of the elderly lady's house. Paul fell down some stairs and broke his backside, empathised with as an extremely painful exercise. Don fell not so painfully asleep on the toilet; Fernando got over his kinkajou episode to then have another episode accusing me pulling one of the volunteers he fancied, when she wasn't even there; a six a.m. rafting session on the lake and watched some world cup qualifiers, that all cumulated in partying for over a full day solid. It was a crazy drunken session where we only really seemed to achieve what it was like to be on the same wavelength as the primates, minus the dexterity and agility. Granted, it's not big or clever, but it was a pretty good way to bow out as a leaving party while living in the jungle.

On the Monday, I woke slightly jaded. I felt tired but remarkably was OK, preparing my things before once again I said my goodbyes to the guys; especially Don and Miguel who I enjoyed working with immensely. Miguel was an absolute Trojan with his efforts and as a small present I gave him my Che Guevara T-shirt that I had bought in Australia, knowing that he was a hero of his and would really appreciate it. I was again really sorry to be leaving, as I loved the place and what it was trying to achieve. Despite many factors, the team ethos and comradery was still there; with Don doing his utmost to make all volunteers helping feel welcome, comfortable and at ease as possible, whilst providing a safe, caring environment for the animals. I have to say it was one of the best times I've had, for exactly the same reasons as before yet arguably better than the previous, only because I now knew the workings of the place, I could start immediately without no fear of the unexpected and just get on without any or much instruction. Also, I could speak better Spanish to integrate more with Miguel, which Don had actually commented on. Leaving, I was really glad I decided to return after a chance meeting as I got to experience first-hand the improvements that have been made there from shelters, integration of animals, feeding procedures and new living quarters that were all solely for the benefit of animals who have suffered trauma and poor quality of life, many of which due to man. I was sad to be leaving yet proud of myself, knowing that I was actually bothered and cared, wanting to make a difference. Initially, the first time there, Miguel stated that he didn't think I would return, and was pleased I had proved him wrong; albeit due to a chance meeting with Don, and was so glad that I did, despite the hard physical work load and extra cost – which in monetary terms actually went to a good cause and wasn't frivolously frittered away, so the only real cost was the actual time spent. But this was more than made up for with the other consolation of now having some photos to remind me of the people, place, animals and the amazing time working there.

My destination for that evening was Cuenca; Ecuador's third largest city. With no direct bus, I had to go from Puyo to Ambato, Ambato to Riobamba, and then from Riobamba to Cuenca. Time was now of the essence and I needed to make some headway south, so unfortunately, I couldn't stop in any of these places and only sampled the delights of each bus terminal during my connections. The day-time journey did provide ample opportunity to gaze upon the stunning mountain views, coupled with the steep drops from the winding roads that never grew old, not to mention the stunning snow-capped Volcán Chimborazo, Ecuador's highest peak and reportedly the highest peak on Earth from the core, due to being on the equatorial bulge. I had enquired with the local friends of Don's about the possibility of taking the train from Riobamba to Sibambe and then carrying on by bus from there to Cuenca. In my guidebook, I'd read that the train ride was a spectacular journey down a passage called the Nariz del Diablo (devil's nose), but unfortunately the train ran only on certain days, which wasn't when I was travelling. The other reason for this was because apparently there was the chance to ride on the rooftop which was actively encouraged, figuring that this would be too good an opportunity to miss as thrill-seeking journeys go; yet was also informed that this had been stopped as two travellers had apparently been decapitated in the process. Any truth to this I did not know, but due to all circumstances I had to make do with the 'not necessarily boring but less death defying' bus journey instead.

Having not made any plans about where to stay, I arrived late in the evening in Cuenca. I'd had cash problems again in Puyo, so had to take money from my credit card to get by, before finally getting in touch with the bank to use my regular card, and withdraw a decent amount from the ATM in the bus station. After pretty much picking the first hotel that was cheap and central, I headed there in a cab to crash for the evening. First thing that was in order in the morning was to shave. A lack of proper facilities, mainly water, had hindered this so I had grown some fuzzy designer stubble on both head and face.

It was early so I headed out to explore what was arguably Ecuador's most beautiful colonial city and I immediately got a good vibe from Cuenca. I wandered around the stone streets, savouring the architecture. Venturing along the river, it was incredibly scenic as some students were taking an art class, and why not in the sunshine? The beautiful surroundings could grace any picture. I happened upon some Inca ruins that were preserved close by, these seemed odd amid the more modern buildings. I took a look around the small museum that accompanied them, before heading back into town, meandering around the shops and appreciating the Parque Calderón, adorned with statues and trees, providing respite for those attending the cathedral or just taking time out to relax in the sun. I wasn't sure how long to spend in Cuenca, but one thing was for sure; there wasn't anything that I wanted to particularly do here, except admire the pretty surroundings. What I did want to do was carry on moving and this involved getting to Máncora in Peru. So, with no reason to hang around, I headed off in the early afternoon; happy to have visited and been impressed with Cuenca's distinct beauty and aware it was somewhere I would like to revisit and take in a little more of its peaceful ambience.

Machala on the south-west coast was where I could get a bus to take me over the border back into Peru. The bus journey provided some of the most diverse scenery yet; ranging from barren, high-ranging mountains that looked like it could have easily been another world, to emerald green trees and vegetation as we headed down to the flat lower lands out of the mountains. Enduring a six-hour- or-so stopover to get my connection allowed enough time to buy my bus border crossing ticket and take a cheap lunch, eating from the vending carts that sold hot kebab meat and potatoes daubed in *aji*. Luckily, here I realised that I had been mis-sold my ticket and managed to exchange it for one that actually stopped in Máncora; my destination. Otherwise, I would have been left stranded. The subsequent bus journey was only around two hours to the border, where I politely declined to pay the 'charge' for a stamp that I already had, so I knew this was another pay for nothing scam. Before we re-boarded the bus in Peru and headed for Máncora; and I left Ecuador for the final time.

I was kind of gutted to be leaving; feeling there was so much more that I wanted to see and do which was quite remarkable given the size of the country compared to others in South America. Yet, I had accomplished so much. Spanish school had given a brilliant introduction to the Latin way of life and provided me the basics and confidence to interact with the locals in their native tongue, which I thought was so important. Not to mention, the people whom I had met, from locals to travellers to fellow students, who due to the length of time spending together became good friends and formed an important part of my memories of adventures and education here. The best thing about Ecuador for me personally was that it was hard work, not the place itself or the travelling but the sheer effort that I had to put in to get the most out of the place, from learning Spanish and extra study to the physical hard work and long hours of the refuge centre and the climbing of Cotopaxi, which was my greatest physical achievement to date. It was my first real experience of South America and it created such an endearing image and now some of my greatest memories and a special kinship with the place that I knew I would always hold dear. It was reported as one of the poorer countries in South America and there were problems involving poverty and that was plain to see and hard to accept, but I loved the place, culture, sights, activities and people making many friends and bonds which would definitely ensure my return at some point.

Due to my wait in Machala, amid buying wrong tickets and eating kebabs, I also had the common sense to book myself into a hostel. So upon my subsequent arrival in Máncora, I had a place to stay, a bed and no issues. I had a plan now somewhat; firstly though was to chill here for a few days and take in some sun and mainly rest and recoup again. Much like in Montañita, I whiled away the days, not doing much around the pool and on the beach, watching the fish jump in and around the surf and braving the mighty 8ft plus waves breaking from the Pacific Ocean, where numerous times I found myself ducking under at the last minute from being nearly wiped out, providing some good fun, exercise and an element of respect for the sheer volume of water thundering in. It was easy to see why this place had such a reputation to attract travellers; with many bars and restaurants, it was somewhat of a party place. I got involved with the others from the hostel but tried to keep it relatively low-key; not wanting to waste too much money drinking and more so because I predominantly needed to relax. Also, unfortunately, here there seemed to be more of a sinister side than in Montañita; with frequent reports about muggings on the streets and being dangerous to go to the beach at night, with locals apparently coming here to take easy pickings off the many tourists. On one particular night out with a few others, one of the guys come running back into the bar in a mad panic, after they insisted on walking back alone and nearly got mugged; and this after being told not to as it was a bad idea. So I sort of got the impression that it was rife from the stories that people were bounding around. After a four-day pit stop, Máncora had served its purpose and I'd had enough sunning myself, recharging batteries and watching my back, so embarked on a journey which was to be my longest yet.

Fly-Bys, *Nacho Libre* and the Most Dangerous

I was more than used to the long journeys at this point and had adapted to be able to get some sleep on the sometimes bumpy, winding ride of an overnight bus, but this was still no substitute for a welcoming bed. So prior to setting off, I smoked a pre-journey joint to relax me and take the edge off the impending thousand or so miles ahead. My destination was Bolivia, but that would require some two days' travelling on the bus, getting from the north-west to the south of Peru, pretty gruelling in anyone's book. So, I made do with putting in a thirty-six-hour journey straight back through to Arequipa with a four-hour stopover connection in Lima. Here, I would finally cotton on to my nickname of '*pelon*' when beckoned by one of the conductors. Seemingly commonplace to call someone by their description, having also heard '*flaco*' (skinny) and '*gordo*' (fatty) also being called forth; I can only assume '*señor*' (sir) was a bit too 'formal' or even 'polite' so the obvious childish school playground nickname description was the easiest way of initiating contact. Although bizarre, nobody seemed to care, so I wondered, *Is that just the way it is here?* I wasn't overly offended and probably wasn't supposed to know what it meant, but did find myself initially thinking, *Did that cheeky fucker just call me baldy?* As I was told to get on the bus.

There was nothing more in my itinerary that I particularly wanted to do in Peru except for possibly in Arequipa; where I never got the chance to raft or do anything for that matter. Also, this was a good stopping point as I knew from the time there previously I could get a bus to the Bolivian capital La Paz. It made perfect sense to stop for a couple of nights, as it provided the opportunity to do what I really wanted. Having quenched my desire to go rafting, I figured it would be pointless doing this again. So, upon my arrival, I booked for the next day; a three-day, two-night trek through the Colca Canyon that called for a two thirty a.m. start the very next morning.

The three a.m. air was freezing cold when we headed north-west out of Arequipa to the canyons and mountains, and I shivered constantly bumping against the frosted windows of the bus, fainting in and out of an uncomfortable sleep. A situation that instantaneously prompted me to buy a llama wool jumper from some of the indigenous locals when stopping off at a village for a toilet and snack break, feeling it could be really sound investment; especially if it was to be as cold overnight because much like other trekking excursions, all that was required was a small backpack with few change of clothes that for me included jeans, shorts, t-shirts and my thin now not very waterproof jacket. Once more, though, as the sun had risen over the mountains, the lack of cloud cover brought with it almost instantaneous heat that required the need to remove clothing, leaving the woollen jumper stuffed in the backpack for later. Our next stop was at Cruz del Condor. Purpose-built walkways high up atop the huge cliffs of the mighty Colca Canyon, with a cross embedded upright in a rock base surrounded by many floral offerings as the last postings between us and a colossal open chasm cut into the earth; where on the far side, imposing jagged cliff faces towered up high as an impassable entity to the distant snow-capped mountain peaks that graced our view beyond.

If this wasn't impressive enough, on our side perched on the end of a rock plinth, over-looking the some 2000m-deep canyon stood two giant bird creatures. They didn't resemble anything I had seen before in the wild, but distinguishable by the vast amount of ruffled feathers, small dark unattractive balding head with a large beak that made them incredibly vicious and ugly looking, coupled with the thin legs propping up the mass made them undeniable to the species and the biggest indicator to what these were. Crowds from the visiting buses quickly gathered around to take photographs of the unique spectacle of having the fabled emblem of South America so close by; the Andean condor. I thought that I might have seen them previously in the wild cruising high in the mountains of Ecuador, but on this evidence, I was wrong; those before definitely weren't condors if only because these were enormous – easily three times the size and absolutely massive. I couldn't believe how lucky we were to have not only one but two perched so near; a few metres or so from the guardrail as soon as we disembarked from the bus. More so as we had been warned that it was the luck of the draw as to whether they would be seen or not. Yet, *Boom!* There they were. Due to the rarity of the spectacle, hastily more and more people arrived and as I had managed to take some photos, I decided on moving down to a lower terrace further away from the crowd along the ridge; a decision which was to prove inspired.

Viewing the birds and the growing crowd from around 50m away, there was motion as one decided that it was time to abandon its perch, having had enough of the ever-growing horde of gawking paparazzi. With one virtually effortless movement, the wings opened and it fell off the craggy plinth into immediate flight mode, heading along the ridge to where few others including myself had gathered. I had noticed its instinctive movement towards us and hoped it would carry on its trajectory. Within seconds, it had covered the distance and passed over some 6m above our heads. I have never seen anything so big in the air in all my life. That was alive, anyway. The wingspan was around 3m wide, ridged with long feathers towards the tips spread out to a fan shape that never beat or flapped; it was clear why the wings didn't move, as the strength required would need great energy-sapping effort from the now streamline body as it passed right over. The sound was immense as any aircraft aerofoil as the cool morning air cut, creating a very loud and obvious *whoosh*, with the size and natural shape of the wings providing all the elevation and direction for efficient gliding flight these magnificent creatures needed to move so effortlessly. It then veered off inward towards the vastness and far side of the gaping canyon.

The sheer size and grace in flight was just something to behold. I watched in awe as it became a comparatively small speck riding higher then lower, patrolling circles in the middle of the two towering sides that now brought the gap between the two cliff faces into huge perspective; and I felt like we all witnessed something special. Even our guide Hernan was taking photos himself as he had never seen anything like it either. This was truly a unique spectacle that happened so quickly, unexpectedly and soon after arriving; seeing one of the largest birds on the planet, in its natural environment, fly-by at such close quarters was beautiful, despite slating their somewhat aged aesthetics. This was a privilege, made all the more so because unfortunately these are now endangered species that only live in certain environments and have to hunt as scavengers, with many of their natural prey killed off by man. It has been reported that they sometimes have to venture hundreds of miles, as far off as the coast in search of food. I'd also seen them at the zoo in Cali and those now seemed smaller too, probably from being in captivity for this very reason; their preservation – yet, sadly, those couldn't grace the skies and were a showcase, but this was a thrilling spectacle to witness and left me sincerely hoping more could be done to protect them.

We hung around for about a further thirty minutes or so, watching mesmerised by the gliding giants as they drifted in and around the canyon.

There were three in total, providing a show for the lucky few that day and I was so happy having now officially seen them in their natural habitat. The day had started brilliantly. The sun was well and truly up and we got back onto the bus to head to our base town to get ready to trek down into the deep canyon. Unfortunately, we had to get ready sooner than we thought, having to all disembark from the bus about a kilometre out of town. This was because the incredibly bumpy dirt track road would provide more excitement.

While gazing out of the window on the way there, I looked ahead and I couldn't quite believe what I saw ahead of the bus standing in the pasture to the roadside. A two-headed donkey? *What the fuck? How?* I looked again; yep, two heads front and back. I couldn't believe it. I scrambled to get my camera to capture the strangest spectacle yet. I was just ready to snap when the bus shifted angle as we passed, to realise that it wasn't quite the freak of nature I thought; a second donkey exactly the same colour came into view standing behind the first, creating the illusion that another head was at the arse end of the one in front. It looked really cool and trippy, from the initial glance at the perfectly aligned beasts and I laughed as it wouldn't surprise me being as South America was a pretty crazy place, where anything could and did seem to happen. Disappointed with my slow reaction time, I put my camera away. Big mistake; moments later, continuing to gaze out of the window I looked down to see something odd. As we were quickly overtaken by a small black cylindrical object. This time, it was obvious what it was; and it was also obvious to the bus driver, as he brought us to an abrupt halt. A wheel and tyre had bounced past us and off down the road, this was strange in the sense that there was nothing else near us for it to come from. That's because it was one of our wheels that had become detached while we were still moving and fucked off down the road, leaving one side to the rear of our bus propped up by the remaining inside wheel; I'm no mechanic, but I figured it a bit more practical and safer to have all four wheels rather than just three attached to our rear axle.

The driver also thought the same; as he got out and hilariously chased after it, seeing it had bounced and rolled into a ditch by the roadside, from where he retrieved it, rolled it back and proceeded to reattach it. Unbelievable, we hadn't even reached base town and I had already acquired a new cheap genuine llama wool sweater, saw some of nature's most spectacular endangered wonders – which included condors and a two-

411

headed donkey – and now the wheels were literally coming off the bus. This was turning out to be one of the most surreal adventures yet and we hadn't even started. We all stripped off, ready to walk into the town of Cabanaconde in the now blazing sun; everybody headed off down the dirt track road except for our group as Hernan insisted, we wait for some unknown reason for the wheel to be reattached to be driven there.

A French couple called Heidi and Stefan, and a Spanish girl called Monica, plus myself made up our group; for a change it was nice being only a few as everyone got to know each other quite quickly amid all the shenanigans and messing around. After lunch in the early afternoon, we set off out of town, making our way along the dusty road to the edge of the canyon where we stopped for photos of the impressive backdrop. The canyon was vast in size, tiny villages with formed terraces were visible deep down on the far side and due to the contours and depth, it was impossible to see the very bottom even from the edge at the top, where this could only offer the far-side rock face, blended mountainous horizon and brilliant blue cloudless sky that now caused the sun to scorch down relentlessly from high; and was wildly impressive nevertheless.

We made our way down into the canyon via a narrow, dusty trail that just seemed to get steeper and steeper. After a while, I had done my usual trick of putting the headphones in and started listening to music, zoning out from the others to concentrate on the task at hand and take in the amazing surroundings. The pathway had changed to loose rubble that zig-zagged down into the canyon, causing the footing underneath to be frictionless and slippery, giving way on numerous occasions, causing a nerving unbalance at the temporary loss of control and increased expectancy of a hard fall. Halfway down, I started to suffer, as my thighs ached badly from each jolt of the energy-sapping downhill steps, but this was mild in comparison to the blisters that were forming fast on my toes due to the foot being shoved forward hard, causing constant rubbing against the inside shoe, where every step now became a painful exercise that was only overcome by maximum concentration, will and desire to avoid steep drops from the jagged cliff side that awaited one wrong move. The villages on the opposite side neared as I gradually drew to eye level with them, where after about three hours we reached the bottom to be greeted by a running river and a bridge crossing. Here, I sat and rested my aching thighs and burning sore feet while waiting on the others' arrival.

Sitting, I noticed that the canyon had drawn in at the bottom with both sides much closer together in an enormous 'V' shape; so much so, it was now impossible to see where we had come from, or the top of either side. The still brilliant bright sun was much lower now but light billowed directly down through the canyon creating shadowy effects before again illuminating the far walls. The others turned up and with a wearily soreness, I got to my feet as we proceed over to the other side of the canyon. Making our way scaling over some huge boulders, I banged my head on a particularly large overhanging rock; that added to the aching legs and blistered feet by also hurting like hell.

A few minutes later, my headache subsided and we arrived in camp. A pleasant little resort owned by locals who lived in the canyon, surrounded by trees and fabulous rock formations striated in appearance millions of years in the making. There was running water to get a shower and stone wall huts to sleep in. Hernan briefed us about the evening events and told the French couple that they had the matrimonial suite; I decided to put my arm around Monica and said that we would have the matrimonial suite as well. Fortunately, she and the others laughed at my abrupt pre-empted marriage proposal, despite only having hung out for all of a day. But I had been getting on well with Monica; she instantly came across as having an unpretentious, naturally cool persona; fun, bubbly, didn't take herself too seriously and could recognise a joke, which thankfully was the case as it would have been rather awkward. We had initially taken a stroll together around Cabanaconde, before setting off and chatted freely, where I tried to impress her with my Spanish that just left her looking quizzical and confused. I could only assume this was because she was from Barcelona and her native tongue was Catalan – and definitely not because my Spanish and Latin American Spanish at that, was shit. But, still, she was very endearing, my instincts were founded and I liked her. The plan for the evening was simple; get cleaned up, chill out, eat dinner, bed. Sounded like a plan to me, because I was in pain, hungry and knackered so this ticked all the relevant boxes.

The room was empty when I woke the next morning, with Monica up and gone.

"Monica!" I shouted. Nothing. "MONICA!" again, I yelled. And again. And again.

Some ten minutes later, Hernan came along and unlocked the door so I could get out. Monica being the kind little diamond that she was had locked me in from the outside. I found her under the canopied area happily tucking into breakfast, absolutely oblivious to the seven a.m. commotion she had caused.

"Where you been? You not take breakfast?" she said in her accompanying Spanish accent.

"I would love to take breakfast, Monica, but someone locked me in the room from the outside," I said in a smiling, sarcastic manner and sat watching, as the penny refused to drop as to what I was talking about. So, eventually, I had to explain; to which she burst out laughing whilst trying to offer a sincere giggling apology, which just made it funnier. After my hasty breakfast, we set off.

Having put plasters and bindings on my feet, I found the terrain easier going as these helped prevent more rubbing. Also, because we were at the bottom of the canyon and we traversed along it, so this meant there wasn't much downhill force being exerted. Even when we had to scale up over, this was much easier than trudging down as toes were refrained from being crushed into the shoe. Along the way, Hernan informed us about some of the plants, such as cactus from the area and how the villagers used them for medicinal and other practical purposes; this provided an interesting insight to how available resources were used within village life of the canyon. We passed through three villages in total, one of which a surprisingly a large community given we were in a massive crevasse deep in the earth crust. It was old with white-washed stone buildings and a larger area towards the centre of the canyon reserved for growing fruits and vegetables with this area being flatter and subject to most sunlight. But like in most places in South America, no matter where it was, there would be a church and a football pitch. Guaranteed, and here was no different. Oddly, though, there were very few inhabitants around and we were informed that people would be out working tending to crops or the livestock. Due a break, we happened upon an indigenous lady selling fresh fruits, so we took time out here also to sample them, refresh and shelter from the sun.

Pressing on, taking ever more photos of the imposing yet impressive walled surroundings, the trail headed downhill and I trudged slowly and wearily along the dusty track. Reaching a brow, relief and happiness overruled an increasingly bedraggled state, as I could see our destination deeper into the canyon. The clustered campsite of Sangalle had wooden bungalows obscured by the trees. I knew this was where we were headed as one thing gave it away; the inviting blue swimming pool that I couldn't wait to get into. Now around one p.m., we had trekked for some five hours. Immediately on my arrival whilst waiting for the others, I took the opportunity to remove my increasingly damaged shoes and socks to immediate relief of my feet. When the others arrived, we found our camp ground and were given our shared wooden bungalows; where like a true gent, I allowed Monica the first choice of not having to sleep in the bed that was remarkably shaped like a hammock.

Not a second wasted, I stripped off to my shorts, grabbed a towel and headed straight out for a swim, where I dived in to the cold yet amazingly refreshing water. Despite the searing sun's elevated status overhead, it hadn't warmed the large pool, this was hardly surprising as actual sunlight on the campsite ground was only around eight hours in the day, before the sun would be too low, so the high ridges either side would then douse the bottom of the canyon in shade. Still this didn't matter; the cool elixir-like liquid instantaneously started to revitalise my worn appendages, muscles, joints and skin. It felt amazing and they all thanked me for submerging them in the less gravitational, denser, soothing massage of water as I swam around.

I spent the rest of the afternoon not doing an awful lot; relaxing and jumping into the pool from the purpose-built rock formations next to it. Monica was reading a book that I didn't recognise; literally translated from Spanish it was the 'Nine Predictions'. When she explained what it was about, I realised that it was *The Celestine Prophecy* the same book that I'd come across, gave away, then regained, eventually read again and had now passed on to another traveller. We chatted about its content. I found it odd and wondered why this book had come back to me in another way, with another person, and in another language; but mainly it only helped reaffirmed my instincts were right and why I liked Monica. I hadn't really been reading anything new at this point; last book being *Yes Man*, which I finished quickly in Peru on my first visit. Again, it centred around the author saying 'yes' to everything asked of him and the consequences that brought. It resonated with me because from then on, I was making things up as I went along, finding myself saying 'yes' (although not to the extreme he was, that would be dangerously reckless in a place like South America!) was indeed making things happen, opening doors and creating opportunities, especially after saying 'yes' to going to Colombia with everything being unscripted and nothing pre-planned. It seemed 'yes' was true, possibilities became exponential and this little word it became the catalyst for going out there, having adventures, being and feeling alive.

Evening quickly drew in cold and we ate by candlelight at the communal area with other groups, and spent the rest of the time sat around wood-carved tables and chairs formed from tree stumps, playing card games and drank a bottle of some potent Peruvian spirit, shared about by those who were either particularly good or bad at drinking games, depending on which way you look at it; before another early night.

Although an early start in the morning, we would be graced with the actual hard work being finished in a relatively short time. But this was still a three hour constant uphill slog back to the top of the canyon along a shorter but no less steep trail. It was still dark and visibility just started to become more apparent as we headed up over at around six a.m. I trudged off again in a world of my own, as I found a rhythm to the gradient walk, along the dust-addled and seemingly never-ending winding tracks. It was hard going and I had to stop to take a breath, but this did provide chance to witness the beautiful spectacle of the sun break over the canyon and send rays of light streaming down, slowly eradicating shadow from the sheer walls of rock on the far side and deep within the crevasse, looking almost heavenly in its brilliance. I eventually made it to the top in a good time of just under three hours, where again I relaxed on a rock savouring the morning light on a stunning setting.

Others arrived and we made our way across the tracks in the fields before getting back to Cabanaconde to take breakfast. Everyone was pleased that the hard work for the day was complete, yet the itinerary not so. Making our way back to Cruz del Condor, we stopped for one last glimpse of the majestic creatures patrolling the area high in the sky, before visiting a site where tombs of former tribe leaders had been carved high into the rock face, overlooking a vast site of villages and farming terraces further up towards the end of the canyon. We stopped in the provincial capital Chivay where disappointingly there wasn't enough time to sample the local hot pools that my muscles and joints would have really appreciated, but instead wandered around the local market looking at the vast array of clothing, arts and crafts before eating lunch in the food hall area that most market places seemed to have; where for a cheap price, a variety of things could be found on the menu that included the usual meats, stews, vegetables, pastas, rice, beans etc. to the more exotic delicacy around these parts of guinea pig. I was at the point now where I could eat most things and wasn't being as fussy with what I wanted or craved, having grown accustomed to eating what was being placed in front of me, yet what was more noticeable was that I was definitely finding myself eating less. And this extended to giving guinea pig a miss.

Early in the afternoon, the bus headed back to Arequipa, this time stopping at the desolate barren landscape of Altiplano. Here at 4800m elevation harboured virtually no plant life due to the terrain and altitude. There were small turrets of rocks that had been placed as an offering to the gods in the event of a loved one's demise, and some with painted indicators giving a name and direction of the various volcanoes and mountains that could be seen, as well as a stone cubicle building billed as the highest official toilets in Peru, if not South America. Not needing the bathroom, I didn't go in. Despite where we were, chances are they were probably still a mozzie pit. And it wasn't as if there was a janitor hanging around keeping them clean either.

I was getting nervous on the way back, because we were late and I had to pick up my bus tickets I'd bought prior to the Colca Canyon trek; because I didn't need to stick around and wanted to get to Bolivia. But if the shop closed, I would be stuck and have to pay for another night's accommodation or buy more bus tickets, as it would be classed that I was a no-show, therefore null and void. As soon as we arrived in town, I hastily said quick goodbyes and ran to the tour shop, which was just up from the main plaza and luckily found the owner just about to leave, so I still managed to get my tickets. It was a risk and by now I should know how these things can run over time. The time frame quoted is usually an estimate if not just a guess by the travel agents. Same as with a lot of things; it seemed if someone in South America didn't know an answer, they would make one up for you, so it looked like they were helping you and didn't lose face by not knowing. I found it was always best to sometimes get a second or even third opinion; something that could still leave you none the wiser as you would be given three different answers.

Luckily, though, I was fine and still managed to head out and have dinner with Heidi, Stefan and Monica to say goodbye properly before I moved on. I was really pleased about this as I would have been disappointed to have missed them. Despite the small group, I had lots of fun being around and chatting with them amid our endeavours; especially Monica who with her fun mannerisms and quirky capers – like 'borrowing' an indigenous lady's hat at the market and posing for photos in it like they were 'best friends' – made me laugh. But due to our routes, it was unlikely we would catch up again, and not randomly either like what had happened before; which was a shame as I was heading in the opposite direction. Regardless, I took their contact details, hopeful that we would maybe get chance to meet up again sometime in the future.

Four a.m. was much earlier than expected to arrive once again back in Puno bus station. I didn't venture out and just hung around, watching dubbed English movies in the hard, uncomfortable seats, and donated some food and spare soles of money I had left over to an old man wandering around the cold terminal. At seven thirty a.m., the bus left to head for the nearby border crossing to Bolivia, as we drove around the south shoreline of the majestic sea-like Lake Titicaca. Again, the weather was favourable, allowing sunlight to reflect wildly off the calm blue water and managed to catch a glimpse of one of the early-morning cattle markets, where a poor donkey received a whack across its arse to obey instruction and a Volkswagen campervan came out of the gateway with a llama sitting down nonchalantly on the roof rack. I couldn't help but stare in wonder, but wasn't surprised. It was just another of a growing list of random strange things that I had witnessed as part of my travels. The ethos in many of the poorer countries I had visited was to get something done by any ways or means; regardless of having the adequate resources or not. But I couldn't start to fathom how on earth they managed to get a llama on the roof? Clearly, the owner's stick was a little bit more persuasive than that of the donkey's owner.

Stopping at Yunguyo on the Peruvian Bolivian border, we disembarked and completed the passport formalities before crossing by foot through a large stone archway into Bolivia. Again, we were subject to immigration before we were allowed to head to Copacabana. Back on board the bus, we were once more stopped and some 'officials' – and I use the term loosely – boarded and tried to charge everyone entry. Some paid but many complained and refused. After a few minutes of frantic discussions between the coach driver and the 'officials', we were on our way. I never paid and I thought it was a scam, but not that I was asked to pay either. After a stopover, something to eat and much confusion about which was our bus and when it was leaving, having been transferred to another Bolivian transport company, we headed off to La Paz, the Bolivian capital. In doing so we had to crossing over a small stretch of Lake Titicaca on a passenger boat at San Pedro de Tiquina; where, to some Bolivian dog owner's embarrassment, their puppy shit all over the deck, yet they still didn't bother to clean it up, while some locals struggled furiously to get another less-than-willing donkey aboard a rather small boat, offering an entertaining spectacle for those watching over the side of our vessel before we set off towards the final leg of the journey.

I had now officially finished in Peru, after my whirlwind dash through the country for the second time; both experiences leaving good and bad impressions of the place. I had witnessed mystical ruins, ventured on to the world's highest lake, flown over the mysterious signs and lines that this age's greatest thinkers can't accurately explain, met shaman, seen one of nature's most endangered species in the wild at close quarters and rolled with some of the biggest waves crashing in from the pacific. Surely these would have been enough to ensure the best time of my travels to date? Yet for me and my own experiences this hadn't happened. Granted, being robbed at knife-point had left a sour taste in the mouth, but this could have happened anywhere as there was plenty of opportunist crime in most places that I visited, and it was just down to circumstance that this had happened here. But there were other factors, such as getting injured which seemed to happen worst in Peru, stopping me doing some of the things that I wanted. Again, this was down to circumstances of my own doing and hardly the places fault itself, but both factors adding to negative times that I personally would associate with Peru, where others wouldn't. But I'd come through these things unscathed and recovered, the bad things were going to happen and proved a test of resolve, and figured these should be welcomed as such as a vital part of the learning and growing from experience as much as the good things. Yet, there were other factors, like the fact that this was easily the most tourist laden place I had been, with the country cashing in ahead of other countries from the money that foreigners would bring, utilising their culture and resources to attract this, expanding through many western commercial outlets such as fast food chains. It could be argued that this was both a positive with money entering the economy, to provide jobs for the poor etc. But was this actually helping them? Another argument could also be to a detrimental effect; well publicised that Machu Picchu is gradually getting destroyed because of its popularity. Now, I'd been part of all this.

Don't get me wrong, I loved the time as I fast realised when travelling things were never going to go plain sailing, and it was a question of taking the rough with the smooth and overcoming problems, accepting and learning from them. But I also felt that some of the people at times resented the fact that many tourists would come here, and locals could be a lot ruder and condescending than I had experienced in other countries, feeling that those visiting were more recognised as a target, where as more of a novelty in Ecuador and Colombia; although, I do have say that this wasn't everyone.

Over all, the sights available to see are phenomenal and were really worth it and I was glad I visited, no question about that; achieving many long-term ambitions and all things considered, circumstance and my own doing predominantly dictated what had happened to me. But I wouldn't have changed it for the world. Purely because things could have been much worse, but I was still here having a great time and the bad just added to the thrills of travelling, easily compensated by the wondrous experiences of what was on offer.

It was pretty obvious I had arrived in La Paz, Bolivia's capital. As it was possible to see from the elevated road side, virtually the whole city sprawled out within a valley. It looked fantastic as the buildings encroached upwards in all directions. Settling in, I wasted no time in getting out and about, having a look around and immediately feeling the effects of the 3600m elevation, sharp becoming short of breath when having to walk up the steep streets; because despite all the time spent at altitude prior this was much higher and when travelling around I'd also been back down closer towards sea level for a fair while. The thin air here also seemed to taste of smog which probably wasn't helping matters either.

I found out that some of the others from the hostel were heading out to an activity that frankly I couldn't believe I hadn't already done, as it was everywhere but just timing was more the issue. Virtually, every country in South America was mad about one thing; football. I had an unsuccessful kick about in Colombia, but the opportunity to actually go to a proper game hadn't risen; until now. Local Club Bolivar were taking on Wilstermann in the Sunday afternoon kick-off in the Estadio Olímpico La Paz, which was a ten-minute walk away from the hostel and where the Bolivian national team had thrashed former world champions and neighbours Argentina 6-1 recently; a famous victory made all the more subject to conjecture due to the elevation factor and the Bolivians being more acclimatised. Despite any indifference towards the game and any disappointments from back home, this was right here and now and I'd never experienced a game abroad before, let alone on another continent. And as 'away' games go, you couldn't get more away. That was it; I was there.

Arriving at the stadium, traffic had to be stopped outside in the plaza due to the volume of people wandering around the streets and on the roads, plus a vast amount of vendors had set up a makeshift market selling all kinds of partisan paraphernalia to the revellers. Some had their face painted in club colours, whereas I on the other hand made an investment in a light blue and white Club Bolivar Mexican wrestler style mask. It looked brilliant and I was over the moon with my purchase and was possibly the best £1.50 that I had ever spent to help me get into the spirit of the game, which frankly I didn't need to do, as the outside spectacle of noise and waving banners was immense and easily enough. The tickets cost an unbelievable £2 and a fraction of the cost back home for good seats. Inside, the atmosphere was constantly raucous, with drums beating like a tribal ritual that caused fans and supporters to shout, sing and chant, as fixed blue and white bunting billowed down from the fittings in the stands. When the teams eventually came out, toilet rolls were thrown about from within the crowd as makeshift streamers and ticker tape fluttered everywhere as the place erupted; it was excellent. Apart from the actual game itself, which putting it mildly was a poor spectacle, played on a pitch best described as a ploughed field that eventually finished 0-0.

Despite the result and lack of goals, it was really worthwhile going as this was a football event; not just a match, being something more than I had ever witnessed before. With the fans constantly singing and jumping around to the drums' beat, the seats were pretty much redundant especially at times when a conga line would start. Mexican waves washed around the stands, vendors brought food and drinks (beer!) to people in the seats like American sports instead of having to queue on the concourse. I saw at least two people who had brought their dogs with them and armed police heavily guarded the perimeter fence and at the final whistle had to be deployed with riot shields to protect the referee off the pitch, as hundreds of disgruntled fans hurled any amounts of fruit and vegetables at him, as a show of their displeasure at not awarding a blatant penalty for the home team towards the end of the match. It was absolutely insane and I had not experienced anything like it at a game before; where I would never be allowed into the ground if I was wearing a Lucha Libre wrestler mask. But here, this type of behaviour was actively encouraged. Regardless of the game itself, we all loved the South American carnival atmosphere that was generated by the vocal, animated, and crazy passionate fans and one thing was for certain, all definitely wanted to get to another game. It was too much fun; even if the match itself somewhat played second fiddle. So I wondered what it would be like if there were lots of goals? Or the home team won? Or lost for that matter? Absolute pandemonium, I guess.

The next day, I was up and about early to sort out some of the things that I wanted to do, while having a look around the city. Liam, one of the Irish lads who had been to the football, joined me and we toked on a cheeky joint before we went out to take the edge off another wise lazy day. The sun was hot in La Paz, but the air cool and crisp due to the altitude, making a bit of a conundrum what to wear when out and about. First point of call was to locate where I was to be picked up from the next morning, which was promising to be another exhilarating excursion and one I'd been looking forward to for some time. It immediately struck me whilst wandering about that there seemed to be a more traditional element to the people here in La Paz; particularly the older ladies wearing the colourful woven ponchos and pork pie hats that I had seen frequent occasions before when near and on Lake Titicaca. Yet not so much in other larger cities and this helped create the illusion of a more authentic Andean city despite quite a few new high-rise buildings. Heading to the opposite side of the city, we came across the lovely San Pedro plaza which was also the location of the notorious San Pedro prison.

I had heard so much about the prison from other travellers who had been inside. This was after paying the guards to enter to then see the inmates and how the place operates. It was referred to as a locked-away community, with families of inmates apparently living there with them in an environment that was virtually run by the inhabitants, where drugs were rife as a way of life and it was apparently possible for anyone who had entered as a visitor to consume as much cocaine as they wanted, for a price that included plenty of cigarettes and alcohol for those within. Speaking to Kevin whom I went rafting with, said he had been inside for this purpose. But there had been a clamp down on that day and numerous reporters were waiting outside for tourists to come out, so they could expose what was going on and said he had been kept inside, being told they may have to spend the night in there, before being let out a back door sometime later and I'd also heard stories that an inmate had recently attacked a tourist visitor. I didn't know to what extent any of this was exact but I could believe it, only because so many other travellers were reporting what was happening from having been in and were all saying the same thing. All I knew was, on this day the doors and gates to gain entrance were now well and truly locked, to stop what was going on.

Honestly, I would not want to visit even if it was possible. I could only imagine that people visiting were only doing so for the apparent supply of cheap drugs. To justify it as 'research', out of 'curiosity' or even 'helping' as humanitarian excuse would be tenuous at best, as I'd doubt these people were involved in a prisoner outreach or pen pal scheme anywhere else, so saying there was any sort of Good Samaritan intention by visiting seemed very futile. Personally, I couldn't think of anything much worse than hanging around in a prison, full of Bolivia's most dangerous inmates and then getting off your face. Paranoid or what? I dare say it would be interesting to see how the place operated and what conditions had to be endured. Yet, I still couldn't get my head around all this. It clearly was exploitative by seemingly all concerned, from prisoners to guards to visitors, as people were in there for a reason and the whole operation seemed to be very underhand and unethical, let alone illegal. It was probably a sign and a good thing that the doors were now firmly closed and under close scrutiny, as I know only far too well how good I was at making some stupid decisions.

In parts, the roads narrowed and became a pedestrianised cobbled street, as we had entered El Mercado de las Brujas or La Hechicería, known as 'the Witches Market'; where lots of open stalls sold a vast array of carved artefacts, natural herbs, potions and remedies to cure many ailments from bad stomachs to bad spirits. It was quite baffling tying to work out what some things were, never mind what they were actually for; especially things like dried lamb foetuses, where many were just hung up ready to be bought on a whim. Close by was the Museo de la Coca. A museum dedicated to the coca plant; here, like Peru, are only two countries in South America where the coca plant is legal and from which cocaine can be derived which is actually illegal (and probably why inmates of a lawless prison can manufacture it so readily). Unfortunately, this would have to wait for another day as it was being refurbished when we arrived. We wandered aimlessly around the city, surviving the incredibly slippery worn steps of the steep streets before we chilled out back at the hostel to psych ourselves up for the big quiz in the bar on the evening.

Arriving at the cafe in the morning, it was just getting light and we met up with others participating and our guides from mountain biking company. Getting organised, we all jumped into the buses and headed out from La Paz to La Cumbre, at around 4800 metres up in the arid landscapes of the cordilleras mountains. Our destination for the day was some 3300 metres downhill over a 60km course along the self-titled 'World's Most Dangerous Road' or 'Death Road', hopefully finishing up near Coroico and not a splattered mess.

There were at least two casualties in the hostel when I left that morning, sporting a dislocated shoulder, busted leg and any amounts of missing skin. This was just over the last two days from what could be described as a dangerous, if not deadly, activity that I was just about to participate in. I had heard so much about the barely five-metre-wide road that rolled down with the contours of the mountain to the town below from travellers and what I had seen on TV. In particular, the dirt and gravel roads twists and turns, with no barriers, and the sheer drops from the cliff sides of up to four hundred metres at points. This called for two things; total concentration and the utmost respect. Any form of bravado could swiftly be punished, as people had perished along the way and our guide Stu had told us that only a month prior, an unfortunate participant had gone too fast and ended up over the edge, reported as still alive when they got to him but he died some hours later. With this information in mind, those left injured and decrepit in the hostel had escaped lightly.

Nervous and apprehensive, I still wanted to do this as many had made the journey down, surviving with fantastic tales of death-defying adventure. I was more than capable of riding a bike competently and was not intent on trying to break any world records (or anything else for that matter). Sticking to my game plan, I could easily do this and have a likewise thrilling tale to tell. It was cold due to brisk winds on the open-top plain car park high on the mountain; we kitted up, donning warm clothing, helmet, goggles, high-visibility vest and the bikes were prepped for personal adjustments. After being encouraged to cycle around to get used to the bikes, we then had some final instruction from the guide – which was tantamount to don't go too fast – and we headed off.

The first part of the road was on asphalt and quick, as we immediately started to descend along the modern winding road that cut a swathe through a ravine in the mountains, having to take care with the passing traffic. It was exhilarating ripping through still air at speed, creating a loud rush, all the while cautious of what could happen after stopping to look over the edge, to peer at the rusting, battered old remains of a bus that lay perished some 50m down over, as evidence of what we were about to undertake was all too real. We continued on through the army checkpoint and then negotiated up two sparsely mentioned inclines, before we arrived at a right-hand turn off.

Here was where the old 'Death Road' began; a new safer tarmac road had been constructed, continuing over the other side of the valley. But we were now switching to dirt track road to head towards the cliff sides and the real deal. Most traffic would be using the new route and this old road would be predominantly used by the biking companies, but we were warned that cars and trucks were still allowed to use the road and they did. So if anything came along, we were instructed to move over to the side where there was mountain wall and not sheer drop cliff; obvious sound reasoning. We had already started to descend quite rapidly in towards the huge crevasse. Now thick with green vegetation, the air temperature and humidity increased at a remarkable rate due to the close confine of trees and mountainous shelter, this required the opportunity to remove the long pants and jacket we had started in, to continue in shorts and t-shirt as it was only going to get hotter. We were given another briefing before we now started to make our way along the perilous part of the unforgiving mountainside track.

Almost immediately, handling the bike became trickier, as loose gravel easily gave way under the tyres from less resistance and lack of friction compared to the solid tarmac and dirt track. This took a bit of time to adjust to. Eventually, handling became easier as desired speed was attained, so that going too fast wasn't dangerous and going too slow would inevitably mean falling off, leaving the only things to worry about: the road itself, a few meandering local dogs and of course, the close by edge. From our high precipice, lots of early morning, low-lying clouds blanketed the gorge, obscuring any view. Although I would've loved to see the magnificent surroundings and cavernous valley, right now at the beginning of the trail it was a distraction so I only had total concentration for the road ahead and an uneasy wariness of the murky grey abyss a few feet to the left-hand side, where ironically the left-hand side of the road was the side, we were instructed to ride on. Seemingly counterintuitive, this though made turning the impending corners more visible, enabling to see what was coming and the severity of the bend ahead, therefore making the course safer and easier, because the 'safer' more natural right side of the mountain made the corners blind, sharper and harder to turn.

It was possible to build up plenty of momentum and speed on the road to many thrill-seekers' joy, but some of the hair pin bends, curving around points in the mountain were absolutely brutal, and could easily end it all for anyone with a blasé and reckless attitude. There was not much room to play with for what was at stake; at best, there was only a very small grass verge between the road and going over the side. I took a nice steady pace, building up momentum when the road was clear and covering the brakes early when bends approached. We paused at regular intervals, allowing us to regroup, be briefed for the next phase and any particular points of interest that mainly concerned the most dangerous of sharp turns.

Stopping for lunch allowed time to relax, chill, take on board some refreshments and admire the scenery that really wasn't possible while moving, due to the high concentration levels fixed firmly on the road. Having descended far enough down, the clouds had dispersed and clearly in view were long drops of wild growing vegetation all over the mountains that stretched far out for miles down the contours of a disappearing chasm. It both looked and felt brilliant to be on this notorious road; the support bus carrying our things allowed us to have cameras, to take fabulous pictures of 'post card corner' where the road seemed to abruptly end, disappearing around a bend to show off the sheer cliff severity that dropped away at a ninety-degree angle from the road, with the mountain range background just helping illustrate how high the elevation and created the wonderful view its moniker proudly boasted.

We negotiated the narrow, barely two-car wide road, that in parts was made more treacherous by small slippery streams that formed due to water cascading down from the lush vegetative side. Other bikers had to be avoided as many other groups participated and was perilous to cycle or bunch too close together, not knowing how the person nearby would react, and when traffic would want to pass, the only safe option was to stop and huddle to the inside of the shrubbery and right-hand cliff face. The varying yet constantly dusty terrain kicked up smouldering dirt clouds from bikes and vehicles, where at times visibility was severely reduced and the air around the face was tantamount to being in a sandstorm, with the only saving grace being the goggles provided and the dust blocking snood covering the nose and mouth; although, sporting such attire did make it look like those involved knew what they were doing and a bit hard core. When the terrain shallowed out, it was possible to pick up more speed, as the roads had longer, straighter stretches with less severe curves, and now only 40m drops to worry about as we descended further out of the mountains into hot blazing sun. Stu continued to regale us with points of interest whilst waiting for everyone to regroup; notably about one of the very few properties that we had passed; this being a former home and hide out of a Nazi general who fled to Bolivia after defeat in the Second World War.

Some five hours later, we finally completed the trail safe and sound, in and around the close heat and humidity of stifling jungle. A few people had fallen off but with no real damage, only few small cuts and scrapes. My worst incident came when the bike skidded approaching a corner a little too fast; thankfully, I held my nerve and managed to gain control before falling, yet the split second where unintentionally the tyres of the bicycle going out from underneath me, next to a steep drop, was heart-stopping enough to create a mad burst of nerve-jangling adrenaline, that left me with only one slight brown trouser moment.

We were all over the moon about completing as was the guide, because everyone had made it down relatively unscathed. This, in his own words, was purely down to the fact that everyone had listened to his instructions well and took them on board, acting on them when needed, as they had to be told to us prior and not whilst in motion. There were no egos within the group who thought that they knew better; which was usually the reason for many of the accidents and unfortunate fatalities, as many people think they can handle a bike when it's not the bike that needs handling; it's predominantly the unforgiving terrain. The guide had been taking tours down the road for a long time and was adept at handling the bike, the conditions and knew the road like the back of his hand, yet didn't carry an ego either and still had respect for the course, this alone should be enough to tell anyone everything they needed to know regardless of skill level or handling ability, and that was nice to see.

I was really pleased that I chose to cycle down the death road. I found it exciting and breathtaking, both for the physical, unnerving, not knowing what was going to happen next experience and the views alike. The company I used were professional, well-equipped and good fun. They were arguably the most expensive option, but in comparison to what you were paying in British money, this was only about £10 more than other companies; who many were opting for due to the cheaper price. Granted, this was a couple of nights' accommodation and a session on the piss in Bolivia, so it was understandable why people were going for the budget option. But their safety record was excellent. Apparently when the guy went over the edge the month prior, the company whom he cycled with had to wait for these guys to come along and assist, as they never had any of the correct rescue equipment. So what price was death or excruciating injury? Plus, there were other added extras such as having a camera man filming action shots and taking photos of our descent, the dust roll neck snood to keep and 'I survived the world's most dangerous road' t-shirt all included in the price. But for me personally, there was another very good reason and ulterior motive why I wanted to ride with these guys, as their trip also offered something quite unique.

Heading back, we stocked up on some beer in the bus before making our way back; that was disappointingly safer via the new tarmac road. We had a good laugh returning, as inevitably efforts like this act as great team-bonding exercises, allowing people to make new friends and for me like many times before this was no different. Personally, though, I was really pleased with efforts of the twelve cycling. One other person and I completed the whole course, as most opted to get back in the bus supporting us when the tarmac inclines came about early in the day, but I wanted the full hard work and exercise. Making the satisfaction of completing what many may not do, or get to do all the more exhilarating. It was dangerous, but thrilling and enthralling at the same time and essentially all down to the individual riding, as the instructor cannot help you while moving so having concentration, some wits about you and utter respect was paramount. I believe anyone could complete it if approached with the right attitude. It offered once again some stunning views, scenery and completed another 'must do' for my ambitions.

After saying goodbye to the group and to our guide Stu – who at the time I didn't realise how much I was going to get to see. I ventured into the bar of the hostel; tired yet feeling almost triumphant, I was greeted by a chorus of "You're alive!" from the Irish lads Liam and his mate Peter, whom

I had also gotten to know. I proceeded to explain about the day that I'd had and how much fun it all was. This conversation must have happened every day at some point in every bar in La Paz as people returned from their gravity-assisted antics. Yet, I suspect some versions would differ greatly to others; mine though was very positive. As was their response which I particularly liked.

"Hey, when you left last night, we only went on to win the fuckin' quiz! There's free beer over the bar for ya!"

Well, if that just didn't cap off a brilliant day. I had left Liam, Peter and a couple of the girls doing the quiz around eleven p.m. the previous night, chipping in with my fair share of answers. As our team had gone on to win and now being all-too-familiar with the bar staff, they had put my share of drinks behind the bar for me when I returned; top folk. So with this and my day's activity, I proceeded to get royally pissed for the rest of the night, jumping around playing air guitar with the pool cues, and watching while others let off fireworks in the street, where another person staying there nearly set fire to himself, much to the drunken amusement of everyone else. A messy evening in itself that was nearly as perilous as riding down 'the World's Most Dangerous Road'.

Crazy Living at the Explosive Matrix

After the raucous entertainment of the previous night, nothing really happened the next day, as everyone involved tried to get rid of hangovers in the darkened confines of the TV room, watching *Father Ted* and movies in a comatose state. But what was to be my final full day in the hostel the day after proved to be somewhat more productive as Liam, Alison and Mica the two girls who did the quiz, and I headed out into town again, where this time we managed to visit the coca plant museum that provided a fascinating insight learning about the history, native use, medicinal properties and how it came to be used within the multi-national beverage industry, providing a great educational experience regarding this native South American plant that the locals revere as a stimulant even before being derived into the malevolent powder form; cocaine. We looked around plaza Pedro D Murillo and its surrounding buildings including; the cathedral, National Congress and Governmental Palace, noting how some on the outside were riddled with bullet holes from revolutionary days past, while we relaxed in the sun eating ice cream, as the world and pigeons whirled around us before finishing at the National Museum of Art to explore the various sculptures and canvas works of local and indigenous artists.

It was quite the relaxed affair back at the hostel. Peter was on the computers while Liam and I wandered into the bar and ordered early afternoon drinks for what turned out to be a seminal moment; one of those 'do you remember where you were when?' happened. Peter burst into the bar and left everyone dumbstruck by shouting at the top of his voice, "Quick, get the TV on; Michael Jackson's dead!"

Liam and I just turned around looking at him with a 'started on the sauce early, have you?' expression on our faces.

"He fuckin' is! Get the TV on!" he continued before running out of the bar back to the computer. Not quite believing what we had just heard, we had the TV put on behind the bar; where indeed CNN had the breaking news that Michael Jackson had been found unconscious and not breathing. Again, I'm no doctor, but that indicated to me that there might have been some validity in what our outspoken friend might've be alluding to. So that was us set for the rest of the day, in the bar with the hot topic of conversation to anyone who entered, before somehow, we ended up inexplicably drunk, with free shots being dished out to ensure playing air guitar with the pool cues again to 'I Bet You Look Good on the Dancefloor' where somehow the pool table itself evolved to become the impromptu dancefloor; much to the displeasure of the owners. There was a brilliant crowd at the hostel and it was far too easy to keep getting pissed up in the bar, as a few drinks inevitably turned into mad sessions amongst friends, with a quite addictive atmosphere that just grew and grew. Unfortunately, though, all good things have to end and the next day just before the weekend, I had made plans to head out.

Still very much wanting to experience working in another rescue facility, I had been put onto a contact of where this was possible but hadn't had much luck getting a response, probably due to the short time available from when I wanted to arrive, but more so what also appeared to be an issue was the amount of time required for a commitment period, which was two to four weeks depending on the types of animals being cared for. It wasn't looking too promising as time was now pressing on and I had put my flight back for the final time and set my return to the UK and it left me a total of seven weeks remaining. Although this sounded plenty, I was powering through, trying to cram as much in as possible, fitting in everything in Bolivia and still had to get to Rio de Janeiro with a bunch of stuff to do in between, so it was pretty much now or never.

Fortune once again, though, disguised itself in another form. The other reason for booking the mountain biking with this particular company was because it came with a surprising bonus. Upon finishing the 'Death Road', we spent a couple of hours in the afternoon at a wildlife rescue centre; just on the outskirts of Coroico. They were the only biking company who worked in conjunction with the refuge, and were allowed to use the facilities there to chill out and recoup, whilst being fed and having a couple of beers after the days downhill drama. Interaction with the animals was also actively encouraged and I immediately got a good vibe from the place. After having chatted with some of the volunteers while there, I found out that I could also volunteer, which I was more than willing to do. So, I got the email address of the owner and she kindly agreed to let me help out for a week or so as I already had experience in a similar environment; otherwise, there was the familiar two-week minimum. I was elated, so I packed my things and headed up over the cordilleras once more for another stint of helping care for some animals and couldn't wait to get started.

Here was smaller in comparison to the one in Ecuador, but nevertheless just as beautiful. Predominantly situated in the middle of a river system, at the end of the valley that the Cordilleras range formed with heaving mountains either side, enshrouded by many trees, out of the way and somewhat secluded from other civilisation; with a ten minute car ride to the nearby town of Coroico. The location created a beautiful, peaceful and idyllic setting. The place seemed to be broken up into three parts; entering over a wooden bridge that crossed the river and walking through the winding tree-encrusted pathway, the space opened up to a large grass field, where there were cabins for people to stay in and dorm residencies for volunteers, plus another larger building that was in the middle of construction to be used as rest and living area for future visitors. Following the path around to the right, there were open areas on both sides and two buildings further on. The one on the left was showering and changing facilities. On the right, a wooden frame structure that was the communal dining and seating area for staff, volunteers and guests, which was covered in mesh to keep the more familiar 'guests' out. Following the path along through the trees, another wooden bridge crossed a smaller subsidiary stream which ran around the back of the complex to meet with the main river and a pathway led up to the owner's house, swimming pool and rest area.

Here, they cared for primates such as capuchin, spider and squirrel monkeys which I had worked with in the past, but also another species; a brilliantly auburn howler monkey, instantly recognisable when making an absolute racket from up in the trees. And again the familiar coatis, many more macaws and parrots plus other varieties of bird including guinea fowl and ducks, also snakes, rabbits, guinea pigs, tortoises, cats and dogs thrown into the mix and all living together in harmony; well, most of the time. There were less species of animals than previous, but more of the similar types to what I was used to working with and enticingly those that I hadn't encountered before.

As well as a lesser variety of species, in comparison to Ecuador, here also included other differences; despite the smaller premises there were more staff both permanent and voluntary, working to keep an eye on events and what was happening on a day-to-day basis, plus guests were not allowed to just turn up for a look around, they had to pre-book in advance to enter or stay. Therefore due to these factors, this allowed for more of the animals to roam free at will; the exceptions being that most of the smaller birds and parrots were in cages, the tortoises in a designated pen and the adult capuchin monkeys, although not in cages, were tethered on long running lines bar one noticeably larger alpha male who was caged for the protection of some of the smaller monkeys – all in a separate space that only people working there were allowed to enter.

Understandably the operational differences and the daily routines of how the animals were cared were the most obvious. Here there were no designated days off as these were just agreed with the owner at their discretion; for me, this wasn't an issue, being I was only going to be there for a relatively short period anyway. Days, again, started at eight a.m. but the animals were fed straightaway. This was usually a quick operation as volunteers would split into two groups; one taking care of feeding the birds and wandering animals by chopping fresh fruit and distributing it with seeds around the grounds, while also providing vegetables for the tortoises, rabbits and guinea pigs and feeding the cats and dogs. The second group, would head to see owners Marco and Vivienne; a lovely Bolivian couple who lived on site as they prepared morning porridge for each variety of monkey. The tethered capuchins were easy enough as food was placed in their area but those roaming free like the spider monkeys proved slightly more difficulty, having to try ensure that each had enough to eat and none were left out, because feeding would sometimes turn into a frenzy despite portions being on enough designated bowls; this could cause havoc and the proverbial chimps tea party would ensue, where food would end up everywhere. But we couldn't and shouldn't expect anything less really.

Feeding amounts were smaller but would happen three times a day at breakfast, lunch and dinner. After every three days, the volunteers would then swap around to add variation to the days and allow for experience dealing with all the animals, another thing I was fine with not really having a preference which I dealt with, being there to gain experience and help wherever was needed. After each feeding session, the volunteers could eat. All meals during the day for either human or animal alike were prepared in the kitchen by the locals who worked there. In total, there was around seven full-time staff including the owners, and during the time I was present there ranged anywhere from six to ten volunteers, as people came and went throughout. Other set duties included the clean down of the animal stations after each of the feeding times and involved picking up any debris, crap and included the compulsory wash and scrub routine.

It was possible to locate someone nearly all the time here. Whether local worker or volunteer, this made operations and finding things out that much easier. But with more animals running around freely, this inevitably made things more interesting and unexpected. During the course of the day, the spider monkeys would come along making sweet *cooing* noises, hold your hand and want some interaction that would generally mean they would climb all over you, which was fun as they were very playful and not at all intimidating with their slender frame, long limbs and friendly calm nature, but this also seemed to double up as a cunning ruse and nothing short of a distraction technique just so they could try to make their way to the communal building with the promise of food on the agenda, causing a constant running battle to keep them out of the kitchen and dining area. And this wasn't just confined to here.

This was especially difficult at around four p.m. as part of the volunteer duties, the 'Death Road' cyclists would arrive as had I previously; they would be given a beer and briefed about the place, with what was to be expected and the regulations they were to adhere to, such as; you will get jumped on, don't have loose things about you that you don't want to lose and don't feed the animals, to name a few. But now, it was me giving the briefing with the others and usually when in full oratory flow; curiosity would overcome Osico the coati and as if by clockwork he would appear from nowhere and start rummaging through guests' bags, much to the amusement of those who had arrived. The bike company were easy to work with in this respect and I got to know some of the other instructors, as well as seeing Stu again a couple of times and they never rested on their laurels and responsibilities whist at the resort, helping ensure the cyclists abided by the rules and what was asked, as they all understood the importance of the place and what it was trying to achieve.

But where there are people and animals, there is potential for chaos and here was no exception; the main entrance doors to the changing rooms and shower cubicles would normally be locked during the day, but these were opened when the 'Death Road' cyclists arrived to offer the chance of getting washed and refreshed. The spider monkeys were all too well aware of this, and somehow seemed to make an art form of slipping past whoever was guarding the doors, thinking nothing of running in either male or female changing area for a good old nosey to see what was being paraded around while people were getting showered. Most people would see the funny side of getting cleaned up in the presence of a pervy primate. A volunteer would have to chase in after them and bring them out by the hand, telling them off like a naughty child. This would happen at least once a day.

Not like Osico and his mischievous ways, he was a full-time regular nuisance. Limon the older golden retriever was really lovely and timid and would often lie down to relax in his dotage. Unfortunately, though, this was 'a red rag to a bull' allowing randy little Osico the chance to come charging over to him, start biting his ears and humping his head. He would literally have to be dragged off Limon at least six times a day and be taken away much to his displeasure; so much so, he would instantly come running back for more, no matter how far away you would put him. The others and I found ourselves being bitten on more than one occasion by him for our efforts protecting poor old Limon. Even to the extent that if you weren't paying attention, he would happily bite you just to let you know he was there and 'a bit of twat'. I liked Osico though; he made the days interesting, as you just didn't know what he would be up to next and I found him just a bored, misunderstood, sex pest coati.

Even so, anarchy wasn't just confined to monkeys with a desire to see naked people and a sexually confused coati; at times, we would find parrots climbing on the inside of the mesh of the kitchen dining area, having somehow negotiated their way through constantly shut doors and would have to get a branch for them to perch on, so they could be removed back outside. There was a macaw who people had to be warned about when walking past because they were protecting a covered egg and viewed anyone close by as a threat; therefore, toes on show became prime pickings for the razor-sharp bill. It was amazing fun though and helping out really did require having eyes in the back of the head. I was really impressed by the team ethos again and those both working and volunteering were good fun and easy to get along with as were the kitchen staff and regular, full-time employees. It was actually mid-week though before I finally managed to actually meet Vivienne the owner. She had been away on business when I arrived but told the others that I was arriving; she was lovely, warm and friendly like Marco, her husband. It was brilliant to finally meet her and put name to a face; especially after having the pleasure of looking after her 'baby' before I even met her.

There were two private areas that were not open to general viewing; the first was behind the owner's house where they had a large cage with a margay inside – again due to the teeth, claws and volatile nature, we never dealt with him and Marco looked after on his own. The other was out the back of the homes of the employees who lived on site and over the stream. Hidden behind the bushes was an electric wire fence that headed off up the forested hill and into the trees. This was where Aruma lived. He was Vivienne's 'baby'. Only open to viewing for visitors with permission and accompanied by volunteers, although to be honest, it seemed to happen quite often. I had started looking after Aruma when asked by Keith, one of the other volunteers there.

"Do you want to help me feed the bear?"

"Bear? What bear? Have we got a bear?"

Aruma was a spectacled Andean bear and after preparing his morning feed, we headed to a part of the site that I didn't even know existed. Approaching the fence, we called his name. Almost immediately, the trees started moving and rustling, he could be heard but it was hard to see, eventually making out a big, dark object balancing out on a branch that had no right holding the weight it did, as it looked almost ready to snap. Food on the morning was usually some jam and bread, fruit, a whole coconut, a few full heads of corn and with good reason a load of peanuts. Hearing voices, with great cumbersome dexterity he would swiftly appear from his leafy abode and come over. It was a two-man job feeding him; the coconut and corn would be thrown around the enclosure for him to rummage around for and find over the rest of the day. One would swiftly go in, clean his covered patio feeding area, by taking in water from the stream to wash and scrub any food debris and big turds that were there, then leave his jam and bread and fruits to eat for breakfast or porridge with an egg in at dinner. After which, the person inside would make a hasty retreat, all while the other outside would cause a distraction by feeding him bear 'candies', otherwise known as peanuts.

As there were plenty of volunteers, generally Keith and I would feed Aruma first then join up with the others. This was my favourite part of the day. Aruma was absolutely beautiful. He had been rescued from the black market in La Paz when he was two months old, and been literally given a new life here where he was now a healthy two-year-old. Not that you could tell; I thought he was older because he was big. Standing on his hind legs, he towered over my 5'10" frame. It was an amazing, unique experience getting to look after and feed him. Putting my hand through the mild electric fence just enough so that his wet nose didn't touch the wires, so he could sit and happily munch peanut after peanut, taking them daintily from fingers through the wire, holding them in his massive, sharp, powerful claws that looked brutal. It was evident that with one swipe, any man wouldn't really stand a chance. His size alone meant he was more than capable of harm. It was quite the nerve-wracking operation when in his pen and we had to quickly clean up and put down his feed, all the while hoping that he was being kept preoccupied enough. There was lots of communication going on between distracter and the one in the pen without too much being said. No one would want to be caught by him in his territory; he wasn't a pet and demanded respect through the simple fact he was a bear. He was very placid though and wasn't at all aggressive when being fed, probably through being used to humans and he would always come over to see people; many of the visitors with us were given the chance of feeding him peanuts too, which after some coercing due to his intimidating size, they loved and I was pleased that they also got to appreciate a unique opportunity and see how fantastic he was.

Quickly, I was finding out that there was always something to do in these types of places, when not feeding, cleaning, looking after visiting cyclists or generally keeping the animals in check. Some of the others were refurbishing a foosball table, which I helped with until proceedings came to a grinding halt as we were missing a vital part – the pitch – and couldn't find a piece of hardboard or wood to fit which made the project pretty much redundant until that was rectified.

Feeling the need to keep busy, I moved on to another project that some had again already started; many signs needed attention and placing in situ around the site when done. So with some help, we spent a few days redrawing, painting and varnishing notices of what the animals were, instructions, warnings and general information, before spending a further two days armed with various tools wandering around the site, digging holes, erecting, hanging and nailing the new signs in the correct place, before finally then taking some remaining paint to spruce up and highlight the information that had faded on existing ones. A job not as easy as it seemed on paper; due to the spider monkeys coming over abound with curiosity to what was happening and stopping proceedings before they could grab the paint and create an unholy mess. As I really didn't fancy explaining to Vivienne and Marco why Wara and Sambo were looking like me at a full moon party and now requiring a shower for real! Upon finishing, I was really quite proud of my efforts. I had some help making and reconditioning notices but put the vast majority of the fifteen or so I put in place myself. It felt good to stand back and appreciate the fruits of the labour. Also, Vivienne and Marco saw the work done and were pleased and grateful, saying a hearty 'thank you' that made me feel good and only helped confirm how nice, kind, warm and appreciative people they were.

The days were long, but they went quickly and were seldom boring. We would generally finish around six p.m. after patrons had left and the animals were fed, taking a spot of downtime and having a kick around with a football to exercise the dogs, before cleaning up to get ready for dinner, then spending the nights relaxing over few beers laughing about the day's activities while playing cards. The other volunteers were from various parts of the world while I was there; made up of Americans, Aussies, Canadians, Israelis and Brits. They were a kind, friendly group who all brought something to the proceedings and were a pleasure to work with as it was good to have such freely available help on a large scale.

Obviously, there were a few annoyances and nervy moments which had to be dealt with. A few days in, I contracted an eye infection that I hoped wasn't anything too bad, as my right eye was swollen red, sore and continually ran. Thankfully, this cleared up after a couple of days and I was OK, but right from the off the sand flies were a nightmare, their bites leaving incredibly itchy red blisters that took an age to clear and I could only use less-effective Deet free insect repellent so as not to harm the animals with chemicals, but on the plus side we were provided with uniforms shirts that covered the arms which helped, if only to ensure clothes didn't get filthy like before. As far as the animals went, I didn't have many problems. Escaping wasn't really an issue here, as many were roaming free, much like the local dogs who I managed to have a run in with when on a walk to the nearby shop, as one tried to bite my leg, only to move out of the way just in time, leaving a puncture mark through my long trousers. Also peanuts weren't cutting it one day distracting Aruma, and I had to get Keith out of the feed area quickly before he decided enough was enough about having someone in his territory, and a similar fate for myself with the one of the larger male capuchin monkeys that charged at me with wild eyes during feeding, only for it to be stopped in its tracks by the tether a matter of a foot away; a close call. But that was the point. They would be territorial and aggressive in the wild, so why not here? Again, they weren't pets and many had come from brutal backgrounds, where they been subject to many forms of cruelty, leaving them psychologically damaged and not trusting humans. At least now, they had a chance to recover in a safe, environment away from harm. Which was the main purpose to rehabilitate them as naturally as possible, not condition them as pets, so it was important to have your wits about you at all times, as certain instances could be quite dangerous. Despite these, though, there was nothing as disturbing as a capuchin monkey looking at you, with a big cheesy grin on its face, eyes wide open and motioning its eyebrows up and down while on heat. Now that's more unnerving than any raging animal.

My time to leave again came around all too quickly. I actually stayed longer than anticipated. This in part caused by not passing the opportunity to have a bonding night out with the other volunteers in Coroico on Saturday evening, at a concert in the local stadium watching bands perform. It was an awesome ten days total, having a brilliant time experiencing a different animal rescue centre's operation, which still encompassed the exact same goals and ethos that had enamoured me before; the presiding care and welfare of vulnerable, abused, harmed or mistreated animals who were now safe. It was heart-warming to see that people like Vivienne and Marco cared so much; along with the other staff and volunteers who carried out the daily tasks with the same passion and verve that they possessed, it was an infectious feeling and I was proud to have helped out and done my bit.

Honestly, I didn't have a preference between each rescue centre. It would be unfair to pick one as both were special to me in their own way. The circumstances of each place and daily operations was the main difference, but both set out to achieve the same goals and objectives; which they both successfully did, so having thought about this question, it became somewhat irrelevant. It was apparent that here was more established and money from volunteer and other contributions had been spent well. Not only that, but each were set up to provide a source of income to locals and education to the community, which was equally important if a place as such was to survive and thrive. The different perspective it provided me, I hoped, would stand me in good stead for the future, as I would love to get another opportunity to work at such a place, to meet other like-minded interesting people and help by donating a little money, time and effort to help protect and conserve the wonderful creatures cared for.

I spoke to Vivienne when I was leaving and explained how much I loved it here and had an amazing, rewarding time, especially finding out about the place by accident; only wishing it could have been longer and again promising to return, if only to live in the best accommodation I'd had yet. Due to the amount of volunteers, there weren't any beds available in the dorm when I arrived; so, I spent the ten days living in a purpose-built tree house and when beds did become available, I didn't want to move out of anyway, because it was so incredibly cool. Each day, I would walk up the embankment trail towards the back of the site, cross a slated rope bridge to reach my peaceful dwelling, expertly crafted into a large tree some five metres from the ground; there wasn't much inside but a couple of bunk beds, and a large window allowed light to stream inside to fully appreciate the view of where I was. This easily provided enough for the experience of living somewhere that was both amazing and unique. Little realising, it wouldn't take long before my living arrangements were to again become as equally unorthodox.

Vivienne, in turn, was very gracious and thankful, asking me to stay longer, but I really couldn't. It was a shame but unfortunately, I had to say my goodbyes to her and the other volunteers, knowing that I was going to miss everyone, the place and the animals, particularly Aruma, who was also the best animal that I'd had the privilege to work with. I caught up with Stu and he let me get a lift with that days' biking group in the bus back to La Paz.

I laughed as it reminded me about the time I left there, after I had biked. I almost forgot to pay my beer tab. The others from the group saying how they "couldn't believe that I was going to run out on an animal refuge centre when they need the money!" and "I'd have gotten away with it if it wasn't for you meddling kids" my retort, sensing the piss-taking tone. It was a genuine mistake and I did forget, but definitely not this time. I paid in full for the accommodation and the large tab accrued from drinking beer and pop over the space of ten days, and I made my return back to La Paz. But I had the unexpected 'bonus' of having to cope with barrier-less 400m drops from the road side as the bus swerved mercilessly close to the contours of the mountain edge, this time taking the 'Death Road' back. So, I managed to revisit the desperate route that never occurred to me I would get to endure again; albeit, this time being able to admire the views and peer over the too-close-for-comfort edge, from the confines of the mini-van window where the only saving grace was putting all faith and hope in the skills of our steely nerved intrepid driver.

La Paz was a night and day fleeting visit to catch up with a few friends who were still there and not doing a lot; with the predominant reason being to book my next engagement. After doing so, I then took another night bus to get me to Uyuni, where I could then get to experience another amazing natural wonder that had me intrigued and excited.

Uyuni was at a slightly higher elevation than La Paz; so when I arrived tired after a bumpy, dark, cold journey with minimal sleep, I was feeling somewhat cranky and unenthused at six a.m. Not helping matters, it was also freezing cold, my llama wool sweater amongst the many layers was indeed now a shrewd investment while I waited in a little tea room at the bus stop, till the tour operator opened some three hours later. At least, I was able to get warm and have a hot beverage while I engaged in more seemingly endless time sitting around waiting; probably the one singular activity that I had participated in more than any other when travelling. Eventually, I was met by a representative of the company and went to the office, where I was able to leave my bags, get some breakfast and invest in some gloves that were a godsend.

At eleven a.m., the Land Cruiser that we were to spend the next three days touring in arrived; already on board were five Spanish friends who had also booked the tour. Although I wasn't fluent, I now could get by with Spanish and try my level best to communicate with them. The thing was, though, their actual Spanish sounded different to South American Spanish, which in turn differed still from country to country; so where I would learn one set of words and get used to an accent, this would change with the crossing of a border and would leave me confused, not to mention the person who I was trying to talk to. But when in Rome, I persevered and obliged with trying to speaking the lingo as I still needed to practise, but was helped out by some of those who could speak a little English when needed.

They seemed like a nice group and I was happy to be on board. But I was still feeling tired and slightly run down, so was quiet as we set off to tour the unique salt flats. First stop was early at a train grave yard situated on the outskirts of the town. Fortunately, this involved a bit of group interaction as we were able to clamber all over and inside the rusting masses; the steam locomotives were huge, covered in graffiti and left there from an industrial time long finished with the potential to be quite dangerous, as slipping off the smoothed weather-worn metal of the chamber and falling a very real possibility. There was no way this would be allowed in Britain; the health and safety officer would have another heart attack (having had numerous already with some of the things I'd been up to and how they were carried out), as many people balanced on top of the trains posing elaborately for photos. This was actually quite good as the interaction instantly started to bring us as a group together more and I liked it, before we set out along the dusty track roads out of town. We stopped on the edge of the Salar for a brief look around the museum of elaborate salt carvings and indigenous arts and crafts that were on sale; we then headed off into the vastness.

I had heard much about the 'Uyuni salt flat' or Salar de Uyuni, from the many people who I had spoken to on the way to getting here and had to see it for myself; as the conversations had left me baffled and intrigued by some of the descriptions. The simplicity of what surrounded us was easy to describe yet hard to comprehend. After speeding for miles in the Jeep, we got out and stepped onto the flat salt desert that had formed after a prehistoric lake dried up. For miles in every direction as far as the eye could see, there was uninterrupted nothing. A brilliant flat white blanket of nothing; far off into the distance on the horizon, the white stopped and changed to a vivid blue from the cloudless sky, which allowed the unobstructed sun to radiate everywhere, giving an intense gleaming reflection of light off the harsh, coarse surface. This had to be seen and experienced to be believed. Never mind stepping into another world, it was more like stepping into another dimension and probably the nearest actual thing on Earth to being in a matrix where all reality is removed. Humans are conditioned to constantly having objects around their persona, from birth throughout the course of a daily existence, but this was something else; a wonderful surreal sensation of vast nothing, except for flat white earth and open blue sky that strangely felt energising being here in a true natural wonder. The fabulous two-tone backdrop provided excellent photo opportunities. Everyone started to experiment with perspective, creating

442

awesome illusionary images of being able to hold a small person in the palm of the hands of a giant; by posing uninterrupted both near and far from the lens. I was already delighted that I had come here and we had only just started.

Pressing on, we drove further for hours into the wilderness before eventually on the horizon a small dot increased in size to reveal the large rock; La Isla de los Pescadores protruded out of the white plateau like an island in an ocean. We were then given an opportunity to explore along the trails around the craggy mass, decorated with enormous cactus that looked like huge aerial antenna easily towering over twice that of a human. Due to the perspective and nothing for the brain to compare it to, the (fisherman's) island was much bigger than it actually looked and from the very top allowed a brilliant shimmering view, where white hazed to blue from the rising heat, creating what looked like an evaporated shoreline. We took lunch here prepared by our guide and driver Juan and had the chance to sample llama meat for the first time, which was incredibly tender and flavoursome, considering it had been prepared in an oasis in the middle of nowhere.

After driving for some time during the course of the afternoon, we arrived at our hotel for the evening just before dusk. This was just off the salt flat plain in a town of small dwellings. There was one thing unique about this place as it wasn't a conventional hotel, because it was made entirely from salt.

Floor, walls, furniture, everything all cut from huge blocks except the fixtures and fittings. We had stopped at a previous 'salt hotel' actually on the flats that I had read about, but being an illegal structure refrained from using the facilities. So, I was happy that we had come to this recently built and not yet fully finished one to stay overnight, experiencing the surreal surroundings of walking around the off-white decor that created the illusion that it was icy and frozen over inside and handed me yet another strange, unconventional abode in a matter of days.

Here, Juan once again played master chef after we had been outside to witness the amazing striated red sunset over the silhouetted mountains. We ate dinner and all chipped in to buy wine, relaxing with others from different groups by candlelight, as the electricity had gone off, before going to sleep on our blocks of salt; layered with masses of blankets to make surprisingly warm and comfortable beds. Despite the sun, it was still very cold due to the elevation and on the evenings, this was even more apparent; wrapping up with layer upon layer and getting in the borrowed sleeping bag allowed for a good night's sleep, still feeling the effects from the previous night's bus journey.

In the morning, though, despite a decent night's sleep and rest, my stomach felt bad with a sickly churning sensation and I was barely able to hold anything in at both ends; and now I had definitely picked up a bug of some sorts. My relentless tiring exploits had started leaving me vulnerable to infections; like in my eye, which I suspected was a virus working its way through my system, leaving me feeling more and more run down. So, I ate a very minimal breakfast that I could keep inside, and took some diarrhoea tablets to block me up, because being this way created an unfortunate predicament; feeling nauseous, having the shits and being in a Jeep all day with total strangers. Friends would be bad enough.

The second day was much more of a stop – start affair, as we now crossed the rugged tracks of the harsh, barren, flat landscape to get up to the surrounding mountains. Here, we appreciated driving around and exploring dormant volcano sights that had left large precipices to clamber up and borax enriched Laguna Colorada, which was an obscure shade of red and brown from the sunlight that not only altered the water colour, but in turn the perception of how unnatural it looked. Yet, it still attracted a huge flock of wild flamingos that stood gracefully in the waters; their plumage apparently turned pink from the mineralised water as they waded and bathed together, a remarkable sight having never actually seen these birds in their natural habitat where en mass they created a beautiful, welcome addition to events. The terrain changed to a more conventional, desolate desert, powering up and over the large dunes that were scarred with wind-addled symmetrical lines, and explored strange rock formations and petrified trees that had been sand-blasted over time into forming unconventional, obscure, twisted masses as the set mountains in the background transformed from one shade of rock colour to another that added depth to a naturally unnatural landscape. It was wonderfully beautiful, where my surroundings were nothing like I had ever seen or witnessed before and felt like we had entered a walk-in surrealist installation that any artist would have been proud just to envisage. Before sunset, we reached our destination for the evening; a hostel in a tiny little village high up in the mountains, where we again ate and huddled around a fire in the quarters, keeping ourselves warm against the biting cold night air.

Five a.m. in the morning, it was still dark and absolutely freezing cold when we got up, as any accrued body heat rapidly escaped when rising from a well-wrapped sleep and was just before dawn when we arrived at our first stop; Sol de Mañana – an incredibly noisy, steaming geyser that blasted pressurised gas high into the air from the ground that dispelled as quickly as it was momentarily blown out, but despite the seeming ferocity, it wasn't hot, so I couldn't resist the opportunity to have my photo taken with my hand in it when erupting. We carefully explored the area of muddy pools and lakes, as the stench of sulphur saturated the air that reminded me of Rotorua when it bubbled up from within, as light started to break over another of our otherworldly landscape settings. Moving on, we weren't finished with nature's thermal wonders, as a new sun highlighted the haze of our morning bath, taking the opportunity to strip off and submerge in some of the natural, hot water springs close by. This warmed and invigorated against the freezing crisp surrounding air, causing steam to rise tantalisingly enhancing the beauty of a rising sun behind the dark, leeward mountain backdrop. After a twenty-minute soothing soak, we got out and hastily dried off, putting many layers back on in record speed to counter against a plummeting body temperature, before taking a still early breakfast in a nearby cabin.

Surrounded by mountains and volcanoes, Laguna Verde was the last point of call; a lake with a dazzling green hue to it where we took time to appreciate the scenery and take some last photos together as now, we were very near the Chilean border. Unfortunately, I had to say goodbye to the Spanish guys as they continued their journey into Chile and I was staying in Bolivia. They were a really nice, welcoming, friendly group and I appreciated the chance to improve my Spanish with them, which they helped with via the modem of rock band Maná on the stereo that I had been introduced to some time ago in Ecuador; they were a great bunch and I was happy to have met them. I now had the prospect of a day travel back in the van with just me and Juan; or so I thought.

Back at the hostel we stayed at the previous night, we took lunch. Before setting off, a friend of Juan's joined us for a lift back to Uyuni with her baby. We took a different route back driving through the mountains, indigenous villages and large open plains, where we could witness local wild life of llamas, ostriches and the somewhat disturbing sight of a donkey that had collapsed by the roadside, where all that remained was a propped-up decomposed skeleton of the beast, testament to the harsh arid landscape we traversed. We then stopped to pick up a mother and her two daughters and I couldn't quite believe what was happening as I didn't realise that we were running a local bus service and could feel myself becoming annoyed at seemingly being taken advantage of by not being told or consulted about this and then even more so as the baby started to wail and cry relentlessly; each screech cut through the ears, body and soul, increasing the angst within that created a frustrating situation where nothing could be helped or done.

We stopped off in the dusty little town of San Cristóbal and I was relieved to get out of the Jeep for some respite, while Juan refuelled by standing on the roof rack from where the fuel was being carried. I offered to help but he said, 'No, it's OK.' So, I just watched as he used gravity to dispense the gas and thought to myself, *that's just how it's done here.* Oddly, that statement helped me get my head around what was happening; having a Jeep full of people that hadn't paid and a wailing infant, it put things into perspective. I was lucky, very lucky. These people were not going to get the chance to see or do any of the things that I had, they were poor people with hard difficult lives, in comparison to my relatively pampered existence. And I felt ashamed and bad for my thought process. Had I not learnt anything? We were helping them out with a kind deed and we should; because we could. What was it costing me? Nothing; except a minor inconvenience, if that. We were providing assistance to people less fortunate, with no real means of infrastructure or funds to get about to where they wanted or needed to go. So, I came to the realisation that it wasn't a big deal and be happy to help my fellow man; particularly because it wasn't me deciding the terms of how and when to offer assistance, so I should appreciate another person giving a helping hand, be happy to help in some small way and stop being a self-absorbed arsehole. This became more apparent when we arrived back in Uyuni where the people got out of the Jeep and said 'Thank you' to both Juan and I with big smiles on appreciative faces – which was really nice and endearing and left me hoping that I had learnt a lesson. Especially when putting things further into perspective, I should've just been glad that I didn't actually shit my pants over the course of the three days.

Not making any excuses but my physical well-being wasn't helping matters. I'd definitely picked up a stomach bug of some sort and the food I ate waiting for my bus left me feeling nauseous. This seemed a vicious circle. Tiredness and fatigue was causing my immune system to weaken, yet I could hardly eat anything, let alone keep it in and irritation again wasn't far away; finding myself annoyed and frustrated when out of the blue a small child kicked me in the leg while waiting to enquire about bus ticket. The ticketing agent and kid's mum couldn't have cared less. I just bit my tongue and walked away to be stared at relentlessly by locals, when finally getting tickets from another agent instead. This had happened lots of times previously and never bothered me before as it was to be expected; the rich random white guy shuffling around lesser known parts of the world. But now looking almost ghostly in a drained forlorn state in the outback of Bolivia, I was going to be stared at, but this time it just left me feeling like I wanted to tell everyone to fuck off and leave me alone. Getting on the bus, I tried to chill out and relax but couldn't relax so much as to fart, because it wouldn't end well.

The Jeep tour of the salt flats was amazing, and was so exhilarating to see that many different, natural wonders in such a small space of time, and arguably the most diverse I had seen in one go. This made the journey more than worthwhile; plus the group I was with only added to the experience. But after travelling pretty much relentlessly for around ten-and-a-half months, and with all that I had done physically, it was taking its toll. With the eye infection that I think had moved through body system to the stomach, plus tiredness, I wondered how much more I could take. Before leaving, I never once envisaged that I would've done or accomplished so much. That said, I never expected to be in Bolivia. But with the way that I was feeling and Bolivia being one of the poorer nations in South America, I was finding it a hard slog to travel through with bumpy dirt track roads, cramped buses, high altitude, blistering sun and freezing night temperatures to name a few issues, but more positively I was still determined now more than ever and wanted to make the most out of the dwindling days left and still cram in as much as possible and didn't care if it killed me. Good attitude to adopt really because at my next point of call, there was the possibility that it could do just that.

One of the first nights out in Beijing, I met an Aussie lad who showed me photos of some Bolivian mines that he had visited. At the time, I thought that I would love to do that, but also at the time I never imagined that I was going to get the chance. Now the chance was handed to me on a plate, and as part of that there was something in particular that I wanted to do as a stunt which could look pretty cool; provided, it didn't go wrong.

Arriving really early in the morning, Potosí was a desolate ghost town, understandable, considering the only things it was really renowned for were the mining industry and the altitude of 4060m, making it one of if not *the* highest city in the world. Getting a cab to the hostel that I'd managed to book, I was ushered to a room and told the wrong bed by a disgruntled, clearly pissed off to be rudely woken night porter, before eventually collapsing into a less-occupied bed to swiftly fall asleep. But, I found myself waking on numerous occasions only to make a mad dash for the toilet. This continued till the afternoon when completely empty, hunger got the better of me, so I eventually managed to wander into the town, in search of some small sustenance to try and keep inside for more than thirty seconds; while having a brief look about the small, narrow, cobbled streets and colonial architecture of the city centre. It was a Sunday and quiet, I managed to eat a little yet was still unenthused and none too clever, so I returned to the hostel to recuperate more. But I did manage to book myself on a tour of the working mines which was what I was there to do, hoping that I would feel better the next day.

After plenty of rest, I was up early and reserved a place on the bus for the evening; more importantly, I was feeling much better but still took some diarrhoea tablets just to be on the safe side before the bus came around to pick me up along with others to go to the mines. After meeting our guide, we went to the office and got equipped with jump suit, hard hat, boots and head light. Suitably geared up, we headed to the local market to buy some supplies; where it was teeming with people going about their Monday morning business, kitted out in similar attire. The supplies purchased were for the working miners who we would meet, as this was an operational mine and it was a given to provide gifts for them in their place of work; these involved the usual cigarettes, chocolate and sodas but also the not-so-usual coca leaves for chewing stimulus along with fuses, detonators and dynamite that we readily purchased as well, like sweets in a sweet shop. We then gave these to the guide. This alone was pretty insane. I don't think I can recall ever being able to buy unrefined cocaine plant leaves, dynamite and the kit and caboodle to make it go boom over the counter before. Nope, haven't done that; probably because sales of such items are illegal everywhere else;

448

being dangerous as fuck.

In the bus, it was obvious where we were headed; the mineral refinery of Cerro Rico or 'Rich Hill', a large, dome-shaped mountain overlooking the city that now apparently resembled a human warren of tunnels on the inside from years of excavation. On arrival, the outside offices were splattered with darkened dried llama blood, done so previously as superstitious offerings for safe and prosperous mining. From here, we were also given final safety instructions about dos and don'ts of being in the mine.

Entering the shaft leading directly into the mine, it was narrow with a low ceiling and we had to bend down continuously while walking over the rusting, narrow trolley tracks, amid the damp and pools of water that had formed, that straightaway signalled the less-than-pleasant conditions to be constantly endured when in here by the miners. There was a statue of a deity where offerings of coca leaves, cigarettes and beaded necklaces had been left to decorate its presence by those who had come down here in exchange for protection and safe passage. The icon wasn't beautiful or ornate as you may expect but grotesque and macabre; this was Tio the underworld god and it was deemed his realm and jurisdiction, so it was him who the miners were to give offerings to within these hellish confines.

Continuing on in the dark further into the mine, the hardhat was coming in exceptionally useful as I found my head banging on the low beams above on more than one occasion, as I crouched and hunched forward, unable to stand up straight, which made running that much more awkward when we had to move quickly to get to a side bay as a full trolley of excavated rock and minerals was being pushed up to the surface. The miners were not stopping, we had to move or get hurt; they didn't care. We'd paid to be there for a tour, so had to be careful and obey the rules, the miners had to be there as it was the main source of income for so many from the region.

We were shown the lines of minerals within the rock that the miners were following to excavate, this included the precious silver; one of the main reasons for the inception of the mines, which led to its and the city's success hundreds of years prior. Unfortunately, though, inside it looked like the methods used were still from the same age, as any form of health and safety seemed non-existent with slippery surfaces, rickety ladders, arcing live electrical wires and most of the work done manually by hand, in dimly lit, unventilated and sweltering conditions for extremely long hours. I could easily feel the effects of being down there within half an hour, sweating

449

profusely and tasting the unsavoury air when attempting to have a go at shovelling some of the rubble as part of the duties, that only amplified the harshness and left the miners laughing, commenting how shit I was at it. Sitting and talking to them emphasised greatly the perilous and torrid conditions that the workers have to endure, where accidents are constantly prevalent and chances of contracting a pulmonary disease from long exposure to the toxic dust and gases is almost guaranteed. In stark contrast to money made, this was far from guaranteed being only what each can excavate. Older, younger, age was not an issue if you were a good worker. We met a boy of fifteen working in there trying to earn some money so that he was able to go to college. Others were there just for the chance to earn to survive. The mine was the only real job opportunity; at times, pay could be good, other times non-existent, it depended on how lucky you were. It portrayed a truly harsh and dangerous existence with no guarantee of survival, let alone reward. It really brought home the extent of brutality and risk that had to be endured by these people, just for themselves and families to get by, with no legislation, union or insurance for protection against the worst-case scenario. It was all or nothing here.

Hand on heart, I can honestly say that I could not work down there; it was horribly dangerous, backbreaking work with minimal chance of big money. Having been in there for only two hours was easily enough to convince me of this. I'm not claustrophobic nor suffer from asthma or the like, but just witnessing the conditions was enough to leave me once again thankful for the luck and privilege I'd had bestowed on me of being where I was from and left me feeling a great respect and empathy for those who have to work in there despite the conditions, with it being the only real means to make a living and pay their way in life, having little to no other options available. A harrowing, thought-provoking experience to witness.

Coming out of the mine, eyes squinted with dazzling bright light of the sun and everyone agreed how good but in a bad way, the tour was and left everyone touched with the same empathy. Next on the agenda was an active demonstration, but there was a problem, as our guide didn't want to head to the designated area to show how dynamite was primed and detonated, quoting that it was against his principles as too much dynamite was set off around the place. This was odd as it was advertised as part of the itinerary and he initially asked if we had the aforementioned articles, which he knew we didn't because he had donated the dynamite, fuses and detonators we bought to the miners. No one was happy with this turn of events as his principles were not indicated prior to starting out. Arriving back at the office, we changed back into our clothing and ended up compromising that if we bought one more stick of dynamite, a fuse and a detonator, then one of his co-workers would take us to carry out the explosion for a small tip. So, it was agreed. I couldn't fathom exactly where the guide was coming from with this, as he seemed to contradict himself somewhat with what he said and his actions. But during the tour, his attitude changed after shouting at a girl on the tour at least twice; for not running fast when instructed to and for nearly falling on a ladder. He was swearing and becoming more rude and disrespectful afterwards, seemingly directing frustrations at all there; quoting how his reputation was on the line (not that we knew what his reputation was because the miners working there were taking the piss out of him) but shouting "I don't give a fuck about you" during his rant to the poor girl was unnecessary. This was a shame especially as nothing bad actually happened and he made the tour more about him, which provided the one downside to an insightful, eye-opening, real-life tour.

So, one of his cohorts of his took us out instead. We headed out of town and up to a hillside view of the city, arriving atop of a flat, massive mound of gravel. The dynamite was primed by breaking it into smaller pieces, packing it together and adding the detonator; the fuse was about a metre in length and then lit. Giving around two-and-a-half minutes with cameras at the ready, we hastily had it passed around to whoever wanted to hold it and have their photo taken. Something which; I of course, did. The fuse *crackled* menacingly as I wished my photographer be quick about pressing button. Not stopping to check to see if the picture was OK, I swiftly passed the deadly item back to the guide. When everyone had pictures done, he scurried about 20m away towards the edge of the mound and placed the primed package in a small hole in the ground. We waited with cameras on video for about a further thirty seconds.

BANG! A sharp, loud din reverberated around us, the trees and out over the city from our elevated level, disrupting a small plume of smoke and gravel about 10m into the air as the device went off after what seemed like an age. And that was it. Wasn't cover-the-ears-extremely-loud and certainly no worse than any large firework, but it was enough to tell you not to be in the way, and was exciting waiting with the anticipation of not knowing the extent of how big the explosion was going to be and exactly when. Not to mention, holding it just prior; this wasn't a kids' toy, it was deadly, dangerous, primed and lit device, and what the miners had to use in confined areas, underground, adding to their already perilous conditions and readily available in the shops, which was all rather unbelievable and hard to fathom. Afterwards, we thanked and handed tips to our new guide who was grateful and returned everyone to their residencies satisfied with another one-of-a-kind demonstration.

That evening, I continued moving on by taking the night bus on the long journey to the border town of Villazón. All was fine until around twelve-fifteen a.m. when the bus started driving very slowly and was apparent that we had a problem. We ambled to the nearest town in the pitch black before finally it gave up completely and broke down. I didn't have a clue where I was or what was going to happen. People frantically disembarked and grabbed their things and the driver made phone calls. Fortunately, within moments, a passing bus pulled over, the doors opened and a mad clamour erupted as people tried to get on. I was close by to where it stopped, so I passed my big bag to the attendant who squashed it into the hold and I joined in the rabble to board. The bus was only half full so I managed to get a seat, which was a bonus. This was short-lived though as the rest of the people squeezed on, and I gave up my seat to an elderly lady and made do with lying in a hunched-up ball at the front of the isle, using my smaller pack as a pillow. Looking around, the bus must have been well over maximum capacity. There were bodies everywhere with seats all full, people sitting on knees, the isle further back had many others' standing and bags seemed to be jammed everywhere. Under the circumstances, I made do with the limited room where I was and amazingly fell asleep squashed on the hard floor.

It was quite the achievement managing to get around four hours sleep in before we arrived at Tupiza where many got off and the congestion eased and I took a seat again. But despite the now apparent comfort of a seat, the floor prior was the only sleep I got, because the terrain changed from asphalt to another bumpy, uneven dirt track road, that I felt I'd already traversed across numerous times in Bolivia, another showcase of the country's poorer infrastructure where the large bus slowly, cumbersomely and at times violently leaned to the sides as if about to tip over. Making matters worse, the journey was made all the more uncomfortable because I started to need a piss from all the rocking and there wasn't a toilet on board, a stop in sight or a bottle at hand. We rolled slowly but surely towards our destination that I hoped was Villazón, and more importantly to somewhere I could empty my bladder and be in one piece while I did it.

Return of the Vulture

The next time we hit solid tarmac was arriving into the dusty one-street border town of Villazón; an uninspiring place where the sole aim seemed to be getting people into Argentina or elsewhere in Bolivia. As I disembarked, I hastily dashed at break neck speed to the nearest toilet and while doing so noticed a tour operator offering tickets to Salta – my next destination. Not really sure what was best; either buy a bus ticket from here or in La Quiaca just over the border in Argentina, I decided to sort it out here and see what would happen – figuring, if anything, it would be cheaper. After negotiating the deal I wanted that mainly involved choosing the type of bus required – because many operators assumed luxury was the preferred option, but not in this case; I pretty much wanted the cheapest – I was then taken with a representative to the close by border crossing, apprehensively passing a pack of local dogs fighting wildly over some morsels of discarded food in the middle of the street.

Formalities completed, upon exiting, I walked the short bridge crossing no man's land and waited patiently in line at Argentine immigration, all the while watching locals pass back and forth across the border seemingly at will. Even though I had no problems with the official-dome and entered Argentina hassle-free, this all seemed very odd and I wanted to enquire what was going on as the only people who appeared to have any issues were four Bolivians; who did get stopped, questioned and searched as they tried to cross. Hardly surprising though; as they were carrying a coffin with them, which finally raised the seemingly slackest of border suspicions, while everyone else appeared to go about their day-to-day border business without a cadaver casket for a shopping trolley.

First thing I noticed crossing into Argentina was a huge billboard that had *Las Malvinas son Argentinas* or 'The Falkland Islands are Argentine' emblazoned on it. Obviously, a politically contentious issue still rumbling here about how Britain has sovereignty over the Falkland Islands yet Argentina still claiming ownership of them which resulted in an Argentine invasion and subsequent war between the two countries back in 1982, that

I remember being in the news and seeing on TV as a young boy. Being from the UK, I wondered how I would be received here and hoped there wouldn't be any problems of nationalistic nature; especially as this seemed something out of my immediate remit to do anything about and apart from being a UK citizen, had nothing to do with.

I took a taxi to the bus station in La Quiaca where to my surprise from over the border my ticket for the bus was valid and legit so I hopped on board and made my journey immediately south. Coming from Bolivia, the roads and buses in Argentina were smooth, quiet, spacious and comparable to floating on air. I had spent nearly three weeks in Bolivia and was some of the hardest travelling that I had done, although not necessarily because of any vast distance. Numerous factors had made the time spent there more gruelling and tough; mainly because it felt like I hadn't stopped cramming in the things that I wanted to do; the 'Death Road', the rescue centre, the salt flats and the mines were my objectives and I had completed them but at a price of running myself into the ground and my health was suffering as part of the consequences. Plus, partying in La Paz hadn't helped and set a precursor of being drained before I had even started, as I seamlessly got caught up in the raucous hostel atmosphere. But this was easily one of the best places that I had stayed in and those there were brilliant and so much fun. And that was one of the beautiful things about travelling; meeting other like-minded people, which was there to be equally embraced. This was all part of my downfall, because there were other factors I never really took into account, such as the altitude when pretty much going from sea level to 3600m in only a matter of days, plus the poorer infrastructure made it much more of a struggle to get any sleep or rest over bumpy track roads on cramped buses. So when all combined together these amplified being run down, increased the chances of getting sick and intensified the need to stop or at least slowdown.

Thinking about it I should have stopped for a while, recovered, recharged and got used to the altitude again. Still having time to get where I needed to be, but I found myself delving into the opportunities as they came thick and fast; to ensure I never missed out with my increasingly diminishing time. And having no structured planning to the activities and taking them as they arose always left me that bit more depleted and with niggling thoughts that I still wanted to have enough time to make the most of Argentina and Brazil; which, from their area size would never be enough anyway. In the end, I exited with the stupid, misguided notion that I may not have made as much of the time in Bolivia that I could have, which was bullshit really as I achieved what I wanted and more; mainly on a wing and a prayer. I think this was because I didn't visit other places less travelled and pretty much stuck to the tourist trail. But it was still fascinating and diverse, offering some of the most beautiful and wonderful surroundings unlike anywhere else on Earth and I found the people whom I interacted with lovely and friendly. Others I had spoken to had differing views, but the same could be said of my opinion from when in Peru. Thing was, though, I felt it was worth it. Yes, it was hard going, but only due to my circumstances. Would I return? In an instant, and I have every intention to do so, if only to go back to the rescue centre. Now knowing what to expect and not taking for granted the elevation and that places may not be as developed as others I'd been in, inadvertently created a truer depiction of travelling life and how much a person has to adapt to this was a lesson in itself, that I had now learnt, again the hard way, but I knew it would make me a better person and traveller for the experience.

The scene outside the window looked like it was straight out of a western movie. An arid dry dusty landscape littered with bushes and large protruding cactus, where the sunset created a fantastic orange hue through the gaps in the clouds, to increasingly darkened distant mountains, aptly fitting the description of cowboy country as our bus sped towards my next destination of Salta. South America's second-largest country Argentina was obviously only going to be a fleeting visit in comparison to its size, and I was only going to have a couple of weeks at best there. As heading further south to somewhere like Patagonia seemed pointless; I would be moving further away from my final destination, and also for the first time since I left Chile some six months prior, I was to leave the tropics and being winter now in the southern hemisphere would only get colder. So, I pretty much decided not to bust a gut and stick to northern parts of the country, do some things in this region to facilitate me in heading to Brazil in a timely fashion, and hopefully finish off with some beach and warmer weather.

Speaking to one of the other volunteers I was told that Salta was beautiful and well worth a visit; also with it being the first main destination in proximity of the border, I decided this would be a good stopping point. Wandering around the next day, I wasn't disappointed; Plaza 9 de Julio in the city centre was indeed beautiful; a square made up of arch way strewn colonial buildings including; the cathedral, museums and nice swish restaurants that surrounded walkways, fountains, monuments and lots of trees within the middle, for the town's inhabitants to while away the sunny day in the shade amid a peaceful green setting. There were lots more modern shops in the conventional European sense here with brand names splashed everywhere, and it instantly reminded me that I hadn't really come across this commercialism before when in South America, creating the illusion and a feeling that I suddenly wasn't on the continent any more, it felt more like Europe. Despite ambling around and taking in the surroundings, I did want to find something to do so I called into a local activities centre, but only left with a brochure to ponder over because many of the activities on offer; like bungee and rafting I had already done so they were not really enticing me as a must do. One possibility was maybe to do a trek on horseback as something different but only regarded this 'maybe' as having never been riding before and I generally had enough trouble communicating with people, never mind a horse.

Overlooking the city was the Cerro San Bernardo, a huge hill graced with religious monuments and offering a spectacular view of the city and valley. The afternoon was sunny but had a chill in the air, yet I still took the opportunity for some exercise by walking to the foot of the hill and then scaling the hundreds of stairs to the top, and not bothering with the *Teleférico* cable car. The forty-five-minute climb was worth it though, as the complex at the top provided an amazing panoramic view of the sprawling city that seemed to merge with the sky in the far-off horizon. I was still undecided what to do for the next day, after continuing to wander about exploring, having decided not to do any of the activities on offer as I was finding it hard to justify the prices. These were now much more, for pretty much everything, compared to that of the other countries I had visited and for things I felt I'd already experienced. Unbeknownst though at the time, my rational thinking theories were going to be proven well and truly wrong.

In the end, here I kept things nice, cheap and cultural by visiting one of the museums in the city centre, which nevertheless still proved to be quite the macabre experience as it harboured five-hundred-year-old mummified human remains that had been found at the top of a volcano. Thought to be part of an Incan ritual sacrifice, the exhibits had hair, teeth and facial features still preserved in a gnarled human form due to the bindings and techniques used. It was very interesting and fascinating to see, even though some were children; and their tomb now was an environmentally sealed, protective case to be stared at, studied and pondered over by the masses from a time they surely could never have envisaged being a part of.

Salta was a really nice place and a city that I really liked and would maybe like to stay a little longer as I was sure it had more to offer. The slower pace I adopted here was welcome, but I decided on the evening of the second day there to move on again in the hope of seeing more and doing as much as possible elsewhere. Transport in Argentina was easy to organise, as the buses were regular, punctual, clean and comfortable, plus reasonably cheap for the distances travelled. The *semi-cama* or 'half bed' seats provided easily enough comfort for the long overnight journey and allowed arriving in a new place adequately rested, having managed to get some sleep and also saved the money of a night's accommodation. Heading further south, my next destination was Córdoba; Argentina's second-largest city and this was more than evident on my arrival, being greeted by the usual barrage of high-rise buildings associated with a concrete metropolis. Finding the hostel that I'd arranged to stay at, I was given the immediate opportunity to visit Alta Gracia that afternoon, as the hostel already had a dual-purpose trip organised to the famous pilgrimage site.

Situated about 30km to the south-west of Córdoba, we entered the colonial town of Alta Gracia; in the main square was the first stop of our excursion which was a Jesuit monastery, now preserved into a museum, offering an interesting insight into how the founding Jesuit fathers used to live, but this was just a passing stop – the main reason why I and most other people were on this tour lay in less grandiose settings of an ordinary house, on an ordinary street. But no ordinary person used to live there because when he was a boy, this was the former home of Ernesto 'Che' Guevara and Villa Beatriz had now been transformed into the museum Casa del Che or 'House of Che' dedicated to the former revolutionary. In the yard, there was a statue of Che as a child and how he would sit on the porch, plus a bust of the fully grown Che in now iconic, traditional pose.

The inside of each room was dedicated to different phases of his life, incorporating plenty of actual photos, documents and memorabilia to portray his story; including telling how he was sick suffering with asthma as a child, gained a doctorate, his political stance, how he met Fidel Castro and became a Cuban revolutionary, travelled under aliases to end up fighting in the Congo and his ultimate death in Bolivia. Also, inside there was even a replica of the Norton bike, made famous from *The Motorcycle Diaries* biopic movie about his travels around South America and startling still, the house had fixtures and fittings in place, such as the fireplace and bathroom as exhibits, where I thought it best to refrain from using Che's toilet figuring it again was probably another no-no. Outside in the back garden, it was hard not to imagine little Che playing as a boy despite the fact that storage buildings had now been converted to a gift shop.

The whole experience took me back to buying the T-shirt in Australia; I realised that I actually didn't know much about Che except for the fact that he was a revolutionary leader and that purchase was more out of pop culture than actually making some form of statement, so I was actually glad that I gave the t-shirt to Miguel as Che was an actual hero of his and more befitting. Now I understood much more about the man. The empathy from the poverty he witnessed, his passion for what he believed in and that he was willing to fight for this and others, but also how learned and intelligent he was from the books he wrote, and not to mention hating imperialism and being a Marxist made him a bit of a capitalist nightmare. Thinking about Che, I wondered if he was actually someone I could relate to? Should I wear the shirt bearing his face? Because to many it makes a statement about political views, where from a certain stance some might regard this man as a communist terrorist, albeit from an era when ideals and attitudes were much different. The problem being, like a lot of other things I'm no politician, nor would I want to be one and I don't have any particular affiliation towards any party or political leanings. I generally try to just go with what's ethically and morally correct, forward thinking and for the greater good, not what the best investment opportunities are or where the most money is for the few. What I did like about Che was that he wanted to actually help the poor, had a conscience, his insights and that he was willing to fight for change; although I cannot necessarily agree with some of his methods. So, yes, he was a person I would like to relate to in this sense and I was really pleased that I took the opportunity to come here and learn about this man whose image as a cultural icon, words and ideals still resonate with many people to this day long after his death. This time, I thought it better to only buy a key ring with his image on, because under all the circumstances it was more befitting and I certainly wasn't going to ask for the t-shirt back.

The rest of my time I concentrated in and around the city, perusing around the shops, taking in the numerous plazas and parks. Parque Sarmiento the most notable as it is huge; so much so that it incorporated a zoo. I decided to have a look inside to see and find out about some interesting animals, hopefully finding them and the place in good order. Here, there were many more species of animals than in Cali, plus some of the much larger variety that included an impressively terraced big cat enclosure, where the tigers patrolled around freely and with menace. I'd never seen hippopotamus before in the flesh and they were much bigger than I imagined, not to mention the size and amount of turd they produced which was nonchalantly swatted away from the rear end by a flapping tail. With numerous llamas, birds, alligators and bison, it was good and the animals seemed to be in decent health but again not for the first time I found myself wondering if some of the cages and enclosures were appropriate for the size of animal, some looked dirty and lacked stimulus inside. If humans are going to keep animals, then surely, it's a moral duty to have them in the best conditions possible. I may be wrong, but I felt that there could have been improvements somewhat. But I would probably feel the same visiting any exhibit such as this, and if I were going to visit these, I would have to accept that I would come across these issues and what I perceived less-than-favourable size or state that the inhabitants would or could be in. And therein lies the whole argument and reasoning behind why keep animals captive and in relatively small confined spaces in the first place; Research? Entertainment? Education? None seem an adequate really with the exception maybe protection or rehabilitation. Especially as the inevitable ignorance displayed by people visiting would show blatant disregard for the animal anyway. It seemed that no matter how much information and safety signs are put up, people will still feed them or put hands inside cages; where on numerous occasions, I again witnessed parents encouraging their kids' ill behaviour, as well as their own when they should know better. If it wasn't bad or stressful enough being locked up, it surely adds insult to injury being gawked at, harassed by, shouted at and possibly poisoned by a moron.

After leaving, I did feel that I had learnt something; on the whole, zoos are generally shit. At best, I was finding them an educational source not only with the information provided, but more so how humans like to dominate other species. Many of the creatures seen within these places aren't endangered or need protecting, so for me, it's just unnecessary as it creates a depressive experience; as they literally act like a jail that only allows the animal to live in its meekest of form, a place where it can't be itself or behave how it truly would in the wild. They are subjected to the same confines day after day with minimal natural interactions and stimulus, offering nothing really of a true existence and only forms a negative reality for the animal. What's wrong with being out in the wild on reservations etc., in habitats that are, well, basically not cages or confining enclosures? The visit here left me with an abundance of questions, as I obviously thought back to the methods used by the rescue centers I worked at and sanctuaries I visited, and it could be argued that they were just the same. At least they were for animal protection, rehabilitation and where they could be released after, plus many roamed free, but a zoo just seems more oppressive with the focus being on money through the door and entertainment for the masses. Still not knowing or understanding the full facts, I was sure there would be other issues to consider which would create plenty of food for thought and the morality of it all to ponder.

No such problems with the morality of the next place; because all the animals were dead. Good job really because it would have been bloody chaos with dinosaurs and the like running around the science museum. It was only small, but I wandered around the building's circular multilayer format, perusing the million-year-old fossils, animal bones and learning about the Earth's creation. Well, as much as I could fathom with all information in Spanish, but that didn't leave me half as confused as when staring at the random crossed-eyed stuffed animal exhibits, they looked bizarre and I could only assume the taxidermist was pissed on the job. Finally, I finished the day off at the Museo Superior de Bellas Artes Palacio Ferreyra. An art gallery which incorporated both fine and modern genres, on canvas and textiles, three of which – *Days of Work, Segment Cubes* and *Painting of Mallorca with Light* – were my favourites, less so the exhibition of sketch drawings that depicted graphic scenes of abuse that included aftermath of rape; which frankly was horrific.

I started to regret not taking time to go trekking on horseback in Salta, as it became quite frustrating that although tour operators in town ran similar excursions, it was turning out to be quite difficult to get on them. Not because they were fully booked; exactly the opposite as they were number dependent and being the middle of winter there weren't enough people and were getting cancelled. This proved more frustrating still as any cancellation would happen the day before I was due to go, only to be told that there weren't enough participants, so I'd missed out on an opportunity; but saying that there was no guarantee that the tour would have happened in Salta either. One thing that I had learnt was, as one door closes another opens and this was no exception. It was still early when I heard that the riding wasn't going ahead so I had a day to kill. I saw a poster in the tour agency of the hostel that caught my eye which I could easily do instead. And as I thought about it, despite all reassurances about the conditions, by not horseback riding I had arguably spared the prospects of participating in an activity where I may have been left feeling awkward about the treatment or condition of the horses, or more to the point one that would have had to carry my fat arse around for half-a-day. So, I decided it wasn't to be and now something else would have the pleasure of carrying me; this though would be for a much shorter time and be much more nerve-jangling.

There and then, I asked the assistant if it was possible to go skydiving. Having already done one of these earlier, I had a fair idea what would be happening; me falling to earth at literally break neck speed, filling my pants, all the while attached to someone, who I hoped knew what they were doing with a solid instinct of self-preservation. So, I wasn't too concerned with the ins and outs of what to expect. What I was more concerned about was having already overcome my fear once, what would be the point of not doing it ever again? Because; if I never, then the fear or concern would still be there and I hadn't overcome my fear. Plus I thought that I enjoyed it, but did I? It was easy to say "yes, I did" after it was done and I was OK and full of adrenaline and relief. So, I decided I wanted to test this theory.

Finishing on the phone, the assistant turned around and said that they would pick me up at ten a.m. Within the hour, I was about to find out, whereby putting my new hypothesis to the test and at such short notice I had impressed myself already. Although the skydive was going to cost easily more than what I was intending to pay or initially wanted to do, I justified it by having the chance to put what I believed in into practise and see whether I could live by it. Also the price here was only just over £100, so relatively speaking it was much cheaper than I would pay anywhere else. Therefore, right time and right place came to mind so I took the opportunity as it came, a theory which I equally wanted to live by. I trusted the Argentineans to throw a British guy out of a plane. Why wouldn't I?

As promised, within the hour, the bus arrived and took us to an air field just outside Alta Gracia. The conditions were again near perfect with low wind and sun shining in an empty but for a few clouds sky, as two other jumpers and myself prepared to take the plunge. The setup was slightly different here; first, we were introduced to our tandem instructor who was German and used to be part of the display team in the army and with over 1800 jumps to his name – this obviously boded well. Then we had to decide what order we wanted go, as we were to be taken up individually in the small plane, jump out and come back down to earth. The instructee would celebrate whilst instructor would kit up with another chute to take the next person up. The altitude this time was to be from 10000ft, shorter than before but in the grand scheme of jumping out of planes, still high enough and allowed free falling for around thirty seconds, before deploying the parachute to savour the views and land gracefully back to earth, as with most events like this all filmed by a camera man. I volunteered to go first which oddly the others didn't have a problem with, as they mainly vied for second or third spot. I put on my yellow *Kill Bill* jump suit, went through the routines, procedures, last checks and had my photo taken in front of the plane as Aerosmith's 'Living on the Edge' blasted out from the stereo in the hangar. Indeed, we were.

The small craft sped along the grass with just the three of us in the back this time, all the while picking up momentum until we cleared the ground and began to climb in a circular motion. The air field below shrank into oblivion, engulfed by the growing landscape of town, fields and mountains. After about fifteen minutes, we arrived at the desired altitude with final checks completed, hand signals then indicated everyone was OK and ready. No time wasted, the somewhat dim drone of the plane was overwhelmed by the deafening rush of air with the opening of the side door below the overhead wings.

Shuffling to the open hatch, the camera man headed out first to film us by balancing precariously, using the wing stanchion as the gale force winds grabbed hold of the jumpsuits. At the door edge, the instructor and I readied ourselves with minimal pause. *Uno, dos, tres,* we tumbled forward into the open sky. Quickly, we resumed position from our disorientating foetal spooring position to facing downwards, head back, legs bent and arms stretched out, to catch some minimal air resistance. Once again, the overwhelming sensation of rushing air numbed the senses to the idea of falling and induced the false sense of flying. Looking ahead and only really concentrating on the camera in front, I waved and gesticulated frantically, trying to look cool despite the cheeks rippling in unflattering waves across the face from the forces of wind. In what seemed a very short time and possibly the fastest thirty seconds of my life, the chute was deployed causing the body to jolt into a vertical position, as we slowed with the greater resistance and as the canopy opened fully, my nether regions once again bore the brunt of being brought to a thankfully abrupt halt. Mission accomplished.

As the critical points of the jump had passed without problem and frenetic wind rush had subsided, the second part allowed time to chill and drift calmly down to earth, appreciating the glorious view of the landscape that merged a blurred horizon of fading fields to a perfectly blue sky, and marvel at gazing across to the top of the Sierras de Córdoba mountains, whose craggy, textured surface looked like it was moulded out of putty and could be squashed with the palm of the hand. For the full experience, we spiralled down to earth in large swooping motions; large lakes became more apparent, residencies came into view, easily spotted by those with light blue swimming pools, that stood out against the tapestry of greens, browns and yellows of surrounding fields and getting a bird's eye view of the little dots running around the pitch playing a game of football before we raised the legs to swoop in for landing back at the air field.

With the adrenaline gone, I was rinsed with the contentment of completion as I trudged back to the hanger. This was instantly broken as I started answering the barrage of questions from the others about the jump who themselves were only moments away from heading up for their own experience that would blot any of my words into insignificance. The whole jump had lasted again just over five minutes but was easily a worthwhile exercise and I was glad that I took the opportunity, as I felt that I had proved something to myself and despite the nerves I really did enjoy it. I liked the rush, the adrenaline, the sensations, the unbelievable views and the idea that I was letting go and putting my faith in all the science of physics and those charged with ensuring these rules and laws are adhered to. It would be almost impossible to not get nervous, but this time with the uncertainty of what would happen regarding the wind, harness and procedures not a factor, I felt I was able to appreciate and enjoy the jump more, as adrenaline had mostly driven the euphoria when in New Zealand. Interestingly, here, the time between the canopy being deployed, to fully opening and stopping also seemed to happen that much faster than before, so it did make me wonder about the other jump as I Sat back and waited for the others to return and regale their experience, regardless I felt really pleased, happy and proud at proving a point to myself and glad to have taken the opportunity to jump again at such short notice.

The next day, I had my tickets booked to leave Córdoba overnight and head east towards Bueno Aires, the capital. Thing was, though, I woke late after check out had passed and had to pay for another evening because I got absolutely post-tandem skydive *borracho* on some potent Argentinean beer, celebrating my free-falling escapades, so didn't get up in time which wasn't unsurprising as I didn't have a clue what really happened after six p.m. All I knew was this beer was brown and lethal. Not being in a position, or for that matter any condition or state of mind to argue, I settled the bill and spent the rest of the time bumbling around the shops and eating food, with the idea that fresh air and sustenance would help bring me round. As the weather wasn't great, this only persuaded me to then crash in front of the TV for the rest of the afternoon to watch movies at the hostel, before early evening I left for the bus station.

Buenos Aires, like most capital cities, was massive and slightly overwhelming in the sense of where was best to stay. My priorities being to see as much as possible within the space of three full days. I opted for smack in the centre of the city amid the hustle and bustle. Upon arriving, I was left slightly out of sorts with the weather; as it was cold, grey, raining and miserable and something I wasn't used to. Here, it actually felt like it was winter being further south and, on the coast, compared to inland and north that still seemed to benefit from warmer climate. This resembled autumnal Britain that pretty much made any outdoor plans quite unappealing.

For a brief period, the rain eased and I headed out but never actually made it very far, only managing to venture down the massive multi lanes of Avenida 9 de Julio, where only a sprint would seem to ensure getting to the opposite side and avoid the roaring onset of speeding traffic, but it was worth it to marvel at the 200ft towering obelisk in the centre of the Plaza de la República built in 1936 to commemorate the founding of the city. Aimlessly wandering, I noticed again that the architecture here seemed to have more European feel to it and could easily associate a Spanish-Italian influence with the way that the older stone facades of buildings seemed to be crafted. Not that I can claim to know much about architecture as the European vibe could easily have come from the fact that at around two p.m., everyone out and about or working seemed to down tools and take a siesta till around five p.m. which to be honest I was very much in favour of. But to make things that bit more obviously Argentinian, tango seemed to be everywhere and I don't mean crappy fizzy drinks.

The cultural dance form originating from here was advertised everywhere; theatres, shows, classes and the place seemed to ride on tango fever and embraced it like its dance partner; so my two left feet toyed with the idea of giving it a go but thought it only romantic idealism, as I'd probably only guarantee making a fool out of myself trampling on some poor *señorita's* toes and ending her fledgling career with a rose clamped between my teeth. So, I put it on the maybe pile. A little less obvious though; while walking, I started noticing little intricate pieces of art-cum-graffiti around the city – on walls, behind posts, on the kerbs and they ranged from flowers to mushrooms to animals to slogans. Some were very cool and added an element of colour and interest to otherwise normal city scenario. It was like the city had a Banksy job. Some might complain and moan about vandalism, but I liked it. It's not like they were someone's shitty tag emblazoned in 6ft-high running spray paint on governmental buildings; they were quite subtle and small, so found it fun and interesting trying to spot them, which seemed to be everywhere I looked.

With one last stop in Argentina before I headed to Brazil, I booked my bus for what was now two days' time, having pretty much lost a day due to the weather. The next day was more beneficial because along with the bus, I decided to participate in a cycle tour of the city, figuring this would be a good way to explore, see more and also get information from a guide. Arriving at the Plaza San Martín, I met the guide Annabel who conducted the tour in both Spanish and English. This was a welcome bonus because now the Spanish in Argentina was spoken much faster and with more of a lisp, like that from their European counterparts (which also was adding to the euro vibe), so I was struggling somewhat more than in other countries to understand what was said, but I persevered and we seemed to understand one another, which was cool and I could get by only using English when needed for the harder words or explanations I didn't quite understand.

Before we even started, it was apparent that I had made a mistake. Not thinking, I put on shorts, T-shirt and rain jacket that left me slight on apparel, because the day itself weather-wise was fine but freezing cold and I couldn't wait to get peddling to warm up. No sooner setting off, we stopped almost immediately and it left me cold and shivering in the brisk windy air. Not only that, it proved to be quite an awkward moment as well, as the first point of interest we were at was the Falkland war memorial and I was the token English person on the tour. Albeit sombre, it was actually well-informed about what happened and paid tribute the mostly young, ill-trained Argentinean forces who lost their lives during the conflict with a permanently lit beacon. Hopefully, this could act as a reminder to both sides and any government for that matter the somewhat futility of war, the devastating effects and the sacrifices that always have to be made which rarely seem to be by any governmental figure. Then we were shown a clock tower close by that had been a pre-war present from the British, which after the conflict was renamed to indicate the ill feeling, rather than being taken down or removed, which struck me as quite odd. To lighten the mood somewhat, we pressed on to visit and ride around the regenerated dockland area of the city before heading to the barrio that I wanted to visit, which was La Boca.

'The Mouth' proved more of a working-class district of Buenos Aires that swapped the newer high-rises of the centre for older, smaller buildings. The actual centre of La Boca was really cool and vibrant, awash with colour, murals and interesting pieces of art both painted and sculpted everywhere. This was a haven for artisans who proudly displayed their works for sale in the street. The name here made famous by the football team Boca Juniors and its legacy of legendary players like Diego Maradona and Gabriel Batistuta; whose faces graced the Stars Wall of Fame outside the ground, situated in a residential area that in parts made it look small and compact, much like the older grounds back home where the stands tower on one side of the street opposite to regular homes on the other. Supposedly, this could be a dangerous place to be if in the wrong place on match day because of the fanatics who go there, but it was out of season so there was no chance of catching a game. This was obviously a less affluent part of the city that we had entered and real people lived here. It was clear there were some unsavoury sorts around, attracted by lots of tourists and their money that had come to visit, but it was beautiful, very charming and I liked it.

Heading back up into the city centre, we stopped at Casa Rosada; a beautifully ornate, palatial building designated as the official office of the Argentinian president, situated at the east end of Plaza de Mayo close by where I'd wandered the day before but now had the pleasure of finding out the historical past, involving Juan and 'Evita' Peron and protests that happened there prior by families wanting answers concerning loved ones who went 'missing' during the dirty war of Videla's military coup during the seventies, before finally tottering around numerous other small parks and plazas to finish early in the afternoon. After this, at the hostel, I took the longest, hottest shower imaginable, in some way to try and remove the chilblains from the bitter wind that had enveloped me all day. The tour was a great informative way to get around and see the city. Even though biking in and around the busy metropolitan streets was quite the hazardous affair with cars pulling out and pedestrians stepping onto the road in front of you, regardless of your or their own safety; so much so, like in Shanghai, it could easily be a video game. But I was glad I went and it set me up nicely for the evening by working up an appetite as I found myself sampling the famous Argentinean steaks from one of the recommended restaurants – something that I wanted to do, having heard so much about how delicious they were. I wasn't disappointed; really tender and succulent rib eye, cooked medium that cost only around £20 and included a 'buy one get one free' bottle of wine to ensure it was washed down well. *Muy rico.*

I checked out the next day; being nice and sunny, with time to spare, I made off on foot in the opposite direction to the day previous, winding through the parks and streets to the Recoleta district. Being in the more exclusive area of the city, I found the high-walled cemetery to famous Argentinians from the past and parks with lovely monuments that honoured these people and sculptured artworks; notably, a giant silver flower, surrounded by water that shimmered brilliantly in the cold, bright sun. This was next to the National Art Museum that harboured a fantastic array of famous works by known artists such as Cezanne, Monet, Toulouse Lautrec, Degas, Rodin, Picasso and Jackson Pollock. I wandered around for ages, it was easily the best gallery I had been in and made the miles of walking well worth the effort, and I felt very much in awe at the amazingly beautiful pieces I was witnessing. Returning, I gathered my things for my journey. Whereby taking the another night bus meant that I was definitely missing out on some tango lessons and not seeing some of the fantastic scenery that Argentina had to offer, but time was of the essence so something had to give. My destination though was going to hopefully make up for that being another natural wonder of the world.

The journey wasn't short either; I headed north for seventeen hours so deciding to travel overnight was an easy choice to make to get to Puerto Iguazú; a small inland town on the border with Brazil. The majority of the day gone; it was about three p.m. as I wandered around town getting my bearings. There were plenty of bars and restaurants due to the constant stream of tourists who were there to cross the border or see the Iguazú falls. But in my case, this was both.

Another early start, the next morning ensured that with only a forty-minute drive, we arrived at the Parque Nacional Iguazú before the expected masses. I had gone with another person from the hostel, an Aussie called Ben who I had met the day previous and also wanted to see the falls. We entered and instantly made our way along the sign-posted pathways carved through the lush, green, humid forest. It was possible to sense that the falls were imminent, as a slight unabated rumbling noise increased in a crescendo that could be felt, and coincided with a fine misty haze that started to fill the air. Opening up from the paths, a huge chasm gaped between us and Brazil on the far side; where in-between frantic raging torrents of water toppled over from huge, terraced, spectacular falls just upriver. White water roared from multiple channels, split by foliage into hypnotic rhythmic cascades as it barrelled relentlessly down over to reconvene as the river below. The pummelled rocks at the bottom only exacerbated the noise and forced the swirling spray into the air, creating constant, perfectly arced rainbows in all direction as the glistening sunlight refracted from within. This was nature being both spectacularly powerful and effortlessly beautiful at the very same time and a true wonder to witness.

As the waters wild energy dissipated, the river was somewhat calm and it was possible to explore around the lookout points of nearby San Martín Island at the base of the first terrace. This provided closer examination of the massive tiers and due to the proximity, it made the tumbling water even more impressive and imposing, emphasising the sheer size and magnitude of nature's ferocity. But also, here, there was a more hair-flattening experience (not in my case, but in general) and getting wet was obviously going to be part of proceedings. As we paid to ride aboard an open speed boat that took tourists on a white knuckle ride to the edge of the thundering white falls, skimming perilously close to the cascading mass, where raging noise and crashing water overwhelmed the senses so much, it was hard to fathom that one wrong move would see the boat and all who sail her smashed to oblivion. All to the sheer terror and unrelenting joy of excited revellers; who like us returned from the experience a saturated but exhilarated soggy mess.

Wildlife teemed around the lush forests of the park and wild coatis tried to pilfer food from unsuspecting diners that made me laugh with a knowing recognition of their mischievous ways. The beauty of the park was that this was only the lower half of a divided river system. After a short train ride or long walk upstream; purpose-built trails had been made around the top of the falls to get an equally impressive view from the highest viewing points. This included the park's main feature, lengthy metal gangways allowing access to the middle of the river to witness the water topple over at Garganta del Diablo or 'Devil's Throat'; Where a semi-circular shape had been eroded by the relentless flow, that billowed down toward the tiered mid-section and the constantly moving brown-white flurries of water caused a reeling hypnotic effect when stared at. Also the view from up here at the very precipice looking downstream was spellbinding; Argentina on the left and Brazil on the right, with the river in the centre glistening in the mist and sunlight, creating an everlasting view with camera ready to capture such a stunning sight! *Click!*

We spent all day in the park wandering around, taking photos and generally having a good time. I had visited Niagara Falls before and although technically bigger, higher and more famous, here definitely gets the recognition it deserves, as it provided a much more picturesque, protected and natural setting that had far less damage incurred on it, especially not being surrounded by civilisation, commercialism, hotels and masses of people. There was more of the falls to see and from many more interesting and somewhat obscure vantage points, plus a vast array of wildlife that I felt provided more substance. We had also been lucky because the weather only seemed to enhance its elegant beauty accumulating in a fantastic day out and a privilege to see such a scenic marvel at its finest.

That evening; after dinner, a local tango jazz band played some tight numbers that I really enjoyed as we chilled over a few beers in the hostel. Needless to say, after a few refreshing beverages, the band instantly became the greatest thing since sliced bread and like 'an A&R man looking for the next big act', I had to buy the CD they had on sale. At least in the cold light of the following day, listening to them sober confirmed that they were actually very good and my feet and hands weren't just tapping along due to wasted euphoria, and my purchase acted as another small reminder of the whistle-stop ten or so days that I'd spent in Argentina, where to be honest I'd made it through the country quicker than expected by taking night buses, the not a very packed agenda and a hankering for warmer weather further north. Due to winter time, there was no way and no point in heading further south as I didn't have the clothing or the desire for that matter, despite being heartily reassured that Patagonia was a sight to behold. But like other things, it would have to wait. Nevertheless, I left Argentina content with the culture vulture activities that I saw and experienced which were still very unique within the few places I visited, these created amazing, lasting memories and impressions of a country that I would love to return to and do justice to its vast size. It might have been very short, but it was very sweet.

The Swan Song

On the first day I arrived in Puerta Iguazú, I booked a bus to take me through into Brazil. It was easier to do this because I could get from here straight to my destination, rather than arrange to go to the border, cross over and then sort transport. Also, I had no real desire or need to stop in Foz do Iguaçu over the river, having already seen the falls from the more prominent and accessible Argentinian side where the largest parts of the cascades were. Besides, I'd read the Argentine buses were both cheaper than in Brazil and generally regarded as better, so this made all the more sense as my plans had changed slightly after speaking to the girls in reception. When I mentioned that my next destination was going to be Florianópolis on Brazil's south-east coast, they questioned this; stating that the weather was only going to be the same as here, not necessarily sunny and more likely to be chilly. After looking on a map, if anything it did look like I would be heading slightly further south. I wasn't having any of that, and decided to cut any losses there and then. I was hellbent having my last two weeks or so hopefully drenched in sunshine; also, the last time I indulged in doing naff all on a beach was back in Máncora, Peru. That seemed ages ago now, as the vast majority of the time spent crossing the continent, it felt like I was constantly busy running around doing stuff, plus this was at altitude and even if it was sunny, most of the time the air was cold. After almost a year of chasing the sun, I was well and truly a lover of its warm, cheery glory. There was only one place that could hopefully solve this dilemma; straight back into the tropics and head to Rio de Janeiro.

Managing to get through immigration with no problems, I changed my money to Reais, but refrained from trying to off-load a fake 50 peso note that I had annoyingly been passed; I didn't know where I got it but comparing it to other notes it was bad; wonky print, faded colour, on shit paper and I didn't want to get busted this late in the day passing forged notes. So, I put it down as a loss and kept it as crap souvenir. What lay ahead was just twenty-two hours or so on a bus, I didn't mind, it wasn't as if I hadn't done this length of journey before, and this now would be the last long stint travelling I would have to do.

At least with such long journeys, movies generally play back to back as entertainment; one of which here included *Marley and Me*. It's about a family and their misbehaving dog and when it finished, looking around there wasn't a dry eye on the bus, as people couldn't control their tugged heartstrings, tearfully and relentlessly sniffing runny noses at its sad end, everyone having bought into two hours of the loveable pets hilariously annoying antics; I only realised the traumatised state of the passengers because I looked around embarrassed, hoping it wasn't just me. The extended time also gave me the chance to read up on the new book that I had bought in Córdoba which contained thought-provoking single-page anecdotes with philosophical and enlightened meanings, that I was drawn to when wandering around a bookstore, its content resonated instantly and now I was pleased with my purchase, as it helped rationalise any ill feeling about the fake money and being lumbered with it but more so my last long-distance journey; which more than anything indicated that I was practically at the end of my travels, because heading straight to Rio was also where I was due to fly home from.

My intention though was to stay at a few places within Rio state first, further along the coast but only an hour or so between each. This was far and away a better idea; to visit different resorts with a relatively short distance to one another along the coast from Rio de Janeiro itself – relative in respect to Brazil being absolutely massive and I'd be missing out on a hell of a lot, and I wasn't going to see or experience a vast amount that surely the biggest country on the continent had to offer. But after everything that had happened and I had done, much like Argentina, then so be it. Something's always had to give so I was happy where I was heading and what was happening.

I arrived in Rio four hours late at around two p.m. and literally jumped straight onto another bus to head out of town, and crossed over the massive bridge that spanned Guanabara bay that the Portuguese explorers had mistaken for a river mouth centuries ago; they arrived in the January so erroneously named the place Rio de Janeiro, or 'River of January'. Except, it wasn't a river it was a bay and by the time they realised they fucked up, it was too late and the place was already established. That's what happened to the best of my knowledge. Makes sense, though, as the bay is huge and an easy mistake to make I suppose; especially back then. We continued over the watery expanse that allowed for first glimpse of the famous Christ the Redeemer statue perched atop the towering hunchback peak, it looked wondrous and instantaneously I had ideas of seeing it at close quarters. The bus headed east along the coast, and passed through the coastal mountains that held blanketing clouds over their edge like a thick duvet covering a bed, and local children played perilously close to the main roads, trying to fly their kites; where just through sitting on a bus staring out of a window for a matter of hours I had noticed this seemed to be a pastime of choice for the young in Brazil; although, I imagined that a football of sorts couldn't be too far away.

Saquarema offered a mellow ambience, being a former fishing village with an inlet lagoon from the ocean for locals to fish in. This was ideal for a couple of days where I didn't achieve much, except for a redeveloping tan from hours whiled away on the beach, a sore chest after a huge wave from the Atlantic picked me up and dumped me unceremoniously on the coarse sandy shoreline and a larger-than-expected hostel bill, as I accidentally dropped and broke the owner's stereo. Couple of days later, I took the local bus and headed further up the coast to Arraial do Cabo for more of the same; relaxing on powdery white sands to catch a glimpse of an enormous stingray patrolling behind huge wall of water waves that eventually broke into a dissipating white rabble; unlike me, though, the stingray was a bit more adept in the ocean and didn't end up a groaning mess on the beach.

Being winter, the weather was three days sun to one day overcast and rain, so my idea of heading this way was working out, as I managed to take advantage of a less-than-favourable day to travel further along the coast. Travelling on the local buses, I was finding the Brazilians polite and helpful, waiting patiently while my bag would get stuck in the turnstiles during boarding and then assisting me when trying to communicate with the driver. Small, I know, but I found these gestures lovely and thanked them, having quickly mastered *obrigado* 'thank you' to offer some slight form of respect now being in a Portuguese-speaking country. After six months being conditioned to the Spanish-speaking part of the continent, I was now once again like a fish out of water, not like the above but certainly in regards to the language. I could sort of read what signs were (or at least thought I could) but understanding what was said – not a chance. Words were rattled at me far too quickly and when pronounced, to my untrained ear, didn't sound like what they were referencing and my pronunciation for that matter was nothing short of terrible. On numerous occasions, I'd subconsciously find myself slipping into Spanish, something that I didn't want to do as not to offend anyone. You wouldn't speak to a French person in Spanish and expect them to understand? For the simple fact it isn't their language. So, as a cop out and natural disclaimer, I tried to make sure I told people I could only really speak Spanish and English before any conversations, to try and avoid any embarrassing miscommunications and fuck ups on my behalf. But for the first time in ages, I had a language barrier problem to deal with, which was like when I started out; it was great as the Brazilian's being cool just laughed most of the time at my inevitable garbled mix of Spanish, English and little Portuguese, as I constantly fluffed my lines trying to get by. They seemed so laid back as if by law, with a really relaxed attitude to, well, seemingly everything. Many were happy to chat (kind of) with the funny-looking foreigner and complete stranger on the bus for nothing in return, which was a really positive thing that struck me early on in my arrival to Brazil.

My penultimate destination was Búzios, described by some as Brazil's answer to St Tropez after being made famous by French movie star Brigitte Bardot apparently hanging out there in the sixties. Chatting away to a Brazilian girl on the bus, I missed the stop to get off for the centre and ended up at the far end of town, having to walk back along the sea front. Despite lugging my bags, this was quite the pleasant experience as I got to see how beautiful and pretty the place was; immaculately clean and tidy with rough-cut stone paving the tree-lined streets of countless boutiques, bars, restaurants and numerous statues and other pieces of artwork littered everywhere. Immediately, it became apparent why this was a favourite place among well-to-do Brazilians. I never really envisaged coming to a place like this with its upmarket demeanour; but was glad that I did.

I pretty much carried on here as I had done at the other two resorts; just pottering around on my own, hanging out with people from the hostel, visiting the various beaches around the peninsula where we were situated and venturing out into the bars for drinks on the evenings. There, I only managed to make a fool out of myself again by coolly leaning on a wall behind me; to find there wasn't a wall there and I fell straight on my arse. I wouldn't care but I was in the middle of chatting to the girl whom I met on the bus; a bit embarrassing to say the least, so after my 'Del boy impression' I made my excuses and left soon after.

A couple of girls called Alison and Kerry arrived whom I had met at the hostel in Buenos Aires and were probably the reason why I didn't end up having some tango lessons on an evening, as we spent the time together getting to know you drunk. We hadn't arranged to meet up and I wasn't expecting to see them, so I was happy with the lovely surprise of catching up again; as all being a bit British it meant we would party. We took some kayaks out onto the calm, serene waters of the sheltered bay that the hostel backed on to, gently weaving in and out of the anchored vessels, before joining the low-key festivities on the hostel terrace that was an ideal setting for the beautiful sunset with early evening drinks. There was a really cool, chilled ambience about the place, where everyone there just got to know each other from relaxing in a warm, friendly atmosphere that oozed inclusivity and welcomed newcomers ad hoc, who all just seemed to go with the flow of hanging, having fun and making sure there wasn't anything too hectic on the agenda to do.

I had spent literally the first ten days in Brazil doing basically nothing, messing about in some big waves, relaxing on lovely powdery beaches, getting a twenty-four-carat tan and on the odd occasion making an idiot out of myself. It didn't bother me one iota that I was doing nothing; it was ideal and just what the doctor ordered after the rigours of the last eleven or so months, while also managing to keep everything relatively cheap and cheerful in the more expensive Brazil; where things were proving more expensive than the rest of South America. Thing was, though, my new-found cheap and cheerful lazy arse mantra was about to change for one last time.

With time pushing on, I had booked my flight back to the UK for 13 August, so I needed to be in Rio. I had heard many fantastic things about the place from fellow travellers and nobody seemed to have a bad word to say about it. Despite being my last place of call and a major city; I was excited to be heading there, particularly as I had a somewhat large itinerary of things that I wanted to do. I figured that if it all had come to this, it all had to come to an end, and I had to go, I was not going to go quietly. So, first thing was to book myself into one of the prominent party hostels in Copacabana.

Rio was massive. Split into various districts divided by the hills and mountains of a rolling landscape and seemed to offer everything. Beautiful long sweeping beaches of Copacabana and Ipanema, the towering buildings of Centro, tree-lined roads of swanky Leblon, street parties of Lapa, the unmissable favelas, amazing views, culture, hot weather, hotter women plus numerous other activities involving whatever to excite the senses and soul. When I arrived, I headed out to meet Ben who I had been to Iguazú falls with and had now arrived in town. Copacabana beach was enormous, sweeping for miles in length, before a peninsula point connected it with Ipanema beach. Hundreds of people strolled up and down the promenade from all walks of life, while those on the beaches played football and volleyball at purpose-made venues when not relaxing on the powdery sand or getting ragged about in the rolling white water crashing in from the ocean. We just hung around at the peninsula, basking in the sun, watching people trying to fish, while kids effortlessly disrupted this by jumping in the water from the rocks. Here was a hive of activity; so much so that watching the world go by could be an event in itself, encompassed by world-famous, beautiful surroundings that attracted arguably the most diverse range of people that anywhere in the world could wish to offer.

I arranged to meet Ben the next day as Rio's famous footballing sons Flamengo were playing Corinthians from Sao Paolo; it offered up a bit of a grudge match for bragging rights between two big teams from two big cities. Wanting again to experience South American football, I had to go. It was still out of season in Argentina so there were no games on; but here in Brazil, the league had started and there seemed to be games on all the time. And where better to catch another game? Nowhere; as this was in Brazil where the country lives and breathes football and would be in the world-famous Maracanã Stadium. It was opened for the hosting of the World Cup in 1950, its size emphasised by the still world record of nearly 200,000 people attending the final, that Brazil unbelievably lost to Uruguay; but now due to seating, the ground a more modest 80,000 capacity, but still large nevertheless and where the history alone would entice anybody with a mere inkling about football to catch a game. When outside, the place reverberated with energy as the stadium loomed large above a carnival atmosphere of shouting, chanting, cheering fanatics in partisan shirts, whistling and hooting horns, waving scarves and flags; all eagerly supplied by vendors of food, drink and merchandise, that were keenly kept in check by a large police presence. It felt like match day was always going to be a special event here, literally for every game.

The stadium inside looked only half full, but the atmosphere still echoed around the bowl-shaped ground, as dominant home fans jumped up and down, waved massive flags and banners, beat and blared drums and horns relentlessly, and the game hadn't even started. Already the noise and expectancy was fever-pitch. As the teams rolled out, the masses of ticker tape showered around upon everyone, so much so that for a brief moment, looking across the huge crowd in the home end, all but a few were obscured from sight by a blanket of fluttering, glistening white and silver. I couldn't help but wonder how the crowd was going to react should and hopefully when Flamengo would score. And really hoped Corinthians wouldn't.

The afternoon sun was directly overhead in the air-trapped stadium and temperatures easily reached into the 30s as there was no breeze and it got much hotter early in the second half, as finally after much anticipation and seemingly from nowhere, Flamengo scored at the far end. I didn't see it and not much thereafter as the place just erupted. People roared, frantically waving their arms, jumping up and down, banners and flags were lofted, ticker tape showered everywhere once more as the excited masses burst into a chorus of pro-Flamengo chants amid the drums and trumpets. It was a fantastic sight and one that was well worth the wait in seeing, and being a part of the euphoria was electric and everyone celebrating together was addictive. The game itself wasn't much of a spectacle, but so what? With the goal and ultimate win, the atmosphere and the crowd themselves made going to the game unbelievably worthwhile. This time though with the favourable result, everyone left the stadium in the early evening in a celebratory fashion, as did we, stopping for a couple of beers before I once again said goodbye to Ben, as he was leaving early the next morning.

I spent the next day in relaxed fashion on Copacabana beach in 30°C sunshine. Whiling away a few hours on the powdery white sand, messing about in the ocean and being hypnotised by the spectacle of people wandering by. A nice chilled affair, as the only thing I had to do was wait for mid-afternoon to come along, having enrolled on an excursion to visit the most iconic of Rio's many sights and fulfil a promise to myself.

Taking the bus booked though the hostel, we made our way through the streets and up to the steep roads of 'hunchback' or Corcovado peak where at 700m and towering majestically, open armed, seemingly embracing all before it the amazing statue of Cristo Redentor or 'Christ the Redeemer'. Made from soap stone and concrete, the statue was completed in 1931 and stands nearly 40m tall. Although solid-looking, it is actually hollow to allow for maintenance. An absolutely magnificent structure that I thought was a brilliant piece of architectural sculpture with it not being too ornate or gregarious. That was the beauty of it, it didn't have to be something outlandish as the pose and what it represented played its part perfectly, to a city which was growing on me all the time with its lovely inhabitants, countless things to do and stunning views and in particular the one which was now directly in front of me.

Despite the hoard of people understandably on the terraces at the top, it was still impossible to not appreciate the fabulous 360-degree view of the city below, now looking a minuscule toy town of varying components that were bathed in the warm late afternoon sun that included the bay with its many shipping vessels and bridge that I'd crossed earlier; the city centre; the iconic Maracanã; the beaches; the huge lake; the favelas that encroached up the hillsides; Sugarloaf Mountain which lolled directly ahead into the ocean and the tropical forests, all encapsulated together into a sprawling metropolis that blanketed everywhere, forming what a truly remarkable place this was. Not only did it seem possible to do anything here, it felt possible to see everything as well, all in one go from this amazing vantage point. Little wonder why the statue has become such an iconic structure for those of religious reasoning, art lovers and people who just like to marvel at incredible views. I was really happy about taking the tour not only for the view and seeing the statue close at hand, but it was really informed and I managed to learn quite a lot, not only in its construction but about the city itself, and a figure that left me quite taken aback was how around 95% of Rio's inhabitants live below the poverty line, a figure I couldn't quite believe or possibly didn't want to believe, not wanting the gloss to be removed from having such a good time, in such a cool city. But I knew it be true because this came mostly from in and around the favelas and cheap housing that seemed to be massing in all directions.

That evening, I was greeted by Bruno, a local who ran Capoeira classes. After the football the day previous, I'd watched a free exhibition of the Brazilian martial art within the relatively small confines of the hostel bar. I was impressed by the agility, grace, movement and co-ordination of the instructors; and me being suitably oiled and possessing none of these attributes, I decided that I would like to try it and take part in a proper lesson, rather than rolling around on the bar floor, something which I knew I could do quite well, although not necessarily performing Capoeira. The lesson though was now and immediately getting in from the statue, I headed straight back out again with our instructor and two others from the hostel, jumped onto the bus and made our way to the other end of the city to the Rocinha favela.

On arrival, I immediately knew that we were in one of the most densely populated, poorest and dangerous parts of the city. The public buses didn't go into the favelas, so we were dropped off at the bottom of the huge hill on the main road, by some makeshift market stalls set up in front of where all the homes started. We each jumped onto the back of some motorbikes organised by our guide, and sped off into the night, up into the favela. I held on to the base of the seat, as our bikes roared around the steep upward-winding road, in and out, narrowly avoiding other traffic and the pedestrians that crossed the street. The hastily built, unfinished, sometimes-decaying random buildings were made from solid brick and mortar, but I had to wonder how? And for how long? They looked like they were being held together by a networked mass of electricity cables that radiated in all directions, to at least provide some light and power to the down-beaten premises now in the dark. At the top, we were privileged to more than just the Capoeira lesson; first, we visited one of the local community centres where many of the local children were playing football in the hall and then onto the rooftop view, via more winding streets, for a glimpse of the city at night, that was a blanket mass of white, yellow and orange illuminations, cascading down and about a darkened, already-dense silhouette of a city.

Making our way to the studio, our instructor and guide was stopped by locals wanting to know who we were. He calmly explained that we were students of his which they readily believed and let us go about our way. It was intimidating and obvious there and then that these were no ordinary streets, and we as strangers were only OK here because we were with him. On the way up, I had noticed more than enough people carrying weapons to mention, and they in turn had noticed us.

Within the gymnasium, there was usual but basic weight lifting and exercise equipment; nothing fancy, but easily enough for anyone to readily work out with. Upstairs was the studio where for the next hour we trained, performing stretches followed by a series of kicks, blocks, spins and sweeping leg and arm movements that pushed my piss poor flexibility, co-ordination and balancing skills to the limit. Finishing, we were treated to a display by the local children who showed us 'how it's done', performing with much more poise and grace than the three of us together. Next, it was back onto the motorcycles where we were whisked down the main road though the favela to a barbeque dinner at one of the local restaurants, to dine on chicken beans and rice. Even though I wasn't that hungry, I obliged and ate as it was already arranged and I wanted to pay into the community, while not wanting to appear rude. Finally, our guide had us brought down to the main road where we all headed back once more on the bus.

It was good fun but hard work and I was tired. But I felt it was worth it especially as I came out feeling that I had learnt something and also thought that I easily could take up Capoeira. It was dynamic, fluid martial art form that seemed great all-round exercise that didn't necessarily seem to focus on kicking the shit out of someone. And I liked that, as I could only imagine I'd be the one getting the shit kicked out of me, within some other discipline.

The experience of actually going into the favela was something else though. I didn't know we were heading inside here. We were only told that the class would be at the studio and we would be taken there. I dare say not many people had done this and especially at night and I wouldn't or couldn't if it wasn't with our instructor. The simple fact is; outsiders who come into the favela run the very high risk of getting into serious trouble. Even the police do not come into these parts. Due to the social and economic status of these communities, they are somewhat outside of the law and run by the people within, which sadly are mainly drug gangs and they dictate what happens; so much so that when we were on the bikes, someone went past us openly holding upwards an automatic weapon that directly emphasised the harsh reality of where we were.

Strange thing was, though, the people we met and were introduced to were really nice and friendly, happy to see us. It was obvious that Bruno was a respected member of the community and many people knew him. I was impressed that he had set up the gym and classes here. It showed he cared, he wanted to make a difference and improve the lives of those who he lived with, especially the children, showing them another way and providing options, rather than that of drugs and crime, yet he wasn't begrudging towards us or condescending to those from there and he showed us an all-too-brief humble way of life, that many had to endure as these were clearly the cheapest homes and poorest people within the city suburbs. I was really glad that I had visited, especially as our fee went straight into the community to the running of the gym, and had been given and shown so much more than a martial arts lesson.

I thought I sort of knew what to expect, having seen the movie *City of*

God; widely regarded as true depiction of life in the favelas but this is still an art form telling a story. Having experienced the reality myself, I was fascinated by the brief outline of the lives that I had seen and wanted to learn more. The next day, I booked myself on another tour into the favelas. This was another opportunity to go back, this time in day time and with a guide again to fully enter the Rocinha favela. Before starting, we were told about the rules of dos and don'ts but mainly that of no photography in main areas as there may be people working for the gangs who would be watching us, where we went, our movements and they may not take too kindly to a snap-happy outsiders taking random photos of people within, while at the same time advertising their expensive cameras. These were perfectly understandable and reasonable rules, and pretty much the same as we were told the night before; so, I figured today wouldn't be any different.

This time, we made our way through the tiny, narrow alley network dividing the people's homes and shops that had been put together with no cohesion, creating tricky paths and steps, amid the piles of rubbish and constantly flowing water in the alleys that people could use to top up on water supplies to homes. Being on a hillside, the further up people live then they have access to cleaner water, unfortunately this causes problems further below where the poorer live as they only have access to the reconstituted water from above as it moves downhill creating an unsanitary mess at the bottom to become a breeding ground for pests and disease. It was hard to imagine having to live here, yet people with nothing or minimal incomes have to, with no other options and here being the only affordable accommodation. It was fascinating and harrowing at the same time wandering through, noticing methods people would use to get by. This included not only the possibility of having to take the dirty water for washing clothes, but then having laundry hanging out to dry on the endless electrical myriads of cables, that many had tapped for electrical power from the mains and created the jumbled mass outside with natural sunlight being sparse within such tight-knit abodes.

Within, we also visited a local gallery where some brilliant works of art were showcased – central to Rio and the favelas – plus a children day care centre which was a nice surprise to see as the many infants played happily inside with their carers; it looked well-managed and a welcome addition of security and safety for children, so parents were able to go out to work. Yet, I couldn't help but feel that these were the lucky few who had

481

this type of care during the day, because this couldn't be all the children that needed looking after. So, I feared many wouldn't be able to afford this service. And not just that, there simply wasn't enough room, as most of the buildings that we were invited into were all small spaces, narrow passages and low ceilings; space inside and out being a luxury in such a condensed, ever-growing community. The rooftops allowed to look out down the favela, fully appreciating now the mass of home and buildings there, harbouring over 200,000 people and evidence of how the local children entertain themselves with kite battles; a game of sorts involving shards of glass attached to the line of a kite, the winner determined by severing the cord of the other so it floats away to lodge on a rooftop or in one of the few trees. The sheer amount of discarded 'lost' kites alone was testimony itself to anyone having or playing a video game console here being a distant dream.

Despite the unsavoury conditions and hardship, the place was vibrant with colour and activity and the people who we met were again friendly and polite, more so to our guide Renato himself from the favela whom people knew. I had sampled a brief insight into Rio's poorest inhabitants, a place where those less well-off have the hills and amazing views, but this was scant consolation and a far cry from anything affluent. These were people with next to nothing and I tried but I couldn't imagine living here and especially not out of choice. Danger clearly lurked in many guises from the drugs, violence and poor sanitation to the design and aesthetics of the place. Unfortunately, these areas are only going to grow and get bigger, as people have to make do with the minimal things that circumstance says that they can have. I was again left humble at how lucky I was and it provided an unforgettable experience which I hoped would make me carry on wanting to help others, and keep my feet on the ground when I have problems that essentially are pale in comparison to these, and remember the happy attitude that many still with no obvious good reason seemed to purvey.

This was turning quite into the action-packed couple of days, trying to make the most out of my time left and I still had a few things that I wanted to do. I needed to arrange to meet a friend of a friend, so I could hopefully set up a meeting for my last day; so went ahead and got this sorted. Also, having seen some of the spectacular views around the city was impressive, but I wanted to go one step further and do something exhilarating so I decided to go all out and combine the two by going hang gliding. I hadn't ever done this before so thought it would be pretty cool as a stunt to finish off with and let's face it, not many better places really.

Obviously, there wasn't anything wrong with the place as the setting would be fantastic; the problem was that morning it was cloudy and raining which was going to spoil the view a little and put a dampener on things, so I was a little surprised when it was confirmed as being on, as I initially wondered if it would even happen. But turns out, the only thing really needed is the wind to be blowing in the right direction to make launching a possibility, which made sense. So off we went. Located at 500m cliff of Pedra Bonita where we were met by the pilot Jurgen, who unlike me was more excited with the conditions.

At the top, the rain had eased off somewhat and was now just overcast, but I already resigned myself to not having perfect condition and can't have or do everything and it was what it was. I was more concerned now with the sloping ramp hanging off the edge of the cliff and that I was moments away from launching myself off it while attached to a big kite; also known as a hang glider. Again, I was nervous, but right up for the challenge. Somehow, with all the dumb shit that I had put myself through, this seemed easy; probably because there was no falling or the sensation of the ground fast approaching involved. All I wanted to do was make sure that I got the instructions right. These were basically; don't jump, don't skip and whatever you do, don't stop. Just hold the bar of the frame and run in time with the instructor as fast as possible off the edge of the cliff. Super easy, I hoped.

Probably out of necessity to get a feel for the clients he was dealing with, Jurgen and I had a few practices dry runs to make sure the timing of our run would be OK. I could envisage some might try this and not realise they would have to run (I didn't) and if you don't have enough speed and fall off the edge, it could turn into a bit of a shit show. But as far as I was concerned, I can run – OK, it's not fast and usually it's not far, but I can run – so we didn't have a problem with the timing. Everything was set and with an almost instantaneous 3-2-1, holding the bar of the glider, we sprinted together, as fast as possible for around 15m towards the edge.

The platform slopped away to nothing and the feet disengaged automatically from the board, but instead of falling the harness kicked in and the body was automatically tilted forward into a downward lying position; it was so cool traversing from running to flying in one smooth, swift natural motion that made me feel like the condor. We started gracefully gliding out away from the mountain side. It was a fantastic feeling gliding around with nothing but a large wing and fancy framework keeping you up. It was surprising how noisy it was though as we cut through the wind, having imagined a more gentle serenity to it all. This was a bit odd as I had experienced paragliding and parachute jump and they both had loud, fast winds rushing around the ears and face, so I don't know why I thought this would be any different. Maybe because this was a beautifully relaxing sensation, in a supine pose; à la Superman, and the nearest thing to being a bird and really liberating flying about so high in the open, where once again I didn't have to do anything except admire the stunning scenery, revel in the manoeuvres and try to look cool for the camera. The ground below was beautiful green forests with smatterings of homes that got gradually smaller, as the winds were providing excellent conditions that took soaring up to over 600 metres, where turning around, we looked down over to the now small speck on the brow of the mountain where we had launched from.

We headed out towards the coast as our landing strip was to be the beach. To the left, we could see the massive Rocinha favela that I had visited and greyer clouds loomed further over more central Rio where it was clearly still raining. Now I was more than willing to compromise with not having sunny weather, as the flight had lasted a relatively long time of about twenty-five minutes, playing in the air currents that Jurgen couldn't resist elevating on, to put us in some deep swoops and fast turns that likened to being on a rollercoaster. We descended in a huge spiral motion, circling around the apartment buildings on the seafront, not resisting the opportunity to fly-by the windows of the penthouse suites. I suspected this was a regular thing as we passed about three times; probably to check to see if anyone was inside wandering around naked, or just an elaborate way of casing the joint. With one last swoop, we speedily came in to land. All I had to do was put my feet down and start running; which I managed with good grace thankfully, because there was a group of spectators watching from the beach front and I didn't want to be the newest star on 'Brazil's best ball's-up's'.

I had to wait while Jurgen went back to the top to take another from the hostel for their flight down, but this wasn't an issue as I had again the satisfaction of doing something different and a new exciting experience that I really enjoyed. I was also pleased that the other participant, Alan, had enjoyed it as well because he was by his own admission really nervous, but having completed it he too was thrilled and we chatted enthusiastically, reliving our time in the air when being taken back to the digs. The days and nights had rolled along unabated and my departure was almost imminent. I couldn't help but have to party somewhat. On the last day of the last night, the Aussies; Mal and Dev, were about and we spent it hanging at the beach as a precursor to getting completely fucked up on the evening, where we and some of the ladies there drank beer, played pool, drank some more beer, did the quiz, dropped some acid, drank some more, laughed a lot, watched the walls and pissed people, wobble, pop and move more than usual, hang out on the roof terrace, smoke some weed with the tunes on, all the while making an absolute fucking racket till the wee hours, that saw us absolutely trashed and almost flung out of the hostel. It was a pretty wild night and a shit tonne of fun. The next day; I checked out, put my bags into storage and headed out for some sun, before going for my meeting; my final swan song before I headed home.

The best picture I had seen of 'Christ the Redeemer' wasn't from a camera or in a souvenir shop. It was when I met Liam in La Paz and we had gotten to talking about tattoos, playing 'I'll show mine', 'you show yours'. Mine turned out to be a piffling effort compared to his, which happened to be a massive 'Christ the Redeemer' with angels and text tattooed across his back and shoulders. It looked amazing. And it turned out that he had it done by a guy staying in his hostel in Rio. I had been contemplating getting another tattoo as I knew of a couple that I wanted, but the opportunity hadn't arisen; until now. Impressed with the handy work, the Irish lads passed on his details. This was the friend of a friend I'd gone to meet prior; finding the hostel, I met artist Kel, sorted what I wanted and arranged to return on my last afternoon to have it done.

After spending the day on the beach, I went for my tattoo and spent an hour-and-a-half wincing as the speeding vibrating needle ground into my right-hand side on the flesh and bone; as I had a poetic song verse running vertically down my side permanently etched onto my persona. I also wanted another, which was some small text from one of my books. Because it was quick and easy, Kel offered to do this for free; which was rather cool of him to have a buy one get one free offer when I was there. He was as nice a bloke as I was led to believe and we chatted about travelling, music and mutual friends. He let me have a smoke of some weed before putting me through the buzzing heap of grimacing pain; on a random lounger; in a random hostel; in random Rio.

I arrived back at the hostel to show off my really sore, freshly inked skin to the rest of the guys and gals, had a quick beer in the bar with them, before saying many goodbyes after having an amazing time and lots of fun in a somewhat blur that was Rio. Nearly a year later from when I started out travelling, I took a taxi to the airport to take my final journey that would see me return to the UK; but not for the first time, it would be in some discomfort as I could only rest on one side, and likewise not for the first time, it was all of my own doing.

Brazil and Rio were like Argentina; in that it was a relatively fleeting visit and in no way did I get to fully appreciate the country as you could easily spend six months there and still not see everything due to the size. The problems of having such short amount of time left in each, it became a balancing act of where to be and what to do, which was exasperated by the funds getting low and I myself being tired and worn down. This was probably why I seemed to do even less in Brazil than in most other places I'd visited, as the end was nigh, dossing around relaxing along the coast of Rio state was very enticing and just what I needed.

What I did do and experienced I thoroughly enjoyed and I didn't regret a thing; because Brazil and Rio de Janeiro in particular was an incredible send-off that had everything, and those last five days all but summed up and encompassed virtually the whole of my travels. Amazing scenery, cultural activity, thrilling 'see me off' stunts, wonderful people who were in less than wonderful situations that kept my whole reality of everything that I was experiencing and doing on a grounded level, to empathise with their plight, support their cause and be ever so thankful for what I had and who I was. I'm not a big lover of big cities, but here was special. I loved it and it could have been a mini vacation in its own right that was a rocking whirlwind adventure. Here would now always be emblazoned with fond memories in my heart and somewhere I would always recommend anyone to visit; not just Rio but the other locations in Brazil also, as the locals were so friendly and helpful, which like many of the places I'd been to made my experience so memorable and all the more worthwhile. It was almost like the next word on everyone's lips seemed to be 'party?' – The buzz word that carried the culture in many countries, but never more so than here. It was like everyone knew I was leaving so had to have an amazing send off.

I would definitely love to return (lots of other places too for that matter) just because I simple hadn't seen or experienced enough and there was so much more. I didn't even get to see or go to carnival for one thing.

It didn't feel like I was going home, which I was. I'd set off on 22 August 2008 and arrived back home on 14 August 2009. After some fifty-one weeks, I finished my year travelling. I didn't take in the full year only so that I could do one last thing, this was to be kindly picked up from Heathrow Airport by my old mate Kenny, who I was at university with and driven the length of the country, so I'd arrive home unannounced a week early to surprise my family, having told them I would be back pretty much a year to the day. My journey and travels were now finished, but I didn't feel too bothered, fazed or upset. I thought I would have to be dragged on the plane kicking and screaming. It was a strange sensation, like I was doing what had to be done, the inevitable facing the music as it were; knowing now that all good things must come to an end. If I could have carried on, I would, but I didn't have unlimited resources or funds, so if I missed my flight that would expire after the 21st and not gone back, then I would have been stranded and it would have felt more like running away. It could be argued that not returning would have been the greater adventure but I couldn't and didn't want to push my luck. If I was meant to have been somewhere, then I would have been there. I had learnt so much about the world during the course of my travels, but in particular about myself. And I knew that this had to happen and was willing to face what now lay ahead. I didn't know what was going to happen; I was going back to the western world, the rat race where everything moves so fast with the prospect of little money when settling my debts and having to find a job in the middle of the worst recession in decades. I was looking forward to seeing friends and family again, sure, but that was about it and how long would that last? A week or two? But then what?

The thing was though, with all the activities that I had done, each had played their part in their own unique way in shaping me to be much less fearful and to believe in myself and what could be achieved. But not only that; counter intuitively, this also included negative things that happened as they equally played their part in helping create this new thought process and idea of myself. Everything came together in building a more confident, relaxed and unfazed persona. I had to willingly face everything as part of what was happening and what would happen. As easy as it was to graciously accept the good things, I equally as graciously had to accept the bad things. They may have been opposite ends on the emotional spectrum but were all equal in teaching a life lesson, to use them as a learning exercise and to grow strength from them. Many of the things I did voluntarily, knowing and calculating the risks involved, which offered personal gains and wondrous experiences that I knew I would benefit from by doing them. But many of these were out of my control; not deciding that these things should happen but they did, so I had to deal with them. These unplanned for or less envisaged incidents always had the potential for unknown outcomes, but by facing them head-on and treating them like a surmountable challenge that could be overcome, they ended up acting as unexpected bonuses that founded the basis for the different person that had now returned, and left me much less fearful of the unknown, which combined with a confident resilience made this prospect for the future ahead an already easier task.

With this, I felt I had gone through a radical mental transformation. Being away from home and my comfort zone for so long meant that I wasn't bothered any more about the things in life that I may have once regarded as important; things that I used as a form of escapism that I had no real influence over. So I started subconsciously quantifying things to how really important they were in my life and a function to my life on the whole; how much attention they would get and whether to just regard these things as a distraction – something for me to use, to switch off and enjoy and not be so engrossed with to the point of obsession, while still realising and recognising importance of these with the unifying properties that a show, movie or professional sport could bring when, say, bonding with others, but not just to fit in. I had seen that life can be different for me now.

With this, I realised I didn't need to have lots of money. Just enough would do. I had witnessed lots of people live a cheery existence with comparable little to others who were miserable yet had lots. The reality dawned on me that you can't take it with you and having it doesn't necessarily say anything positive about you. But what you do with money, privilege, power and what you do with yourself can speak volumes. This allowed and inspired me to also become more conscious of the people around me, wanting to do better by my fellow man, to be and act a better person and hopefully be able to set an example; born from the wonderful kindness show by people I knew to complete strangers that manifested itself in various, ways, shapes and forms. Each was special because when the chips were down, they offered help, assistance and recognition of what was required even if I may not have asked, and it was the most welcome of gifts – and one that I would dearly love to be able to give back or pay forward going in to the future.

Travelling gave me the impetus to want to do things, get out there and see the world regardless of what it entailed and whether it was for me or others. I was motivated and active more than I ever have been in my life. Granted, many of these things produced fabulous experiences and memories for my own pleasure, gratification, wellbeing and self-worth; such as climbing Cotopaxi but even when not so for myself, like the voluntary work, where I would be on the go all day and I seemed to want to push myself and give as much as I could. Here, subconsciously, I think this was because I wanted to see if I actually liked what I was doing and maybe find out if I would like it as my own profession, but I also was inspired by others' drive and commitment to their cause. It was incredibly endearing seeing someone work for a worthy goal; even with the jobs that were hard, physical work, it made me not want to let them down and help as best I could, because if I didn't give my all, I knew I would have let myself down as well, something that I didn't want to do.

With both the positive and negative things, I was determined to make the most out of every situation and scenario, especially as I realised early on that this was what I was supposed to do. Travelling quickly felt like the most natural thing in the world, probably why I never really missed anyone or anything from home while away. Don't get me wrong, I thought about people and things but tried not to let this distract me from my endeavours too much, as what I was doing was for me and something very important. I was lucky enough to be able to provide myself with the opportunity to follow a dream. I took it and if I was going to take it, I was grabbing it with both hands and running. I swiftly came to the conclusion that I would try to immerse myself in anything and everything that I was interested in and that came my way, no matter how weary, scared, tired or difficult the task as I may never have or be given the opportunity to do it ever again. There are millions in the world who couldn't do or experience even half of the things that I had, so I regarded this as a blessing and sort of felt it my duty to want to make the most of it; I should because I could – whether for myself, for others or other things.

Seeing others in poorer nations had a profound effect on me, and left my conscience reeling, the amount of times that I was left humbled at the hardship and poverty that has to be endured by young and old was incredible, especially when you would see these people smiling and actually having fun, yet having next to nothing. And it left me wondering what true happiness is? Was it more a frame of mind? Seemingly it cannot be bought. Yet, I was spending like it was going out of fashion and having an amazing time. I knew I had saved and sacrificed for this and many things were to serve a self-purpose, education and research etc., but it made me want to pay into the communities, to help where and when I could, whether this was via teaching, donating time or even handing out some food or loose change. The worst thing that struck me was that every human has the capacity to recognise suffering or struggle and surely there must be some way and means to alleviate this between the haves to the have nots regardless of race, colour, creed or orientation. Looking at it simply, we are all made up the same biologically, but the odds of you being you and in your circumstance are billions to one. It's surely just luck dictating the opportunities between having and not having; most people unfortunately do not have. It was heartbreaking the hardship and poverty of the masses, in numerous counties and at times everywhere I looked, especially where children were concerned; putting myself in these less-affluent, unfamiliar surroundings enabled me to grow in compassion, kindness and understanding as it was impossible for me to ever fully appreciate the reasons why other people behave like they do, especially when desperate people have to resort to desperate measures just to be able to survive. A statement that resonated with me was when a football manager, who was being interviewed before a big game, was asked about the pressure having lost the two previous fixtures. His reply was, "Pressure? Pressure is millions of people in the world; parents with no money to buy food for their children…that's pressure."

Wondering about all these things, I started to ask myself other big questions; like being the most developed species on the planet, surely this would lead us to having a moral duty to help other animals and species who we share our planet with? Especially as many are vital to our own existence and Earth isn't exclusively ours and certain species have been around a hell of a lot longer than humans. I always loved animals and was interested in them. Yet, I had never actually done anything in regards to helping or working with them – lack of opportunity? Maybe. Fearful of working with something I couldn't reason with and had no control over? Certainly. This was why I specifically wanted to educate myself and assist where possible to improve the wellbeing of these creatures, and now I had a chance. Sadly, though, I found many who suffered unnecessary cruelty, abuse, mistreatment and/or exploitation by man, with simply no need. I saw it many times on many levels; from the rescue centres I helped out at, the poorly maintained and inadequate zoo habitats, to the shows and tricks performed by magnificent creatures like dolphins, elephants and crocodiles. That could even extend to a person level from the photos and rides I had with some animals and many would also argue the horses at the track; where I was only there not for any educational or moral reason but only for my own entertainment and to reinforce negative vices like drinking and gambling; so these would only be construed as being part of any problem and slightly hypocritical. Other more prominent and more abundant instances were where people would abandon the no-longer-cute, easy-to-look-after puppy because now it is a large boisterous problem. It's not the animal's fault. Human ignorance is the problem. Such as the reckless harvesting of the oceans with unsustainable things like mass trawler fishing, which massively and unnecessarily decimates fish stock levels; affecting all marine life at every level as tonnes of unwanted by-catch such as sharks are just discarded as dead waste when caught up in the nets. Furthermore the unnecessary destruction and brutality also extends to menu 'delicacies' such as shark fin soup; where fins are cut off only to add texture to a dish with no flavour or nutritional value. Still alive, the stricken shark is thrown back into the water to die as it can't swim, making the whole disgusting, barbaric process; gluttonous and pointless. Yet sadly, people want to be rid of things like sharks just because they think they will be attacked if they go in the water. It's ridiculous. Everything is vital to the ocean food chain which in turn is vital to life on land. If the oceans die we die. All animals deserve the same protection that we all do, because their survival within Earths eco-systems might just in turn save us. Even sometimes counterintuitively; being pollinators, a food source and where only certain species bite humans this could also extend too mosquitos – the little wankers.

Yet still, I'm well aware of the argument of nature's balance and species need to be culled, but surely not unnecessarily, brutally or out of complete ignorance. Who knows what untold damage may be done? Also, I'm well aware of the possible two-faced irony and hypocrisy that I'm not a vegetarian; the idea interests me as something that I should try. May be help justify my love of animals and nature; but I would have to want to do this properly because of the morality involved, rather than something haphazard where I would fail due to missing meat in my diet. But if I personally had to kill an animal to eat, could I do it? I don't think I could. I'd be living on a diet of plants and leaves or I'd have to go fishing – and that would still probably leave me enjoying a nice hearty bowl of cabbage soup afterward. But these were now the things that I started to ask of myself all the time. In Thailand; one of the things that intrigued me most about Buddhism, is that all life is sacred and a monk practicing at the highest level would never knowingly kill another animal; whereas, some people just don't have that luxury of choice in life, whereas I do. So, maybe I should at least cut down my intake? Or eat only anything humanely dispatched, sustainable and locally sourced? At the very least, this would cut down the carbon footprint. Therein provides another gregarious irony; having in the end flown around the globe with a total of eleven flights and thousands of miles covered within the year, an environmental piss-take to say the least. Something; with hindsight I need to address as being way too much, unnecessary and that I should and do apologise for. In future, I need to definitely think about this impact and try to travel in a more reasonable, sustainable and environmentally friendly way, and that extends to being careful about visiting places which are susceptible to the detrimental effect of an increased tourist footfall.

Everything that I was learning, doing, witnessing or was happening seemed to be providing me with some form of lesson or food for thought; even from the books I read to the movies I saw. Making me wonder how my destiny was shaping before me and everything that was happening was for a reason. This allowed me to become very conscious of the things that were happening while I travelled, and the more I travelled life seemed somewhat amplified – coincidences, opportunities, excitement, drama, good things and bad things. At home within the day-to-day existence, life can pass you by in routine. But out in the big wide world, opportunities come thick and fast, which also would include difficult experiences. Here, though, there were fewer distractions and fewer places to hide. This, therefore, made these opportunities easier to embrace being out of the loop, regarding friends, family and entertaining distractions. It was easy meeting other people, because most are in the same scenario, offering common ground that generally tends to mean many are like-minded. It was great hanging around with random strangers whenever it suited or moving on to do your own thing. Being a lone traveller out on the road provided a very self-centred way of life, doing what you wanted, when you wanted and not having to worry about others. But this was the whole point for me; who else was it for? It offered total freedom and something different to that of living in a democratic society where you are regarded free, but bound by the quietly dictated, covert constraints of society like; families, friends, possessions, obligations and distractions. As I had nothing or minimal of those things, this, therefore, gave me a new feeling and that was incredibly energising. I had tasted it and loved it.

Long hours' travelling provided me with many opportunities to broaden my knowledge, finding myself thinking more about the world, life and where I was heading in all this. I believe that everything that I did, everyone I met and everything that happened served a purpose whether positive or negative, some became clear while others not so, and I found myself having to willingly accept these. If I'm truly honest, I was looking for answers; including where do I want to be? What do I want to do? Can I meet someone special to share this with? Honestly, I thought that I would get all these (or at least one), but never did. People may think this a shame, but life isn't written by a Hollywood writer. I didn't find the ideal job, in the idyllic location and I didn't meet the girl. I only got more questions. As the world, life and travel opened my eyes and mind, I came to realise I was quite ignorant and naive to think there would be any easy answers. As there rarely is and, frankly, these are obvious questions that everyone wants the answer to anyway. Looking back, though, I received so much more than the answers to these questions; I had received first-hand lessons about struggle, hardship, empathy, compassion, kindness, gratitude, honesty, love, real happiness, true values and what's actually important finding that these things are priceless as they cannot be bought.

Another more obvious change that had happened was physically easier see, upon my return I had lost nearly two-and-a-half stone (35lbs), and had acquired a physique that I never thought possible; all the activities, working, training, altitude, sun and heat, and strangely sometimes stress and illness had taken a very positive toll on my body – I felt great. But why was this? I hadn't gone away travelling with the sole purpose to return feeling and being physically fitter than I ever have done. What had happened? There was no way that this would've been possible back in the UK because of the way I was with my mental attitude. Yet, the rigours and excitement of travelling, incorporating tonnes of activity had a real beneficial by-product of massively improving my physicality, which in turn had a massive, positive, knock-on effect on my mental wellbeing also. It was nice being slim, it was nice being athletic, it was nice being ache-free and it was nice to lock down and see my dick without holding my belly in.

Travelling was easily the best thing that I have ever done. The vocational things, the personal achievements, incredible views, surreal sights, fabulous people, the feel-good factor trying to make a difference, overcoming difficult times, overcoming personal fears, making new friends all encompassed to creating a brilliant personal adventure that left me exhilarated, proud and worthy of myself; all the while knowing that I helped make a small difference to those less fortunate, yet still missed out so much, unable to do it all and visit everywhere which just left pages unwritten for new adventures. At times, I was angry, frustrated, scared, lonely and/or worried but something always seemed to happen at the right moment to help elevate this and something positive would happen, like everything was perfectly in balance with everything that did happen. Looking back, I wouldn't change a single thing even if I could, purely because it wouldn't have helped create the person that I am now or show me the person I could or can be. And I say 'could' or 'can' be because despite all this personal growth, there is always an element of darkness to address.

Throughout my journey, I was very aware of the demons I carry and how they easily can manifest when inspired by the devil making use of idle hands. Put simply, I'm quick to bask in the escapism of getting drunk. This is usually and more often is for no good reason and way too much; excessive to the point where I don't know what is going on or happening around me. Normally I'll revel in a joyous frame of mind; but by not having an off switch and moderating or stopping my consumption of alcohol, sometimes my mood can alter in a negative way or I'll drink so much that I just blackout or pass out. Sadly, getting so fucked up the knock-on effects of the next day are worse, as the depressant booze can leave me horribly hungover unable to recall what happened. Even if I haven't done or said anything bad, I don't want to talk to anyone or do anything; except maybe feel the urge to have another drink starting a vicious cycle. So, I need to change these habits, because I don't like it when I feel that way, and manage my alcohol intake to sensible levels where I stay in control or don't drink at all. And that isn't easy, especially when caught up in the moment of everyone else drinking, partying and being susceptible to another societal dictatorship that is peer pressure, which in many other instances is something I easily reject, but drinking and its effects have a malevolent hold. Yet, what is strange; when I'm occupied or busy, I can go days without feeling the needing to drink. But when I do, it's never a few, it's all or nothing. Somewhat less problematic is drug use, because I'm not around them or actively seek them to soothe an addiction. But as soon as the opportunity arises, I have a tendency to take them (especially if drink is involved) simply because I can; usually no questions asked as – like with drinking – I want the rock 'n' roll buzz of the unknown. Especially unknown is what's happening to me mentally and physically; put simply, it isn't good. On all counts; it's a sad state that with these escape mechanisms, sometimes, I will push these limited boundaries.

As a strange twist, drugs were one of the reasons I ended up breaking loose and heading on this travelling path; point and case being that few years prior it was a drug offence that I was arrested for, being caught with cocaine in my possession. And this is what showed up on my caution. Then more ironically with all the butterfly effect events, a few years later, I ended up wandering around cocaine central Colombia and South America. Did I try the powder? Of course, I did; because at times I am really stupid. It was a couple of times in powder form and a few times munching the leaves. But if I could say anything to anyone about being the best and being the person that you want to be, don't drink alcohol (or at least only in limited moderation) and don't take drugs. By avoiding these vices, chances are you will make it and be how or what you want to be. The time and energy saved alone can create focus needed to make things happen a shit tonne quicker and with a lot less angst. I can say this now I've seen I don't necessarily need these in my life for enjoyment or fulfilment; if anything, I actually need them out of my life for enjoyment and fulfilment. The experiences I've had and following interests alone provided this and why I have tried not to embellish or focus too much on what happened when on the drink or drugs - I don't really remember that much to be honest! - as a glamourous or major feature within the story; they played a part usually for socialising and bonding purposes, but they are what they are, which was nothing that noteworthy except for sometimes the trouble, idiocy and waste they can cause to lives from the many different negative levels and aspects that come with their consumption.

Also writing this itself, has brought enjoyment and fulfilment and allowed me to achieve another ambition. I've written it mainly because it was the wildest, most profound, surreal and educational experience that allowed me to live what felt a whole life's worth of adventure in a year, where I never once envisaged that what would happen could stretch the realms of possibility so far. So far, in fact, that I felt the need to share it; as I did when sending emails to people, telling them about my exploits, which each of these chapters are an elaboration on. I've changed or omitted some names to protect the innocent or not-so-innocent and haven't included hoste names and companies so as not to prejudice people from using or not using these, because I would like to think that this could prove inspirational to anyone wishing or hoping to go out there and do something similar – although I wouldn't expect anyone to do what I have done, far be it from me to tell people what to do. This was my own personal journey, but that's the beauty; everything is out there to enhance your own life and existence to get out of it what you will, by your own means and the things that inspire or you are passionate about most. And I can't emphasise how much it could change a person, especially for the better. As you could live out your craziest of dreams and ideas; but it does come at a price that's not just about monetary cost. You have to embrace the unknown, accept fear, don't not run away and be aware that unfavourable things will happen, but if you are prepared to do this and deal with them, the rewards can be beyond your wildest ambitions and can truly feel like you have lived your life and felt alive. You will have to take a deep breath, throw caution to the wind and go for it. Nobody else can do it for you, nor should you want them to.

As for me, who knows? Nothing now is guaranteed and I don't know what the future has in store, much like when I left. But now, I'm more than equipped to deal with whatever life has to throw at me, as I'm now a stronger person in every aspect, yet, still with no real direction in life; that said, I'm not sure when, but, I know there's one thing I really want to do…